# DRUGS, CRIME, AND JUSTICE

# DRUGS, CRIME, AND JUSTICE

## CONTEMPORARY PERSPECTIVES

**Larry K. Gaines**
*Eastern Kentucky University*

**Peter B. Kraska**
*Eastern Kentucky University*

WAVELAND

PRESS, INC.

Prospect Heights, Illinois

For information about this book, write or call:
Waveland Press, Inc.
P.O. Box 400
Prospect Heights, Illinois 60070
(847) 634-0081

Printed in the United States of America

7  6  5  4  3  2

# Contents

## The Drug Industry

## Policing Drugs

---
## The Courts and Drugs
---

---
## Drug Criminalization Debate
---

# Preface

The drug phenomenon occupies an ambiguous position within crime and justice studies. Students and professors could legitimately question whether graduate and undergraduate level courses on drugs belong in a criminology/criminal justice program. After all, why should breaking drug laws hold any more importance for study than breaking burglary laws, family violence laws, or homicide laws—topics which are rarely included on permanent curriculums? It could be argued that the recent surge in scholarship and interest in this area merely reflects another fleeting "fad."

The personal experiences of the editors offers one justification for including this topic in the curriculum and for the importance of a reader like this one on drugs, crime, and justice. Despite having taught and researched the drug issue for seven years, we perceived the full impact of its importance while teaching "Advanced Criminal Justice Studies." The four books and numerous articles used in the course were chosen to illuminate the major theoretical, ideological, and practical issues facing contemporary society and the criminal justice system. No matter which direction our focus turned—social inequality, media coverage of crime, criminal justice as industry, racism, crime causation, prison overcrowding, or expanding police powers—we bumped into substance abuse and drug wars as an influential dimension for each. It became clear that understanding crime and justice issues in the 1990s requires a sound understanding of the nature of substance abuse itself and our society's reaction to it.

As the first three articles in this collection illustrate, politicians and bureaucrats over the last one hundred years have fumbled and stumbled their way into a response to the problem of substance abuse guided by the rhetoric and ideology of "war"—the same ideology which underlies "war on crime." Although tremendous ideological pressure distorts our perceptions, the act of altering one's state of consciousness using a chemical or organic substance differs substantively from stealing a car, killing a bar-room patron, or sexually abusing a child. Government officials, with help from the media, have linked punishment-oriented drug control efforts with the never-ending "war on crime." Unlike any other form of criminality, however, the government orchestrates autonomous strikes against drug use and distribution. These coordinated efforts can involve federal agencies (including the armed forces), state and local agencies, and special task forces. In some instances separate court and correctional facilities (see the articles on drug courts and drug boot camps) are enlisted to address the problem of drugs. Because the criminal justice system can take proactive measures and round up as many drug users and distributors as it wants (versus, for example, burglars or robbers), these wars yield tremendous "results" in the form of massive numbers of drug arrests, drug convictions, and drug incarcerations. This characteristic of limitless results, along with the relative autonomy of drug control efforts, renders drug wars in and of themselves a vital area of study.

This autonomy of pursuit does not mean, however, that drugs, crime, and their attendant wars are not interrelated. As mentioned above, they are interwoven. One of the most misunderstood dimensions of this interrelationship is the drug-crime connection (see articles 4, 5, and 6). The misguided, simplistic belief—"drugs cause crime"—has helped justify our current drug war. It was perhaps the most important public justification for criminalizing certain mind-altering substances. Again, there is nothing intrinsically criminal about using a mind-altering substances; what justifies its criminalization is the perceived criminogenic consequences stemming from its use (see Lusane and Musto's account of the criminalization process). Research and logic tell us that although drug use itself (especially alcohol use) may contribute to crime, the crime associated with drugs may be better explained as (1) caused by drug *laws* themselves and/or (2) the result of a third variable such as inequality. Understanding the complexities of the drug/crime connection is critical for understanding crime and justice issues in general.

Drugs and the enforcement of drug laws are integral issues in the day-to-day operations of each component of the criminal justice system. Criminal justice practitioners confront both the immediate effects of drugs themselves and the consequences of substance abuse. Even if these substances were not illegal (alcohol provides a prime illustration), they still pose significant health, psychological, and criminal justice related problems for the police officer, juvenile justice practitioner, corrections officer, and probation officer. Criminalization superimposes a sticky moral and legal dimension which most practitioners confront daily. This book attempts to provide students—both as members of society and perhaps as future criminal justice practitioners—with the factual, theoretical, and philosophical information necessary to understand the multifaceted dimensions of drugs.

# Introduction

The first section of President Clinton's 1995 National Drug Control Strategy states:

> No community in America can escape the problems surrounding illicit drug use and its consequences . . . According to the most recent National Household Survey on Drug Abuse, roughly one in three Americans has used an illicit drug sometime in his or her lifetime, and roughly one in nine Americans has tried cocaine at least once.

These types of statistics are a popular way to discuss the "drug problem" in the United States. What do they mean? What exactly does one in three Americans using illegal drugs sometime in their lives indicate about the "consequences" and "surrounding problems" of illicit drug use? The intended purpose of such statistics is to expose the pervasiveness of the criminogenic practice of large numbers of people altering their states of consciousness. Much of the public might even conjure up images of 86 million people (one-third of the population of the United States) being either former or current drug fiends—predisposed, as the characterization goes, toward crime. If accurate, that image is indeed ominous.

What does "one in three Americans" tell us in reality? Statistics tucked away in a table from the same report indicate that out of the 37 percent of Americans who have tried illegal drugs sometime in their lives, marijuana was the drug of choice in 91 percent of these cases. Translated into common language: one-third of our fellow citizens have smoked pot at least once in their lives. Should this alarm anyone to the point of wanting to wage *war*? The report does not mention that only 4 percent of Americans have used marijuana in the last month, and only 9 percent have used it in the last year. What about cocaine? "One in nine Americans" on cocaine would be an epidemic. However, only .6 percent of Americans report using cocaine in the last month, and only 2.2 percent in the last year. It requires a seasoned and critical reader to notice in this report that the government's trenches in this war exist not throughout the drug-using public but almost exclusively in poor urban and rural neighborhoods.

The point here is not to deny the existence of a substance abuse problem. The abuse of mind-altering substances is a major concern in the mosaic of social problems our society faces. Recent trends in drug use show an increase in the use of heroin, LSD, methamphetamines, marijuana, and alcohol in high schools and colleges (Feldkamp, 1995). In addition, women are catching up to men in consumption of alcohol and the use of drugs (Kotulak, 1996). We highlighted the presidential rhetoric because it illuminates an often taken-for-granted ideology about drugs, substance abuse, and how to minimize their negative consequences—something often referred to as "drug war ideology" (Kraska, 1993; Johns, 1994). The gripping power of this ideology masks the complex, tangled mixture of assumptions, beliefs, morals, and ideas about drugs in the United States. Untangling the web of facts and fiction is a requisite foundation for understanding why the criminal justice system is the front line of attack for an intractable social problem and how current policy might be altered to ameliorate rather than exacerbate that problem.

Statistics are not the only misleading elements in this country's approach to drugs. Contradictory examples abound. A sampling of three ironic outcomes of current policy follow. When Lee Brown was appointed drug "czar" (the title alone is ironic in a democratic country), his post was elevated to a cabinet position but his staff was slashed from 146 to 25 and $231 million was subtracted from his budget. When he was replaced by Barry McCaffrey, the staff and budget were reinstated with a small increase. Drug czars may be important symbolically, but opinions about support services and monies required for the department to function fluctuate erratically.

In order for countries to qualify for U.S. aid, the president must certify that they are cooperating fully with combatting illicit narcotics trafficking. As Senator Dodd noted in a 1996 controversy over certification of Mexico, "If we subjected our own country to this test, we wouldn't pass it." The State Department acknowledged that "no country in the world poses a more immediate narcotics threat to the United States than Mexico." Mexico was, however, certified as cooperating fully with the U.S. effort to combat drugs (*Chicago Tribune*, 1996).

In the 1980s more than twenty states created a marijuana tax as a means of depleting the profits of drug dealers. Typically, the state issued a dealer's license which gave holders the right to buy tax stamps to affix to each bag of marijuana sold. Although the legislators had no qualms about passing a regulatory tax for something you cannot legally own, they did take the precaution of stating on the license that it did not authorize dealing or protect the purchaser from prosecution. If caught selling the drug, the dealer could also be charged with tax evasion. The absurdity of applying for a license to buy tax stamps for the sale of an illegal product in order not to be charged with tax evasion was not lost on most dealers, who simply did not sign up. The laws were intended to give law enforcement another weapon against drug dealers, but the constitutionality of the laws has been challenged. Supreme courts have ruled in several instances that adding a punitive tax to the threat of jail violates the protection against being punished twice for the same crime. In 1994 the U.S. Supreme Court had established that precedent by ruling against the state of Montana. In Arizona, criminal drug charges were dismissed when a defendant produced his official drug-dealer's license and a receipt for the money he had paid the state for it (Dellios, 1996). The tool designed to give law enforcement two opportunities to punish drug dealers ended up functioning as a pass for the defendant.

Although drug war ideology is marked by misinformation and illogic, it is by no means dysfunctional. The cumulative missteps have combined to form a very effective means of continuing current policy. The circular argument of the prevailing ideology uses criticism as proof of the necessity to increase efforts. Opposition to the drug war enterprise, no matter how reasonable or factually based the specific arguments, is quickly labelled as an attempt to legalize drugs—a solution assumed by the ideology to be so reprehensible that it can be rejected without further examination. Anything labelled as legalization is immediately rejected—a "legalization garbage can" that eliminates the need for reasoned discussion (Henry and Milanovich, 1991). Jocelyn Elders lost her position as surgeon general for suggesting the need for *discussion* about legalization.

One book cannot completely comb through and detangle drug war ideology and activities. We will focus on drugs and substance abuse as they relate to crime and the government's drug control efforts. Each article treats one facet of the problem from a criminal justice vantage point. The purpose of this introduction is to introduce you to a potpourri of issues, concepts, and ideas that will act as a contextual map and (we hope) intellectual stimulant for critical thinking as you read through the rest of the articles. Without some background for the genesis of criminal justice responses to the use of illegal substances, it is difficult to judge whether those responses are adequate, effective, and proportional to the harm. We need a factual record of previous experiences that is not colored by fears, prejudice, and exaggerated accounts about the effects of mind-altering substances. As David Musto points out in the first article, the ebb and flow from recurrent enthusiasm for recreational drugs to campaigns for abstinence do not leave accurate recordings of previous experience. Rather, the ideologies of zealous adherents battle each other for dominance.

## Defining Drugs

Imprecise terminology obscures precise analysis. Part of the power of drug war ideology stems from the catch-all term "drugs." Most people do not question the political/media cries to do something about our "drug" problem; to wage wars on "drugs"; or that "drug use" destroys a person's, or even an entire community's, well-being. Drug war ideology lulls us into assuming a number of properties about *drugs*. We refer to certain drugs, for example, as being criminal, or needing to be criminalized, as if they were little demons committing crimes. Waging wars on drugs—as if the drugs themselves constitute our "drug problem"—allows us to overlook the underlying reasons why people abuse these substances. We can place blame on the seductive powers of an object—avoiding responsibility for ourselves and the society which we have created. This would be equivalent to waging war on food, versus discovering psychological, sociological, or genetic reasons for overeating. The language of the ideology fools us into thinking that we're waging war against drugs themselves, not real people—many of whom have no more drug addiction than the social drinker who frequents "happy hour" after work. Conversely, someone dependent on illegal substances is not granted the same tolerance or assistance as the alcoholic. Groups have worked diligently to link alcoholism with disease, whereas other interests have adamantly rejected a therapeutic approach to the use of illegal drugs.

Mention our "drug problem" to the average person and notice how the immediate link is to our *illicit* drug problem—possibly just the "crack" problem. Most people do not classify alcohol and cigarettes as drugs. They are legal substances available for sale to anyone who meets the age restriction. Since they are socially sanctioned, few people compare the depressant/stimulant properties of these two substances with other drugs. Our society clearly has numerous drug problems—beyond those that occur among lower socioeconomic groups. More than one-half million people a year die due to alcohol use and cigarette-related diseases; less than 2 percent of this number die per year due to the use of all illegal drugs combined. In addition, the psychoactive properties of alcohol are strongly associated with violent crime; little evidence supports the same conclusion for most illegal drugs (Abadinsky, 1993; Goode, 1993). Mark Kleiman notes alcohol is the drug on which kids "are most likely to get pregnant, commit crimes, get in fights or drive recklessly" (Chapman, 1996b: 15).

Our society has an enormous prescription "drug problem" as well. Not only do billions of dollars of prescription drugs reach the black market, the medical industry (reminiscent of the early days of its profession) legally overprescribes numerous antidepressants including Prozac and tranquilizers such as Valium or Xanax (*Consumer Reports*, 1993). A report by the Center on Addiction and Substance Abuse at Columbia University found that 21.5 million women in the United States smoke, 4.5 million are alcoholics, 3.5 million abuse prescription drugs, and 3.1 million regularly use illegal drugs (Kotulak, 1996). Since the figures for men are slightly higher, the totals for abuse of legal substances far outstrip the totals for illegal substances. Political and media cries to wage war on our "drug problem"—as if there were only one clearly definable entity—are hypocritical, exploitative, and dangerously misleading.

*Drug*, as a generic descriptor, ignores important distinctions between types of illicit drugs and their effects. The typical citizen may well assume that all illegal drugs have either lethal or highly damaging health consequences, that all illicit drug use constitutes abuse, and that all illicit drugs by definition lead to "addiction." Legal drugs are viewed as different (less harmful and dangerous, aside from their legal status) than their illegal counterparts. Being "high" on a fifth of bourbon versus being "high" from ingesting multiple lines of cocaine is assumed to be radically different. Emotionally, politically, and socially the differences may seem obvious. Behaviorally, few differences exist, except that the bourbon drinker would probably be more physically impaired.

The problem of defining drugs is complicated by the fact that drugs are both physical substances with pharmacological effects and cultural icons with values and behaviors linked to them by the society in which they are found. The values of a particular culture include attitudes toward drugs and beliefs about what they do (Knipe, 1995). We have already explored one of the predominant links (criminogenic) in this society. We will take a look at others later in this introduction.

The first entry in *Merriam Webster's Collegiate Dictionary* (1995) under drugs is: a substance used as medication. This is followed by the definition according to the Food, Drug and Cosmetic Act: (1) listed in official pharmacopoeia, (2) intended for use in the diagnosis and treatment of disease, and (3) substance other than food intended to affect the structure or function of the body. Finally the definition lists "something and often an illegal substance that causes addiction, habituation, or a marked change in consciousness."

The dictionary definition relies on the government's definition of drugs; in reference to illegal drugs, it emphasizes addiction.

## Drug Dependency

We find the same type of bias applied to the often misused terms, "drug abuse," "drug dependence," "addiction," and "drug use." At what point does drug use constitute abuse? Under the prevailing philosophy, drug abuse is redundant; any *use* of an illegal drug constitutes *abuse* and leads to dependence. In actuality, abuse varies with the individual. Abuse occurs when the use of the drug—whether aspirin, beer, caffeine, cigarettes, marijuana, diet pills, or heroin—becomes a psychological, social, or physical problem for the user. Contrary to commonly accepted opinion, most people avoid *abusing* marijuana, amphetamines, cocaine, and even heroin, just as most people avoid the abuse of beer or wine. Indeed, although rates of compulsive abuse vary from drug to drug, it ranges from about 7–20 percent—meaning that even for cocaine (1 in 10 become behaviorally dependent), the bulk of illegal drug users are not abusers (Kraska, 1990).

What does it mean to be a compulsive user or to be "addicted" to a drug? The literature prefers the term "dependence." "Addiction" stems from the traditional approach to compulsive abuse: any drug which leads to physiological dependence and results in physical withdrawal symptoms is considered "addictive." Goode (1993:29) explains the reason behind the shift in emphasis to the term "dependence":

> The intent of the drug experts who devised this terminology seemed to be ideological: to make sure that a discrediting label was attached to as many widely used drugs as possible. Under the old terminology of "classic" addiction, it was not possible to label a wide range of drugs as "addicting." It thus became necessary to stigmatize substances such as marijuana and LSD. . . .

The concept of "psychological dependence" has proved useful in understanding drugs such as cocaine which cannot be classified as "physically addictive" but can result in compulsive and destructive abuse. Most literature now uses the term dependence and makes a distinction between psychological dependence and physical dependence, although the two are often interrelated. The interrelationship highlights an important aspect of any discussion about drugs. As discussed earlier, the prevailing tendency is to elevate the substance to a status capable of generating its own action and effects. That would clearly favor a one-way causal relationship of physical properties creating predictable effects in users. This approach denies the influence of culture and society on individuals. The values and beliefs taught to members of society affect one's perceptions and expectations. In this case, the effects of drugs would be viewed as psychogenic—originating in the mind and affecting the body, or psychosocial—involving both psychological and social aspects where social conditions affect responses. Throw differences between individuals into the mix and separating cause and effect becomes even more difficult. Careful analysis of issues requires a consideration of multiple factors— and a healthy suspicion of simplistic linear causality.

Dependence then usually involves a combination of physiological or psychological craving for a substance. It also often involves a tolerance for the drug which requires larger doses to ease the craving. The substance becomes a primary focus in the life of someone dependent on it; the dependency is frequently accompanied by denial about the amount used and the degree of dependency.

Applying the label "drug abuse" reinforces the distinction between sanctioned and illegal drugs. Prescriptions grant positive connotations to drugs. Therapeutic value is acceptable; recreational is not. This society, in general, rejects the use of intoxicants for pleasure—with the exception of alcohol. Recreational drug users are viewed at best as hedonistic threats to the moral and social order—antisocial people leading wasteful lifestyles. At worst, they are dangerous fiends looking for every opportunity to lead innocents to a criminal lifestyle. To understand how well socialization processes work on attitudes, we need only compare advertisements for alcohol with public attitudes toward drugs. A recent series of advertisements proclaims, "It would be weird without beer." An older campaign proclaimed, "It doesn't get any better than this." Imagine a similar campaign for marijuana. We accept the use of alcohol as a mood enhancer, aid to relaxation, and symbol of sociability. Of course, we oppose underage drinking and assume that any problems magically disappear once the legal age limit has passed. Another example of the socialization process is the willingness of some parents to administer Ritalin, a Schedule II drug (see next section) to their children. The legitimacy of a prescription overrides the horror parents would feel if another Schedule II drug—opium, for example—were suggested by someone on the street.

## Types of Drugs

Just as definitions of drugs vary according to the perspective one holds, so do classifications of various substances. Medical personnel focus on the utility and therapeutic effects of substances. The government, police, and courts focus on illegality. The Controlled Substances Act specified five hierarchical categories—ranked by potential for abuse; medical use, if any; and dependency. Schedule I drugs have the highest potential for abuse and no currently accepted medical use in the United States. Curiously, in place of a dependency description there is a remark that there is no accepted safe use of the drug under medical supervision—seemingly unnecessary since it was already labelled as having no medical utility. Heroin, LSD, Ecstasy, and marijuana are Schedule I drugs. Schedule II drugs are listed as having high abuse potential, accepted medical use under very specific conditions, and severe psychological or physical dependence. Copies of prescriptions must be filed in Washington, D.C., the capital of the state in which it is prescribed, and in the physician's office. No refills are permitted. Drugs must be stored in a vault. Schedule II drugs include opium, morphine, methadone, codeine, cocaine, Ritalin, and amphetamines. Schedule III drugs are listed as having less potential for abuse and moderate or low physical dependence or high psychological dependence. Schedule III drugs may be prescribed without copies filed; prescriptions are refillable with some restrictions. Schedule IV drugs have low potential for abuse with limited physical or psychological dependence. Most tranquilizers are Schedule IV, including Librium, Xanax, Valium, and Prozac. Schedule V drugs are ranked even lower than the previous category in potential for abuse and dependency.

An alternative classification is by effects on the central nervous system. Depressants slow down signals through the system thereby reducing sensitivity. As a result, they decrease pain and anxiety. The action of analgesics may be similar to naturally occurring endorphins in the body (Abadinsky, 1993). Narcotics include opium derivatives such as heroin, morphine and codeine and synthetics such as methadone. Alcohol is the most widely used depressant. Barbiturates, tranquilizers, and sedatives all belong in this category. Depressants can produce both physical and psychological dependency. Analgesics also include aspirin, ibuprofen, and acetaminophen, which are neither psychoactive nor addictive.

Stimulants amplify signals passing through the central nervous system. By stimulating sensation, they elevate mood and produce feelings of well-being. As such, they are similar to three neurotransmitters in the body: dopamine, norepinephrine, and serotonin (Abadinsky, 1993). Caffeine, nicotine, amphetamines and cocaine are all stimulants. While there is rarely physical addiction as commonly defined, psychological dependence on stimulants can produce unpleasant, discomforting experiences.

Hallucinogens include LSD, PCP, mescaline, the peyote cactus, and Ecstasy. Hallucinogens produce such exhausting yet inconsistent experiences and last for such an extended period of time that they are usually used only occasionally. They are neither physically nor psychologically addicting (Goode, 1993). Many of the conceptions about hallucinogens are based on society's reaction to Timothy Leary's mantra in the 1960s to "Turn On; Tune In; Drop Out." His championing of LSD as a means of elevating the senses beyond the rigid rules prescribed by society was anathema to thousands of parents who feared losing their children to the drug subculture.

The last category is cannabis—marijuana. It is not only the most frequently used illegal drug, it is possibly the most misunderstood. As noted above, the government classifies it as having no medicinal use, although it has been approved for just such use in half the states (Goode, 1993). It is a Schedule I drug yet is far less likely to be a factor in violent criminal activity than alcohol. Marijuana is frequently charged with inducing the use of other drugs. While a correlation can be established between the use of marijuana and the use of other drugs, a *causal* relationship is difficult to prove. Is there a chemical "hook" in marijuana that implants the desire to try another substance? Are the influences more likely sociocultural or psychological? Two legal drugs are correlated with marijuana—cigarettes and alcohol. Is the link the same? In general, both the subjective effects and physical repercussions of marijuana use are minimal.

## Effects of Drugs

The difficulties of classifying drugs are compounded because effects are not uniformly measurable. They vary depending on the chemical properties of the drug, the setting in which it is ingested, the method of ingestion, the potency and quantity, the frequency of use, and the specific biological and psychological traits of the user. Expectations about what will happen and the reactions of others all affect results. Analysts often refer to the effective dose of a drug. Since experiences are subjective, effective dose is measured by administering the drug to a number of people and observing at what dosage similar effects can be noted in a certain percentage of the subjects. However, the laboratory experience cannot replicate ordinary experience. The clinical setting imposes its own context on the experiment and—at least for certain aspects of experience—cannot be extrapolated to nonclinical settings. In addition, dosages and purity levels are known quantities in the laboratory. Since many drugs are illegal, buyers on the street have no means of confirming the purity of the drugs purchased. Thus, survey results depend on reported quantities—unverified data. Illegality colors the results of most analyses. Lethal incidents are confirmable through autopsies and do provide more reliable data under those extreme conditions.

Drug war ideology glosses over the differing consequences of various drugs and treats all illegal drugs as uniformly dangerous for the user and for society. The fact is that an illegal drug such as marijuana has few of the health consequences that we would find for heroin. Inhaling the smoke of a burning marijuana plant does have health risks (as does taking diet pills). A wealth of research has attempted to document the severity of these risks, but no research to date concludes that it is a "dangerous" drug, especially when compared to numerous legal drugs (Goode, 1993; Kappeler et. al., 1996). This is not to say that it does not have any social implications. The subculture of some teenagers develops a less than "productive" mind-set that revolves around inhaling marijuana smoke; they can become psychologically dependent (although our cause-and-effect discussion applies here in that it is impossible to determine if the mind-set is caused by the marijuana use itself).

Current research claims that marijuana use is increasing among the young, and the stigma associated with it during the Reagan-Bush drug war is diminishing (*U.S. News & World Report*, 1995). In the 1993 high school survey by the National Institute on Drug Abuse, 26 percent of high school seniors reported the use of marijuana in the previous 12 months, compared to 21.9 percent in 1992. Marijuana use in the previous month was 15.5 percent compared to 11.9 percent (Bureau of Justice Statistics, 1995). Indeed, some popular musical groups lend status to the drug. Dr. Dre's rap album was entitled "The Chronic"—slang for a strain of marijuana twenty times more potent than others. The Black Crowes perform with a pro-marijuana sign on stage. Caps and shirts decorated with the marijuana leaf are popular. Researchers at the University of Michigan found that marijuana use among high school students doubled from 1991 to 1994. (*U.S. News & World Report*, 1995). Marijuana is not toxic to the body (no documented case of death exists); it has few demonstrable health risks (decline in respiratory functioning with chronic use is one); and it is more likely to inhibit, rather than incite, someone from committing acts of violence. On each point, the same could not be said of the legal drug, alcohol.

Heroin use, in and of itself, also has few health consequences (Abadinsky, 1993; Goode, 1993). The most extreme danger comes from overdosing, an effect not generally sought by the user. Overdoses are due mainly to heroin users self-administering the drug in less than controlled conditions; fluctuations in black market purity levels are common. Other health consequences stem from the impurities found in the black market product and the transmission of hepatitis and AIDS through shared needles. Being "high" on heroin does not, according to the research, predispose someone to criminal activity. Criminality, however, is highly correlated with heroin addiction; addicts often resort to crime to generate the income necessary to support their expensive habit (Inciardi, 1979; see also article 5). Remember that the price of illegal drugs results primarily from the illegality. Profits are high because of the risks of providing a black market substance. An ounce of cocaine costs $3.50 to produce in the Andes; it retails for $3,500 in Chicago. Joseph McNamara, former police chief in Kansas City and San Jose, states:

> All the cops, armies, prisons and executions in the world cannot impede a mar-
> ket with that kind of tax-free margin. It is the illegality that permits the obscene
> markup, enriching drug traffickers, distributors, dealers, crooked cops, law-
> yers, judges, politicians, bankers, businessmen. (McCarron, 1996).

Of course, that profitability is itself criminogenic in that battles over turf and supplies are frequently waged with firearms.

Examining the differing individual and societal consequences of marijuana and heroin should demonstrate the importance of placing each drug into its proper context. Drug war ideology, in fixating on the evils of illegal drugs, neglects social and psychological contexts. Zinberg (1984) developed a conceptual model that helps to re-contextualize drugs and their use by taking into account: (1) the pharmaceutical properties of the intoxicant; (2) the attitude and personality of the user (referred to as "the set"); and (3) the physical and social setting in which drug use takes place (referred to as the "setting"). Out of the three, the "setting" receives the least attention. It also has the highest potential for undermining the mythology associated with drug war thinking. As Zinberg repeatedly points out, placing drug use in its social context provides the keys to understanding how some societies and groups of people are able to have moderate rates of drug use, with low rates of drug abuse. In other words, the social group provides the key to "responsible" drug use. Current philosophy rejects any such approach. However, our brief look at alcohol advertising provides a small illustration of this type of socialization. Viewing drug issues through a social filter forces us to look beyond the possible evils of the drugs or the psychologically aberrant drug user.

Social filters help explain how once-accepted behavior can be converted to deviance. As McBride and McCoy point out in article 4, the Harrison Act of 1914 created a criminal subculture by labelling drug use a criminal act. Today most people view the use of narcotics as predominantly occurring in lower socioeconomic groups (although the heroin-related deaths of the actor River Phoenix and the rock star Kurt Cobain served to alarm the public that heroin use was an increasing danger). At the turn of the century, people addicted to legally available narcotics were most likely to be middle-aged women from a wide geographical spectrum, not limited to large urban areas. When the Harrison Act was originally passed, doctors simply prescribed maintenance dosages to their patients who were addicted. However, the police began pursuing physicians, and the Supreme Court ruled in a number of cases between 1919 and 1922 that maintenance of an addict was outside the scope of medicine and was illegal (Goode, 1993). Although those rulings were later reversed, most physicians were unwilling to risk arrest in order to treat addicts. As Erich Goode points out, officials must have been somewhat aware of the bind they had created because 44 clinics were opened to treat addicts. Having little experience, some clinics primarily dispensed drugs—which often ended up in the newly created black market. Journalists published sensational stories, the public was outraged, and prohibitionists successfully enlisted support for punitive sanctions over a medical approach (Goode, 1993). The public image of a narcotics addict was successfully transformed from white, female, middle-class dependency to criminal, immoral, and depraved.

The history of cocaine and marijuana is similar. As Lusane points out in article 2, cocaine was sold door-to-door in the late 1800s. It was distributed to employees for a productivity boost. Coca leaves were used in Coca-Cola until 1903 when they were eliminated because of expressed concerns by southerners that blacks would have access to cocaine in this form (Goode, 1993). The Harrison Act mistakenly classified cocaine as a narcotic. Marijuana was routinely used until the Hearst papers successfully linked sex and race with marijuana. As Lusane points out, hemp offered a cheap alternative for paper supply, which threatened one of the activities of the Hearst empire. Economic motives may have ignited the fire to prey on public fears for private ends.

## Where We Are

The preceding discussion briefly introduces some basic drug issues and the power of drug war ideology to obfuscate alternative ways of viewing the use of mind-altering substances. A conglomerate of varying interests, most well-intended and some not, operate collectively to sustain and promote the drug war enterprise. Viewing the drug war as "industry" (see Christie, 1994) requires distance from its myriad justifications, the rhetoric of politicians, and the cheerleading of the media (who would be reluctant to risk a sensational story by contradicting the policies of officials on whom they depend for information). This view portrays the entire enterprise as a unified industrial venture—its central purpose being its own growth—despite a failure to ameliorate the problem. Just as Harry Anslinger masterfully orchestrated the rapid growth of the Federal Bureau of Narcotics (the precursor to the Drug Enforcement Administration) through greatly exaggerated claims about the evils of certain drugs and the minorities who used them, so now we see a mutually reinforcing system of politicians, media, police, military, numerous private enterprises, corrections facilities, and others, pursuing growth relentlessly. Although some claim the drug war industry's physical and ideological power has waned in the last few years, drug wars over the course of their 100-year history have gained strength with each resurrection.

There exist "no natural limits" to the drug war industry because it is shrouded in moralism—a disgust, disdain, and fear of "drugs," their users, and their sellers (Christie, 1994:87). Even compared to crime, illicit drugs evoke a particularly virulent strain of moralism. They have come to symbolize our society's most pressing social problems; for many, our very survival depends on eradicating the drug problem.

> Does the "drug crisis"—something that many see as a reoccurring socially constructed myth—constitute an authentic threat to the state's legitimacy? Standing alone, the answer is probably not; but it is critical to recognize that the "war on drugs" symbolizes more than just the consequences of substance abuse. It carries with it and has tacitly been given responsibility for a wide range of the state's most pressing social problems such as chronic poverty, family violence, high rates of violent and property crime, gang violence, inner-city decay, a breakdown in community, and a general decay in moral standards (Kraska, 1993:196).

Drug control efforts carry tremendous symbolic clout. If the link to the issues mentioned above were substantiated, the government would be viewed as irresponsible not to pursue extreme measures to solve the problem. The link, however, is tenuous. In addition, the measures chosen—incarceration in ever-increasing numbers, employing all branches of the military both domestic and abroad, and widespread use of asset forfeiture by police—yield primarily symbolic results for politicians. Two symbiotic purposes are served: sustaining the material growth of private and public bureaucracies within the industry, and generating symbolic currency. Despite the ubiquity of the "drug problem," the urban and rural poor provide the bulk of the raw material—as is the case with the war on crime. The condemnation of the lifestyles and character of the poor comprises a powerful element in the moralistic fuel which feeds the drug war industry. The association of feared or hated groups with drugs or dangerous drugs with dangerous people has been exploited throughout this century. Drugs function perfectly as an all-purpose scapegoat for social problems (see article 3 by Brownstein).

The drug war is unique, as compared to the crime war, in that it can proactively generate an almost limitless supply of raw materials (Barnett, 1987). Imagine if the police decided to wage a crackdown on robbery—how many additional robbers do you think they could arrest in a given month? They would likely use stake-outs at key locations, waiting for a robbery to occur; logic and research prove this to have little effect on the number of arrests (Marx, 1988). Now imagine a crime in which all players engage in their criminal transaction voluntarily. The police have only to pose as one of the players—buyer, seller or supplier—and arrest those they deceive. Considering the numbers of people involved in these transactions at any given time, police can arrest users and small-time dealers with little effort—compared to victim-based crimes. Christie and others note that prison populations in the last decade have skyrocketed largely due to the crackdown on illegal drugs, not because the drug problem has worsened (Irwin and Austin, 1994). In an attempt to expedite the push for more raw material, the system has been developing a specialty area within the crime war with its own police subsystem (e.g., drug task forces), court subsystem (e.g., drug courts), and corrections subsystem (e.g., boot-camps).

The "raw materials" of proactively generated arrests have a companion benefit. Under the Comprehensive Forfeiture Act of 1984, any assets—cash, residences, vehicles, businesses, etc.—used in connection with illegal drug activity may be seized. The defendant—in a direct reversal of the innocent until proven guilty concept—must prove the assets were *not* involved. Forfeiture generates income for agencies (the DEA made 16,690 such seizures in 1993 for a total value of $680 million); it also embroils agencies in functions that are inherently contradictory and at odds with basic tenets of justice. As article 13 points out, forfeiture subordinates justice to profits.

We must not overlook, however, the interconnectedness of the wars on drugs and crime. Despite the class and race underpinnings of the criminalization of certain drugs (see Lusane), the most fundamental factor in the criminalization of any drug is the ability to create the perception that it is directly connected to "real crime." The use of drugs targeted for criminal justice action must be linked with some sort of harm to someone beyond the individual user (e.g., criminalizing smoking by accentuating the dangers of second-hand smoke). With drug-using behavior and crime behavior so closely associated, both industries flourish. As Wisotsky points out in article 15, narcotics legislation has a history of turning the screw of criminal machinery: detection, prosecution, and punishment. The unintended consequences of this approach are that it creates additional—equally insoluble—problems.

## The Participants

As mentioned earlier, federal, state and local agencies share responsibility for enforcing drug laws. Most arrests occur at the state and local levels. Federal agencies consist of four departments plus the postal service (which made 2,193 arrests for controlled substances mailed in 1993). The Department of Justice agencies include the FBI, DEA, Immigration and Naturalization Service (INS), and Marshals Service. The Controlled Substances Act granted the FBI concurrent jurisdiction with the DEA for drug-law enforcement and investigation. The DEA administrator reports to the FBI director. The FBI employs 10,075 agents who investigate 250 types of federal crimes; the DEA employs 2,800 officers who enforce regulation governing the manufacture of controlled substances, investigate narcotics violations, and engage in activities to prevent drug trafficking (Bureau of Justice Statistics, 1995). INS supports efforts to intercept drugs from other countries, and the Marshals

Service manages forfeited property and the witness protection program. The Department of Defense includes all the armed forces. The Treasury Department oversees the activities of the ATF, IRS, and Customs Service. The latter collects duties on imports and can inspect vehicles or persons crossing international boundaries without establishing probable cause. The Coast Guard is part of the Department of Transportation and can board vessels without probable cause in their efforts at drug interdiction.

Multi-agency task forces benefit from the expanded powers of federal agencies—including fewer restrictions on probable cause and wiretaps. Task forces frequently use informants, surveillance, and undercover operations (Bureau of Justice Statistics, 1995). Drug-related law enforcement activities include arrests, seizure of drugs, laboratory testing of drugs, drug education, and drug testing. In 1995, the federal drug control budget was $13.2 billion—compared to $1.5 billion in 1981. Of those monies, $5.9 billion went to the criminal justice system; $1.8 billion for international interdiction and intelligence; $2.9 billion for treatment; and $2.1 billion for education. State and local government totals exceed federal expenditures. In those budgets, police activities comprise about 26 percent of the monies; judicial and legal 9 percent; corrections 43 percent, treatment 17.5 percent, and education 3 percent.

## Results

How do we measure the results of these efforts? Do we count the number of arrests? In 1993, arrests for drug possession, sale or manufacturing reached 1.1 million. Do we count the number of prison inmates convicted of drug offenses? In 1993, 61 percent of inmates in federal prisons were there for drug convictions. In 1991, 21 percent of state prisoners were serving time for drug offenses. Women were more likely to be incarcerated for a drug offense than men (33 percent versus 21 percent); Hispanics were the most likely to serve time (33 percent) versus blacks (25 percent) and whites (12 percent) (Bureau of Justice Statistics, 1995).

Should we pay attention to the numbers of drugs seized? (Think of photographs in newspapers of large quantities of drugs being inspected by an agent.) The 1993 Bureau of Justice Statistics sourcebook of criminal justice statistics lists a number of results:

- 286 clandestine drug laboratories seized; 83 percent of them manufactured methamphetamines
- 393 million marijuana plants destroyed by DEA agents
- 133,665 pounds of cocaine; 1,590 pounds of heroin; 39 pounds of opium; 2.8 million dosage units of hallucinogens; 80.5 million units of stimulants confiscated by the DEA

- 507,249 pounds of marijuana; 175,318 pounds of cocaine; 17.9 dosage units of LSD and barbiturates seized by the Customs Service
- 48,441 pounds of marijuana; 32,313 pounds of cocaine seized by the Coast Guard

*After* enumerating all these figures, there is a notation in the report that drug seizure data should not be added together because if more than one agency participated in the operation, they *each* reported the total. (There is another reporting system, Federal-wide Drug Seizure System, which eliminates duplicate reporting.)

The results of the educational part of the budget are even more difficult to quantify. The best-known component is the DARE (Drug Abuse Resistance Education) program. Those initials appear on bumper stickers and banners across the United States. A few parental groups allege that the program uses the "touchy-feely" psychology of the 1970s to attempt social engineering in schools which should be spending their time on academic pursuits, but most accept the concept. The program consists of local police officers visiting schools for 17 weekly sessions lasting about one hour with fifth- and sixth-grade students. The National Institute of Justice commissioned a three-year, $300,000 study to evaluate the program. The Justice Department refused to accept the key finding that the program is statistically insignificant in preventing drug use (Monroe, 1994). Critics say the fifth- and sixth-graders were the wrong group to study since they rarely use drugs—yet they are the target group. As one of the researchers pointed out, without a booster session to reinforce the original program, the effects of drug-use-prevention programs decay over time.

DARE is an excellent example of the use of symbolism to reinforce attitudes. Symbols are most useful for a public that prefers simplification. Many people cannot tolerate ambiguous situations. Symbolism reassures and induces feelings of well-being. Legal and political institutions are permeated with rituals which promote conformity and reaffirm beliefs in the rationality of the system. The influence of symbolism on regulatory policy is to reassure the public that a problem is under control. Success is measured by the public's response to the ideal of the policy—not the actual consequences. DARE is the perfect program to fulfill these goals. It rallies support to "do something" about drugs (with a population that offers little resistance); it links parents, community, schools, and law enforcement. Politicians thrive on linkages with highly visible, popular programs. DARE is the ideal symbol—marked by automatic approval and legitimacy by incorporating all the traditional authority figures.

## Where Do We Go from Here?

A tourist in Amsterdam approached a police officer stationed across the street from a coffee shop where marijuana was one of the items on the menu. The tourist said, "We found out in the States that doing drugs has consequences for everyone. . . . we need values, ethics, self-discipline, denial." The officer's response after listening politely was, "What about the money spent for your war on drugs? Did it solve the problem?"

There are unquestionably harmful effects from some drug usage: physical impairments, criminal acts to pay for drugs, unsafe streets, health endangerment, possible overdoses. Is the harm balanced by the efforts to suppress? There are also harmful effects from the drug war: imprisoning people does not improve the chances that they will lead productive lives, families are separated, enormous expense on punishment eliminates resources for treatment. What price are we willing to pay for what benefits?

Is zero tolerance a realistic goal? The rhetoric feeds the zealousness of proponents while the idealistic goal stymies the search for a more workable solution. The previous discussion has sketched how illusory most aspects of the drug issue are. Article 17 reminds us that when outcomes are unpredictable, the usual choice in the face of frustration is incarceration. It disengages the decision from feedback about effectiveness. Punishment is the goal; prison is punishment; end of discussion. A spokesperson for the Amsterdam Health Service stated, "I know a country that tried to prohibit the trade of alcohol. . . . you ended up with Al Capone."

Does the current system discriminate? Those who can afford to visit a psychiatrist can obtain prescriptions; those who can't risk the criminal label for self-medication. Methadone treatment offers another example of discrimination. Studies have shown that people on methadone commit less crime, are less likely to contract AIDS, and pose less of a danger to themselves and others (Chapman, 1996a). The treatment is so regulated that it costs more than is necessary, and many addicts are so discouraged by the restrictions that they give up on the process. Currently, methadone may only be dispensed at special clinics; the addict must visit the clinic daily to obtain the treatment. Ethan Nadelman and Jennifer McNeely of the Lindesmith Center, a drug policy think tank, point out that patients in methadone maintenance may stay in treatment for 20 years and are subject to stricter supervision than convicted parolees. Critics of methadone programs claim such controls are necessary to keep methadone from reaching the black market—and because they disapprove of trading one opiate addiction for another. The National Academy of Sciences found that current policy "puts too much emphasis on protecting society *from* methadone and not enough on protecting society from the epidemics of addiction, violence and infectious diseases that methadone can help reduce" (Chapman, 1996a:21).

We have seen how fear has activated much of public concern over drugs. There is no symbol more easily linked with fear than children. Erich Goode (1993) recounts the factors contributing to a public fixation on crack babies. After the crack cocaine fears in the late 1980s, there was concern about effects on babies whose mothers used crack while pregnant. Initial findings reported devastating, seemingly irreversible conditions. The media widely published the findings accompanied by heartbreaking stories of pathetic, helpless children caught in the web of their mothers' addiction. Public response followed traditional paths—criminal penalties for transferring illicit drugs to a minor (the fetus) during pregnancy. In the early 1990s, medical evidence indicated that the original research was flawed. There had been no controls to check for the contribution of other factors, such as alcohol, tobacco, sexually transmitted diseases, malnutrition, and lack of medical care. In addition, the effects reported seemed to have no long-lasting consequences and the "crack babies" had normal development six years later. The media did not display the same fervor in reporting the facts as it had with the sensational aspects of the original research. Even if it had, what is the likelihood that distress caused to infants by alcohol consumption or smoking would elicit the same cries for criminal penalties? Goode concludes his discussion with a quotation from a doctor who partially attributed the "media hit" of crack babies to the fact that crack is not used "by people like us" (1993, p. 57).

If the punishment model isn't the answer, what is? The last three articles address possible solutions. As with any intractable problem, there is no panacea. What will be the costs and benefits of new policies to which groups? How do we balance economic costs and human casualties? Will the moral stance change to accommodate workable approaches? Will the country accept the European approach that drugs are essentially a health and social problem? Can we change our focus to treatment and to reducing the disease and crime that accompany the illegal trade in drugs?

As we mentioned at the beginning of the introduction, sorting through alternatives requires the ability to look past conditioned responses. Do drug dealers turn kids on to drugs? Most drug use is initiated by friends. Whether it is an invitation to get high together as social relaxation, an attempt to establish solidarity, to escape, to break taboos, to be rebellious, or myriad other reasons, drug use is rarely initiated by a sinister deviant attempting to criminalize the innocent. Goode (1993) points out that there may even be a hierarchy of competition—a contest of daring and bravado as in who can drink the most liquor.

In this sense, drug use is a mirror of society's emphasis on success and competition. As Robert Samuelson (1996) tells us:

> America's glories and evils are tightly fused together. The things that we vener-
> ate about America—its respect for the individual, its opportunity, its economic
> vitality, its passion for progress—also breed conditions that we despise: crime,
> family breakdown, inequality, cynicism, vulgarity and stress, to name a few.
> Naturally optimistic, Americans reject any connection between our virtues and
> vices. . . . The same emphasis on individual striving, success and liberty can also
> inhibit social control and loosen people's sense of communal obligation. Crime
> becomes just another path to "making it."

The ambivalence, hypocrisy, and irony woven through the quilt of drug issues result from the double-edged values described above. They also help explain how so moralistic a society is one of the world's most violent. An atmosphere that promotes material acquisition carries enormous potential for disappointment. Whether trying to resolve peer pressure to belong or a drug dealer's quest for profit, we cannot reduce the problem of drugs to a simplistic view of deviant behavior to be punished. If we do, our children will find the twenty-first century repeating the same mistakes as the twentieth.

Does drug use cause crime? As noted earlier, little evidence supports the contention that being under the influence of most illegal drugs (versus being under the influence of the legal drug, alcohol) predisposes people to crimi-nality. What might be the "cause" of the strong association between drugs and crime? The following articles explore the drug-crime connection, how the police and courts approach the issues, corrections/treatment, and policy. A range of approaches and perspectives are included to stimulate thinking and discourse. We hope you develop your own antennae to tune in to the propositions being presented. Is there a hidden agenda? Are the evidence and arguments presented based on a solid foundation or do they rest on assumed but unproven assumptions? The issue of drugs, crime, and justice is important and complex. It requires discerning analysis and synthesis. We hope this collection inspires you to be a well-informed participant in the debate.

## References

Abadinsky, H. (1993). "Drug Abuse: An Introduction." Chicago: Nelson-Hall Pub-
lishers.

Associated Press (1996). "Mexico Drug War Questioned." *Chicago Tribune*, March
29, Sec. 1, p. 6.

Barnett, R. (1987). "Curing the Drug-Law Addiction: The Harmful Effects of Legal
Prohibition." In *Dealing with Drugs: Consequences of Governmental Control*,
ed. R. Hamowy. San Francisco: Pacific Research Institute for Public Policy.

Bureau of Justice Statistics (1995). *Drugs and Crime Facts, 1994*. Washington, DC: U.S. Government Printing Office.

Chapman, Stephen (1996a). "Facing the Ugly Facts." *Chicago Tribune*, May 26, Sec. 1, p. 21.

———. (1996b). "The GOP's Bogus Drug Attack." *Chicago Tribune*, May 25, p. 15.

Christie, N. (1994). *Crime Control as Industry: Toward Gulags, Western Style*. New York: Routledge.

*Consumer Reports* (January 1993). "High Anxiety." New York: Consumers Union of the U.S.

Dellios, Hugh (1996). "Marijuana Licenses Backfire in Court." *Chicago Tribune*, March 11, Sec. 1, p. 4.

Feldkamp, R. H. (1995). "Heroin Use Expanding to Teens, Females and Middle-Income Americans Says New U.S. Study." *Crime Control*, 29, 11:1.

Goode, Erich (1993). *Drugs in American Society*, 4th ed. McGraw-Hill, Inc.

Inciardi, J. A. (1979). "Heroin Use and Street Crime." *Crime and Delinquency* 25:335–46.

Irwin, J. and J. Austin (1994). *It's About Time: America's Imprisonment Binge*. Belmont, CA: Wadsworth.

Kappeler, V. E.; M. Blumberg and G. W. Potter (1996). *The Mythology of Crime and Criminal Justice*, 2nd ed. Prospect Heights, IL: Waveland Press.

Knipe, Ed (1995). *Culture, Society, and Drugs*. Prospect Heights, IL: Waveland Press.

Kotulak, Ronald (1996). "Women Narrow Gender Gap in Drug, Alcohol Abuse." *Chicago Tribune*, June 6, p. 1, 30.

Kraska, P. B. (1990). "The Unmentionable Alternative: The Need for and the Argument Against the Decriminalization of Drug Laws." In *Drugs, Crime, and the Criminal Justice System*, ed. R. Weisheit. Cincinnati: Anderson Publishing.

McCarron, John (1996). "Finding the Cure." *Chicago Tribune*, January 24, p. 15.

Monroe, Sylvester (1994). "D.A.R.E. Bedeviled." *Time*, October 17, p. 49.

*Merriam Webster's Collegiate Dictionary*, 10th ed. (1995). Springfield, MA: Merriam Webster.

*National Drug Control Strategy* (1995). Washington, DC: Office of the National Drug Control Policy, Executive Office of the President.

Samuelson, Robert (1996). "In Perspective: Connecting the Social and Economic Dreams and Nightmares of America." *Chicago Tribune*, March 8, p. 17.

*U.S. News and World Report* (1995). "Kids and Marijuana: The Glamour is Back." January 2, p. 12.

Zinberg, N. E. (1984). *Drug, Set, and Setting: The Basis for Controlled Intoxicant Use*. New Haven: Yale University Press.

# 1

# Opium, Cocaine and Marijuana in American History

## David F. Musto

Dramatic shifts in attitude have characterized America's relationship to drugs. During the 19th century, certain mood-altering substances, such as opiates and cocaine, were often regarded as compounds helpful in everyday life. Gradually this perception of drugs changed. By the early 1900s, and until the 1940s, the country viewed these and some other psychoactive drugs as dangerous, addictive compounds that needed to be severely controlled. Today, after a resurgence of a tolerant attitude toward drugs during the 1960s and 1970s, we find ourselves, again, in a period of drug intolerance.

America's recurrent enthusiasm for recreational drugs and subsequent campaigns for abstinence present a problem to policymakers and to the public. Since the peaks of these episodes are about a lifetime apart, citizens rarely have an accurate or even a vivid recollection of the last wave of cocaine or opiate use.

Phases of intolerance have been fueled by such fear and anger that the record of times favorable toward drug taking has been either erased from public memory or so distorted that it becomes useless as a point of reference for policy formation. During each attack on drug taking, total denigration of the preceding, contrary mood has seemed necessary for public welfare. Although such vigorous rejection may have value in further reducing demand, the long-term effect is to destroy a realistic perception of the past and of the conflicting attitudes toward mood-altering substances that have characterized our national history.

The absence of knowledge concerning our earlier and formative encounters with drugs unnecessarily impedes the already difficult task of establishing a workable and sustainable drug policy. An examination of the period of drug use that peaked around 1900 and the decline that followed it may enable us to approach the current drug problem with more confidence and reduce the likelihood that we will repeat past errors.

Until the 19th century, drugs had been used for millennia in their natural form. Cocaine and morphine, for example, were available only in coca leaves or poppy plants that were chewed, dissolved in alcoholic beverages or taken in some way that diluted the impact of the active agent. The advent of organic chemistry in the 1800s changed the available forms of these drugs. Morphine was isolated in the first decade and cocaine by 1860; in 1874 diacetylmorphine was synthesized from morphine (although it became better known as heroin when Bayer Company introduced it in 1898).

By mid-century the hypodermic syringe was perfected, and by 1870 it had become a familiar instrument to American physicians and patients (see "The Origins of Hypodermic Medication," by Norman Howard-Jones; *Scientific American*, January 1971). At the same time, the astounding growth of the pharmaceutical industry intensified the ramifications of these accomplishments. As the century wore on, manufacturers grew increasingly adept at exploiting a marketable innovation and moving it into mass production, as well as advertising and distributing it throughout the world.

During this time, because of a peculiarity of the U.S. Constitution, the powerful new forms of opium and cocaine were more readily available in America than in most nations. Under the Constitution, individual states assumed responsibility for health issues, such as regulation of medical practice and the availability of pharmacological products. In fact, America had as many laws regarding health professions as it had states. For much of the 19th century, many states chose to have no controls at all; their legislatures reacted to the claims of contradictory health care philosophies by allowing free enterprise for all practitioners. The federal government limited its concern to communicable diseases and the provision of health care to the merchant marine and to government dependents.

Nations with a less restricted central government, such as Britain and Prussia, had a single, preeminent pharmacy law that controlled availability of dangerous drugs. In those countries, physicians had their right to practice similarly granted by a central authority. Therefore, when we consider consumption of opium, opiates, coca and cocaine in 19th-century America, we are looking at an era of wide availability and unrestrained advertising. The initial enthusiasm for the purified substances was only slightly affected by any substantial doubts or fear about safety, long-term health injuries or psychological dependence.

History encouraged such attitudes. Crude opium, alone or dissolved in some liquid such as alcohol, was brought by European explorers and settlers to North America. Colonists regarded opium as a familiar resource for pain relief. Benjamin Franklin regularly took laudanum—opium in alcohol extract—to alleviate the pain of kidney stones during the last few years of his life. The poet Samuel Taylor Coleridge, while a student at Cambridge in 1791, began using laudanum for pain and developed a lifelong addiction to the drug. Opium use in those early decades constituted an "experiment in nature" that has been largely forgotten, even repressed, as a result of the extremely negative reaction that followed.

Americans had recognized, however, the potential danger of continually using opium long before the availability of morphine and the hypodermic's popularity. The American Dispensatory of 1818 noted that the habitual use of opium could lead to "tremors, paralysis, stupidity and general emaciation." Balancing this danger, the text proclaimed the extraordinary value of opium in a multitude of ailments ranging from cholera to asthma. (Considering the treatments then in vogue—blistering, vomiting and bleeding—we can understand why opium was as cherished by patients as by their physicians.)

Opium's rise and fall can be tracked through U.S. import-consumption statistics compiled while importation of the drug and its derivative, morphine, was unrestricted and carried moderate tariffs. The per capita consumption of crude opium rose gradually during the 1800s, reaching a peak in the last decade of the century. It then declined, but after 1915 the data no longer reflect trends in drug use, because that year new federal laws severely restricted legal imports. In contrast, per capita consumption of smoking opium rose until a 1909 act outlawed its importation.

Americans had quickly associated smoking opium with Chinese immigrants who arrived here after the Civil War to work on railroad construction. This association was one of the earliest examples of a powerful theme in the American perception of drugs: linkage between a drug and a feared or rejected group within society. Cocaine would be similarly linked with blacks and marijuana with Mexicans in the first third of the 20th century. The association of a drug with a racial group or a political cause, however, is not unique to America. In the 19th century, for instance, the Chinese came to regard opium as a tool and symbol of Western domination. That perception helped to fuel a vigorous antiopium campaign in China early in the 20th century.

During the 1800s, increasing numbers of people fell under the influence of opiates—substances that demanded regular consumption or the penalty of withdrawal, a painful but rarely life-threatening experience. Whatever the cause—overprescribing by physicians, over-the-counter medicines, self-indulgence of "weak will"—opium addiction brought shame. As consumption increased, so did the frequency of addiction.

At first, neither physicians nor their patients thought that introduction of the hypodermic syringe or pure morphine contributed to the danger of addiction. On the contrary, because pain could be controlled with less morphine when injected, the presumption was made that the procedure was less likely to foster addiction.

Late in the century some states and localities enacted laws limiting morphine to a physician's prescription, and some laws even forbade refilling these prescriptions. But the absence of any federal control over interstate commerce in habit-forming drugs, of uniformity among the state laws and of effective enforcement meant that the rising tide of legislation directed at opiates—and later cocaine—was more a reflection of changing public attitude toward these drugs than an effective reduction of supplies to users. Indeed, the decline noted after the mid-1890s was probably related mostly to the public's growing fear of addiction and of the casual social use of habit-forming substances rather than to any successful campaign to reduce supplies.

At the same time, health professionals were developing more specific treatments for painful diseases, finding less dangerous analgesics (such as aspirin) and beginning to appreciate the addictive power of the hypodermic syringe. By now the public had learned to fear the careless, and possibly addicted, physician. In *A Long Day's Journey into Night*, Eugene O'Neill dramatized the painful and shameful impact of his mother's physician-induced addiction.

In a spirit not unlike that of our times, Americans in the last decade of the 19th century grew increasingly concerned about the environment, adulterated foods, destruction of the forests and the widespread use of mood-altering drugs. The concern embraced alcohol as well. The Anti-Saloon League, founded in 1893, led a temperance movement toward prohibition, which later was achieved in 1919 and became law in January 1920.

After overcoming years of resistance by over-the-counter, or patent, medicine manufacturers, the federal government enacted the Pure Food and

Drug Act in 1906. This act did not prevent sales of addictive drugs like opiates and cocaine, but it did require accurate labeling of contents for all patent remedies sold in interstate commerce. Still, no national restriction existed on the availability of opiates or cocaine. The solution to this problem would emerge from growing concern, legal ingenuity and the unexpected involvement of the federal government with the international trade in narcotics.

Responsibility for the Philippines in 1998 added an international dimension to the growing domestic alarm about drug abuse. It also revealed that Congress, if given the opportunity, would prohibit nonmedicinal uses of opium among its new dependents. Civil Governor William Howard Taft proposed reinstituting an opium monopoly—through which the previous Spanish colonial government had obtained revenue from sales to opium merchants—and using those profits to help pay for a massive public education campaign. President Theodore Roosevelt vetoed this plan, and in 1905 Congress mandated an absolute prohibition of opium for any purpose other than medicinal use.

To deal efficiently with the antidrug policy established for the Philippines, a committee from the Islands visited various territories in the area to see how others dealt with the opium problem. The benefit of controlling narcotics international became apparent.

In early 1906 China had instituted a campaign against opium, especially smoking opium, in an attempt to modernize and to make the Empire better able to cope with continued Western encroachments on its sovereignty. At about the same time, Chinese anger at maltreatment of their nationals in the United States seethed into a voluntary boycott of American goods. Partly to appease the Chinese by aiding their antiopium efforts and partly to deal with uncontrollable smuggling within the Philippine Archipelago, the United States convened a meeting of regional powers. In this way, the United States launched a campaign for worldwide narcotics traffic control that would extend through the years in an unbroken diplomatic sequence from the League of Nations to the present efforts of the United Nations.

The International Opium Commission, a gathering of 13 nations, met in Shanghai in February 1909. The Protestant Episcopal bishop of the Philippines, Charles Henry Brent, who had been instrumental in organizing the meeting, was chosen to preside. Resolutions noting problems with opium and opiates were adopted, but they did not constitute a treaty, and no decisions bound the nations attending the commission. In diplomatic parlance, what was needed now was a conference not a commission. The United States began to pursue this goal with determination.

The antinarcotics campaign in America had several motivations. Appeasement of China was certainly one factor for officials of the State Department. The department's opium commissioner, Hamilton Wright, thought the whole matter could be "used as oil to smooth the troubled water of our aggressive commercial policy there." Another reason was the belief, strongly held by the federal government today, that controlling crops and traffic in producing countries could most efficiently stop U.S. nonmedical consumption of drugs.

To restrict opium and coca production required worldwide agreement and, thus, an international conference. After intense diplomatic activity, one was convened in the Hague in December 1911. Brent again presided, and on January 23, 1912, the 12 nations represented signed a convention. Provision was made for the other countries to comply before the treaty was brought into force. After all, no producing or manufacturing nation wanted to leave the market open to nonratifying nations.

The convention required each country to enact domestic legislation controlling narcotics trade. The goal was a world in which narcotics were restricted to medicinal use. Both the producing and consuming nations would have control over their boundaries.

After his return from Shanghai, Wright labored to craft a comprehensive federal antinarcotics law. In his path loomed the problem of states' rights. The health professions were considered a major cause of patient addiction. Yet how could federal law interfere with the prescribing practices of physicians or require that pharmacists keep records? Wright settled on the federal government's power to tax; the result, after prolonged bargaining with pharmaceutical, import, export and medical interests, was the Harrison Act of December 1914.

Representative Francis Burton Harrison's association with the act was an accidental one, the consequence of his introduction of the administration's bill. If the chief proponent and negotiator were to be given eponymic credit, it should have been called the Wright Act. It could even have been called a second Mann Act, after Representative James Mann, who saw the bill through to passage in the House of Representatives, for by that time Harrison had become governor-general of the Philippines.

The act required a strict accounting of opium and coca and their derivatives from entry into the United States to dispensing to a patient. To accomplish this control, a small tax had to be paid at each transfer, and permits had to be obtained by applying to the Treasury Department. Only the patient paid no tax, needed no permit and, in fact, was not allowed to obtain one.

Initially Wright and the Department of Justice argued that the Harrison Act forbade indefinite maintenance of addiction unless there was a specific medical reason such as cancer or tuberculosis. This interpretation was rejected in 1916 by the Supreme Court—even though the Justice Department argued that the Harrison Act was the domestic implementation of the Hague Opium Convention and therefore took precedence over states' rights. Maintenance was to be allowed.

That decision was short-lived. In 1919 the Supreme Court, led by Oliver Wendell Holmes and Louis Brandeis, changed its mind by a 5–4 vote. The court declared that indefinite maintenance for "mere addiction" was outside legitimate medical practice and that, consequently, prohibiting it did not constitute interference with a state's right to regulate physicians. Second, because the person receiving the drugs for maintenance was not a bona fide patient but just a recipient of drugs, the transfer of narcotics defrauded the government of taxes required under the Harrison Act.

During the 1920s and 1930s, the opiate problem, chiefly morphine and heroin, declined in the United States, until much of the problem was confined to the periphery of society and the outcasts of urban areas. There were exceptions: some health professionals and a few others of middle class or higher status continued to take opiates.

America's international efforts continued. After World War I, the British and U.S. governments proposed adding the Hague Convention to the Versailles Treaty. As a result, ratifying the peace treaty meant ratifying the Hague Convention and enacting a domestic law controlling narcotics. This incorporation led to the British Dangerous Drugs Act of 1920, an act often misattributed to a raging heroin epidemic in Britain. In the 1940s some Americans argued that the British system provided heroin to addicts and, by not relying on law enforcement, had almost eradicated the opiate problem. In fact, Britain had no problem to begin with. This argument serves as an interesting example of how the desperate need to solve the drug problem in the United States tends to create misperceptions of a foreign drug situation.

The story of cocaine use in America is somewhat shorter than that of opium, but it follows a similar plot. In 1884 purified cocaine became commercially available in the United States. At first the wholesale cost was very high—$5 to $10 a gram—but it soon fell to 25 cents a gram and remained there until the price inflation of World War I. Problems with cocaine were evident almost from the beginning, but popular opinion and the voices of leading medical experts depicted cocaine as a remarkable, harmless stimulant.

William A. Hammond, one of America's most prominent neurologists, extolled cocaine in print and lectures. By 1887 Hammond was assuring audiences that cocaine was no more habit-forming than coffee or tea. He also told them of the "cocaine wine" he had perfected with the help of a New York druggist: two grains of cocaine to a pint of wine. Hammond claimed that this tonic was far more effective than the popular French coca wine, probably a reference to Vin Mariani, which he complained had only a half a grain of cocaine to the pint.

Coca-Cola was also introduced in 1886 as a drink offering the advantages of coca but lacking the danger of alcohol. It amounted to a temperance coca beverage. The cocaine was removed in 1900, a year before the city of Atlanta, Georgia, passed an ordinance (and a state statute the following year) prohibiting provision of any cocaine to a consumer without a prescription.

Cocaine is one of the most powerful of the central nervous system euphoriants. This fact underlaid cocaine's quickly growing consumption and the ineffectiveness of the early warnings. How could anything that made users so confident and happy be bad? Within a year of cocaine's introduction, the Parke-Davis Company provided coca and cocaine in 15 forms, including coca cigarettes, cocaine for injection and cocaine for sniffing. Parke-Davis and at least one other company also offered consumers a handy cocaine kit. (The Parke-Davis kit contained a hypodermic syringe.) The firm proudly supplied a drug that, it announced, "can supply the place of food, make the coward brave, the silent eloquent and . . . render the sufferer insensitive to pain."

Cocaine spread rapidly throughout the nation. In September 1886 a physician in Puyallup, Washington Territory, reported an adverse reaction to cocaine during an operation. Eventually reports of overdoses and idiosyncratic reactions shifted to accounts of the social and behavioral effects of long-term cocaine use. The ease with which experimenters became regular users and the increasing instances of cocaine being linked with violence and paranoia gradually took hold in popular and medical thought.

In 1907 an attempt was made in New York State to shift the responsibility for cocaine's availability from the open market to medical control. Assemblyman Alfred E. Smith, later the governor of New York and in 1928 the Democratic party's presidential candidate, sponsored such a bill. The cost of cocaine on New York City streets, as revealed by newspaper and police accounts after the law's enactment, was typically 25 cents a packet, or "deck."

Although 25 cents may seem cheap, it was actually slightly higher than the average industrial wage at that time, which was about 20 cents an hour. Packets, commonly glycine envelopes, usually contained one to two grains (65 to 130 milligrams), or about a tenth of a gram. The going rate was roughly 10 times that of the wholesale price, a ratio not unlike recent cocaine street prices, although in the past few years, the street price has actually been lower in real value than what it was in 1910.

Several similar reports from the years before the Harrison Act of 1914 suggest that both the profit margin and the street price of cocaine were unaffected by the legal availability of cocaine from a physician. Perhaps the formality of medical consultation and the growing antagonism among physicians and the public toward cocaine helped to sustain the illicit market.

In 1910 William Howard Taft, then president of the United States, sent to Congress a report that cocaine posed the most serious drug problem America had ever faced. Four years later President Woodrow Wilson signed into law the Harrison Act, which, in addition to its opiate provisions, permitted the sale of cocaine only through prescriptions. It also forbade any trace of cocaine in patent remedies, the most severe restriction on any habit-forming drug to that date. (Opiates, including heroin, could still be present in small amounts in nonprescription remedies, such as cough medicines.)

Although the press continued to reveal Hollywood scandals and underworld cocaine practices during the 1920s, cocaine use gradually declined as a societal problem. The laws probably hastened the trend, and certainly the tremendous public fear reduced demand. By 1930 the New York City Mayor's Committee on Drug Addiction was reporting that "during the last 20 years cocaine as an addiction has ceased to be a problem."

Unlike opiates and cocaine, marijuana was introduced during a period of drug intolerance. Consequently, it was not until the 1960s, 40 years after marijuana cigarettes had arrived in America, that it was widely used. The practice of smoking cannabis leaves came to the United States with Mexican immigrants, who had come North during the 1920s to work in agriculture, and it soon extended to white and black jazz musicians.

As the Great Depression of the late 1930s settled over America, the immigrants became an unwelcome minority linked with violence and with growing and smoking marijuana. Western states pressured the federal government to control marijuana use. The first official response was to urge adoption of a uniform state antinarcotics law. Then a new approach became feasible in 1937, when the Supreme Court upheld the National Firearms Act. This act prohibited the transfer of machine guns between private citizens without purchase of a transfer tax stamp—and the government would not issue the necessary stamp. Prohibition was implemented through the taxing power of the federal government.

Within a month of the Supreme Court's decision, the Treasury Department testified before Congress for a bill to establish a marijuana transfer tax. The bill became law, and until the Comprehensive Drug Abuse Act of 1970, marijuana was legally controlled through a transfer tax for which no stamps or licenses were available to private citizens. Certainly some people were smoking marijuana in the 1930s, but not until the 1960s was its use widespread.

Around the time of the Marihuana Tax Act of 1937, the federal government released dramatic and exaggerated portrayals of marijuana's effects. Scientific publications during the 1930s also fearfully described marijuana's dangers. Even Walter Bromberg, who thought that marijuana made only a small contribution to major crimes, nevertheless reported the drug was "a primary stimulus to the impulsive life with direct expression in the motor field."

Marijuana's image shifted during the 1960s, when it was said that its use at the gigantic Woodstock gathering kept peace—as opposed to what might have happened if alcohol had been the drug of choice. In the shift to drug toleration in the late 1960s and early 1970s, investigators found it difficult to associate health problems with marijuana use. The 1930s and 1940s had marked the nadir of drug toleration in the United States, and possibly the mood of both times affected professional perception of this controversial plant.

After the Harrison Act, the severity of federal laws concerning the sale and possession of opiates and cocaine gradually rose. As drug use declined, penalties increased until 1956, when the death penalty was introduced as an option by the federal government for anyone older than 18 providing heroin to anyone younger than 18 (apparently no one was ever executed under this statute). At the same time, mandatory minimum prison sentences were extended to 10 years.

After the youthful counterculture discovered marijuana in the 1960s, demand for the substance grew until about 1978, when the favorable attitude toward it reached a peak. In 1972 the Presidential Commission on Marihuana and Drug Abuse recommended "decriminalization" of marijuana, that is, legal possession of a small amount for personal use. In 1977 the Carter administration formally advocated legalizing marijuana in amounts up to an ounce.

The Gallup Poll on relaxation of laws against marijuana is instructive. In 1980, 53 percent of Americans favored legalization of small amounts of marijuana; by 1986 only 27 percent supported that view. At the same time, those favoring penalties for marijuana use rose from 43 to 67 percent. This reversal parallels the changes in attitude among high school students revealed by the Institute of Social Research at the University of Michigan.

The decline in favorable attitudes toward marijuana that began in the late 1970s continues. In the past few years we have seen penalties rise again against users and dealers. The recriminalization of marijuana possession by popular vote in Alaska in 1990 is one example of such a striking reversal.

In addition to stricter penalties, two other strategies, silence and exaggeration, were implemented in the 1930s to keep drug use low and prevent a recurrence of the decades-long, frustrating and fearful antidrug battle of the late 19th and early 20th centuries. Primary and secondary schools instituted educational programs against drugs. Then policies shifted amid fears that talking about cocaine or heroin to young people, who now had less exposure to drugs, would arouse their curiosity. This concern led to a decline in drug-related information given during school instruction as well as to the censorship of motion pictures.

The Motion Picture Association of America, under strong public and religious pressure, decided in 1934 to refuse a seal of approval for any film that showed narcotics. This prohibition was enforced with one exception—*To the*

*Ends of the Earth*, a 1948 film that lauded the Federal Bureau of Narcotics—until *Man with a Golden Arm* was successfully exhibited in 1956 without a seal.

Associated with a decline in drug information was a second, apparently paradoxical strategy: exaggerating the effects of drugs. The middle ground was abandoned. In 1924 Richmond P. Hobson, a nationally prominent campaigner against drugs, declared that one ounce of heroin could addict 2,000 persons. In 1936 an article in the *American Journal of Nursing* warned that a marijuana user "will suddenly turn with murderous violence upon whomever is nearest to him. He will run amuck with knife, axe, gun, or anything else that is close at hand, and will kill or main without any reason."

A goal of this well-meaning exaggeration was to describe drugs so repulsively that anyone reading or hearing of them would not be tempted to experiment with the substances. One contributing factor to such a publicity campaign, especially regarding marijuana, was that the Depression permitted little money for any other course of action.

Severe penalties, silence and, if silence was not possible, exaggeration became the basic strategies against drugs after the decline of their first wave of use. But the effect of these tactics was to create ignorance and false images that would present no real obstacle to a renewed enthusiasm for drugs in the 1960s. At the time, enforcing draconian and mandatory penalties would have filled to overflowing all jails and prisons with the users of marijuana alone.

Exaggeration fell in the face of the realities of drug use and led to a loss of credibility regarding any government pronouncement on drugs. The lack of information erased any awareness of the first epidemic, including the gradually obtained and hard-won public insight into the hazards of cocaine and opiates. Public memory, which would have provided some context for the antidrug laws, was a casualty of the antidrug strategies.

The earlier and present waves of drug use have much in common, but there is at least one major difference. During the first wave of drug use, antidrug laws were not enacted until the public demanded them. In contrast, today's most severe antidrug laws were on the books from the outset; this gap between law and public opinion made the controls appear ridiculous and bizarre. Our current frustration over the laws' ineffectiveness has been greater and more lengthy than before because we have lived through many years in which antidrug laws lacked substantial public support. Those laws appeared powerless to curb the rise in drug use during the 1960s and 1970s.

The first wave of drug use involved primarily opiates and cocaine. The nation's full experience with marijuana is now under way (marijuana's tax regulation in 1937 was not the result of any lengthy or broad experience with the plant). The popularity and growth in demand for opiates and cocaine in mainstream society derived from a simple factor: the effect on most people's physiology and emotions was enjoyable. Moreover, Americans have recurrently hoped that the technology of drugs would maximize their personal potential. That opiates could relax and cocaine energize seemed wonderful opportunities for fine-tuning such efforts.

Two other factors allowed a long and substantial rise in consumption during the 1800s. First, casualties accumulate gradually; not everyone taking cocaine or opiates becomes hooked on the drug. In the case of opiates, some users have become addicted for a lifetime and have still been productive.

Yet casualties have mounted as those who could not handle occasional use have succumbed to domination by drugs and by drug-seeking behavior. These addicts become not only miserable themselves but also frightening to their families and friends. Such cases are legion today in our larger cities, but the percentage of those who try a substance and acquire a dependence or get into serious legal trouble is not 100 percent. For cocaine, the estimate varies from 3 to 20 percent, or even higher, and so it is a matter of time before cocaine is recognized as a likely danger.

Early in the cycle, when social tolerance prevails, the explanation for casualties is that those who succumb to addiction are seen as having a physiological idiosyncrasy or "foolish trait." Personal disaster is thus viewed as an exception to the rule. Another factor minimizing the sense of risk is our belief in our own invulnerability—that general warnings do not include us. Such faith reigns in the years of greatest exposure to drug use, ages 15 to 25. Resistance to a drug that makes a user feel confident and exuberant takes many years to permeate a society as large and complex as the United States.

The interesting question is not why people take drugs, but rather why they stop taking them. We perceive risk differently as we begin to reject drugs. One can perceive a hypothetical 3 percent risk from taking cocaine as an assurance of 97 percent safety, or one can react as if told that 3 percent of New York/Washington shuttle flights crash. Our exposure to drug problems at work, in our neighborhood and within our families shifts our perception, gradually shaking our sense of invulnerability.

Cocaine has caused the most dramatic change in estimating risk. From a grand image as the ideal tonic, cocaine's reputation degenerated into that of the most dangerous of drugs, linked in our minds with stereotypes of mad, violent behavior. Opiates have never fallen so far in esteem, nor were they repressed to the extent cocaine had been between 1930 and 1970.

Today we are experiencing the reverse of recent decades, when the technology of drug use promised an extension of our natural potential. Increasingly we see drug consumption as reducing what we could achieve on our own with healthy food and exercise. Our change of attitude about drugs is connected to our concern over air pollution, food adulteration and fears for the stability of the environment.

Ours is an era not unlike that early in this century, when Americans made similar efforts at self-improvement accompanied by an assault on habit-forming drugs. Americans seem to be the least likely of any people to accept the inevitability of historical cycles. Yet if we do not appreciate our history, we may again become captive to the powerful emotions that led to draconian penalties, exaggeration or silence.

## Further Reading

*American Diplomacy and the Narcotics Traffic, 1900–1939.* Arnold H. Taylor. Duke University Press, 1969.

*Drugs in America: A Social History, 1800–1980.* H. Wayne Morgan. Syracuse University Press, 1981.

*Dark Paradise: Opiate Addiction in America Before 1940.* David T. Courtwright. Harvard University Press, 1982.

*The American Disease: Origins of Narcotic Control.* Expanded Edition. David F. Musto. Oxford University Press, 1987.

America's First Cocaine Epidemic. David F. Musto in *Wilson Quarterly*, pages 59–65; Summer 1989.

Illicit Price of Cocaine in Two Eras: 1908–14 and 1982–89. David F. Musto in *Connecticut Medicine*, Vol. 54, No. 6, pages 321–326; June 1990.

**2**

# Racism and the Drug Crisis

## Clarence Lusane

*. . . around the country, politicians, public officials, and even many police officers and judges say, the nation's war on drugs has in effect become a war on Black people.*

—Ron Harris, journalist[1]

While the facts show that the majority of drug users and drug profiteers are White, the nation and the world are bombarded with images of young Black males who are handcuffed, lying on the ground dead, or herded behind prison walls—all due to trafficking or abuse of illegal drugs. The racist myth is that most inner-city, young Black males are gun-toting, crack-smoking criminals-in-waiting. From the days of slavery to the trumped-up cases of the Scottsboro boys and the Willmington Ten, to the death by a White mob of Yusef Hawkins in New York, the very presence of young Black males is seen as a threat to White society. This perspective, repeated in countless ways, is an objective truth for many schoolteachers, judges, police officers, politicians, and journalists.

Reprinted by permission of South End Press, Boston, from *Pipe Dream Blues: Racism and the War on Drugs* © 1990.

Although the incidence of trafficking and drug abuse is relatively the same for Blacks and Whites, their resources and political capacity to confront the problem differ. Inner-city and poor communities, disproportionately people of color, are locked into a cycle of poverty, illegal drug trafficking and abuse, and increased poverty.

The question of political power becomes essential because illegal drugs have such a powerful economic and social impact in these communities. Efforts to address problems, such as Black-on-Black crime and AIDS, are shaped by the political perspectives of those who seek to address them. While observers from either end of the political spectrum would agree that Black-on-Black crime, of which the current drug crisis is the most representative expression, is one of the most serious issues facing African Americans, few would agree on its causes, impact, and resolution.

Conservatives, both Black and White, argue that a moral revival is needed to reestablish the kinds of values that would prohibit drugs in the Black community. From their perspective, primary concern for the victim necessitates more prisons in which to house drug dealers who prey on the Black community. Many conservatives argue that crime causes poverty. Businesses are hesitant to locate in high-crime areas, they argue, and residents in these areas are intimidated from participating in crime-fighting, community-building projects. Leading conservative voices from Thomas Sowell to Robert Woodson have stated that Black civil rights leaders benefit from the perpetuation of poverty and, therefore, intend to do very little to eliminate it.

At first glance, this line of reasoning may seem compelling and attractive. Surely, the values of community and charity have disappeared in many of our neighborhoods, Black and White. Individuals must take responsibility for their actions, as conservatives demand, and all the racism in the world does not excuse the brutal gunning down of a sixty-five-year-old grandmother in order to get money to buy drugs, or the rape of a fifteen-year-old junior high school student by a drug dealer seeking payment. But for conservative thinkers, jail and "just say no" slogans are adequate and appropriate responses to the danger posed by drug traffickers and drug users.

Their answers are inadequate to resolving a situation that in many sectors of the Black community has developed over generations: the culture and material reality of poverty. The reproduction of self-destructive behavior was neither sudden nor benign. After years of facing brutality, conscious divide-and-conquer political tactics, and marginalization into depressed communities, Black Americans have developed a conditioned response. For every strong individual who has risen above those conditions, many more did not and could not. While many have chosen not to sell or abuse drugs, too often drug dealing is the only means of economic or mental survival.

While it is difficult to pinpoint why a particular individual abuses drugs, many addiction experts target a low level of self-esteem as a critical factor. In recent history, intellectuals such as Karl Marx and Richard Wright have noted that the crushing impact of poverty leads to alienation and low self-esteem. Consequently, when a whole community faces this condition, in an atmosphere that promotes identity through material consumption, social deterioration becomes inevitable. Alienation shatters the spirit and destroys the ability to love oneself and others. The escalation of violence and the devaluation of life is rooted in the isolation and nihilism symptomatic of our consumer society.

Former California assemblywoman and activist Maxine Waters, now a member of Congress, speaks to the conservatives' flawed analysis. She writes,

> In the face of this horror story, we have the rationalizations of police and national officials that the "disintegration of the family" or "lack of values" are responsible for what is the colossal failure of local and federal officials to wage an effective war against drugs—one in which the strategy of prevention would be clearly defined and underwritten by the necessary resources in money and man- and womanpower and coordinated with respected community activists capable of contributing to the detection and apprehension of those who prey on the community from within and without.[2]

With an amazing blindness, conservatives of all colors dismiss a long history of denial of opportunity and resources to the poor sectors of the Black community. They refuse to acknowledge that whole generations are being victimized by systemic factors. They have abandoned hope that the loss of so many young Black males to drugs and violence is preventable.

Beverly Coleman-Miller, special assistant to the Commissioner of Public Health in Washington, D.C., dramatically points out that in the District of Columbia, a young Black male is dying every sixteen-to-twenty hours.[3] Such figures are socially determined and socially driven. In 1969, the National Commission on the Causes and Prevention of Violence astutely wrote,

> To be young, poor, male; to be undereducated and without means of escape from an oppressive urban environment; to want what society claims is available (but mostly to others); to see around oneself illegitimate and often violent methods being used to achieve material success; and to observe others using these means with impunity—all this is to be burdened with an enormous set of influences that pull many toward crime and delinquency. To be also Black, Puerto Rican or Mexican-American and subject to discrimination adds considerably to the pull.[4]

If we are to rescue the generations of Black and Latino youth and the inner-city poor who are the most trapped in the ravages and destructiveness of the drug lifestyle, we need to first grasp the historic development of drug trafficking and abuse. What has been popularly described as a boom in drug trafficking and abuse in the Black community, as one writer put it, can more rightfully be called an echo of the past.

# In the Beginning

In traditional African cultures, as in most of the rest of the world, alcohol use was common. Palm wine was a regular part of the diet, an important part of community and of medical use against measles and dysentery. It was also used as a medium of exchange. Traditions dictated when, where, how, and how much alcohol was consumed. Natural substances, such as kola nuts and guinea corn, were used as intoxicants, but with moderation.[5] In southern Africa, marijuana was used as an intoxicant as well as for other purposes. It was used by women to ease childbirth and as an ingredient in breads and soups. It is speculated that the plant was probably brought to the Mozambique region by Arab traders centuries ago.[6]

The link between deadly drugs and African Americans began in the era of the slave trade. During the seventeenth, eighteenth, and nineteenth centuries, many of the companies that controlled the trafficking of slaves from Africa to the New World, such as the British East India Company, were also the companies that would later come to dominate the world's opium trade.[7]

Large-scale production of sugar led to the development of molasses and rum. Rum became a key part of the triangular slave trade that took ships carrying captured Africans from West Africa to the Caribbean and North America in exchange for raw materials and commodities produced by the colonies that were then taken to Europe, where they were sold for large profits. Rum exports from the Caribbean islands grew from 58,000 gallons in 1721 to more than two million gallons by 1765.[8] The sales from rum accounted for one-quarter of all products sold from the islands. New England rum traders eventually monopolized the trade, however, and by 1770 controlled four-fifths of all exports to Europe and Africa.[9] Rum was traded to Black slave dealers in exchange for the captured Africans. This noxious and ruinous type of trading became so popular that two distilleries were opened at Liverpool just to provide rum to dealers going to Africa.[10] In addition to its value as a commodity, traders often gave rum to Black dealers to get them drunk, making it easier to swindle and cheat them.

Portuguese slave trafficking gave rise to tobacco addiction on the part of Africans on the West Coast. In Guinea, for example, slave traders would sell captured Blacks for as little as six or seven seventy-five-pound rolls of Brazilian tobacco.[11] By the late seventeenth century, addiction was so pervasive that a slave or a farm animal could be traded for as little as a single length of twisted leaf.[12]

Slaves found alcohol easy to obtain or make despite laws forbidding alcohol consumption. Yet African patterns of consumption, marked by moderation, persisted during slavery. According to Eugene D. Genovese in *Roll Jordan Roll: The World the Slaves Made*:

> Slaves maintained relative sobriety, especially when compared to Whites and Indians of the period. Slaves neither often drank to excess nor acted upon their knowledge of the narcotic effects of hemp. Rarely, apart from holiday frolics, at which getting drunk became a test of manhood for the young men, did widespread drunkenness occur among slaves, although it did among masters, overseers, and neighboring poor Whites.[13]

This view contradicts the views propagated by slave owners that drinking was a serious problem among slaves. Researcher Denise Herd writes that "the rhetoric of slave holders emphasizing the problems of Black drinking must be seen as a function of social and political reality rather than as a reflection of actual conditions. The legal measures prohibiting Blacks from using alcohol were a means of asserting social dominance and an attempt to tighten social control mechanisms in order to preserve the tenuous institution of slavery."[14]

In the seventeenth century, African slaves brought the hemp plant, which produces marijuana, with them to the New World, where it grew wild and plentiful in Jamaica and other countries, including the United States.[15] Hemp was widely used in colonial America to produce many products, from paper to clothes to rope. To what extent marijuana was used by slaves is not well documented; but given their knowledge of the plant, it probably was used as an intoxicant at certain ceremonies or rituals.

For more than two centuries, hemp was one of the most important crops in the United States. In 1619, generally noted as the year the African slave trade began in the United States, the Jamestown colony in Virginia passed a law forcing farmers to grow hemp.[16] Both George Washington and Thomas Jefferson cultivated the plant.[17] Hemp was legal tender from 1631 up until the 1800s. A number of areas were so dominated by the plant that they named themselves after it—such as Hempstead, Long Island; Hempstead County, Arkansas; and Hempstead County, Texas.[18]

Although hemp grew all over the South, Kentucky and Missouri were the chief growing areas. Slaves were forced to plant and harvest this valuable product. The buds, roots, stems, seeds, and leaves were all commonly used ingredients in hundreds of medicines that were prescribed for ailments such as asthma, glaucoma, nausea, tumors, epilepsy, back pain, insomnia, and stress. Ship sails, ropes, food oils, textiles, paints, and many other products were made from hemp by slaves.[19]

In other parts of the country, natural intoxicants were used by native people mainly, but not solely, for religious and spiritual purposes. For example, indigenous people in the Western hemisphere had used peyote, a hallucinogenic plant, for centuries. The use of peyote and other plants came under attack with the introduction of alcohol.

Guns, diseases, and alcohol were used by White colonialists in the war to conquer Indian lands. Just as tobacco and opium addiction were used against the Africans and Chinese, respectively, alcoholism was introduced among Indians and became a problem among the poorer and nomadic tribes. Researchers believe that while alcoholism among Indians was not initially genetic, heredity was a key factor in their susceptibility to addiction. Indians produced less of the enzymes that break down alcohol and, therefore, were more susceptible to alcoholism.[20]

In the mid-1800s, the biggest drug problem facing the American population was opiate addiction. Due to the wide dissemination of opium derivatives, including laudanum, morphine, codeine, and other drugs as medicine, many people became "medical" addicts. During the Civil War, for example, many of the injured soldiers who were injected with morphine to ease pain became addicted. This addiction became so widespread that it became known as the "Soldier's Illness."[21]

The medical profession used opium, morphine, and codeine in its medicines as painkillers and relaxers. In the era before nonaddictive painkillers such as aspirin and bufferins, opiates were the only relief available and were broadly distributed to the ill and infirm, especially the elderly. In addition, many older, middle-class White women who could afford prescribed medicine became addicts. It did not take long before many thousands of addicts were created. One out of every 400 people in the United States was addicted to opium derivatives. It was estimated that about 250,000 people were addicted to opiates by 1900.[22]

In the nineteenth century, in the years following slavery, few references to Black drug use can be found. There certainly was no evidence of disproportionate use or of significant abuse among Blacks.

Surveys and studies done at the end of the last century concluded that most opiate users (morphine, heroin, etc.) came from the middle and upper classes. An 1885 Iowa study stated that the majority of opiate users "are to be found among the educated and most honored and useful members of society." In 1889, a survey of druggists and physicians reached the same conclusion. Both druggists and physicians reported that the middle and upper classes comprised the overwhelming bulk of their customers and patients.

During this period, users also tended to be middle-aged or older. An 1880 Chicago study reported that the average age for male opium users was 41.4 years of age and for women 39.4 years. The Chicago study also concluded that female users outnumbered male users three to one. The 1885 Iowa study reached a similar conclusion with its estimate that women were 63.8 percent of all opiate users.[23]

In the 1850s, when many Chinese came to the United States in response to the gold rush in California, there was little record of opium use. A significant amount of this first wave of Chinese came from the merchant class and engaged in commerce. By 1852, Chinese immigrants had investments of more than two million dollars in California. The growing wealth of Chinese small businesses and manufacturing enterprises threatened White businesses. A second wave of Chinese came to the United States in the 1860s and 1870s to work on the railroads. Some Chinese were even brought to Mississippi to work in the rice fields to displace Black sharecroppers. As the economic downturn of the mid-1870s grew worse and wages fell, White laborers began to see Chinese laborers as competition for scarce jobs. It was in this period that opium use began. It was mainly the poor Chinese who smoked opium, and its use was encouraged by the Chinese merchant class. As the small merchants began to suffer from the economic recession of the 1870s, they turned to prostitution, gambling, and drugs as critical sources of income.[24]

It did not take long for racial prejudice against the Chinese to arise and for their drug use to become a target. A number of racist laws were passed, including the Chinese Exclusion Act of 1882. In 1887, the federal government outlawed opium importation and smoking among Chinese Americans, although White citizens had no such restrictions.[25]

England had its own opiate abuse problem. In England, opium use affected all classes, but especially the impoverished working class crowded into cities. Karl Marx wrote in *Capital* about the horrific rate of death of working-class children—26,000 per 100,000 in 1861—partially due to the habits of parents of "dosing with opiates" their ill children.[26]

At the turn of the twentieth century, opiate addiction in the United States was to some degree fueled by the domestic production of opium. Opium was legally and abundantly grown in the United States in the eighteenth and nineteenth centuries. At least ten states cultivated the crop, including Vermont, Connecticut, California, Arizona, Virginia, Tennessee, South Carolina, Georgia, Florida, and Louisiana.[27]

Along with the morphine and opium addicts, there was an increasing number of cocaine users. Its use for illicit and pleasurable purposes was small and initially restricted to lower-class White males and Chinese immigrants. Cocaine use expanded dramatically as cocaine found its way into many commercial products.[28]

According to drug historian Dr. David Musto, pure cocaine was first taken from the coca plant by Austrian chemist Albert Niemann in 1860.[29] U.S. physicians, and Dr. Sigmund Freud, at first thought that cocaine could be used to cure morphine and alcohol addiction. The medical profession and astute commercial interests saw the financial potential of capitalizing on cocaine's energy-enhancing properties.

In the late 1800s, pharmaceutical companies, many of which have grown to become some of the large corporations of today, became involved in the importation and dispensation of cocaine and its by-products; these included Squibb, Merck, and Parke Davis. Merck sold Sigmund Freud his first gram of cocaine for $1.27. Rather than just rely on unknown importers, the Parke Davis company sent botanist Dr. H. H. Rusby to Bolivia to purchase coca leaves directly. Rusby is credited with first coming up with the idea of refining the cocaine at its source and then shipping the more portable product to the United States. He later wrote a book, *Jungle Memories*, on his experiences.[30]

Unconstrained by any regulations, salesmen sold cocaine door-to-door. It was often distributed free by employers to their workers to give them a productivity boost. The American Hay Fever Association made cocaine its official remedy due to the product's ability to drain the sinuses. By 1885, cocaine-based products were being sold as cigarettes, inhalants, crystals, tablets, ointments, sprays, teas, and liquor. Coca wines and soft drinks containing cocaine appeared, such as the legendary Coca-Cola and other soft drink brands with provocative names such as Rocco Cola, Koca Nola, Nerv Ola, and Dope.[31]

Coca-Cola originally contained not only cocaine, but an extract of the African kola nut that also had intoxicating properties. By the time of the 1906 Pure Food and Drug Act, Coca-Cola was being made from decocainized coca leaves; that is, the cocaine alkaloid was removed.[32]

As the importation of opium, morphine, and cocaine increased, and their distribution within the country expanded, harmful addictions to these drugs became too obvious to ignore. By 1900, the first mass anti-drug campaign was in full swing. The major targets of the first anti- drug campaign were rural White males, the largest group of addicts and users; immigrant groups, in particular Chinese opium smokers; and, as the campaign grew, southern Blacks. The first federal anti-drug law, passed on February 14, 1902, was somewhat bewildering, but indicative of things to come. The law made it a punishable offense to supply opium for nonmedical purposes to any aboriginal native of any Pacific island lying between the 20- degree north and 40-degree south latitude, and between 120-degree east and 120-degree west longitude. The law, however, only applied to islands "not in the possession of any civilized power," revealing that addiction was not the lawmakers' only motivation.[33] It wasn't long, though, before the anti-drug campaigns started in earnest.

The American Pharmaceutical Association, pharmacist organizations, and drug companies at first fought any effort at regulation and reform. When it became clear that regulation of drugs was inevitable, these groups success- fully sought to shape the new laws. After much fighting, a compromise was reached and, in May 1906, Congress passed the District of Columbia Phar- macy Act, the first federal drug control law.

In June 1906, Congress passed the Pure Food and Drug Act, requiring manufacturers to list addictive drugs contained in their products. The law was apparently successful, for within a few years sales of those products dropped by one-third.[34]

Within a few years, Washington, D.C. would become the center of both the national and international war against opium. In 1909, President Theodore Roosevelt appointed Washington, D.C.-based physician Dr. Hamilton Wright to lead a commission to an international conference on stopping the opium trade in Asia. The administration's political goal was to increase the U.S. influence in the Far East.

Wright created the strongest anti-drug regulations ever in the United States and earned the title "Father of America's Drug Laws." According to Musto, Wright felt that the United States had to set an example of strident anti-drug laws in order to convince other nations to do the same. In order to accomplish this goal, Wright used two dishonest but successful tactics: he exaggerated addiction figures and played on the racism of Whites.[35] Although the number of opium addicts was shrinking, as was the importation of opiates, Wright used wildly inflated figures to scare Congress and the nation. Most of the older addicts, many of whom were Civil War veterans, were dying, as were the doctors who relied on opiate remedies. Wright sup- pressed this information.[36]

In 1910, he issued his *Report on the International Opium Commission*. This report was noteworthy not only for its blown-up figures, but also for its racist myths and lies about drug use among Blacks. The document described in hor- rifying detail the supposed superhuman strength and extreme madness expe- rienced by Blacks on cocaine, and explained that cocaine drove Black men to rape.[37] Rumors circulated at the time went so far as to claim that cocaine made African Americans bullet proof.[38] Contrary to the report, no evidence exists of disproportionate opiate use among Blacks in the nineteenth century or the early part of the twentieth century. In fact, studies done in Florida and Tennessee around the time of World War I found a lower proportion of opi- ate use for Blacks than for Whites.[39]

Yet, article after article appeared that claimed that Blacks were using cocaine at alarming levels. One article that was written in a medical journal complained about the "disastrous use of cocaine among the negroes and lower-class Whites who were snuffing cocaine and lying around in every con-

ceivable state of depravity" in Chattanooga. Another article written in the
*New York Times,* titled "Negro Cocaine 'Fiends' Are a New Southern Menace," stated that southern sheriffs had switched from .32-caliber guns to
.38-caliber pistols to protect themselves from drug-empowered Blacks. The
article was subtitled "Murder and Insanity Increasing Among Lower Class
Blacks Because They Have Taken to 'Sniffing' Since Deprived of Whiskey by
Prohibition."[40]

In the United States, the concerted effort to paint all addicts as drug-
crazed Blacks or Chinese led to the most critical anti-drug legislation in the
early part of this century: the Harrison Narcotics Act of 1914. This act was
written as a tax law and effectively eliminated the use of morphine, opium,
heroin, and other addictive drugs through strict regulation and harsh penalties. Although cocaine is not considered to be in the narcotic family of drugs,
it was included in the Act. Physicians tried to get around the law by opening
clinics that would dispense opiates in compliance with the Act, but they were
shut down by the early Twenties. Armed raids by Treasury agents rapidly discouraged doctors who tried to continue the distribution of opium-based medicines.

Racist fabrications were not limited to the United States. In 1911, the
White South African government outlawed marijuana, known as "dagga," in
an effort to stop the growing radicalization of Blacks. Dagga was blamed for
making Blacks rebel and fight back against racist laws and growing White
power. White South Africans continued to allow Black miners to smoke it
because Whites believed that it made Black workers more productive. South
Africa led the international fight to ban hemp and had direct and significant
influence over White political leaders and legislators in the U.S. South.[41]

The racial fears played upon by the anti-drug campaigns worked in har-
mony with the general wave of racial attacks that were sweeping the country.
The legacy of lynching that had seen over 1,000 Black victims by the end of
World War I went into high gear after the war.[42] In 1917, thirty-eight Blacks
were lynched. By 1918, the number had risen to fifty-eight and a year later,
after the war had ended, more than seventy lynchings were recorded. At least
ten of the Black men hanged in 1919 were still in uniform.[43] The "Red Summer" of 1919, as writer James Weldon Johnson termed it, became even more
deadly for Blacks as the nation experienced twenty-five race riots.[44]

The Ku Klux Klan and other racist groups enjoyed a free hand as J. Edgar
Hoover's newly organized FBI focused on eradicating the communist threat.
The Klan grew from a small group of racists in the early 1910s to over 100,000
by the early 1920s. In the first year following the end of the war, the Klan
made over 200 public appearances in twenty-seven states.[45] To add to the
racial fires, the Black community saw an alliance formed between temperance groups and racist organizations such as the Klan. In the past century,

temperance organizations had forged ties with abolitionists and been reliable friends to the ex-slaves following the Civil War.[46] In a number of cases, the leadership of the two movements had been identical. However, as attitudes changed and tolerance for drinking grew in the 1910s and 1920s, the movement sought and accepted allies from any quarter.[47]

W.E.B. Dubois wrote about the problems of alcoholism and of prohibition:

> Nothing demonstrates more clearly the limitations of half-baked minds than the present discussion of the United States concerning liquor. We are not, in fact, discussing liquor at all. We are discussing laws. Laws depend for their enforcement upon public opinion. There is no royal road to manners and morals. They cannot be established by an act of Legislature or royal proclamation. They can only be instilled by parental advice, the love of friends and human contact. All other methods have failed and will fail. We are a drunken land and drunken race. Not because of prohibition or the open saloon but because we have ceased to teach temperance to the young.[48]

After World War I, large numbers of Blacks moved to northern cities in search of employment opportunities and to escape the terrorism of southern Whites. Most Blacks, while finding the North to be somewhat more secure, found little opportunity to enter the economic or social mainstream.

The development of a Black underground economy led to the rise of Black bootleggers during the 1920s. This development, in turn, led to a dramatic increase in Black alcohol consumption and related problems. The rate of deaths due to alcohol among Blacks grew every year from 1918 to 1927.[49] Often seen as folk heroes who outfoxed the law and White competitors, Black bootleggers plied the community with rivers of hard liquor.

The war against marijuana after World War I also became a vehicle for attacks on the Black community. Although marijuana had existed in the United States for centuries, it wasn't used primarily as an intoxicant until the early part of this century. One of the first recorded incidents of marijuana smoking occurred in the famous Storyville section of New Orleans, which became a major marijuana-importation and distribution center.[50] Most of the marijuana came from Mexico, Cuba, the Caribbean, or Texas. From Louisiana, it traveled across the country to other major cities.

Many of the Black, White, and Mexican dock workers became smokers as shiploads of the weed came into New Orleans. As they moved on, they took as much marijuana as they could carry with them and helped to spread its use across the nation.

At the same time, New Orleans had become the magnet for jazz musicians as the new music form began to grow and develop passionate followers. Both

Black and White jazz musicians smoked marijuana and came to enjoy the headiness and pleasure that it gave.

By the mid-1920s, however, a full-scale anti-marijuana campaign was in full swing. In 1925, Louisiana made marijuana possession and use a felony. Many other southern and southwestern states soon followed suit. Blacks and Mexicans became the main targets of this new wave of anti-drug fever.

In 1931, jazz great Louis Armstrong became a victim of this campaign. He was arrested in Los Angeles for marijuana possession and served ten days in jail. He was then released with a six-month suspended sentence. One year earlier he had recorded "Muggles," a song about marijuana.[51]

Black jazz and blues musicians in the Twenties, Thirties, and Forties wrote many songs about drugs. From well-known artists such as Cab Calloway, Bessie Smith, Fletcher Henderson, and Leadbelly to hundreds of unknowns, they joyfully and woefully sang about getting high on "reefer" (marijuana), "dope" (heroin), and "caine" (cocaine). Some of the songs that were recorded include "Pipe Dream Blues" (1924), "Cocaine Habit Blues" (1930), "Reefer Man" (1932), "Kickin' the Gong Around" (1933), "Take a Whiff on Me" (1934), "Dopey Joe" (1938), and "Dope Head Blues" (1941). One of the most popular packages of cigarette papers used for rolling marijuana cigarettes was called *blanco y negro* (White and Black) and featured a Black saxophonist on the cover.[52]

Hysterical newspaper headlines and radio broadcasts blamed marijuana-intoxicated Blacks and Mexicans for many heinous crimes they claimed were being committed against Whites. According to these stories, similar to earlier ones about cocaine, marijuana gave Blacks superhuman strength and extraordinary and violent sexual desires.[53]

Linking sex, race, and drugs seem to touch the deepest nerves of the American people. The suppression of interracial socializing by government decree and racist organizations had been strong since the days of slavery. The fear of miscegenation re-emerged, with rising interracial sex and drug use, and drove many Whites to near-hysteria. The proliferation of heroin use, as in the past, found cultural expression in many of the popular pulp novels of the time. Numerous books about White women who were seduced into drugs and sex by men of color were published, including *Marijuana Girl* by N. R. de Mexico (1951), *Narcotic Agent* by Maurice Helbrant (1953), *The Dream Peddlers* by Floyd Miller (1956), *Rock `N Roll Gal* by Ernie Weatherall (1957), and *The Needle* by Sloan M. Britain (1959). These books sold in the tens of thousands as White and Black Americans continued to be fascinated by the image of interracial sex and drug use.

The Hearst newspaper empire was the chief vehicle for the spread of these racial tales. It was the Hearst papers that first popularized the term "marijuana."[54] Few realized until it was too late that the evil marijuana cigarette being attacked in the Hearst papers and by federal authorities was the same hemp plant that had provided so many useful and essential products for decades.

William Randolph Hearst's antagonism toward Mexicans and Blacks was rooted in both his own racist world outlook and in the service of his own greed. He was more than a little upset when Pancho Villa's army seized about 800,000 acres of his land during the Mexican revolution.[55]

Also, hemp's use as a high-quality paper substitute threatened the lumber and newspaper industries controlled by Hearst, especially after the invention of state-of-the-art, affordable hemp-stripping machines in the 1930s. The USDA was predicting that hemp would be the number-one crop in America, and even as late as 1938, one year after marijuana was outlawed, *Popular Mechanics* referred to hemp as the $1 billion crop.[56] Hearst, along with the Dupont chemical companies, which had just invented a wood-pulp process of their own, formed an alliance to outlaw hemp.[57]

The federal side of this campaign was orchestrated by Harry Jacob Anslinger, who had made his reputation as a hard-line law enforcer during prohibition. In 1930, he became director of the Federal Bureau of Narcotics and remained so for the next thirty-two years. Anslinger's agents helped to spread the rumors and tales about the dangers of Black and Mexican drug use.[58] Success came for Anslinger in the Fall of 1937 when the Marijuana Tax Act, which made use and sale of marijuana a felony, became law.[59]

Anslinger's hatred of people of color was legendary. In official memos to his staff, he would refer to a Black person as a "ginger-colored nigger."[60] He testified before a southern-controlled Congress that "coloreds with big lips lured White women with jazz and marijuana."[61] In the 1940s, he ordered files to be kept on all jazz and swing musicians. This included jazz greats such as Duke Ellington, Thelonius Monk, Dizzy Gillespie, Cab Calloway, and Count Basie. Even White performers who were close to Blacks, such as Jackie Gleason, Milton Berle, and Kate Smith, came under his scrutiny.[62]

Anslinger hated the way jazz artists boldly defied social and cultural values he held dear. Interracial sex, drug use, and bohemian lifestyles were taboos that directly contradicted the conservative social and political views of Anslinger.

Anslinger became friends with right-wing Wisconsin Senator Joseph McCarthy and participated in the anti-communist witch hunts of the 1950s. Their fierce and frenzied battle against drugs and communists was the height of disingenuousness. Anslinger admits in his autobiography that he had supplied McCarthy with morphine for many years. His ludicrous and hypocritical justification was that he was protecting the junkie senator from communist blackmailers who could exploit his addiction.[63]

## The Heroin Surge: Black Power vs. White Powder

The Mafia Dons sit around the table. The room is as dark as the tone of the men who occupy it, and a deadly seriousness pervades the atmosphere. The issue is how to end the battle over whether or not to deal drugs that has led to internecine war among the "families" and with outsiders. Don Corleone expounds on morals versus profits to be reaped by entering full-scale into the drug trade. He proposes a compromise that everyone agrees on: organized crime will move into drug trafficking, but will only sell to Blacks.

This scene, from *The Godfather*, had its duplicate in real life. Prior to the Forties, illegal use of light drugs (marijuana) and hard drugs (heroin and cocaine) was restricted to a small segment of society, including the African American community. Jazz greats Charlie Parker and Billie Holiday were infamous heroin addicts, but for the most part, hardcore drug abuse was small and isolated. By 1951, however, due to the Mafia's marketing focus, over 100,000 people were addicts in the United States, many of them Black.[64]

Heroin traffic in the Black communities of the East Coast was controlled by New York's big-five Mafia families, in addition to the French-Cuban connection run by Florida-based gangsters: the Joseph Bonanno family, which was the most deeply involved; the Carlo Gambino family; the Vito Genovese family; the Thomas Lucchese family; and the Profaci-Maglioco family.[65] Reportedly, these five families had taken over from the Jewish mob, which up to the Forties had controlled the drug and numbers rackets in Harlem and other Black areas. The Black street name for heroin was "smack," that came from the Yiddish work *shmeck*, meaning "smell."[66]

Jewish dominance over the rackets had begun in the bootlegging days of the 1920s. The legendary Arnold Rothstein, famous for bribing the Chicago White Sox to throw the 1919 World Series, controlled a significant portion of all illegal liquor in New York City. In the early 1930s, Jewish gangster Dutch Schultz took control of most of the illegal activities in Harlem that were being operated by Harlem's scattered Black and Puerto Rican crime figures. He controlled the area up until his death in 1935, after which the Italian mobsters took over.[67]

The decision by the organized crime families to sell hard drugs almost exclusively to the Black community created a heroin addiction crisis of stunning proportions. This crisis was facilitated by the pay-offs to police officials, judges, politicians, and other White power brokers who had little interest in the welfare of the Black community. As addiction grew, burglaries, robberies, and other crimes were being committed as junkies attempted to finance their habit. Although figures were exaggerated to show an increase in drug-related crime, they were sufficiently frightening to convince New York legislators to pass the strongest anti-drug laws in the country. Unlawful possession of a hypodermic needle, for instance, carried a six-month automatic sentence.[68]

Every major city with a substantial Black population suffered a heroin epidemic. The Black nationalist organization, Nation of Islam (NOI), found many of its recruits in the clutches of heroin addiction and grew from a small religious group into one of the major organized forces in the Black community of that period. Malcolm X describes in his autobiography his easy access to heroin, cocaine, and marijuana. Known as Detroit Red, he eventually became a drug dealer in Boston and New York:

> I kept turning over my profit, increasing my supplies, and I sold reefers like a wild man. I scarcely slept; I was wherever musicians congregated. A roll of money was in my pocket. Every day, I cleared at least fifty or sixty dollars. In those days . . . this was a fortune to a seventeen-year-old Negro.[69]

Most of NOI's work with drug addicts was done by Muslims who themselves had been junkies. With amazing success, the NOI turned hundreds of addicts into disciplined Muslims and members of the growing nationalist group. The NOI's anti-drug program, as Malcolm X described it, was a six-stage process.[70] Ostensibly, it was not a recruitment program, but those who went through the process were informed that the only way to really stay drug-free was to join the NOI.

In the first stage, as advocated by other treatment programs, the addict first had to admit that he or she was addicted to drugs. Although ex-addicts worked with the individual to take this first step, it often could take months of work. Stage two involved coming to grips with why a Black person in America used drugs in the first place. In the nationalist rhetoric of the NOI, Black drug use was an attempt to escape or blunt the hurt of racism. For the Muslims, this was the critical distinction between their anti-drug work and the work being done by others.

This led to the punch line of stage three, where the addict was told that the only true freedom was to join the NOI and submit to Elijah Muhammad. The addict candidate would begin the rites of initiation, including visits to Muslim establishments and discussions about Islam. In stage four, after association with the NOI and its positive values and strong beliefs, the addict would have accumulated enough self-esteem to begin to believe in himself. This new self-worth provided the strength to go to the next stage.

Finally, in stage five, the addict went through the merciless and brutal process of non-chemical detoxification. Muslim brothers (or in the case of a woman addict, Muslim sisters) helped the addict go "cold turkey."

The sixth stage came full circle when the newly initiated, drug-free brother or sister went out and found another addict, usually an old acquaintance from the drug scene, and began the process of transformation with them.

During this period, a number of Black heroin dealers wrestled away distribution networks from the Italian, Cuban, and Jewish mafias. Prior to this time, if a Black drug dealer wanted to buy some drugs, he had to go through one of organized crime's chosen Black middlemen. In New York, the most infamous dealer was Ellsworth Raymond "Bumpy" Johnson, who was immortalized in the movie *Shaft*. Well-dressed, smooth-talking Bumpy was the most powerful Black underworld figure in New York from the late Forties to the mid-Sixties. Yet he was always beholden to the Italian mobsters who sponsored him.[71]

Some low-level Black dealers operated around the time of the Korean War. Bap Ross was credited with bringing innovative distribution and marketing techniques to street-level dealing. He established a system whereby pushers to whom he distributed would only be told by one of his workers where to pick up the heroin. The heroin package would be hidden in a hallway or behind a radiator by another of Ross's operatives. Although Ross was eventually caught, these techniques demonstrated the creative ways that dealers could avoid the law and minimize risks.[72] Another Black dealer, John Freeman, worked with Joseph Valachi up until the time Valachi was arrested.[73] None of these dealers, however, had any real independent power. That changed with the arrival of Frank Matthews, the first Black drug kingpin of the modern era.

Matthews, born in Durham, North Carolina, in 1944, got involved in numbers running in New York City. Through this work he had come into contact with drug bigshot Louis Cirillo, one of the Mafia's biggest distributors on the East Coast.[74] When Matthews decided to go independent in 1967, he was told in no uncertain terms by the Mafia that they would tolerate no competition, especially from a Black man. Undeterred, Matthews made contact with the French connection on his own and installed his network of numbers runners and operatives as his base. Pool halls, candy stores, laundries, and other businesses in New York's Black communities soon became retail outlets for Matthews's heroin. Within a year, he controlled all or a significant amount of distribution in Black communities in every major city in the country, including Philadelphia, Baltimore, Cleveland, Detroit, Cincinnati, Chicago, Kansas City, Las Vegas, and Los Angeles.

Despite threats from the Mafia and the emergence of local rivals, Matthews was never overthrown. Between 1967 and 1971, he grossed over $100 million, making him a multi-millionaire before he was thirty.[75]

Matthews hired hundreds of people and set up operations all over New York to cut and bag heroin and later cocaine. He started a number of innovations that did not exist at other heroin "factories," such as eight-hour shifts and the wearing of surgical masks by workers so that they would not inhale the drugs as they worked. However, these steps were taken more out of a concern for efficiency than for workers' rights.

Matthews even had CIA connections, according to a "Top Secret" Justice Department report written in 1976. According to the report, nine persons indicted for supplying drugs to Matthews had drug importation charges dropped because of their ties to the CIA.[76] In mid-1971, Matthews's heroin supplies from the suffering French connection began to dry up, and he came under more scrutiny from law enforcement agencies. His dealers and his contacts with the Cuban Mafia, some of his key suppliers, started to squeal. He was arrested in Las Vegas on New Year's Day in 1973, his bond set at $5 million.

Matthews was eventually released when the bond was dropped to $325,000, and he returned to New York. By July 1973, Matthews had reportedly converted nearly $20 million in assets into cash. On July 2, 1973, Matthews, a bodyguard, a mistress, and the money vanished and were never found.[77]

Other major Black drug dealers came on the scene following Matthews's disappearance, including his New York successor, the legendary Nicky Barnes, and Los Angeles' so-called "Magnificent 7," the West Coast's first major grouping of Black distributors.[78] Barnes's stature grew even larger than that of Matthews, his mentor, who had taught him the ins and outs of a sophisticated drug operation. As he won well-publicized and numerous acquittals on gun, narcotics, bribery, and murder charges, Barnes's reputation expanded. *The New York Times* dubbed him "Mr. Untouchable."[79] It was not long before Barnes was at the top of the Drug Enforcement Agency's and New York Police Department's target list of key dealers to take down. Barnes proved to be a formidable enemy, however, and, although he was followed and wiretapped, he remained untouched for a number of years. Matthews was one of the first independent big dealers to see the value of laundering drug profits. Barnes followed his example, but his lucky streak came to an end when the White man who washed his money turned out to be an FBI informant. On January 19, 1978, Barnes was found guilty of a 1971 law specifically aimed at big-time criminals who operated "continuing criminal enterprises," and sentenced to life imprisonment and a $125,000 fine.

The Vietnam War created thousands of Black addicts who would eventually become some of the key sources for drugs from Southeast Asia. With roadside access to heroin, opium, and hashish in Vietnam, many Black soldiers became addicts within a few months of their tour of duty. Although there was clear evidence that drug abuse among both combat and support soldiers was growing, the U.S. Armed Forces refused to implement any serious treatment program or make an effort to halt trafficking.[80]

The stress and fears created by war and the racism of the armed services pushed many Black and Latino soldiers to drugs. Black and Latino soldiers served disproportionately on either the front lines or in menial janitorial positions, often under the command of racist officers. Drug use became a way of coping with the dehumanizing treatment they received.

The CIA's collaboration with organized crime and anti-communists guaranteed that the area known as the Golden Triangle, where Laos, Thailand, and Myammar converge, would become the center of heroin production worldwide, meeting the demand being created back home. At the height of the French connection, no more than eight tons of heroin a year reached the United States. During the peak of the Vietnam War more than sixty tons a year of heroin was coming to the United States.[81]

In the early- to mid-Sixties, many of the Black youth gangs, particularly in Los Angeles, Chicago, New York, and Philadelphia, became involved in the Black freedom struggle. In Los Angeles, gangs like the Businessmen, the Gladiators, the Swamp Boys, and the Slausons became the nucleus for many community and political organizations. The Slausons were the base of a Black Panther chapter. Other gangs became involved with Maulana Ron Karenga's United Slaves (US) organization, which rivaled the Black Panthers. The FBI, under the direction of racist J. Edgar Hoover, decided that one effective way to stop the anti-war and Black liberation movements was to go after leaders and activists on drug charges. Numerous activists were set up by narcs and given stiff sentences for the possession of often tiny amounts of marijuana.[82]

The Panthers and other Black radical organizations of the period expressly forbid drug use among their members. In an effort to follow the revolutionary principles exercised by guerrillas in Cuba, Africa, and Vietnam, drug use was seen as counter-revolutionary and destructive to the community. The Panther leadership issued explicit orders that no party member could have in their possession or use any "narcotics or weed" while doing party work.[83] In the Panther lexicon, narcotics were any drugs except marijuana, which was considered benign. Any member found shooting narcotics, meaning heroin, was to be expelled. Orders were also issued against being intoxicated. No member was to have a weapon in their possession while drunk or high. Most Panthers were not addicted to drugs, and anti-drug rules were only rarely enforced.

Similar patterns developed in other ghetto areas. In Chicago, the Blackstone Rangers became an organized, militant force against Mayor Richard Daley and his political machine and for the advancement of Black politics in the city. In the Eighties, under the name El Rukn, they turned back to their old, gang habits of intimidation and petty crime. They eventually became some of Chicago's largest drug traffickers.[84] In the Seventies and Eighties, many (but by no means all) of the Black youth gangs that developed became involved in drug dealing and drug-related violence.

## Crack, Crime, and Crisis in the Black Community

I never ever ran from the Ku Klux Klan and I shouldn't have to run from a Black man.

—Kool Moe Dee from the rap song "Self-Destruction"[85]

The destructive impact of illegal narcotics on Blacks, Latinos, and poor people has become murderous. Indeed, whole communities are being destroyed from top to bottom as children take over the role of family breadwinner, mothers become addicts who barter sex for drugs, and drug-addicted, abandoned babies strain already overburdened city hospital services.

Ironically, government solutions to the drug crisis increasingly assume the posture of attacks on the civil and political rights of the Black community. Plans to build more prisons, the barrage of media images portraying young Black males as addicts and criminals, and efforts to physically cordon off entire Black neighborhoods all reek of racism.

In the Black community, the "war on drugs" has raised the question of "war against whom?" One ominous sign of the government's real aim is the Federal Bureau of Prisons' announcement that it plans to build 20,000 new prison cells over the next fifteen years.[86] It is obvious who is expected to fill those jails; at the beginning of the 1990s, African Americans were almost half of the prison population.[87]

The prison population of the United States, partly a result of increased Black incarceration, has nearly doubled in the last ten years. In 1980, there were 329,821 in America's prisons. By 1989, that number had risen to 627,402. In 1980, the rate of prisoners per 1,000 population was 139. By 1988, it had shot up to 256.[88] State after state saw extraordinary growth in incarceration rates.

According to the Washington, D.C.-based Sentencing Project, as of 1990, the United States had the highest incarceration rate in the world (426 per 100,000), which was higher than that of South Africa (333 per 100,000). More than one million U.S. citizens were in jail.[89] The Sentencing Project also released the study that documented that about one in four young Black males in their twenties were either in jail, on parole, or on probation. Only 6 percent of White males in their twenties were in a similar situation, and for Latinos it was about 10 percent.[90] At the same time, only 13 percent of Black youth were in higher education.[91] In Washington, D.C., 16 percent of all Black males under twenty-one would be arrested and charged with selling drugs.[92] By 1994, in Florida, almost half of all Black men between the ages of eighteen and thirty-four would be incarcerated or placed under court supervision.[93]

Even women's prisons, traditionally underpopulated, were overflowing with Black women.

By mainly going after street-level dealers, drug enforcement officers perpetuate the myth that the majority of traffickers and users are people of color. In 1988, however, the FBI and the National Institute for Drug Abuse concluded that Blacks constitute only 12 percent of the nation's drug users.[94] Whites comprise 80 percent of all illegal drug users.[95]

According to the National Institute on Drug Abuse's (NIDA) 1990 figures of the estimated 13 million regular users of illegal drugs, Blacks make up 15 percent, Latinos make up 8 percent, and Whites make up 77 percent.[96] The percentage of drug use is relatively the same for each race. For Blacks, Latinos, and Whites, the figures are 8.6 percent, 6.2 percent, and 6.6 percent, respectively.[97] Even William Bennett recognizes the disparity between myth and fact. He stated that the typical coke user is "White, male, a high-school graduate employed full-time and living in a small metropolitan area or suburb."[98]

Whites are not only the majority of drug users; they are also the most common drug sellers. Contrary to mainstream media images of young Black men spread-eagled on the ground or handcuffed in the latest high-profile drug raid, Whites dominate the drug trafficking industry. Whites also get the lion's share of profits, as they deal narcotics wholesale and behind the security of closed corporate doors.

Although Whites are the majority of drug users, they are not the majority of those convicted for drug use. In 1988, Blacks were 38 percent of those arrested on drug charges. In 1989, that figure grew to 41 percent.[99] In New York, Whites are 47 percent of the clients in state- funded centers, but less than 10 percent of those committed to prison.[100]

The mandatory sentencing laws enacted by Congress and many states in response to citizens' outcry regarding street trafficking and its accompanying violence have resulted in discriminatory arrest and sentencing patterns against Blacks. Since low-level street dealers in urban areas are predominantly Black, they are easier to arrest than the big kingpins, meaning Blacks will go to jail at a greater rate than Whites.

Laws passed by Congress further this bias by giving harsher mandatory sentences for crack cocaine, which is more likely to be found on the Black street dealer, than for cocaine powder. For example, distribution of five grams or more of crack, worth only about $125 on the street, is a five-year mandatory term in prison. In contrast, it would take 500 grams of powder cocaine, worth about $50,000, to receive the same sentence.[101] One gram of crack has roughly become the equivalent of 100 grams of cocaine powder.[102] In response to this blatantly obvious inequity, Seattle federal public defender

William Hines stated, "I cannot say with any authority that the law was intended to be racist, but the effect of that law is racist."[103]

Drug laws are also discriminatory at the local level. In Minneapolis, Minnesota, in December 1990, a law was thrown out that gave four years to first-time crack users, but only probation to first-time cocaine powder users. Figures showed that 92 percent of those arrested for crack possession were Black, while 85 percent of those arrested for possessing cocaine powder were White.

The Black community is also victim of the violation of civil liberties due to the Bush Administration's drug war. In Washington, nearly 200 evictions of mostly Black citizens took place on the word of landlords who claimed that these residents were dealing drugs. Although few drugs were found, using warrantless searches, it turns out that most of these tenants were in rent disputes with their landlords.[104]

In numerous Black communities, police departments have launched what are essentially full-scale military assaults. With the logistics of the kind usually reserved for invasions of other nations, police raid Black neighborhoods weekly. Kicked-in doors, ransacked homes, mass arrests, and other brutal tactics are common in these raids. These campaigns have macho-sounding names such as Memphis's Operation Invincible, Los Angeles's Operation Hammer, Chicago's Operation Clear Sweep, Atlanta's Red Dog Squad, and New York's TNT. Not a single White community has been the target of these assaults, although drug use may be of crisis proportions there, too.

Increased police presence in the Black community has meant general increase in arrests and charges against Blacks. In one Black housing project in Atlanta where drug dealing had become a serious problem, the subsequent police focus on the neighborhood resulted in a disproportionate rise in traffic violations. Although only about 10 percent of Atlanta's residents lived in the project, in the month following the decision by the police to target their community they received more than half of Atlanta's traffic tickets. The same neighborhood was the victim of one-third of the cars towed in the city. Of the 4,800 charges filed against residents in the area, more than 4,300 were either minor traffic charges or misdemeanors.[105] In other cities, citizen groups, civil libertarians, and even law enforcement officials report similar situations. According to David Meyers, Assistant Director of the Los Angeles County Public Defender's Office, "The number of drunk driving arrests go up. They pick up people they wouldn't otherwise get on petty misdemeanors that are not drug related."[106]

The threat to the civil liberties of Blacks is real. The use of unconstitutional legal tactics echoes centuries of unequal treatment of Blacks by the U.S. justice system. The racist application of the death penalty and inappropriately harsh sentences have historically been challenged by a strong movement for judicial fairness; amendments to the Constitution that have guaranteed equal rights and civil liberty protection were won after hard-fought battles. The American Civil Liberties Union has gotten behind the Black community in a number of instances to stop the erosion of their civil liberties caused by the drug war. In Chicago, the ACLU stopped police raids on Black public housing units after complaints that the Chicago Housing Authority was requiring identification for residents and banning overnight guests.[107] In Boston, the ACLU was involved in a case where Superior Court Judge Cortland Mathers determined that there was an official "search-on-sight" policy against men in the Black communities of Roxbury, Dorchester, and Mattapan.[108] In one incident, a Black man was "accidently" shot by Boston police during one of their street searches.[109] Atlanta citizens in one public housing unit also filed legal suits and raised loud complaints against illegal police tactics. They objected to roadblocks being set up at entrances to their unit and being asked for identification just for being in that neighborhood.

The fight to stop civil liberties abuses against the Black community has been complicated by the fact that many Blacks are willing to relinquish some of those civil liberties in the name of the war against drugs. Many in the Black community who experience the violence much more directly than Whites want relief and are ready to accept brutal law enforcement tactics as a short-term solution.

Chicago's Father George Clements, a national and local anti-drug leader in the Black community, stated unequivocally that he did not care if a few rights were stepped on if it meant ridding the community of drugs. He said, "I'm all for whatever tactics have to be used. If that means they're trampling on civil liberties, so be it. I feel that they're not being strict enough. For me, the bottom line is death."[110]

## Drugs and Economic Genocide

The current upsurge in drug trafficking and abuse in the Black community has mainly been driven by a complex web of economic need meeting economic opportunity. It's impossible to grasp the dynamics of the current drug problem without grasping the impact of economic changes on the Black community during the Reagan era. Black males, particularly young ones, have been trapped in a cycle of poverty and unemployment, nothing less than economic genocide. A 1985 Field Foundation study asserts that one-half of all Black men between the ages of sixteen and sixty-five are chronically unemployed.[111] Black youth unemployment has officially hovered around 45 percent or higher for the last decade, and in reality is much higher.[112]

Since 1960, Black youth have suffered the sharpest increases in unemployment and the worst poverty. At least 45 percent of all Black children live in poverty.[113] When Black youths become unemployed, they are unemployed much longer than their White counterparts.[114]

Black family per capita income continues to be a fraction of White income and even has fallen behind the income of Latinos. In 1990, Black family median income was 54 percent of Whites, where it was about thirty years ago. In the mid-1970s, it was 62 percent of Whites.[115] One-third of Black Americans, 9.7 million, lived in poverty in 1990, an increase of 700,000 since 1986. Meanwhile, the poverty level for Whites actually decreased between 1986 and 1987 from 11 percent to 10.5 percent.[116] In 1989, 11.9 percent of all Black families earned less than $5,000 annually compared to 6.7 percent in 1976.[117]

The small increase in income among middle-class Blacks is dramatically offset by the growth of poverty in too many Black communities. Indeed, according to an important study done by *Money* magazine in December 1989, racial discrimination continues to prevent the Black middle class from achieving parity with its White counterpart. Among the conclusions drawn by the study were: Blacks earn 10 percent to 26 percent less than Whites with similar educational backgrounds; the median income for Black male college graduates was $26,550 compared to White male college graduates' median income of $35,701; and Black professionals and managers are twice as likely to be unemployed as their counterparts.[118]

Cuts in aid for higher education in the past ten years, under the knife of then-Education Secretary William Bennett, blocked one more avenue out of poverty. In the mid-1970s, when almost twice as much federal grant money for higher education was available to the Black community, the percentage of Black high school graduates who attended college (33.5 percent) was higher than that of Whites (33 percent).[119] Between 1985 and 1990, the impact of Bennett's cuts was a fluctuation in Black college enrollment between 26 percent and 30 percent. Over the same period, White enrollment of high school graduates averaged about 36.6 percent.[120] At the high school level, the drop-out rate for young Blacks is nationally about 25 percent, and is much greater in many urban areas.[121]

During this period, the coca leaf production glut made cocaine plentiful and, therefore, cheaper. A kilogram that sold for $50–60,000 in 1980 goes for as little as $10–12,000 today. The development of crack cocaine, which sells for as little as $2.00 a "rock" in some cities, was the final step in turning cocaine from a faddish drug used predominantly by a small coterie of affluent Whites and some Blacks to a mass product used by hundreds of thousands of people of all races.

Poor Black communities became the ideal market for crack. They provided a ready-made distribution network of existing or easily created street gangs of unemployed youth who could retail crack and other drugs. These communities also had consumers who would purchase the cheap, but potent, product. It's no accident that Los Angeles, Miami, Chicago, and New York, cities that have historically had large Black street gangs, are the major points of drug distribution. In Los Angeles, for example, it's estimated that there are between 80,000 and 100,000 gang members, many of whom deal in drugs.[122]

As a result of the increase in street marketing, the illegal narcotics industry has become a major (perhaps the major) employer of Black youth. Illegal drug trafficking is the major economic activity in many Black and Latino neighborhoods. In the era of Reagan budget cuts, large cash flow into these communities was quite welcome. Due to income derived from drug trafficking, people can buy food, pay rent, and live materially better lives. Black youth can easily make $100 a day or more simply by watching for the police or steering customers in the right direction. A study by the Urban Institute underscores the economic imperative for many young people. The study indicates that more than two-thirds of those who sell drugs don't use drugs.[123]

The Reagan-Bush administrations have made much of the supposed many jobs available to Black youth at fast-food places such as McDonalds. However, McDonalds' low wages and boring work are not an effective alternative to the more lucrative drug trade earnings, and, for those who do choose the fast-food job path, discrimination is a major factor.

A study done in Philadelphia by the Philadelphia Unemployment Project discovered that McDonalds was paying inner-city workers an average of one dollar less per hour than their suburban counterparts: $3.82 versus $4.82. The inner-city workers were overwhelmingly Black and Latino (77 percent) while the suburban workers were majority White (67 percent). In the city's poorer sections, such as North Philadelphia, the gap was even larger.[124]

## Chemical Warfare

Blacks are spending between $16 and $20 billion a year on illegal drugs, according to *Ebony*.[125] In every area of Black America, drug abuse is growing. The impact of these developments has been staggering and deadly. The drug epidemic has initiated a wave of violence and a community health crisis of genocidal proportions. One in thirty Black males will be a murder victim.[126] The frequency of accidental murders of citizens caught in the crossfire of drug deals gone sour has demoralized communities across the country.

The drug crisis in the Black community has been labelled by some analysts as "chemical warfare" against Black people. Blacks make up 50 percent of those admitted to emergency rooms for heroin; 55 percent of those for cocaine, and 60 percent of those for PCP.[127] Blacks comprised 31 percent of all people with drug emergencies in 1985 and 25 percent of those in treatment for drugs in 1987.[128]

Heroin use has accelerated the spread of AIDS in the Black community. Heroin addiction, declining prior to the 1980s, has risen again, as many crack addicts also use heroin. It's not just heroin that is spreading AIDS. Many cocaine users are also injecting, and, because the addiction is stronger than that of heroin, users are injecting more frequently, thereby increasing the chance of becoming infected. Blacks constitute 37 percent of all those who contracted AIDS through needles and 48 percent of those who contracted AIDS through partners who use dirty needles. These patterns of transmission largely explain why Blacks are 27 percent of all people with AIDS, and Black women are 52 percent of all women with AIDS.[129]

## Community Dope Busting

In lieu of constructive government action, the Black community has aggressively taken the struggle into its own hands. From Dick Gregory's work in Louisiana to the Muslim Dope Busters in the nation's capital, community-based groups have fought drug dealers on their own turf as well as launched successful education and prevention projects. These groups have also taken the lead in demanding more treatment centers and more local, state, and federal resources.

In the 1980s, Muslim organizations, Black men's groups, and community activists in New York, Detroit, Washington, Atlanta, and other major cities decided to confront street-level dealers and crack-house operators directly. By aggressively challenging the corner dealer for his turf, these groups caused many pushers to switch rather than fight. Although no particular organization took credit for it, crack houses were burned down in some cities. While some local police authorities decried these endeavors as vigilantism and citizens taking the law into their own hands, most of the residents in those Black communities cheered their work, honored their successes, and wondered aloud why the police had been previously unable to get rid of these dealers.

These displays of courage and action forced other players in the Black community to move. The major civil rights organizations have marshalled their resources and joined in the fight and revamped their work to end drug trafficking and abuse in the African American community. The Urban League, which has historically spoken out against the destructiveness of Black-on-Black crime, in 1989 declared its determination to rid the Black community of drug pushers. Urban League President John Jacob, speaking at the organization's seventy-ninth annual convention, compared the dope dealer with the Ku Klux Klan. He said, "Drugs kill more Blacks than the Klan ever did."[130]

Tilting towards the get-tough banter reminiscent of the Reagan administration, Jacob attempted to prepare the Urban League for a campaign that would take it back to the streets. The anti-drug programs previously run by the Urban League had not been successful in reaching the hard-core addicts or street traffickers. Jacob advocated a program that included closer cooperation with law enforcement agencies, photographing people who openly sold drugs, and support for tougher laws and penalties for drug-related crimes.[131]

The Southern Christian Leadership Conference (SCLC) also started a new anti-drug program. The national program, known as "Wings of Hope," was started on April 18, 1989, and focuses on organizing through the churches.[132] Wings of Hope provides churches and community groups with training in drug prevention through health professionals who are treatment experts. The program also gives training in parental skills and spiritual guidance. Black actor Louis Gossett, Jr., came on board as the national spokesperson for the campaign. The program earned kudos from William Bennett and has been cited by his office as one of the top fifteen community-based, anti-drug programs in the nation.[133] Significantly, SCLC National President Joseph Lowery has not let Bennett's praise mute his criticism of how the federal drug war is being waged. Lowery has been disparaging of Bennett's war on drugs and said that it would not succeed "unless it offers substantial economic assistance to desperate people plagued by the despair of poverty, high unemployment, and homelessness."[134] Rev. Richard Dalton, National Program Director of Wings of Hope, is equally adamant about the need to address the social causes of the drug problem. He sees not only users as victims, but, to some degree, young pushers as well. "Crack dealers are not born, they are made!" he says.[135] The NAACP's *Crisis* magazine has published a number of thought-provoking articles that have called for more of a balance between law enforcement, on the one hand, and decriminalization and treatment on the other.[136]

In order to more effectively unite forces within the African American community against the drug crisis, a number of important national conferences were held in 1989 and 1990 that brought together activists, professionals, and concerned citizens. The largest of these conferences was organized in the Spring of 1989 and 1990 by Rev. Cecil Williams of Glide Memorial Church in San Francisco.[137] The conference was titled "The Black Family/Community and Crack Cocaine: Prevention, Treatment, Recovery—The Death of a Race" and was attended by thousands from around the country. The most important thing to emerge from these meetings was the construction of regional networks where people could share experiences and, when possible, work together in joint projects.

In the written statement welcoming participants to the 1989 conference, Rev. Williams stated, "As an African American, I had not envisioned that we would be involved in yet another era of slavery. Crack cocaine has become the 'master' and we have become 'slaves' of this intensively addictive drug. Our lives are at stake. Our children's lives are at stake."[138] In an earnest and deeply felt call to arms, he went on to say:

> It is at the "bottom" that we are most victimized, and from the bottom we must rise up. Now is the time to call for the Freedom Train. The Freedom Train that freed us once is the train that will free us again. The Conference is the call for us to be the engineers to lead our people to liberation. Prevention, intervention, and recovery are tickets for the train. We must realistically, honestly, actively, and spiritually come together in unity and solidarity to confront the crisis of crack cocaine. We must engage in networking that will ensure our connection, and bring our brothers and sisters back home.[139]

While most African American leaders have been reluctant to embrace radical solutions such as "clean" needle distribution, legalization, and decriminalization, there are a few notable exceptions. Baltimore Mayor and former prosecutor Kurt Schmoke, in a speech before the U.S. Conference of Mayors, called for "a national debate on decriminalization."[140] Schmoke, whose city faces one of the most intractable heroin and crack epidemic problems of any in the nation, says, "I'm convinced that we can't prosecute our way out of this problem. All that we do when we get tough on drugs is inflate the price on the street, and cause more addicts to break into more houses and mug more people."[141]

Former Congressman and judge George Crockett (D-MI) has also spoken out favorably for expanding the discussion about legalization. Crockett, who has a long record of standing strong on progressive issues, believes that legalization could undermine the criminal elements at the root of the violence associated with drug trafficking. He argues further that resources being used against the Black community in the drug war could be put to better use in treatment and prevention programs.[142]

# Conclusion

A mass political movement is needed in the Black community. As in the past, we now need Black mass movements, a flowering of organizations and opinions, of ideas and identity, of actions and audacity. But the new conditions and realities of the Nineties must be acknowledged.

Distinct from the past, power—political, economic, social, or cultural—must be delivered to those who toil every day in the service industries, manufacturing sectors, and the public sector of our society. People need to be organized as workers, as communities, and as recipients of the resources of our nation. Homeless unions, tenant organizations, free health care advocacy groups, and many other underfunded causes should continue to be coordinated and advanced.

The struggle against racism lost much of its focus after the death of King and the end of *de jure* segregation. Too often, the interests of the Black middle class—tax relief, political appointments, higher education opportunities, small-business development—were projected as the immediate interest of all Blacks. But the trickledown notion that benefits to a few Blacks will eventually accrue to the race as a whole is flawed. Important Black middle-class gains in education, employment, and politics have been offset by cutbacks, increased discrimination against poor people, and the inability to translate political positioning into economic power. In the Nineties, the needs of poor people in the Black community will have more in common with other people of color and poor Whites than with Blacks in the middle class.

At the same time, the institutional and systemic racism that continues in the United States will not only have an impact on African Americans, but on other people of color as well, thereby demanding a unity of interests across racial lines. A rainbow coalition neither hurts Black unity or dilutes the struggle against racism. But that rainbow will only be successful to the degree that it acknowledges and understands the complexities of class and race politics of the current era.

It is not just the potential of Blacks as individuals that is being threatened by the drug crisis. Entire communities are being destabilized as the drug epidemic reaches into every sector of the community. Women who traditionally have not been as caught up in the grips of addiction are becoming addicted in the largest numbers in history. The toll on the Black community is devastating.

## Notes

[1] Ron Harris, "Blacks Feel Brunt of Drug War," *Los Angeles Times*, 22 April 1990, p. A1.

[2] Maxine Waters, "Drugs, Democrats, & Priorities," *Nation*, 24 July 1989, p. 142.

[3] Katherine McFate, "Black Males and the Drug Trade: New Entrepreneurs or New Illusions," *Focus*, May 1990, p. 5.

[4] Arnold S. Trebach, "Can Prohibition Be Enforced in Washington?" *The Truth Seeker*, Sept/Oct 1989, p. 22.

[5] Vivian Rouson Gossett, *Alcohol and Drug Abuse in Black America,* Institute on Black Chemical Abuse, Minneapolis, MN, 1988, p. 2.

[6] Edward M. Brecher and the Editors of Consumer Reports, *Licit and Illicit Drugs*, Little, Brown, Boston, 1972, p. 398.

[7] Eric Williams, *Capitalism and Slavery,* Andre Deutsch Limited, London, 1964, p. 37; Henry

Hobhouse, *Seeds of Change*, Harper & Row, New York, 1985, pp. 116–117.

[8] Ibid.; Williams, pp. 78–79.

[9] Ibid., p. 80.

[10] Ibid., p. 79.

[11] Jerome E. Brooks, *The Mighty Leaf*, Little, Brown, Boston 1952, p. 105.

[12] Ibid.

[13] Eugene D. Genovese, *Roll Jordan Roll: The World the Slaves Made*, Vintage Books, New York 1986.

[14] Denise Herd, "We Cannot Stagger to Freedom: A History of Blacks and Alcohol in American Politics," *Yearbook of Substance Use and Abuse,* Vol. 3, Human Science Press, New York, 1983.

[15] Jack Herer, *The Emperor Wears No Clothes*, Queen of Clubs Publishing, Van Nuys, CA, 1990, p. 65.

[16] Ibid., p. 1.

[17] Ibid.

[18] Ibid.

[19] Kenneth M. Stamp, *The Peculiar Institution*, Vintage Books, New York, 1956, p. 49.

[20] "Native Americans Declare War on Alcohol," *The Newsletter*, Fall 1988, p. 11.

[21] Patrick Anderson, *High in America,* Viking Press, New York, 1981, p. 48.

[22] Alvin Moscow, *Merchants of Heroin*, The Dial Press, New York, 1968, p. xiv; David Musto, "The History of Legislative Control Over Opium, Cocaine, and Their Derivatives," *Dealing With Drugs*, Pacific Research Institute, San Francisco, 1987, p. 62.

[23] Ibid.; Brecher, pp. 17–19.

[24] John Helmer, *Drugs and Minority Oppression,* Seabury Press, New York, 1975, pp. 18–33.

[25] *Great Decisions 1989*, New York: Foreign Policy Associates.

[26] Karl Marx, *Capital*, Vol. 1, New World Paperbacks, New York, p. 398.

[27] Ibid.; Brecher, p. 4.

[28] Daniel Kagan, "How America Lost Its First Drug War," 20 November 1989, *Insight,* p. 10.

[29] Ibid.

[30] "Miscellanea: Pioneers in the Cocaine Trade," *The Forensic Drug Abuse Advisor*, September 1989, p. 7.

[31] Ibid.; Kagan, p. 10.

[32] Ibid.; Brecher, p. 271.

[33] *Drug Trafficking in the Washington Metropolitan Area*, Oversight Hearing, Subcommittee on Fiscal Affairs and Health, Committee on the District of Columbia, 99th Congress, 17 April 1985, p. 314.

[34] Ibid.; Kagan, p. 11.

[35] Ibid.; Kagan, p. 12.

[36] Ibid.; Kagan, p. 13.

[37] *Opium Problem: Message From the President*, 61st Congress, 21 February 1910, p. 50.

[38] Ibid.; Kagan, p. 13.

[39] Ibid.; Brecher, p. 18.

[40] Edward Hunting Williams, "Negro Cocaine 'Fiends' Are a New Southern Menace," *New York Times*, 8 February 1949, sec. 5, p. 12.

[41] Ibid.; Herer, p. 68.

[42] John Hope Franklin, *From Slavery to Freedom*, Vintage, New York, 1969, pp. 439–440.

[43] Ibid., p. 474.

[44] Ibid., p. 480.

[45] Ibid., p. 479.

[46] Ibid.; Gossett, p. 4.

[47] Ibid.; Gossett, p. 4.

[48] W. E. B. Dubois, "Drunkenness," October 1928, *Crisis,* No. 35, p. 348.

[49] Ibid.; Gossett, p. 4.

[50] Ibid; Herer, p. 65.

[51] Ibid., p. 66.

[52] Liner notes from album *Pot, Spoon, Pipe and Jug*, Stash Records, Tenafly, NJ.

[53] Ibid.; Herer, pp. 67–68.

[54] Ibid., p. 23.

[55] Ibid.

[56] "New Billion-Dollar Crop," *Popular Mechanics*, February 1938, pp. 238–239.

[57] Ibid.; Herer, p. 23.

[58] Ibid.

[59] Oversight Hearing, p. 316.

[60] Ibid.; Herer, p. 25.

[61] Ibid., p. 26.

[62] Ibid., p. 66.

[63] Ibid., p. 27; Brecher, pp. 36–37.

[64] Norman Riley, "The Crack Boom is Really an Echo," *Crisis,* March 1989, p. 27.

[65] Newsday Editors, *The Heroin Trail,* Signet, New York, 1973, p. 199.

[66] Ibid.

[67] Stephen Fox, *Blood and Power*, Penguin Books, New York, 1989, pp. 25–26, 163–165.

[68] Ibid.; Riley, p. 27.

[69] Malcolm X, *The Autobiography of Malcolm X,* Ballantine Books, New York, 1965, pp. 99.

[70] Ibid., pp. 259–261.

[71] Francis A. J. Janni, *Black Mafia*, Pocket Books, New York, 1975, pp. 101–102.

[72] Ibid.; Newsday Editors, p. 196.

[73] Hank Messick, *Of Grass and Snow,* Prentice-Hall, Englewood, CA, 1979, p. 15.

[74] Ibid., pp. 24–35.

[75] Newsday Editors, pp. 194–195.

[76] Jefferson Morley, "The Kid Who Sold Crack to the President," *City Paper,* 15 December 1989, p. 31.

[77] Ibid.; Messick, pp. 36–37.

[78] Michael Covino, "How the 69th Mob Maximized Earnings in East Oakland," *California Magazine*, November 1985, p. 87.

[79] Ibid.; Messick, p. 148.

[80] Congressmen Morgan Murphy and Robert Steele, *The World Heroin Problem*, U.S. Government Printing Office, 1971.

[81] *Washington Star,* 4 May 1980.

[82] Ibid.; Anderson, p. 54.

[83] Gene Marine, *The Black Panthers,* Signet Books, New York 1969, pp. 45–46.

[84] Tom Brune and James Ylisela, Jr., "The Making of Jeff Fort," *Chicago*, November 1988, p. 208–210.

[85] Nelson George, *Stop the Violence*, National Urban League publication, Pantheon, New York, 1990, p. 44.

[86] "Prisoners in 1988," *Bureau of Justice Statistics Bulletin,* April 1989, U.S. Department of Justice.

[87] "Profile of State Prison Inmates 1986," *Bureau of Justice Statistics*, January 1988, Special Report, U.S. Department of Justice.

[88] Ibid.

[89] Sharon LaFraniere, "U.S. Has Most Prisoners Per Capita in the World," *Washington Post*, 5 January 1991, p. A3.

[90] "Young Black Men Most Likely to Be Jailed," *Washington Afro-American*, 10 March 1990, p. A1.

[91] Ibid.

[92] Ibid.; McFate, p. 5.

[93] Raymond M. Brown, "NACDL, the Black Community, and the War on Drugs," *The Champion,* November 1990, pp. 18–20.

[94] Ron Harris, "Blacks Feel Brunt of Drug War," *Los Angeles Times*, 22 April 1990, p. A26.

[95] Ibid.

[96] "Drug Use Down Report Says," *USA Today*, 20 December 1990, p. 6A.

[97] Ibid.

[98] *Intricate Web*, General Board of Global Ministries, The United Methodist Church, 1990, p. 5.

[99] Jack Kelley and Sam Vincent Meddis, "Critics Say Bias Spurs Police Focus on Blacks," *USA Today,* 20 December 1990, p. 6A.

[100] Letter from Jim Murphy, Director of New York State Coalition for Criminal Justice, *City Sun*, 27 September to 3 October 1990.

[101] Gerry Fitzgerald, "Dispatches From the Drug War," *Common Cause*, January/February 1990, p. 16.

[102] Ibid.

[103] Harris, p. A26.

[104] Michael Hasty, "Drug War Targets Civil Liberties," *Washington Peace Letter*, September 1989, p. 4.

[105] Harris, p. A27.

[106] Ibid., p. A26.

[107] Ibid.

[108] Ibid.

[109] Ibid.

[110] Ibid.

[111] Ibid.; Gossett, p. 13.

[112] National Research Council, *Common Destiny,* National Academy Press, Washington, D.C., 1989, p. 302.

[113] Ibid., p. 8.

[114] Ibid.

[115] Press Release, U.S. Department of Commerce, Bureau of Census, 31 August 1988.

[116] Ibid.

[117] Walter L. Updegrave, "Race and Money," *Money*, December 1989, p. 154.

[118] Ibid., p. 152.

[119] Ibid., p. 170.

[120] Ibid.

[121] *Common Destiny*, pp. 335–337.

[122] *Drug Trafficking: A Report to the President*, U.S. Department of Justice, 3 August 1989, p. 33.

[123] Carlos Sanchez, "A Fifth of Poor in Study Involved With Drugs," *Washington Post*, 29 July 1989.

[124] Paul Choitz, "McBoycott Against Unfair Wages," *In These Times,* 21 March 1990.

[125] "Drug Economy in Black America is Between $16 Billion and $20 Billion," *Ebony*, August 1989, p. 108.

[126] Patrick Welsh, "Young, Black, Male and Trapped," *Washington Post,* 24 September 1989, p. B4.

[127] David R. Gergen, "Drugs and White America," *U.S. News & World Report,* 18 September 1989, p. 79.

[128] Ibid.; Stone, p. 18.

[129] Ibid.; Stone, p. 18.

[130] George Curry, "Urban League Declares War on Drug Pushers," *Chicago Tribune*, 7 August 1989, p. 1.

[131] Ibid.

[132] Khali Abdegeo, "Wings of Hope," *SCLC National Magazine*, March/April 1990, p. 40.

[133] Ibid.

[134] Ibid.

[135] Ibid., p. 41.

[136] Gary Kamiya, "The Crack Epidemic: The Season of Hard Choices,"*Crisis*, March 1989, p. 32.

[137] Cecil Williams, Conference Welcoming Statement, April 1989.

[138] Ibid.

[139] Ibid.

[140] Walter W. Morrison, "An Interview with Mayor Kurt L. Schmoke, Baltimore," *Crisis,* March 1989, p. 31.

[141] Ibid.

[142] Congressman George Crockett, "A 'Helping Hand'—Not Jail—For Drug Use," *The Detroit News*, 11 February 1990.

# 3

# The Media and the Construction of Random Drug Violence

## Henry H. Brownstein

From 1986 to 1990, the news media in New York City constructed a compelling picture of a reality in which drug-related violence was spreading and becoming random in its selection of victims. In so doing, it encouraged a belief in the growing vulnerability of white, middle-class people in the face of such violence. This case is an example of how the media, operating in a particular political context, effectively supported the movement of government policies toward the right. The relationship of that construction to public policy is discussed, as is its grounding in erroneous premises and its potential for harmful social consequences.

Reprinted by permission of *Social Justice* from Vol. 18, No. 4, pp. 85–103, © 1991.

# The Media and the Construction of Reality

The reality of everyday life is a social construction (Berger and Luckmann, 1966; Schutz, 1962). When the news media report stories as news, they objectify reality (cf. Lichter et al., 1986; Koch, 1990). Naturally, then, the newsmaking process is subject to some measure of distortion (see Lee and Lee, 1939; Lee, 1978, 1988; Gans, 1979; Schiller, 1981; Chancellor and Mears, 1983; Walker, 1983; Lichter et al., 1986; Broder, 1987; Koch, 1990).

This process of making news inevitably is value-based (cf. Barak, 1988:573). Lichter and his associates interviewed 240 journalists and concluded that these people, whom they call the "media elite," distort the news in a liberal direction (1986:294). Others have argued that news is actually constructed in a particularly conservative direction (see, for example, Lee, 1978, 1988; Barak 1988; Koch, 1990). The case of news about drugs in New York City in the second half of the 1980s supports the latter conclusion.

# The Context of Newsmaking

The contemporary American news media is both an institution designed to inform the public and a business, the primary purpose of which is to make a profit (see Lee, 1973, 1988; Mayer, 1987; Koch, 1990). Thus, news reporting is as likely to sensationalize events as it is to report them, as likely to serve as an instrument of propaganda as it is to be a source of information, and as likely to be a creator of myth as it is to be a purveyor of truth (cf. Lee and Lee, 1939; Lee, 1978; Barak, 1988; Reinarman and Levine, 1989; Koch, 1990).

To obtain the information needed to make news, the media rely on experts and public officials whose control over knowledge makes them the gate keepers of that information. To construct news that is not favorable to those with power and authority over knowledge is to risk being cut off from the information that is needed to be able to construct news at all. Consequently, news is necessarily constructed in a political context.

Reinarman and Levine (1989) demonstrate how the current drug crisis in America is a construction of the news media within a conservative political context. After establishing that official claims about "a pandemic [crack] 'crisis' endangering the lives of 'a whole generation' of youth are at odds with the best official data," they suggest, "the crack 'crisis,' like previous drug scares, is in part the product of the association of 'dangerous drugs' with a 'dangerous class' [of people] and of the peculiarly fertile features of politics in the current context" (*Ibid.*: 554–555). Specifically, they argue that in the 1980s, the New Right and Ronald Reagan used drugs as an "all-purpose scapegoat with which they could blame an array of problems [that had been exacerbated by social and fiscal policies of the Reagan administration] on the deviance of the individuals who suffered them" (*Ibid.*: 562). Further, they argue that normally liberal Democrats responded to the political pressure created by the drug "crisis" by moving to the right on social issues (*Ibid.*: 563). Notably, the prominence of drugs as an issue "dropped sharply in both political speeches and media coverage after the 1986 [congressional] election, only to return during the 1988 [presidential] primaries" (*Ibid.*: 564).

In New York State, the political context in relation to drugs was shaped in 1986 by the growing concern about crack, a refined and smokable form of cocaine (see the Governor's Office of Employee Relations, 1986a; 1986b). In his annual address to the New York State legislature in January 1987, just after his election to a second term, Governor Mario Cuomo told the legislators:

> This year, we must intensify our efforts as never before in the face of the emergence of crack—the extraordinarily potent, highly addictive, and relatively inexpensive cocaine derivative. The lightning speed with which this lethal drug has spread through society is evident in substantial increases in drug-related deaths and demands for treatment by drug users. Crack has also been accompanied by rising incidents of violent crime, including robberies and murders. We must attack this new menace by enacting stiffer penalties for its sale and possession (1987:39).

With this statement the governor identified the major themes of a campaign against crack and other drugs as follows:

1. Crack is a particularly lethal and addictive drug;
2. The use of drugs, especially crack, has reached epidemic proportions;
3. Drugs, especially crack, are largely responsible for the increasing rates of crime and violence; and
4. The proper response to the crack menace is enhanced enforcement of drug laws.

In a press release dated May 5, 1986, the governor identified a fifth theme: drug education or prevention and treatment programs are also important responses to the crack problem.

By January 1989, a "Campaign Against Drug Abuse" was the highlight of the governor's annual address to the state legislature. He opened his remarks by telling the legislators that New York's three most serious problems were "drugs, drugs and drugs" (Cuomo, 1989). He then announced the formation of a Statewide Anti-Drug Abuse Council that would coordinate statewide efforts through the Office of the Lieutenant Governor.

A major function of the Council was to develop a statewide drug strategy. The first "State of New York Anti-Drug Abuse Strategy Report" was issued at the end of 1989. Of 110 recommendations in the report, 41 were enforcement-oriented, 38 were in the area of prevention, and 31 in the area of treatment (Statewide Anti-Drug Abuse Council, 1989).

The drug strategy in New York tried to balance conservative and liberal elements. But given the belief in a drug crisis brought on by the introduction of crack, both the government and the public showed greatest interest in law-and-order responses to "dangerous" drugs. The news media supported this reactionary position and added its own theme: drug-related violence as random violence. The random violence theme mobilized the white middle class against drugs and thereby invited an even more repressive response than might otherwise have been possible.

## Making the Case for Random Drug Violence

Between 1986 and 1990, there were countless news stories about crack, other drugs, and drug-related criminal violence. A review of printed news stories about these phenomena during this period in New York City reveals how the media, operating within a predominantly conservative political context, took the government's notions about crack, pursued these themes, and constructed a "reality" in which drugs, crack in particular, were identified as responsible for widespread and random drug-related street violence.[1]

Given its reliance on public officials for information, from the beginning the news media took its cues from state government in its campaign against crack and other drugs. There were few articles about either the accuracy or validity of the assumptions on which the government themes were based or on their appropriateness. Discussions of alternate strategies, such as legalization, when they were reported at all, were left to the editorial columns.

Shortly after the governor's May 5, 1986, press release, the news media in New York began to report on the problem of crack. On May 18, 1986, *The New York Times* published an article called "Opium Dens for the Crack Era" on page one. The article described the "scene" at a particular crack house, highlighting the experience of a:

> 17-year-old girl from Queens who, together with two friends, brought $200 to a Manhattan base [crack] house and smoked it in less than an hour. To get more crack, she said, she had sex with the operators of the base house and the customers.

The themes of the article, the growing use of crack and its pernicious and addictive qualities, were grounded in quotes from "officials."

On July 31, 1986, *The New York Times* published an article about a meeting between state and city government officials at which they jointly issued a number of proposals calling for more state judges, more courtroom space, more federal judges to handle drug cases, the deportation of illegal aliens convicted of drug offenses, mandatory jail sentences for repeat misdemeanor drug offenders, and increased state penalties for possession or sale of crack.

The next day, August 1, *The New York Times* published an article under the heading, "Rise in Major Crimes in City Continues, the Police Report." The article provided statistics to support the argument that crime was increasing and reported on deployment of a special unit of the New York City Police Department to help in precincts with soaring homicide rates. The author wrote, "police officials yesterday attributed many of the increases in reported murders, robberies, and other crimes to drugs, particularly the rapid proliferation over the past several months of crack, a potent cocaine derivative."

In 1986, there were congressional elections in the United States and a gubernatorial election in New York. In 1987, not an election year, considerably less emphasis in the media was placed on drugs (cf. Reinarman and Levine, 1989:536). Still, the media kept the reactionary drug themes alive, maintaining a focus on the link between drugs and violence.

At the end of 1987, a New York City police officer was shot and wounded. The *Daily News* on December 14 used a two-inch headline on its cover: "BLOODBATH." Headings of the related articles were: "Machine-gunner wounds cop; drug war kills 2 men," "In Bedford-Stuyvesant . . . Business as usual—B'klyn crack den" . . . "A Drug War Bloodbath—Cop is shot in Brooklyn—Was probing double murder," and "Don't worry, Mom." The year 1987 was over and 1988, a congressional election year, was about to begin.

The year began with straightforward, general interest reports. Then, at the end of February 1988, a young police officer was shot point-blank while guarding the home of a witness in a drug case in Queens. At first, the newspapers simply reported the event. Yet as the cold-blooded nature of the attack, the youth of the officer, and the involvement of the perpetrators in the drug trade became widely known, the reports began to focus more generally on the violence committed by users and dealers of crack and other drugs.

During March, *The New York Times*—the New York paper least likely to sensationalize the news—ran the following articles: "Machine Guns and Unpredictability Are the Hallmarks of Crack's Violence" (March 8) and "Brutal Drug Gangs Wage War of Terror in Upper Manhattan" (March 15). In April, *The Times* ran a series of three articles on the drug war, ending with an article called "In the War on Illegal Drugs, Main Battle Is on the Home

Front" (April 12, 1988). The series focused on drug trafficking and interdiction efforts as well as on law enforcement and corruption.

During this period, the New York City Police Department reported that the murder rate in Queens had increased by 25 percent over the previous year. *The Times* reported this on April 20 and the next day published an article with the headline, "Drug Violence Undermining Queens Hopes" (*The New York Times*, April 21, 1988). The page B1 article began with the words:

> Queens officials and residents said yesterday that a police report showing that the borough's murder rate, fueled by crack, has increased 25 percent for the second year in a row confirmed their worst fears: that drug violence is threatening the very stability of what has long been considered New York's most middle-class borough.

The threat to the middle class was the subject of the article, and it was noted that the "hardest-hit section is predominantly black middle-class southeastern Queens."

During the middle of the year, it was quiet, but toward the end of the year, during election campaigns, things picked up again. In September, the police announced that murder and manslaughter rates were up and this was dutifully reported. That month a story about a drug dealer who was set ablaze by three men on a Manhattan street corner was also widely reported.

In December, the New York City news media summed up the drug story of the year: in 1988 the city had experienced a record number of violent crimes and a notable percentage of these were considered by law-enforcement officials to have been drug related. A December 30 article entitled "Crack Whips Killing Toll" in the *Daily News* covered the police announcement on the year's record-setting murder rate. On December 27, 1988, *The Times* ran a short article on page B3 called "Police Term Homicide Data Too Raw and Not Definitive." However, the uncertain nature of the figures on which the big story was based was not given much attention.

Early in 1989, the random drug violence theme first appeared. In its Sunday edition on January 22, 1989, *The New York Times* included an article entitled "Drug Wars Don't Pause to Spare the Innocent." Citing "experts," it was about the "killing of innocent bystanders, particularly in the crossfires of this nation's drug wars." It is suggested that such killings had "suddenly become a phenomenon that greatly troubles experts on crime." Drug-related violence was spreading and now even "innocent" people were at risk.

There was some evidence that innocent bystanders had been shot in the crossfire of drug battles. In the January 22 article, *The New York Times* estimated that in New York City there bad been eight such cases in 1988. In a companion piece, *The Times* reported that a 12-year-old girl had been killed when she "was talking with a group of friends less than a block from her home when she inadvertently walked into a drug-related dispute on a sidewalk in Brooklyn."

For the first few months of the year, the random violence theme continued to be promoted by the media. On January 23, the *Daily News* published an article about the spread of crime into previously "safe" neighborhoods. Called "IT'S CALLED SPILLOVER, Silk-stocking areas share run on crime," the article quoted a "community leader" from Brooklyn who said, "there are no safe neighborhoods anymore." The article gave statistics showing the level of violent crime in each police precinct in the city. On February 2, the *New York Post* gave an example under the dramatic heading, "HUMAN SHIELD—Snatched tot wounded in Brooklyn gun battle." The story was about a three-year-old boy who was "critically injured yesterday when a teenager snatched him from his mother's grasp and used him as a human shield in a gun battle."

There were also reports that drug-related violence had spread beyond the boundaries of New York City, threatening the smaller cities of upstate New York. The Rochester Democrat and Chronicle reported on January 15, 1989, that the per capita murder rate in that city was as high as that of most large urban centers. The headline read, "Rochester faces image of violence—12 drug-related killings last year were the highest ever in the city."

During this period, the national media continued to view drug-related violence as being focused on inner-city neighborhoods. On January 16, 1989, Newsweek published a story called "A Tide of Drug Killing." The article emphasized the reactionary themes that drugs were behind a record-breaking level of violent crime and that crack was "uniquely evil." Yet it also clearly suggested that drug-related violence was concentrated in poor and minority communities and went as far as to include the subheading, "The crack plague spurs more inner-city murder." On April 10, 1989, U.S. News & World Report published a similar article. The main heading was "DEAD ZONES," and the subheading was, "Whole *sections* of urban America are being written off as anarchic badlands, places where cops fear to go and acknowledge: 'This is Beirut, U.S.A.'" (emphasis added).

An incident in April 1989 accelerated the objectification of the random drug violence theme. A young, middle-class white woman was jogging through Central Park in Manhattan when a large group of younger black males attacked her and brutally raped and beat her. After reporting the story, the news media followed up with articles suggesting that innocent victims were increasingly likely to become victims of violence. For example, on April 25 *The New York Times* ran an article called "Gang Attack: Unusual for Its Viciousness." The article stated:

> The random, apparently motiveless rampage in Central Park last week that the suspects call wilding was an extraordinarily ferocious version of group delin-

quency that usually takes less vicious forms, according to law-enforcement officials and psychologists.

The people of the city were angry about the Central Park attack and the news media fueled this anger. Though the question of a racial motive was occasionally raised—the victim was white and the suspects Black—it was doubted. However, when an African-American woman was found brutally murdered in Fort Tryon Park a few weeks later, only the *New York Amsterdam News*, the newspaper that gives "The new Black view," argued on May 6 that the two cases should be treated in a similar fashion. It was suggested in the article that African-American women are frequently the victims of violence, but their victimization is never given the same attention as that of white women.

While the Central Park case was not necessarily drug-related, it was violent and it did draw attention to the vulnerability of white, middle-class people. Throughout the remainder of 1989, the news media continued to develop this theme, bringing in mention of crack whenever possible. On May 28, *The New York Times* published a full-length, double-column editorial called simply, "Crack." It was subheaded "A Disaster of Historic Dimension, Still Growing," and claimed, "Crack poses a much greater threat than other drugs. It reaches out to destroy the quality of life, and life itself, at all levels of American society." The theme of the editorial, a call for government action, was that crack is uniquely destructive and that as crack "spreads to middle America," the "fabric of society" itself is at risk.

On October 1, 1989, an article called "Crack's Destructive Sprint Across America" appeared in *The New York Times Magazine*. Its author argued that "now, in smaller communities, too, crack is striking with swift fury. From rural woodlands to shady suburbs, prairie townships to Southern hamlets, no community seems immune" (Massing, 1989:38). Also in its Sunday edition, *The Times* began a two-part series with a front-page article entitled "The Spreading Web of Crack" that stated: "Crack, which has been devastating entire inner-city neighborhoods, has begun to claim significant numbers of middle- and upper-class addicts, experts have found."

The year ended again with reports about the record number of homicides in the city. On December 31, *The New York Times* reported, "More Americans Are Killing Each Other." On December 17, the *Daily News* took a different angle by headlining: "Thugs rule subway." The *News* went on to provide a "log" of the crimes that took place on the subways, a common means of transportation for most New Yorkers.

The year 1989 began with an article in *New York* magazine that clearly explained the random violence theme. In "Fighting Back against Crack," the author wrote:

For two years after the crack plague struck New York in 1985, people who lived in solid neighborhoods around the city thought they could remain insulated from the havoc wreaked by the drug—at first crack was largely confined to the poorest neighborhoods, and many people thought it would be just another dreadful thing they read about in the tabloids or watched on the news.

It hasn't turned out that way. Although there are a few parts of town where people still think of the crack epidemic as something distant and alien—the area around Gracie Mansion [the mayor's residence] would seem to be one—most neighborhoods in the city by now have been forced to deal with either crack or its foul by-products: if not crack houses and street dealers or users, then crackhead crimes such as purse snatchings, car break-ins, burglaries, knife-point robberies, muggings, and murders (Pooley, 1989:32).

By 1990, the theme of random violence had been objectified, and the news media continually argued for that position and reported stories that supposedly demonstrated its validity. An unusually high number of such incidents in the summer of that year fueled the argument, and the random violence theme was brought to a new level of sensationalism. During one month of the summer of 1990, nine children in New York City were hit by stray bullets. Five of them died. The mayor compared New York to the television image of Dodge City. The news media were suggesting that now innocent bystanders were the targets of drug-related violence.

On August 5, the *Daily News*, which calls itself "New York's Picture Newspaper," gave the cover of its Sunday edition to the following headline in two-inch high letters: "ENOUGH!" Just below the headline were white-bordered pictures of two of the latest "innocent" victims of the violence. Articles about each followed. One victim was a 33-year-old man who was shot to death "in a botched robbery" while he was making a call from a public telephone on a street corner of New York's Greenwich Village. The other, a nine-month-old boy, was killed while standing in his walker when bullets meant for his uncle came through the door of their home. One of the many articles that followed carried the headline, "Innocent is slain by the damned." On August 12, *The New York Times* Sunday edition included an article with the title, "Bystander Deaths Reshape City Lives."

Even *USA Today*, with its national focus, on July 31 featured an article about the shootings of bystanders in New York City. The article was called, "New NYC fear: Stray bullets."

The innocent bystander motif of the random drug violence theme gained important symbolic support when a tourist to New York City was killed on a subway platform while trying to help his mother. On Labor Day, a young man visiting New York from Utah was killed when, according to the *New York Post* on September 4, he "tried to protect his mother from the bloodthirsty bunch stalking the 7th Avenue IND station at 53rd Street." Newspaper headlines highlighted the theme that, as had always been feared, even tourists to New York were potential victims of the city's widespread and random violence. For example, the *Post* article was called "TOURIST SLAIN PROTECTING MOM."

The national news media also gave attention to the random nature of drug-related violence in New York. On September 17, for example, *Time* magazine had the headline on its cover, "The Rotting of the Big Apple." Inside was an article called "The Decline of New York," followed immediately by the sub-heading, "A surge of brutal killings has shaken the Big Apple to its core." The author wrote:

> A growing sense of vulnerability has been deepened by the belief that deadly violence, once mostly confined to crime-ridden ghetto neighborhoods that the police once wrote off as free-fire zones, is now lashing out randomly at anyone, even in areas once considered relatively safe (Attinger, 1989:38).

On December 31, 1990, *The New York Times* again reported a record number of killings in New York City. On the first page of its Metropolitan Section was an article called "Record Year for Killings Jolts Officials in New York." The author wrote:

> Crime in New York in 1990 was defined primarily in two ways, both of which tended to heighten anxiety. One was the large number of shootings of bystanders, whose victims were often children—crimes that frightened by their casualness and unpredictability. The other was crime that seemed to follow a pattern—like the Zodiac shootings and the livery-cab killings.

The first "way" referred to innocent bystanders as victims. The second referred to the innocent victims of a person who had frightened the entire city for a time by shooting at people for no apparent logical reason and to attacks on innocent taxi cab drivers. In effect, the newspaper was suggesting that violent crime in the city in 1990 was defined by the innocence of its victims and the randomness of their selection for victimization.

Reporting on drugs between 1986 and 1990, the news media in New York took its cue from the conservative political context of the state and nation. Then news makers developed their own theme, one that had the sensational quality that could attract people to buy the news. That theme said that drug-related violence in the city was widespread and random. A picture of reality was drawn in which all people were purported to be equally and indiscriminately subject to drug-related violent victimization.

## Official Statistics and Research Findings

Drug scares are independent phenomena, not necessarily related to actual trends or patterns in drug use or trafficking (Reinarman and Levine, 1989:537). In New York in the late 1980s, the alarm over random drug-connected violence was not related either to what was known about street crime and violence through official statistics or to research findings.

A sample of people is considered *random* when that sample "has the property not only of giving each individual an equal chance of being selected, but also of giving each combination of individuals an equal chance of selection" (Blalock, 1960:109). Even news reporters knew in the late 1980s in New York that the observed increase in officially recorded drug-related violence was not truly random (see, for example, Greenberg, 1990).

Official statistics, to the extent they are themselves an accurate reflection of actual conditions, show that not all people in New York City in the late 1980s faced the same risk of violent victimization—drug-related or otherwise. The conclusion that officially defined violent crime increased in New York City during this period is compelling.[2] The argument that the extent to which such violence was randomly distributed, however, is not.[3]

Besides official crime statistics, the findings of a study on homicide by the national Centers for Disease Control support these conclusions (CDC, 1990). Using official mortality data, the study examined homicide as a cause of death in the United States between 1978 and 1987. As the authors of the report found:

> From 1978 through 1987, annual homicide rates for young black males were four to five times higher than for young black females, five to eight times higher than for young white males, and 16 to 22 times higher than for young white females. Since 1984, the disparity between homicide rates for young black males and other racial/sex groups increased substantially (CDC, 1990:870).

In addition, they reported, "despite common perception that the victims of homicide are usually killed by unknown assailants during robberies or drug-related crimes, more than half of all homicide victims are killed by persons known to them" (*Ibid.*: 871–872).

Police statistics from New York City directly address the question of innocent bystanders. Despite the alarm, the number and proportion of victims of violence who are actually innocent bystanders remain very small. On August 5, 1990, *The New York Times* informed readers that the police had reported 1,051 homicides in New York City during the first six months of the year. The

New York City Police Department (NYPD) officially identified 15 of those cases as having involved victims who were innocent bystanders. Thus, according to official statistics, during the first half of 1990 in New York City, 1.4 percent of all homicide victims were innocent bystanders.

Recent studies of homicide provide additional empirical support for the conclusion that only a low percentage of homicide cases involves innocent bystanders. One study of 414 homicides in New York City in 1988 found that only 1.2 percent involved innocent bystanders as victims (Brownstein et al., 1989). Another study of random shootings of bystanders in four U.S. cities between the years 1977 and 1988 concluded that "bystander shootings are a rare event" (Sherman et al., 1989:303).

There is much research that shows the link between the observed violence and drugs, particularly crack (see, for example, Office of the Attorney General, 1989; Goldstein et al., 1989; Mieczkowski, 1990; Belenko, 1990). Given the characteristics of crack itself and the nature of the crack market, however, this research suggests that the violence is a product of drug-market instability and is aimed primarily at people who participate in, or whose lives touch upon, that market.

The research on drugs and violence suggests that most drug-related violence is confined to people who, by choice or circumstance, live in or near drug communities and neighborhoods (cf. Brownstein, 1991). Further, very few people are likely to be innocent-bystander victims of the violence. Yet the media was able to suggest otherwise, since even a few cases of innocent people being victimized by violence has great symbolic value. As Sherman and his associates wrote:

> Bystander deaths violate the routine assumptions necessary for conducting daily life. . . . An increase in such killings, even a small proportion of all homicide, suggests a threat of spillover of street violence from the underclass to the middle and upper classes (1989:299–300).

In other words, poor and minority people should expect to be victims of violence and violent crime. Middle- and upper-class people, on the other hand, should not be expected to tolerate any increase in their risk of violent victimization.

It is safe to say that official statistics do show an increase in the incidence of street violence over the past few years in New York City. Yet that violence has not become random. It continues to be directed at the same people it always has victimized: minorities, women, and probably the poor and the young as well. This point is not meant to minimize or debase the great personal tragedy that any and every victim of violence is likely to suffer. It does suggest, though, that in New York City, if not elsewhere, all people are not equally likely to become the victims of street violence, drug-related or otherwise.

## What's the Harm?

Reinarman and Levine pose an interesting question: "Given the damage that drugs can do, what's the harm in a little hysteria?" (1989:567). They propose two answers.

"First," Reinarman and Levine write, "drug scares blame individual immorality and personal behavior for endemic social and structural problems, and they divert attention and resources from those larger problems" (*Ibid.*: 567). Such has been the case in New York. The fear of random drug violence, which invites policies that are tough on drug offenders (cf. Fox, 1983), bolstered and supported a major expansion of law enforcement, highlighted by a prodigious prison-expansion program. Such policies place the onus on individual drug users and dealers, who are viewed primarily as potential perpetrators of violent crime and thus in need of control by the criminal justice system.

The federal strategy toward drugs and drug-related problems has been largely reactionary, with about 70 percent of all dollars being proposed for spending on law enforcement and supply-reduction programs (Office of National Drug Control Policy, 1989; 1990; 1991). In New York State, where much more consideration has been given to treatment and prevention (Statewide Anti-Drug Abuse Council, 1989), official statistics show extremely large increases in the number of felony drug arrests, indictments, convictions, and sentences to prison from 1983 to 1988 (Ross and Cohen, 1988; Division of Criminal Justice Services, 1988).[4] From 1983 to 1990, the New York State prison population grew from approximately 30,000 to about 55,000 inmates, with drug offenders accounting "for 45 percent of the total system growth since 1980 and 75 percent of the growth since 1986" (Statewide Anti-Drug Abuse Council, 1989:7).

As noted earlier, in his message to the state legislature in 1989, Governor Cuomo told legislators that the three most serious problems faced by the state were "drugs, drugs, and drugs" (Cuomo, 1989). What about homelessness and AIDS, illiteracy and unemployment, or racism, ageism, and sexism? And what about the abuse of our children and the destruction of our environment? During a period when people believed the greatest threat to their well-being to be random violence perpetrated by drug users and traffickers—a notion constructed by the media—attention and resources were diverted from the more intractable social and structural problems.

The second response to the question of harm, according to Reinarman and Levine, is that "drug scares do not work very well to reduce drug problems and that they may well promote the behavior they claim to be preventing" (1989:568). The failure of the tactics flowing from the War on Drugs strategy is well documented (see, for example, Nadelmann, 1988, 1989; Ostrowski, 1989; Brownstein, 1990) alongside evidence indicating that policies and programs that address the larger and more basic social and structural problems would be more effective (see, for example, Schur, 1962; Joint Committee on New York Drug Law, 1977; Trebach, 1982; Curtis, 1989; Milton S. Eisenhower Foundation, 1990).

Social scientists, political analysts, and even news reporters have acknowledged that drug abuse, the drug trade, and drug-related violence have not been reduced to acceptable levels, even in those areas where enforcement and interdiction efforts have been strongest (Schur, 1962; Joint Committee on New York Drug Law, 1977; Falco, 1989; Weisheit, 1990; Miller, 1990). In fact, these efforts have resulted in several unintended and undesirable consequences.

As noted earlier, the War on Drugs has overwhelmed federal, state, and local criminal-justice systems (Austin and McVey, 1989; Nadelmann, 1989), including those in New York City (Ross and Cohen, 1988; Belenko, 1990). In addition, the war has contributed to the erosion of civil liberties, as is true of the congressional amendment to the Posse Comitatus Act (Wisotsky, 1986) and its assault on the Bill of Rights (Finkelman, 1990).

In some ways, the reactionary policies of the enforcement emphasis have exacerbated the very problems they were designed to solve. In his study of marijuana trafficking, Kleiman argued that marijuana enforcement "acts as a protective tariff" and thereby encourages "domestic commercial production [that] tends to be quite violence-intensive" (1989:73, 119). Similarly, findings from a New York City study of homicides suggest:

> Given that most drug-related violence is related to conflicts over market share, violence is likely to increase as [inexperienced, young crack] dealers [with no links to any stabilizing organizational structure] compete for control of territories left unserved and unprotected as a result of successful enforcement activity (Brownstein, 1990:117).

In his study of prostitution and drugs, Goldstein wrote, "when no social harm exists, there can be no justification for repressive legislation" (1979:2). This insight remains true even in relative terms. The extent of repression in public policy should not exceed the harm caused by the problem being addressed by the policy. By promoting the myth that citizens are all equally at risk of violence, especially at the hands of drug users and traffickers, the news media is at least in part responsible for encouraging the ill-founded and illogical expansion of law enforcement and the contraction of civil liberties in contemporary American society.

# Conclusion

The reactionary agenda toward drug users and traffickers resulted from a constellation of forces. Liberal government officials in New York reacted to a perceived drug crisis by calling for a variety of programs. The news media, pursuing a sensational story that would sell the news and not contradict the policies of officials on whom they depended for information, mobilized the white middle class with an emphasis on the theme of random drug violence. Faced with an alarmed voting public calling for law and order, government officials promoted a drug scare that would permit spending on law-enforcement programs during a time of fiscal crisis and overcrowded prisons.

The drug scare around crack allowed the development of a conservative agenda even in a liberal political environment. In cases like this, social scientists should play a more active role (cf. Barak, 1988; Brownstein, 1991). For example, they can use their skills and positions to provide information through government and through the media, to clarify the debate. In this case, for example, social scientists could have shown empirically that the fear of random drug violence, especially among white middle-class people, was unrealistic.

# Epilogue

Thanks largely to the drug scare generated by government officials and the media, the prison inmate population in New York State doubled during the 1980s. Late in 1990, an article in *The Times Union of Albany* asked whether it is "proper" to continue to build prisons to satisfy "intense public demands to get tough on crime, particularly drug offenders." An "expert" and reform advocate from Washington, D.C., is quoted as having said, "the bills are coming due they are quite large. At some point, it will force an examination of how much incarceration we can afford."

Just days before publication of the article, Governor Cuomo had announced that the state was facing a major fiscal crisis, one that would cost the Department of Correctional Services alone an estimated $27 million during the current fiscal year. On the eve of the 20th anniversary of the prison uprising at Attica in upstate New York, the newspaper's sudden interest in the costs of incarceration was not surprising. It is only interesting.

## Notes

[1]From 1986 to 1990, I clipped and saved articles on drugs, drug policy, drugs and health, drug treatment and prevention, crime and drugs, and violence and drugs from *The New York Times*, the Albany *Times Union*, and *Newsweek* regularly and from *The New York Post*, the *New York Daily News*, and other magazines and newspapers when relevant articles or events were brought to my attention. During the same period, a bureau at the New York State Division of Criminal Justice Services regularly clipped and circulated to staff articles about crime and criminal-justice practices and policies (including those about drugs, drug policy, and so on) from the major New York newspapers. Both sources were used for this analysis. Articles from *The New York Times* were oversampled, since that is the only major mainstream New York City newspaper that is not a tabloid, and therefore least likely to sensationalize the news.

[2]Uniform Crime Report (UCR) statistics show that, overall, the level of violent crime in New York City did increase during the late 1980s. From 143,413 reported violent offenses in the city in 1986, there were 169,616 reported for 1989. In terms of the rate per 100,000 population, the increase was from 1,997.5 in 1986 to 2,301.6 in 1989. Comparing the first quarter of 1990 to the first quarter of 1989, the number of violent offenses reported declined from 37,443 to 29,833 (DCJS, 1990a; 1990b).

[3]National Planning Association population estimates and Supplementary Homicide Data for New York City for the period 1987 to 1989 show: (1) between 33 percent and 34 percent of the people in the city were non-white, but 55 percent of the victims of homicide were Black; and (2) about 53 percent of the people living in the city were female, yet women accounted for less than 15 percent of all homicide victims.

[4]Between 1983 and 1987, the number of felony drug arrests in New York State increased by 118 percent, indictments by 207 percent, convictions by 210 percent, and sentences to prison for drug convictions by 220 percent (Ross and Cohen, 1988). From 1987 to 1988, felony drug arrests increased by an additional 23 percent, indictments by 12 percent, and sentences to prison for drug convictions by 22 percent (accounting for 37 percent of all sentences to state prison in 1988) (Division of Criminal Justice Services, 1988:197). For New York City during the period from 1983 to 1987, the number of felony drug arrests increased by 122 percent, indictments by 305 percent, and sentences to prison for drug convictions by 237 percent (Ross and Cohen, 1988).

## References

Attinger, Joelle
  1989    "The Decline of New York." Time (September 17): 36–41, 44.
Austin, James and Aaron D. McVey
  1989    "The 1989 NCCD Prison Population Forecast: The Impact of the War on Drugs." NCCD Focus. National Council on Crime and Delinquency (December).
Barak, Gregg
  1988    "Newsmaking Criminology: Reflections on the Media, Intellectuals, and Crime." Justice Quarterly 5:565–587.

Belenko, Steven
　1990　"The Impact of Drug Offenders on the Criminal Justice System." R. A.
　　　　Weisheit (ed.), Drugs, Crime, and the Criminal Justice System. Cincinnati,
　　　　OH: Anderson Press: 27–28.
Berger, Peter L. and Thomas Luckmann
　1966　The Social Construction of Reality. Garden City, NY: Doubleday.
Blalock, Hubert M., Jr.
　1960　Social Statistics. New York: McGraw Hill Book Company.
Brownstein, Henry H.
　1991　The Social Construction of Public Policy: A Case for Participation by
　　　　Researchers." Sociological Practice Review 2:132-140.
　1990　"Demilitarization of the War on Drugs: Toward an Alterative Drug Strat-
　　　　egy." A. S. Trebach and K. B. Zeese (eds.), The Great Issues of Drug Pol-
　　　　icy. Washington, DC: The Drug Policy Foundation:114–122.
Brownstein, Henry H., Paul J. Goldstein, Patrick J. Ryan, and Patricia A. Bellucci
　1989　"Homicide and Drug Trafficking." Paper presented at the annual meeting
　　　　of the Society for the Study of Social Problems, Berkeley, California
　　　　(August).
Broder, David
　1987　Behind the Front Page—A Candid Look at How the News Is Made. New
　　　　York: Simon and Schuster.
Centers for Disease Control
　1990　Homicide among Young Black Males—United States. 1978–1987." Mor-
　　　　bidity and Mortality Weekly Report 39 (December 7): 869–873.
Chancellor, John and Walter R. Mears
　1983　The News Business. New York: Harper and Row.
Cuomo, Mario M.
　1989　Message to the Legislature. Albany, New York (January 4).
　1987　Message to the Legislature. Albany, New York (January 7).
Curtis, Lynn A.
　1989　The National Drug Strategy and Inner City Policy. Testimony before the
　　　　Select Committee on Narcotics Abuse and Control, U.S. House of Repre-
　　　　sentatives (November 15).
Division of Criminal Justice Services
　1990a　"Uniform Crime Reporting—Index Offenses Reported—Final Counts for
　　　　1989." Office of Justice Systems Analysis Bulletin (August). Bureau of
　　　　Criminal Justice Statistical Services. Albany, New York: vii, 2.
　1990b　"Crime and Justice Trends in New York State: 1985–89." Office of Justice
　　　　Systems Analysis Bulletin (August). Bureau of Criminal Justice Statistical
　　　　Services. Office of Justice Systems Analysis. Albany, New York.
　1988　Crime and Justice Annual Report. Bureau of Criminal Justice Statistical
　　　　Services. Albany, New York.
Falco, Malthea
　1989　Winning the Drug War—A National Strategy. A Twentieth Century Fund
　　　　Paper. New York: Priority Press.

Federal Bureau of Investigation
  1990   "Crime in the United States." Uniform Crime Reports
  1989.   Washington, DC: U.S. Department of Justice (August 5).
Finkelman, Paul
  1990   "In War Civil Liberties Is the Second Casualty: The War on Drugs and the
         Bill of Rights." Paper presented at the annual meeting of the American
         Society of Criminology. Baltimore, Maryland (November).
Fox, James G.
  1983   "The New Right and Social Justice: Implications for the Prisoners' Move-
         ment." Crime and Social Justice 20:63–75.
Gans, Herbert J.
  1979   Deciding What's News—A Study of CBS Evening News, NBC Nightly
         News, Newsweek, and Time. New York: Pantheon.
Goldstein, Paul J.
  1979   Prostitution and Drugs. Lexington, Massachusetts: Lexington Books.
Goldstein, Paul J., Henry H. Brownstein, Patrick J. Ryan, and Patricia A. Belluci
  1989   "Crack and Homicide in New York City. 1988: A Conceptually Based
         Event Analysis." Contemporary Drug Problems 16:651–687.
Governor's Office of Employee Relations
  1986a  "Crackdown on Crack." GOER News 2 (August): 16 (Governor's Page).
  1986b  "Crack—The Deadliest Cocaine of All." GOER News 2 (September): 11–
         12.
Greenberg, Jonathan
  1990   "All about Crime." New York (September 3): 20–32.
Joint Committee on New York Drug Law Evaluation
  1977   The Nation's Toughest Drug Law: Evaluating the New York Experience,
         Final Report. New York: The Association of the Bar of the City of New
         York, Drug Abuse Council, Inc.
Kleiman, Mark A. R.
  1989   Marijuana—Costs of Abuse, Costs of Control. New York: Greenwood
         Press.
Koch, Tom
  1990   The News as Myth—Fact and Context in Journalism. New York: Green-
         wood Press.
Lee, Alfred McClung
  1988   Sociology for People—Toward a Caring Profession. Syracuse, NY: Syra-
         cuse University Press.
  1978   Sociology for Whom? New York: Oxford University Press.
  1973   The Daily Newspaper in America—The Evolution of a Social Instrument.
         New York: Octagon Books.
Lee, Alfred McClung and Elizabeth Briant Lee
  1939   The Fine Art of Propaganda—A Study of Father Coughlin's Speeches.
         New York: Harcourt, Brace and Company.
Lichter, S. Robert, Stanley Rothman, and Linda S. Lichter
  1986   The Media Elite. Bethesda, MD: Adler and Adler.

Massing, Michael
  1989 "Crack's Destructive Sprint across America." The New York Times Magazine (October 1): 38–41; 58–62.
Mayer, Martin
  1987 Making News. Garden City, NY: Doubleday & Company.
Mieczkowski, Tom
  1990 "Crack Distribution in Detroit." Contemporary Drug Problems 17:9–29.
Miller, Mark
  1990 "A Failed 'Test Case': Washington's Drug War." Newsweek (January 29): 28–29.
Milton S. Eisenhower Foundation
  1990 Youth Investment and Community Reconstruction—Street Lessons on Drugs and Crime for the Nineties. Final Report, The Milton S. Eisenhower Foundation.
Nadelmann, Ethan A.
  1989 "Drug Prohibition in the United States: Costs, Consequences, and Alternatives." Science 245 (September): 939–947.
  1988 "U.S. Drug Policy: A Bad Export." Foreign Policy 70 (Spring): 83–108.
Office of the Attorney General
  1989 Drug Trafficking—A Report to the President of the United States. Washington, DC: U.S. Department of Justice, compiled by the United States Attorneys and the Attorney General of the United States.
Office of National Drug Control Policy
  1991 National Drug Control Strategy. Washington, DC: Executive Office of the President.
  1990 National Drug Control Strategy. Washington, DC: Executive Office of the President.
  1989 National Drug Control Strategy. Washington, DC: Executive Office of the President.
Ostrowski, James
  1989 "Thinking about Drug Legalization." Policy Analysis. Cato Institute, No. 121 (May 25).
Pooley, Eric
  1989 "Fighting Back against Crack." New York Times (January 23): 31–39.
Reinarman, Craig and Harry G. Levine
  1989 "Crack in Context: Politics and Media in the Making of a Drug Scare." Contemporary Drug Problems 16:535–577.
Ross, Richard and Marjorie Cohen
  1988 New York Trends in Felony Drug Offense Processing. Albany: New York State Division of Criminal Justice Services.
Schiller, Dan
  1981 Objectivity and the News—The Public and the Rise of Commercial Journalism. Philadelphia: University of Pennsylvania Press.
Schur, Edwin
  1962 Narcotic Addiction in Britain and America—The Impact of Public Policy. Bloomington, Indiana: University Press.

Schutz, Alfred
  1962   Collected Papers I—The Problem of Social Reality. Edited and introduced
         by M. Natanson. The Hague: Martinus Nijhoff.
Sherman, Lawrence W., Leslie Steele, Deborah Laufersweiler, Nancy Hoffer, and
         Sherry A. Julian
  1989   "Stray Bullets and 'Mushrooms': Random Shootings of Bystanders in Four
         Cities, 1977–1988." Journal of Quantitative Criminology 5:297–316.
Statewide Anti-Drug Abuse Council
  1989   State of New York Anti-Drug Abuse Strategy Report. The Governor's
         Statewide Anti-Drug Abuse Council. Albany, New York.
Trebach, Arnold S.
  1982   The Heroin Solution. New Haven: Yale University Press.
Walker, Martin
  1983   Powers of the Press—Twelve of the World's Influential Newspapers. New
         York: The Pilgrim Press.
Weil, Andrew
  1986   The Natural Mind (Revised Edition). Boston: Houghton Mifflin Company.
Weisheit, Ralph A.
  1990   "Civil War on Drugs." R. A. Weisheit (ed.), Drugs, Crime, and the Crimi-
         nal Justice System. Cincinnati, OH: Anderson Press:1–10.
Wisotsky, Steven
  1986   Breaking the Impasse in the War on Drugs. New York: Greenwood Press.

# 4

# The Drugs-Crime Relationship
## An Analytical Framework

Duane C. McBride
Clyde B. McCoy

The relationship between drug using and criminal behavior has been a primary concern of researchers, policymakers and the general public for most of this century (see McBride & McCoy, 1982). Both the scientific and popular media have tended to view the existence of the drugs-crime relationship as the basis of the public concern about drug use, as well as of national and international drug policy and the current infrastructure of drug law enforcement, treatment, and research. Although in the public mind, the relationship be tween drugs and crime is often seen as fairly straightforward—with drug use being viewed as directly causing criminal behavior—critical research analysis has indicated that the relationship is conceptually and empirically quite complex. Given this, it is the purpose of this article to suggest an organizational paradigm for examining the literature on the drugs-crime relationship, to use that paradigm to review relevant literature, and to examine the policy implications of recent research on the drugs-crime relationship.

Reprinted by permission of Sage Publications, from *The Prison Journal*, Vol. 73, Nos. 3 & 4, pp. 257–278, © 1993 by Sage Publications, Inc.

---

## An Organizational Paradigm

---

Although the phrase "drugs-crime relationship" is commonly used, it often masks the variety of substances that are included under the concept of *drugs*, and the specific types of violations of the criminal law that is encompassed by the term *crime*. In addition, the phrase does not elucidate issues of the etiology of the relationship. It might be helpful if an analysis of the relationship between drug using and criminal behavior were organized within the following framework:

1.   the historical underpinnings of current perspectives
2.   types of drugs and types of criminal behavior
3.   the statistical relationship: the extent and type of criminal behavior among various types of drug users and the extent and type of drug use among various types of criminals
4.   the etiological nature of the relationship, including such issues as causality and interaction
5.   theoretical interpretations of the relationship
6.   the policy implications of research conclusions

---

## Historical Underpinnings of Current Perspectives

---

### The 19th-Century National Drug Culture

During the late 19th century, American society had a fairly laissez faire attitude toward what were called "patent medicines." These medicines, often containing opium, were touted as cure-alls for whatever ailed a person, from general aches and pains to sexual dysfunctions. They were available through a variety of means, including private physicians, the Sears catalog, and the traveling medicine show. The claims of one patent medicine, Hamlin's Wizard Oil, well illustrate the exaggerated assertions. The advertisement for the Hamlin product claimed that "there is no sore it will not heal, no pain it will not subdue." The oil was "Pleasant to take and magical in its effects" (Inciardi, 1992, p. 4). The makers and distributors of patent medicines were effective entrepreneurs organizing themselves as the Proprietary Medicine Manufacturers Association in 1881. For over two decades they successfully prevented any attempt to limit their enterprise. They effectively marketed their products in most of the mass and professional media and catalogs of the era. The development of the hypodermic needle in the middle of the 19th century and advances in chemistry resulted in the development of more potent drugs that could be delivered in the most efficacious manner. As David Musto (1973) observed, "Opiates and cocaine became popular—if unrecognized—items in the everyday life of Americans" (p. 3). Although exact figures on the consumption of opium during this time period are not available, the U.S. Public Health Service estimated that between 1859 and 1899, 7,000 tons of crude opium and 800 tons of smoking opium were imported in the United States (Kolb & Du Mez, 1924).

The turn of the century seemed to initiate a broad-based social reform movement in a wide variety of areas of American culture. The developing American Medical Association (AMA) began questioning the effectiveness claims of the patent medicines. As a result of the failure to scientifically verify the claims, the AMA removed advertisements for patent medicines from their journals. By this means, the professional physicians began to disassociate themselves from the medicine show. Perhaps as a result of these professional critiques of patent medicines, journalists also began to focus on the industry. One of the most noted series of articles was in the national weekly magazine *Collier's*. For about a four-month period during 1905 and 1906, a *Collier's* reporter, Samuel Adams, chronicled the fraudulent claims of the patent medicine sellers, the toxic ingredients they contained (often high dosages of opium and cocaine), and the consequences of their use. Adams claimed that the use of these medicines made criminals of young men and harlots of young women (see Young, 1967, p. 31).

Although the *Collier's* articles on the patent medicine industry did cause a great deal of discussion in the popular press, it was the impact of Upton Sinclair's *The Jungle* on legal policy that most affected the patent medicine industry. As a result of the documented filthy conditions in the American meatpacking industry, Congress passed the Pure Food and Drug Act in 1906. Although this act did not outlaw patent medicines, it did require that the ingredients and their proportions be listed on each bottle. This, coupled with persistent media focus on the horrors of opium and other drug use, appeared to prepare the public and the Congress for further restrictions on the industry. Within the next few years, many states severely restricted the distribution of narcotics through physicians and pharmacists or over the counter (see Musto, 1973, p. 18). The distribution was further restricted by the Harrison Act of 1914. In spite of what is popularly thought, this act did not make the manufacture, distribution, or use of opium, cocaine, or marijuana illegal. What it did was require that individuals and companies that manufactured or distributed these substances register with the Treasury Department and pay special taxes. The Treasury Department's interpretation of the Harrison Act and subsequent Supreme Court decisions served to make a wide variety of

narcotics and other drugs illegal to manufacture, distribute, or even pre-
scribe.

## Perceptions of Drugs and Crime in the Early 20th Century

Some critics have argued that the Harrison Act turned law-abiding users of
patent medicines into criminals (King, 1974). Although this is probably an
oversimplification, the Harrison Act did culminate and strongly support a
popular social reform movement that increasingly defined drug use as criminal and often the cause of violent, bizarre behavior.

The medical literature of the early 20th century, by contrast, viewed the
opiate user as lethargic and less likely to engage in violent crime. Whatever
criminal behavior resulted from drug use was seen as occurring to obtain
money to buy drugs. Shoplifting and other forms of petty theft were seen as
the primary types of criminal behavior. Many observers noted that debauch-
ery, laziness, and prostitution were the primary deviant behavioral consequences of opiate use—not violent predatory crime (see Kolb, 1925;
Lichtenstein, 1914; Terry & Pellens, 1928). Overall, the medical and psychiatric literature of the early 20th century viewed opiate use as debilitating and
a cause of petty property crimes or prostitution, but not as a cause of violent
crime.

Some medical practitioners did consider cocaine to be different from opiates in its behavioral consequences (Kolb, 1925). Kolb's observation was that
cocaine tended to make individuals more paranoid and that consequently, a
cocaine user might strike out violently at an imagined pursuer. Although
cocaine was used in many patent medicines and was included in the Harrison
Act, the official government position seemed to conclude that cocaine use,
although potentially a cause of crime, was relatively small and therefore of
insignificant consequence (U.S. Treasury Department, 1939).

Although the medical literature did not see opiate use as a prime cause of
violent street crime or crime in general, there were many popular lecturers
who did. Perhaps the most prolific and popular antinarcotic lecturer was
Richmond P. Hobson. He founded a number of anti-narcotics-use organizations and both published and lectured extensively on the violent crimogenic
nature of narcotics use. Throughout the 1920s, Mr. Hobson argued that most
property and violent crimes were committed by heroin and other types of
drug addicts. He further argued that the continuity of civilization itself
depended on the elimination of narcotics use (Hobson, 1928). With his frequent radio broadcasts, he played a significant role in creating a national perception of the direct link between all types of drug use and all types of crime.

Somewhat surprisingly, the primary drugs-crime connection portrayed in
popular and government media involved marijuana use. On July 6, 1927, the

*New York Times* reported that a family in Mexico City had become hopelessly insane by eating marijuana leaves. The epitome of the marijuana-causes-crime perspective was probably the Hollywood production of the film, *Reefer Madness*. This film was strongly influenced by the Commissioner of the Treasury Department's Bureau of Narcotics, Harry J. Anslinger. *Reefer Madness* portrayed marijuana as the great destroyer of American youth. Marijuana, it was shown in the film, not only caused young people to become sexually promiscuous but also violently criminal and prone to suicide. Marijuana was viewed as the most dangerous substance in America and one that, unless stopped, would lead to the violent downfall of Western civilization. It was not only in the movies that marijuana was portrayed as causing violence. Anslinger and his colleagues at the Bureau of Narcotics published a number of books focusing on the direct violent criminal behavior caused by narcotics, particularly by marijuana use, and on the involvement of criminal gangs in the distribution of illegal drugs (Anslinger & Oursler, 1961; Anslinger & Tompkins, 1953). In all of his work, Anslinger listed cannabis as a narcotic and always described its consequences as the most violent and dangerous. For example, in *The Murderers*, he claimed that "All varieties (of Cannabis) may lead to acts of violence, extremes, madness, homicide" (p. 304). In this book, Anslinger provided many examples of the criminal honors committed by those who had smoked even one reefer. The most gruesome illustration was the case of a seventeen-month-old White female raped and murdered by a cotton picker who had smoked one marijuana cigarette (Anslinger & Tompkins, 1953, p. 24). The popular book entitled *Dope* argued that "when you have once chosen marijuana, you have selected murder and torture and hideous cruelty to your bosom friends" (Black, 1928, p. 28). Popular periodicals such as *American Magazine* also told in lurid detail about ax-murdering marijuana-intoxicated youths on rampages (Sloman, 1979, p. 63).

A crucial implicit and often explicit aspect of the portrayal of the relationship between drugs and crime was the strong antiforeign feelings and racism of the 1920s and 1930s. Many of the horror stories that focused on the violence and degradation of narcotics users centered on African Americans, Mexicans, and Chinese. All of the illegal drugs were portrayed as foreign imports brought in by dark- or yellow-skinned outsiders wanting to corrupt White youth, seduce White women, and/or overthrow Northern European ascendancy. The drugs-crime relationship was thus an important asset of a popular racial and national isolationist perspective (see Inciardi, 1992; Musto, 1973).

During the 1930s and 1940s, and even into the 1950s, the American government and the popular media seemed to work closely in continuing to create the image of the "dope fiend" as a violent, out-of-control sexual predator who accounted for a large proportion of America's heinous crimes. By the late 1950s, this image had been strongly challenged by a wide variety of academic and other critics. However, these formative images of the bizarre, violent dope fiend continue to provide at least a background schemata that affects cultural perceptions of the drugs-crime relationship.

## The Intersection of Typologies

Although the historical and current discussions of the drugs-crime relationship often assume a particular intersection between specific types of drugs and specific types of crime, that intersection is generally not explicit or examined in a logical, sequential manner. As McGlothlin (1979) noted, if the drugs-crime relationship is to be examined logically, it is important to use typologies of both types of behaviors and proceed to review how each type of drug use relates to each type of crime. Drug abuse and crime are complex issues that include a multitude of specific behaviors.

### Types of Drugs

At the turn of the century almost all drugs were called narcotics—including opium, marijuana, and cocaine. However, as is apparent, each of these substances has a very different chemical structure and a different psychopharmacological effect. Thus each potentially has a very different relationship to various types of criminal behavior. During the 1960s and 1970s, the term *drug abuse* primarily seemed to mean heroin use and, to a lesser extent, LSD use. Today, the term probably conjures up images of cocaine use. Regardless of what specific drug the term may be most associated with, an analysis of the drugs-crime relationship must conceptually use the major specific categories of drugs.

Generally, it has been recognized that the various types of illegal drugs have different possible relationships to criminal behavior, based on their chemical structure, subculture of use, cost, or differential patterns of control. Over the last decade, major national surveys on illegal drug use have tended to develop a list of drug types that are routinely included in questionnaires (for example, see Clayton et al., 1988; Johnston, O'Malley, & Bachman, 1993; Liska, 1990). These are

1.  narcotic analgesics: including heroin, Demoral, Percodan, and Dilaudid
2.  stimulants: including cocaine in all of its forms and amphetamines
3.  hallucinogens: for example, LSD, PCP and MDA

4.  inhalants: including gasoline, paint thinner, glue, other volatile hydrocarbons and amyl/butyl nitrites
5.  sedatives: for example, barbiturates and methaqualone
6.  major and minor tranquilizers
7.  marijuana (although the effects of this drug combine some aspects of sedatives, tranquilizers, and hallucinogens, it is usually placed in its own separate classification)
8.  steroids and other types of hormonal substances designed to build muscle or increase aggressiveness.

In some research projects, these categories might need to be expanded to include more specific drugs within each category. However, these are the general categories used in drug research.

---

## Types of Crime

---

Types of criminal behavior also need to be constructed in drugs-crime research and conceptual understandings. For the last two decades, researchers have explicitly argued that drugs-crime research needs to work within common parameter definitions of categories of criminal behavior (see Inciardi & McBride, 1976). Traditionally, criminologists have had a major focus on the construction of criminal behavior typologies. The aim has been to construct mutually exclusive homogeneous categories (see Hood & Sparks, 1970). Typically, typological constructions in criminology have been based on legal categories, such as the Uniform Crime Reports (UCR) (1993), the public's perception of the severity ranking of specific criminal behaviors (Rossi, Waite, Bose, & Berk, 1974), the social psychology and behavioral characteristics of offenders (Duncan, Ohlin, Reis, & Stanton, 1953), or combinations of all of the preceding (Clinard & Quinney, 1967). Recent criminology and criminal justice texts have tended to use the categorization of the UCR, which includes a sense of public and official views of seriousness plus elements of social psychological characteristics (see Inciardi, 1993). The following categories of crimes are commonly used in criminal justice research:

1.  crime against persons: including homicide, manslaughter, rape of all types, aggravated assault, assault and battery, and child molestation
2.  armed robbery
3.  property crimes: including breaking and entering, larceny, auto theft, arson, forgery, counterfeiting, passing worthless checks, buying, concealing, and receiving stolen property, vandalism

4.  income-producing victimless crimes: including prostitution, commercialized vice, and gambling
5.  violation of drug laws: including the possession or sale of dangerous drugs or the implements for their use
6.  other offenses: for example, disorderly conduct, vagrancy, loitering, and resisting arrest.

Sequentially examining each of the specific intersections between each type of drug and each type of crime could help build a systematic body of knowledge about the totality of the drugs-crime relationship.

## The Statistical Overlap

Historically, and currently, one of the major arguments for the existence of a drugs-crime relationship is the high level of drug use among populations of criminals and the frequent involvement in criminal activities of street-drug users. About 40 years ago Anslinger and Tompkins (1953), as a part of their argument that drug use was a component of a criminal culture, claimed that a large proportion of federal prisoners were users of illegal drugs. During the late 1960s and early 1970s, many epidemiologists, and certainly the popular culture, believed that the United States was undergoing a drug epidemic. The evidence for the epidemic was large increases in drug overdosages, drug-related arrests and drug treatment admissions (see O'Donnell, Voss, Clayton, Slatin, & Room, 1976). One of the major perceived consequences of increased drug use was the perception of an associated increase in street crime. This apparent epidemic stimulated the development or reinvigoration of a vast drug treatment, enforcement, and research endeavor culminating in the establishment of the National Institute on Drug Abuse (NIDA) in 1974. In 1971, during an address to Congress on June 17, President Richard M. Nixon called the drug epidemic a national emergency. The Federal Strategy Report of 1975 noted that the crime associated with drug use was a major reason for the national attention focused on drug abuse in that era.

### Drug Use in Populations of Criminals

One of the tasks of the newly created NIDA and the National Institute of Justice was a series of studies and symposiums on the drugs-crime relationship (see Inciardi & McBride, 1976; Gandossy, Williams, Cohen, & Harwood, 1980). As these study groups documented, many research projects conducted in a variety of urban areas during the early 1970s found that somewhere between 15 percent and 40 percent of arrestees and prisoners were users of illegal drugs—mostly marijuana and heroin (see Eckerman, Bates, Rachal, & Poole, 1971; Ford, Hauser, & Jackson, 1975; McBride, 1976). These findings were seen, at the time, as dramatic evidence of the existence of the drug/crime connection and the need to integrate the criminal justice system with the drug treatment system. One of the outcomes of these types of studies was the establishment of the Treatment Alternatives to Street Crime (TASC) program, which attempted to identify drug users in populations of offenders, assess their treatment needs, and refer them to appropriate treatment facilities (see Inciardi & McBride, 1991).

Recent research has shown an even more extensive use of drugs in a variety of criminally involved populations. In a study of nonincarcerated delinquents in Miami, Florida, Inciardi, Horowitz, and Pottieger (1993) found that some three-fourths of male and female delinquents used cocaine at least weekly. Further, the Drug Use Forecasting (DUF) program collects and analyzes urine from arrestees in 24 major cities across the United States. In most, over 60 percent of the male and female arrestees are positive for illegal drugs. The lowest rates for males were in Omaha and San Antonio, where only 48 percent were positive for an illegal drug. The lowest rate for females was 47 percent in New Orleans. The highest for females was 81 percent in Manhattan, and the highest rate for males was 80 percent in Philadelphia. In almost all of the cities in the study, cocaine was the most common drug found through urinalysis, followed by marijuana and opiates (see DUF, 1993; Wish, 1987).

Surveys of incarcerated populations show a similarly high rate of illegal drug use just prior to incarceration. In 1990, for example, the Bureau of Justice Statistics found that over 40 percent of state prison inmates reported the daily use of illegal drugs in the month prior to the offense that resulted in their incarceration. A comparison of these data to that of criminally involved populations in the 1970s shows a much higher rate of illegal drug use in the current criminal justice population and a dramatic shift from heroin and marijuana to primarily cocaine and marijuana. These data also suggest a virtual saturation of the criminal justice system by illegal drug users who mostly consume cocaine in some form.

There is also a body of research that indicates a high level of drug use among incarcerated individuals. In a study of Delaware prison inmates, Inciardi, Lockwood, and Quinlan (1993) found that 60 percent of the respondents reported the use of drugs, mostly marijuana, while in prison. However, urinalysis found only about a 1 percent positivity rate. A random sample of urine collected in Wisconsin discovered a rate of 25 percent positive, mostly marijuana (Vigdal & Stadler, 1989). There is also some ethnographic evidence that drugs are integrated in the prison culture as a part of control, management, and reward systems (see Hawkins & Alpert, 1989; Inciardi, Horowitz,

& Pottieger, 1993). Although there is no evidence that drug use is rampant in jails and prisons, the high use rates in the population prior to incarceration as well as the level of continuing use while in prison have stimulated the development of drug treatment services in prisons throughout the United States (Hayes & Schimmel, 1993).

## Criminal Behavior in Populations of Drug Users

Examinations of drug-using populations for the last few decades have found similarly high rates of criminal behavior. Surveys of populations of illegal drug users in the late 1960s and early 1970s generally found that a large majority had extensive criminal histories (see Defleur, Ball, & Snarr, 1969; Voss & Stephens, 1973). Recent local and national research has confirmed these early findings. In a population of over 400 street-injection-drug users in Miami, Florida, for example, McBride and Inciardi (1990) found that over 80 percent had been in jail in the last 5 years and about 45 percent had been incarcerated within the last 6 months. An analysis of over 25,000 street-injection-drug users from 63 cities found that some two-thirds were in jail in the last 5 years, with over one-third currently on probation or parole or awaiting trial (Inciardi, McBride, Platt, & Baxter, 1993). Consistently, examinations of populations of nonincarcerated drug users clearly show a high level of current involvement with criminal behavior and with the criminal justice system.

## The Statistical Overlap in the General Population

General-population surveys also show the overlap between drug using and criminal behaviors. In 1991, the National Household Survey of drug use conducted by the NIDA included questions on criminal behavior. Analysis of that data showed a correlation between drug use and engaging in criminal, particularly violent, behavior. Less than 5 percent of those who drank alcohol only or who consumed no substance engaged in a violent or property crime during the last year. About 25 percent of those who had used marijuana and cocaine in addition to alcohol admitted to the commission of a violent and/or property crime in the last year (Harrison & Gfroerer, 1992).

Analyses of data from the National Youth Survey also show a strong correlation between serious drug use and serious delinquent behavior. The National Youth Survey is a longitudinal study initiated in the late 1970s and was designed to survey a variety of behaviors, including substance use and crime (see Huizinga, 1978, for a description of the survey and its methodology). In an analysis of these data, Johnson, Wish, Schmeidler, and Huizinga (1993) found that only 3 percent of nondelinquents used cocaine, whereas 23 percent of those with multiple delinquency index crimes were current cocaine users. Examining the data from the perspective of drug-using behavior, they found that only 2 percent of those who used alcohol only had multiple index offenses compared to 28 percent of the cocaine users. Overall, these researchers found a correlation of .53 between the delinquency and drug use scales.

Although the complexity and causal nature of the drugs-crime relationship is open to considerable debate, there is little contention about the statistical correlation between drug use and crime. For a number of decades, the existence of the empirical relationship has been documented by researchers as well as by criminal justice practitioners and drug treatment professionals. The size of the relationship between using drugs and criminal behavior is a daily reality in criminal justice systems and drug treatment programs throughout the United States. This reality has stimulated a wide variety of critical thinking and research projects designed to sort out the nature of the drugs-crime relationship and policies that could be used to reduce the extent of the relationship.

# The Etiological, Nature of the Drugs-Crime Relationship

## Which Came First?

The issue of behavioral and causal priority in the drugs-crime relationship has been a primary research focus of numerous investigators. For the past 20 years, researchers have consistently found that individuals who frequently use illegal drugs such as cocaine, heroin, or marijuana have engaged in criminal behavior prior to or concurrent with the initiation of any stable illegal drug use pattern (see Anglin & Speckart, 1988; Huizinga, Menard, & Elliot, 1989; Inciardi, Lockwood, & Quinlan, 1993; O'Donnell et al., 1976; Stephens & McBride, 1976). Rather than innocents seduced or propelled into criminal activity by their drug use, existing data and research indicate that drug abuse and criminal activity are a part of a broader set of integrated deviant behaviors involving crime, drug use, and, often, high-risk sex. Although a variety of empirical data indicate that drug use does not appear to initiate a criminal career, a large volume of research clearly indicates that frequency of drug use has a strong impact on the extent, direction, and duration of that career.

## The Impact of Drug Use on Frequency of Criminal Behavior

A wide body of research indicates that although criminal behavior may be initiated prior to or concomitant with the genesis of illegal drug use, once illegal drug use is initiated it has a dramatic effect on the amount of criminal activity (Anglin & Hser, 1987; Anglin & Speckart, 1988; Ball, Rosen, Flueck, & Nurco, 1981; Chambers, Cuskey, & Moffett, 1970; Chaiken & Chaiken, 1990; Stephens & McBride, 1976). Particularly the work of Ball and his colleagues (1981), using longitudinal data, and Anglin and his colleagues (Anglin & Hser, 1987; Anglin & Speckart, 1988), using a life history method, clearly indicate the effect of narcotics use on rates of criminal behavior. These researchers found sharp decreases in criminal activity during periods of abstinence from heroin and large increases in criminal activity during periods of increased heroin use (see Anglin & Speckart, 1988; Ball et al., 1981; Ball, Shaffer, & Nurco, 1983).

The expense of cocaine and heroin use and the fact that most frequent users of these drugs are unemployed result in a high level of criminal activity in user populations. Inciardi, McBride, McCoy, and Chitwood describe what they call an amazing amount of criminal activity involving over 100,000 criminal acts (excluding drug law violations) committed by some 700 cocaine users in the 90 days prior to being interviewed. Johnson and his colleagues (1985) reported that over 40 percent of the total income of a population of street-drug users was generated from illegal activity. Using a variety of methodologies, including life histories, surveys, and longitudinal data, the existing research literature suggests that the frequent use of illegal drugs is clearly a part of the motivation for an increase in criminal activities that are designed to obtain funds for drugs or as a part of other activities designed to access, possess, and use drugs. In addition, the available data suggest that, rather than a simple linear relationship between drugs and crime, both may emerge at a similar time period and that the two behaviors may have a recursive element to their relationship. That is, drug use may be involved in increasing criminal behavior, but the initiation of criminal behavior may also result in subcultural participation and individual-risk decision making that involves taking high-risk drugs (see Clayton & Tuchfeld, 1982).

## The Impact of Drug Use on Sustained Criminal Behavior

There is some evidence that frequent hard-drug use may be involved with a sustained criminal career. Longitudinal research indicates that most delinquents cease their illegal activity by late adolescence or early adulthood (e.g., see Kandel, Simcha-Fagan, & Davies, 1986). Traditionally, getting a steady job, getting married, and having children was viewed as a sign of maturation and as increasing an individual's stakes in conformity and therefore decreasing rates of illegal behavior. The UCR indicates a sharp drop in arrest rates for populations over 25 years of age. A wide variety of research data indicates that frequent drug use may severely interfere with that maturation process and consequent reduction in crime. National (Elliott & Huizinga, 1985) and local studies (Dembo et al., 1987) have indicated that chronic serious delinquent offenders are more likely to become involved with hard-drug use, which, in turn, relates to continued participation in a criminal subculture and high rates of criminal behavior. Life history research (Faupel & Klockars, 1987) also documents the recursive relationship of using drugs and criminal behavior.

The recursive nature of the drugs-crime relationship appears to act to reinforce continued drug use and crime. Ethnographers have described this as "taking care of business" (Hanson, Beschner, Walters, & Bovelle, 1985). Essentially, the argument is that the subcultural values that emerge in street-drug-using cultures encompass crime as a means to obtain drugs and as a cultural value itself in opposition to the straight world of legitimate low-paying jobs. Using drugs and criminal behavior become well integrated within the cultural/social role of the street-drug user (see Stephens, 1991). From this perspective, drug use does not directly cause crime, but, rather, is an integral part of the street-drug subculture. To focus only on drug-using behavior as a primary means to reduce crime misses the intertwined complexity of the drugs-crime relationship.

## Drug Use and Type of Crime

Probably as a result of images created by decades of government and media messages about the violent dope fiend, the public has been concerned about the types of crime in which drug users engage. The particular concern has been that the use of many types of drugs causes extreme violence. As noted earlier in this article, many years ago, Kolb (1925) argued against the prevailing popular view of the crazed dope fiend. From a psychopharmacological perspective, he contended that the biochemical effect of opiate use was to make a user lethargic and less likely to engage in violent crime, at least while under the influence of the drug. This original perspective continued to find empirical support for decades. For example, Finestone (1957) claimed that heroin users were much more likely to engage in petty property crime to support their vice than in noneconomically productive violent crime. In fact, he observed that as street groups initiated and increased heroin use, the rate of violent crime decreased and their rate of property crime increased. These types of research findings continued through most of the next two decades. Basically, heroin users were found to be overrepresented among property criminals and underrepresented among those charged with crimes of violence (see Inciardi & Chambers, 1972; Kozel & DuPont, 1977; McBride, 1976).

In the late 1970s, researchers began to report an increase in violence in the street-heroin-using subculture, particularly among younger cohorts of users

(Stephens & Ellis, 1975; Zahn & Bencivengo, 1974). During the 1980s, epidemiological data indicated a rapid increase in cocaine use. As has been noted, DUF (1993) data indicate a virtual saturation of cocaine use in arrested populations. This rapid rise in cocaine use and in rates of violent behavior has stimulated a variety of speculation and research about the impact of cocaine on criminal behavior and on the world of the street-drug user. For most of the last decade, researchers have been reporting that increased cocaine use was related to violent confrontational crime for men and women (Datesman, 1981; Goldstein, 1989; Simonds & Kashani, 1980; Spunt, Goldstein, Bellucci, & Miller, 1990). Research has also indicated that cocaine use may be related not only to being a violent offender but also to being a victim of violent crime. McBride, Burgman-Habermehl, Alpert, and Chitwood (1986), in an analysis of homicides in Miami, Florida, found that after alcohol, cocaine was the most common drug found in the bodies of homicide victims. Almost 10 percent of homicide victims had cocaine in their bodies at the time of death. This was more than 8 times the rate of any other illegal drug. Goldstein, Bellucci, Spunt, and Miller (1993), in a study in New York City, found that increased cocaine use was associated with being a victim of violent crime for women.

Paul Goldstein (1989) has proposed a very useable framework for interpreting the relationship between drugs and violence that seems particularly appropriate to interpreting the relationship between cocaine and violence. He calls this paradigm "a tripartite scheme." Goldstein sees this scheme as involving psychopharmacological, economically compulsive, and systemic aspects. Essentially, a part of the violent behavior of cocaine users may relate to the psychopharmacological consequences of cocaine use. This effect includes a strong stimulant impact, long periods without sleep, and increased paranoia. All of these effects could result in an increased willingness on the part of those using cocaine (and other stimulants, such as amphetamines) to engage in aggressive behavior or to put themselves into situations where aggressive behavior is more likely to occur. The economic demands involve the cost of heavy cocaine or crack use that may result in violent predatory behavior designed to obtain the most money. The systemic aspect of the model involves violent subcultural behavior patterns that are integral to being a street-drug user and those violent behavior patterns that are a part of the street distribution of cocaine. Other researchers (McBride & Swartz, 1990) have suggested that the drugs-violence and cocaine-violence relationship is also occurring within the framework of a rapid increase of heavy armaments in general society. That is, our whole society has undergone an increase in the availability and distribution of powerful automatic weapons. This general availability of weapons has also become a part of the street-drug-using culture. Rather than drug use being a direct cause of violence, it might be important to recognize that the drug culture has adapted the weaponry of the general culture and has used it for its own purposes. Regardless of the exact nature of the relationship, the existing data suggest that, increasingly, drug use, particularly cocaine use, has become integrated with a high level of international, national, and local street violence. The extent of cocaine use among felony offenders and the perceived relationship between cocaine and violence has played a major role in the reinvigoration of the debate about national drug policy and the issue of the decriminalization of drug use.

# Some Theoretical Perspectives on the Drugs-Crime Relationship

From every conceivable methodological perspective, data consistently show that there is a strong correlation between drug use and criminal behavior and that increases in drug use are related to increases in crime. However, the theoretical analysis of the relationship has not been as extensive. Some perspectives argue that the interpretation of the empirical relationship might be very different from what the data initially suggest.

## Subcultural, Role Theory, and Ecological Perspectives

Ethnographic and role theory analyses have tended to view the crime and drug relationship as associated with subcultural roles that include what general society would call extreme deviant behavior (Hanson et al., 1985; Stephens, 1991). High frequencies of drug use, high rates of crime, and extensive high-risk sexual behavior are seen from this perspective as "taking care of business" or an integral part of the social role of the street-drug user. This type of conceptual analysis suggests that the drugs/crime relationship may not be directly linear in cause, but, rather, drug use and crime exist as a part of an intertwined mutually reinforcing subculturally contexted set of behaviors.

Ecological theoretical analysis has suggested that the drugs-crime relationship appears to be related because both types of behavior are caused by similar environmental conditions, such as poverty and lack of social control and economic opportunity. In that sense, some observers have concluded that drug use is spuriously related to crime. That is, there is the appearance of a statistical causal relationship, but that relationship may be an artifact of common etiology (Fagan, Weis, & Cheng, 1990; McBride & McCoy, 1981). Drugs and crime occur together because they share a similar set of causal variables and they are a part of the same subcultural value and role system. From these ecological and subcultural theoretical perspectives, the drugs-crime relationship is not so much affected by attempts to stop or reduce drug use but, rather, by attempts to address the common underlying initiating and sustaining causes of both behaviors.

## A Radical Interpretation of the Drugs-Crime Relationship

Another major theoretical critique of the apparent drugs-crime relationship comes from radical theory. This perspective maintains that the drugs-crime relationship is an artifact of legal policy since 1914. From this viewpoint, the existence of a drugs-crime relationship simply resulted from laws that effectively criminalized a variety of drug-using behaviors. As the result of the Harrison Act and subsequent law, American society created a criminal subculture where none existed; drove up the cost of drugs, thereby providing an economic motivation for drug-related crime; and left the distribution of drugs to organized criminal networks. These, in turn, grew immensely wealthy and powerful through the distribution of the much-in-demand and now-expensive illegal drugs. The current violence, corruption, and civil rights issues associated with drug use and drug law enforcement are seen, from this perspective, as the inevitable result of the social construction of deviance. Radical theorists argue that the drugs-crime relationship can best be disentangled by decriminalizing drugs and treating drug abuse and addiction as mental and public health problems that are best addressed through psychological counseling and social work case management. The drug policy of the Netherlands is often advocated as an example of an enlightened, less criminogenic strategy (see Lindesmith, 1965; Nadelmann, 1989; Trebach & Inciardi, 1993).

There is considerable evidence that much of the crime committed by drug users involves only violations of drug laws involving possession and distribution of illegal drugs. For example, Inciardi et al. found that during the 90 days prior to being interviewed, their sample of some 700 cocaine users had committed over 1.7 million criminal acts with well over 95 percent of them involving violations of drug laws. Further evidence exists in examinations of the current operation of drug courts. Originally, these courts were designed to focus on the increasing number of drug-involved cases coming before the court. However, these courts may be increasing the focus on drug users who are involved only in drug law violations and not implicated in other types of crime and thereby furthering the appearance of a relationship between drug use and crime, particularly among African Americans in the inner city (Klofas, 1993).

The radical perspective does provide a valuable insight into how society may create by law that which it is attempting to avoid by law, and there may be some applicability to the interpretation of the drugs-crime relationship. The perspective is, however, often built on the notion that somehow the relationship between drug use and crime would virtually disappear if drugs were just decriminalized, that there would be no or minimal increase in drug use, and that any increase would have virtually no impact on violence or crime. Such a view would seem to ignore psychopharmacological aspects of the relationship, the fact that criminal behavior generally precedes drug use, and the findings that both behaviors arise from similar etiological variables and act in a mutually reinforcing manner.

In a recent analysis of the drugs-crime relationship in Amsterdam by Grapendaal, Leuw, and Nelen (1992), it was shown that 53 percent of a sample of 148 polydrug users engaged in acquisitive crime during an average month, and those 79 individuals netted almost $66,000 per month from their property crimes to buy drugs. Further, it was found that property crime accounted for 24 percent of total income in the sample. This was the second highest percentage of total income after welfare payments. During 1991, the city of Zurich, Switzerland experimented with the decriminalization of drugs and experienced an increase in property and violent crimes. Public pressure forced a reversal of Swiss policy (see the *New York Times*, February 11, 1992, A10). Although, as Grapendaal and his colleagues (1992) noted, the extent of drug-related crime in the Netherlands may not be as extensive as in New York or other American cities, there is a significant relationship even in a highly tolerant city. These researchers also noted that the policy of tolerance has created a permanent underclass whose crime may only be lessened by a generous welfare system but not eliminated. Just as the perspective arguing that drug use seduced innocent youth into a life of crime has been shown to be simplistic, so the perspective that drug laws throw otherwise peaceful citizens into a life of criminal violence that can be eliminated if drugs are just decriminalized may also be more simplistic than is warranted by the facts (for perspectives against decriminalization see Inciardi & McBride, 1989; Wilson, 1993).

## Policy Implications of the Drugs-Crime Data

Although the drugs-crime data and conceptual understandings may be complex and even contradictory, there appear to be three major common implications from current knowledge.

1. There is a strong need for treatment services for drug-using, criminally involved populations. This would include both those who are incarcerated as well as those on probation or in a diversion program. Regardless of the complexity of the data, there is a clear indication that levels of drug use relate to levels of criminal activity. Reducing drug demand through treatment has a strong possibility for reducing levels of crime. Increasing treatment

resources at all levels of the criminal justice system to eliminate waiting lists, as well as increasing recruitment outreach in criminal populations, has a significant potential to reduce the level of crime in a community.

2. The ecological and subcultural perspectives remind our society that the drugs-crime relationship is at least in part the result of a history of differential social, political, and economic opportunity. The development of oppositional subcultures in which drug use and crime are an integrated part will be addressed only by major efforts to provide educational and economic development opportunities. Social and economic progress in communities with high rates of drug use and crime must be a local and national priority.

3. The radical perspective reminds us that in any application of drug policy, civil rights must be protected, that there are severe limits to the effectiveness of law enforcement, and enforcement practices can increase the appearance of the drugs-crime relationship well beyond the framework of psychopharmacology, economic demand, and subcultural roles. Drug laws and policy should focus on demand reduction at least equal to supply reduction. Drug law enforcement must never be an excuse for a retreat on hard-won legal and civil rights, and drug law and policy must rest on a strong public support base.

## References

Anglin, M. D., & Hser, Y. (1987). Addicted women and crime. *Criminology, 25,* 359–397.

Anglin, M. D., & Speckart, F. (1988). Narcotics use and crime: A multi sample, multi method analysis. *Criminology, 26,* 197–233.

Anslinger, H. J., & Ourlser, W. (1961). *The murderers.* New York: Faaar, Straus & Cudahy.

Anslinger, H. J., & Tompkins. W. F. (1953). *The traffic in narcotics.* New York: Funk & Wagnall.

Ball, J. C., Rosen, L., Flueck, J. A., & Nurco, D. N. (1981). The criminality of heroin addicts: When addicted and when off opiates. In J. A. Inciardi (Ed.), *The drugs-crime connection* (pp. 39–65). Beverly Hills: Sage.

Ball, J. C., Shaffer, J. W., & Nurco, D. N. (1983). The day-to-day criminality of heroin addicts in Baltimore: A study in the continuity of offense rates. *Drug and Alcohol Dependence, 12,* 119–142.

Black, W. (1928). *Dope: The story of the living dead.* New York: Star & Co.

Bureau of Justice Statistics. (1990). *Drugs and crime facts.* 1989. Washington, DC: Author.

Chaiken, J. M., & Chaiken, M. R. (1990). Drugs and predatory crime. In M. Tonry & J. Q. Wilson (Eds.), *Drugs and crime* (pp. 203–239). Chicago: University of Chicago Press.

Chambers, C. D., Cuskey, W. R., & Moffett, A. D. (1970). Demographic factors associated with opiate addiction among Mexican Americans. *Public Health Reports*, *85*, 523–531.

Clayton, R. R., & Tuchfeld, B. S. (1982). The drug-crime debate: Obstacles to understanding the relationship. *Journal of Drug Issues*, *12*, 153–166.

Clayton, R. R., Voss, H. L., Loscuito, L., Martin, S. S., Skinner, W. F., Robbins, C., & Santos, R. L. (1988). *National household survey on drug abuse: Main findings, 1985*. Washington DC: U.S. Department of Health & Human Services.

Clinard, M. B., & Quinney, R. (1967). *Criminal behavior systems*. New York: Rinehart & Winston.

Datesman, S. (1981). Women, crime, and drugs. In J. A. Inciardi (Ed.), *The drugs/ crime connection* (pp. 85–104). Beverly Hills: Sage.

Defleur, L. B., Ball, J. C., & Snarr, R. W. (1969). The long-term social correlates of opiate abuse. *Social Problems*, *17*, 225–234.

Dembo, R., Washburn, M., Wish, E. D., Yeung, H., Getreu, A., Berry, E., & Blount, W. R. (1987). Heavy marijuana use and crime among youths entering a juvenile detention center. *Journal of Psychoactive Drugs*, *19*, 47–56.

Drug use forecasting. (1993, May). Washington, DC: National Institute of Justice.

Duncan, O. D., Ohlin, L. E., Reis A. J., & Stanton, H. E. (1953). Formal devises for making selection decisions. *American Journal of Sociology*, *58*, 537–584.

Eckerman, W. C., Bates, J. J. D., Rachal, J. V., & Poole, W. K. (1971). *Drug usage and arrest charges*. Washington, DC: Drug Enforcement Administration.

Elliott, D. S., & Huizinga, D. (1985). The relationship between delinquent behavior and ADM problems. *Proceedings of the Prevention Research Conference on Juvenile Offenders with Serious Drug, Alcohol and Mental Health Problems*. Washington, DC: Alcohol, Drug Abuse and Mental Health Administration, Office of Juvenile Justice and Delinquency.

Fagan, J., Weis, J. G., & Cheng, Y. T. (1990). Delinquency and substance use among inner-city students. *Journal of Drug Issues*, *20*, 351–402.

Faupel, C. E., & Klockars, C. B. (1987). Drugs-crime connections: Elaborations from the life histories of hard-core heroin addicts. *Social Problems*, *34*, 54–68.

Federal strategy for drug abuse and drug traffic prevention. (1975). Washington, DC: U.S. Government Printing Office.

Finestone, H. (1957). Narcotics and criminality. *Law and Contemporary Problems*, *9*, 69–85.

Ford, A., Hauser, H., & Jackson, E. (1975). Use of drugs among persons admitted to a county jail. *Public Health Reports*, *90*, 504–508.

Gandossy, R. P., Williams, J. R., Cohen, J., & Harwood, H. J. (1980). *Drugs and crime: A survey and analysis of the literature* (National Institute of Justice). Washington, DC: U.S. Government Printing Office.

Goldstein, P. J. (1989). Drugs and violent crime. In N. A. Wiener & M. E. Wolfgang (Eds.), *Pathways to criminal violence* (pp. 16–48). Newbury Park, CA: Sage.

Goldstein, P. J., Bellucci, P. A., Spunt, B. J., & Miller, T. (1993). Volume of cocaine use and violence: A comparison between men and women. In R. Dembo (Ed.), *Drugs and crime* (pp. 141–177). New York: University Press of America.

Grapendaal, M., Leuw, E., & Nelen, H. (1992, Summer). Drugs and crime in an accommodating social context: The situation in Amsterdam. *Contemporary Drug Problems*, pp. 303–326.

Hanson, B., Beschner, G., Walters, J. M., & Bovelle, E. (1985). *Life with heroin: Voices from the inner city.* Lexington, MA. Lexington Books.

Harrison, L., & Gfroerer, J. (1992). The intersection of drug use and criminal behavior: Results from the national household survey on drug abuse. *Crime & Delinquency, 38,* 422–443.

Hawkins, R., & Alpert, G. P. (1989). *American prison systems: Punishment and justice.* Englewood Cliffs, NJ: Prentice-Hall.

Hayes, T. J., & Schimmel, D. J. (1993). Residential drug abuse treatment in the Federal Bureau of Prisons. *Journal of Drug Issues, 28,* 61–73.

Hobson, R. P. (1928). The struggle of mankind against its deadliest foe. *Narcotic Education, 1,* 51–54.

Hood, R., & Sparks, R. (1970). *Key issues in criminology.* New York: McGraw-Hill.

Huizinga, D. H. (1978). *Sample design of the National Youth Survey.* Boulder, CO: Behavioral Research Institute.

Huizinga, D. H., Menard, S., & Elliot, D. S. (1989). Delinquency and drug use: Temporal and developmental patterns. *Justice Quarterly, 6,* 419–455.

Inciardi, J. A. (1992). *The war on drugs II.* Palo Alto, CA: Mayfield.

_____. (1993). *Criminal justice.* Fort Worth, TX: Harcourt Brace Jovanovich.

Inciardi, J. A., & Chambers, C. D. (1972). Unreported criminal involvement of narcotic addicts. *Journal of Drug Issues, 2,* 57–64.

Inciardi, J. A., Horowitz, R., & Pottieger, A. E. (1993). *Street kids, street drugs, street crime.* Belmont, CA: Wadsworth.

Inciardi, J. A., Lockwood, D., & Quinlan, J. A. (1993). Drug use in prison: Patterns, processes, and implications for treatment. *Journal of Drug Issues, 23,* 119–129.

Inciardi, J. A., & McBride, D. C. (1976). Considerations in the definition of criminality for the assessment of the relationship between drug use and crime. In Research Triangle Institute (Ed.), *Crime and drugs* (pp. 123–137). Springfield, VA: National Technical Information Service.

_____. (1989). Legalization: A high risk alternative in the war on drugs. *American Behavioral Scientist, 32,* 259–289.

_____. (1991). *Treatment alternatives to street crime (TASC): History, experiences. and issues.* Rockville, MD: National Institute on Drug Abuse.

Inciardi, J. A., McBride, D. C., Platt, J. J., & Baxter, S. (1993). Injecting drug users, incarceration, and HIV: Some legal and social service delivery issues. In *The national AIDS demonstration research program.* Westport, CT: Greenwood.

Inciardi, J. A., McBride, D. C., McCoy, H. V., & Chitwood, D. D. Recent research on the crack-cocaine/crime connection. *Studies on crime and crime prevention.*

Johnson, B. D., Goldstein, P. J., Preble, E., Schmeidler, J., Lipton, D. S., & Miller, T. (1985). *Taking care of business: The economics of crime by heroin abusers.* Lexington, MA: Lexington Books.

Johnson, B. D., Wish, E. D., Schmeidler, J., & Huizinga, D. (1993). Concentration of delinquent offending: Serious drug involvement and high delinquency rates. In R. Dembo (Ed.), *Drugs and crime* (pp. 1–25). Lanham, MD: University Press of America.

Johnston, L. D., O'Malley, P. M., & Bachman, J. G. (1993). *Drug use among high school seniors, college students and young adults, 1975*–1990 (NIH Publication No. 93-3597). Washington, DC: U.S. Department of Health and Human Services.

Kandel, D. B., Simcha-Fagan, O., & Davies, M. (1986). Risk factors for delinquency and illicit drug use from adolescence to young adulthood. *Journal of Drug Issues, 16*, 67–90.

Klofas, J. M. (1993). Drugs and justice: The impact of drugs on criminal justice in a metropolitan community. *Crime & Delinquency, 39*, 204–224.

Kolb, L. (1925, January). Drug addiction in its relation to crime. *Journal of Mental Hygiene*, pp.74–89.

Kolb, L., & Du Mez, A. G. (1924, May 23). The prevalence and trend of drug addiction in the United States and factors influencing it. *Public Health Reports*.

Kozel, N. J., & Dupont, R. L. (1977). *Criminal charges and drug use patterns of arrestees in the District of Columbia*. Washington, DC: U.S. Government Printing Office.

King, R. (1974). The American system: Legal sanctions to repress drug abuse. In J. A. Inciardi & C. D. Chambers (Eds.), *Drugs and the criminal justice system* (pp. 17–37). Beverly Hills, CA: Sage.

Lichtenstein, P. M. (1914, November 14). Narcotic addiction. *New York Medical Journal*, pp. 962–966.

Lindesmith, A. R. (1965). *The addict and the law*. Bloomington: Indiana University Press.

Liska, K. (1990). *Drugs and the human body*. New York: Macmillan.

McBride, D. C. (1976). The relationship between type of drug use and arrest charge in an arrested population. In Research Triangle Institute (Ed.), *Drug use and crime* (pp. 409–418). Springfield, VA: National Technical Information Service.

McBride D. C., Burgman-Habermehl, C., Alpert, J., & Chitwood, D. D. (1986). Drugs and homicide. *Bulletin of the New York Academy of Medicine, 62*, 497–508.

McBride, D. C., & Inciardi, J. A. (1990). AIDS and the IV drug user in the criminal justice system. *Journal of Drug Issues, 20*, 267–280.

McBride, D. C., & McCoy, C. B. (1981). Crime and drug using behavior: An areal analysis. *Criminology, 19*, 281–302.

———. (1982). Crime and drugs: The issues and literature. *Journal of Drug Issues, 12*, 137–151.

McBride D. C., & Swartz, J. (1990). Drugs and violence in the age of crack cocaine. In R. A. Weisheit (Ed.), *Drugs, crime and the criminal justice system* (American Academy of Criminal Justice Series, pp. 141–169). Cincinnati, OH: Anderson.

McGlothlin, W. (1979). Drugs and crime. In R. L. DuPont, A. Goldstein, & J. A. O'Donnell (Eds.), *Handbook on drug abuse* (pp. 357–364). Washington, DC: National Institute on Drug Abuse, Office of Drug Abuse Policy.

Musto, D. F. (1973). *The American disease.* New Haven, CT: Yale University Press.

Nadelmann, E. A. (1989, September). Drug prohibition in the United States, costs, consequences, and alternatives. *Science,* pp. 939–947.

O'Donnell, J. A., Voss, H. L., Clayton, R. R., Slatin, G. T., & Room, R. G. W. (1976). *Young men and drugs—A national survey* (National Institute on Drug Abuse Research Monograph 5). Washington, DC: U.S. Government Printing Office.

Rossi, P. H., Waite, E., Bose, C. E., & Berk, R. E. (1974). The seriousness of crimes: Normative structure and individual differences. *American Sociological Review, 31,* 324–337.

Simonds, J. F. & Kashani, J. (1980). Specific drug use and violence in delinquent boys. *American Journal of Drug and Alcohol Abuse, 7,* 305–322.

Sloman, L. (1979). *Reefer madness : A history of marijuana in America.* Indianapolis: Bobbs-Merrill.

Spunt B. J., Goldstein, P. J., Bellucci, P. A., & Miller, T. (1990). Race/ethnic and gender differences in the drugs-violence relationship. *Journal of Psychoactive Drugs, 22,* 293–303.

Stephens, R. C. (1991). *The street addict role.* New York: State University of New York Press.

Stephens, R. C., & Ellis, R. D. (1975). Narcotic addicts and crime: An analysis of recent trends. *Criminology, 12,* 474–488.

Stephens, R. C., & McBride, D. C. (1976). Becoming a street addict. *Human Organization, 35,* 87–93.

Terry, C. E., & Pellens, M. (1928). *The opium problem.* New York: Bureau of Social Hygiene.

Trebach, A. S., & Inciardi, J. A. (1993). *Legalize it? Debating American drug policy.* Washington, DC: American University Press.

U.S. Department of Justice, Federal Bureau of Investigation. (1993). *Uniform crime reports.* Washington, DC: U.S. Government Printing Office.

U.S. Treasury Department, Bureau of Narcotics. (1939). *Traffic in opium and other dangerous drugs.* Washington, DC: U.S. Government Printing Office.

Vigdal, G. L., & Stadler, D. W. (1989, June). Controlling inmate drug use: Cut consumption by reducing demand. *Corrections Today,* pp. 96–97.

Voss, H. L., & Stephens, R. C. (1973). Criminal history of narcotic addicts. *Drug Forum, 2,* 191–202.

Young, J. H. (1967). *The medical messiahs: A social history of health quackery in twentieth- century America.* Princeton, NJ: Princeton University Press.

Wilson, J. Q. (1993). Against the legalization of drugs. In R. Goldberg (Ed.), *Taking sides* (p. 25). Guildford, CT: Dushkin.

Wish, E. D. (1987). *Drug use forecasting: New York 1984–1986.* Washington, DC: U.S. Department of Justice.

Zahn, M. A. & Bencivengo, M. (1974). Violent death: A comparison between drug users and non drug users. *Addictive Diseases, 1,* 293–298.

# 5

# Drugs-Crime Connections
## Elaborations from the Life Histories of
## Hard-Core Heroin Addicts

## Charles E. Faupel
## Carl B. Klockars

The debate over the nature and extent of the relationship between heroin use and criminal activity is a long-standing one which has generated a voluminous literature. A 1980 survey (Gandossey et al., 1980) lists over 450 citations to books, articles, and research reports which directly or indirectly bear upon the heroin-crime relationship. Since 1980 the study of this relationship has continued, and several large-scale quantitative studies (Anglin and Specart, 1984; Ball et al., 1981, 1983; Collins et al., 1984, 1985; Johnson et al., 1985) generally support the thesis that an increase in criminality commonly

Reprinted by permission of the University of California Press from *Social Problems*, Vol. 34, No. 1, pp. 54–68, © 1987 by the Society for the Study of Social Problems.

occurs in conjunction with increased heroin use in the United States. These studies, together with a host of others preceding them (e.g., Ball and Snarr, 1969; Chein et al., 1964; Inciardi, 1979; McGlothlin et al., 1978; Nash, 1973; Weissman et al., 1974) have moved the focus of the debate from the empirical question of whether or not there is a heroin-crime connection to empirical and theoretical questions about the dynamics of that connection.

In particular, two hypotheses, neither of which is new, currently occupy center stage in the drugs-crime controversy. The first, stated by Tappan a quarter of a century ago, maintains that the "addict of lower socio-economic class is a criminal primarily because illicit narcotics are costly and because he can secure his daily requirements only by committing crimes that will pay for them" (1960:65–66). This hypothesis maintains that heroin addict criminality is a consequence of addiction, albeit an indirect one. As physical dependence upon and tolerance for heroin increase, and the cost of progressively larger dosages of heroin increase proportionally, the addict is driven to criminal means to satisfy his or her habit. Empirically, this hypothesis predicts a linear increase in heroin consumption and a corresponding increase in criminal activity necessary to support it. In contrast, a second hypothesis maintains that the "principal explanation for the association between drug abuse and crime . . . is likely to be found in the subcultural attachment" (Goldman, 1981:162) comprised of the criminal associations, identifications, and activities of those persons who eventually become addicted. The basis for this hypothesis can only be understood in the context of the contemporary socio-legal milieu in which narcotics use takes place. Since the criminalization of heroin in 1914, the social world of narcotics has become increasingly intertwined with the broader criminal subculture (Musto, 1973). Consequently, would-be narcotics users inevitably associate with other criminals in the highly criminal copping areas of inner cities, and, indeed, are often recruited from delinquent and criminal networks. Through these criminal associations, therefore, the individual is introduced to heroin, and both crime and heroin use are facilitated and maintained. Empirically, this second hypothesis predicts increases in heroin use following or coinciding with periods of criminal association and activity.

A shorthand title for the first hypothesis is "Drugs cause crimes"; for the second "Crimes cause drugs." Each, as we shall see below, is subject to a number of qualifications and reservations; but each, as we shall see below, continues to mark a rather different approach to understanding the drugs-crime connection. Furthermore, each hypothesis has quite different policy implications associated with it.

# Methodology

Our contribution to understanding the dynamics of the drugs-crime connection is based upon life-history interviews with 32 hard-core heroin addicts in the Wilmington, Delaware area. We purposely selected the respondents on the basis of their extensive involvement in the heroin subculture. All of the respondents had extensive contact with the criminal justice system. At the time of interview, 24 of the 32 respondents were incarcerated or under some form of correctional authority supervision (e.g., supervised custody, work release, parole, or probation). While this places certain limits on the generalizations that can be made from these data, the focus of this study is the dynamics of addiction among heavily-involved street addicts. For example, controlled users or "chippers" will not have experienced many of the dynamics reported here. Similarly, physicians, nurses, and middle class "prescription abusers" are not typically subject to many of the constraints experienced by lower-class street users. Hence, it is important to emphasize that the findings we report here are intended to describe "hard-core" urban heroin addicts.

Women are slightly overrepresented, constituting 14 of the 32 respondents. Ethnically, the sample consists of 23 blacks and nine whites; Hispanics are not represented because there is not a sizable Hispanic drug-using population in the Wilmington area.

Respondents were paid five dollars per hour for their interview time, which undoubtedly contributed to the 100 percent response rate. The interviews ranged from 10 to 25 hours in length, with each interview session averaging between three and four hours. With a single exception, all of the interviews were tape recorded and transcribed. Respondents were promised confidentiality and, without exception, they spoke openly of their drug, crime, and life-history experience.

The incarcerated respondents and most of the street respondents were selected with the aid of treatment personnel who were carefully instructed regarding the goals of the research and selection criteria. This strategy proved invaluable for two reasons. First, by utilizing treatment personnel in the screening process, we were able to avoid the time-consuming task of establishing the "appropriateness" of respondents for the purposes of this research; the treatment personnel were already intimately familiar with the drug-using and criminal histories of the respondents. Second, the treatment personnel had an unusually positive relationship with Wilmington-area drug users. The treatment counselor in the prison system was regarded as an ally in the quest for better living conditions, appeals for early release, etc., and was regarded as highly trustworthy in the prison subculture. His frequent confrontations with prison authorities over prisoner rights and privileges enhanced his reputation among the inmates. Similarly, the treatment counselor who aided in the selection of street respondents was carefully selected on the basis of his positive involvement with street addicts. His relationship with area addicts is a long-standing and multifaceted one. His reputation among street addicts was firmly established when he successfully negotiated much needed reforms in one of the local treatment agencies. Because of the long-standing positive relationship they had with area addicts, this initial contact by treatment personnel greatly facilitated our establishing necessary rapport.

After a few initial interviews were completed, several broad focal areas emerged which formed the basis for future questioning. Respondents were interviewed regarding: (1) childhood and early adolescent experiences which may have served as *predisposing factors* for eventual drugs/criminal involvement; (2) *initial encounters* with various types of drugs and criminality; (3) the *evolution* of their drug and criminal careers; (4) their patterns of activity during *peak periods* of drug use and criminality, including descriptions of *typical days* during these periods; (5) their *preferences* for types of crimes and drugs; (6) the *structure of understanding* guiding drug use and criminal activity; and (7) their perceptions of the nature and effectiveness of *drug treatment*. Structuring the life-history interviews in this way insured that most relevant career phases were covered while at the same time it permitted the respondents a great deal of flexibility in interpreting their experiences.

## Drugs Cause Crimes Versus Crimes Cause Drugs

One of the earliest strategies for testing the Drugs-cause-crimes versus Crimes-cause-drugs hypotheses involved trying to establish a temporal sequence to drug use and criminal behavior. If it can be established that a pattern of regular or extensive criminal behavior typically precedes heroin addiction, that finding would tend to support the crimes-cause-drugs hypothesis. Conversely, if a pattern of regular or extensive criminality tends to develop after the onset of heroin addiction, that finding would tend to support the Drugs-cause-crimes hypothesis. Previous research on this question is mixed, but mixed in a systematic way. Most of the early studies found little criminality before the onset of opiate addiction (Pescor, 1943; Terry and Pellens, 1928). Later studies, by contrast, have shown a high probability of criminality preceding heroin addiction (Ball and Chambers, 1970; Chambers, 1974; Jacoby et al., 1973; Inciardi, 1979; O'Donnell, 1966; Robins and Murphy 1967).

Our life-history interviews are consistent with the findings of the recent studies. All of our respondents reported some criminal activity prior to their first use of heroin. However, for nearly all of our respondents, both their criminal careers and their heroin-using careers began slowly. For the respondents in our study, a median of 3.5 years elapsed between their first serious criminal offense and subsequent involvement in criminal activity on a regular basis. Likewise, all of our respondents reported at least occasional use of other illicit drugs prior to their first experience with heroin. Moreover, many of our respondents indicated that they spent substantial periods of time—months and even years—using heroin on an occasional basis ("chipping" or "chippying"), either inhaling the powder ("sniffing" or "snorting"), injecting the prepared ("cooked") mixture subcutaneously ("skinpopping"), or receiving occasional intravenous injections from other users before becoming regular users themselves. Perhaps most importantly, virtually all of our respondents reported that they believed that their criminal and drug careers began independently of one another, although both careers became intimately interconnected as each evolved. In the earliest phases of their drug and crime careers, the decision to commit crimes and the decision to use drugs were choices which our respondents believe they freely chose to make and which they believe they could have discontinued before either choice became a way of life (also see Fields and Walters, 1985; Morris, 1985).

## Drug and Crime Career Patterns

From our interviews it appears that two very general factors shape and influence the drug and crime careers of our respondents, not only during the early stages of each career but as each career evolves through different stages. The first of these factors is the *availability* of heroin rather than the level of physical tolerance the user has developed. "The more you had the more you did," explains "Mona," a thirty-year-old female. "And if all you had was $10 then that's all you did. . . . But if you had $200 then you did that much." Addicts are able to adjust to periods of sharply decreased availability (e.g., "panic" periods when supplies of street heroin disappear) by reducing consumption or by using alternative drugs (e.g., methadone). They are also able to manipulate availability, increasing or decreasing it in ways and for reasons we discuss below.

As we use the term, availability also means something more than access to sellers of heroin who have quantities of the drug to sell. By availability we also mean the resources and opportunities to buy heroin or obtain it in other ways as well as the skills necessary to use it. In short, availability is understood to include considerations of all those opportunities and obstacles which may influence a heroin user's success in introducing a quantity of the drug into his or her bloodstream.

The second general factor shaping the drugs and crime careers of our life-history interviewees is *life structure*. By "life structure" we mean regularly occurring patterns of daily domestic, occupational, recreational, or criminal activity. Recent ethnographic accounts of heroin-using careers in several major cities reveal that, like their "straight" counterparts, most addicts maintain reasonably predictable daily routines (Beschner and Brower, 1985; Walters, 1985). Throughout their lives our respondents fulfilled, to one degree or another, conventional as well as criminal and other subcultural roles. In fact, during most periods of their crime and drug careers, our interviewees spent far more time engaged in conventional role activities than in criminal or deviant ones. Many worked conventional jobs. Women with children performed routine housekeeping and child-rearing duties. Many leisure-time activities did not differ from those of non-addicts. These hard-core addicts spent time grocery shopping, tinkering with cars, visiting relatives, talking with friends, listening to records, and watching television in totally unremarkable fashion.

Life structure in the hard-core criminal addict's life can be also provided by some rather stable forms of criminal activity. Burglars spend time staking out business establishments. Shoplifters typically establish "runs," more or less stable sequences of targeted stores from which to "boost" during late morning, noon, and early afternoon hours, saving the later afternoon for fencing what they have stolen. Prostitutes typically keep a regular evening and night-time schedule, which runs from 7 P.M. to 3 A.M. Mornings are usually spent sleeping and afternoons are usually occupied with conventional duties.

It is within this structure of conventional and criminal roles that buying ("copping"), selling ("dealing"), and using ("shooting") heroin take place. For example, shoplifters typically structure their runs to allow times and places for all three activities. Likewise, prostitutes seek to manage their drug use so that neither withdrawal symptoms ("joneses") nor periods of heroin-induced drowsiness will interfere with their work. In order to meet the demands of criminal or conventional roles, addicts in our sample often used other drugs (e.g., marijuana, barbiturates, alcohol, amphetamines, methadone) to alter their moods and motivations, saving heroin as a reward for successfully completing a job or meeting other obligations.

## A Typology of Career Patterns

These two dimensions—*availability* and *life structure*—are critical to understanding the dynamics of addict careers. According to our respondents, differences in the ways addicts manage these functions and variations in these two dimensions that are beyond the control of addicts combine to produce fairly distinct patterns, periods, or stages in their careers. The interaction of availability and life structure may be understood to describe addict career phases that are familiar to participants or observers of the heroin scene.

In Figure 1, we identify four such familiar career phases, each of which is marked by a different interaction of heroin availability and life structure. It is important to note that while each denotes an addict type, none of the "types" imply a single career pattern. That is, throughout their drug-crime careers, addicts typically move through periods in which they may at one time be described as one type and later another. In our discussion of each type, we describe some of the ways in which transitions seem to occur.

## Figure 1:   A Typology of Heroin Use Career Phases

| Availability | Life Structure | |
| --- | --- | --- |
| | *High* | *Low* |
| *High* | The Stablized Junkie | The Free-Wheeling Junkie |
| *Low* | The Occasional User | The Street Junkie |

*The Occasional User—Low Availability/High Life Structure.* Initiates into the heroin-using subculture typically begin as occasional users. For the beginning heroin user, a variety of factors typically serve to limit the availability of heroin. The initiate has usually not spent enough time in the heroin subculture to develop extensive drug connections. In addition, the beginner must be taught how and where to buy heroin, and also must learn how to use it. Moreover, the typical beginning heroin user is unlikely to have sufficient income to maintain any substantial level of heroin consumption, and is most unlikely to have either the connections or the knowledge necessary to increase availability through low-level dealing or through shrewd buying and reselling as experienced addicts sometimes do.

In addition to these factors which tend to limit the availability of heroin to the beginning user and hold him or her to an occasional user role, a variety of factors related to life structure also tend to oblige the beginning heroin user to play an occasional user role, or at least to do so until that life structure can be modified to accommodate a higher level of heroin use. In many cases beginning heroin users are young, dependent, involved in school, and bear family roles and obligations which are not easily changed. Likewise, adult role obligations, such as full-time employment, housekeeping, and child rearing, can be altered so as to be compatible with occasional patterns of heroin use, but not without considerable difficulty if those patterns include high or even moderately high levels of addiction.

One of our respondents, "Belle," explained how she and her husband, "Taps," maintained a very long period of occasional use, due largely to Taps' determination to keep his full-time job:

> I know of people that does half a bag generally. Do you understand what I'm saying? That they automatically live off of half a bag and got a jones. Like I said, Taps worked—and he would shoot no more than half a bag of dope at any time he took off and wouldn't do no wrong. He would not do no wrong. He worked each and every day. And this is what I told you before—I said I don't know how he had a jones and worked, but he worked every day.

Moreover, Belle went on to explain that when the life structure Taps provided for her lapsed—and availability increased—she did not remain an occasional user:

> Taps had me limited a long, long time. I mean a long time limited to nothing but half a bag of drugs, until he completely stopped hisself. Then when he stopped, I went "Phwee!"—because I didn't have anybody to guide me. I didn't have to take half a bag and divide it in half for him. And I went from one bag to more.

"Ron," another addict in our sample, played the role of "occasional user" without interruption for nearly eight years. During this period he consumed an average of $10–15 in street heroin per day, while holding down a full-time job and living with his mother, who refused to allow him to use drugs in her home. Toward the end of the eight-year period he became a "tester" for a local drug dealer, a role which increased the availability of heroin. At about the same time, he also lost his job and moved out of his mother's home. Having lost the support of the stable routine imposed by his job and living arrangements at the same time heroin became more readily available to him in his role of "tester," his drug use escalated dramatically within a very short time.

Interestingly, the low availability/high life structure pattern of occasional use, which typically marks the beginning addict's entrance into the drug-using world, is characteristic of many addicts' attempts to leave it. Many formal drug rehabilitation programs impose conditions of low (or no) heroin availability combined with high life structure upon addicts enrolled in their programs (Faupel, 1985). Likewise, as Biernacki (1986) and Waldorf (1983) have extensively demonstrated, addicts who attempt to quit on their own often seek to do so by limiting or eliminating altogether their contacts with addict friends, self-medicating with "street" methadone, and devoting themselves intensively to some highly demanding routine activity such as a full-time job or caring for young children.

*The Stabilized Junkie—High Availability/High Life Structure.* For the occasional user to become a stabilized junkie, heroin must become increasingly available in large and regular quantities, and his or her daily structure must be modified to accommodate regular heroin use. Making heroin regularly available in sufficiently large quantities is not only a matter of gaining access to reliable sources of supply of the drug; it also involves learning new and more sophisticated techniques for using and obtaining it as well as getting enough money to be able to buy it regularly.

During the time beginning addicts play occasional user roles, they typically learn the fundamentals of copping, cooking, cutting, and spiking. These are all drug-using skills that take time to learn. It was not uncommon for addicts in our sample to report that a sharp increase in their level of heroin use followed their learning to shoot themselves. When an occasional user learns to self-inject and no longer requires the more knowledgeable drug-using friends to "get off," this new level of skill and independence, in effect, increases the availability of heroin.

Likewise, copping skills and contacts which might have been sufficient to support occasional use require upgrading to support the needs of the stabilized junkie. The would-be stabilized junkie who must rely solely on low-quality, "street" heroin, who gets "ripped" by paying high prices for "bad dope," or who is totally dependent on what quality or quantity of heroin a single supplier happens to have available must seek to stabilize both the quantity and quality of regularly available heroin. Doing so seems to require extending and developing contacts in the drug subculture. In the words of one of our respondents:

> . . . you got to start associating with different people. You got to be in touch with different people for the simple reason that not just one person has it all the time. You got to go from one person to the other, find out who's got the best bag and who hasn't. . . . You want to go where the best bag is for your money, and especially for the money *you're* spending. You got to mingle with so many different people.

Making, developing, and maintaining the contacts that are helpful if not absolutely necessary to stable heroin use seem to invite natural opportunities for the most common modification in the stabilized junkie's life structure: dealing. From the point of view of the would-be stabilized junkie, dealing has two major advantages over most other forms of routine daily activity. First, it can be carried on in the course of the stabilized junkie's search for his or her own supply of drugs and, second, it can be a source of money for the purchase of drugs or a source of drugs itself. Dealing can be rather easily accommodated to the needs of both availability and life structure.

All of our respondents reported that at some time in their drug-using careers they had played the role of dealer, if only occasionally. Becoming an occasional dealer is almost an inevitable consequence of becoming a competent, regular users. A stabilized junkie will not only be approached to "cop" for occasional users and addicts whose suppliers are temporarily out of stock, but the stabilized junkie will come to recognize occasions on which especially "good dope" can be purchased and resold at a profit to drug-using friends.

Because the work of dealing drugs on a small scale does not require much more time or effort than that which goes into buying drugs regularly for one's own use, dealing also has another advantage which makes it an attractive activity for the stabilized junkie. Namely, it can be carried on as a source of drugs or income without undue interference with whatever other "hustle," if any, constitutes the stabilized junkie's additional source of support. This is particularly true if, in the course of carrying on the hustle—be it theft, shoplifting, pimping, prostitution, bookmaking, or dealing in stolen property—the stabilized addict is likely to come into regular contact with other drug users.

The extent to which dealing can be carried on along with other hustles depends, of course, both on the nature of that hustle and on the extent of the dealing. The stabilized junkie will tend to divide his or her hustling efforts between dealing and other hustles with an eye toward which one delivers the highest profit. However, dividing those efforts will also involve other considerations such as the stabilized junkie's personal preference for one type of work, life style and community reputation considerations, opportunities to practice one type of hustle or another, and the physical demands each type of hustle tends to require. Among female heroin users, a rather common accommodation to the profits and opportunities of dealing and those of other hustles is a live-together arrangement with a male user. In this division of labor each tries to conduct their outside hustle during hours when the other can be at home to handle dealing transactions. An important feature of this arrangement is that, if necessary, it can be structured so as to permit the stabilized female junkie to be at home for housekeeping and child-rearing duties as well as dealing.

*The Free-Wheeling Junkie—High Availability/Low Life Structure.* Although most heroin users spend some portion of their drug-using careers as stabilized junkies and many manage to live for years with high heroin availability and highly-structured daily routines, at least two properties of the stabilized junkie's situation tend to work against the maintenance of stability. One is the pharmacological property of heroin. It is a drug to which users tend to develop a tolerance rather rapidly, although as Zinberg (1984) has demonstrated, such tolerance is neither necessary nor universal. Moreover, as we have pointed out earlier, numerous factors in the social setting of heroin use mitigate the destabilizing effect of the drug. Work routines, household duties, and even subcultural roles all serve to structure drug consumption. However, in the absence of external structures of constraint, or when such routines are temporarily disrupted, the pharmacological properties of heroin tend to destabilize the lifestyle of the addict further. In sum, contrary to popular belief, heroin use does not inevitably lead to a deterioration of lifestyle. Rather, the physiological dynamics of narcotics use tend to be most destabilizing under conditions where life structure is already weak and incapable of accommodating the physiological demands imposed by increased tolerance.

The other property of the stabilized junkie's life which tends to undermine stability is the hustle the junkie uses to finance his or her habit. According to our respondents, it is not hard times or difficulties in raising money through hustles which tend to destabilize the stabilized junkie's life. "You can adjust yourself to a certain amount of drugs a day," explained Belle, "that you don't have to have but just that much." In addition to reducing their drug consumption, stabilized junkies accommodate themselves to such lean periods by substituting other drugs for heroin, working longer and harder at their hustling, or changing the type of hustle they work.

On the contrary, it is the unusual success, the "big sting" or "big hit," that tends to destabilize the stabilized junkie's high degree of life structure. The "big sting" or "big hit" can come in many forms. One of our respondents— an armed robber who usually limited his robbing to street mugging, gas stations, and convenience stores—"hit" a bank, which to our respondent's surprise, produced a "take" of over $60,000. He increased his heroin consumption dramatically and, while doing so, abandoned virtually all the stabilizing routines which marked his life prior to his windfall take. In another instance, a relatively stable junkie dealer was "fronted" several thousand dollars of heroin on consignment. Instead of selling it as he had agreed to do, he absconded with it to another state, shot up most of it himself, and gave the rest away. In still another case, a relatively low-level burglar/thief came across $10,000 in cash in the course of one of his burglaries. He took the money to New York where he intended to cop a "big piece" that he could bring back to the city in which he lived and sell for a nice profit. However, instead of selling it, he kept it for his own use and his habit rapidly increased from a stable three bags per day to nearly a "bundle"—25 bags per day.

Although the "big hit" or "big sting" appears to be the most common precipitator of the transition from the status of stabilized or occasional heroin user to the status of free-wheeling junkie, many other variants of similar destabilizing patterns are common. The stabilized junkie may not be the one who makes the big sting. It may be his or her spouse, roommate, paramour, addict friend, or regular trick who receives a windfall of drugs or money and invites the stabilized junkie to share in the benefits of good fortune. "Goody," a part-time street prostitute, moved in with a big-time drug dealer who provided her with all the heroin she wanted in exchange for domestic services, sexual favors, and some modest help in cutting and packaging drugs. Although her supply of drugs was virtually limitless, she took her child-raising obligations and responsibilities very seriously and they kept her to a modest level of use. However, after a year of domestic living she began to miss the "street" life and the friends she had there and to resent her total ("bag bitch") dependence on her dealer boyfriend. She returned to the street and used the money she earned from "hoing," and "ripping" her tricks to purchase drugs in addition to what she got at home for free. This behavior not only destabilized her drug use, but it also disrupted her home life to such an extent that she parted with her dealer and returned to the street full-time. Interestingly, this return to prostitution, theft, and robbery as her sole means of support forced her to develop a new life structure and abandon the free-wheeling pattern into which she had drifted when she had a dual source of supply.

Unless heroin addicts are disciplined by a life structure to which they are so committed and obligated that it effectively prevents them from doing so, they will expand their consumption of heroin to whatever level of use the availability of drugs or funds to buy them makes possible. What marks the career stage of the free-wheeling junkie is the almost total absence of structures of restraint. In the words of "Little Italy," who described a "free-wheeling" stage of his addict career:

> I can remember, I wouldn't be sick, I wouldn't need a shot. . . .And some of the guys might come around and get a few bags [and say] "Hey man, like I don't have enough money. Why don't you come down with me?" . . . I'm saying [to myself], "Oh-oh, here I go!" and I would shoot drugs I didn't even need to shoot. So I let it get out of control.

The problem for the first free-wheeling junkie is that the binge cannot last forever and is typically fairly short-lived. After a month or two of free-wheeling heroin use—during which time the free-wheeling junkie may have no idea of how much heroin he or she is consuming daily—not only is a modest usage level unsatisfying but the life structure within which he or she might support it is likely to have been completely abandoned or at least be in severe disrepair.

***The Street Junkie—Low Availability/Low Life Structure.*** At the point in a free-wheeling junkie's career when heroin availability drops precipitously and life structure does not provide the support necessary to stabilize heroin use, the free- wheeling junkie may manage to rebuild that life structure and accommodate to a new and lower level of availability. To the extent that this rebuilding and accommodation can be managed, the free-wheeling junkie may be able to return to the life of a stabilized junkie. However, if the rebuilding of life structure cannot be managed, the free-wheeling junkie may become a street junkie.

Street junkies most closely approximate the public stereotype of heroin addicts, if only because their way of life—both where and how they live—make them the most visible variety of heroin addict. Cut off from a stable source of quality heroin, not knowing from where his or her next "fix" or the money to pay for it will come, looking for any opportunity to make a buck, getting "sick" or "jonesing," being pathetically unkempt and unable to maintain even the most primitive routines of health or hygiene, the street junkie lives a very difficult, hand- to-mouth (or more precisely arm-to-arm) existence.

In terms of our typology, the street junkie's life may be understood as a continuous but typically unsuccessful effort to stabilize life structure and increase heroin availability. The two problems are intimately related in such a way that, unless the street junkie can establish a stable life structure, he or she will be unlikely to increase the availability of heroin. Likewise, unless the street junkie is able to increase the availability of heroin, he or she will be unlikely to establish a stable life structure.

To illustrate how this relationship works in less abstract terms, it is helpful to begin with a description of what low life structure means in the life of the street. Goldstein (1981:69) captures the tenor of the street junkie's situation nicely when he observes that

> [if] any single word can describe the essence of how street opiate users "get over," that word is *opportunism*. Subjects were always alert to the smallest opportunity to earn a few dollars. The notion of opportunism is equally relevant to predatory criminality, nonpredatory criminality, employment, and miscellaneous hustling activities.

The cause of the street junkie's opportunism is his or her failure to establish a stable life structure which regularly produces enough income to support an addiction. Consequently, the street junkie's life is a series of short-term crimes, jobs, and hustles. Street junkies steal or rob when opportunities arise to do so. For a price or in exchange for heroin, they will "cop" for an out-of-towner, "taste" for a dealer, "tip" for a burglar, rent their "works" to another junkie, sell their "clinic meth" and food stamps, or share their "crib" (accommodations) with a junkie who needs a place to "get off" or a "hoe" who needs a room to take her "tricks." They will do odd jobs, wash cars, paint apartments, deliver circulars, move furniture, carry baggage, or snitch to the police. The problem is not only that this opportunistic crime, hustling, or legitimate work pays very little, but that none of it is stable. While one or more of these activities may produce enough income today, none of them may be counted on to do so tomorrow. Moreover, because typical street addict crimes pay so little, because such crimes must be repeated frequently to produce any sizable income, and because they are so unpredictably opportunistic, the chance that the street addict will be arrested sooner or later is very, very high. This was the unfortunate experience of Little Italy who, after falling out with his supplier, was forced to discontinue drug sales as a major means of income and turned to armed robbery to support his use.

> I know today, I can say that if you don't have a plan you're gonna fuck up man. . . . Now those robberies weren't no plan. They didn't fit in nowhere . . . just by the spur of the moment, you know what I mean? I had to find something to take that place so that income would stand off properly, 'cause I didn't have a plan or didn't know anything about robbery . . .

As Little Italy's experience demonstrates, street junkies' lives are further complicated by the fact that "big dealers"—vendors of quantities of good quality heroin—often refuse to sell to them. The reasons they refuse are directly related to the instability of street junkies' lives. Because street junkies can never be certain when and for how much they will "get over," they are frequently unable to afford to buy enough drugs to satisfy their "jones." In the face of such a shortage they will commonly beg drugs from anyone they know who might have them or have access to them, try to "cop short" (buy at less than the going rate), attempt to strike a deal to get drugs loaned or "fronted" (given on consignment) to them on a short- term basis, or, if necessary, engage in opportunistic hustling. Also, because street junkies are the type of addict most vulnerable to arrest they are also the most likely category of addict to be "flipped" by police into the role of an informant. Usually street junkies will be promised immunity from prosecution on the charge for which they were arrested if they "give up" somebody "big." Given the frequency with which street addicts "come up short," the relatively small amount of profit to be made in each individual transaction with them, and the higher than normal risk of police involvement, few "big dealers" are willing to put up with all of the attendant hassles and hustles that dealing with street junkies typically involves.

While there are exceptions—the most common being big dealers who are relatives of street junkies or their friends of long standing—street addicts are mainly limited to "street dope," heroin that has been repeatedly "stepped on" (diluted) as it is passed from the highest level of dealer to the lowest. In fact, some studies (Leveson and Weiss, 1976:119) have shown that as much as 7 percent of street dope may have no heroin in it at all, while other studies (Smith, 1973) show a heroin concentration of from 3 to 10 percent in street dope as compared with an average concentration of nearly 30 percent in bags seized from "big dealers." The irony in this situation is that, as a consumer of "street dope," the street addict pays a higher per/unit price for heroin than any other person in the distribution chain. Furthermore, this very low and often unpredictable quality of heroin available to the street junkie serves to destabilize his or her life structure further.

## Research and Policy Implications

The life-history data presented here have some important research and policy implications which merit brief consideration. Particularly relevant are the implications for: (1) the nature of the drugs-crime connection itself; (2) drug law enforcement; and (3) treatment policy.

### The Drugs-Crime Connection

As we have pointed out above, early studies examining the relationship between drug use and crime have utilized the strategy of establishing the temporal priority of the onset of drug use versus criminality. While the earliest of these studies tended to find that drug use preceded the onset of criminal behavior, virtually all of the studies conducted since 1950 have found a reverse pattern, thus posing once again the perplexing question of the theoretical nature of the relationship between drug use and criminal behavior. Because the methodologies employed in these "sequence" studies are incapable of examining the dynamic nature of this relationship over time, they have succeeded in raising theoretical questions which continue to beg for explanation. More recent studies—particularly those of Ball et al. (1981, 1983) and Johnson et al. (1985)—have moved beyond the sequence issued by examining drug-using and criminal behavior on a daily or weekly basis over a period of time. These longitudinal methodologies represent a major breakthrough toward establishing the dynamic nature of the drugs-crime relationship.

This study further contributes to the emerging "post-sequence" literature by examining the drugs-crime nexus in the broader context of addict careers. Perhaps the most significant finding to emerge from our data is that the relationship between heroin use and crime is not necessarily consistent throughout the career of the addict. During the "occasional user" phase, for example, the issue is a moot one for many addicts; their limited level of drug use is quite affordable with a legitimate income, and any criminal activity that does take place is often quite spurious to drug use. During the "stabilized junkie" and "free-wheeling junkie" periods, the level of drug use seems to be largely a function of availability, typically enhanced through criminal income. Rather than *drug use causing crime*, however, it seems more accurate to suggest that *crime facilitates drug use* during these periods. Quite the reverse is the case during the "street junkie" phase, where availability through normal channels is lacking but the addict lacks the necessary structure to regulate his or her drug needs. Under these conditions the drug habit does indeed appear to "cause" crime in the manner commonly depicted.

Moreover, the life history data reveal that the relationship between drugs and crime is more dynamic than phrasing the issue in terms of "cause" typically suggests. In addition to providing necessary income for the purchase of heroin, criminal activity also serves to *structure* the drug using behavior of the addict. Crime thus provides the addict with a daily routine which for many addicts actually serves to limit or at least regulate their drug use.

In short, the respondents in this study have revealed that the relationship between drug use and criminal behavior is far more complex and dynamic than previous research has suggested. While in any given instance, it may be possible to specify a causal sequence, our data suggest that any generalizations suggesting a simple cause-effect scheme fail to capture the complexity of the drugs-crime connection throughout an addict's career.

## Drug Law Enforcement

Since the passage of the Harrison Act in 1914, drug law enforcement in the United States has been dominated by the "criminal model" of drug use (Inciardi, 1974). While variously articulated, this model understands drug use as primarily a *criminal* issue which should be addressed by imposing criminal sanctions on both users and dealers, and by taking steps to prevent the import and distribution of heroin. Insofar as there is a relationship between drug use and other criminal behavior, the narcotics user is understood to be a criminal, first and foremost, whose drug using behavior is an important and contributing component in an extensive pattern of related criminal behavior.

Not surprisingly, the criminalization of heroin has profoundly affected the dynamics of the drugs-crime nexus. Virtually all of the post-1950 studies have found that criminal histories preceded expensive drug-using histories of the respondents in their samples as suggested by the subculturally based "Crimes cause drugs" model. Our life-history data support and qualify the implications for the criminal model suggested by these studies. While our respondents do report criminal involvement prior to their first exposure to heroin, the drug-using histories began quite independently of their criminal involvement. Throughout their early "occasional use" phase, most of these individuals were supporting their drug use without relying on a stable income from systematic criminal activity. As their careers progressed, however, they cultivated criminal skills and associations which played an important role in facilitating a greatly expanded level of heroin use.

However, our research suggests that even if such enforcement efforts rightly characterize the drugs-crime connection, enforcement approaches may not have their intended effects of controlling or suppressing drug use or the crimes related to it. We find no reason to conclude that enforcement efforts may have an effect on very early periods in addict careers. During the period of occasional use, addicts can easily adjust to dramatic variations in the level of supply of heroin and our respondents report little need to support such occasional use through systematic criminal activity. Even in those periods of the hard-core addict's life history which we have described as characterized by a "stabilized junkie" model, our respondents report being able to adjust to periods in which heroin supplies are sharply reduced, only to return to previous levels of use when their channels of supply are restored. Moreover, our respondents report that during stabilized junkie periods in their life histories they cultivated a variety of sources of supply. Given this variety, not only could they choose vendors who appeared to offer the best quality product, but they could adjust relatively easily to the temporary or permanent loss of a supplier. Unless enforcement efforts managed a simultaneous elimination of virtually all of these sources of supply, we would not anticipate that they would have much effect on the stabilized junkie's pattern of stable use, nor on the criminal activity which the stabilized junkie typically pursues to support it. Likewise, enforcement efforts may not be expected to have much impact on hard-core addicts during "free-wheeling" phases in their life histories. Particularly insofar as these periods are precipitated by "big scores" or "big hits" and marked by short-term, unlimited availability of drugs or the money to purchase them, enforcement is already too late.

The street junkie, by contrast, faced with the lack of ready availability of adequate supplies of heroin and without the necessary life structure to constrain his or her felt need for drugs, is most vulnerable to law enforcement activity. Indeed, our data would suggest that the effectiveness of current law enforcement efforts is largely limited to this career phase. The addict in this situation is often confronted with the alternative of arrest or informing on other addicts. Either alternative almost inevitably imposes a criminal transition in the career of the addict. Arrest typically culminates either in treatment or incarceration, both of which impose a disengagement from street routine. Even if the addict subsequently returns to the street, the conditions of availability and life structure will be profoundly altered. While informing on other addicts may buy more time on the street, this alternative will only further alienate the street junkie from the subculture. While such a strategy of "flipping" informants may be helpful in locating "big dealers," its overall impact in limiting the availability of drugs to nonstreet junkies appears negligible unless, as we have suggested, all major dealers are "hit" simultaneously. Unless our drug policies give balanced weight to educational and treatment efforts, law enforcement effectiveness appears relegated to the already vulnerable "street junkie."

## Treatment Policy

Narcotics treatment in the United States has also been characterized by an overriding concern with the anti-social behavior associated with heroin use. Methadone maintenance is currently the dominant model of treatment, and has generated a voluminous literature addressing its effectiveness as a deterrent to crime (see, for example, Dole et al., 1968, 1969; Gearing, 1974; Judson et al., 1980; Lukoff and Quatrone, 1973; Newman and Gates, 1973). These and other studies have reported widely varying effects of methadone treatment upon criminality ranging from a 99.9 percent reduction (Gearing, 1974) to an actual *increase* in crime following admission to treatment (Lukoff and Quatrone, 1973). Unfortunately, our understanding of the effect of methadone maintenance on criminality is severely limited because of the many methodological difficulties associated with these studies (Faupel, 1981).

However, our data suggest that to the extent that a long-term reduction in criminality is a central goal of drug treatment, treatment policy must attend to more than simply the physiological demand for heroin. Drug-free residential programs, in particular, attempt to reduce availability by imposing abstinence for a substantial period of time. Beyond simply curtailing access to heroin, however, successful treatment will require provision for an alternative life structure which facilitates and rewards conventional behavior, thus reducing demand as well. We would argue that such an agenda not only requires renunciation of past routines but also the facilitation of long-term alternative behavior patterns through a concerted effort at community reintegration (see Dembo et al., 1982; Faupel, 1985; Goldbart, 1982; Hawkins, 1979). Involvement in conventional employment, voluntary associations, and even organized leisure-time activities should tightly structure the addicts' daily routine. Just as importantly, since access to drugs is largely a function of social networks, renunciation of "street" relationships and subsequent integration into supportive conventional social networks should serve to reduce availability and demand simultaneously.

# References

Anglin, M. Douglas and George Speckart
1984 Narcotics Use and Crime: A Confirmatory Analysis. Unpublished Report, University of California Los Angeles.
Ball, John C. and Carl D. Chambers
1970 The Epidemiology of Heroin Use in the United States. Springfield, IL: Charles C. Thomas.
Ball, John C., Lawrence Rosen, John A. Flueck and David Nurco
1981 "The criminality of heroin addicts when addicted and when off opiates." Pp. 39–65 in James A. Inciardi (ed.), The Drugs-Crime Connection. Beverly Hills, CA: Sage Publications.
Ball, John C., John W. Shaffer and David Nurco
1983 "The day to day criminality of heroin addicts in Baltimore: A study of the continuity of offense rates." Drug and Alcohol Dependence 12: 119–42.
Ball, John C. and Richard W. Snarr
1969 "A test of the maturation hypothesis with respect to opiate addiction." Bulletin of Narcotics 21:9–13.
Beschner, George M. and William Brower
1985 "The scene." Pp. 19–29 in Bill Hanson, George Beschner, James M. Walters and Elliot Bovelle (eds.), Life with Heroin: Voices from the Inner City. Lexington, MA: Lexington Books.
Biernacki, Patrick
1986 Pathways from Heroin Addiction: Recovery without Treatment. Philadelphia: Temple University Press.
Chambers, Carl D.
1974 "Narcotic addiction and crime: an empirical overview." Pp. 125–42 in James A. Inciardi and Carl D. Chambers (eds.), Drugs and the Criminal Justice System. Beverly Hills: Sage Publications.
Chein, Isidor, Donald L. Gerard, Robert S. Lee and Eva Rosenfeld
1964 The Road to H: Narcotics, Juvenile Delinquency, and Social Policy. New York: Basic Books.
Collins, James J. Robert L. Hubbard and J. Valley Rachal
1984 Heroin and Cocaine Use and Illegal Income. Center for Social Research and Policy Analysis. Research Triangle Park, NC: Research Triangle Institute.
1985 "Expensive drug use and illegal income: A test of explanatory hypotheses." Criminology 23:743–64.
Dembo, Richard, James A. Ciarlo and Robert W. Taylor
1983 "A model for assessing and improving drug abuse treatment resource use in inner city areas." The International Journal of Addictions 18:921–36.
Dole, Vincent P., Marie E. Nyswander and Alan Warner
1968 "Successful treatment of 750 criminal addicts." Journal of the American Medical Association 206:2708–11.

Dole, Vincent P., J. Waymond Robinson, John Orraca, Edward Towns, Paul Searcy and Eric Caine
  1969    "Methadone treatment of randomly selected criminal addicts." New England Journal of Medicine 280:1372–75.
Faupel, Charles E.
  1981    "Drug treatment and criminality: Methodological and theoretical considerations." Pp. 183–208 in James A. Inciardi (ed.), The Drugs-Crime Connection. Beverly Hills: Sage Publications.
  1985    "A theoretical model for a socially oriented drug treatment policy." Journal of Drug Education 15: 189–203.
Fields, Allen and James M. Walters
  1985    "Hustling: supporting a heroin habit." Pp. 49–73 in Bill Hanson, George Beschner, James M. Walters and Elliot Bovelle (eds.), Life with Heroin: Voices from the Inner City. Lexington, MA: Lexington Books.
Gandossy, Robert P., Jay R. Williams, Jo Cohen and Hendrick J. Harwood
  1980    Drugs and Crime: A Survey and Analysis of the Literature. National Institute of Justice. Washington, DC: U.S. Government Printing Office.
Gearing, Frances R.
  1974    "Methadone maintenance treatment five years later—where are they now?" American Journal of Public Health 64:44–50.
Goldbart, Stephen
  1982    "Systematic barriers to addict aftercare program implementation." Journal of Drug Issues 12:415–30.
Goldman, Fred
  1976    "Drug markets and addict consumption behavior.": Pp. 273–96 in Drug Use and Crime: Report of the Panel on Drug Use and Criminal Behavior. National Technical Information Service publication number PB-259 167. Springfield, VA: U.S. Department of Commerce.
  1981    "Drug abuse, crime and economics: The dismal limits of social choice." Pp. 155–81 in James A. Inciardi (ed.), the Drugs-Crime Connection. Beverly Hills: Sage Publications.
Goldstein, Paul
  1981    "Getting over: Economic alternatives to predatory crime among street drug users." Pp. 67–84 in James A. Inciardi (ed.), The Drugs-Crime Connection. Beverly Hills: Sage Publications.
Hanson, Bill, George Beschner, James M. Walters and Elliot Bovelle
  1985    Life with Heroin: Voices from the Inner City. Lexington, MA: Lexington Books.
Hawkins, J. David
  1979    "Reintegrating street drug abusers: Community roles in continuing care." Pp. 25–79 in Barry S. Brown (ed.), Addicts and Aftercare. Beverly Hills: Sage Publications.
Inciardi, James A.
  1974    "The vilification of euphoria: Some perspectives on an elusive issue." Addictive Diseases 1:241–67.
  1979    "Heroin use and street crime." Crime and Delinquency 25:335–46.

Jacoby, Joseph E., Neil A. Weiner, Terence P. Thornberry, and Marvin E. Wolfgang
   1973   "Drug use in a birth cohort." Pp. 300–43 in National Commission on Mari-
       juana and Drug Abuse, Drug Use in America: Problem in Perspective,
       Appendix I. Washington, DC: U.S. Government Printing Office.
Johnson, Bruce D., Paul J. Goldstein, Edward Preble, James Schmeidler, Douglas S.
       Lipton, Barry Spunt and Thomas Miller
   1985   Taking Care of Business: The Economics of Crime by Heroin Abusers. Lex-
       ington, MA: Lexington Books.
Judson, Barbara, Serapio Ortiz, Linda Crouse, Thomas Carney and Avram Goldstein
   1980   "A follow-up study of heroin addicts five years after admission to a metha-
       done treatment program." Drug and Alcohol Dependence 6:295–313.
Leveson, Irving and Jeffrey H. Weiss
   1976   Analysis of Urban Health Problems. New York: Spectrum.
Lukoff, Irving and Debra Quatrone
   1973   "Heroin use and crime in a methadone maintenance program: A two year
       follow-up of the Addiction and Research Corporation Program: a prelimi-
       nary report." Pp. 63–112 in Gil J. Hayim, Irving Lukoff and Debra Qua-
       trone (eds.), Heroin Use in a Methadone Maintenance Program.
       Washington, DC: U.S. Department of Justice, National Institute of Law
       Enforcement and Criminal Justice.
McGlothlin, William H., M. Douglas Anglin and Bruce D. Wilson
   1978   "Narcotic addiction and crime." Criminology 16:293–315.
Morris, Richard W.
   1985   "Not the cause, nor the cure: Self-image and control among inner city black
       male heroin users." Pp. 135–53 in Bill Hanson, George Beschner, James M.
       Walters and Elliot Bovelle (eds.), Life with Heroin: Voices from the Inner
       City. Lexington, MA: Lexington Books.
Musto, David
   1973   The American Disease: Origins of Narcotic Control. New Haven, CT: Yale
       University Press.
Nash, George
   1973   "The impact of drug abuse treatment upon criminality: A look at 19 pro-
       grams." Upper Montclair, NJ: Montclair State College.
Newman, Robert G., Sylvia Bashkow and Margot Gates
   1973   "Arrest histories before and after admission to a methadone maintenance
       treatment program." Contemporary Drug Problems 2:417–24.
O'Donnell, John A.
   1966   "Narcotic addiction and crime." Social Problems 13:374–85.
Pescor, Michael J.
   1943   "A statistical analysis of the clinical records of hospitalized drug addicts."
       Public Health Reports Supplement, 143.
Robins, Lee N. and George E. Murphy
   1967   "Drug use in a normal population of young Negro men."American Journal
       of Public Health 570:1580–96.

Smith, Jean Paul
  1973   "Substances in illicit drugs." Pp. 13–30 in Richard H. Blum and Associates
         (eds.), Drug Dealers—Taking Action. San Francisco: Jossey Bass.
Tappan, Paul
  1960   Crime, Justice and Correction. New York: McGraw-Hill.
Terry, Charles E. and Mildred Pellens
  1928   The Opium Problem. New York: The Haddon Craftsman.
Waldorf, Dan
  1983   "Natural recovery from opiate addiction: Some social-psychological pro-
         cesses of untreated recovery." Journal of Drug Issues 13:237–80.
Walter, James M.
  1985   "'Taking care of business' updated: A fresh look at the daily routine of the
         heroin user." Pp. 31–48 in Bill Hanson, George Beschner, James M.
         Walters and Elliot Bovelle (eds.), Life with Heroin: Voices from the Inner
         City. Lexington, MA: Lexington Books.
Weissman, James C., Paul L. Katsampes and Thomas A. Giacienti
  1974   "Opiate use and criminality among a jail population." Addictive Diseases
         1:269–81.
Zinberg, Norman E.
  1984   Drug Set and Setting: The Basis for Controlled Intoxicant Use. New Haven,
         CT: Yale University Press.

This research was supported in part by DHEW Grant No. 1 RO1 DA 01827 from the
Division of Research, National Institute of Drug Abuse. Correspondence to Faupel:
Department of Sociology, Anthropology, and Social Work, Auburn University,
Auburn University, AL 36849-3501.

**6**

# Prostitutes on Crack Cocaine
## Addiction, Utility, and Marketplace Economics

## Thomas E. Feucht

## Introduction

A small mountain of research has accumulated regarding prostitution and drugs. Some of the earlier research focused on narcotics, especially heroin, as the drug most widely used by prostitutes (e.g., Chambers, Hinsley, and Moldestad 1970; Cushman 1972; Goldstein 1979; James, Gosho, and Wohl 1979; Miller 1986). More recently, attention has turned to the rapid spread of cocaine use—particularly crack cocaine—and its relation to prostitution. The urgency of this research has been heightened by growing concerns about the spread of human immunodeficiency virus (HIV) through heterosexual contact. For instance, the Centers for Disease Control (1987; 1988) report that increases in the incidence of sexually transmitted diseases (STDs) can be linked to prostitution and contact with prostitution. STDs have been identified as important "multiplier" risk factors for HIV infection because

Reprinted by permission from *Deviant Behavior*, 1993, Vol. 14, pp. 91–108. Published by Taylor & Francis, Inc., Washington, DC. All rights reserved.

they create lesions through which the HIV can more easily enter the body (Kerr 1988; *The Economist* 1989). In addition, prostitutes frequently associate with intravenous drug users (IDUs) or are IDUs themselves. As a result, prostitutes constitute a primary vector of HIV transmission to others who are not themselves IDUs (Friedman, Dozier, et al. 1988).

These two simultaneous developments—the arrival and spread of HIV and the rapid rise in the popularity of crack cocaine—are closely related, and prostitution appears to be the platform on which the crisis is being built. Many have suggested that the widespread use of cocaine—especially crack cocaine—has accelerated the spread of HIV and other STDs through prostitution and heterosexual contact in general (Abramowitz, Guydish, et al. 1989; Fullilove and Fullilove 1989; Aral and Holmes 1990: Fullilove, Fullilove, et al. 1990; Rolfs, Goldberg, et al. 1990). A review of the literature reveals two related characterizations of cocaine that link it to sex and ultimately to prostitution. These characterizations are cocaine as a highly addictive substance and cocaine as an aphrodisiac or sexual stimulant.

Some early research on cocaine focused on the reputation of the drug as an aphrodisiac or sexual stimulant (Grinspoon and Bakalar 1976; Parr 1976). Although most of these reports were from subjects who used cocaine intranasally, similar characterizations have been reported by people who smoke cocaine (Kerr 1988; MacDonald, Waldorf, et al. 1988; Bowser 1989; *The Economist* 1989; Bowser, Fullilove, et al. 1990). There is some psycho- physiological evidence for this purported effect of cocaine. Buffum (1982, 1988) states that increases in the release of dopamines to the brain have been associated clinically with heightened sexual drive. Because cocaine promotes the production of dopamines, it could well act as a sexual stimulant in some users.

Of course, many dispute the characterization of cocaine as a sexual stimulant or aphrodisiac. Some researchers suggest that male users are more likely than female users to describe cocaine as a sex-enhancing drug (Friedman et al. 1988), whereas others have reported that chronic use of crack eventually results in a lessened interest in sex altogether (Cregler 1989; Fullilove and Fullilove 1989; Inciardi 1993).

In any event, a prostitute's libido may be rather irrelevant to her conducting business, and she may have no desire to increase or enhance her feelings of sensuality or her sexual drive. There are, however, other reputed benefits of cocaine for people involved in prostitution. For example, although subjects in Wesson's (1982) study of masseuses in the San Francisco area often dismissed the sex-enhancing effects of cocaine, they did report that using cocaine made their work more enjoyable by heightening their awareness, suppressing negative feelings, and assisting them in staying awake for long nights of work. Furthermore, clients frequently offered cocaine to the masseuses as a supposed sexual stimulant, confirming that cocaine has at least the reputation of being a sex drug. Thus, even if a prostitute were to deny the aphrodisiacal effects of cocaine, allowing clients to associate her with the drug might make her seem sexier to them, thereby enhancing her reputation and increasing her value in the prostitution marketplace.

Finally, although the aphrodisiacal properties of cocaine may be exaggerated, at a minimum, the use of crack may at least lower inhibitions and provide a subcultural context in which greater sexual activity is acceptable or even expected (Kerr 1988; Abromowitz et al., 1989; Leigh 1990).

A second factor in the increased concern about the risk of HIV infection among crack-using women arises from the popular belief regarding the extremely addictive nature of cocaine. Many studies have identified the need to support a crack habit as a primary factor leading to entry into prostitution (Inciardi and Pottieger 1986; Friedman et al. 1988; Bowser 1989; *The Economist* 1989). Further evidence of the addictive nature of crack cocaine is drawn from the increasingly common practice of exchanging sex for drugs directly. This is by no means a new phenomenon (see Goldstein, 1979, for a discussion of heroin-addicted "bag-brides" who frequently exchanged sex for drugs). However, the proportions to which the behavior has expanded among crack-using women seem unprecedented (Cooper 1988; Inciardi 1989; Isikoff 1989; Minerbrook, 1989).

In addition to these two characterizations of cocaine, researchers have noted several significant developments in the prostitution marketplace that may be direct consequences of the increased use of cocaine. Apparently, the steady influx of women into prostitution has created rather competitive conditions for prostitutes and has changed some aspects of the way in which business is conducted. For instance, *The Economist* (1989) reports that the value of sex has dropped precipitously, and in some places, sex can be purchased at unprecedented low prices. Lower prices and increased competition apparently have resulted in some women engaging in extreme and degrading forms of sex (Bowser et al. 1990), and bartering sex for drugs—a relatively uncommon practice among narcotics-using prostitutes—has become increasingly popular, especially with younger crack-using prostitutes (Fullilove and Fullilove, 1989; Inciardi 1989; *The Economist* 1989; Aral and Holmes 1990; Bowser et al. 1990; Fullilove et al. 1990). In addition, Shedlin (1990) suggests that as more women have entered prostitution to support their crack habits, competition for clients has reduced the use of condoms due in part to clients' disfavor for them in spite of their effective protection against the spread of diseases. Shedlin cites the unwillingness of some prostitutes to spend their earnings on condoms. Instead, oral sex has become the modal form of sex because of its perceived greater safety from infection as well as the speed and ease with which it can be performed. Finally, the increasing competition seems to have forced some women out of the profession entirely: Although prostitutes who use crack have become increasingly active, older prostitutes are reportedly retreating from the streets to avoid the dangers associated with the crack trade (Shedlin 1990).

Though some important work has been done on a typology of prostitution (Winick and Kinsie, 1971), including those who exchange sex for drugs (Goldstein 1979), the body of recent research suggests that prostitution is undergoing a dramatic transformation as a result of the widespread use of crack cocaine. This study reports findings from recent research on crack-using prostitutes that describe three aspects of prostitutes' orientations to crack cocaine. A discussion of the findings focuses on how the deviant roles of prostitute and crack addict are related.

## Methods

Intensive interviews were conducted by the author with 39 women who used crack and had multiple sex partners within the week preceding the interview.[1] Interviews were conducted in an office affiliated with a local drug education and outreach project and lasted approximately 1–2 hrs. Subjects were paid $25 for their participation.

The subjects' age averaged approximately 32 years, and about half stated that they had less than a 12th-grade education. Thirty-three subjects were black, and six were white. Though only one was legally employed at the time of the interview, subjects averaged a monthly income of nearly $2,000.

Information was obtained regarding the subject's drug history (particularly her introduction to and use of crack cocaine), her experiences as a prostitute, and other related matters. Tape recordings of the interviews were transcribed by a research assistant, and relevant responses were categorized and coded by the author. Inductive techniques were used to classify subjects' statements about their use of crack cocaine and the relation of the drug to their involvement with prostitution.

## Results

An analysis of subjects' statements regarding their use of crack cocaine and its relation to their involvement in prostitution led to the identification of three primary characteristic responses: addiction, utility, and marketplace economics. These responses define the ways in which the role of crack user and prostitute are integrated. All three types of integration were evident in the responses of many of the subjects, and most subjects manifested at least two types to some degree. The implications of this overlap are discussed below.

## Addiction

Of the various expressions given by subjects for describing their use of crack cocaine and its link to prostitution, none was represented so frequently in the responses as the image of crack addiction. This type of response was typically characterized by straightforward statements of the subject's addiction to crack cocaine. Prostitution was viewed simply as a means—a typically reliable and relatively lucrative means—of securing funds needed to purchase the drug.[2] (Other means included other illegal activities, legal employment, public aid, and financial assistance from family and friends.) Like these other activities, prostitution was typically described as merely a means to obtaining and doing crack.

The responses indicative of this form of role integration clearly place drug use or drug addiction near the center of the subject's identity. Prostitution (as well as many other roles) is secondary. For example:

> I smoke every day, all day . . . It's like that every day. I just got out of the ward, and it's been like that . . . I've been smokin' ever since I started. Every day, all day. And the only time I miss smoking is when I'm locked up. [On prostitution:] I'll be anxious to get it over with so I can go get a rock. I'll be like I wish you would hurry up, don't take so long 'cause I got to go. (Respondent #1238)

This woman went on to state that her need for crack cocaine made it likely that she would have sex without using condoms, something she knew she should not do:

> The majority of the time I use condoms. I may just find myself sometimes without, you know just to get what I want . . . Because I'm a coke addict. I just want to get me some cocaine. Just do it, just to go get me some more cocaine so I don't have to look for more money. (#1238)

Others gave similar expressions of their overwhelming desire to obtain the drug:

> The rock is the pimp . . . We go out there, we do all this, we get all this money, first person we run to is to the dope man. The rock is the pimp . . . So that's why they call us strawberries, 'cause we get the rocks and we will have oral sex, have you, have your brother too, all at the same time to get this cocaine. (#1221)

> When you're using these drugs sometimes you'll do just about anything to get it. (#1217)

> I really didn't want to be with them, but I wanted to get high, so I just went
> ahead and had sex with them to get the money and go on and buy my [rock].
> [Q: So, why do you have sex?] So I could get high. (#1240)

When asked whether using crack cocaine had increased their sexual activity,
29 (78.4 percent) of the 37 women who answered the question responded
affirmatively. Many said the only reason they were hustling dates was in order
to obtain crack.

Although addiction is perhaps the most prevalent motivation for continuing to engage in prostitution, it rarely appeared to be the dominant factor in
a respondent's initiation into prostitution. Respondent #1226 was representative of many women who began "dating" (soliciting sex) in order to make
money for general living expenses. At the time, her use of drugs was limited
and only subsequently did her crack cocaine use become her primary
expense. Others suggested that as their use or addiction rises and falls so does
their prostitution (#1229). Nearly everyone stated flatly that if she was not
using crack cocaine she would not be dating.

In light of their addiction to crack cocaine, the distinction between a sex-
for-cash exchange and a sex-for-drugs exchange is one that matters little to
many women. One woman stated that it did not matter whether she got cash
or rocks as payment for sex because "that [crack cocaine] is what I'm gonna
get anyway" (#1208).

## Utilitarianism

For many subjects, the relation between their prostitution activities and their
use of crack cocaine cannot be characterized solely in terms of an addiction
model. In particular, there are some connections between the two roles that
might at first appear rather incidental but on closer examination are shown
to be important facilitating links between the two. Consistent with earlier
reports from cocaine users (e.g., Grinspoon and Bakalar 1976; Parr 1976),
statements from these women suggest that there is still a fairly widespread
perception of cocaine as at least an ameliorating, if not sexually stimulating,
drug. For many women, cocaine facilitated the business of prostitution,
enabling them to cope with difficult work conditions. For instance, some
women reported that smoking crack made them feel sexy and reduced their
inhibitions about having sex. Many also reported that smoking made the customer more relaxed, though some stated that crack often interfered with the
customer's ability to achieve orgasm, thus unduly prolonging the session.
Overwhelmingly, women shared the general view that doing cocaine was at
least somewhat useful in their particular line of work:

> I don't think I could do it [have sex with a john] if I wasn't high . . . A lot of the
> time I'm smoking while I'm having sex." [She stated that she was high approxi-

mately 80–85 percent of the time that she had sex.] (#1217)

[After the initial high] there is something in the drug that gives you that sexual desire. (#1224)

Approximately 75 percent of the time coke is involved with the date. It's the drug of choice [among johns]. Why, I don't know, but it's the drug of choice. I always go, yeah, that's what you're supposed to do. (#1231)

[How much of the time are you high when you're having sex?] All the time. [Laughs.] No, mostly all the time I been had some saved and I hit it before I have sex. [Has cocaine ever increased your desire to have sex?] Yeah, it makes you feel sexy. (#1221)

Many women attempted to counter possible criticism of their admitted dependence on cocaine by citing its usefulness. One respondent, acknowledging this two-sidedness of cocaine, stated that her dependence did not interfere with her ability to work:

When I'm high though, I usually don't let it affect me, so that I can't take care of my business. It just makes me funky and better. (#1238)

Again, this type of facilitating link between crack use and prostitution is independent of the level of addiction experienced by the women. A few of the women were nightclub dancers or had been dancers in the past. The two occupations of dancer and prostitute were clearly related in the minds of these women. Just as in prostitution, cocaine had a use for the role of dancer:

The girls that get into drugs real heavy, they get up on stage and do what they have to do. (#1230)

Another useful aspect of doing crack is that the prostitute regularly interacts with "dope men" who have a lot of money, although reports of their willingness to part with it vary. These dope men are good, wealthy clients, but their acquaintance is valuable in other ways as well, as discussed in the next section. One subject spoke repeatedly of the significance of this acquaintance during the interview:

[Describing some of her better dates, one where a couple of johns went in together and paid her well in rocks:] Usually it be like the dealers, and a couple of guys, usually be the dealers you know, and that's how you get more rocks 'cause usually a person that, unless they done got paid, that would be the only person buy you that many rocks, other than that we can get that many rocks from a dealer. (#1221)

## Marketplace Economics

The third characterization of subjects' use of crack and its relation to prostitution is one in which subjects described their procurement of crack and their selling of sex as fundamental marketplace processes. Responses often exhibited the subject's shrewd understanding of how to thrive in a competitive marketplace. Many of these women engaged in prostitution as a livelihood long before they began using crack cocaine. Specific aspects of their marketplace role relations include: prostitutes as drug couriers, common market interest of prostitutes and crack sellers, frequent sales and bartering between prostitutes and crack sellers, and the social and symbolic benefits of the relation.

## Prostitutes as Drug Couriers

The first aspect of the role relation evolves from the common practice among drug buyers and sellers of using women (and young boys) as couriers. This is a frequent practice among drug suppliers and users because women are thought to be less likely to arouse the suspicion of the police. Even though they may possess a certain notoriety vis-à-vis the police, prostitutes would be especially well-suited to this task because they already possess a certain intrepid street savvy. As a result, these women would regularly find themselves in possession of significant quantities of crack. Receiving (or taking outright) some of the contraband as payment for their courier services could be expected to occur rather often. For many women, profits from this work are likely to be as important as those derived from their prostitution activities:

> Uh-huh, I be showin' 'em where, you know, like what area to go in. And then I'll be getting my money, you gonna give me $2 or $3 for shown' 'em . . . Over the weekend I do it every night. (#1240) [She went on to indicate that this was a function of her being out on the street, hustling.]

> Somebody came by and asked me if I had a stem [a pipe for smoking crack] and did I know where to cop. But they knew, you know, where to get it and everything, but they all gave me the money. (#1238)

Thus, although cocaine was often defined as an aid in the performance of the business of prostitution, it was clear from the interviews that a woman's pursuit of cocaine is well served by her role as a prostitute. For instance, although prostitution constitutes a major source of income and enables many addicted women to purchase crack cocaine, it is often the case that prostitution activities merely provide somewhat serendipitous access to crack. In many ways, prostitution is apparently perceived as a central role in the deviant street network, affording the prostitute knowledge of and access to a wide range of profitable and ostensibly exciting activities. Many prostitutes develop a high profile on the street and are often well connected in the deviant community. These characteristics make them popular choices as sources of information and as couriers for others wishing to purchase drugs. Performing these minor services for other drug users will frequently net the prostitute a share in the drugs. Sometimes she is given a portion of the drugs; other times she skims part of it without the buyer's knowledge. As a courier, some women reported establishing a price with the occasional drug buyer for a certain amount of drugs. Subsequently, the prostitute is able to arrange a more desirable deal with the supplier and keeps the difference for herself. Twenty (51 percent) of the women in the sample reported having served as drug couriers or "coppers" in the previous week, often handling hundreds of dollars of crack cocaine in a single deal. For these women, their street role as a prostitute was extremely useful in their ability to locate, obtain, and profit from cocaine to be delivered to others.

In addition, prostitution sometimes brings women into contact with customers who are in possession of large quantities of drugs. These special customers may occasionally bestow special attention on the prostitute, giving her free gifts of crack or bargain rates, and may provide a certain measure of protection or security because she is often viewed as an important link in the drug information and supply network. Women who take advantage of this fortuitous facilitation of crack use that prostitution provides may or may not be heavy users, and thus, this aspect of the interrelation between the two activities is distinct from the addiction model described above.

## Common Market Interests of Prostitutes and Crack Sellers

Because prostitution and crack constitute two major commodities in the inner city, crack dealers and prostitutes are likely to have overlapping markets. Like more conventional retailers who form associations to preserve their market interest, these illegal entrepreneurs have common interests in the marketplace that they no doubt wish to protect, including the stability of prices, the encroachment on established territory by outside vendors, the freedom of the marketplace from police interference, and even the credit ratings of various customers. Regular interaction between prostitutes and crack sellers to exchange information and safeguard their areas of enterprise would be a part of the natural course of doing business:

> They call us little ladies of the night, and the little ladies of the night is out there, of them they surely takes good care of us 'cause they know we gonna go get the money and come back to them 'cause see sometimes when you ask them for something and maybe I have time or maybe I want to have sex with you then, they will give you some because if you are spendin' with them all the

time, know what I'm saying, and bring customers to them all the time, oh they'll look out for you before they'll look out for anybody. (#1221)

## Frequent Sales and Bartering of Goods and Services

As a natural extension of drug dealers' and prostitutes' common market interests, it is likely that members of these two groups frequently engage in direct sales and exchange of goods. Both crack dealers and prostitutes would at times probably find it expedient to exchange one commodity for the other. For instance, during the days and weeks immediately prior to the mailing of government support checks (e.g., Aid to Families with Dependent Children, social security, etc.) there is often a widespread shortage of cash in neighborhoods where this monthly influx of capital is of significant proportions. Given that easy credit may be difficult to secure from prostitutes and drug dealers, goods and services like crack and sex (as well as food and other necessities) may be available during such times only through bartering. Though by no means a recent phenomenon in the drug culture, bartering has reached impressive dimensions in the crack trade. Goods and services of all sorts can be exchanged in this cashless market:

> [Describing how she let a dealer use her apartment for his business:] If I got a lot of money I might buy me like three rocks. I try not to go with three rocks 'cause usually, I hook up with some of the boys and they *give* it to me. See, you know come in my house and cut up dope and some, they leave me some. They do that too, you know. Well, if they want to sell some out of your house for the day and, um, they'll throw you out some like that too, just to use your house for the day . . . I had one guy stay there for a whole week. And I had to buy nothing. I just got it free all that week. (#1221)

The economics of prostitution and cocaine are probably as complex as any other illegal market. There are relatively simple issues to resolve such as the quality of the drug being sold and the advantage of buying in quantity. Other issues such as procuring cocaine with cash versus exchanging sex for it are not so straightforward. Some respondents stated that it made more sense to them to be paid by their johns in cash and then purchase drugs with the cash:

> I prefer being paid in cash . . . 'cause you can do with it what you want. I may not want to buy $200 worth of rock. I might want to buy [something else] and some rock, you know. Whereas, if you turn a date for drugs and you take drugs you might tell yourself you're gonna sell it but you're not gonna sell it . . . So I would prefer to be paid with cash. (#1217)

This sentiment was echoed by another who said that all her dates are cash dates, and she buys her rocks. Being paid in cash allows her to "do what I want to do" (#1234). Other women were more willing to accept rocks in payment for sex. Often, this willingness is partly a function of their current need to get high. One respondent who gave considerable evidence of being addicted to cocaine reduced the issue of cash payment versus bartering to a truism: It did not matter, because "that's [crack] what I'm gonna get anyway" (#1208). Even when addiction or immediate need for the drug was apparently not a factor, several women suggested that it was wiser to accept rocks for sex rather than money if the quality of the rocks was certain.

A range of factors impinge on the economic decisions of these women. Some have children to support whereas others cited routine household expenses. The salience of these factors varied. For instance, one woman's children had recently moved in with her mother. This arrangement meant that she required significantly less cash in payment for sex. Other women indicated that the depletion of their public assistance funds by about the middle of each month made for a significant change in the level of their solicitation activities and put a premium on cash dates during the last weeks of the month.

> Well, first of all I really didn't have no place to stay, . . . and I needed somewhere to stay . . . so I walking down the street, in the street rather, and the guy stopped me and said, um, are you dating today? And I thought he was the police so I wouldn't say nothing and kept going. And then he came back around the corner and he said "I got $20," like that, and I said god, I need this $20. I did it with him in the car. And I got the $20, and then I said well, I can get me some more money, you know, like this . . . . It started becoming a regular thing when I needed a place to stay for good to sleep, something to eat, and clothes and stuff to wear, and just money to get around, you know. (#1221)

Other aspects of this woman's purchasing habits and her sex marketing practices show all the sophistication of a savvy entrepreneur:

> Sometimes I get two rocks, sometimes I don't. Sometimes I may do good they may give me four rocks. The least I ever took was two rocks. They know I ain't going below that. I'll go make me some money, buy my own. (Laughs.) I mean I'm sorry to say that but I will . . . . They so cheap. [Describing customers who pay in cash, she complained about how little they paid:] About $25, I'll say $20. See they give you more rocks they only gonna give you less money. They give you more rocks you don't get that much money. Sometimes you just get those rocks and you don't get money at all. (#1221)

## Social and Symbolic Benefits

Finally, beyond general economic concern, it is possible that relationships between prostitutes and crack sellers serve other functions as well. For instance, prostitutes willing to exchange sex for crack sometimes seek to establish a fairly stable relationship with a dealer (or several), particularly one who sells "weight" (significant quantities of cocaine) in order to ensure a regular supply of the drug. In lieu of cash payments, crack sellers engaged in such bartering might derive a form of symbolic status by having in their debt women willing to do almost anything for them. The perception of such women as a type of chattel would be consistent with the prevailing low esteem in which "strawberries" are typically held by those inside as well as outside the drug trade.

The issue of surviving in the competitive marketplace (as a supplier in the prostitution market and as a consumer in the cocaine market) underscores the need to establish reliable contacts with others, especially clients, drug users, and drug dealers. Most of the women sought to maintain a regular sex clientele, seeing several customers on a weekly basis. The same reliability was sought in their source of cocaine as well as in opportunities for supplemental income (e.g., by copping drugs for others).

## Discussion

Nearly all the women interviewed for this study gave some incidence of being addicted to cocaine. However, the link between prostitution and cocaine is more complex than this. It involves specific utilitarian aspects of the drug (e.g., its stimulant effect) as well as the general symbolic value of cocaine as a "sex drug." In addition, prostitution and consumption of cocaine are parts of larger economic processes that are not unlike those of a more typical worker: occasional changes in expenses and other sources of income, the need to anticipate cash flow needs, the liquidity of assets, and the importance of good credit and reliable marketplace contacts. These economic concerns form the foundation of an important role relationship between prostitutes and others who traffic in cocaine.

Recent reports have suggested that crack sellers frequently target women as a sizable and important market for the drug. Fearful of intravenous use of drugs but desirous of something more potent than marijuana, many women find crack an agreeable alternative (Massing 1989). Even street terminology reflects users' and sellers' sensitization to certain gender implications of the drug, sometimes referring to cocaine as "girl" and heroin as "boy."

The data presented here reveal a multidimensional relation between cocaine and prostitution, but they do not provide a basis for establishing a conclusive priority among the ways in which the relation can be characterized. It seems clear that the effect of cocaine on the libido and acute addiction do not alone explain the high rates of cocaine and crack cocaine use among prostitutes. Rather, the data relating prostitution to the use of cocaine seem to suggest that this use partly reflects specific economic relationships that link prostitutes and crack dealers.

As concern grows regarding the spread of HIV, more attention has been focused on prostitution as a vector of transmission. Increasingly, the examination of prostitution has uncovered how closely related prostitution is to the problem of substance abuse, particularly crack cocaine abuse. As a result, solving the public health problem posed by unsafe sex with prostitutes depends to a great extent on getting a grip on the problems posed by unchecked distribution and consumption of crack cocaine. Traditional substance abuse treatment may remedy the problem of substance addiction, but it does not provide solutions to marketplace processes that, for many, are exploitive and ultimately destructive. These solutions require a more wholistic understanding of the cocaine-abusing prostitute and her economic relationships than typically has been the case.

## Notes

[1]Women were recruited for the study by outreach workers of a drug-counseling agency in Cleveland, Ohio. The parameters of the population from which subjects were recruited were women who used cocaine at least three times in the week prior to the interview and had at least three different sex partners during the same week. Because the study was exploratory in nature and because of the lack of shared meaning of labels such as "prostitute" or "strawberry," it was not required that subjects identify themselves *a priori* as either to be included in the study. In response to a question in the interview, all the women in the sample agreed that they would label themselves as either prostitutes or strawberries. (The term "strawberry" is slang for a woman who accepts drugs—especially crack—as payment for sex. One subject informed the interviewer that the term was meant to indicate that such women were "easy pickin's," willing to perform nearly any sort of sexual act for as little as a "bump" or a puff off a crack pipe.)

[2]Of course, for some women, prostitution was a means for obtaining crack directly. Though some have suggested that bartering sex for drugs is an indication of the degree of addiction, it is apparent that other marketplace issues also figure in whether women seek and receive cash in payment for sex or whether they accept drugs in direct exchange. These marketplace issues are discussed later.

## References

Abramowitz, A., J. Guydish, W. Woods, and W. Clark. 1989. "Increasing Crack Use Among Drug Users in an AIDS Epicenter: San Francisco." *Fifth International Conference on AIDS Abstracts*: 1:764.

Aral, Sevgi O., and King K. Holmes. 1990. "Epidemiology of Sexual Behavior and Sexually Transmitted Diseases," Pp. 19–36 in *Sexually Transmitted Diseases*, edited by King K. Holmes, Willard Cautes, Jr., Stanley Lemon, and Walter E. Stamm. New York: McGraw Hill.

Bowser, Benjamin P. 1989. "Crack and AIDS: An Ethnographic Impression." *Journal of the National Medical Association* 81:538–40.

Bowser, Benjamin P., Mindy Thompson Fullilove, and Robert E. Fullilove. 1990. "African-American Youth and AIDS High-Risk Behavior: The Social Context and Barriers to Prevention." *Youth and Society* 22:54–66.

Buffum, John. 1982. "Pharmacosexology: The Effects of Drugs on Sexual Function— A Review." *Journal of Psychoactive Drugs* 14:5–44.

———. 1988. "Substance Abuse and High-Risk Sexual Behavior: Drugs and Sex— The Dark Side." *Journal of Psychoactive Drugs* 20:165–8.

Centers for Disease Control. 1987. "Antibody for Human Immunodeficiency Virus in Female Prostitutes." *Morbidity and Mortality Weekly Report* 36:157–161.

———. 1988. "Relationship of Syphilis to Drug Use and Prostitution—Connecticut and Philadelphia, Pennsylvania." *Morbidity and Mortality Weekly Report* 37:755–64.

Chambers, Carl D., R. Kent Hinsely, and Mary Moldestad. 1970. "The Female Opiate Addict." Pp. 222–39 in *The Epidemiology of Opiate Addiction in the United States*, edited by John C. Ball and Carl D. Chambers. Springfield, MA: Charles C. Thomas.

Cooper, Mary H. 1988. "The Business of Illicit Drugs." *Congressional Quarterly Editorial Research Reports* May 20:258–71.

Cregler, Louis. 1989. "Adverse Health Consequences of Cocaine Abuse." *Journal of the National Medical Association* 81:27–38.

Cushman, Peter. 1972. "Methadone Maintenance Treatment of Narcotic Addiction: Analysis of Police Records of Arrests Before and During Treatment." *New York State Journal of Medicine* 72:1752–69.

*The Economist*. 1989. "American Survey: The AIDS Plague Spreads." 312:23–4.

Friedman, S. R., C. Dozier, C. Sterk, T. Williams, J. L. Southeran, D. C. Des Jarlais. 1988. "Crack Use Puts Women at Risk for Heterosexual Transmission of HIV from Intravenous Drug Users." *Fourth International Conference on AIDS Abstracts* 2:396.

Fullilove, Mindy Thompson, and Robert E. Fullilove. 1989. "Intersecting Epidemics: Black Teen Crack Use and Sexually Transmitted Disease." *Journal of the American Medical Women's Association* 44:146–53.

Fullilove, Robert E., Mindy Thompson Fullilove, Benjamin P. Bowser and Shirley A. Gross. 1990. "Risk of Sexually Transmitted Disease Among Black Adolescent Crack Users in Oakland and San Francisco, California." *Journal of the American Medical Association* 263:851–5.

Goldstein, Paul. J. 1979. *Prostitution and Drugs*. Lexington, MA: Lexington Books.

Grinspoon, Lester and James B. Bakalar. 1976. *Cocaine: A Drug and Its Social Evolution*. New York: Basic Books.

Inciardi, James A. 1989. "Trading Sex for Crack Among Juvenile Drug Users: A Research Note." *Contemporary Drug Problems* 16:689–700.

Inciardi, James A. 1992. "Kingrats, Chicken Heads, Slow Necks, Freaks, and Blood Suckers: A Glimpse at the Miami Sex for Crack Market." Pp. 37–67 in *Crack Pipe as Pimp*, edited by Mitchel Raener. Lexington, MA: Lexington Free Press.

Inciardi, James A., and Anne E. Pottieger. 1986. "Drug Use and Crime Among Two Cohorts of Women Narcotics Users: An Empirical Assessment." *Journal of Drug Issues* 16:91–106.

Isikoff, Michael. 1989. "Crack Holds Many Inner-City Women in Its Grip." Pp. A–18 in *The Washington Post* August 20: Reprinted on the NIJ Conference electronic BBS.

James, Jennifer, Cathleen Gosho, and Robbin Watson Wohl. 1979. "The Relationship Between Female Criminality and Drug Use." *International Journal of the Addictions* 14:215–29.

Kerr, Peter. 1988. "Syphilis Surge With Crack Use Raises Fears on Spread of AIDS." *The New York Times* June 29:B1.

Leigh, Barbara Critchlow. 1990. "The Relationship of Substance Use During Sex to High Risk Behavior." *The Journal of Sex Research* 27:199–213.

MacDonald, Patrick T., Dan Waldorf, Craig Reinarman, and Sheila Murphy. 1988. "Heavy Cocaine Use and Sexual Behavior." *Journal of Drug Issues* 18:437–55.

Massing, Michael. 1989. "Crack's Destructive Sprint Across America." *New York Times Magazine* October 1:38–41 and 58–9.

Miller, Eleanor. 1986. *Street Women*. Philadelphia: Temple University Press.

Minerbrook, Scott. 1989. "A Night in a Crack House." *U.S. News and World Report* April 10:29.

Parr, Denis. 1976. "Sexual Aspects of Drug Abuse in Narcotic Addicts." *British Journal of Psychiatry* 71:261–8.

Rolfs, Robert T., Martin Goldberg, and Robert G. Sharrar. 1990. "Risk Factors for Syphilis: Cocaine Use and Prostitution." *American Journal of Public Health* 80:853–7.

Shedlin, Michele. 1990. "An Ethnographic Approach to Understanding HIV High-Risk Behaviors: Prostitution and Drug Abuse." *National Institute on Drug Abuse Research Monograph Series* 93:134–49.

Wesson, Donald R. 1982. "Cocaine Use by Masseuses." *Journal of Psychoactive Drugs* 14:75–6.

Winick, Charles, and Paul M. Kinsie. 1971. *The Lively Commerce*. Chicago: Quadrangle.

# 7

# Worldwide Drug Scourge
## The Expanding Trade in Illicit Drugs

## Stephen Flynn

Now that the Cold War is over, calls for a greater emphasis on the American domestic agenda have reached a crescendo. The problem of illicit drugs is invariably mentioned as one of the leading domestic ills deserving the full measure of the federal government's attention. But the drug issue is no more purely a domestic problem than are ozone depletion and disease control. As with greenhouse gas emissions and the AIDS epidemic, the drug scourge is a global phenomenon, and it is expanding at an alarming pace. Further, even the most aggressive domestic response cannot insulate the United States from the political, economic, and social fallout associated with the explosive growth in illicit drugs worldwide.

In the Central Asian republics, for instance, thousands of acres have been given over to the cultivation of opium poppies and cannabis. Over the past year, Hungary and Czechoslovakia have become major transit countries for Asian heroin destined for West Europe. Recently, Polish health officials warned that a dramatic rise in intravenous drug abuse in Warsaw has

Reprinted by permission of the Brookings Institution from *The Brookings Review*, Winter, 1993, pp. 6–11.

unleashed an AIDS epidemic. Especially ominous are reports of expanding organized criminal networks engaged in drug trafficking with the former Soviet Union, Central Europe, and Latin America.

The surge in the illicit narcotics trade in Eurasia and elsewhere has been first and foremost fueled by its tremendous profitability. Today drugs are a $100 billion a year transnational industry. The illicit stockholders and operatives come from every continent and include Colombians, Mexicans, Italians, Nigerians, Poles, Turks, Chinese, Lebanese, and Georgians.

Second, the recent unraveling of socialism and the move toward freer trade among industrialized countries has created a fertile environment for international businesses—even illicit ones—as deregulation and integration gather momentum. As commercial banks, investment firms, insurance companies, full-service brokers, and asset managers have all globalized their operations, the menu of financial institutions through which both clean and dirty money can be moved has never been so extensive. With the North American Free Trade agreement, EC '92, the Asia-Pacific Economic Cooperation effort, and the collapse of the Iron Curtain, torrents of people, goods, and services are pouring across borders. In their midst, drug shipments can move with little risk of detection by customs authorities.

Third, the colossal social and economic dislocations connected with both the implosions of the communist world and the desperate standard of living in much of the third world are creating the ideal climate for widespread drug production and abuse. In the third world, the loss of superpower benefactors, declining rates of per capita GNP, unstable commodity prices, and rising domestic and foreign debt make the hard currency and profits connected with the drug trade almost irresistible. For many of the destitute and disaffected survivors of impoverished third world states and once rigidly controlled communist societies, drugs offer a seductive reprieve from an unpleasant world.

Finally, the recent resurgence of ethnic, religious, and nationalistic conflict slows or precludes altogether the development of new regional and international regulatory regimes to control illicit activities within the global community. It also hampers intelligence sharing and cooperation among neighboring law enforcement agencies, a development of which criminal drug organizations are a direct beneficiary.

The results: the production of heroin, cocaine, cannabis, and synthetic drugs is at a record high and will continue to rise; narcotics traffickers are moving drugs and money throughout the international economy with virtual impunity; and drug consumption is exploding in many countries that had hitherto escaped the drug scourge.

## Global Drug Production

Because drug production is illicit, estimating its worldwide extent can be no more than an exercise in guesswork. But clearly the production of opium poppy, coca, and cannabis is on the rise. According to U.S. government estimates, in 1991 cocaine production in Latin America grew by 85 tons—a 7 percent increase over 1990. Opium production was estimated to be 4,200 tons in 1991, a 33 percent increase since 1988. Hashish production from the four major producing countries grew 65 percent between 1990 and 1991 to 1,244 tons.

More disturbing than the rise in global drug production is the sudden proliferation of producers. Within Peru, the world's leading producer of coca, illicit cultivation has spread out of the Upper Huallaga Valley into the Cuzco, Ayacucho, Pasco, and Puno Departments. New coca cultivation has been reported in remote regions in Brazil, Ecuador, and Venezuela. Cocaine refinement, once restricted to Colombia, now takes place in Peru, Bolivia, Venezuela, Argentina, Ecuador, and Brazil. Brazil's involvement is particularly ominous since it is the only South American country where acetone and ether, the chemicals used to turn coca base into cocaine, are manufactured in industrial quantities. Over the past year, European authorities have even discovered cocaine processing laboratories in Portugal, Spain, and Italy.

Opium cultivation has spilled over the traditional production regions of Mexico, the Golden Triangle (Burma, Thailand, and Laos), and the Golden Crescent (Pakistan, Afghanistan, and Iran). Guatemala and Colombia are now major source countries in the Western hemisphere. U.S. officials estimate that Colombia may have produced about 4 tons of heroin in 1992—close to Mexico's 6.8 tons in 1990. The Colombians almost certainly have the means to become the chief world heroin suppliers of the 21st century.

In Eurasia, extensive opium poppy cultivation has been reported in Poland, Ukraine, Moldova, the Caucasus, and Central Asia. In January 1992 Sergey Tershchenko, the prime minister of Kazakhstan, legalized the cultivation of the opium poppy. The government of Kyrgzstan toyed with the idea, but backed away. In Central Asia, per capita income is approximately 40 percent below, and unemployment nearly 70 percent above, the average of the other former Soviet states. The economic incentives for poppy production will be even greater when Moscow ends its annual subsidy of billions of rubles to the region. Central Asia could very well become the "Andean region" of Eurasia.

Opium cultivation has also reemerged in China after being virtually eliminated by the communists when they seized power in 1949. Law enforcement authorities have spotted poppies in at least 13 of China's 23 provinces and 5 autonomous regions, with the largest plots in the remote southern province of Yunnan and in the northern province of Inner Mongolia.

Among traditional source countries for cannabis (the United States ranks second), production fell in 1991 because of bad weather and stepped-up eradication efforts. Still, the capacity for large-scale cultivation is spreading quickly. Brazil has become a major producer, with illegal cultivation taking place in at least 20 of its 26 states. In the former Soviet Union, cannabis plants grow freely on more than 2.5 million acres, mostly in Kazakhstan, Kyrgzstan, Siberia, and the Far East. Cannabis is being grown throughout Africa. Hashish production soared in 1991, with Lebanon increasing its total production almost sixfold over 1990.

Production of synthetic narcotics also appears to be spreading. Laboratories in Taiwan and South Korea are the chief source of "ice," a high-purity methamphetamine developed during the mid-1980s. Poland has recently become one of the largest producers of amphetamines for the European market. According to police lab analyses, in 1991 some 20 percent of the amphetamines seized in West Europe and 25 percent of those seized in Germany originated in Poland. Underground laboratories for synthetic drugs have been discovered in Moscow, St. Petersburg, Sverdlovsk, and many other large cities in the former Soviet Union. Methaqualone ("mandrax") is produced throughout India, primarily for the large market in Southern Africa.

## Spreading Like Weeds

Neither geography nor laboratory technology can constrain the cultivation of illicit drugs. Poppy, coca, and cannabis can be grown almost anywhere, and the ability to refine them or to produce synthetic drugs is widely available. All the coca and opium poppy plants being grown in the world would fill a space not much larger than the Eastern Shore of Maryland. The global capacity for cultivating these drugs is virtually untapped.

Illicit drug production is taking root most quickly in areas with few other meaningful economic options. Sub-Saharan Africa, Inner Mongolia, southern China, Central Asia, Afghanistan, and northeastern Brazil are among the most remote and impoverished places on the planet. Although peasants rarely get rich growing coca, poppies, or cannabis, they can earn up to 10 times what they can by growing traditional farm products. That can mean the difference between providing for the most basic needs of one's family or exposing it to life-threatening poverty.

Throughout much of the developing world, national currencies are nonexchangeable and worthless. Businessmen trying to finance capital improvements, insurgents and terrorists seeking the weapons and resources to fight their causes, and governments struggling to keep their economies afloat are in desperate need of hard currency at a time of global capital shortage. For them, too, the drug trade is almost the only answer.

The temptation to produce drugs may also prove almost irresistible in Eastern Europe and the former Soviet Union. One-third of the people in Hungary now live below the poverty level. By the end of 1991 unemployment in eastern Germany was 30 percent. In Russia as many as 10–11 million people, or 15 percent of the work force, may be unemployed by the year's end.

Drugs are usually produced where they are most difficult to stop—generally in remote areas safely outside a government's reach, often in territory under the sway of insurgency groups. The criminal organizations that support drug production have the resources to corrupt, intimidate, or bypass the authority of governments that, in addition, often face political problems that are more pressing than drugs or cannot take effective enforcement action because of a lack of political legitimacy.

## The "Big Business" of Drug Trafficking

In essence, drug trafficking is a form of commodities trade conducted by transnational consortiums. Acquiring chemicals to produce drugs, transporting the drugs to wholesale distributors, and laundering the profits require interacting with and blending into legitimate markets. The size and complexity of these operations mandate that the drug industry pattern itself after the modern multinational corporation. Yet unlike traders in oil, automobiles, or microchips, traders in illicit drugs must outwit a dynamic enforcement environment designed to defeat them. Consequently, over the past two decades the drug trade has undergone something of a Darwinian evolution, the survivors of which have developed into sophisticated and highly flexible organizations. As one senior American drug enforcement official put it, "Lee Iacocca could learn a heck of a lot from these people!"

For those in the business of moving illicit drugs and money, the post-Cold War era has much to offer: a trend toward privatization and liberalization; an increase in the volume and diversity of world trade; the deregulation of national economies; the integration of global transportation, communications, and financial systems; and increasingly open and unmonitored borders between states. And since trafficking organizations are not bound by the legal constraints of domestic and international commerce regulation, they are particularly well placed to respond rapidly and with considerable ingenuity to these changes in the international economic system.

A prime example of the modern drug trafficking organization is the Cali "cartel." Like its better known counterpart from Medellin, the Cali cartel is a loose conglomeration of Colombian families based in a major Colombian city. But unlike the often violent Medellin cartel, which conjures up images of well-heeled thugs surrounded by private armies, the Cali cartel operates more like the senior management team at Exxon or Coca Cola. Its transportation, distribution, and money-laundering networks cover the globe. Outside the Western hemisphere, Cali operatives work in Japan, Hungary, Czechoslovakia, Poland, Germany, Italy, Spain, Portugal, the Netherlands, France, and Great Britain.

Because the huge U.S. and European markets are so far from coca production areas, transportation is critical to the cocaine business. Contrary to popular belief, most drugs do not cross American borders on low-flying Cessnas or aboard fast-moving "cigarette" boats. Most reach their markets by way of commercial conveyances. Containerized shipments, bulk cargo, false documentation, and front companies conceal the movement of cocaine by water. By land, most cocaine crosses the U.S.-Mexican border in hidden compartments of tractor trailers and other vehicles or in commercial cargo itself. For these border crossings, the Cali cartel relies on Mexican smugglers.

The Cali organization uses international shipping centers in Central and South America, particularly in Brazil, Venezuela, Surinam, and Panama, to ship cocaine by sea to Europe and to the eastern United States. It conceals the drugs in a variety of imaginative ways, one of the most creative of which was to hide 15.7 tons of cocaine in 2,000 concrete cement posts (U.S. authorities seized that shipment in September 1991). Occasionally drugs are shipped to the United States circuitously, passing through Europe or Canada before arriving.

When commercial airliners are used for shipping cocaine, the drug is hidden on the plane itself, or it is carried by human "mules," who swallow condoms containing pellets of cocaine. It is also concealed in luggage with false bottoms, in aerosol cans, and sneakers with hollowed-out soles. Sometimes it is converted to liquid and smuggled in bottles of shampoo, mouthwash, and liquor.

By blending shipments within the growing volume of international trade, the Cali cartel greatly reduces the chance of discovery. Interdicting drugs has always been a "needle-in-a-haystack" exercise for customs authorities, but when those drugs are hidden among general merchandise or on the person of international travelers, the task becomes overwhelming. In 1991, for example, 1.8 million containers arrived in the Port of Newark alone, but U.S. customs inspectors there were able to search thoroughly only 15–18 containers a day.

## Getting the Goods to the Wholesalers

Once the drug arrives, it must be distributed. The Cali cartel has set up wholesale distribution networks throughout the country and exercises complete control over the New York and Washington, D.C., markets. If a load of cocaine arrives at Kennedy International Airport or at the Port of Newark, one of the 10 to 12 Cali distribution cells in New York receives it. Each cell, made up of 15–20 Colombian employees who earn monthly salaries ranging from $2,000 to $7,500, conducts an average of $25 million of business a month. Each cell is self-contained, with information tightly compartmentalized. Only a handful of managers know all the operatives. The cell has a head, bookkeeper, money handler, cocaine handler, motor pool, and 10 to 15 apartments serving as stash houses.

Communications are conducted in code over facsimile machines, cellular phones, and pay phones. To eliminate any risk of interception, cellular phones are purchased and discarded, often two or three times a week. When a wholesale customer wants to make a purchase, a cell member is notified by a pager system. That cell member proceeds to a public phone and arranges a rendezvous site. He then gets, from the motor pool, a rental car that is returned to the rental agency after the transaction. The transaction itself, including any travel receipts, is logged by the bookkeeper, and the money is turned over to the money handler to be shipped to the financial network set up by the cartel to hide and invest it. A favorite way to ship within the United States is the U.S. Postal Service's "Express Mail."

Such tactics stretch traditional law enforcement surveillance to the limit and beyond. Most national police authorities are finding themselves completely "outgunned" by technologies that are relatively cheap for organized crime but financially out of reach for the law enforcement community. The situation in Poland is suggestive. Between 1990 and 1991, Poland's police budget fell 13 percent. The use of patrol cars was limited to 60 kilometers a day, and police abandoned plans to modernize their vehicles or buy new car radios. Throughout the country only 30 police officials were assigned full-time to antidrug operations.

Once the cartel has received the money for its drug sales, it moves it into and through the legal financial system to conceal its origins. If the Cali cell broken up by federal authorities in December 1991 is typical, the Cali financial network must launder up to $300 million each year per cell. Money laundering typically involves three independent phases. First, drug proceeds are "placed," or used to make deposits or to purchase monetary instruments or securities that can be turned into cash elsewhere. Second, the money is "layered," or sent through multiple electronic funds transfers or other transactions to make it difficult to track and blur its illicit origin. Finally, the source of the money disappears as it is "integrated," or invested into seemingly legitimate accounts and enterprises.

The revolution under way in the global financial and banking markets has made all three of these jobs easier. Drug traffickers have a vast new array of possibilities for the placement of funds as national currencies become convertible and new and largely unregulated private banking institutions spring up throughout the former Soviet bloc and the third world. Many of the new banks have primitive accounting practices, no computers, and little or no experience with international banking practices. The integration and increased efficiency of the global banking system allows money launderers to layer money with virtual impunity. The sheer volume of electronic funds transfers makes them almost impossible to track. In 1991, for example, the Clearing House Interbank Payment System handled some 37 billion transactions worth $222 trillion. Finally, the sudden shift away from state to private ownership throughout the former communist world provides launderers with an array of "front" organizations to integrate their money into seemingly legitimate enterprises. The Cali cartel set up a number of such companies in Hungary, Czechoslovakia, and Poland in 1991.

Of course, the Cali cartel is not the only beneficiary of the changing international business environment. Italian, Polish, Turkish, Georgian, Chinese, Vietnamese, Lebanese, Pakistani, Nigerian, and many other transnational trafficking organizations are profiting as well.

## Trends in Global Drug Consumption

Predicting with any precision the character and dimension of the global drug market is difficult. Most drug abuse research has been done on population groups within advanced societies, and epidemiologists are understandably hesitant to apply these findings to the developing world. Too, drug epidemics typically refuse to stay within tidy political, cultural, or geographical boundaries. Islamic fundamentalism seems to help explain why drug abuse is uncommon in Saudi Arabia, but not why more than a million Iranians and 1.7 million Pakistanis use drugs.

But although it may not be possible to anticipate precisely which specific locations are likely to suffer from widespread abuse and when, forecasting the overall trend in global drug consumption is less problematic. The prospect for growing drug abuse worldwide can be correlated with the prevalence of its three requisite ingredients: an awareness of drugs, access to them, and the motivation to use them.

The awareness of drugs has become almost universal. In the third world, demographic pressures are forcing millions of people out of their isolation in remote villages and into large cities, where it is impossible not to know about drugs. And the collapse of the communist regimes in the former Soviet bloc has ended the state's monopoly on information and has made it possible for people to travel freely both at home and abroad. Word of a drug that has acquired popularity somewhere can spread quickly almost everywhere.

Access to drugs is also increasing with the projected rise in production and trafficking. Further, if democratization and economic liberalization persist, individuals will have greater personal freedom, mobility, and control over their personal incomes, facilitating contacts with drug distributors and their purchases.

People in most third world societies are also increasingly motivated to use drugs. For one thing, the population of the developing world is growing younger. More than half the people in Nigeria and Kenya, and more than 40 percent in Latin America, are under the age of 20—an age group known for risk-taking behavior and the willingness to challenge social conventions. In addition, rapid population growth rates are causing people, particularly young men, to move to big cities. Separated from their families, often unemployed or underemployed, and with little opportunity for schooling, more and more of these disillusioned young people are at great risk of taking up drugs.

Peer pressure and the mass media also can push vulnerable young people to become drug users. Many European and American movies and television programs—even programs like "Miami Vice" and movies like *Scarface* that presumably show that "drug crimes don't pay"—portray drugs as luxury goods consumed by wealthy Americans. As such, drugs end up serving as status symbols, or as one Nigerian addict recently put it, as a way to "become like an American."

Finally, the dislocations associated with the end of the socialist experiment and the desperate economic plight of much of the third world are increasing the willingness of people, young and old, to violate the law.

## Drug Use on the Rise

What evidence is there that global drug consumption is in fact on the rise? Although the data are soft, health officials around the globe are becoming increasingly alarmed. In Poland, 75 percent of all alcoholics are also addicted to either licit or illicit drugs. Most of these drug abusers in Poland are infected with the AIDS virus as a result of sharing intravenous needles. In Yugoslavia there are 300,000–400,000 addicts, with more than 15,000 in Belgrade alone. Estimates of drug abuse in the former Soviet Union range anywhere from 1.5

million to 7.5 million people. In all three areas, the spread of drug abuse is worst among the young. Almost two-thirds of Polish drug abusers are under 21 years of age.

In Eastern and Southern Asia nearly every country is reporting rising drug abuse. As the Burmese heroin trade has spilled increasingly into the subcontinent, Nepal, Bangladesh, and India all confront burgeoning user populations. In Pakistan, heroin users have grown from a few hundred to more than a million in little over a decade. Drug use in Thailand appeared to be stabilizing after an initial surge in large-scale opium poppy production in the 1970s, but new reports indicate that many villagers are shifting from traditional opium consumption to the more debilitating heroin addiction. As noted, opium and heroin are making a comeback in China, where police estimate that 300,000 use drugs, despite a relentless enforcement effort that featured the public execution of 250 drug traffickers in 1991.

In the barrios of Central and South America, cocaine addiction is becoming more prevalent, with the most worrisome trends in Colombia, Peru, Bolivia, Brazil, Ecuador, and Panama. One of every three secondary school students in Peru uses drugs. In Chile, Argentina, and Brazil, drug consumption is rising most dramatically among young people from upper-income families.

Africa represents the greatest unknown in the consumption picture, though it has virtually all the high-risk factors. Nigeria, Kenya, and South Africa, the wealthiest countries on the Sub- Saharan continent, are witnessing a rising incidence of drug abuse. In South Africa the drug of choice is "mandrax," a synthetic drug imported from India. In Nigeria and Kenya cannabis is the most widely abused drug, although there have been a growing number of reports of cocaine and heroin use.

The seductiveness of mood-altering substances is age-old and virtually universal. As the conditions that support widespread abuse become more prevalent within much of the global community, the prospect of expanding drug markets appears almost inevitable.

## Needed: An International Response

The profound changes connected with the passing of the Cold War era have transformed the drug trade into a transnational challenge of the first order. As with other such challenges—weapons proliferation, disease control, migration, ozone depletion—states can do little on their own to stand up against the rising tide of drug production, trafficking, and consumption.

Acknowledging that the drug trade has become a transnational activity that is outstripping the traditional tools available to governments to combat it has important implications for current U.S. drug control strategy. In 1992, 93.6 percent of the $11.9 billion national drug control budget was spent on domestic enforcement, demand reduction, and border control. Of the rest, 6.3 percent went to bilateral programs to help governments in source and transit countries fight illicit narcotics. One-tenth of one percent ($15.5 million) of the total budget supported multilateral drug programs.

What these budget allocations tell us is that U.S. policymakers see drugs as essentially a domestic problem that can be resolved with a national response. At home, it is assumed that large doses of law enforcement, prevention, and treatment programs will erode the market for illicit narcotics. Likewise, along the borders, we seem to believe that a full-scale investment in interdiction will keep traffickers at bay. Overseas, selected governments are enlisted in an American effort to disrupt the production and transit of drugs destined for our shores.

Even if a national strategy to combat the scourge of drugs were to succeed at home, Americans would still face the effects of a flourishing drug trade overseas. As recent events in Peru illustrate, large-scale drug production can disrupt national economies and destroy democratic institutions. When drug trafficking can infiltrate with virtual impunity the commercial conveyances, migrant labor forces, banks, and securities markets that service a global economy, it provides fuel for protectionist forces who seek to slow or reverse the global trend toward greater economic liberalization. Finally, the reduced worker productivity and the public health consequences, including the spread of AIDS, associated with widespread drug abuse jeopardize further the limited development prospects of many third world countries, weakening their potential to become strong U.S. trading partners and stable allies. The surging global drug epidemic requires an international drug control response and sooner rather than later.

# 8

# The Social Structure of Street Drug Dealing

## Jerome H. Skolnick
## Theodore Correl
## Elizabeth Navarro
## Roger Rabb

## Introduction

We undertook a small, descriptive two-month crash study—in effect, a research probe—during the summer of 1988 to investigate five issues:

1.  How is drug distribution in California related to the gang phenomenon?
2.  How are dealers socialized into the drug business?
3.  How is street drug dealing organized?

Reprinted by permission from the *American Journal of Police*, Vol. 9, No. 1, pp. 1–42, 1990. Published by Anderson Publishing Co., Cincinnati.

4.   What financial and contractual arrangements are associated with street drug dealing?

5.   What is the market?

The questions were stimulated by increasing interest on the part of the general public and the law enforcement community in the rapid rise of "crack," or rock cocaine, street drug dealing in California and the violence associated with its sale.

## Methods

Given the two-month time constraint, the sample was limited. Nevertheless, more than 80 interviews were conducted, 39 with inmates and wards at four California correctional institutions—two in southern California and two in northern California. One was an adult prison, and the other three were run by the California Youth Authority. Forty-two interviews were conducted with city and county police, state narcotics officers and correctional officials. Without the cooperation of those from whom we learned so much, the study could not have been completed.

Some further comments about methodology and resources are in order here. Given our time constraints and limited resources, there were many things we were not able to do. For example, we were able to retrieve some quantitative data on drug use by race for those who failed probation drug testing, but we simply did not have the resources to follow up this important data source around the state. Furthermore, we acknowledge that our sample does not represent the universe of those who sell drugs. Our sample is open to at least four criticisms:

An initial criticism could be leveled at the universe of drug dealing our data represents. We describe neither dealers in affluent communities, who may not come to the attention of police, nor higher-ups in the drug business. A richer and better rounded portrait of the social structure of drug distribution might be obtained by interviewing federal agents and prosecutors, plus defense attorneys who operate at both the state and federal level. The study could also be expanded to interview inmates in federal prisons who were convicted of drug- related offenses. Such a study was attempted by Peter Reuter of the Rand Corporation, and was limited in its success at generating information from these dealers.

Second, to what extent does our ward and inmate sample represent the universe of street drug dealers? Those who chose to interview with us were self-selected. They were approached initially not by us, but by institutional gang counselors and prison officials. After they agreed to talk with us, they were told that we wanted information on the above questions, and that information would be kept confidential by us. We showed each informant a letter to that effect, plus a consent form. We told them we weren't interested in having them "snitch" on anyone, but were only interested in general patterns in relation to the above questions. We told them that their names would be kept confidential and that they were, in effect, reporters about the drug scene in their gang or neighborhood, and how it worked. We also told them they could stop talking to us at any time.

Those inmates and wards who agreed to be interviewed may indeed differ both from other wards and inmates, and from others in the street who sell drugs. Their descriptions of the street drug scene and associated processes were, however, quite consistent with each other and were also essentially consistent with the descriptions of law enforcement officials. One could argue that consistency between the picture painted by police and inmates may not count for much, since the information of law enforcement officials is derived from a similar population—persons in trouble with the law.

Moreover, we acknowledge that our interview numbers are light, and could be enhanced with more inmate interviews. Although that would not solve the self-selection problem, the more interviews, and the more consistency among them, the more confidence we would have in our data. We did not try to conduct interviews with probationers and parolees since, we were advised, many of them are currently involved in the drug trade, and would have been even more apprehensive than inmates. Given this consideration, plus time limitations, we decided to forego probationer and parolee interviews.

Teachers and community youth workers are another useful data source that we did not have the time or resources to use. This population might offer a somewhat different picture of the centrality of gang identity to inner city youth. Our sample of incarcerated youth may be more "hard core" than others in the neighborhood, even others who sell drugs.

A third criticism could be directed at the richness and depth of our interviews. Most interviews lasted around one hour, and there were no reinterviews. We could have made, and hopefully in the future will make, more use of the case study as a research tool. This could be done especially with key informants, who might be persuaded to tell us more about their lives and their entry into the drug business.

Fourth, although this sort of study does not lend itself to much quantification, certain statistics which we did not gather are available, and should be collected systematically. For example, we should be able to obtain data, through time, on probation and parole revocation for drugs by type of drug and ethnicity as one indicator of the persistence of "the drug problem." We do not know much about drug substitutability, that is, the extent to which individuals are committed to particular drugs, and to what extent this commitment varies through time. This is a very significant issue for law enforcement strategy. Unfortunately, local law enforcement is usually afforded only the time and resources to make tactical decisions about problems that happened yesterday and might happen tomorrow.

Given the acknowledged limitations of our database, our report proceeds to address the questions above, with the clear understanding that further research is needed in this area. This report should be considered exploratory in two respects: (1) we need more data along the lines indicated above; (2) drug markets, marketing practices and gang formations are dynamic phenomena, and may change rather quickly. A 1988 study's findings may not be applicable in 1990 or, for that matter, even in 1989.

## How Is Drug Distribution Structurally Related to the Gang Phenomenon?

To ask the question presupposes some preexisting relation between gangs and drugs, or that in some way, gangs are synonymous with drugs. Our data suggest this is not true, nor should it be assumed that just because gang members participate in the sale or use of controlled substances, they have some preestablished arrangement to distribute drugs. Our research indicates that the relationship between the traditional or neighborhood-based gang—which we call the cultural gang—and drugs is not so causal. That is, traditional neighborhood gangs, especially Chicano gangs in Los Angeles, do not organize for the specific purpose of distributing drugs.

On the contrary, the cultural gang is strongly grounded in a neighborhood identity which may extend through generations. This is not to suggest that the cultural gang is uninvolved with crime or drugs or that it may not sometimes be opportunistic. Still, the idea of territory is deeply rooted in the cultural gang. Loyalty to the neighborhood is virtually indistinguishable from loyalty to the gang. We designate these gangs as "cultural" to distinguish them from opportunistic groups of young men who also may call themselves "gangs" or "mobs" and are organized primarily for the purpose of distributing drugs.

These sorts of gangs dominate the drug trade in northern California where gangs do not entertain such a developed ideology of neighborhood loyalty. Such gangs are usually regarded by their members as "organizations" and are considered a strict "business" operation. They are organized primarily to engage in criminal activities. We call these "entrepreneurial" gangs in the sense that the fealty of membership depends on the opportunities offered by leaders, usually those who can claim a reliable connection to a source of drugs. Northern California gangs are thus less neighborhood-centered and more business-focused, although recruitment usually occurs within an identifiable neighborhood or housing project. Like any other capitalist enterprise, the "organization" is motivated by profits and the control of a particular market or markets. But unlike many capitalist enterprises, not all drug organizations strive for growth or expansion. They often perceive themselves as local businesses. Some may merely seek to control drug sales and distribution within delimited territorial boundaries, such as a part of the city or a housing project.

Our data suggest that mob-associated violence in northern California also tends to be entrepreneurial; that is, for the purpose of controlling a drug-selling territory, or for enforcing norms of loyalty to the organization. By contrast, Los Angeles drug dealers engage in violence—called "gang banging" as a symbolic aspect of gang loyalty and social identity. But the situation of the Los Angeles gangs, as we shall explain, seems to be changing, indeed dynamically so, as the values associated with drug marketing come to dominate members.

## Socialization into the Drug Business

Although we did not find a causal relationship between gangs and drug distribution, our research did indicate that most, if not all, cultural gang members had their first contact with drugs, either as sellers or users, as members in the gang or the set. For the most part, gang or set members started off as users, using drugs with other gang members, first smoking marijuana and then moving on to more potent or sophisticated drugs, such as PCP, cocaine or heroin. One gang member recalled:

> I started smoking pot with my homeboys, kickin'. It was part of being in the gang with the homies, everyone did it.

The cultural gang social milieu facilitates the use of drugs and, in many instances, the sale of drugs. Drug use is common in the neighborhoods where entrepreneurial gang members grow up, but it is not so clearly involved with gang identity. We found no cultural gang member who did not use or sell drugs while a member of that gang. In both sorts of gangs, older members assist younger ones to sell drugs. This is considered to be a friendly gesture, a measure of economic opportunity. An older "homeboy"—both north and south—may help out a younger one with little income by consigning or "fronting" some drugs to him. Since most of the gang members come from economically depressed communities and backgrounds, the drug-selling business is very appealing, especially in Los Angeles where the protection of the gang is also assumed. There are more youngsters, we were told, who want to sell drugs, than can be accommodated.

The introduction of younger boys to the drug business often serves to establish membership criteria and respect in the cultural gang. An individual may prove that he is worthy of respect and trust if he can show that he can sell for one of the "homeboys" and be trusted with the merchandise. This establishes respect, especially when the individual can sell his product and return with the money. Drug sales and distribution within gangs have their roots in such apprenticeship processes.

Once the individual is accepted into the cultural gang, participation in the drug business can facilitate upward mobility within the gang structure. To advance one's position in a gang, it is important to show that one is willing to take risks, is fearless, is willing to hurt and be hurt, and can be trusted. Drug-related activities—especially inter-gang violence for black gang members—present some of the most risky, and therefore the most highly valued, of gang activities. Through this avenue, cultural gang membership escalates involvement in the use and sale of drugs, and the commission of crimes which facilitate these activities. At the same time, the gang structure is supported when one "homeboy" initiates a younger one to sell drugs. In sum, the cultural gang is not organized for the express purpose of selling drugs, but gang organization facilitates that activity.

It should also be noted that gang members find it hard to quit a gang. The only way to pull away, short of moving out of town (which might not even work), is to "fade out," to slowly disassociate oneself from the gang's activities. Yet our interviews show that, particularly for the cultural gang, if a member fails to fulfill gang obligations, the gang will take retribution. Furthermore, and this is the case for both cultural and instrumental gangs, even if a member were able to "fade out," rival gang members, as well as police correctional officials, will likely continue to identify the former gang member as an active member. Thus, gang members tend to believe that membership is permanent. In the words of one member who had tried to quit his gang: "If I'm going to be identified as a gang member anyway, I might as well really be one." And in the words of another:

> It's the age where if you was ever in a gang, it's not like you could just stop. There's probably something you did to somebody or one of their buddies a long, long time ago, when you was in the gang—this is probably five or ten years later, you probably successful in life—and he remembers your face . . . somebody always consider you in.

In the following section, we further elaborate the distinction between the Los Angeles cultural and the northern California instrumental gang. As the discussion should make clear, the "cultural-instrumental" pattern variable represents contrasting endpoints. Each end of the continuum represents an ideal type or construct, but any given gang may contain features of the other. And we shall also conclude that black cultural gangs in Los Angeles are increasingly being dominated by instrumental drug-dealing values.

## How Is Street Drug Dealing Organized?

Gangs that are organized solely for the purpose of distributing drugs often refer to themselves as "organizations," because they have a direct relationship to the distribution and sales of drugs. Members enter the organization for instrumental reasons—because of their interest in earning money via drug sales. Since these organizations may be territorially based, that feature alone does not distinguish them from what we are calling the cultural gang.

The distinction between the cultural gang and the entrepreneurial gang is highlighted by the different priorities of neighborhood and criminal activity, such as dealing drugs. Although entrepreneurial gangs may be organized around a territory or even a neighborhood, their neighborhood connection is far less salient than their financial goals. A northern California dealer reports that he always had an opportunity to get into a gang to sell drugs. That was the purpose of the gang, to be a business:

> They (the higher ups) liked me because they seen I know how to make money. And they trusted me. They knew my brothers. But trust came from when I got to the point where I was an asset. You know what I am saying? They knew I could make the money.

Cultural gangs, by contrast, are not initially organized for financial reasons. Criminal activities, such as stealing hubcaps or cars, and committing burglaries, have traditionally been a contingent feature of the southern California cultural gang. As Joan Moore (1978:39) points out, "In the poverty environment, small scale extortion was (and is) fairly common among teenagers to obtain public consumption ends." Klein's (1971) earlier study of an east Los Angeles gang shows similar patterns of delinquency—theft, truancy, status offenses such as incorrigibility—as a minor part of gang life. Moreover, gangs have always formed some important part of the illegal economy, with the sale of drugs, particularly marijuana, heroin, and PCP, as part of an "innovative" response to economic deprivation and restricted economic opportunity in the larger society.

Nevertheless, in contrast to the entrepreneurial gang, the cultural gang exists prior to and independently of the illegal activities in which it is engaged.

At least on an ideological level, gang and neighborhood values dominate over pecuniary ones. Thus, a young man who describes himself as a "rollin' 60s Crip" denies that his organization is primarily a drug-dealing gang, that drug dealing is incidental to the requirements of gang membership:

> Nah, it's for fun. It's part of being bad and being part of the neighborhood. Like if someone come shooting up our neighborhood, we go back and shoot up theirs. If we kill somebody, we kill somebody. But you don't have to sell drugs. People sell drugs for the money, not because they have to to belong to the gang. The only thing you have to do is protect the 'hood.

So the concept of loyalty to neighborhood prevails in the cultural gang, at least on an ideological level. Members of cultural gangs refer to themselves as an extended family, as a community. Notions of brotherhood, sisterhood, loyalty and respect, especially for those who are more experienced or older, were cited as important values by our respondents. These values are frequently described as "sacred" and form the backbone of the gangs' organizational structure. Thus, the gang or the set is considered as a familial resource, with strongly held values of attachment and loyalty. The cultural gang is a place where individuals can turn to "homeboys" for financial support, physical protection, and other assistance when necessary.

Significant ethnic differences are also apparent among Los Angeles neighborhood gangs. Family and community ties are most apparent among Chicano gangs, which sometimes are traceable back through several generations. The individual gang member is expected to assist other gang members in times of need and to uphold the neighborhood gang name. Relationships among the members evolve around familial notions of togetherness, respect and loyalty. These Chicano gangs have a history that predates involvement with contemporary drug trafficking. For these gangs, drug selling is usually an incidental feature of gang life. Traditional gang values of machismo and being a "warrior for the barrio" still appear to dominate.

Black gangs are different, although organization is also based on family notions of respect, loyalty, and brotherhood. One difference is in tenure of origin. It is almost as if black gangs in the southern California area were loosely modeled upon Chicano gangs, but do not have their stability and rootedness in history. Another is in neighborhood solidarity. Although black gangs identify with neighborhoods, they do not seem to command the solidarity and traditional values of local Chicano neighborhood gangs. Police are especially skeptical of the cultural basis of black gangs in Los Angeles, particularly as these are increasingly involved in the crack cocaine trade. Police we interviewed on the whole maintain that Chicano gang members practice their ideology of loyalty, while black gang members are in actuality less tied to expressed gang and neighborhood norms than to financial incentives and other forms of self-interest. These are said to include "dealing" with police and informing on others.

Indeed, some of our interviews suggest that neighborhood gangs are being organized primarily for instrumental reasons. Individuals are being attracted to gangs, not for what they represent to others in the neighborhood, nor for that matter what they represent to other gangs, but rather for what they represent in opportunities for drug dealing. Thus, one respondent comments:

> Some people say they get walked on the set or jumped on the set . . . Now it's different . . . there's dudes that I see here that be telling me they're from my neighborhood, and I'm sayin', I don't know you. When did you get in our neighborhood? But it's different because you got drugs—cocaine.

> People joining, I figure myself, they join the gangs, because in the gangs, I guess if you got a gang behind you, you stronger. It's easier to distribute cocaine if you got a lot of people to sell to or to sell for you. It's safer because there's one person that come in our neighborhood that want to sell cocaine, if nobody know him, then whatever he got . . . it's going to be ours . . .

Still, black gangs also identify with an overall gang structure associated with the larger neighborhood. The largest gang structure is the Crips, and its rivals are the Bloods. The concept of rivalry seems significant for these cultural gangs, with violence as a symbol of personal and neighborhood respect and identity, especially in the neighborhood "set." A Crip will fight a Blood for reasons seemingly similar to those which might motivate a Serbian to fight a Croatian because of a perceived traditional rivalry. Youngsters grow up and distinguish themselves in "gang banging," that is, in fighting with other gangs over matters that are seen as central to identity.

By contrast, the predominantly instrumental gangs in Oakland and San Francisco do not, on the whole, recognize or give deference to such traditional rivalries. This does not mean that they will refuse to engage in violence. On the contrary, they can be pitilessly savage. However, when such violence occurs, it seems primarily to be instrumental—the gang seeks to maintain or expand its territory, to enrich its economic opportunities or to protect its authority. One northern California informant described having participated in three gang wars. When asked how these wars came about, he said:

> Disrespect. Turf. Selling dope on our turf. One war even came about within my own circle. (He describes how a younger member of his gang tried to cheat him out of ten kilos.) He's a gangster too, but you can never underestimate anybody in a dope gang. You always have got to watch out for the motherfuckers. They're always looking to take your position. They will cross you out to the penitentiary or cross you out to the graveyard.

Whenever possible, northern gangs prefer not to fight for territory. As self-perceived organized criminals, they prefer to develop understanding of territorial boundaries, an almost rational sharing. Of course, rational sharing does not always happen, anymore than it does among traditional Mafia families.

But youthful "gang banging" of the sort engaged in between Crips and Bloods is viewed disdainfully. A northern California drug dealer describing Los Angeles Crips and Bloods says:

> They're sick. They're stupid. They don't got no intelligence. They follow colors and shit. They just out there for the glory of the thing.

When asked if he would engage in violence, he replied:

> Without a doubt. Ain't no question. But you try to stay away from violence, because the violence brings publicity. In a dope gang, violence is the worst thing. The police is not the worst thing for the dope gang. It's the media and the public. Drive-by shootings brings in a public outcry and the media. And that quite naturally means that the police have got to step up their investigations.

He concluded,

> San Francisco, northern California is much different from Los Angeles.

In Los Angeles, dress code or the use of a particular color distinguishes black neighborhood "sets" from Chicano gangs. Black gangs dress according to colors while Chicano gangs have not traditionally associated themselves with any particular color symbol or gang, but that may be changing. One of our respondents reported a degree of association between Chicano and black gangs:

> They be Mexicans that are Crips and they be some that are Bloods. They really just come down for their friends 'hood, like say their friends are Crips and they be in trouble, then the Mexican gang come down too and then others call them a Crip gang, but they really a Chicano gang. That's all it be.

Set members usually identify their local set or gang with a particular street, and wear red or blue "rags" or bandanas to symbolize their association with the Crips or Bloods gang, although other colors are sometimes worn as well.

Almost all the interviewed respondents, members from neighborhood gangs and drug-dealing organizations, agreed that an individual becomes part of a neighborhood gang, set, or organization by "growing up in the neighborhood." The "homeboy" serves an important function in both the entrepreneurial and the cultural gang. Since each gang will freely engage in illegal activities, the "homeboy" offers protection against any sort of infiltration, either by the police or rival gangs. "Homeboy" status is everywhere a symbol of trustworthiness, but neighborhood identity is most significant in the Chicano cultural gang. Moore (1979:35) explains that the territorial basis of gang membership is almost a truism "because young male peer groups all tend to be based in some local network." And she adds:

> But for Chicanos the territoriality is very deep. For gang members the word for gang and for neighborhood is identical. "Mi barrio" refers equally to "my gang" and "my neighborhood." This complete intermingling of peer group and neighborhood identity is a core characteristic of the Chicano gang, and extends even to the gang member who resides in a different barrio.

Black gang members whom we interviewed also claimed and expressed strong neighborhood ties. It is difficult to say whether these are as symbolically meaningful as those of Chicano gang members. Certainly there are recognized neighborhood affiliations which black gang members are willing and expected to risk their lives to defend. One of our black respondents commented on how an individual becomes socialized into becoming a "Blood" in his neighborhood:

> You just grow up in the neighborhood. If you ain't a member you will be one. Everybody part of the 'hood, not everybody be down and all that, but when you growing up, like age ten or something, your brothers be saying "Blood" to you and all this, homeboys saying, "Hey, Blood" because that's what we say when we talk to the homeboys . . . you know . . .

But not everyone growing up in the neighborhood is considered part of the gang or the set. In the gangs of northern California, "homeboys" develop reputations by performing economic services, such as acting as lookouts for police while drug dealing is in progress, or steering customers to drug dealers. Many Los Angeles gangs, by contrast, require each member to satisfy some pre-established membership criteria before he can be considered a "homeboy" or an official member. Membership criteria may include anything from getting beaten on (often referred to as getting "jumped") to selling drugs, even killing a rival gang member. "Getting jumped in" is a common membership practice among Chicano gang members, while "riding" on a rival gang territory or participating in "gang banging" against a rival gang establishes membership in most Los Angeles black gangs.

Generally, individuals acquire membership by proving themselves in some form of physical violence or prowess to other members, especially the older gang members, referred to as OGs (Original Gangsters), or the most respected members. The individual must be respected as a reliable and loyal fighter to qualify as a gang member. Indeed, the combination of toughness, ability as a fighter, and loyalty seem to form the basic membership criteria as well as the normative grounding of the gang. The gangs view themselves, and are seen by other gangs, as urban warriors who must neither admit nor exhibit fear as an emotion. One gang member reports:

> We just expected to stay down for mine, stay on, don't be a punk. See . . . most of the people, ordinary people, see . . . they punks. They can't fight or nothing, you know what I'm talking 'bout? Like in a gang, most people know how to fight 'cause you be fighting with the homeboys and messing around . . . and you do it all the time, it ain't going to stop. You just got to stay down and stay hard.

Another concurs that members must:

> . . . stay down for the gang and not be a sissy, so that when the shit comes down, we's all down and ready to fight back.

The initiating process differs according to the structure and the inherent values of each gang, set, or organization. For example, as a more fundamental requirement, neighborhood gangs require loyalty and respect from their members, and members must prove that they can fight and defend the neighborhood against any outsiders, especially gang rivals. Through a combination of fighting and associated behavior, the gang member pledges allegiance to the familial values of the neighborhood.

Entrepreneurial drug-dealing organizations also require some sort of membership criteria, but the requirement is a willingness, indeed a motivation, to participate in a lucrative and, more importantly, a risky and often dangerous business. The desire to make money and the individual's disposition to take the risks associated with the business fulfill some of the mandate, but respect and loyalty and proof of the two are also involved.

An individual must show that he can be trusted, that he is a worthy business person. One way of establishing trustworthiness is simply by having grown up in or lived in the neighborhood where the organization operates or sells its merchandise. There the individual can make his connection into the drug business. The connection alone presupposes some trust; for the individual would not have made the connection had there not been some trust already established. Membership criteria within the drug-dealing organization serves the purpose of protecting the drug-dealing business, as well as promoting its success and prosperity.

One can also attain the status of a "homeboy" through adoption if one successfully sells drugs for another higher ranking "homeboy." One of our respondents told how the adoption mechanism worked:

> If they sold dope for me, that would be my homeboy and if he's my homeboy then he's everybody's homeboy. As they say workers, or whatever, that's my worker, so . . . he's in with everybody. Something happen to him, it's all our responsibility just as it's his responsibility.

Family ties are important everywhere. Having an uncle, a cousin, or a relative in a gang, set, or organization facilitates membership and serves as *prima facie* evidence of character and reliability. Trust and respect easily follow. We were told that gang members with very strong kinship ties to the gang might not have to fulfill any additional criteria; kinship alone will suffice. Thus, one respondent reported that he did not have to meet any of the required membership criteria, like being "jumped in" or having to fight with other "homeboys," because of his kinship association with the OGs (Original Gangsters). He stated:

> You got to do something to become official, like hurt somebody, like our enemies, or get jumped and getting to fighting with the other homeboys, but not me. My relatives set me up. I didn't need to do nothing.

Family ties and close associations are just as important within entrepreneurial drug-dealing organizations. Since the business is so risky and dangerous, family ties often lessen the strain of maintaining trust. A member will trust his brother over a non-relative. Furthermore, the individual with family ties will find it easier to participate in the business and make more money, not only by having members to trust and rely on for information and other assistance, but by using family ties to advance in the hierarchy of the gang.

Overall, both cultural gangs and entrepreneurial gangs require each member to prove himself in some form or other. The major difference is in what the "gangster" is supposed to prove, depending on the organizational purpose of the gang. The cultural gang stresses the survival and protection of a community and a neighborhood, while the entrepreneurial gang demands proof of ability to protect a lucrative and often dangerous business.

## Violence

This difference in organizing purpose—between sustaining neighborhood identity for the cultural gang and pursuing business profit for the entrepreneurial gang—is also importantly evidenced both in the use of violence by gang members and in the pattern of their drug involvement. Violence is certainly a central aspect of both types of gang activity. But our data indicate that violence is used for differing purposes as between the gang types. Purpose, in turn, affects the frequency of the incidence of violence, the resources gangs are likely to have for engaging in violent activity, and ultimately, the degree to which gang violence is susceptible to control by law enforcement efforts. The violence of cultural gangs has traditionally centered on retribution and the assertion of neighborhood gang identity. Entrepreneurial gangs, by contrast, employ violence to control or expand their drug business and markets. Thus, depending upon the stability of the market, the entrepreneurial gang may be more or less violent than the cultural gang. The cultural gang protects its neighborhood, a stable area. It engages in violent activity for two reasons: to protect the turf identity and the drug market. As the latter sort of violence occurs in the cultural gang, it begins to look more like the entrepreneurial gang.

The frequency of entrepreneurial gang violence depends on territorial stability. If the market is stable there is little violence. But if the market is destabilized, whether by a rival gang or by law enforcement, then violence is likely to erupt, as it did in Oakland after the arrest and conviction of three major drug dealers and their lieutenants. At the same time, there appears to be an inherent instability in entrepreneurial gang markets, provided the gang seeks to expand, or provided another gang seeks to cut into its territory. In Oakland, in May 1988, one gang group invaded the Acorn housing project to kill the leader of the gang controlling that territory.[1] Thus, the entrepreneurial character of the gang may compound both the frequency and severity of violence because violence is ultimately the basis of its effectiveness; the gang only exists and thrives insofar as it can control a market and intimidate its competitors. By contrast, the authority of the leaders of cultural gangs rests on tradition as well as on power.

This could possibly have important implications for law enforcement strategies. Law enforcement efforts might be able to limit and inhibit the violence of cultural gangs by arresting leaders or depleting the number of gang members. But imprisoning entrepreneurial gang leaders may destabilize markets, with new entrepreneurs employing violence to assert control over the lost markets. Yet we must caution that, as cultural gangs begin to develop into entrepreneurial gangs, the distinction may be less significant. One of our respondents reports that traditional cultural gang identities are becoming less salient as cultural gangsters are motivated to become organized drug criminals, that is, as persons for whom rational economic motives come to replace traditional neighborhood ties and associated values:

> When I was coming up . . . either you was a Crip or you was a Blood, and if you was a Crip, Bloods was your enemies. Nothing in between. No friendship or nothing. No understanding. But now you might see a neighborhood that is Blood and Crip together. But that's because they got something going on with drugs. They got some kind of peace because of drugs.

## What Marketing Arrangements Are Associated with Street Drug Dealing?

In many commercial transactions which tend to deal with large sums of cash, the degree to which an individual is trusted—perceived as a good risk—will determine whether credit will be extended. Our research indicates that this holds true for those transactions involved in the street dealing of cocaine as well. At various points during the trafficking enterprise, it is not uncommon for cocaine—in whatever form—to change hands without payment being made at that time. As should be expected, however, the prevalence of this varies according to the relationship between the individuals involved.

In the early stages of cocaine procurement, in those transactions which generally involve two wholesalers and large quantities of the drug—usually a kilogram or more—we find some evidence that drugs may be offered on consignment. For example, we found at least two reported instances where dealers were able to obtain large quantities without paying for them simultaneously. The first involved a San Francisco dealer whose family appears to have had strong connections with organized crime and the drug supply business. The second involved a Los Angeles area supply system which would allow dealers to pick up four tires full of cocaine at a dock, drive them back to their neighborhood, deliver three, and keep the fourth as payment for making the delivery. In the first example, long-established family ties made consignment a low risk; in the second, the deliverer simply performed a service for which payment was made in cocaine.

However, interviews with Los Angeles area street dealers suggest that by the time the drugs reach the neighborhood where they are ready to be put on the streets for sale, credit transactions are common. Neighborhood dealers often have in their employ several people from the same neighborhood who work on the streets as retailers. These street dealers are often given on consignment a certain quantity of drugs by the dealer they work for and are told to bring back a certain amount of cash, usually amounting to three-fourths of the total value of the drugs. Our respondents indicated that these amounts might be as low as $100 worth of crack, with $75 being returned to the supplier and $25 being kept by the seller. This seems to be the low end, however. Normally, drugs offered on consignment might have street values varying between $700–$800 and $3,000–$4,000. Three-quarters of the street value must be returned to the seller. The remainder of the drug is usually sold by the street dealer and the profits either spent, saved, or reinvested in the drug business, although occasionally it is simply consumed by the seller.

Our interviews indicate, however, that almost without exception, known cocaine users are not trusted enough by dealers to be given this type of responsibility. Indeed, several of the dealers we interviewed spoke derisively of users. One respondent said:

> People who buy the drugs . . . we call them "cluckheads," "caneheads," "crack-heads," things like that. You can't sell drugs and use dope at the same time, 'cause you won't get nowhere. You're not going to make no money. So, basically, I try to keep myself away from people who sell and use drugs, 'cause otherwise you come up short for money.

The trust needed to make street-level consignment purchases generally evolves in one of two ways: either the street seller is kin or a close personal friend of the supplier, or the street seller has shown through past business transactions with the supplier that he or she is dependable and can be trusted with more responsibility.

Similar trust is rarely extended to street consumers by sellers. Buying on the street usually requires cash to be paid at the time of purchase. This is sometimes attributable to a lack of personal knowledge of the buyer, which precludes the building of the necessary trust, and sometimes to the simple fact that the buyer is a cocaine user and as such is perceived to be unreliable.

Some exceptions to this general picture can be found. At least one seller indicated that he would sometimes extend credit to a buyer he knew would be receiving either an unemployment check or a welfare check within a few days. More common than this type of credit allowance, however, is the situation where a buyer will try to exchange other goods for drugs. Several sellers related stories of buyers offering sellers guns in exchange for drugs. And one seller described a veritable black market where food stamps are commonly exchanged for drugs at a rate of half their face value. Another dealer reports that he was approached by a woman interested in exchanging a child's bicycle for drugs, although the offer in that instance was refused.

## Individuals or Gangs?

It is possible to be—indeed, we spoke with some dealers who were—"self-employed." In these instances, connections necessary to maintain a supply of drugs came from family involvement or from personal friendships made within the setting of organized gangs. These connections usually emerged from friendships which developed over time and often lasted past the period of active gang participation or engagement in drug trafficking. Individual sellers may be socialized in gangs, but may also prefer to sell on their own. One respondent described the process by which this happens:

> If a person wants to sell drugs on his own, he sells drugs on his own. You see people growing up together selling drugs together, but then one say, "Fuck it, I want to sell on my own." He figures he can come up with more on his own.

The individual seller does not actually need a gang to sell drugs. He can still protect himself from competition or contractual breach, although probably not as effectively as those who belong to an organized gang. Weapons are as available to an individual as they are to a group. However, areas controlled by established drug organizations would appear to be effectively off-limits to any but the most inconsequential competition. This appears to be true in the streets of Los Angeles, where gangs may sometimes dominate, albeit not entirely control, the illegal drug market. Where that occurs, organized street gangs may serve as protective organizations when called upon to do so by the member engaged in drug selling.

Thus, the organized gang offers several advantages to the drug dealer who is a member: First, the gang member can rely on his "homeboys" for protection if anything were to happen to him inside or outside gang turf. Second, gang members enjoy easy control and access to territorial markets. They can sell drugs in their own neighborhood without intruding upon the turf of others. In return, they can exclude others from selling on their turf—and this territorial monopoly is backed by force since the gang automatically protects against outside intruders. Third, trust inheres in the "homeboy" relationship, so gang members are expected not to betray other members to the police or rival gangs. Fourth, gangs offer a rich source of shared marketing information. Information about who sells what for what price and who has which drugs available is more easily communicated along gang lines.

Individual drug dealers—and there are some—do not enjoy the same advantages. They must establish their own turf and be careful not to intrude upon gang turf. In addition, they must establish their own clientele. But they do also enjoy the advantage of not having to fulfill gang obligations, which in Los Angeles may result in serious injury or in death.

Law enforcement officials believe that street gangs dominate the rock cocaine traffic in Los Angeles (Baker, 1988). This perception was recently challenged in a study by Malcolm W. Klein and Cheryl L. Maxson (1988). Based on an analysis of 741 cocaine sale arrests made in five sections of Los Angeles where gangs are thought to dominate, the study found that in 75 percent of the cases no gang member was arrested as a suspect.

Is it possible to reconcile the Klein and Maxson findings with law enforcement perceptions? We think it is: the report studied the years 1983 to 1985, the first years in which sizable amounts of "rock" cocaine began to be sold in Los Angeles streets. If the study was done today, researchers might find more gang involvement as rock cocaine has become more popular. Yet Klein and Maxson seem to reject that interpretation because, despite a huge 375 percent increase in cocaine sales arrests between 1983 (233) and 1985 (1,114), the proportion of cocaine sales arrest data with at least one arrestee identified as a gang member increased by only 213 percent. Indeed, they argue that, to the contrary, gang involvement might well diminish over time.

Based on our interviews, however, plus a careful reading of the Klein and Maxson study, we conclude that police perceptions of gang involvement are probably more accurate than those of Klein and Maxson because their underlying assumptions systematically tend to understate gang involvement.

The Klein and Maxson statistics were generated from Los Angeles police gang files. When a young man is arrested for selling cocaine in Los Angeles he may or may not be identified as a gang member by an arresting officer. If so identified, his name is entered into a gang member data base. It is not known what percentage of the Los Angeles gang members who do sell crack will find their way into this data base. Los Angeles Police Department officers familiar with the files, whom we interviewed, estimated that no more than 50-60 percent of Los Angeles gang members have been identified in police files. Generally, we were told, gang members are reluctant to identify themselves. This factor might in itself explain an undercounting of gang involvement in cocaine sales.

If police files contain less than 60 percent of Los Angeles gang members, two other inferences might be drawn. One is that the remaining 40–50 percent of unlisted gang members do not sell drugs. That is possible but unlikely. Alternatively, they might not have been caught. Although we do not actually know whether gang membership increases or reduces a drug seller's chances of being arrested, gang members who are not arrested and identified cannot be processed into the files.

More importantly, the Klein and Maxson study seems to assume that both drug sellers who do belong to gangs and those who do not, have similar chances of being caught. As we point out above, gang members tell us they enjoy numerous advantages over individualized sellers in the crack cocaine trade ranging from control of markets to reliance on gang members to protect against intruders, including the police, using kids as lookouts. Experienced drug dealers are more effective at identifying undercover police. Thus, a significant advantage of gang membership might well be the capacity to evade arrest while selling drugs, even as police are actively trying to arrest gang members. By contrast, individual drug dealers are less organized and less stable entrepreneurs.

Klein and Maxson assume a constant ratio of drug sales to drug arrests, irrespective of gang membership. But if gang members are, on the average, more efficient drug sellers, and engage in significantly more sales than non-gang members, they would be arrested less frequently than non-gang members per unit of sale. Suppose that, for every hundred sales, gang members are arrested once, while non-gang sellers are arrested twice or even three times as often. This factor alone—an inconstant relationship between sales and arrests—could easily account for police perceptions of high gang involvement, while Klein and Maxson would find low gang involvement per unit of arrest for selling cocaine.

Certainly all three factors—change in time, the limits of gang file identification processes and the drug-selling efficiency of gang members—could help explain the difference between the Klein and Maxson findings and law enforcement perceptions of gang domination. The Klein and Maxson statistical study is by no means badly done. On the contrary, it is an able study using a limited data base. Our own qualitative research is likewise limited. On balance, however, we think that law enforcement perceptions of gang involvement in the drug trade are sharper than the Klein and Maxson statistical study suggest. But both studies show how difficult it is to make precise claims about the facts of the drug trade, and why we need a variety of research methods to understand the complexities of illicit drug use and distribution in our society.

## Effects of Imprisonment

Correctional facilities are a fertile ground both for developing drug business contacts during incarceration and for affirming the identity of gang members. A recent article (Sagar, 1988) on gangs in Venice, California concludes:

> Being respected for going to jail is only one aspect of a curious system of beliefs in Venice. It seems as if the social stigma that most of America attaches to things like killing, going to jail and being addicted to drugs is not attached to such things here.

Prisoners say, and correctional officials confirm, that drugs are routinely marketed even in prisons. Our informants differ primarily on the extent to which they acknowledge that guards are involved in drug smuggling. As might be expected, prisoners we interviewed claim that guards are seriously involved, while prison officials maintain that prisoners grossly exaggerate guard participation in the prison drug trade. In any case, both agree that drugs are routinely smuggled into prison by relatives, wives, and girlfriends. These civilian visitors pass the drug through physical contact with prisoners, who in turn conceal the drugs in body cavities.

Correctional institutions also affirm the identity of gang members through well-intentioned and seemingly rational administration of the institutions. Correctional officials seek to identify the putative gang affiliation of every inmate and ward, as a means of avoiding conflict and bloodshed among rival gangs. In one institution in which we interviewed, drug dealers from northern

California had no connection with southern California street gangs. Correctional officials referred to them, and they to themselves, as 415s—the area code for the San Francisco Bay area.

Ironically, by structuring inmate assignments along gang lines, the correctional system inadvertently confirms the gang identity of inmates. Moreover, the identification of one's self as a person who has served time affords the inmate an alternative kind of "homeboy" status—the prison becomes a kind of neighborhood. Today's California correctional institutions, overcrowded as they are with parole violators, have become, in effect, schools for advanced drug dealing connections. Drug dealers who leave prison are rarely, if ever, reformed. On the contrary, imprisonment for drug dealers, both gang and individual, may well serve functions similar to those conventions perform for business people and scholars—as an opportunity for "networking."

## What Is the Market?

Why do people buy and use drugs? An obvious answer might be that people use drugs because they induce pleasurable feelings. There is something to that answer, but it has limited explanatory force. First, large numbers of people do not use drugs, as perhaps most readers of this report do not—even though they are abstractly aware of the psychoactive pleasures that drugs may offer.

Second, drugs do not necessarily offer pleasure, at least initially. First use may be unpleasant, even painful. Thus, many readers of this report who have never used heroin or cocaine may well be familiar with effects of cigarettes and alcohol. Cigarette smokers rarely, if ever, begin a smoking pattern because cigarettes initially offer pleasure. On the contrary, a smoker's first cigarette usually induces coughing, nausea, dizziness, and so forth. Similarly, few first-time users of alcoholic beverages find the taste of whiskey, beer, or wine pleasurable and often describe the initial taste as harsh or bitter.

The moral of the story? *Initiates who smoke or drink must learn to define the experience as positive.* Cigarette smoking or drinking is rarely initially pleasurable, but is defined in peer groups as *socially* desirable, that is, as a sign of masculinity, feminine independence, maturity, and so forth. Initiates have to learn, and are taught by peers or role models, to ignore initially negative sensations and to *appreciate* the experience of smoking or of drinking alcohol.[2]

We use the example of harsh-tasting cigarettes and alcohol—particularly cigarettes—to illustrate the subtle yet extraordinary influence of peer and similar social influences, such as movies and television, on adolescents to engage in what virtually introduces itself as health-destructive behavior. After cigarette smokers smoke for some time, they typically develop a physiological and psychological addiction that can be very hard to escape. But the essential point is that the unpleasant feelings generated by the initial inhalation of smoke, followed by a continuation of smoking, is testimony both to how a reality can be socially constructed and to the powerful influence of peer pressure and wider social pressures, especially for adolescents, but for adults as well. Harvard Medical School Professor Norman Zinberg (1984:83) reports that marijuana initiates are often fearful, but their apprehensions are tempered by friends and associates who guide the initiate to use the drug "correctly—and safely." In sum, drugs and their effects must be understood sociologically as well as pharmacologically.

## Cocaine

The focus of this report is on cocaine, particularly crack cocaine. According to the National Institute of Drug Abuse (Virmani et al., 1988), the number of people in the United States who use cocaine has increased dramatically from 5.4 million in 1974 to 21.6 million in 1982 to approximately 25 million in 1986. Why has the market for this drug increased so dramatically? One part of the answer has to be its affiliation with socially attractive people. Cocaine tends to be associated with use by fast and successful people—film stars, jazz, rock and sports figures. As the movies of the 1940s portrayed heroes and heroines as cigarette smokers and cocktail drinkers, the movies of the 1970s and early 1980s largely showed a positive picture of cocaine use, often with a wink at its potentially addictive side. In any case, the combination of social desirability with euphoria—not sputtering or coughing—suggests why increasing numbers have tried the drug.

What are the drug's effects? These vary, depending upon dosage. But in contrast to the effects of cigarettes and alcohol, effects are rarely unpleasant to the initiate. Two leading authorities describe its consequences as ". . . the pleasant stimulation that makes it a recreational drug" (Grinspoon & Bakalar, 1976:78). High dosages are said by other authorities to produce an "intense euphoria" (Smith & Wesson, n.d.). The combination of euphoric effects plus association with glamor and prestige render cocaine a very attractive drug, despite its illegality. People use it partly for its effects, but begin to use for reasons similar to those inclining individuals to initiate cigarette, alcohol, and marijuana use—their friends introduce them to the drug and praise its properties. One of our respondent drug dealers reports how he was introduced to free base cocaine:

> Like I said, I learned from older dudes that used to hand out in my neighborhood, that used to hand out at the corner. One night they told me there was a this new kind of hot. So I tried the shit.

The new kind of "hot" was called "wet base" in the street. It is a form of cocaine nearly free of adulterants. It was called "wet" because the adulterants were released by heating ether with the powder cocaine. Ether is, however, highly flammable. Actor Richard Pryor suffered severe burns as a result of freebasing with ether.

Sometime in the early 1980s an underground chemist (nobody we interviewed knew precisely who, where or when) figured out how to freebase safely by adding baking soda to the powder and heating the mixture on a stove, or in a gas or microwave oven. The result is a dry form of cocaine called "crack" or "rock." This is nearly pure, heat stable cocaine, suitable for smoking. "Absorbed across the pulmonary vascular bed," write the neurologists Golbe and Merkin (1986:1602), "it produces a more intense euphoria and more precipitous withdrawal than cocaine HCl and is therefore more addictive. It has come into widespread use since 1984." Indeed, it makes sense to consider *crack* cocaine as a kind of designer drug. After all, powder cocaine has been available since the nineteenth century. Crack cocaine is an underground designer's method of purifying the agricultural product, combining low cost with high absorption through smoking. (Nasal ingestion limits cocaine's impact because cocaine constricts small blood vessels and slows absorption.)

Whether cocaine is addictive depends upon how addiction is defined. Smith and Wesson write that "Many clinicians describe cocaine as non-addicting because of the absence of a well-defined withdrawal syndrome. We define addiction as compulsion, loss of control and continued use of a drug in spite of adverse consequences. Using this definition, cocaine is definitely addicting." One of our respondents, who used to freebase, describes the sensations of crack:

> It's not addicting like your body craves it. You're not going to get sick and shit by not smoking. Only thing that craves crack is your mind. It's like an illusion. You hit the pipe, you are whatever you fantasize you want to be. Like you *are* Al Capone. You're into basketball, you *are* Magic Johnson. Say you're into music and you're basing. You feel like you *are* James Brown or Stevie Wonder or Michael Jackson. It makes you feel like what you really want to be.

This same dealer also describes selling crack cocaine as a "money-making machine . . . because they got to have it."

## What is the Market?

Who are "they"? Even a cursory knowledge of cocaine use and sale suggests that there may be several markets and therefore different commercial organizational networks to service. Can it be that the same organizational patterns of wholesaling, distribution, and sale apply in Bel Air and East Los Angeles, in Sausalito and in Oakland? If not, an important distinction may need to be drawn in regard to the social positioning and relationships between dealers and users. The "drug problem" may also need to be desegregated according to violence proneness. Much concern has been expressed by inner-city residents over street drug dealing because of the violence that has come to accompany it. Who buys in the street? Are they the peers of the dealers or are they working-class people who lack the connections to buy in the pricey hills?

Our research in this area is, unfortunately, limited. Although we do have a reasonably clear idea of who sells in the street (i.e., how the distribution, wholesaling and retailing of crack cocaine work in the inner city), we are less aware of how cocaine is sold in the suburbs, upper-class neighborhoods, to business people. We interviewed, north and south, inner-city dealers but we should not assume that this is the only cocaine market, either for powder or crack cocaine. The other dealers, those who deal to the affluent, seem to be able to escape law enforcement, and in any case do not belong to street gangs. Inner-city dwellers are not the only people using cocaine in our society. Our research is confined to the inner city, but it would be wrong and misleading to generalize from our findings to the entire cocaine market (see Adler, 1985; Morales, 1989).

An inner-city crack cocaine marketplace is graphically described by cultural anthropologist Benjamin Bowser (1988) in the Bayview-Hunter's Point area, a low-income, predominantly black section of San Francisco, where Bowser conducted an ethnographic survey and observed crack sales. One can scarcely summarize or improve upon his vivid description, so we reproduce it here:

> In Bayview-Hunter's Point, there is both a high visibility crack trade and a less obvious crack trade. The primary, headline-grabbing crack dealing involves young black men in their late teens to early twenties who sell the drug to people who drive into the community to buy it. These young salesmen, who are the most visible members of the sales network, are assisted by three other groups. First, there are "near-in-lookouts" who double as guards: they look out for undercover police, rip-offs, rival gangs and any other threat. Then there are "runners" who carry new supplies of crack from off-street locations to the curbside dealers. Finally, there are the "far-out guards" who provide long range warnings. The curb-side dealers are the mature elite, alert and physically trim. They are the most visible, take the most obvious risks and handle the money. The ones I talked to or learned about did not use crack. One stated, "I can't touch this s___ and stay out here. It's too dangerous to have your mind all messed."

> The secondary, and less obvious, crack trade goes on in the alleys, hallways and apartments that adjoin the curbside dealership. The young people conducting

this secondary trafficking cater to local customers. They are younger, less disciplined and potentially more dangerous to local residents than the curbside merchants. Many are selling crack to support their own habits. These secondary salesmen take payment in money or in sex. I asked one trafficker why there were no women selling crack. I fully expected he would tell me it was "too dangerous." Instead he answered, "They don't have to . . . they have to 'give it up' as part of their payment." An older man who stood watching sales from a distance told me that he had caught several couples high on crack "doing it" in the hallway of his building. I asked if this was more common now with crack than before. He laughed and said, "Man, where you from? These girls used to have boyfriends of sorts. Now, with this crack thing, they'll do anybody, anytime and anywhere. All they want is that dope and sex, dope and sex."

We found nothing to contradict Bowser in our interviews, including crack cocaine's effect on women. On the contrary, one finding of his and ours is especially important and needs to be repeated both to understand the rationality of drug marketing and the addictive properties of crack cocaine. *Neither the primary sellers he observed (whom we call entrepreneurial gang sellers) nor the ones we interviewed—also primary sellers—regularly used crack cocaine.* Successful dealers consider regular use a business impediment. In one dealer's words:

I never use cocaine; it's not real when they say that a person that sells ends up using his drugs; that's not true, he's like an outcast . . . you get beat up, dogged out; nobody respects you anymore, it turns you scandalous; the shit will make you steal from your mama.

This suggests that however compelling the drug, those who try it and use it are not necessarily "hooked." Consistently in our interviews we found gang member-drug users who had entirely given up any drug use that would impair their ability to function in their business or maximize profits. So drug dealers, who have as much access to the drug as anyone, are able to defer its gratifications in the interests of doing business. For them, the entrepreneurial ethic appears to outweigh the pull of the drug.

Another interesting marketing finding is this: in 1988 crack cocaine selling seems to be associated primarily with black youth. There seems little disagreement about the lack of involvement by Chicano youth in the crack cocaine trade in Los Angeles. To the extent drug trafficking occurs, drugs of choice for both sale and use appear to be PCP (angel dust) and marijuana. PCP is often sold in the form of "Sherms" which are Nat Sherman brown cigarettes dipped in the drug. Brown cigarettes are preferred to escape detection, since the drug stains white cigarettes.

We have not discovered, nor has anyone—police, psychiatrists, sellers, users we interviewed—been able to offer a compelling explanation of why drug sales and use vary with ethnicity. Individuals in all groups apparently use alcohol, cigarettes, and marijuana. When we explore harder drug use, however, all of our subjects across the spectrum report that whites prefer speed and nasal cocaine and some heroin; Mexicans use PCP and heroin, and may be beginning to use crack;[3] while blacks use heroin, crack cocaine, and some PCP. Even in San Quentin, we were told without exception by prison officials, psychiatrists and prisoners that whites used "crank" (amphetamines); blacks, "crack"; and Mexicans, PCP.

Heroin seems, however, no longer to be a drug of choice among younger users in any ethnic group. As heroin users die off, we may well find a sharp decline in heroin use over the next decade. On the other hand, some crack users are turning to heroin to "adjust" the crack high. Crack cocaine appears to have replaced heroin as the drug of choice, especially in the black community.

With the cooperation of the Alameda County Probation Department we were able quantitatively to verify, to a degree, ethnic variation in drug choice. In Oakland, where probationers are predominantly black, 62 percent of those who tested positive for drugs in 1988 tested positive for cocaine. (Probation officers told us that this in fact is "crack" rather than powder cocaine.) Only 5 percent tested positive for amphetamines, 6 percent tested positive for marijuana, while the remainder tested positive for opiates (heroin, methadone). In suburban Livermore, where probationers are predominantly white, only 14 percent tested positive for cocaine, 55 percent for marijuana, 27 percent for amphetamines, and none for opiates.

The contemporary drug distribution pattern suggests something about drug markets that we also know from history; that drug preference, the epidemiology of drug use, seems much less related to the intrinsic properties of the drug than to the social definition of a particular substance as the drug of choice. A genetic explanation should be ruled out for any number of reasons, but one is particularly compelling. We have seen a generational preference shift in the black community from heroin to cocaine. This shift cannot be ascribed to genetic differences between generations. Drug preference must instead be analyzed as a sociological preference, a fad or a fashion—long skirts over short, narrow collars over wide, or the reverse—rather than as physiologically or genetically driven.

## Profitability

Why is crack cocaine so profitable? Consider that coca leaf is an agricultural product. It is, in effect, psychoactive lettuce. A head of romaine lettuce weighs something like a kilogram (2.2 lbs.) and costs us less than a dollar at the supermarket. A kilo of cocaine sells for substantially more.

During the so-called "war on drugs" years the price of cocaine has dropped considerably. A kilo of cocaine reportedly sold for $50–60,000 in Miami in 1982. Narcotics investigators in Los Angeles and Atlanta told us in the summer of 1988 that a kilo of 87 percent pure cocaine cost around $12,000 in Miami or Los Angeles, and 20 to 30 percent more as it made its way north. We have a report that a kilo of cocaine sold in Oakland in October 1988 for $16,000. That still leaves room for considerable profit, but most of the profit is made when the cocaine is distilled into "rocks" and retailed on the street. When broken down into rocks, drugs can retail at 8 to 10 times the wholesale price depending on whether the rocks sell for $5, $10, $20, or $50.

One of the larger dealers we interviewed declines to sell by the kilo. When asked how many rocks he could get out of ten kilos, he replied, "depends on how you sell it. Like with me I sold straight rocks. I don't like to sell weight too much, because you lose money in selling weight. Plus, I had the manpower to sell on the street." We asked this dealer to break down the pricing structure and he reported the following: There are 1,000 grams of cocaine per kilo. Each $20 rock is .20 gram; that is, $100 per gram. Thus, a kilo will *retail* for approximately $100,000. Alameda County authorities report that the rocks they have confiscated range in size from .08 to .33 grams.

Typically, a dealer will consign 20 rocks to a street dealer, to be sold at $20 per rock. The street dealer is expected to return $300 to the middle dealer. If he fails to carry out his end of the bargain, he will be physically punished and more importantly, his supply will be cut off. We were told that this rarely happens, but when it does it is because the dealer "smoked up" the product, which is another reason why dealers try to avoid the product they sell.

## Market Expansion

Dealers also told us that wholesaling is generally considered to be safer than retailing, although less profitable, since law enforcement is most limited at that level. Thus, Los Angeles gangs have taken to becoming wholesale distributors throughout the western part of the United States. Eastern cocaine, we were told by Atlanta narcotics police we interviewed, is smuggled through Florida and other points south, and makes its way up the east coast (see Penn, 1982).

This is not to suggest that wholesaling is without risk and considerable anxiety, not so much from being caught as from being killed or injured by other drug dealers. As one of our higher-level dealers said:

> About selling dope, it's money, you have a good life. But the worst thing about it is buying it. When you sitting up there in a little motel room and everybody got guns, holding guns, and counting money, you sweatin'. No windows open—

nothin' can be open 'cause you got all that dope. And you're talkin' about price. Then I say, "Well, I can only give you 17 for this right here." And he says, F____ that, on the phone you told me different." You don't want to look weak and he don't want to look weak. All that tension. If I could ever find a way where I didn't have to buy nothing, just trust somebody with all that money, I'd never buy again.

Any discussion of the business arrangements of street drug dealing requires mention of the several alarming ways drug dealers—particularly cultural gang dealers—are developing increasingly sophisticated business practices. Many of these practices comprise "tricks" of the trade which are most readily and easily passed between gang members and hence must be seen as yet another advantage such gang dealers enjoy over the independent street drug dealer.

First, since a dealer has a drug-selling organization at his disposal, lower-downs in the organization can be, and routinely are, employed to handle the high-risk work of drug handling. In one dealer's words:

I don't like touching it . . . even with it in your hand you get a dirty (parole drug) test. Coke is potent, it gets through your hand, you have a dirty test. So I can't really touch it. I just leave it in the plastic . . . and let other people deal with it.

Second, the gangs have learned to employ novices in the drug business to distribute drugs around the country:

We'd have somebody else, you know that wasn't on probation or parole, that didn't have no kind of record—if they were stupid enough to take a chance and do it. Anyhow, they got paid for it.

Third, they have learned that law enforcement is well aware of color identification of gangs, and so they report that gang dealers have learned to avoid colors, switch colors, or wear neutral colors when completing drug deals. This is also a way of avoiding gang identification by police.

Fourth, they have also learned that it is better to have an effective lawyer:

On the street, they know for a fact, $2,000 for a lawyer, you outta here if you're caught with less than eight ounces. Anyhow, everybody knows that the better your lawyer, the better you do in the courts.

Fifth, in general, dealers are aware of, legal risks and associated penalties. Thus, they generally dislike dealing from houses, because "there's too much drugs in there if you get caught." At the same time, there is less fear of being caught on the street:

The police just give theyselves away. You just know them when they come, you know, undercover. It's just instinct from being a street person. They catch somebody, they catch little naive people with three or four rocks, and they be out of jail right away.

A Los Angeles police lieutenant confirmed how difficult it is for undercover police to buy drugs on the streets. He describes police in a disguised surveillance van observing the undercover police. The sellers will not sell to the undercover police but they will sell "all around us in the van" to "legitimate" buyers.

## Supply and Interdiction

How do dealers obtain their drugs and why has the price of cocaine dropped so sharply? Dealers would offer only the murkiest answers to the first question. Generally, they would say things like, "You have to be plugged," that is, to have connections to higher ups. They seemed candid about how their own operations worked, but wary about describing those from whom they purchased "weight." In any case, drugs seem plentiful, as evidenced by the fact that the wholesale price of a kilo of 87 percent pure cocaine has dropped precipitously. It is virtually impossible to identify another product—oil, real estate, wheat—whose price has declined by two-thirds to three-quarters in five or six years. This is true even in the face of a government policy designed to disrupt supply through interdiction.

The drop in price can be accounted for by any number of reasons including increased efficiency of smugglers, rise in demand bringing a larger number of competing producers into the market, or police corruption. Whatever the contribution of any of these factors, the possibility of substantially reducing supply through interdiction seems extremely remote—a point which the RAND Corporation makes clear in its study of the economics of interdiction. One reason has to do with the relation between smuggling costs and pricing structure. Actual transportation costs for shipping five kilograms of cocaine is a few dollars. Interdiction practices tax these transportation costs and transform them into smuggling costs. But smuggling costs amount to roughly 10 percent of wholesale and 1 percent of retail prices in the United States. RAND economist Peter Reuter (1988:6) writes, "Fully 99 percent of the price of the drug when sold on the streets in the United States is accounted for by payments to people who distribute it." Thus, if a kilo costs $15,000 wholesale, the cost of smuggling is around $1,500. Military interdiction might, at considerable cost to the taxpayer, double smuggling costs. But that would raise the wholesale price only by an additional ten percent, and the retail price by one percent (Reuter et al., 1988).

Regarding the limits of interdicting cocaine traffic to California, RAND economists (Reuter et al., 1988) make an even more compelling observation in connection with their discussion of the importation of Mexican heroin. They say:

> Interdiction of Mexican heroin appears to be very weak because the U.S.-Mexican border can be crossed at many points (there is little channeling at point of exit or entry), and a high value crossing can be accomplished very suddenly by a single individual in a large crowd of similar individuals (i.e., a low-profile target). Consequently, Mexican heroin can be smuggled at a low unit cost.

Since cocaine is presently being illegally imported into California from Central America through Mexico, a similar observation can be made for the difficulty of interdicting cocaine. A state narcotics agent (of Mexican background) whom we interviewed made the point simply and directly when he said, regarding the possibility of interdicting the cocaine supply into California:

> Four hundred thousand of my people cross the border illegally every year. How can you stop a much smaller number who carry a kilo or two of cocaine on their back?

## Is Demand Stable?

But suppose we could successfully interdict cocaine or even destroy Central American cocaine fields? Would we assuredly solve our drug problem or perhaps make it worse? The answer depends on our assumptions about the creative potential of underground chemists and the stability of drug choice for any population or cross section of potential users.

We already know much about the creative potential of underground chemists simply from the fact that crack cocaine was unknown in the 1970s. This suggests that there is always a potential for the development and marketing of new or variant drugs. This might be especially so if the supply of currently used drugs were to be eliminated.

We also know that lurking in the background are what the *Journal of the American Medical Association* (1986:3061) has described as "A Growing Industry and Menace: Makeshift Laboratory's Designer Drugs." The *Journal of the American Medical Association* describes much more potent synthetic drugs that might eventually replace cocaine and other agricultural products. These include fentanyl, for example, which is around 100 times as powerful as morphine and 20 times stronger than heroin. Fentanyl's medicinal analogs, sufentanyl and lofentanyl, are 2,000 and 6,000 times stronger than morphine. These drugs can produce bizarre, destructive, and unpredictable toxic effects.

Fentanyl, called "China White" in the street, may be more widely used than we now know, because it cannot be detected by law enforcement drug tests.

Moreover, underground chemists can synthesize powerful narcotics relatively inexpensively and with readily available materials. PCP (Angel Dust) is a synthetic drug which, we were told by Compton gang and vice officers, may be becoming more popular among black youth, accompanied by less interest in crack cocaine. These officers speculated that gang drug marketing beyond the Los Angeles area may in part be attributable to a declining market in Los Angeles. Since drug gangs are not incorporated or publicly traded, their actual economic decisions will always be subject to rumor and speculation. Still, based on what we already know about drug markets, shifting drug preferences, and the creativity of underground chemists, it seems a mistake to base drug enforcement strategies and policies on the assumption that drug markets and preferences are stable.

## Summary and Conclusion

### The Relation Between Gangs and Drugs

We distinguish between the entrepreneurial and the cultural gang. Cultural gangs are not organized for the purpose of selling drugs as a business of the gang. These gangs are typically found in the Mexican-American community, and stress loyalty to neighborhood and to other gang members. For these gangs, loyalty norms may even interfere with organized drug selling, since those who possess drugs might be expected to share with other gang members. By contrast, the entrepreneurial gang is organized primarily for the purpose of selling drugs. Such gangs predominate in northern California and perceive themselves as organized criminals. Although neighborhood ties often form the basis for recruitment, the individual's commitment to life-of-crime values is the key requirement for membership.

The cultural gang, it should be recalled, is not initially organized for the purpose of selling drugs. Its association with drugs begins once members, out of their own self-interest, begin to sell drugs. The instrumental gang also employs "homeboys" for the same sort of reasons that the cultural gang does. That is, to socialize "homeboys" into norms of trustworthiness and loyalty. Drugs seem to have become a more significant aspect of black cultural gangs in Los Angeles, than of Chicano gangs, where selling is incidental to gang membership.

Possibly, that is connected to a puzzling yet persistent sociological finding: that drug sale and use are related to class and ethnic background. All of our informants—drug dealers, police, psychiatrists—report that working-class whites prefer crank or speed, blacks prefer crack cocaine and Mexicans prefer PCP or angel dust. This is true of drugs within prison walls as well as on the streets.

Since crack cocaine appears to be the most profitable drug (for reasons we discussed earlier), and since crack cocaine is sold mainly by black street drug dealers, the sale of that drug seems to have blurred the distinction between the cultural and the entrepreneurial gang. Black Los Angeles cultural gangs, which were never as tightly identified with the neighborhood as Chicano gangs, are becoming increasingly entrepreneurial. Black gangs seem to prize individual initiative and ambition as indicia of status. As a result, the black Los Angeles cultural street gangs seem increasingly to look like gangs designed for the sale of drugs. Moreover, unlike northern California instrumental gangs, Los Angeles gangs are expanding their marketing throughout the western United States. Hispanic gangs, by contrast, are both local and cultural. They tend to be characterized by stricter authority, leader control and communal loyalty, while black gangs seem more individualistic, less hierarchical, and more economically oriented. They, rather than individual drug sellers, are coming to dominate the street drug market.

## The Future of Drug Markets

Our findings also point to a significant feature of drug use and sale patterns in California—their potential transience or instability. We cannot confidently predict the future by examining today's problems. David Musto (1987) observes that American attitudes toward drugs from the nineteenth century to the present have always been cyclical, subject to change. It is hard to say whether the same demand patterns we have described will continue, and for the same drugs. In a decade we may be facing a designer drug problem as serious as the crack cocaine problem we face today. Crack cocaine might be replaced in popularity by another "champagne" drug or just another drug. Some of our law enforcement interviewees thought that the crack cocaine phenomenon had peaked in southern California, and that this accounted, at least in part, for gang expansion into other territories.

This research has convinced us how important it is to expand our systematic knowledge of drug sales and use beyond easily visible or surveyable populations, such as high school students. Such surveys are valuable, but limited. We also need to develop methods for studying suburban drug markets and higher-ups in the importation business. We need to chart changes in parole and probation violation patterns. We also need to track the incidence and prevalence of various kinds of drug use and drug marketing as accurately as possible; and how these vary in response to differing law enforcement and other initiatives, including imprisonment and education. For this, we will need to be imaginative in our methodologies, employing both quantitative and qualitative research methods.

At the same time, anti-drug use education, heightened law enforcement and a climate of opinion shift may lower drug demand and reduce the drug problem. Although in this report on gangs and drugs we have focused on black street gangs, we should also point out that illegal drug sales and use are by no means confined to the inner city, although drug marketing is more visible there. The visibility of selling, coupled with attendant violence as gangs fight for control over public area markets, generates fear, apprehension and anger among law-abiding area residents. Black community representatives all over the state have provided the strongest possible grass roots leadership in combatting drug use and dealers. Their concerns may exercise considerable influence within the community itself, and may well help to turn the problem around.

In a larger sense, the drug problem implicates both the national society and the local community. There is no longer any question that drugs constitute a national problem that manifests itself at the local level all over the country. To fight the drug problem, communities will need to have resources, not just for exiling offenders to prison, but for creating a social and economic climate where the drug business is not the major avenue of economic opportunity. Viewed from that perspective, as an illegal yet lucrative business, drug enterprising will not disappear unless significant alternatives are made and are seen to be available. The inner-city drug dealers we talked with can be dangerous, sometimes violent criminals. But they can also be described as rational, calculating, enterprising entrepreneurs. Our challenge as a society is to figure out how to turn that energy and intelligence into socially constructive channels.

## Notes

[1]A witness to the shooting, when asked for its motive, told the investigating officer that "Emanuel Lacy sent underlings there (to the Acorn project) supplied with his rock cocaine with instructions that they sell it to addicts. Mr. Russell (the witness) says that Kenneth Winter's people ran them off the property . . . this did not sell well with Lacy." Sergeant Michael Sitterud, search warrant affidavit, Oakland Municipal Court, May 16, 1988, p. 4.

[2]There is substantial sociological literature on the learning associated with becoming a marijuana user, but not much on the possibly more problematic use of cigarettes and alcohol. For the former see generally the writings of Howard S. Becker, David Matza and Erich Goode, plus the National Commission on Marijuana and Drug Abuse (1974).

[3]Sagar (1988) describes Chicano gang youth who are addicted to crack, but do not sell it.

# References

Adler, P. (1985). *Wheeling and Dealing*. New York: Columbia University.

Baker, B. (1988). "Black Gangs' Role in Drug Trade Overblown, Study Finds." *Los Angeles Times* (September 8).

Bowser, B. (1988). "Crack and AIDS: An Ethnographic Impression." *MIRA Quarterly Newsletter* 2 (Spring).

Golbe, L. I. and M. D. Merkin (1986). "Cerebral Infraction in a User of Free-Base Cocaine ('Crack')." *Neurology* 36, 12 (December).

Grinspoon, L. and J. B. Bakalar (1976). *Cocaine: A Drug and Its Social Evolution*. New York: Basic Books.

*Journal of the American Medical Association* (1986). (December 12).

Klein, M. W. (1971). *Street Gangs and Street Workers*. Englewood Cliffs, NJ: Prentice-Hall.

Klein, M. W. and C. L. Maxson with L. C. Cunningham (1988). "Gang Involvement in Cocaine 'Rock' Trafficking." Center for Research on Crime and Social Control, University of Southern California.

Linberg, N. E. (1984). *Drug, Set, and Setting*. New Haven: Yale University.

Moore, J. with R. Garcia, C. Garcia, L. Cerda, and F. Valencia (1978). *Homeboys: Gangs, Drugs and Prison in the Barrios of Los Angeles*. Philadelphia: Temple University.

Morales, E. (1989). *Cocaine*. Tucson: University of Arizona.

Musto, D. F. (1987). *The American Disease: Origins of Narcotic Control*, expanded edition. New York: Oxford University.

National Commission on Marijuana and Drug Abuse (1974). *Drug Use in America: Problem in Perspective*. Washington, DC: Author, Technical Papers Volumes 1–4.

Penn, S. (1982). "Joint Agency Effort is Curbing Smuggling of Drugs Into Florida." *Wall Street Journal* (August 5).

Reuter, P. (1988). "Can the Borders Be Sealed?" *RAND Note* (August).

Reuter, P., G. Crawford, and J. Cave (1988). *Sealing the Borders: The Effects of Increased Military Participation in Drug Interdiction*. Santa Monica: RAND Corporation.

Sagar, M. (1988). "Death in Venice." *Rolling Stone* 535 (September 22).

Smith, D. E. and D. R. Wesson (n.d.). "Cocaine Abuse." In *Treatment and Management of Cocaine*. Vacaville, CA: Center for Accelerated Learning, STC #628-4431.

Vitznani, Robinowitz, Smialek, and Smyth (1988). *American Heart Journal* 5 (May).

# 9

# Crack Dealing on the Street
## Crew System and the Crack House

## Tom Mieczkowski

Widespread public attention has been focused on the use of crack cocaine and the problems associated with it. Yet many aspects of the crack phenomenon remain unexplored. Some researchers have described the current media images of the crack culture as "caricatures" (Reinarman and Levine 1989). Others examining the scientific literature available on crack and crack distribution have noted the tendency to characterize crack as more dangerous or more threatening than other forms of cocaine, even though the empirical data do not support such a view (Fagan and Chin 1989).

Reports on the organization of crack selling are limited. Johnson and his associates (1990, 1991) have developed a model of crack distribution. Mieczkowski (1989a, 1989b, 1990a, 1990b) has written on crack distribution. Hamid (1990) and Bourgois (1990) have published ethnographic descriptions of crack sellers in New York. Bourgois deals mainly with social psychological

Reprinted by permission of the Academy of Criminal Justice Sciences from *Justice Quarterly*, Vol. 9, No. 1, 1992.

aspects of crack culture among Hispanics and its relation to the ethos of the barrio. Hamid examines the impact of crack on existing dealing systems; he reports on West Indian dealers who made a transition from marijuana dealing to crack dealing, with emphasis on the aspects of crack that are destructive for their dealing systems.

Some good descriptive research on powder cocaine sales has been conducted in recent years. Patricia Adler's (1985) work focuses on middle-class cocaine users and dealers. Terry Williams's (1989) narrative, *The Cocaine Kids*, is descriptive of Hispanic powder cocaine sellers. Carl Taylor (1990) has produced a descriptive study of Detroit drug-dealing gangs with some ethnographic description. It focuses on the Young Boys, Incorporated and their successors, however, without detailing the types of drugs sold or discussing specific organizational mechanisms of crack selling. Detailed economic information and careful empirical data—such as the landmark work by Johnson et al. (1985) on the economics of heroin distribution—have not been assembled for cocaine, either powder or crack. It has been noted, however, that the lack of ethnography on drug distribution groups hampers our ability to understand this phenomenon (Reuter and Haaga 1989; Reuter, Macoun, and Murphy 1990).

The objective of this article is to report on street-level crack buying and selling. In presenting this description, I evaluate a strategic prediction made in 1986 regarding future styles of street drug sales (Mieczkowski 1986). This material is important for two reasons. First, although ethnographic descriptions of the crack culture are important in their own right, ethnography also creates the basis for interpretative analysis of other sorts of information, such as statistical data (Anderson 1978). Second, effective social responses, such as the evaluation of treatment strategies and social services, require accurate qualitative data to provide interpretation of the worldview of those for whom the services are provided.

The data reported here come from two sources. The first is the Detroit Crack Ethnography Project (DCEP), conducted in 1988 and 1989. The DCEP studied 100 active crack dealers in Detroit; the data base consists of in-depth interviews with crack dealers. These interviews, which were tape-recorded and transcribed into manuscripts, consisted of a structured questionnaire as well as open-ended conversation. Both statistical and text DCEP data are presented here.

The second source is data taken from the Detroit Drug Use Forecast (DUF) Crack Supplement. This information was gathered from arrestees processed in the Detroit DUF, an ongoing drug survey conducted by the National Institute of Justice. The Detroit staff administered a supplemental set of questions on crack use and distribution as an addendum to the national questionnaire. During the structured interviews, the interviewers also made notes and observations. The data in this article are based on 212 DUF cases.

## The Drug Bazaar: Open Street Sales

During the late 1970s and early 1980s, the evolution of youthful street entrepreneurs who openly sold drugs (primarily heroin) at retail became an important element in drug distribution mechanisms in inner-city communities (Geberth 1978; Johnson et al. 1985; Mieczkowski 1986). In Detroit this attention centered around an organization called the "Young Boys, Incorporated" (YBI). The appearance and alleged citywide dominance of the heroin trade by these youths (the terms "young boys," "quarterkids," and "runners" were applied to them) appeared to be a new strategic approach to drug selling. The phenomenon of young operatives selling drugs en masse "on the street" was strikingly innovative. Geberth (1976) first reported this sales style in New York. In fact, these operations were so highly developed that certain areas of Detroit (and other cities) were labeled "drug bazaars" or "open drug markets." In these locales, drug sales were carried out overtly, in plain sight, and with apparent indifference to potential police action or other forms of legal interference.[1] Such open action represented a dramatic departure from earlier "closed" selling strategies, which were characterized chiefly by secrecy, stealth, and the need to develop social entree and "connections" or "contacts" to secure drugs.

This new marketing method consisted of "runners" and their "crew boss," who operated a "runner system" for retailing drugs (Mieczkowski 1986). They worked in relatively large teams or units ("crews"), sold openly and often brazenly, and had an identifiable and effective organizational structure. Post-World War II drug trafficking had been based on a covert system that avoided gross public displays (Courtwright, Joseph, and Des Jarlais 1989). These older retail selling operations used a quiet, private strategy to distribute drugs, primarily heroin. Typically a house or apartment was used as a base. Heroin was obtained by house operators and was "broken down" from wholesale into small retail units of sale. From these base locations, operatives conducted their sales. Customers were referred by social networking; prior knowledge or personal introduction was requisite to making drug purchases.

In sharp contrast to the older procedure, the "crew system" of open-air street sales is based on the active "hawking" of drugs by a staff (the "crew") of out-of-pocket retailers servicing a drive-up or walk-up trade in open public spaces. This departure from the fixed-locale system represents a profound strategic marketing innovation based on rational business concerns, and is a critical functional evolutionary step in the drug distribution business.[2]

The runner system exploits specific marketing advantages, with emphasis on high-volume street sales. It offers a potentially greater profit than the older style. The street crew style of sales offers at least three identifiable advantages:

First, the runner system allows the sellers to escape the confinement of a fixed selling locale, and makes police surveillance and control more difficult. A fixed locale is easier for police to observe, to isolate, and to seize; it represents a catchment of persons and contraband. In contrast, a diffused crew of teenagers, each carrying a little contraband, requires duplicate observational and legal processes. Furthermore, a "flight strategy" is a very effective deterrent to police invasions of the operation: in the event of a police raid or intrusion, crew members simply melt into the surrounding neighborhood. The crew system imposes a heavy burden of duplication on the police and diffuses the cache of contraband in such a way as to reduce the risks of large, simple seizures.

Second, when the trade is taken directly into the streets, a larger volume of sales can be achieved. Thus the economic return is more attractive.

A third advantage is the use of minors as street operatives. Minors strongly dominate the composition of the street crews. This arrangement reduces legal difficulties for syndicate executives, who themselves are adults. In addition, syndicate executives believe that minors work more cheaply and are easier to regulate and control than adult operatives. They are also easy to recruit.

Considering these advantages, we would expect widespread adoption of this sales strategy as time passes. The street "crew system" would become the standard for retail drug sales, at least in those urban communities which are comparable to Detroit and New York in size and composition. With the appearance and the relatively dramatic popularization of crack, one then could hypothesize that this technique would proliferate. It is not within the scope of this article to evaluate the national adoption of the technique, because a deep ethnographic data base does not yet exist for crack selling. Even so, we can evaluate Detroit, one of the origination sites of this system, and can speculate on the likelihood of multi-city adoption.

## Street-level Crack Distribution

The findings from the Detroit Crack Ethnography Project do not support the hypothesis that the open-air street crew system is prominent in the crack marketplace. Several generalizations about the Detroit crack trade are supported by the DCEP data:

First, according to reports by crack sellers, open street sales are not a typical or popular method for selling crack. As an organizational format, this method is a distant third to crack houses and "beeper-men" (who deliver crack to their customers or rendezvous with customers at designated locations).

Second, according to reports by consumers, purchasing crack from street corner or curbside crack vendors is not popular with customers. They strongly prefer to purchase from fixed locales or from established vendors who "work off the beeper."

Finally, although the crew system per se has not survived intact as a marketing device, elements of the process have persisted and have been incorporated into the crack trade. The most prominent of these are the dominant role of youthful managers and a management system that bears similarities to a crew system. It is applied, however, in the management of crack house locations and disparate "beeper" networks.

## The Popularity of the Crack House

Table 1, based on DCEP data, shows customers' preferences for particular sales settings. The most frequent method of purchase is the crack house, which 35 of the respondents named as their principal setting. Twenty others relied upon a "touter" or "beeperman," who delivered the contraband to them. This delivery was reported variously as "home service" (i.e., delivery to the customer's residence) or as a delivery by rendezvous in an agreed-on public locale. Table 1 also shows that 41 respondents reported "combination" purchasing—that is, using both crack houses and beepermen. Only four respondents named the street as their exclusive source for crack.

**Table 1. Buying Preferences, DCEP Sample (N=100)**

| | |
|---|---|
| Crack House | 35% (35) |
| Street Sellers | 4% (4) |
| Beepermen | 20% (20) |
| Combinations | 41% (41) |

Overt street sales of crack have not achieved the prominence and popularity that street sales of heroin reached in Detroit at the end of the 1970s (Mieczkowski 1986). In comparing Detroit DUF data to the DCEP data, we find these buying preferences reaffirmed. Table 2 documents a low regard for buying off the street. In a survey of 211 regular users of crack, fully 64 percent typically bought at a crack house. In contrast, only 10 percent reported making regular purchases from street dealers.

---

**Table 2. Buying Preferences, DUF Sample**

| | |
|---|---|
| Crack House | 63.7% (135) |
| Street Sellers | 10.4% (22) |
| Beepermen | 11.8% (25) |
| Combinations | 14.1% (30) |

---

Overall, the data from these studies show that the system for crack sales is quite different from the heroin sales system. Interview transcripts from the DCEP data show that only 26 informants used street purchasing sites in their lifetime; as noted in Table 1, only four individuals purchased consistently from street sellers. Although the percentage of regular street purchasers is somewhat higher in the DUF sample (Table 2), it still rates as the least popular of all methods, alone or in combination.

---

# Explaining the Patterns

---

The reasons for this pattern are revealed in the characterizations of street sales by DCEP informants.[3] They offer two perspectives on the disadvantageous nature of such transactions. The first is the view of the purchasers of crack; the second is that of the sellers.

## Qualms of the Buyer

The two major issues of concern for crack buyers were quality control of the drug and their personal safety during the purchasing process. Informants reported that crack sold as "rocks" on the street was of very poor quality. This contempt for the quality of the merchandise led them to prefer a fixed locale. They believed that a seller in a fixed locale had to provide good quality because the transaction process was less furtive. If the customer smoked the crack at the locale, the quality would be revealed immediately. Also, the seller at the fixed locale was concerned with continuing business, so he had to pay attention to the quality of the merchandise.

In regard to danger, open street transactions were defined as the least physically secure. One was more likely to be "burned" on the street because the vendor, having no fixed locale, could not be held readily accountable for the quality of the merchandise. The furtive nature of the public sale was not conducive to examining and verifying even the most elementary aspects of the sale, such as adequate quantity, the "look" of the contraband, and similar concerns. Street sales, for example, virtually preclude a sample (a "taste") of the goods. Although sampling is not very common in crack houses, at least it is possible in certain types of crack houses (see Mieczkowski 1990b).

Buying crack on the street had another negative aspect: users reported that reliance on street crack was typical of people who had reached extreme stages of dependence. In effect, one was "reduced" to buying from the street as the craving for crack increased because using other sources required some measure of gratification delay and discipline. For optimum quality control, users ought to "rock up" their own cocaine, but it takes time and effort to "rock up caine." Thus, controlled users stigmatized street transactions as being associated with "fiending": acute, high-rate, compulsive crack use. Buying from the street was a sign that the user was growing imprudent and wasteful. In effect, "only a fool or a fiend" would buy from a street vendor.

## Qualms of the Seller

In general, sellers also viewed open street sales negatively. The negative aspects were the ease of exploitation by both customers and employers, the relatively high degree of violence and exposure to potential violence, and the rate of financial return that resulted from the lack of high-volume "sales organization." The following three accounts by street dealers illustrate these points.

### Interview 12: 27-year-old black male

Interviewee 12 began at the lowest level of sales as a street vendor recruited by a young gang of drug distributors (the "Pony Downs"). Eventually he reached a relatively high level in another gang, was injured seriously in a violent event, spent time in federal prison after conviction on felony drug trafficking charges, and then was severely addicted to crack cocaine. Interview 12 is cited here to demonstrate the concern with violence and the importance of a violent reputation in order to exert control; skill in violence is a necessary asset for a crack retailer. Note that the informant was recruited by the "Pony Crew"[4] because he had a strong reputation for the ability to act violently; thereby he could deter or control predation by customers and his employers. Here he talks about his early days as a seller.

> I come against this, uh, this gang called Pony Crew, you know. And, uh, I had came back and they needed me around the neighborhood anyway cause I always liked to fight. I always liked to go in a disco and start a fight or end up with a fight and come out on top.

> (You had a violent reputation?) Yes. So next thing I know I was with em. I raised up with em so we went to gettin together. First they wouldn't show me

no lotta dope, you know, it was like they was bringin me packs . . . (Nobody tried messing with you?) I wadn't worried about that, you know . . . I ain't got to worry bout em jumpin on me you know cause they knew where I was and what state of mind I was then, you know. Wadn't worried about nothin, you know. (If there) was somebody jumped on me they knew where I'd get back with 'em, you know. Either way, they know if they jumped on me they'd had to kill me, so my reputation was alright far as bein in there . . . .

### Interview 13: 27-year-old black male

A seller's concerns did not focus only on potential violence from customers. In the following excerpt a seller recounts an event arising from competition on the street, which centered around a "turf issue." The visibility of street selling exposes one to observation and increases vulnerability; here the source of concern is retailers, who are in competition for customers. The group in competition to which the speaker refers is a group he once worked with.

One night I'm up on Woodward in Highland Park doin my business, you know. They still doin they business, you know. They watch me pick up money and stuff. I was sellin off a beeper then and, uh, they decide w'elp I got enough money for em to rob tonight, you know, which I didn't have but a couple hundred dollars, you know . . . I had took my car when I broke away from 'em. I also cut 'em short on transportation too cause we was rentin cars. But I had a car also and that car, that I had was for our other activities besides doin drugs. And so they felt in a lotta ways I left em hangin but they had asked me for a ride back over to the joint. But before we got there the guy that I was in prison with asked me to drop him off somewhere, right? So I stopped and let him out the car. But his friend is still in the front seat and when he get out the other guy pulled a pistol on me, you know, sayin you know what time it is, right? But all along he had been tellin me and I wasn't goin for it. I looked at him, I said, "Man I want to talk to" (name), "you know this is the guy . . ." I go to get out my car, and he shot me in the back up under my shoulder blade with a .25. It punctured my lung, ricocheted off my rib cage, and it's in front of my spine. It surprises me cause personally I have killed, and I know I'm not tryin to brag or nothin like that, but I am a killer. If I shoot you I'mmo kill you, you know. I figured he just didn't want to kill me cause from what he was tellin me was just don't come back to Highland Park. It was just a warnin to run me out of Highland Park cause my legs was outside of the car, he put me back in the car, took my money, he coulda killed me, he coulda killed me but he didn't. I'm thankful for that.

### Interview 61: 41-year-old black male

Interviewee 61 reports the "ripoff" of a solo street seller by robbers posing as customers. This particular scenario, robbery by violent predators, is one of the events feared most by the street dealer. This man was stabbed severely.

(Ever get stuck up?) Oh yeah, I got stabbed two or three times. Damn near killed me. One Saturday night we was on the corner and it was crowded that night. There was three different kinds of dope on the corner. Competitors. They say "Hey boy, come on man, walk us around here"—they want to get some. So I ain't thinkin and I ain't scared or nothin. I had been drinkin—I ain't drunk or nothin but I'm high. I walked around the alley and they say "Give it up" with a gun. I thought they was bullshittin and that's when he jugged it.[5] I said "Man don't kill me, here take this bullshit, here take the dope, take the dope." He said "I should shoot your mutherfuckin ass" . . . I said "Man fuck that. Y'all can have the dope, man. I got to go to the hospital." So they took all the dope but not the money. They knew me. One's dead, shot in the head. Started fightin up there on the corner. Somebody came back and shot him in the head.

---

## The Reemergence of the Fixed Locale: The Crack House as a Response to the Crew System

The disadvantages of open street sales and the resulting dislike are understandable when we review these accounts. The use of a crack house (combined to some extent with a beeper network) allows more control over the danger and uncertainty that surround the open street system. The differences between heroin and cocaine markets are important in conceptualizing these dangers and in understanding why the different systems emerged. The following marketing innovations are responses based on several key factors.

First, there is a qualitative difference between the heroin and the crack subcultures, both in selling and using. Elements of relative stability characterize the subculture of heroin users but are largely absent from the crack use world. Informants believe this difference is due to the relative novelty of crack. Long-term normative codes are absent in crack retailing because it achieved its widespread popularity so recently.

The older crew system included a relatively strict prohibition against drug intoxication "on the job," and reports indicated virtually no heroin use among street runners. This restriction, although cited by crack sellers, is less universally accepted and enforced. DCEP data show very large proportions of sellers using crack compulsively and destructively.

Second, the domination of crack sales organizations by youthful operatives stands in relatively sharp contrast to the historic control of heroin sales by adults. One can characterize this youth domination as an outcome of the crew system, in which youths were incorporated as low-level operatives and now have come to be dominant in the business. The YBI system in Detroit, for example, consisted of the recruitment of youths by adults to perform relatively low-level functions (Taylor 1990). Now the youths apparently have succeeded in dominating and commandeering the management of crack sales organizations. The DCEP data contain many cases of adults employed by teenage "bosses." Adults also state frequently that these younger boys are "crazy" or "scandalous" and that they enjoy gratuitous violence.

Third, there are differences in the methods of consuming the substances. Rates of crack use are high, both in Detroit and nationwide, among young black males (DUF 1991). Thus there are more crack users than heroin users, and volumes of crack sales are higher. One possible reason for the transition in sales systems is the addictive potential of crack. The method of crack use (smoking), as contrasted to heroin use (primarily injection), removes an important barrier to use. Therefore the relatively rapid proliferation of crack use has created entrepreneurial opportunities not seen in the heroin market.

Finally, the psychotropic and physiological effects of crack are different from those of heroin and translate into different behaviors. The stimulant and mania-inducing properties of crack cocaine, as contrasted with the analgesic and soporific properties of heroin, represent a major distinction which influences the evolution of marketing structures. The consequences are seen quite clearly in the evolution of different types of crack houses, each with its own peculiar ethos and methods of operation (Mieczkowski 1990b).

All of these elements contribute to the crack market's aura of instability and immaturity, and are compounded by a literal laissez-faire entrepreneurialism and a self-stimulating code of violence. Many of these underlying propensities are aggravated by the psychotropic effects of crack.

## Summary

It appears that the distinctive street-sales technique which emerged in Detroit and other cities during the heroin-dominated 1960s and 1970s has not survived intact in the era of crack cocaine. The crack trade appears to be dominated by a "crack house system" rather than by an expansion of the crew style of street selling. It remains to be seen whether the current constellation of sales methods will stabilize the crack trade, or whether further innovations will emerge from the entrepreneurial actions of crack dealers.

At this juncture it is difficult to generalize the Detroit-based findings of this study. Some elements of Ansley Hamid's (1990) work in New York parallel the Detroit experiences, especially the susceptibility of successful dealers to becoming disablingly addicted to crack. Yet several elements of Hamid's work are also distinctive, notably the domination of the trade by West Indians. The earliest descriptions of the YBI-style heroin gangs in New York by Geberth (1978) and Johnson (1985) showed very striking operational similarities to gangs in Detroit. Bourgois's material on New York Hispanic involvement in crack reflects the violent elements of Detroit, and reports the use of fixed locales (*bodegas* or *botanicas*) as retailing sites.

Until we have more ethnographic data on crack sales over a larger number of urban centers, however, the degree of generalizability of the Detroit experience will be a matter of speculation. Yet even with that restriction, Detroit's experiences with crack serve to inform us; they may prove quite useful to others who examine this behavior in different locales and in somewhat different social circumstances.

## Notes

[1] Joseph Albini (1991) wrote an excellent description of this type of sales activity in New York.

[2] The importance of this innovation motivated this researcher to predict the wholesale adoption of a crew-style system for drug retailing nationwide.

> In this regard it is reasonable to contend that the appearance of YBI-style crews is a rational innovation in the Mertonian sense of accomplishing legitimate social goals, the creation of a profit-generating business, by utilizing socially disapproved means. *Viewed in this fashion it is also reasonable to expect that such a system, if it proves to be a continuing success, will spread as a consequence of its competitive advantages in the drug selling subculture.* (Mieczkowski, 1986; emphasis added)

[3] See Mieczkowski (1989b) for a detailed analysis of expression of preferences regarding types of purchasing circumstances.

[4] The "Pony Crew" also was known around the city as the "Pony Downs." The name came from the brand of athletic shoes preferred by those crew members. Dress style was quite specific among crew members, and distinguished various crews from one another. The dress codes also formed the basis on which entrepreneurs could establish an instant, if fictive, identity as "high rollers" by posing as members of a notorious or "scandalous" crew. The second part of the name, "Downs," came from the phrase "to be down," meaning to be sharp, aware, hip, as in "Meet my man Larry. He be down, man."

[5] "Jugged it" means "stabbed or slashed with a knife." In this case the assailants stabbed the speaker in the lower abdomen at the midline and drew the knife upward to his sternum, inflicting a terrible gash. The informant showed me the scar when I initially hinted that I thought he was exaggerating the injury. He was not.

## References

Adler, Patricia A. (1985) *Wheeling and Dealing: An Ethnography of an Upper-Level Drug Dealing and Smuggling Community*. New York: Columbia University Press.

Albini, Joseph (1991) "The Distribution of Drugs: Models of Criminal Organization and Their Integration." In T. Mieczkowski (ed,), *Drugs, Crime, and Social Policy*, pp. 75–109. Boston: Allyn and Bacon.

Anderson, Elijah (1978) *A Place on the Corner*. Chicago: University of Chicago Press.

Bourgois, Philippe (1988) "Fear and Loathing in El Barrio: Ideology and Upward Mobility in the Underground Economy of the Inner City." Paper presented at the fortieth annual meeting of the American Society for Criminology, Chicago.

_____ (1990) "In Search of Horatio Alger: Culture and Ideology in the Crack Economy." *Contemporary Drug Problems* 16(4): 619–50.

Courtwright, David, Herman Joseph, and Don Des Jarlais (1989) *Addicts Who Survived*. Knoxville: University of Tennessee Press.

Drug Use Forecast (DUF) (1991) *DUF Survey Data: 1988–1990*. Washington, DC: National Institute of Justice.

Fagan, Jeffrey and Ko-lin Chin (1989) "Initiation into Crack and Cocaine: A Tale of Two Epidemics." *Contemporary Drug Problems* 16(4): 579–618.

Geberth, Vernon (1976) "The Quarterkids," *Law and Order* 20(9): 42–56.

Hamid, Ansley (1990) "The Political Economy of Crack-Related Violence." *Contemporary Drug Problems* 17(1): 31–78.

Johnson, Bruce D., Paul J. Goldstein, Edward Preble, Thomas Miller, James Schmeidler, Barry Spunt, and Reuben Norman (1985) *Taking Care of Business: The Economics of Crime by Heroin Abusers*. Lexington, MA: Lexington Books.

Johnson, Bruce D., Ansley Hamid, and Harry Sanabria (1991) "Emerging Models of Crack Distribution." In T. Mieczkowski (ed.), *Drugs, Crime and Social Police*, pp. 56–70. Boston: Allyn and Bacon.

Johnson, Bruce D., Terry Williams, Kojo A. Dei, and Harry Sanabria (1990) "Drug Abuse in the Inner City: Impact on the Hard Drug Users and the Community." In J. Q. Wilson and M. Tonry (eds.), *Drugs and Crime*, pp. 9–68. Chicago: University of Chicago Press.

Mieczkowski, Tom (1986) "Geeking Up and Throwing Down: Heroin Street Life in Detroit." *Criminology* 24(4): 645–66.

_____ (1989a) "Studying Life in the Crack Culture." *NIJ Reports* (Fall): 7–10.

_____ (1989b) "The Detroit Crack Ethnography: Summary Report." Submitted to the Bureau of Justice Assistance, Washington, DC.

_____ (1990a). "Crack Distribution in Detroit." *Contemporary Drug Problems* 17(1): 9–30.

_____ (1990b) "The Operational Styles of Crack Houses in Detroit." NIDA Research Monograph 103. Washington, DC: National Institute on Drug Abuse.

Reinarman, Craig and Harry G. Levine (1989) "The Crack Attack: Politics and Media in America's Latest Drug Scare." In Joel Best (ed.), *Images of Issues: Typifying Contemporary Social Problems*, pp. 115–37. Hawthorne, NY: Aldine.

Reuter, Peter and John Haaga (1989) *The Organization of High-Level Drug Markets: An Exploratory Study*. Santa Monica: RAND.

Reuter, Peter, Robert Macoun, and Patrick Murphy (1990) *Money from Crime: A Study of the Economics of Drug Dealing in Washington, D.C.* Santa Monica: RAND.

Taylor, Carl (1990) *Dangerous Society*. Lansing: Michigan State University Press.

Williams, Terry (1989) *The Cocaine Kids*. New York: Addison-Wesley.

# 10

---

# A Successful Female Crack Dealer
## Case Study of a Deviant Career

---

### Eloise Dunlap
### Bruce D. Johnson
### Ali Manwar

Selling drugs has been defined as a major social problem (Inciardi 1986; Bourgois and Dunlap 1993; Inciardi et al. 1993). Most of the half million prison slots created since 1980 are occupied by persons imprisoned for drug sales, drug possession, or crimes committed to obtain drugs. Among illegal drugs, crack cocaine is recognized as presenting particularly severe social problems, and criminal penalties for crack sales, more severe than those for selling other drugs, are similar to penalties for burglary and robbery (Belenko et al. 1991).

Reprinted by permission from *Deviant Behavior,* 1994, Vol. 15, pp. 1–25. Published by Taylor & Francis, Inc., Washington, DC. All rights reserved.

Several studies have documented the role of females in criminal activity in general and in illegal drug use and sales in particular (Chambers et al. 1981; Inciardi 1986; Inciardi and Pottieger 1986; Sanchez and Johnson 1987; Dunlap and Johnson 1992a, 1992b; Bourgois and Dunlap 1993). The female prison population has doubled since 1980, with drug sales among the most common reasons for arrest (Sanchez and Johnson 1987; Bourgois and Dunlap 1993). Of all drug arrests of females, only arrests for the sale of heroin, cocaine, or crack are likely to result in imprisonment, but convictions since 1985 for such sales—especially for crack sales—account for much of the increase in the number of women in prison (Division of Criminal Justice Services 1988; Bureau of Justice Statistics 1992). Nevertheless, very little is known about females' participation in illegal drug sales, and virtually nothing is known about female crack dealers.

This paper presents a case study of Rachel (a pseudonym), a petite, attractive, outgoing African-American woman with a moderate Afro and fashionable appearance who looks much younger than her 40 years. A successful Harlem crack dealer, Rachel is a deviant among deviants, for several reasons. First, she is female in a traditionally male occupation. Second, her educational level, middle-class background, and professionalism are atypical of drug dealers. Third, her drug-related activities are distinctly different from those of both male crack dealers and other female dealers studied (cf. Dunlap and Johnson 1992a, 1992b; Maher and Curtis 1992): her thriving business serves not the stereotypical young, male addict but the older employed, "hidden" user; and even though her activities occur in the depths of the inner city she conducts her business according to practices common among middle-class dealers. Finally, Rachel is herself an addict who uses sizable amounts of crack several times a day, yet she has avoided both arrest and the usual consequences of personal crack use. Neatly balancing the various roles and competing social expectations placed on her, she stands at the intersection of the straight and drug subcultures, between middle-class and inner-city drug dealers, between drug abusers and more casual users.

Careful analysis of deviant cases often provides important insights, both theoretical and practical, about little understood phenomena (Becker 1963). Particularly helpful are informants who, like Rachel, are articulate enough to discuss their deviant behavior and explain the pressures and rewards that mold it. Rachel's case illustrates how the market for illegal drugs has shifted in the United States from marijuana to cocaine to crack; how drugs permeate inner-city communities, reaching older, better educated, middle-class professional people as well as the young, the uneducated, and the poor; how women fit into a sphere of activity heavily dominated by men; and how drug dealers justify their illegal activities and cope with moral opprobrium.

# Methods

Rachel's story is drawn from an ongoing, large-scale ethnographic research project, the "Natural History of Crack Distribution," designed to develop a systematic understanding of careers in drug (especially crack) sales. Under this project, information was collected on the structure, functioning, and economic aspects of cocaine and crack distribution in New York City, primarily in inner-city minority communities where selling crack has become a major career for many (Dunlap and Johnson 1992b). More than 300 crack dealers were observed and their activities noted in field records. More than 160 (approximately 130 males and 40 females) were interviewed and their responses recorded in field notes and on tape. Other papers provide details of the qualitative and quantitative methods used in the project, including respondent recruitment and interviewing procedures (Dunlap et al. 1990; Lewis et al. 1992), the transcription/retrieval of ethnographic texts for analysis by theme (Manwar et al. 1993), and techniques for assuring personal safety (Williams et al. 1992).

During ethnographic field work between 1989 and 1992, the senior author (Dunlap) developed close relationships with many crack dealers and their families. Her introduction to Rachel, whose cooperation was to prove crucial to the research, was arranged by a dealer for whom several others worked. With a college degree in psychology, Rachel quickly grasped the intent of the study and the importance of the issues to be examined. She was outgoing and friendly, and mutual rapport and trust soon emerged. As well as securing the ethnographer's personal safety (Williams et al. 1992), she also assured fellow dealers of the legitimacy of the research, which encouraged them to participate fully. Her story, elicited over a one-year period in ethnographic interviews and direct observation at her apartment (also her place of business), generated more than 700 pages of transcripts from tapes and field notes. The quoted material below is drawn from these transcripts.

Rachel speaks in a nonstandard English vernacular that combines the syntax used in the South (where she spent her childhood) with New York street talk, and incorporates what linguists call "code shifting" between standard English and African-American speech patterns (cf. Painter 1979). The quoted material below preserves her words, syntax, and speech rhythms, since "language symbolizes as well as expresses the distinctiveness of our personal identity and our most important group memberships and identifications: family ethnicity class, peer group, and lifestyle enclave" (Blauner 1989, p. 328; see also Blauner 1987).

---

# Background

---

## Deviance Versus Legitimacy

Deviant careers are fundamentally different from legal ones. Government helps individuals to gain the resources and skills necessary to become legally employed, produce legal goods and services, and pay taxes, routinely providing legal-regulatory structures and financial support for the agencies (schools, families, employers, etc.) that supervise, educate, train, test, and reward these individuals. No such support is available to those in deviant careers, who "drift" into activities for which no formal training is available, learning "on the job" and receiving informal mentoring from other deviants (Matza 1964). In addition, the state and its social control agents (police, judges, treatment officials, etc.) protect persons pursuing legal careers, but those pursuing careers defined as illegal or immoral must consistently avoid the efforts of both social control agents and ordinary citizens to halt their activities.

In the world of illegal drug sales, the opposition of government and the absence of formal training means that individuals must discover by themselves how to deal with the complex contingencies involved in selling drugs (Faupel 1981; Waldorf et al. 1991). They must learn how to obtain supplies of high quality drugs to sell; create retail sales units; recruit buyers; avoid arrest, incarceration, and violence from competitors or customers; and handle and account for large amounts of cash, while evading both formal and informal sanctions. Individual dealers must develop informal rules or norms of conduct by which to conduct business (Zinberg 1984), determining what kinds of suppliers and customers to seek out; where and when to conduct sales; how to avoid the police and competitors; how to moderate personal crack use; how to spend cash income; and how to obtain shelter, food, and clothing. Perhaps their most difficult challenge, however, is to limit their own drug consumption so that they sell enough to "re-up," or purchase more wholesale units of drugs (Hamid 1992; Johnson et al. 1992).

## Inner-City Versus Middle-Class Drug Careers

The limited literature on illicit drug sales suggests that there are two relatively distinct types of drug-selling careers, which for convenience may be labeled the "inner-city" and "middle-class" career types (Faupel 1981; Adler 1985; Johnson et al. 1985; Carpenter et al. 1988; Johnson et al. 1990; Waldorf et al. 1991; Reuter et al. 1990). Drug dealers representing the two types exhibit both similarities and differences.

In both types of drug-selling careers, dealers are primarily youths and young adults. Dealers themselves are typically among the heaviest users of the drugs they sell (and sometimes other drugs as well), although self-consumption is a rapid route to destitution (Reuter et al. 1990). Sales usually take place on an intermittent basis. Across several years, most dealers report cycles of "success" (characterized by many sales, high income, high levels of personal drug use, and high status in drug-consuming circles) and "failure" (characterized by low or no drug sale income, inability to obtain supplies of drugs, arrest, violence, and economic deprivation). Males dominate the upper level drug-dealing roles (e.g., importer, wholesale dealer, supplier); females typically act as freelancers or work with or for others, usually males (Johnson et al. 1992).

For present purposes, the differences between the two career types are more important than the similarities. Middle-class dealers almost always sell directly to steady customers in private settings—homes, cars, offices—rather than to buyers they do not know personally or who have not been recommended by their steady customers (Adler 1985; Waldorf et al. 1991). They generally get their supplies of drugs from a small number of "connections" and usually sell in relatively large quantities, measuring cocaine by the gram and marijuana by the ounce. Their retail sales average $50 or more. Violence is relatively uncommon, since middle-class dealers tend to avoid threatening situations. Most manage to avoid arrest because their activity is private, and they are rarely incarcerated since they have greater resources for legal defense. Inner-city dealers, in contrast, often lack access to private settings for sales and typically sell in public locations to buyers they do not know. While they may have some steady customers, high customer turnover is common (Johnson et al. 1985, 1990). They typically have numerous suppliers and usually sell smaller retail units at lower prices: $10 to $25 bags of cocaine or heroin, $3 to $20 vials of crack. Violence and the threat of violence, arrest, and incarceration are common among inner city drug dealers (Goldstein 1985).

The most important difference between the two kinds of dealers is probably the disparity in their resources and life skills. As children and young adults, most middle-class dealers had the advantages of relatively stable homes, stronger kinship and friendship networks, and more formal education. As adults, they have access to resources such as permanent housing, telephones, and cars, and to life skills such as literacy, some accounting expertise, and effective interpersonal relationships. Thanks to these resources and skills, middle-class dealers frequently either have legal incomes or access to them. The early family and educational backgrounds of inner-city drug dealers, in contrast, are often found to have been grossly deficient (Dunlap and Johnson 1992c; Bourgois and Dunlap 1993; Ratner 1993). Lacking resources and life skills, they are effectively excluded from legal employment in their late teens and early 20s. Most have left school, are homeless (unless they live with family or friends), and have no legal jobs or sources of income. Effectively, their only economic options are nondrug criminality (robbery, burglary, theft, prostitution) or drug sales, with crack sales being the most profitable (Johnson et al. 1993).

## Women as Crack Cocaine Users and Dealers

Today women constitute a third to a half of all users of illegal drugs in the United States, with cocaine second only to marijuana as their drug of choice (Greenleaf 1989). However, the proportion of women involved in crack dealing—mostly at the lower levels of drug sales—is much smaller (Maher and Curtis 1992; Dunlap and Johnson 1992b; Inciardi et al. 1993). Selling is a career that carries harsh social penalties. In general, female dealers are viewed as having somehow overstepped their feminine bounds. They are stigmatized because, as society's "gatekeepers," they are viewed as being more responsible than males for upholding traditional values. Men often brand crack-using/selling women as "whores," a label resulting from the fact that some women engage in sex for crack or prostitute themselves to earn money for crack (Bourgois and Dunlap 1993; Ratner 1993; Inciardi et al. 1993).

The severe deprivation experienced by the typical female crack abuser and dealer in childhood, adolescence, and young adulthood has been documented elsewhere (Dunlap and Johnson 1992a, 1992b; Bourgois and Dunlap 1993), as have details of the typical careers of inner-city female crack dealers (Dunlap 1992; Dunlap and Johnson 1992a, 1992b). Rachel's childhood and adolescence are described in a companion paper (Dunlap et al. 1993) in which her family life is shown to be more characteristic of middle-class than inner-city dealers.

Generally, female dealers try to avoid violence and are therefore more apt than males to cooperate with competitors instead of confronting them (Dunlap and Johnson 1992b). This tendency makes dealing relatively safer for females than for males. Some report that, faced with choice of dealing crack or prostituting themselves, they prefer the former because drug dealing gives them more control over what takes place, even though the amount of money they make is smaller (Dunlap and Johnson 1992b; Maher and Curtis 1992).

---

## Development of a Drug-Dealing Career

### Rachel's Early Involvement with Drugs

As a child, Rachel moved from Mississippi to Harlem, where at 15 she met her future husband, a heroin and marijuana dealer with several uncles in the illegal drug business. She became pregnant at 16, gave birth to a daughter and married the baby's father a year later. As a teenage mother, Rachel remained uninvolved in drug use or sales, yet through her husband's activities she was introduced to drug dealing and a network of users and dealers. Her husband also provided a model of behaviors that contributed to his success in drug dealing: legitimate employment in addition to illegal activities; separation of drug involvement and family life; and expenditure of extra time and money on family rather than on street life.

After her daughter's birth, Rachel enrolled in an educational program targeting the poor, holding a program-related job as she worked toward her high school diploma. By 20 she had earned a high school equivalency degree. Then, when she was 21 and had been happily married for 5 years, her husband died suddenly of a kidney infection, leaving her to care alone for her 5-year-old daughter as well as her alcoholic mother. Rachel had negotiated adolescence without using drugs, had completed high school, held a legitimate job, lived in a household that was affluent by Harlem standards, and had well-developed household management and child-rearing skills. In short, by 21 she had acquired resources (housing and household furnishings, limited savings, close relationships with her husband's relatives) and skills (household maintenance, budgeting and accounting, child care, interpersonal negotiation) that would be valuable in her future career.

As a single black parent and informal custodian of an alcoholic mother, Rachel's new position placed conflicting demands upon her. In her bereavement, she began going to parties and smoking marijuana.

> With the marijuana, you know it . . . started out as a social situation, you know . . . I would say that for myself, I was probably a late person, in trying any of . . . any of these drugs at all. You could go to a party, you know, when you smoking marijuana, everybody smoking it, you know its, really—uh—nothing that you want to get over, you don't have worry about going into a special room or anything like that, you know. A lot of clubs and places, you know and—um—a lot of people who you knew at the time, any people, say people . . . with money or—you know—like movers and shakers . . . it was all right, it was acceptable, you know?

Rachel's earnings at her poverty program job were insufficient for the lifestyle she wanted for herself and her family. Since she was already familiar with the drug business, she began selling marijuana, obtained from her husband's family.

> And then really it's like—it's a good—you get a little chunk of money. A little boost in your checking account, and as you boost your checking account one time and you know you not planning to do it no more, then something will come up and maybe you want something, you know . . . . You don't be planning

to do it, like be out there, you know. . . . I made good money, okay. . . . I'm
always working, so I always had a good job, okay. Let's say I figure it like this. I
predict what I needed, and if I needed $1,000 then that's what I was gonna get.
If I needed $500 then that's what I was gonna get. See, I'd make whatever I
needed, you know. . . .

Rachel's success with her marijuana customers, most of whom were co-
workers or other working-class drug users, increased her economic reliance
on drug profits. At the same time, however, she was establishing herself as the
provider for her family, a role that increased her commitment to conventional
norms.

You see, it (drug dealing) was about different things then, you know. 'Cause I
wanted to travel, and then—you know—the kid, and we gave her everything
. . . and then [I] gotta look out for my mother and stuff, so it was about—it was
all about business then, you know . . . I wanna give her [daughter] everything in
the world. When she's into college, no struggling, no sleeping in no dorm with
two and three people. You get your own room, your own telephone, your own
refrigerator, your own everything, you know.

## From Marijuana to Cocaine

Thus far, Rachel had used and sold only marijuana, avoiding heroin. However the drug scene—customers, dealing activities, patterns and places of consumption—was changing. By the mid-1970s, cocaine use had begun to
increase among nonheroin drug users in New York (Johnson et al. 1985;
1990). Rachel, still in her 20s, began snorting cocaine at social gatherings,
although marijuana remained her dominant drug of consumption.

I was still working and stuff, you know, and I was still out there doing my thing
(selling marijuana), and I used to deal with—you know—a lot of people of different ethnic origins, okay, and I can remember—I used to go camping a lot.
And we take the van, you know, go upstate, and hustle on back down here to
Manhattan, to the Bronx, get a load of herb, you know, take it up to the camp,
you know . . . and then I noticed, I think it was probably like . . . one of the last
times I went camping . . . we came down in the van and we had $200 and we
(spent it) for cocaine! Instead of, you know, herb . . . Well, um . . . I started—
all right, I started snorting cocaine, okay? But I didn't stop using marijuana on
account of that, you know. Uh, I used marijuana and cocaine, sniffing cocaine,
okay? Uh, a lot together, you know, and still basically under the same social situations. I . . . had a close friend that I worked with, and he got into the habit,
like, um, bringing it to the job, okay? And, you know, we started sniffing a little

bit. But, um . . . I would still primarily (snort cocaine) in a social situation, you know.

By the early 1980s, Rachel, like many other inner-city marijuana users, had begun to consume cocaine more regularly. She continued to sell and use marijuana, although good quality marijuana was becoming hard to find.

> The marijuana . . . it just got to a point where it was hard to get. I mean, it's not hard to get marijuana, herb is—you know—you can still get herb anywhere, but it's just not the same quality, you know. And if you been smoking herb a long time . . . it's nothing compared to what herb used to be. . . . The more cocaine started being utilized in the form of crack, the less good herb seem to be available, okay . . . when I was getting it, you know, for, um, other reasons, other than personal use, you know, there's people that I would get it from, you know . . . (and) the quality just started (going down). 'Til you . . . just start gradually moving away from it, you know.

While she used cocaine in the same social situations as she had smoked marijuana, the setting for cocaine use was slightly different.

> Um, with cocaine, okay, you still . . . supposedly with "in" people, but you know—you kinda—it started moving to the back room a little bit, so naturally you can't—because a lot of places you couldn't go in the place, smoke coke openly, you know, but you could go the ladies room, and, you know, all the ladies—quote ladies—was in there doing it, you know. Or if you went to a party at somebody's house, you know, there was always that special place where you could do . . . a line, you know, snorting a line of cocaine, or you could spoon, you know . . . years ago people used to wear those spoons around their neck, you know, little gold chain thing . . . you would announce it, you know, in a way . . . it was fashionable!

At 24, Rachel enrolled in college, again under a social welfare program, and eventually earned a bachelor's degree in psychology. She was accepted into and began a graduate program, but dropped out to work as a rehabilitation psychotherapist.

## Career and Drug Use Changes

Rachel continued to supplement her legal income with marijuana dealing, always keeping her drug-related activities separate from her family life. Prior to 1985, she had been motivated primarily by the desire to provide her mother and daughter with a comfortable life-style, and her personal drug consumption was limited by her commitment to them. But after her daughter married and moved away and her mother died, her involvement with drugs began to change; she sold drugs more and more to support her own habit. Eventually she left her legal job, although she retained the appearance and attitude of a legitimate professional woman.

> See, I'm, not . . . not so much into it the way I was before, when all I thought about was the dollar. I just feel like being comfortable, you know—um—support my own particular habit, you know keep myself cared for. There was a time when it was a lot different, it was just all about the dollar bill, you know . . . when my daughter was going to college I was dealing, you know, because I needed, I wanted the money, okay? That was my primary thing. After my mother died and . . . my daughter went away to college . . . it was easier to get high and stuff.

As supplies of good quality marijuana became increasingly difficult to acquire, Rachel drifted into crack selling. The switch was accomplished through the same male co-worker who had previously provided her with cocaine.

> This particular friend . . . was also, as it turned out, when I first started dealing with crack and then started, you know, again with the selling a little bit, with the same person, you know, we just escalated (from) one thing to the other . . .

Selling crack as she had marijuana, in an open, convivial, "tea-pad" atmosphere, attracted attention, and Rachel soon recognized that even though she was making "crazy money" she would have to change her style of doing business. News of her high-quality crack traveled so fast that overnight she had lines of people seeking to buy it. Not only did such obvious drug dealing put her in jeopardy from her nondrug-using neighbors, whose friendship she valued, and from the authorities, it also made her more prone to robbery by crack users and other dealers.

> I mean it was like lines of niggers, you know what I'm saying. Oh, God. I remember one time . . . I had the line up from the door. It was like oh, God, I can't do this . . . I mean, it was like, it was really ugly in the beginning, you know . . . . Money was so fast, people so crazy, it was ugly.

Rachel quickly ended such sales, although occasionally she is pressured into dealing with strangers who have heard of the quality of her crack.

> . . . you know, I'm the type of person, I'm friendly with people, you know, so some time it be like, "yo, I heard . . ."—especially when I got that good quality from Long Island, then it be—it's like a nickel, you know, see for $5, somebody gonna go, child—I got this bad [i.e., good] stuff . . . I sell it to them. But that— that's not really what I . . . [have for] my clientele per se.

Since the advent of crack, Rachel's neighborhood has become permeated with crack users and dealers, even though most residents are still working people with families. Shootings, robberies, assaults, and rape have become commonplace. Indeed, rape is so common that most of its victims no longer consider it a reportable crime.

> It's a lot more violence associated with this drug. With cocaine in general, okay. But with crack in particular, you know. I never knew anybody on this— on this block that got killed for cocaine, but I've known, in the last year, three people getting killed for this crack business. They'll pull a gun up to you in a minute. In a minute. The young guys . . . I'm talking about organized drug dealers, okay, the young ones that are really into it and working for real big movers and shakers in the drug business, okay. They have no respect for no one, male or female, okay? And they as soon whip it out on you as anything . . . seem like the taking of a life is not . . . important. . . .

Relationships among crack users are different from marijuana users' social interactions, and Rachel had to readjust her selling strategy to accommodate the particular effects of crack on users. Whereas marijuana consumers enjoy a sociable environment with wine, music, and conversation, many of Rachel's crack customers wanted to be left alone, requiring only a safe, quiet place where they could consume their drug discreetly.

> . . . particularly for older customers, they don't like that feeling of being—you know—like moles under the ground or something . . . if you ever been in a (crack house), it's a awful, awful sight, you know what I'm saying.

Recognizing a need among middle-class crack users for a safe haven, Rachel reorganized her business, developing techniques similar to those of the middle class/professional users and dealers studied by Waldorf et al. (1991) in the San Francisco Bay area. Some of her customers were former marijuana users who, like herself, had grown older and disliked the street crack users who were everywhere evident in the neighborhood.

With the demise of her obligations to her daughter, her mother, and her legal job, Rachel became more involved in drug consumption. In addition, the stress of dealing crack, combined with its easy availability and pleasurable high, encouraged her increased consumption.

> You see, I'm not the gun-toting mama type, you know what I'm saying. So . . . when it was like that, when it was like heavy at that time, it was like—I don't know, I would start to smoking too much my own damn self and then it was just—you know—when it's free . . .

## Rachel in the Ethnographic Present

Four years after entering the crack market, Rachel is one of very few successful female crack dealers in the inner city. A freelancer, she operates as a "house connection"—a dealer who conducts drug sales from her apartment (Johnson, Dunlap, Manwar and Hamid 1992). Most other freelancers are involved in networks of dealers who help one another to avoid robbery, competition, and arrest (Johnson, Dunlap, and Hamid 1992), but Rachel is not a part of any network. Nor does she fit comfortably into the established hierarchy of drug dealers, since she is neither a street dealer or lower level distributor like most other female crack dealers (Johnson, Hamid, and Sanabria 1991; Maher and Curtis 1992; Dunlap et al. 1992b) nor an upper-level distributor.

Rachel's apartment, one of the few places where buyers can both buy and consume crack, is a sixth floor walk-up with bars on the windows and several locks on the door. Unlike the typical crack house, it is immaculate, much like the Harlem home of a typical lower middle-class nondrug user. The living room contains a worn but clean sofa, a coffee table, two end tables, a bookcase full of old books, a portable black and white TV, an ineffective table fan, and an old-fashioned entertainment set (a radio/record player/tape deck combination with a space for albums). A record player, long broken, and a stack of old albums provide evidence of Rachel's former marijuana-dealing days. Pictures of her mother, daughter, grandchildren, and son-in-law decorate the room, and she is eager to show visitors her family photo albums. The bedroom contains a single bed, a wardrobe, and a dresser with a mirror. The kitchen is furnished with an old table and chairs, refrigerator, stove, and a large barrel in one corner.

Rachel had more household possessions and more money when she was selling marijuana to supplement her income. During the early stages of her crack career, she lost possessions such as tape decks and color TVs by admitting "certain types" of customers into her apartment. Now, with her daughter educated and married and her mother deceased, she lives modestly, maintaining her business primarily to pay her rent and bills and to get high.

> So right now it ain't really all about (money) . . . it's like keeping a steady pace, keeping myself on a steady flow and just basically having what I want, you know, like that. And it works out better, and it's a lot easier 'cause it's a lot less headache. . . .

Despite her satisfaction with her current lifestyle, Rachel has occasional feelings of remorse about being "a bad person," a judgment she believes her customers reflect.

> No matter who's buying it, it's like they always wanna look at the person that's selling it . . . therefore that makes me—you know—the dealer is the bad guy . . . I mean . . . it's the fact that you're doing something shady and you're doing something wrong, you know. Especially, like I said, the way most of the time I dealt with it, it was a lot of professional people, people that I worked with and stuff like that. So it's like I'm the shady character, you know—'cause I'm the dealer. So somehow or another, that makes me the shady character.

To counter this view, Rachel and her suppliers, whom she chooses according to the same criteria of adherence to conventional norms as she does her customers, attempt to bolster one another's self-images as respectable professionals.

> They (suppliers) are also human beings who wanna be looked at in another light . . . They wanna be looked at respectable and decent, you know. So you go out to dinner with me, I'm also going with you. I'm making you look good, you make me, and we all pretending that we normal people out here just like everybody else, hob-knobbing downtown and where ever you wanna go, you know. So you feed into each other's egos, because you don't really want to look at yourself as a bad person.

Her relationships with her (male) dealing associates take two different forms. Some treat her as a businessperson, according her the same respect they would give any business owner. But others treat her like a street dealer, making her vulnerable to the violence ordinarily found in drug dealing. Over the years she has developed the expertise required to offset the potential for violence with the ability to handle difficult situations, managing to tread a thin line between being a friendly, accommodating businesswoman and attracting unwanted sexual attention.

> What I dislike . . . men get the wrong idea about you, you know. Even when you straight up . . . they always gotta look at you somewhere lesser than what they are. If they being a businessman, why can't I be being a businessperson too? . . . They always feel like somehow or another—you know—there's supposed to be that little extra fringe benefit in there, you know . . . and especially if you try to treat 'em like a human being, you know, with respect. Oh, then— you know—you think—they start playing on you then, you know. Because if you try, then they wanna, "oh, would you like to go out to dinner." Then the next thing is, "cause you bought me a meal, I'm supposed to go to bed with you." And then that makes you a black bitch and all that kind of stuff . . . and stuck up, you know. Okay I'm friendly, I'm a damn friendly personality, okay, and I like everybody, but then—you know—they read it all out of proportion . . .

## Strategies for a Successful Drug-dealing Career

In conducting her successful drug business, Rachel deviates considerably from the practices of most other drug dealers.

### Catering to Working/Middle Class Users

Rachel's clients represent a hidden element in the world of illegal drugs about whom little is known (cf. Hamid 1992). Many have spouses and children who are unaware of their crack use. Their average age is 30, although many are older, with adult children. Some are newly middle class, the first in their families to have college degrees or to own businesses. Despite their secure, longtime positions, comfortable housing, and material wealth, however, they find themselves in empty households and holding unfulfilling jobs.

> I must say, of the people I know like myself . . . they older people, I have to say that, yeah. They're all older people . . . some of 'em got families and things like that, you know . . . everybody, everybody works. . . . I know some, to be frank, I know some doctors, you know. Two doctors, yeah, and, um, a couple of social workers, you know . . . They got a sense of black identity about them also, okay? And they do believe in something of a higher being, you know. I mean, they know about faith and stuff like that . . . And they get high differently, you know, than the younger crowd . . . they don't get as paranoid, you know. And they don't want to talk about negative things . . . We be getting high but we be keeping talk about religion. What's happening to the black people in general, including ourselves. We can talk about these things, okay. . . .

### Avoiding the Street Market

A key element in Rachel's success is her avoidance of both customers and dealers involved in the street crack market. Normally she declines to sell crack to street users or to anyone who threatens her or others. While she knows street dealers, she stays out of their territory and does not compete for their customers. In this way she avoids violence and maintains the safe, comfortable environment her customers prefer.

> Well, (I) try not to . . . get into no antagonistic situations, you know . . . You try to give a little respect to the neighbors around you, you know, so that they don't get too mad . . . they will tolerate you, you know. You try not to . . . go direct into no one's turf, and stuff like that. In other words, you have to maintain a low profile, you know. That's the main thing . . . And then . . . you know, like—I don't hit nobody, I don't rob nobody, I don't deliberately mess with

people's heads, and I expect the same with them, okay . . . I think it's all in the way you treat people. . .

## Maintaining Good Relations with Neighbors

Most crack users eventually lose their apartments (Dunlap 1992), but Rachel has lived in the same building for some 20 years and has established herself as a good neighbor to other long-time tenants, most of whom are not involved with drugs. Her neighborliness is motivated both by genuine affection for her neighbors and by an awareness that they could destroy her business. She retains their friendship (and avoids detection by the police) by restricting her business to a limited number of quiet, middle class customers.

> This is a quiet building and stuff like that. . . . I got neighbors that I've known, like, a long, long time, and (if I attracted the wrong clientele) I'd be outta here quick fast. 'Cause they got a law now, they kick you out . . . when you selling and they know.

## Providing a Setting Appropriate to Clients' Needs

Aware of her customers' desire for a quiet, discreet atmosphere in which they can smoke crack without having to deal with the dangers of street life, Rachel strives to create a climate of tranquility in her apartment. She also makes much of the fact that she will not sell anything she would not smoke herself, which assures her customers that her crack is of high quality.

> I have it set up in a sense that now it's nice, easy, a social kind of situation. Person comes . . . they bring a certain amount of money, it's payday, you know, and . . . most of the time, they don't want to go out no more. They don't want to be seen, there's a lot of professional people, and they want to feel safe, you know. [I] sell it right to them, point blank period dot, and then smoke it with 'em too. You know what I'm saying? . . . And it's easy, it's subtle, it's quiet. Ain't a whole lot of noise, a whole lot of traffic . . . my main focus is to keep 'em comfortable.

## Managing the Effects of Crack on Customers

Familiar with the negative physical and psychological reactions that crack consumption can cause, Rachel works hard to keep her customers from suffering "tension" (also a street name for crack). Her dimly lit bedroom provides those who prefer not to interact with others a place to be alone and those who are paranoid a place to feel safe.

> You don't know how this shit hits some people . . . If you could see some of the people that I have to tolerate, people come here because they know I have

patience to deal with them, with the looking under the bed, and looking in the closet. They feel safe here . . .

## Managing Customers' Finances

Many of Rachel's customers need help managing their drug habits. She knows when they get their paychecks, and also that if they arrive at her apartment with a full paycheck they may not have paid their bills or set anything aside for necessities. If she is aware that a customer needs money, she may cash his paycheck but then purchase a money order for him to take home.

> Whatever they come with, 9 times outta 10, sometime what I do is I'll take some off the top and—you know—'what did you say you needed?' . . . And I will go to the store and get it, get 'em whatever it is they needed . . . or even give 'em a money order or something. Especially the people that's living with families.

## Controlling Unruly Customers

Rachel is quite capable of holding her own when customers attempt to "try her out" by violating her house rules. Prior to one interview, the ethnographer found Rachel scrubbing blood off the floor of the hall in front of her apartment. She reported that a customer had become violent—an unusual occurrence—and she had settled the matter. Since this was the second time this customer had acted this way, she barred him from returning. She keeps knives in her apartment for emergencies but no longer owns a gun, having devised other ways to discourage rowdy or threatening customers.

> Well, yeah, I got stuff like (knives), you know. I got quite a few of them . . . I just don't have weapons, I don't have a gun anymore, okay, 'cause it's hard for me to keep from not shooting somebody if I really did want to . . . and uh, I just went through last year a thing that—and it's like . . . I tried to kill that man. You don't come here and then bogart me around the house [i.e., act in a rough or bossy manner], okay, you can't do that, you know.

## Choosing Suppliers Carefully

Rachel chooses stable suppliers who, like herself and her customers, lead superficially "normal" lives and have self-images of attachment to conventional norms and behaviors.

> . . . my best person, supplier, is a family man, you know, they have a home, everything. You know, nice people . . . Drive a nice car, nice kids, nice wife, the whole bit. That's the best kind of people to deal with, because they can't go but so far. You know, raunchy people, man, they'll be ready to take you off, you

know, and then you gotta come out a whole 'nother bag, you know. Which I can do that too, but you see, why set yourself up for that?

## Avoiding Unwanted Sexual Attention

Rachel knows that both clients and suppliers are drawn to her as an attractive woman, and she exploits this for business purposes. At the same time, she is aware that no special consideration is given female drug dealers and that the consequences of failing to anticipate and defuse potentially dangerous situations may be sexual harassment or physical harm.

> Being a female—you know, it's good . . . 'cause they always think they gonna get something out the deal other than business, you know. I dress good, look good, you know. . . . (I) let them think whatever they wanna think, you know. It ain't about stringing them on, because when push come to shove, you know what talk more than anything else is the money. . . . Most of the time—you know—you just, you gotta handle it. You either gotta do one of two things . . . 9 times out of 10, you know you can kinda talk your way out of it . . . use that reverse psychology in Psychology 101 on 'em . . . (But) sometime there are— you know—you just have to get downright, like, you just gotta act like a bitch. I mean you gotta get downright nasty, you know. See—but that's always a problem in that, you know—because then you don't want nobody coming back on you, you know. But . . . it depends on the kind of person you are, you know. Because it's like I don't sell my body.

## Avoiding Arrest

By dealing discreetly, catering to a middle-class clientele, and being a responsible neighbor and tenant, Rachel has successfully avoided the police and has no arrest record. The threat of arrest is

> . . . important enough to me to do it (deal) the way I do it, you know. In other words, I'm not looking for the big profits no more, okay . . . it's very, very, very essential that I do not go to jail!

Another of her tactics for avoiding the police is to dress like a working woman when buying cocaine. On one occasion, when she encountered police who had staked out her supplier's apartment, her appearance plus some creative lies helped her to evade arrest.

> It's in the wintertime, right? Put my boots on, had nice leather boots, long coat, you should have seen me . . . I put my makeup on and stuff, like I'm going to work, okay? Earrings and everything, okay? So I get to where I got to go, right. . . . Soon as I went in there [i.e., into the area in which weight cocaine is sold], I felt it. I said, it's too quiet around here, and I turned around to make my move and come on out and they [undercover police] stopped me. Five of

em, okay? But I was looking the part, so they say, "Where you going?" I said, "I'm getting ready to go to work. I heard my girlfriend, she gets in a lot of trouble on the job, and I ain't know whether she had got fired and I came to see about her." . . . He said, "You know about this place," and I said "I've heard terrible, terrible things about this place here, but I was so worried about my girlfriend that I had to take a chance and come anyway." So they said "Well, where?" I say "Apartment one, right over there" . . . They said, "Get the hell outta here."

## Controlling Personal Consumption

For the most part, Rachel has avoided the pitfalls of excessive crack use. She manages to eat properly by requiring her customers to bring food, which she then cooks, serves, and shares with them, and she is careful to set aside money to pay the rent. She also avoids consuming too much of her own supply of crack. Unlike the average consumer, she does not "go on missions"—nonstop 3- to 5-day crack smoking binges without food or sleep. When one of her customers goes on a mission, consuming a substantial part of her supply of crack, she re-ups with money from her next well-heeled customer. She considers herself an intelligent crack user.

> You know, that's all a part of using your head. When you take care of your body, okay, and you put some knowledge up here in your head, if you are doing these things, it's because you want to survive after you do it. . . . See, a lot of people . . . just want to get high, and don't care nothing else other than that. Getting high, okay . . . for me [is] like some people want to take a martini after work, okay? Then you work and you do what you have to do. For me it's delayed gratification, is what I call it, okay?

---

## Lessons from a Successful Drug-Dealing Career

---

Rachel is in many ways unique, a product of her singular personality, life history, and experiences, yet her very uniqueness sheds light on a number of aspects of illegal drug sales and use in the United States.

First, Rachel's career illuminates trends in the history of illegal drug use in New York and the United States. The shifts in her involvement, from one drug to another, were engendered not so much by her personal decisions as by macrolevel social and logistical forces (Johnson and Manwar 1991; Dunlap and Johnson 1992a, 1992b). Her introduction to cocaine in the mid-1970s, for example, was typical of many inner-city drug users of that era, who frequented "after-hours clubs" to snort cocaine when they could afford it (Williams 1978). More broadly, Rachel's business illustrates general shifts in the drug market in New York, from marijuana to cocaine to crack, showing how supply, demand, and consumption feed into one another. Her customers' drug choices and consumption patterns and her marketing practices reflect the availability of certain drugs. Availability in turn influences demand, which drives the market.

Second, Rachel's business illuminates an unknown side of the drug economy: the world of the older, better educated, employed, middle-class, violence-averse drug user (Hamid 1992; Waldorf et al. 1991). In the United States, the stereotypical crack user is young, violence-prone, poorly educated, and unemployed. In addition, entertainers and sports figures are widely viewed as being involved with drugs; actor Richard Pryor provides an example. But Mayor Marion Barry's arrest for crack use came as a surprise to many because his position as mayor of Washington, D.C. was inconsistent with such stereotypes. Middle-class drug users may consume drugs discreetly to protect their jobs and reputations, but they are no less a part of the illegal drug industry.

Third, Rachel illustrates the effects of being female in a profession dominated by males, a subject about which little is known despite recent increases in convictions of female drug offenders. Females are often stigmatized in the world of illegal drugs, but Rachel has managed to turn being female into an asset by cultivating a friendly, accommodating, caring, noncompetitive image. She exploits the fact that males find her attractive, but is able to defuse unwanted sexual attention with professionalism.

Finally, Rachel's attempts to be "normal" suggest the tension inherent in moving between the legitimate world and the world of illegal drugs. Her feelings of remorse, reflected in her need to see herself as other than "a bad person," are assuaged by her ability to justify her actions. She prides herself on providing high quality crack for her customers and a safe, congenial place to smoke it, and on her ability to avoid the police. But most important, she sees herself as a legitimate businessperson with a commitment to conventional norms and chooses associates—suppliers, other dealers, and customers—who share this self-image.

# Conclusion

Rachel's success in her profession can be attributed to a unique combination of historical contingencies, personal qualities, and career choices. On the one hand, she is a product of a particular background and of the macrolevel social forces existing in a particular temporal and geographical context. Yet within this context, her unique personal characteristics—her intelligence, sense of professionalism, commitment to conventional values, skill as a businessperson, and self-discipline—have contributed to her position as a deviant among deviants, as have her surprising personal choices. Formerly a conventional black mother and nondrug user, she became involved with drugs relatively late, after her husband died. She completed high school and college and was clearly capable of graduate work, yet abandoned the promise of a legitimate career for marijuana sales. And not until she was in her mid-30s did she shift from marijuana to crack. Together, these factors have contributed to the ingenious ways in which Rachel controls her environment to the specific strategies she employs, and, ultimately, to her career success.

## References

Adler, Patricia A. 1985. *Wheeling and Dealing: An Ethnography of an Upper Level Drug Dealing and Smuggling Community*. New York: Columbia University Press.

Becker, Howard S. 1963. *Outsiders: Studies in the Sociology of Deviance*. Glencoe, IL: Free Press.

Belenko, Steven, Jeffrey Fagan, and Kolin Chin. 1991. "Criminal Justice Responses to Crack." *Journal of Research in Crime and Delinquency* 28:55–74.

Blauner, Robert. 1987. "Problems of Editing 'First-Person' Sociology." *Qualitative Sociology* 10:46–64.

———. 1989. *Black Lives, White Lives: Three Decades of Race Relations in America*. Berkeley: University of California Press.

Bourgois, Philippe, and Eloise Dunlap. 1993. "Exorcising Sex-for-Crack: An Ethnographic Perspective from Harlem," pp. 97–132, in *Crack as Pimp: An Ethnographic Investigation of Sex-for-Crack Exchanges*, edited by Mitchell S. Ratner. New York: Lexington Books.

Bureau of Justice Statistics. 1992. Drugs and the Justice System. Rockville, MD: Center Clearinghouse. Dec. NCJ-133652.

Carpenter, Cheryl, Barry Glassner, Bruce D. Johnson, and Julia Loughlin. 1988. *Kids, Drugs, Alcohol, and Crime*. Lexington, MA: Lexington Books.

Chambers, Carl D., S. W. Dean, and M. Fletcher. 1981. "Criminal Involvement of Minority Group Addicts," pp. 125–154, in *The Drugs-Crime Connection*, edited by James A. Inciardi. Beverly Hills, CA: Sage.

Division of Criminal Justice Services. 1988. *New York State Trends in Felony Drug Offense Processing 1983–1987*. Albany: DCJS.

Dunlap, Eloise. 1992. "The Impact of Drugs on Family Life and Kin Networks in the Inner-city African American Single Parent Household," pp. 181–207, in *Drugs, Crime and Social Isolation*, edited by Adele Harrell and George Peterson. Washington, DC: Urban Institute Press.

Dunlap, Eloise and Bruce D. Johnson. 1992a. "Structural and Economic Changes: An Examination of Female Crack Dealers in New York City and Their Family Life." Paper presented at the annual meeting of the American Society of Criminology November, 1992. New Orleans, LA.

____. 1992b. "Who They are and What They Do: Female Dealers in New York City." Paper presented at the annual meeting of the American Society of Criminology, November, 1992. New Orleans, LA.

____. 1992c. "The Setting for the Crack Era: Macro Forces, Micro Consequences (1960–1992)." *Journal of Psychoactive Drugs* 24: 307–321.

Dunlap, Eloise, Bruce D. Johnson, and Ali Manwar. 1993. "Rachel's Place: A Case Study of the Impact of Resources on Crack Use and Sales." Paper prepared for Urban Institute, Washington, D.C.

Dunlap, Eloise, Bruce D. Johnson, Harry Sanabria, Elbert Holliday, Vicki Lipsey, Maurice Barnett, William Hopkins, Ira Sobel, Doris Randolph, and Ko-Lin Chin. 1990, Spring. "Studying Crack Users and Their Criminal Careers: The Scientific and Artistic Aspects of Locating Hard-to-Reach Subjects and Interviewing Them About Sensitive Topics." *Contemporary Drug Problems,* pp. 121–144.

Faupel, Charles E. 1981. "Drug Treatment and Criminality: Methodological and Theoretical Considerations," pp. 183–206, in *The Drugs-Crime Connection*, edited by James A. Inciardi. Beverly Hills: Sage.

Goldstein, Paul. 1985. "The Drug/Violence Nexus." *Journal of Drug Issues* 15:493–506.

Greenleaf, Vicki D. 1989. *Women and Cocaine: Personal Stories of Addiction and Recovery*. Los Angeles: RGA.

Hamid, Ansley 1992. "Drugs and Patterns of Opportunity in the Inner City," pp. 209–239, in *Drugs, Crime and Social Isolation*, edited by Adele Harrell and George Peterson. Washington, DC: Urban Institute Press.

Inciardi, James A. 1986. *The War on Drugs: Heroin, Cocaine, Crime and Public Policy*. Palo Alto, CA: Mayfield.

Inciardi, James A., Dorothy Lockwood, and Anne E. Pottieger. 1993. *Women and Crack-Cocaine*. New York: MacMillan.

Inciardi, James A., and Anne E. Pottieger. 1986. "Drug Use and Crime among Two Cohorts of Women Narcotics Users: An Empirical Assessment." *Journal of Drug Issues* 16:91–106.

Jessor, Richard, John E. Donovan, and Francis M. Costa. 1991. *Beyond Adolescence: Problem Behavior and Young Adult Development*. New York: Cambridge University Press.

Johnson, Bruce. 1991. "Crack in New York City" *Addiction and Recovery* XX:24–27.

Johnson, Bruce D., Eloise Dunlap, Ali Manwar, and Ansley Hamid. 1992. "Varieties of Freelance Crack Selling." Paper presented at the annual meeting of the American Society of Criminology, November. New Orleans, LA.

Johnson, Bruce D., Eloise Dunlap, Ansley Hamid. 1992. "Changes in New York's Crack Distribution Scene," pp. 360–364, in *Drugs and Society to the Year 2000*, edited by Peter Vamos and Paul Corriveau. Montreal: Portage Program for Drug Dependencies.

Johnson, Bruce D., Paul J. Goldstein, Edward Preble, James Schmeidler, Douglas S. Lipton, Barry Spunt, and Thomas Miller. 1985. *Taking Care of Business: The Economics of Crime by Heroin Abusers*. Lexington, MA: Lexington Books.

Johnson, Bruce, Ansley Hamid, and Harry Sanabria. 1991. "Emerging Models of Crack Distribution," pp. 56–78, in *Drugs and Crime: A Reader*, edited by Tom Mieczkowski. Boston: Allyn-Bacon.

Johnson, Bruce and Ali Manwar. 1991. "Towards a Paradigm of Drug Eras: Previous Drug Eras Help to Model the Crack Epidemic in New York City During the 1990s." Presentation at the American Society of Criminology November, 1991. San Francisco, CA.

Johnson, Bruce E., Mangai Natarajan, Eloise Dunlap, Elsayed Elmoghazy. "Crack Abusers and Noncrack Abusers: Profiles of Drug Use, Drug Sales, and Nondrug Criminality." *Journal of Drug Issues*.

Johnson, Bruce, Terry Williams, Kojo Dei, and Harry Sanabria. 1990. "Drug Abuse in the Inner City: Impact on Hard-Drug Users and the Community," pp. 9–66, in *Drugs and Crime*, edited by Michael Tonry and James Wilson. Chicago: University of Chicago Press.

Lewis, Carla, Bruce D. Johnson, Andrew Golub, and Eloise Dunlap. 1992. "Studying Crack Abusers: Strategies for Recruiting the Right Tail of an Ill-Defined Population." *Journal of Psychoactive Drugs* 24:323–336.

Maher, L. and R. Curtis. 1992. "Women on the Edge of Crime: Crack Cocaine and the Changing Contexts of Street-Level Sex Work in New York City." *Crime, Law and Social Change* 18:221–258.

Manwar, Ali, Bruce D. Johnson, and Eloise Dunlap. 1993. "Qualitative Data Analysis with Hypertext: A Case of New York City Crack Dealers." Paper presented at the annual meeting of the American Sociological Association. August, 1993. Miami Beach, FL.

Matza, David. 1964. *Delinquency and Drift*. New York: Wiley.

Painter, Neil, Irvin. 1979. *The Narrative of Hosea Hudson*. Cambridge: Harvard University Press.

Ratner, Mitchell S. (ed). 1993. *Crack Pipe as Pimp: An Ethnographic Investigation of Sex-for-Crack Exchanges*. New York: Lexington Books.

Reuter, Peter, Robert MacCoun, and Patrick Murphy. 1990. *Money from Crime: A Study of the Economics of Drug Dealing in Washington, D.C.* Santa Monica, CA: Rand.

Sanchez, Jose E. and Bruce D. Johnson. 1987. "Women and the Drugs-Crime Connection: Crime Rates Among Drug Abusing Women at Rikers Island." *Journal of Psychoactive Drugs* 19:205–215.

Waldorf, Dan, Craig Reinarman, and Shegila Murphy. 1991. *Cocaine Changes: The Experience of Using and Quitting*. Delphia, PA: Temple University Press.

Williams, Terry. 1978. "The Cocaine Culture in After Hours Clubs." PhD dissertation. New York: Sociology Department, City University of New York.

Williams, Terry, Eloise Dunlap, Bruce D. Johnson, and Ansley Hamid. 1992. "Personal Safety in Dangerous Places." *Journal of Contemporary Ethnography* 21:343–347.

Zinberg, Norman E. 1984. *Drug Set and Setting: The Basis for Controlled Intoxicant Use*. New Haven, CT: Yale University Press.

# 11

---

# The Police and Drugs

---

## Mark H. Moore
## Mark A. R. Kleiman

Many urban communities are now besieged by illegal drugs. Fears of gang violence and muggings keep frightened residents at home. Even at home, citizens feel insecure, for drug-related break-ins and burglaries threaten. Open dealing on the street stirs the community's fears for its children.

The police sometimes seem overwhelmed. Occasionally they are outgunned. More often, they are simply overmatched by the resilience of the drug commerce. Furthermore, their potential impact is neutralized by the incapacity of the courts and penal system to mete out deserved punishments.

Urgent problems and limited resources demand managerial thought for their resolution. Thus, police executives facing the drug problem might usefully consider four strategic questions:

- What goals might reasonably be set for drug enforcement?
- What parts of the police department engage the drug problem and to what effect?

*Perspectives on Policing*, No. 11, September 1989. National Institute of Justice, U.S. Dept. of Justice, Office of Justice Programs.

- What role can citizens and community groups usefully (and properly) play in coping with the problem?
- What basic strategies might the police department consider as alternative attacks on the problem?

## The Goals of Drug Enforcement

From a police chief's perspective, the drug problem presents distinguishable threats to community security. Most pressing is the violence associated with street-level drug dealing—particularly crack cocaine.[1] Much of this violence involves youth gangs.[2] Often the violence spills over into the general population, leaving innocent victims in its wake. There is also the worry that the practice in armed, organized violence is spawning the next generation of organized crime.[3]

Also salient is the close link between drug use and street crime.[4] Criminal activity is known to vary directly with levels of heroin consumption.[5] Many of those arrested for robberies and burglaries, use cocaine during the commission of their crimes or steal to support drug habits.[6] Among the small group of the most active and dangerous offenders, drug users are overrepresented.[7] Thus, controlling drug use (and drug users) opens an avenue for reducing the robberies, burglaries, and petty thefts that have long been the focus of the police.

A third problem is that drug use undermines the health, economic well-being, and social responsibility of drug users. It is hard to stay in school, hold onto a job, or care for a child when one is spending all one's money and attention on getting stoned.[8] The families and friends of drug users are also undermined as their resources are strained by obligations to care for the drug user or to assume responsibilities that the drug user has abandoned.

Fourth, drug trafficking threatens the civility of city life and undermines parenting. While parents can set rules for conduct in their own homes, the rules are hard to extend to city streets and urban classrooms where drug trafficking has become a way of life. Although these threats affect all city neighborhoods, they are perhaps worst for those in the most deprived areas. There, the capacity of the community for self-defense and the ability of parents to guide their children are not only the weakest, but also the most in need of public support and assistance.[9]

Fifth, the police executive knows, even before he commits his troops, that the police can accomplish little by themselves. Drug arrests and prosecutions are exceedingly difficult, owing to the absence of complaining victims and witnesses.[10] Even with these limitations, the police can make many more arrests than prosecutors can prosecute, courts can adjudicate, and prisons can hold.[11] Furthermore, drug distribution systems, held together by the prospect of drug profits, will adapt quickly rather than collapse in the face of police action.

Finally, the police executive knows from bitter experience that in committing his force to attack drug trafficking and drug use, he risks corruption and abuses of authority.[12] Informants and undercover operations—so essential to effective drug enforcement—inevitably draw police officers into close, potentially corrupting relationships with the offenders they are pledged to control. The frustrations of the task lead some officers to cynicism or desperate anger. As the police become more cynical or more angry, the dealers will be standing there with cash in their pockets, ready to make a deal. Or they will mock the police with apparent invulnerability and provoke indignant officers to plant evidence or pursue justice through other illegal means.

These threats define the goals of police action against drug trafficking and use. The goals are:

(1) reduce the gang violence associated with drug trafficking and prevent the emergence of powerful organized criminal groups;
(2) control the street crimes committed by drug users;
(3) improve the health and economic and social well-being of drug users;
(4) restore the quality of life in urban communities by ending street-level drug dealing;
(5) help to prevent children from experimenting with drugs; and
(6) protect the integrity of criminal justice institutions.

The operational question, of course, is how best to accomplish these goals. Or put somewhat differently, the question is how best to deploy police resources to produce the maximum contribution to the achievement of these goals.

## Police Organization and Deployment

The narcotics bureau is generally considered the center of the police response to drug trafficking and use. That operational unit aims directly at the source of the problem and mounts the most sophisticated investigations against drug traffickers. It also accumulates the greatest substantive knowledge about drugs in general and in the local community.

Although the narcotics bureau is at the center of the attack, police strategists must recognize that other operating elements of the police department also confront drug trafficking and use. For example, many police departments have established specialized units to attack organized crime or criminal gangs. These units deal with narcotics trafficking because (1) the organized crime groups or gangs that are their central targets are involved in drug dealing; or (2) they have access to informants who can usefully guide narcotics investigations; or (3) they have specialized equipment that can be used in sophisticated drug investigations.

Regular patrol and investigative units also inevitably attack drug trafficking, use, and related violence. Insofar as their efforts are focused generally on street crime, and insofar as drug users commit a large portion of these crimes, patrol units and detectives wind up arresting a great many drug users. Regular patrol and investigative units also end up arresting some drug users for narcotics offenses such as illegal possession and use of drugs.[13] In most cases, the person arrested will not be on probation or parole and must be tried to be punished. In other cases, however, the drug offenses will constitute probation or parole violations that could result in immediate incarceration if the local court system took such offenses seriously.

The patrol bureau will also be engaged in the fight against drugs as a result of calls from citizens complaining about drug dealing in specific locations. Often, in response to citizen complaints or at the initiative of the chief, special drug task forces will be formed to deal with a particularly threatening or flagrant drug market.[14] These operations draw on patrol forces as well as detective units. Typically, they last for a while and then go out of existence.

Somewhat more specialized are those units committed to drug education. Although drug education seems like a significant departure from the usual objectives and methods of policing, increasingly police departments are establishing such programs to fill a perceived void in this important demand-reducing function.[15]

The point of reviewing these different lines of attack is not only to remind enforcement strategists that a police department's overall strategy against drugs includes far more than the activities of the narcotics bureau, but also to raise an important managerial question: who in the police department will be responsible for designing, executing, and evaluating the department-wide drug control strategy? In some cases, the department will make the head of the narcotics bureau responsible for the broad strategy as well as the narrower operational tasks of the narcotics bureau itself. That has the advantage of aligning responsibility for the strategy with substantive expertise. It has the potential disadvantage of focusing too much of the organization's actions against drugs in the narcotics bureau itself, and of limiting the department's imagination about how it can and should engage the problem.

In other cases, a special staff officer might be assigned the responsibility of coordinating department-wide efforts without necessarily being given any line responsibility over the activities. This has the advantage of drawing more widely on the department's operational capabilities. It has the disadvantages of failing to establish clear operational responsibility and of requiring the collection of additional information throughout the department.

In still other cases, the chief might assume that responsibility. That has the advantages of elevating concern for the problem throughout the organization, of giving the department a powerful representative in dealing with other city departments and community groups, and of aligning operational responsibility with authority. It has the disadvantages of focusing the attention of the chief on only one aspect of the organization's fight against crime and disorder and of moving command further from operations.

## The Community's Resources

Police strategists must also consider that the assets available to attack the drug problem are not limited to the money and legal powers channelled through the police department. The community itself has resources to deploy against drug trafficking and use. Indeed, without the community's own efforts at self-defense, it is hard to see how the police can possibly succeed.

The importance of community self-defense is evident in a review of the spatial distribution of drug dealing across a city. In some areas, drug dealers cannot gain a foothold. There are too few users to make dealing profitable and too many vigilant people ready to expose and resist the enterprise. Other parts of a city seem to have yielded to the drug trade. Drug users are plentiful. Drug dealers are an influential social and economic force. Local residents and merchants have lost heart.

Often, these conditions bear no relationship to the distribution of police resources. The areas that are safe rarely hear a police siren. Those that have yielded to the drug trade are criss-crossed by racing patrol cars with sirens blaring. The reason that little policing sometimes produces safe communities while heavy policing sometimes fails to do so is simply that success in confronting drug trafficking depends as much (or perhaps more) on the community's self-defense than on official police effort. Where community will and capacity for self-defense are strong, a little official policing goes a long way to keep the neighborhood free of drugs. Where it is weak, even heavy doses of official policing will not get the job done.

Exactly what communities do to defend themselves varies greatly according to their character and resources.[16] Most communities start trying to control the drug problem by calling the police to complain about drug dealing. Such calls, if they come through the regular 911 dispatch system rather than a dedicated hotline, are very difficult for the police, as currently organized, to handle. They cannot be handled like robberies and burglaries, for those directly involved in the offense (and therefore able to give useful testimony) are reluctant to do so. Moreover, by the time the police arrive, the activity has ceased or moved to a new location. Because a response to these calls rarely produces a successful case, the calls tend to get shifted back and forth between the patrol division and the narcotics unit.

When citizens cannot command police attention through telephone calls, they do what they can to defend themselves individually. They stay in their houses, buy locks and shutters, and fret about their children. This, of course, makes their neighborhoods more vulnerable to the drug users and dealers.

Sometimes citizens take more aggressive action against drug dealers. They harass drug users and sellers at some risk to themselves. They demonstrate against drug dealing in their neighborhoods to rally others to their cause. They invite groups such as the Guardian Angels or the Nation of Islam to help them regain the upper hand against the dealers.[17] On some occasions, they burn down crack houses.[18]

From the perspective of effectively controlling drug trafficking and use, the police must be enthusiastic about direct citizen action against drug dealing. Such efforts extend the reach of social control over more terrain and longer periods of time than the police could sustain by themselves.

On the other hand, direct citizen action poses new problems for the police. Citizens who directly confront drug dealers and users might be attacked and injured. If this occurs, the failure of the police to protect the community becomes manifest. Fearful of this result and solicitous of the welfare of citizens, the police often advise citizens not to take direct action against dealers and, instead, to leave enforcement to the police.

Another risk is that sharp conflict between drug dealers and citizens escalates into large-scale violence. Part of this risk is that the rights of citizens who are suspected by the community of being drug dealers and users will be abused; that is, they will be beaten, their property taken, their freedom of movement and expression limited. Although such threats are rarely taken as seriously as the physical threats to citizen activists, there comes a point when direct citizen action becomes vigilantism, and when the police, as officers of the law and defenders of the Constitution, must defend the rights of suspected drug dealers against mob hostility.

Finally, the police have an interest in maintaining their position as independent experts in controlling crime problems and as the principal suppliers of security services to the communities they police. To a degree, this can be understood as nothing more than an expression of professional pride and bureaucratic self-interest. But, insofar as the community prefers the restraint, expertise, and professionalism of policing to the risks of direct citizen action, the desire of the police to retain most of the responsibility and initiative for crime control is consistent with the public interest as well as their parochial interests.

While such concerns about the consequences of community action against drugs are entirely appropriate, they cannot lead to the simple conclusion that the police should suppress all such action. They particularly cannot justify this conclusion in a situation where the police have nothing else to provide to the communities that feel outraged and frightened. Instead, the police must find a way of accommodating, regulating, and using citizen indignation to help them manage the drug problem.

A crucial first step in managing the potential partnership with the community is to learn how to diagnose the community's capacity for self-defense. This diagnosis begins with a community's own attitudes and practices regarding drug use.

Although it is discouraging, an enforcement strategist must recognize that parts of communities are interested in continuing and facilitating drug use.[19] They include at least the users and the dealers. They may also include people who make accommodations with drug dealing, such as those who run shooting galleries, landlords who milk the economic value of deteriorating properties by renting to drug users who are indifferent to their living arrangements, and local merchants or police who earn money from drug dealers to provide safe havens for drug dealing.

Others in the community do not profit from drug dealing, but nonetheless have stopped fighting it. This group includes ordinary people who no longer use local parks and streets because they are intimidated by drug dealers and users. It could also include local police officers who conclude that dealing with the local drug trade is like shovelling sand against the tide and turn their attention to less frustrating problems.

Nevertheless, however widespread support for drug use seems to be, every community also contains some significant elements opposed to at least some aspects of drug use. This is particularly hard to keep in mind when the public face of the community—what is occurring on its streets and public places of business—seems openly tolerant. The reality is, however, that behind the shuttered windows of local merchants and in the apartments off the streets, many citizens are outraged and afraid of the drug use in the community. What outrages them may not be the same things that outrage the police or violate the laws, but there is some level of opposition to drug use. That opposition is the asset that needs to be assessed and mobilized.

In thinking about how the police and citizens might reclaim territory from drug trafficking and use, police strategists must anticipate a special problem in helping neighborhoods make transitions from one condition to another. A community that has had a long tradition of being clean may find it relatively easy to maintain its tradition.[20] Such a community is likely to discover a drug problem early because the community is vigilant and the drug problem sticks out. It is likely to respond quickly and aggressively because the problem is both outrageous and small. Drug dealers and users, confirming their prior expectation that the community is inhospitable, will go somewhere else. The probe will be quickly routed.

A community that has had a long tradition of being tolerant of drug dealing has the opposite problem. It may have difficulty in changing its image and condition to one of intolerance. Changes in the level of drug dealing may be difficult to notice because it is so commonplace. The response to a campaign against drugs may be ambivalent because of active opposition by some elements of the community and a sense of despair and futility among the others. Even if an attack is successfully mounted, the dealers and users may view it as a temporary state of affairs. Thus, sustained efforts will not necessarily discourage the dealers and the users.

In confronting drug trafficking and use, then, the task of a police department is often to find a way to prime the community's own capacities for self-defense so that police efforts may be effectively leveraged through community self-help. This involves learning enough about the community to know the sources of support for drug dealing and use in the neighborhoods and the potential opposition. It also means finding ways to reach out to those people in the community who are hostile to drug dealing and to strengthen their hand in dealing with the problem. For example, it may be as important to organize community meetings as to make it easier for individuals to call the police over the phone. It may be more effective to organize and support citizen patrols than to chase the drug dealers from one block to another. It may be more effective to organize groups of parents, educators, and youth leaders to resist drug dealing in and around schools than to increase arrests of drug dealers by 20 percent. In short, drug enforcement may be as much a political struggle to get neighborhoods to oppose drug use in small, informal ways every day as it is a technical law enforcement problem that can be solved by more resources or more sophisticated investigations.

## Alternative Strategies

Police departments rely on many different activities to deal with the drug problem. They conduct sophisticated investigations of trafficking networks. They mount buy and bust operations to suppress open drug dealing. They arrest robbers and burglars who also happen to be drug users. They arrest drug users for illegal possession. They conduct drug education programs in schools.

Most departments do all of these things to some degree. In this sense, departments generally have "comprehensive" approaches to the problem. Departments differ, however, in the overall level of activities they sustain and in the relative emphasis they give to each. Some place greater emphasis on sophisticated investigations, while others stress "user accountability." Departments may also differ in terms of how much thought they have given to deciding on their most important objectives, and in terms of the relationship between the overall objectives and the distribution of the activities.

To help police executives think about how to confront the narcotics problem, we describe seven alternative strategies. The strategies are different from activities not only because they typically involve bundles of activities, but also because each strategy is built upon its own assumption of why the effort is appropriate and valuable to pursue.

## Expressive Law Enforcement: Maximum Arrests for Narcotics Offenses

The most common narcotics enforcement strategy could be described as "expressive law enforcement." This differs from other strategies in that it takes all the activities in which the department is engaged and increases them by a factor of two or three. If a city's drug problem is getting worse, the response is simply to increase the resources devoted to the problem. The operational task is to increase the total number of narcotics arrests. The narcotics bureau is expanded and driven to higher levels of productivity. Special task forces are created to deal with brazen street dealing. The patrol force is equipped and encouraged to make more drug arrests. There is much to commend this strategy. First, it is a straightforward approach that citizens, politicians, and police officers understand. It relies on common sense for its justification. It avoids the trap of being too cute, subtle, or sophisticated.

Second, it is what police departments know how to do—namely, enforce the law. It does not make them responsible for outcomes that they cannot control or for activities that they do not do well.

Third, to the extent that the courts and corrections system do their part, the strategy may succeed in bringing drug trafficking and use under control through the mechanisms of incapacitation and deterrence.

Fourth, the all-out, direct attack on the problem sustains and animates a general social norm hostile to drug use. That emboldens and strengthens the hand of those within the community opposed to drug use.

This strategy also has weaknesses. First, it does not admit that police resources, even when multiplied, may not control the problem. It ignores whether the rest of the system can deliver deserved punishments; disregards the scale and resilience of the drug markets; and fails to establish any benchmarks for success other than the promise of a valiant effort to increase arrests.

Second, this strategy rarely examines its impact on the community's own capacities for self-defense. There is a plausible argument that a strong police commitment to aggressive narcotics law enforcement will strengthen the community's resolve to deal with the problem. Under the expressive enforcement strategy, however, no organizational means are created to build community opposition to drugs. Without such efforts, there is the risk that the police action will weaken rather than strengthen community efforts by suggesting that the community has no role to play. Even worse, unilaterally designed and executed drug enforcement efforts may alienate communities from the police rather than build effective partnerships to control drugs.[21] In short, there is the risk that the expressive law enforcement strategy, effective as it may be in its own terms, will fail to develop, and may even inhibit, the development of the self-defense capacities of the communities that must, in the long run, be the route to success.

## Mr. Big: Emphasis on High-Level Distributors

A second common strategy to deal with drug trafficking and use is the "Mr. Big" strategy. Its principal operational objective is to reach high levels of the drug distribution systems. The primary tactics are sophisticated investigative procedures using wiretaps, informants, and undercover activities. Often these investigations also depend on "loose" money to purchase evidence and information. The "story" that makes this a plausibly effective attack on the problem is that the immobilization of high-level traffickers will produce larger and more permanent results on the drug-trafficking networks than arrests of lower-level, easily replaced figures.

Again, there is much to commend this strategy. It is common sense that the impact of drug enforcement would be greater if it could reach the source of the problem, the criminal entrepreneur whose energy, intelligence, greed, and ruthlessness animate and sustain the drug trade. This seems particularly true if enforcement and punishment capacity is limited, and must therefore be focused on high-priority targets.

It also seems more just to focus society's efforts on those who are becoming rich and powerful through the trade rather than on those lower-level figures. While lower-level dealers are hardly blameless, they are arguably less culpable and less deserving of punishment than the high-level traffickers who are the focus of the Mr. Big strategy.

Finally, the Mr. Big strategy is consistent with the development of professionalism within police departments. The strategy challenges the departments to develop their investigative and intelligence capabilities.

There are reasons to worry about the overall effectiveness of the Mr. Big strategy, however. First, it is not clear that current investigative techniques are powerful enough to reach Mr. Big. The time, resources, and luck needed to arrest him are much greater than those needed to reach intermediate targets; therefore, the admittedly greater impact of arresting Mr. Big may turn out not to be worth the special effort.

A related point concerns overestimating the significance of Mr. Big. There may be almost as many potential Mr. Bigs as there are street-level dealers. There may also be a great deal of turnover in the ranks of drug entrepreneurs. The implication is that the value associated with arresting any given Mr. Big in terms of supply reduction impact may be much less than is usually considered. A further implication is that no one may know who Mr. Big is. Or, if we knew who he was six months ago, the situation may now be different. Thus, the greater difficulty of arresting Mr. Big may not be offset by any larger, long-term impact.

The final point is organizational. While it is true that the Mr. Big strategy will challenge the police to develop professionalism in dealing with drug traffickers and thus increase the overall capabilities of the narcotics bureau, it is also true that this particular focus may lead to the atrophy of narcotics enforcement efforts in other parts of the agency. Other units may decide to leave drug enforcement to the narcotics bureau.

## Gang Strategies

Among the most urgent and oppressive aspects of the current drug problem is the violence of gangs engaged in street-level drug distribution. Some of these groups, like the various "Crip" and "Blood" factions now spreading out from Los Angeles, are formed from traditional youth gangs of the type once romanticized in "West Side Story."[22] Others, like the "posses" of New York's Jamaican neighborhoods, simply began gang life as drug-dealing organizations.[23]

Although violence has always been a feature of drug trafficking, to many observers the current level of violence seems unprecedented. As *The New York Times* reported:

> Older drug rings, wary of drawing police attention, generally avoided conspicuous violence. New York's new gangs, like similar groups in Los Angeles and Washington, are composed mainly of undisciplined teen-agers and youths in their early twenties. They engage in gun battles on the street and have been known to execute customers for not leaving a crack den quickly enough.[24]

Indeed, these gangs are held responsible for significant increases in homicide rates in the cities in which they operate.[25] They use violence not only to discipline their own employees and to intimidate and rob their competitors but also to intimidate individual citizens and groups of citizens who resist their intrusion.[26]

Exactly how the police can best deal with this aspect of the drug problem remains uncertain. One approach is to view drug gangs as similar to the youth gangs of the past and to use the same strategies that proved effective in the past.[27] That older strategy was designed primarily to reduce intergang violence, to prevent the extortion of neighborhood citizens and merchants by the gangs and to minimize the seriousness of the crimes committed by gang members. It was not designed to eliminate the gangs, although some efforts were made to turn them to legitimate and constructive activities. It depended for its success on such activities as establishing liaison with the gangs to communicate police expectations and aggressive police action against gang members, their clubhouses, and their activities when the gangs stepped out of line.

Such a strategy does not seem suitable for dealing with the new drug gangs, however. After all, the old gangs were viewed as threatening to society principally through their violence towards one another. Thus, it was possible for the police to make an accommodation: the gangs could remain intact so long as they refrained from violence. No such accommodation seems appropriate with the drug gangs—particularly not with those that are making places for drug distribution through intimidation of local citizens and merchants. Such conduct requires a sterner response.

A second approach is to view the drug gangs as organized criminal enterprises and to use all of the techniques that have been developed to deal with more traditional organized crime. These include: (1) the development of informants through criminal prosecutions, payments, and witness protection programs; (2) heavy reliance on electronic surveillance and long-term undercover investigations; and (3) the use of special statutes that create criminal liabilities for conspiracy, extortion, or engaging in criminal enterprises.

Such tactics work. They can, if executed consistently, destroy the capacities of organized criminal enterprises.[28] However, such efforts are also time-consuming and expensive. Perhaps these elaborate efforts are not required to deal with the relatively unsophisticated street-level drug gangs. Indeed, in the past, relatively superficial undercover approaches seem to have been successful,[29] as were large-scale sweeps targeted on gang members. What seems to be needed to make police efforts succeed once the gangs have been wounded is the willingness of citizens to resist gang intimidation after the police return to ordinary operations.

## Citywide Street-Level Drug Enforcement

A fourth narcotics enforcement strategy, now widely discussed, can be described as "citywide, street-level drug enforcement." The principal objective is to disrupt open drug dealing by driving it back indoors, or by forcing the markets to move so frequently that buyers and sellers have difficulty finding one another. The primary tactics include buy-and-bust operations, observation sale arrests, and arrests of users who appear in the market to buy drugs.[30] The major reasons to engage in such activities include: (1) enhancing the quality of life in the communities for residents who are discomfited by the presence of drug dealers; and (2) discouraging young, experimental users from continuing to use drugs by making it harder for them to score.[31]

At first glance, the limitations and hazards of this strategy seem more apparent than its strengths. To many law enforcement professionals and commentators, the idea that one would invest the enormous amount of time and effort that continuing street-level enforcement requires for nothing more than increased inconvenience to buyers and sellers of drugs seems absurd. It hardly seems worthwhile to send the police out daily to battle street-level drug dealers to achieve nothing other than market disruptions.[32]

Second, the police know that they have nowhere near enough manpower to work at street levels across the city. Moreover, they are reluctant to begin doing this job in any particular place because they know that once they have committed police to a given area, it will be hard to withdraw them.

Third, police executives know from much prior experience that street-level narcotics enforcement is extremely vulnerable to various forms of corruption. Bribery, perjured testimony, faked evidence, and abused rights in the past have accompanied street-level narcotics enforcement. Indeed, it was partly to avoid such abuses that many police departments began concentrating on higher-level traffickers and restricted drug enforcement efforts to special units.

Fourth, the police know that they can arrest many more drug traffickers and users than the rest of the criminal justice system can process. If the practical value and moral vindication of arrests for drug offenses only come with successful prosecutions and suitable punishment, then street-level enforcement is undermined from the beginning, for there is no reasonable prospect for such results. The likely outcome of most street-level arrests is several weeks in jail prior to trial, a bargained guilty plea, a sentence to time served, and a long period of inadequately supervised probation.[33]

Knowing this, the police can take one of two stances: (1) they can recognize that, for narcotics offenses, the process is the only punishment that offenders are likely to receive and choose to load into the process what they consider a reasonable level of punishment; or (2) they can grow cynical and refuse to make street-level arrests. In either case, a kind of corruption sets in. The least likely response is the only proper one: namely, to continue to maintain discipline and poise in making narcotics arrests on the street.

Against these disadvantages, the advantages of street-level enforcement seem small and speculative. The most certain and concrete is that street-level enforcement can succeed in restoring the quality of life in a community and bring a feeling of hope to the residents. It can regain, for those citizens, merchants, and parents who disapprove of drug use, a measure of control over their immediate environment. It can reassure them that they have not been abandoned in their struggles against drug dealers. It can provide a shield that protects them from the intimidating tactics of aggressive drug dealers. That is no small effect, though it might be hard to quantify.[34]

A second benefit, somewhat more speculative, is that the strategy might well succeed in discouraging experimental drug use, particularly among those teenagers who are not yet deeply involved in drugs.[35] Merely increasing the inconvenience to drug buyers may be little deterrent to experienced and committed drug users. They will have enough connections in the drug trade and enough determination to find alternative sources. This same effect may be a significant deterrent for young, experimental users, however. They have less experience with drugs, hence fewer alternative sources of supply and less motivation to keep searching when open drug markets are no longer available. It is also possible that with open drug bazaars effectively closed, parents and neighbors may feel sufficiently emboldened to exercise greater efforts at home and on the street.

A third benefit is that street-level drug enforcement has, on occasion, been effective in controlling street crimes such as robbery and burglary.[36] A crackdown on heroin markets in Lynn, Massachusetts, seems to have substantially reduced levels of robbery and burglary. Operation Pressure Point directed at drug markets on New York's Lower East Side also seems to have reduced robbery and burglary. A similar effort in Lawrence, Massachusetts, however, failed to produce the expected effects. This benefit must be treated as uncertain partly because of measurement problems in identifying the effect, and partly because it seems that the tactic produces this effect only under some special circumstances.[37] On the other hand, it does provide an additional reason for considering the potential value of street-level drug enforcement.

## Neighborhood Crackdowns

A fifth strategy that the police might consider could be called "neighborhood crackdowns." Instead of committing themselves to citywide street-level enforcement, the police might decide to leverage their resources by cracking down on drug offenses in those neighborhoods that are willing to join the police in resisting drug use. Some of these neighborhoods might be those that are just beginning to be invaded by drug dealers. Others might be those that have long been occupied, but have finally reached a stage where they are now determined to rid their area of drugs. Police resources would be attracted to these areas precisely because there is some prospect that the impact of police crackdowns would be prolonged and widened by determined citizens.

News media coverage of the drug problem, particularly the violence associated with drug dealing, suggests that society is handicapped in dealing with the drug problem by a breakdown in the police-community partnership. Wherever there is an opening in a community's self-defense, aggressive young drug dealers seem to find a niche to develop the demand for crack. Sometimes it is a park that the police do not patrol frequently enough and from which other citizens can be driven. Other times it is an abandoned house that can be turned into a shelter for both dealing and using drugs. Still other times it is an all-but- abandoned building whose owner is willing to have anyone pay the rent, and who does not notice that the new tenants arrive with no furniture or clothes, but lots of guns.

Once established, drug dealers send a message that draws customers and other dealers. Many citizens, finding the company no longer to their liking, begin avoiding crack-dealing locales. Citizens who resist are intimidated. Citizens' groups that complain are also threatened. Occasionally violence breaks out among customers, between dealers and customers, or between competing dealers. The violence accelerates the process of intimidation. Eventually, the drug dealers operate alone.[38]

Citizens cannot deal with these situations by themselves. They need laws and law enforcement to oppose the actions of the drug dealers and consumers and to take action against the landlords (both public and private) who allow the drug dealers to operate in their buildings. They need the police to respond to their calls for assistance—including crackdowns designed to break the backs of the drug dealers and reclaim the territory for those not using drugs. They need the police to offer assurances that citizens who resist the drug dealers will be protected from attacks.

It is also clear, however, that the police cannot do this job alone. They have only a certain number of officers and many other duties. Drug cases are hard to make and vulnerable to legal challenges. Police can conduct special operations, but eventually they must leave neighborhoods in the hands of citizens. At that time, whether the drug dealers return or not depends a great deal on what citizens do.

If this analysis is correct, a strategy that uses police crackdowns to break the hold of drug dealing in communities that are prepared to assume some responsibility for holding onto the gains might make sense. The police could conserve resources by focusing on only a limited number of areas for relatively short periods of time. The community, working with the police, could shape a police intervention that would be most effective in helping them reclaim their streets. Each would know what would be expected of the other.

The results would be the same as those anticipated in a citywide, street-level drug enforcement strategy: namely, an improved quality of life in the city, reduced experimentation with drugs among young people, and conceivably even reduced street crime in those neighborhoods that succeeded in keeping drugs out.

Just such efforts seem to lie behind the most successful cases of drug enforcement. In one particular case in Brooklyn, a neighborhood invaded by drugs managed to drive out the drug dealing by enlisting police efforts to close the buildings that were used for drug dealing, and then mounting patrols through a local branch of the Nation of Islam.[39] The police were willing to put resources on the line to go after the problem with an aggressive approach that was discussed in advance with the community. The community was prepared to try to hold onto the gains by taking disciplined action on their own that stopped well short of vigilantism. The police promised to back up the citizen groups in the future if their vigilance, now refined by prior experience, revealed a major new incursion of drug dealers.

The nature of the strategy is captured well by the testimony of two participants. The local police commander commented:

> I think the patrols are going well. We now have almost nonexistent drug activity in the locations that had been hard-core drug areas. This is a good example of what the police and the community can do together.[40]

One of the patrolling citizens also gave grudging support to the concept:

> We still believe there are problems with the police, with racism and corruption within the department. But we feel we can solve the problems together. We learned a lot of lessons during this. The price you have to pay to fight against drugs is ongoing struggle. We had to pay the price by standing in the cold and rain without pay. But the most interesting thing, I think, is that this has given people hope. Apparently, partnerships are hard and chancy enterprises, but when they succeed, they are worth a great deal.[41]

## Controlling Drug-Using Dangerous Offenders

The drug strategies that have been discussed so far have been primarily focused on drug trafficking and use. They are designed to produce arrests for narcotics offenses rather than for street crimes such as robbery, burglary, and assault. This is not to say that drug enforcement strategies have no effect on these crimes. Relationships between drug use and crime are so strong that when the police affect drug trafficking and use, they probably affect street crimes as well. The effect is indirect rather than direct, however.

This suggests a drug enforcement strategy designed to achieve *crime control* rather than *drug control* objectives. Such a strategy would focus enforcement attention on those drug users who are committing large numbers of robberies and burglaries.[42] Studies show that drug users account for a large proportion of those arrested for these crimes and that they are among the most active and dangerous offenders.[43] Further, levels of criminal activity among heroin users are known to be higher when they are using heroin than when they are not.[44] It stands to reason, then, that the police might affect a significant portion of the crime problem by controlling the drug use of those active offenders who are heavily involved with drugs.

The principal operational objectives of this strategy would be: (1) to arrest and convict drug-using criminal offenders for either narcotics offenses or street crimes such as robbery and burglary; (2) to identify such offenders after arrest through a combination of criminal record searches, physical examination for needle marks, urinalysis in the jails, and interviews; and (3) to sentence these offenders to dispositions that work directly on their drug consumption such as intensive probation with mandatory regular urinalysis or compulsory drug treatment.

The primary activities of the police department would be to continue making arrests for narcotics and street offenses, improve the records that would allow them to identify the dangerous offenders among the arrested population, and lobby for the development of urinalysis, intensive probation, and mandatory treatment capabilities. The important claim that can be made for this strategy is that it would address the primary reason that citizens worry about drugs, namely drug-related crime, and would do so more effectively, cheaply, and humanely than approaches that rely only on repeated arrests and costly jails to produce the same effects.

There is a reasonable amount of evidence indicating that this approach would work. In California, mandatory treatment programs for drug users are effective in controlling both crime and drug use, both while the person remains under supervision and afterwards.[45] There are also some reasons to believe that coerced abstinence, imposed as a condition of probation and parole and enforced through a system of mandatory urinalysis, can be effective in reducing street crime.[46]

The strategy would also have benefits for organizational development. It would challenge police departments to reach outside their own boundaries, and outside the boundaries of the criminal justice system, to produce the desired effects. Prosecutors, judges, and corrections officials would have to be persuaded of the merits of the strategy.[47] The drug treatment community would also have to be mobilized, their capacity expanded, and their attention focused on the objective of crime control as well as improving the health of users. Perhaps the most challenging aspect of this strategy, however, is that it would require the police to consider the possibility that their primary interest in controlling drug-related street crime could be achieved more directly, surely, and inexpensively by close supervision on the street rather than by the enormously expensive process of repeated arrests, jail, and imprisonment.

The limitations of this strategy are the opposite sides of its strengths. It does little by itself to suppress drug trafficking or to discourage the spread of drug use, except insofar as it succeeds in suppressing the demand for drugs among those users brought into the network of coerced treatment. Moreover, it seems to reduce police control over the problem by forcing them to rely on cooperation with others to produce the desired effects. Finally, it does not seem like a suitable law enforcement approach to the problem. There is not enough punishment and jail to satisfy those who think that effective law enforcement by itself will be enough to deal with the problem. For these reasons, the police have generally neither adopted nor supported such strategies.

## Protect and Insulate the Youth

A final police strategy for dealing with drugs could be built around the objective of drug abuse prevention. Instead of generally attacking drug trafficking, a police department might concentrate on trying to halt the spread of drug abuse to the next cohort of 16-year-olds. Part of this effort would consist of enforcement operations to suppress drug trafficking around and within schools. Another part might consist of police-sponsored drug education designed not only to impart information about drugs and discourage drug use, but also to create a favorable climate for police efforts to suppress drug trafficking. A third part might consist of police-sponsored efforts to create partnerships among parents, schools, and the police to define the outer limits of acceptable drug use and to establish a predictable community response to drugs.

The country now has operating experience with each of these elements. New Jersey has made a concerted effort to mount enforcement operations in and around schools to disrupt the trafficking networks that serve high school students.[48] The Los Angeles Police Department's DARE program has shown the potential of involving police in drug education programs in the schools and has been widely emulated throughout the country.[49] Massachusetts has experimented with establishing community partnerships to confront children with a consistent set of messages about drug use. None of these approaches has been systematically evaluated, however. Nor do we have any documented experience with combining the different approaches in a concerted strategy to prevent new drug use. Thus, the potential of this strategy remains uncertain.

# Conclusion

Drug trafficking, use, and associated violence challenge today's police executives to find ways of using the limited resources and capabilities of their departments to reduce the violence, halt the spread of drug use, and control drug-related crime. Moreover, they must do so while protecting the integrity of their own organizations and the legal system.

Past approaches that have relied only on police resources seem to be limited in their ability to achieve any of society's important goals in this domain. To reclaim neighborhoods now yielding to drug use, police must find ways to mobilize and use community opposition to drugs. That the opposition to drugs exists is evident in the willingness of many citizens to take direct action against drug dealers. This adds urgency to the task of thinking through a strategy that builds effective partnerships, for it suggests not only that a resource is available to the police, but also that failing to harness it effectively may compound the problem by inciting vigilantism.

It also seems clear that successful approaches to the problem will rely on enlisting the assistance of other public agencies. For dealing with drug-related crime, the urinalysis and supervisory capacities of out-patient drug treatment programs might turn out to be valuable. To prevent the spread of drugs to new cohorts of teenagers, cooperation with schools and parents is essential.

Thus, to a degree, the drug problem requires first-rate professional law enforcement. Quality arrests for drug offenses are an important part of all police strategies. Great investigative sophistication, and no small amount of force, are required to deal with the traditional organized crime groups and the emergent gangs that now dominate the trade.

Yet it is also true that drug trafficking and use represent a problem that must be addressed through remedies other than arrests and through agencies other than police. The police can play an important role in strengthening neighborhood self-defense capacities by cooperating with local demands rather than suppressing or ignoring them. They can play an important role in mobilizing parents and schools. And they might even succeed in focusing the attention of drug treatment programs on their great opportunity to reduce crime as well as achieve other purposes.

In this domain, as well as in dealing with crime and fear, the methods of problem-solving and community policing combine with the methods of professional law enforcement to produce a perspective and a set of results that neither can produce by itself.

# Notes

[1] William G. Blair, "Study urges new measures to combat drugs," *The New York Times*, March 8, 1987. Jeffrey Yorke, "Pr. George's homicides soar," *The Washington Post*, November 16, 1987. Matt Lait, "The battle to control 50,000 gang members on the streets of Los Angeles," *The Washington Post*, March 12, 1988. George James, "Crime totals confirm fears in Queens," *The New York Times*, April 21, 1988.

[2] "Juvenile gangs: Crime and drug trafficking," *Juvenile Justice Bulletin*, Washington, D.C., Office of Juvenile Justice and Delinquency Prevention, September 1988. Cheryl Carpenter, Barry Glassner, Bruce D. Johnson, and Julia Loughlin, *Kids, Drugs, and Crime*, Lexington, Massachusetts, D.C. Heath, 1988. Robert Reinhold, "Gangs selling crack give rise to new wild west," *The New York Times*, June 21, 1988. Sam Roberts, "Ask not for whom the beeper tolls," *The New York Times*, June 2, 1988.

[3] "Juvenile gangs: Crime and drug trafficking," n. 2 above.

[4] Douglas M. Anglin and George Stenkert, "Narcotics use and crime: a multi-sample multi-method analysis," *Criminology*, Spring 1988. John A. Carver, "Drugs and crime: controlling use and reducing risk through testing," *Research in Action*, Washington, D.C., National Institute of Justice, 1986. Mark A. R. Kleiman, "Crackdowns: the effects of intensive enforcement on retail heroin dealing," in *Street-Level Drug Enforcement: Examining the Issues*, ed. Marcia R. Chaiken, Washington, D.C., National Institute of Justice, August 1988. David N. Nurco, John C. Ball, John W. Schaffer, and Thomas E. Hanlon, "The criminality of narcotic addicts," *Journal of Nervous and Mental Disease* 173, 2 (1985): 94–102. Mary A. Toborg and Michael P. Kirby, "Drug Use and Pretrial Crime in the District of Columbia," *Research in Brief*, Washington, D.C., National Institute of Justice, October 1984. Eric D. Wish, "Drug use in arrestees in Manhattan: the dramatic increase in cocaine from 1984 to 1986," New York, Narcotic and Drug Research, Inc., 1987.

[5] John C. Ball, Lawrence Rosen, John A. Flueck, and David N. Nurco, "The criminality of heroin addicts when addicted and when off opiates," in *The Drug-Crime Connection*, ed. James A. Inciardi, Sage Annual Reviews of Drug and Alcohol Abuse 5, 1981.

[6] National Institute of Justice, *Drug Use Forecasting (DUF)*, May 1988.

[7] Jan Chaiken and Marcia Chaiken, *Varieties of Criminal Behavior*, Santa Monica, RAND Corporation, 1982.

[8] Peter Kerr, "Addiction's hidden toll: poor families in turmoil," *The New York Times*, June 23, 1988. Felicia R. Lee, "Breaking up families, crack besieges a court," *The New York Times*, February 9, 1989.

[9] Ronald F. Ferguson, "The drug problem in black communities," Report to the Ford Foundation, working paper #87-01-01, Program in Criminal Justice Policy and Management, John F. Kennedy School of Government, Harvard University, Cambridge, October 1987.

[10] Peter Manning, *The Narc's Game*, Cambridge, Massachusetts, MIT Press, 1980. James J. Collins and Jay R. Williams, "Police narcotics control: patterns and strategies," Research Triangle Park, North Carolina, Research Triangle Institute, RTI Project No. RTI/1302/00-01F, May 1978.

[11] Lynn Zimmer, "Operation Pressure Point: the disruption of street-level drug trade on New York's Lower East Side," Occasional Papers from the Center for Research in Crime and Justice, New York University School of Law, 1987.

[12] Gary T. Marx, *Undercover: Police Surveillance in America*, Berkeley and Los Angeles, University of California Press, 1988. Lawrence W. Sherman, ed., *Police Corruption: A Sociological Perspective*, Garden City, New York, Anchor Press, 1974.

[13] For 1986, there was a national total of 691,882 reported arrests for drug abuse violations. See Bureau of Justice Statistics, *Sourcebook of Criminal Justice Statistics 1987*, ed. Timothy J. Flanagan and Katherine M. Jamieson, Washington, D.C., U.S. Government Printing Office, 1988.

[14] Mark A. R. Kleiman, "Crackdowns," n. 4 above.

[15] Daryl F. Gates, "Project DARE—a challenge to arm our youth," *The Police Chief* 54, 10 (October 1987). Evaluation and Training Institute (ETI), "DARE longitudinal evaluation annual report 1987–88," Los Angeles, July 1988.

[16] Wesley G. Skogan and Michael G. Maxfield, *Coping with Crime: Individual and Neighborhood Reactions*, v. 124, Beverly Hills, California, Sage Publications, 1981. Wesley G. Skogan, "Fear of crime and neighborhood change," in *Communities and Crime*, ed. Albert J. Reiss, Jr., and Michael Tonry, *Crime and Justice* 8, Chicago, University of Chicago Press, 1986.

[17] William K. Stevens, "Muslim patrols fight Capital drug trade," *The New York Times*, April 24, 1988. Sari Horwitz and James Rupert, "Calm returns as police, Muslims patrol in NE," *The Washington Post*, April 29, 1988. Peter Kerr, "Citizen anti-crack drive: vigilance or vigilantism," *The New York Times*, May 23, 1988. Steven Erlanger, "The new show off Broadway: 46th Street," *The New York Times*, June 15, 1988.

[18] Isabel Wilkerson, "Crack house fire: justice or vigilantism," *The New York Times*, October 22, 1988.

[19] Ronald F. Ferguson, "The drug problem in black communities," n. 9 above.

[20] James Q. Wilson and George L. Kelling, "Broken windows," *The Atlantic*, March 1982.

[21] See Philadelphia example cited in Mark A. R. Kleiman, "Crackdowns," n. 4 above.

[22] *Juvenile Justice Bulletin*. "Juvenile gangs . . .," n. 2 above.

[23] Linda Wheeler and Keith Harriston, "Jamaican gangs wage war over drugs, area police say," *The Washington Post*, November 19, 1987.

[24] Selwyn Raab, "The ruthless young crack dealers," *The New York Times*, March 20, 1988.

[25] Blair, Yorke, Lait, and James, newspaper stories cited n. 1 above.

[26] Eric Schmitt, "On a corner in North Amityville, a reign of crack and violence," *The New York Times*, October 13, 1987. Peter Kerr, "Crushing the drug dealers of Washington Square," *The New York Times*, November 9, 1987. Jane Gross, "Weathering the crack storms in Queens," *The New York Times*, March 21, 1988.

[27] For discussion of older gang strategy, see Richard A. Cloward and Lloyd E. Ohlin, *Delinquency and Opportunity—A Theory of Delinquent Gangs*, Glencoe, Illinois, Free Press, 1960.

[28] For full account of successful FBI attacks on organized crime (the Cosa Nostra case), see *Organized Crime 25 Years After Valachi: Hearings Before the Permanent Subcommittee on Investigations*, Senate Hearing 100–906, Washington, D.C., U.S. Government Printing Office, April 1988.

[29] For accounts of undercover and plainclothes successes, see Peter Kerr, "Drug dealers of Washington Square," n. 26, and Michael Wines, "Against drug tide, only a holding action," *The New York Times*, June 24, 1988.

[30] Mark H. Moore, *Buy and Bust: The Effective Regulation of an Illicit Market in Heroin*, Lexington, Massachusetts, D.C. Heath, 1976.

[31] Mark A. R. Kleiman, "Crackdowns," n. 4 above.

[32] Anthony V. Bouza, "Evaluating street-level drug enforcement," in *Street-Level Drug Enforcement*, ed. Marcia R. Chaiken, n. 4 above.

[33] Lynn Zimmer, "Operation Pressure Point . . .," n. 11 above.

[34] Benjamin Ward, comments at the fourth meeting of the Executive Session on Community Policing, Program in Criminal Justice Policy and Management, John F. Kennedy School of Government, Harvard University, Cambridge, November 21, 1986.

[35] Mark H. Moore, "Policies to achieve discrimination in the effective price of heroin," *American Economic Review*, May 1973.

[36] Mark A. R. Kleiman, "Crackdowns," n. 4 above.

[37] Kleiman, above, and see Arnold Barnett, "Drug crackdowns and crime rates: a comment on the Kleiman report," also in *Street-Level Drug Enforcement*, ed. Marcia Chaiken.

[38] See Schmitt and Gross, both n. 26 above; also, Reinhold, n. 2 above.

[39] Patrice Gaines-Carter and John Mintz, "Muslims nurture legacy of power," *The Washington Post*, April 20, 1988; also Kerr, "Citizen anti-crack drive," n. 17 above.

[40] Thomas Morgan, "Muslim patrol helps cut crime in Brooklyn," *The New York Times*, February 25, 1988.

[41] Morgan, n. 40 above.

[42] International Association of Chiefs of Police and Bureau of Justice Assistance, *Reducing Crime by Reducing Drug Abuse: A Manual for Police Chiefs and Sheriffs*, Washington, D.C., Bureau of Justice Assistance and U.S. Drug Enforcement Administration, June 1988.

[43] National Institute of Justice, *Drug Use Forecasting* (DUF). Jan Chaiken and Marcia Chaiken, *Varieties of Criminal Behavior*, n. 7 above.

[44] Ball et al., "Criminality of heroin addicts . . .," n. 5 above.

[45] Carl Lukefield and Frank Tims, eds., *Compulsory Treatment of Drug Abuse: Research and Clinical Practice*, NIDA Research Monograph #86, Washington, D.C., National Institute on Drug Abuse, 1988.

[46] For discussions of experiences and problems with implementing drug testing, see: John A. Carver, "Drugs and crime," *Research in Action*, n. 4; Mark A. R. Kleiman, "Heroin crackdowns in two Massachusetts cities: executive summary," Working Paper #89-01-15, Program in Criminal Justice Policy and Management, John F. Kennedy School of Government, Harvard University, Cambridge, March 1989. For a proposal to control crime through the use of intensively supervised probation and urine testing, see: Mark A. R. Kleiman, Mary Ellen Lawrence, and Aaron Saiger, "A drug enforcement program for Santa Cruz County," Working Paper #88-01-13, Program in Criminal Justice Policy and Management, John F. Kennedy School of Government, August 1987.

[47] IACP/BJA, *Manual for Police Chiefs and Sheriffs*, n. 42 above.

[48] Joseph F. Sullivan, "Jersey takes drug effort into schools," *The New York Times*, January 3, 1988.

[49] Gates, "Project DARE"; Evaluation and Training Institute, "DARE longitudinal evaluation," both n. 15.

# 12

# Proactive Policing Against Street-Level Drug Trafficking

## Lynn Zimmer

## Introduction

Studies of the police have failed to identity any strategies guaranteed effective in reducing crime, and a number of scholars now agree that the mere expansion of traditional policing techniques will have little or no impact on crime rates; they argue that if police departments are to respond more effectively to both crime and citizen fear of crime, they must develop new strategies of policing. Jerome Skolnick and David Bayley (1986), for example, have suggested that urban police departments free more personnel from the reactive mode of operation—where officers respond to criminal "events" as they occur—and deploy them proactively in response to chronic criminal "situations" that exist in specific neighborhoods. Skolnick and Bayley examined a number of innovative strategies being used around the country and concluded that, in spite of shortcomings, they offer a useful and exciting addition to traditional methods of policing.

Reprinted by permission from the *American Journal of Police*, Vol. 9, No. 1, pp. 43–74, 1990. Published by Anderson Publishing Co., Cincinnati.

The New York City Police Department has recently developed a number of special proactive operations, designed to supplement its predominantly reactive system. This paper will describe and evaluate Operation Pressure Point (OPP), a project created to disrupt the drug traffic which had, for several years, been expanding on the streets of Manhattan's Lower East Side. Data for this analysis were obtained through examination of police reports and documents, as an observer on patrol with OPP forces during the summer of 1985, and in extensive, open-ended interviews with community members, drug users, drug treatment personnel, police administrators, and rank-and-file police officers from the Lower East Side.

## Operation Pressure Point as an Innovative Police Strategy

The multifaceted role of the police prevents any complete classification of policing strategies, but two dichotomous schemes of police work are useful for comparing more traditional policing strategies with recent innovations. James Q. Wilson (1968) has categorized police work as oriented toward either "order maintenance" or "crime control;" Albert Reiss (1971) has classified police interventions as either "proactive" or "reactive." Every police department utilizes both proactive and reactive interventions, oriented toward both order maintenance and crime control, but over the last several decades, most urban police departments have emphasized reactive crime-control strategies, hoping they would help in the fight against serious crime. Today, more proactive order-maintenance tactics such as those outlined by Skolnick and Bayley (1986) are being tried as police departments around the country renew their effort to fight some of the criminal "situations" which have proven resistant to strictly crime-control methods.

Fighting serious crime and catching criminals have always been crucial aspects of policing, but before the mid-1960s or so, order-maintenance was an important function as well. Police officers often worked particular neighborhoods for an extended period and helped to enforce community standards of conduct through both moral authority and the arrest of persons engaging in "disreputable" behavior. According to James Q. Wilson and George Kelling (1982:34), "the objective was order, an inherently ambiguous term but a condition that people in a given neighborhood recognized when they saw it."

Maintaining orderly neighborhoods involved proactive, more than reactive, intervention strategies. Rather than waiting for specific complaints from citizens about undesirable or criminal conduct, police officers patrolled the streets and monitored the behavior of persons assumed most likely to violate community standards—strangers, youth, drunks and the like. The police might have requested that such persons alter their behavior or leave the neighborhood, requests that the police could back up with an arrest on charges of vagrancy, drunkenness or disorderly conduct.

There are a number of reasons why the order-maintenance function lost ground to a crime-control orientation in the mid-1960s. For one, the rate of serious crime in the country began to rise, a trend that would continue into the 1980s. Several presidential commissions appointed to study the crime problem consistently pointed to police reform as an important component of any crime-reduction package.[1] Police scholars called for increased profession-alism (Saunders, 1970; President's Commission, 1967b), greater utilization of scientific and technological advances (Clark, 1970; President's Commission, 1967c), and improvements in police response time (President's Commission, 1967), all suggestions oriented toward catching criminals for specific crimes rather than maintaining orderly neighborhoods. Several researchers even sug-gested that the service and order-maintenance functions of the police be turned over to less highly trained personnel, freeing police resources for the fight against serious crime (Cumming et al., 1965, Garmire, 1972; Palmer, 1973; President's Commission, 1967b). This official separation of function did not occur, but most police departments did begin to more systematically dis-patch patrol cars on the basis of the seriousness of a call, a process facilitated by adoption of centralized reporting (often through a 911 system). The National Advisory Commission on Criminal Justice Standards and Goals (1973) urged that special attention be paid to the society's five most serious crimes: homicide, rape, assault, robbery and burglary. The kind of disreputa-ble behavior handled (often informally) within the order-maintenance role was automatically given a low priority in this fight against serious crime, espe-cially as police resources were stretched thin during the urban fiscal crisis of the 1970s.

Order maintenance also suffered with the more general demise of the neighborhood cop during this period. The focus on crime fighting and rapid response time required a mobile police force, unattached to specific commu-nities, allowing officers to respond to reports of serious crime over a wide geographical area. The removal of police officers from regular neighborhood beats was also encouraged by efforts to solve the problem of police corrup-tion (McNamara, 1976; Walker, 1977; Gardiner, 1970). By breaking the close bond between officers and those they policed, law enforcement officials hoped to prevent the charges of corruption that had scandalized several large departments during the 1970s (Goldstein, 1975; Sherman, 1974; Knapp Com-mission, 1972). Removed from daily contact with specific neighborhoods, patrol officers thus lost both the opportunity and motivation to enforce the standards of conduct critical to order maintenance.

The order-maintenance role of the police also became highly politicized during this period. By its very nature, the enforcement of "community standards" requires the police to accept the legitimacy of some citizens' standards over others, and especially in communities divided on the basis of class, race or ethnicity, this can exacerbate, rather than soothe, neighborhood tensions and open the door to charges of discrimination against the police. In some communities, proactive, order-maintenance policing defined the police as an "occupying army" (Wilson, 1972; Silberman, 1978; Rubinstein, 1973), one that may have contributed to the eruption of ghetto riots in the late 1960s (Jacob, 1980; National Advisory Commission on Civil Disorders, 1967). This was simply not a good time for the police to perform a function that required consensus over standards of conduct. Not surprisingly, during this period of turmoil the police willingly withdrew from the communities they served and relinquished order maintenance in favor of a more legalistic, crime-fighting orientation.

The ascendancy of the crime-fighting model—responding to serious crime as it is reported—led automatically to a decrease in proactive policing. Proactive strategies continued to be used, especially in the battle against vice crime (gambling, prostitution, drug trafficking), but such enforcement was largely taken away from regular patrol forces and placed within separate units that, freed from the reactive system, could investigate them more efficiently and could, themselves, be monitored more closely for signs of corruption (Jacob, 1984). The duties of the patrol force, the largest proportion of officers in all departments, became more and more devoted to roving patrol, with cars dispatched to the scene of a crime in response to an incoming call.

It is this general model of policing—professional, highly bureaucratized, technological, legalistic, and impersonal—that was urged by numerous police researchers, reformers, and government commissions over the last few decades. It is also a model that many now realize has failed to reduce crime or the fear of crime substantially (Silberman, 1978; Skolnick & Bayley, 1986; MacGillis, 1983; Wilson, 1985). James Q. Wilson and George Kelling (1982) have urged a return to the order-maintenance function, not only because citizens want more orderly neighborhoods, but because disorder itself, beginning with the "broken window" left unattended, creates an environment in which serious crime can occur more easily. Others have suggested that more police resources be devoted to proactive policing strategies which attack specific crime problems rather than crime in general; Herman Goldstein (1979) calls for "problem-oriented" policing, James Q. Wilson (1985) for "crime-specific" policing, and Ronald Clarke (1983) and Engstad and Evans (1980) for "situational" policing. David Farmer (1984) advocates allocation of police resources by neighborhood, or even by street, in response to the crime problems that plague certain areas.

In the 1980s, the crime problem that plagued many inner-city neighbor-hoods was street-level drug trafficking. As traditional efforts to reduce both the supply of drugs and the demand for drugs failed, public officials increasingly advocated that more law enforcement dollars be deployed proactively, to "take back the streets" from drug buyers and sellers. Operation Pressure Point (OPP) is an early example of this type of innovative, community-oriented intervention against drug trafficking: an aggressive, proactive strategy with both crime-fighting and order-maintenance goals. By disrupting the sale of drugs on the streets of the Lower East Side (a crime itself), the police were also hoping that OPP would decrease drug-related crime, particularly the robberies, burglaries, and violence associated with the drug trade.[2] At the same time, OPP was an order-maintenance strategy, oriented toward improving the quality of life in the community as a whole and enforcing the standards of conduct of the increasingly affluent population that had gradually begun to move into the area. After more than three years of Pressure Point, drug trafficking became much less visible (and almost disappeared in some sections); the official crime rate declined; and people in the community began to feel more comfortable using many of the parks and public areas that were once "owned" by drug sellers, buyers, and other "undesirables." The Lower East Side was far from transformed into an orderly, crime-free community, and the changes which occurred may not be permanent, but the changes were substantial and speak well for the potential of proactive, crime-specific policing to relieve particular communities of particular forms of crime. This does not mean that similar operations would necessarily work as well in the other communities. The following sections will describe OPP in more detail, focusing on its accomplishments, its limitations, and the dilemmas it created for the police.

## Creation of Operation Pressure Point

By the early 1980s open drug dealing on city streets had become a fact of urban life (Beschner & Brower, 1985; Hanson, 1985). On New York's Lower East Side the commerce had become so conspicuous that the area gained a local reputation as a "drug supermarket" and a national reputation as "the most open heroin market in the nation."[3] Police videotapes taken before OPP show long lines of double-parked cars, hundreds of people milling around waiting to purchase heroin and cocaine, sellers shouting out the "brand names"[4] and prices of their drugs, and others openly advertising "works"—hypodermic needles—guaranteed clean for two or three dollars. Enterprising young men and women sometimes searched the crowd, looking for novice customers who might be willing to pay to have someone else "score" for them. When long lines formed behind dealers, waiting buyers at the end of the line were sometimes offered "express service," for a fee. On some blocks, vendors set up their carts, selling hot dogs and sodas to the crowd; portable radios competed with the shouting. The unaware might have thought, for a moment, that they had stumbled upon a block party or street festival.[5]

The Lower East Side of Manhattan has a long history as a "port of entry" neighborhood, having housed the steady stream of immigrants coming into the country during the nineteenth and early twentieth centuries. It was once the location of a variety of poor but fairly stable ethnic communities. By the 1980s, however, the area had been undergoing several decades of decay and decline, as the housing stock deteriorated and many second- and third-generation Americans moved into more middle-class communities. As the local population declined, businesses left the area and entire blocks of old tenements were destroyed, burned out, or simply abandoned, providing an ideal location for expansion of a drug trade that had been there for a long time. Empty buildings were turned into drug warehouses, storefront selling operations, and shooting galleries. Empty streets meant an absence of people to complain about the expanding trafficking in drugs.

At the same time the drug traffic was expanding on the Lower East Side, police attention to street drug trading was declining, in part because of budget cutbacks and decrease in police personnel (Smith, 1984). Between 1976 and 1984 there was a 29 percent decrease in uniformed officers in New York City as a whole, from approximately 24,000 to about 17,000. The Lower East Side precincts[6] fared even worse, going from 733 officers to 492—a decrease of 33 percent.[7] During this same period, the overall crime rate rose substantially,[8] and in an effort to deploy personnel in response to serious crimes, the police gave citizen complaints of drug dealing on the streets a low priority not only on the Lower East Side, but elsewhere in the city as well.[9] The Narcotics Division, devoted to drug enforcement, also lost personnel during this period and, after 1970, began to focus most of its resources on long-term investigations of the high-level distribution system rather than street-level sales (Belenko, 1981). After 1970, a year in which the New York City police made over 50,000 drug-related arrests, the number of drug arrests declined sharply, and for the years 1973 to 1980 averaged between 17,000 and 18,000 (Belenko, 1981). With the waning risk of arrest and prosecution, street-level dealers were able to expand their operations, and as the volume of drug dealing increased, police effectiveness decreased even further. Patrol forces made occasional one-day "sweeps" through the area, making large numbers of arrests, but any individual's chance of arrest remained small. Drug traffic was hardly interrupted, returning to "normal" the following day.

The inability of the police to enforce the law made the Lower East Side particularly attractive to drug buyers. There was already a substantial population of drug users living in the neighborhood where, as in other poor urban areas, heroin use had become more prevalent after World War II (Chein et al., 1964; Waldorf, 1973; Johnson & Lipton 1984). In the 1970s, as the area lost population and began to deteriorate, drug users from elsewhere may have migrated to the Lower East Side, attracted by low rents or the opportunity to live rent-free in one of the growing number of abandoned buildings. This resident-user population provided a ready market for drug sellers and provided the supply of street-level workers necessary for expansion of the drug trade.

The Lower East Side also became an increasingly attractive market for drug consumers who lived outside the area. The area had a reputation for particularly high quality drugs, with higher potency than those available elsewhere in the city (Goldstein et al. 1984). Small-time dealers could reportedly buy drugs on the Lower East Side and, by cutting and reselling them, quickly turn a profit in another district.[10] Individual drug users from other parts of the city and from neighboring states also came to the Lower East Side because it was easily accessible and anonymous. Numerous bridges and tunnels connect lower Manhattan with Brooklyn, Long Island, Staten Island, and New Jersey, making it easy to enter and exit. And because of its ethnic mix, the Lower East Side may have been particularly attractive to out-of-town white buyers who were reluctant to frequent open drug markets in predominantly black areas like Harlem.

For a variety of reasons, then, the Lower East Side was ripe for expansion of the drug trade. Dealers became increasingly blatant, gradually spreading into occupied as well as abandoned blocks, and the area's reputation as a buyer's paradise, offering little threat of arrest and no need for an established connection, rapidly grew. The situation was clearly beyond the capacity of the regular precinct forces to solve, and even the permanent assignment of several Special Narcotic Enforcement Units (SNEUs) to the Lower East Side precincts in 1982 was a matter of "too little, too late." Many officers no doubt felt the frustration and resignation voiced by an officer who had spent nearly thirty years policing the Lower East Side:

> There was nothing we could do. There were some blocks in the precinct that I avoided as much as possible because it was embarrassing to see them; it was embarrassing to be a police officer and see the law broken in front of your eyes and know there was nothing you could do.

The people involved in the drug scene appreciated the impotence of the police. A drug user who occasionally worked on the streets reported:

> There was nothing the police could do. There were more of us than there were of them and for every seller they arrested, there were ten people waiting to take his place on the street. The police were more of a nuisance than anything. I'd think "like, why do they bother coming out here at all?"

Many people in the community had also given up hope that their streets could be recaptured. One long-time resident said:

> I had totally stopped complaining to the police. Every time I called, they said they'd send a car, but I'd seldom see one. Many of my neighbors had moved out, but I had no place to go. There was no choice but to just live with it, day after day, and stay indoors as much as possible.

Not everyone accepted the situation as hopeless, however, and in the early 1980s a number of citizen groups formed on the Lower East Side to confront the problem. In 1983, one such group began to hold monthly candlelight vigils on some of the most drug-infested street corners.[11] They also organized several protest marches, including one that ended at the mayor's residence. Eventually, the media were aroused, and New York newspapers and local television stations ran a series of exposés. *The New York Daily News*, for example, ran a cover story entitled "Is This Any Place for Children?" with a picture of day-care workers and children walking past junkies.[12] Several local politicians, who had for years been fielding the complaints of Lower East Side residents, also voiced outrage. Some residents cynically attributed the politicians' response to pressure generated by real estate interests as certain Lower East Side blocks, after decades of decline, were beginning to show the early signs of gentrification.[13]

Early in 1984, the New York Police Department responded to these various community and political pressures by launching Operation Pressure Point (OPP), a massive police initiative involving the deployment of over 240 additional officers into the high-drug areas of the Lower East Side. Operation Pressure Point was the brainchild of New York's new police commissioner, Benjamin Ward, a man who came into office especially concerned about the problem of drugs and committed to implementing a more community-oriented approach to policing.[14] Operation Pressure Point fit well into Ward's agenda and gave him a highly visible and newsworthy project with which to begin his administration.

## The Operation

Operation Pressure Point forces moved into the Lower East Side with strength and confidence, quickly establishing an imposing police presence in the community. The team was made up primarily of uniformed patrol officers, many just out of the police academy, who swept through the streets, mostly on foot, dispersing the crowds, giving out parking tickets, conducting searches, and making arrests. Extra officers assigned from the Housing Police and the Transit Police used similar tactics on the grounds of the public housing projects and in subway stations within the Pressure Point area. In the first few weeks, mounted police rode through and cleared the parks, and the canine unit was used to empty out the abandoned buildings which had been turned into drug warehouses and shooting galleries. The Organized Crime Control Bureau (OCCB) conducted hidden surveillance operations and engaged in "buy and bust" arrests. Police helicopters sometimes hovered overhead, watching the rooftops for possible counterattacks against the police.

Operation Pressure Point substantially increased the risk of arrest for the drug buyers and sellers who previously had been almost immune. In the first month, the police made over 2,000 drug-related arrests, an average of about 67 per day. After five months, the arrest total was close to 7,000 and after seventeen months, almost 14,000. Not only did OPP increase the risk of arrest, but its leaders also sought severe sentences for those apprehended. The U.S. Attorney for the Southern District of New York agreed to process all arrests made one day each week through the federal court system, where penalties for drug offenses are more severe than those of New York State and where judges have a "street reputation" as being tougher than state court judges. The federal courts did, in fact, hand out substantially harsher penalties,[15] and although it is difficult to quantify their impact, the police believe that rumors of "federal day" produced a notable decrease in the volume of drug traffic.

The police department also raised the cost of Pressure Point arrests by eliminating the Desk Appearance Ticket (DAT) system that ordinarily allows many persons charged with misdemeanors to be released from custody with notice of a court appearance date.[16] A DAT arrest imposes no immediate cost on the offender and may result in no punishment at all if the courts fail to locate defaulted DATs.[17] The elimination of DATs meant that all Pressure Point arrestees were immediately subjected to the full arrest, booking, and arraignment process and, especially in the first few months of mass arrests and backed-up courts, they often had to spend several days in jail before gaining release. Every Pressure Point arrest thus represented not only a first stage in the criminal process, but also an "immediate intervention" (Goldstein, 1977); every arrestee, even those against whom charges were later dropped or who were acquitted, was subjected to some sanction.

Even when unable to make arrests, OPP forces tried to discourage involvement in the drug trade by acting as what Sagarin and McNamara (1972) call a "judicial punitive body." This is a euphemism for harassing suspicious people in a "known drug area" by stopping them, questioning them, searching them, and telling them to "move on."[18] The police find this type of intervention useful because it does not take officers off the street to do the paperwork that accompanies an arrest. The cost to the alleged offender is substantially less when the police harass rather than arrest, but a greater number of interventions per officer can occur.[19]

This harassment strategy became especially useful to the OPP patrol force as the months wore on, not only because manpower was reduced,[20] but also because street selling became less blatant and less frequent in response to the earlier efforts. In the early days of Pressure Point, arrests were guaranteed, but both buyers and sellers quickly altered their behavior in response to the police threat, making early police tactics gradually less effective. Buyers, for example, began to spend less time on the street, trying to decrease the possibility of arrest:

> Buying drugs used to be an all-day affair. You'd hang around, shooting the breeze, maybe picking up a little work [in one of the street operations]. Now, I get my drugs and get out of the area as quickly as possible. Nobody "shoots up" on the block anymore; it's just too dangerous.

Drug sellers also adapted to the police presence by varying the location and time of sales[21] selling in larger quantities,[22] and employing more helpers. "Steerers" began to walk the streets, notifying buyers of the time and location of the next sale; more "lookouts" appeared, sending warning signals when the police drew near. Sellers stayed on the street for only short periods of time, distributing drugs to buyers who had already paid their money to another worker. As the whole drug operation adjusted itself to decrease the risk of detection and arrest, Pressure Point patrol officers turned more and more to monitoring the street population, harassing anyone who appeared to be involved in the drug trade, and encouraging the very changes in drug trafficking that made it more difficult for them to make arrests.

The demise of the blatant "drug supermarket" increased the usefulness of undercover surveillance operations aimed at drug sellers who, because they make only brief appearances on the street, are often able to avoid both arrest and harassment by the patrol force. On a surveillance operation, one officer concealed in an observation post uses binoculars to watch drug transactions taking place and then radios a description of buyers to officers waiting in cars outside the observation area. Several buyers will be arrested as they leave the purchase area before the police move in to arrest the seller. This type of operation can be very effective, but is difficult to organize because it requires considerable manpower, knowledge of possible sale locations, the cooperation of someone in the community to provide the lookout post, and adequate advanced planning—especially coordination with the patrol force to make sure it does not disrupt the sale before it takes place. Even then, surveillance operations are not foolproof and may fail to catch the sophisticated dealer, who can decrease the chance of detection by employing lookouts to patrol surrounding blocks, look for police cars, and report back by walkie-talkie.

Recognizing the limitations of a pure law enforcement strategy for fighting a problem as entrenched as the Lower East Side's drug trade, the police department supplemented it with community-based programs designed to strengthen the neighborhood and increase resident support of the police effort. As part of the Neighborhood Involvement Program (NIP), OPP officials met with church and community groups to develop programs that would encourage residents to report drug sales on their blocks. This eventually led to establishment of a special hotline, allowing callers to bypass the centralized reporting system and telephone anonymous tips directly to the Pressure Point office. The program not only sought to improve enforcement (by providing the police with information), but also to involve Lower East Side citizens more directly in the fight against drugs.

The Police Department's Community Affairs Division also became more active on the Lower East Side, adding extra officers to each of the Pressure Point precincts. This allowed them to expand their work with local community groups and help residents form block associations to plan outdoor activities designed to "recapture" the public spaces "liberated" by the police. In two of the three Lower East Side precincts, Community Patrol Officer Programs were created, and specially selected officers began to work with residents, business people, and community groups to solve the problems of individual blocks and neighborhoods, whether directly related to drugs or not. Police officials also sought the cooperation of other city agencies, encouraging them to demolish city-owned abandoned buildings being used in the drug trade, improve garbage pickup, sweep the streets, and tow away abandoned cars. By promoting general improvements on the Lower East Side, the police hoped to make the streets more attractive to residents who would then use them more, thus making them less available to drug traffickers.

## Impact of OPP on the Drug Trade and Drug-Related Crime

The package of law enforcement and community-oriented strategies making up Operation Pressure Point led not only to changes in how drugs were marketed on the Lower East Side, but also to what all observers agree was a noticeable decrease in the volume of the drug traffic itself.[23] There are a number of possible explanations for this decrease. It may be that OPP forced a reduction in the demand for drugs and that, simply because of the police presence, some drug users stopped buying drugs altogether or decreased their consumption. There is no evidence of Pressure Point putting additional strain on New York City's drug treatment facilities,[24] but both James Q. Wilson (1985) and Mark Moore (1977) suggest that it may be relatively new (and still unaddicted) drug users who can best be deterred by raising the costs of "copping." Bruce Johnson's (1984) research suggests that even chronic heroin users vary their daily intake considerably and occasionally experience days of total abstinence. So, at least some portion of the reduced volume might have been due to a reduction in the number of people seeking drugs on any given day.

A second explanation for the reduced volume of drug buyers on the Lower East Side after OPP is that some portion of the drug traffic moved to other locations. Within a few months of implementation, OPP was expanded to include some neighboring blocks which had not previously been high-drug areas and the police department created two additional, although smaller, operations (Pressure Point II and Pressure Point III) to attack drug traffic in other parts of the city. Some drug operations reportedly moved out of Manhattan altogether, relocating to other New York City boroughs, New Jersey, and Long Island. Established drug markets in Harlem may also have expanded their operations, taking on some of the business deflected from the Lower East Side.[25]

The police take the view that they were especially successful in ridding the Lower East Side of "out-of-town" buyers. Persons residing outside of New York City never constituted a large proportion of arrestees—only 14.2 percent in the first five months of Pressure Point, and 11.6 in the following year. However, a visual survey of the drug traffic two years after implementation, compared with police videotapes of pre-OPP, does reveal a difference in clientele. Pre-OPP, many of the buyers were white, and many appeared to be middle class—men with briefcases, wearing business suits, and women with babies in back-pack carriers. By 1985, white faces were scarce; in fact, police on patrol in high-drug areas of the Lower East Side automatically viewed any white person with suspicion. Cars with New Jersey license plates, which OPP officers report were once double parked along some blocks, had virtually disappeared.

If OPP forced some drug operations to move to new locations, this was probably more a result of police pressure on buyers than on sellers. Drug sellers are accustomed to the possibility of arrest, accepting it as a built-in cost of doing business (Luksetich & White 1982), and even the threat of extraordinarily severe punishments may not deter them. When New York State increased penalties under the "Rockefeller Drug Laws," it did not reduce the number of drug dealers or the supply of drugs available in the state (Japha et al. 1977; U.S. Department of Justice, 1978); and according to data gathered by the New York City Criminal Justice Agency (CJA), the sentences imposed on drug sellers arrested during the first month of OPP and subsequently convicted were not terribly severe.

Of 716 felony sale arrests analyzed by CJA, the large majority were settled in Criminal Court with guilty pleas to misdemeanors; only 131 defendants (less than one-fifth) were convicted on felony charges and only 87 persons were jailed, with almost half of them (40 percent) serving one year or less.[26] Some longer sentences were given out,[27] but these data suggest that the cost of selling drugs (at least in the first month of OPP) may not have been high enough to turn a substantial number of people away from the business. In addition, those who were deterred by the threat of imprisonment (or incapacitated by actual imprisonment) were, in all likelihood, easily replaced. Street-level dealers are a fluid group, made up primarily of drug users who sell to support their own use and local adolescents, anxious to earn easy money. Many work the streets only sporadically and are, as one local user/part-time dealer put it, "a dime a dozen." The arrest of even a large number of street dealers might not force a drug operation to move its location. In fact, perhaps the only thing that could force a drug operation to move is a reduction in buyers. If OPP made buyers afraid to buy drugs on the Lower East Side, then at least some number of dealers might have been motivated to relocate to areas where buyers felt safer.

The increased threat of arrest under OPP might be expected to have more impact on drug buyers than on sellers and, to some extent, buyers were a main target of this operation. Nearly half of all arrests were for misdemeanor possession; another nearly 10 percent were for loitering for the purpose of buying drugs. Conviction on these charges tends not to result in severe punishment, especially compared to the sentences meted out for drug sale: almost half of those arrested on misdemeanor charges were released quickly, with no imprisonment at all; of those who did receive jail time, the large majority (64.8 percent) received a sentence of "time served." Only 3.2 percent were given jail terms of over 90 days.[28] While these dispositions may seem mild, they are perhaps sufficient to deter some drug purchasers, particularly occasional users with legitimate employment and reputations that could be hurt by an arrest record. The police were hoping, in fact, that some buyers could be deterred by traffic summonses and in the first year, gave out more than 62,000 in the Pressure Point area. By harassing drug users—subjecting them not only to arrest and detention, but also parking tickets, towed cars, and the like—the police were hoping especially to discourage "out-of-towners" from buying drugs on the Lower East Side. The decreased volume of the drug traffic and the changes in clientele suggest that some of these buyers did stop buying on the Lower East Side; in some cases, markets may have moved to them.

Drug users indigenous to the Lower East Side were more resistant than outsiders to OPP and more easily adapted to the changes in street dealing that it created. One Lower East Side drug user explained how "scoring" became more complicated and time consuming:

> For the first time in a long time, I had to start worrying about where I was going to get my stuff. Before Pressure Point, it was there any time you wanted it, day or night. Suddenly, I had to make phone calls to get information; then sometimes, you'd go to the spot and no one would be there. Eventually, you'd get your drugs but it might take all day. And right away, you'd start worrying about tomorrow.

To minimize the chance of arrest, local buyers began to stay off the streets as much as possible, but still recognized that buying was riskier than before:

> With Pressure Point, the police would arrest you just for being on the streets. One day I got work transporting drugs for someone; I was carrying a couple of bundles and was scared shitless being on the street. Later that day, when I was perfectly clean, I got busted for loitering just because I was walking in a "known drug area." Everyone I know got arrested during Pressure Point.

Other local users turned to the "inside operations" which are generally unavailable to outsiders:

> I have a lot of connections in the area and have worked with the distributors, so when the police came on strong I avoided the street and started getting my stuff from this guy who works out of an apartment in the projects. He doesn't let you in if he doesn't know you.

Some Lower East Side users may have traveled outside the Pressure Point area to buy their drugs, but this user's attitude may be more typical:

> I'm not going to travel all over the city—riding the trains—just to buy drugs. There's always a risk. Hell, I was arrested probably a dozen times before Pressure Point; it's all part of using drugs.

Not all drug users, then, are deterred from buying by the increased threat of arrest. OPP pushed out out-of-town buyers, but many local buyers remained; the drug trade did not disappear, but it was reduced and made less blatant.

Going along with the decrease in drug trafficking on the Lower East Side was a decrease in the often drug-related property crimes of robbery and burglary. Within two months of Pressure Point's inception, a police department news release claimed a 52.1 percent decrease in robbery and a 35 percent decrease in burglary.[29] Data gathered over the six-month period from January to June 1984 show a slightly lower decrease, although still a substantial one. Table 1 compares the robbery and burglary rates for the Pressure Point area with other areas of the city for 1983 (pre-OPP) and 1984. Since the entire city of New York experienced a decrease in robbery and burglary during this period, not all of the decrease in the Pressure Point area can be attributed to the operation itself. However, the decrease in crime on the Lower East Side was considerably larger than for the city as a whole, and the area immediately surrounding OPP also experienced a more substantial decrease in crime than the remainder of the city.

Although these data regarding the impact of OPP on property crime are interesting, we do not know how much crime was actually deterred and how much was displaced to the other parts of the city (and even beyond) where some of the drug traffic became relocated. These other areas might have experienced some of the crime that, without OPP, would have been committed on the Lower East Side. For the Lower East Side, however, OPP meant not only less drug traffic, but less drug-related crime.

**Table 1. Robberies and Burglaries in OPP Area and Other Areas of New York City***

**ROBBERY**

|  | Jan.–June '83 | Jan.–June '84 | % Change |
|---|---|---|---|
| OPP Area | 67 | 37 | -44.8 |
| 3 OPP Precincts (minus OPP area) | 800 | 629 | -21.4 |
| Borough of Manhattan South (minus OPP area) | 5,301 | 5,089 | -4.0 |
| New York City** | 42,022 | 39,771 | -5.4 |

**BURGLARY**

|  | Jan.–June '83 | Jan.–June '84 | % Change |
|---|---|---|---|
| OPP Area | 519 | 319 | -38.5 |
| 3 OPP Precincts (minus OPP area) | 1,214 | 1,031 | -15.1 |
| Borough of Manhattan South (minus OPP area) | 7,243 | 7,376 | +1.8 |
| New York City** | 72,372 | 64,962 | -10.2 |

*Data supplied by New York City Police Department
**Figures not available for Jan.-June period. Figures for entire year were divided in half to obtain 6-month estimate.

## Impact of OPP on the Community[30]

A 1986 *New York Times* article focusing on the Lower East Side reported that "thanks to Operation Pressure Point, art galleries are replacing shooting galleries."[31] Even a police operation of the magnitude and intensity of OPP could not, single-handedly, produce such a transformation, but the *Times* is correct in its reporting of the change itself. In some sections of the Lower

East Side, property values began to climb, new shops and restaurants (and art galleries) opened up, and entire blocks of apartment buildings became renovated and occupied. OPP did not create these changes, but it did facilitate the process of gentrification. that began on the Lower East Side in the early 1980s, largely in response to the increased demand for residential property in Manhattan.[32] Not all neighborhoods in the Lower East Side have been part of this gentrification process; in particular, the sections bordering Chinatown and those along the East River have changed very little and are still occupied, primarily, by poor and working-class minorities, many of them living in city-owned housing projects. Just as gentrification of the Lower East Side was not uniform across all neighborhoods, neither was the impact of OPP; it was most successful in ridding drug traffic from neighborhoods already in the process of change before OPP began and least successful in the areas which have remained largely untouched by gentrification.[33]

In the first few weeks of OPP, the police successfully "liberated" the most drug-infested streets and parks all over the Lower East Side; the drug traffic did not disappear, but the volume decreased quickly and substantially. Many drug sellers, perhaps hoping that OPP would be nothing more than a temporary interruption, stayed off the streets, waiting for law enforcement to return to "normal" so they could resume operations. It was only with the realization that OPP would continue indefinitely that drug sellers began to reemerge, developing the new marketing strategies that would decrease their risk of arrest. What they also quickly discovered was that some neighborhoods (specifically, those in the process of change and improvement) presented more risk than others. Consequently, as the drug trade began to reassert itself, it became increasingly more concentrated in the most disadvantaged neighborhoods of the Lower East Side.

Poor, run-down neighborhoods hold some advantages for street-level drug dealers. For one thing, there is often a transient population on the streets and in the local parks, making it difficult for the police to identify persons involved in the drug trade. Buyers and sellers often live in the neighborhood themselves and are similar to other residents in terms of class, race, ethnicity, and general appearance, again making them indistinguishable to the police. And as the methods of selling became less blatant, the police became increasingly less effective in these neighborhoods. OPP officers, patrolling on foot and by car, constantly monitored the street population, conducting searches and sometimes making arrests, but seldom witnessed a drug sale in progress. Their presence undoubtedly had some deterrent effect, keeping some buyers out of the area and preventing sellers from returning to pre-OPP ways of doing business.

It is hard to imagine what the OPP team could have done to have more impact in these neighborhoods. Undercover and surveillance operations might have been more effective but a 1985 departmental policy aimed at pre-venting corruption prohibited officers on the regular patrol force (the large majority of Pressure Point officers) from working out of uniform.[34] This meant that all drug-related undercover operations had to be handled by the Narcotics Division, a unit which has limited resources in light of the volume of drug crime in the city as a whole. The Narcotics Division did assist the reg-ular OPP force on the Lower East Side,[35] and if expanded, could have pro-vided more assistance, but this would have made OPP much more costly. Most of the patrol officers assigned to Pressure Point were fairly inexperi-enced (many straight out of the police academy), allowing a massive police presence at relatively low cost. In fact, OPP might not have been created at all were it not for expansion of the New York City force beginning in 1984, and the increased number of recruits available for their first street assign-ment. Operation Pressure Point continued to rely on this steady supply of new officers to fill the ranks and it would have required substantial reorgani-zation and expansion of departmental resources to substitute a highly trained and experienced undercover force for the OPP patrol force.

In contrast to its failure to clear the drug traffic out of the poorest areas of the Lower East Side, OPP substantially reduced (and perhaps even elimi-nated) the street drug trade in the more gentrified neighborhoods. There, the initial liberation of the streets and parks was not followed by the gradual reemergence of drug buyers and sellers. This does not seem to be because the police paid more attention to these areas; they deny any bias in coverage and my own observations during the second year of OPP bear out that police patrols remained heaviest in the poor areas where the drug traffic had become concentrated.

The success of OPP in neighborhoods that were becoming gentrified can probably best be explained in the same way as its failure in poorer neighbor-hoods: by the make-up of the community itself. Once cleared off the streets in the first few weeks of Pressure Point, drug buyers and sellers quickly became "outsiders," their presence readily apparent to OPP personnel and to residents, many of whom were eager to report them to the police. The resi-dent population in these neighborhoods had been changing gradually over a period of years—becoming increasingly middle class and white—a change that was not as apparent when the drug dealers and other "undesirables" occupied the streets and parks. By clearing out these groups, OPP allowed the resident population to "claim" the public areas, both formally (through orga-nizing neighborhood events) and informal—(through their increased willing-ness to be on the streets).[36] Research by Stephanie Greenberg et al. (1985) suggests that residents themselves can reduce crime and other undesirable behavior through informal social control of their neighborhoods, especially by increasing their use of public space. Such informal control is most likely to occur in communities with general agreement concerning social norms, an agreement which perhaps began to emerge in these gentrifying neighborhoods as the police cleared the "street population" away for the first time since the area had begun to change. A new group of people, themselves once intruders into a run-down, sparsely populated neighborhood, began to establish new standards of acceptable conduct and assist the police in enforcing them. Operation Pressure Point thus facilitated a change that had already begun and, by making these neighborhoods even more desirable than before, increased the chance that further gentrification would occur, making it even more unlikely that the drug traffic would return.

## Conclusion

Operation Pressure Point accomplished a great deal: a drastic improvement in some neighborhoods, a more modest improvement in others, but an overall reduction in drug trafficking and drug-related crime on the Lower East Side. Operation Pressure Point was also a tremendous tactical success for the New York City Police Department. In spite of very little advance planning,[37] the whole operation was carried out with very few procedural problems; both the Transit Police and Housing Authority Police were extremely cooperative;[38] coverage by the local media was nothing but favorable;[39] and the response of people in the community was, for the most part, very positive. Community reaction was naturally most favorable in neighborhoods where the impact was greatest, but even in areas with remaining drug traffic, residents appreciated the reduction in volume and the less obtrusive methods of dealing being used. As a neighborhood improvement strategy, then, OPP was a success, even if a limited one, and it shows that the police can develop innovative strategies to fight some of the pervasive "criminal situations" that plague specific urban neighborhoods.

It does not necessarily follow, however, that all drug-infested communities can benefit equally from an operation like Pressure Point. Police officials around the country, understandably anxious for solutions to the problems of drug trafficking and drug-related violence, should be cautious in copying this model. Mark Kleiman (1986) reports that a similar operation in Harlem had very little impact on the open drug market there. In a neighborhood in Queens, the drug trade reportedly returned in full force within days of the dismantling of a nine-month police offensive against crack dealers.[40] Operation Pressure Point worked better on the Lower East Side than similar operations elsewhere probably because much of the Lower East Side was in the early stages of gentrification, on its way to becoming a middle- and upper-middle-class community. In other middle-class neighborhoods, even citizen-patrol groups have recently had some success in reducing drug trafficking simply by acting as an active counter-presence on the street.[41] We should probably expect that neither citizen groups nor the police will have as much impact in the poverty-ridden areas where most of the nation's street-level drug trafficking is concentrated.

There is also, at this point, no reason to believe that operations like Pressure Point can substantially reduce the overall volume of drugs being sold or consumed. In all likelihood, OPP simply displaced much of the drug trade from the Lower East Side to other parts of the city and beyond.[42] This displacement is of value to residents of the Lower East Side who, for a long time, were bearing a disproportionate share of the burden of a drug problem that extends far beyond the boundaries of their neighborhood; they had reason to favor a more equitable distribution of that problem, even it if meant pushing it into other communities. But street-level drug enforcement of OPP's magnitude does not offer a solution to the drug problem itself. It is hard to imagine the resources that would be necessary at the local level to put sufficient pressure on an entire city to prevent displacement and produce a substantial reduction in drug consumption. Anytime the costs of buying drugs are raised, some users will reduce or eliminate their use (Moore, 1973; Reuter & Kleiman, 1986), but by 1988 even New York's Police Commissioner Benjamin Ward was warning that the strategy of neighborhood saturation had been "perhaps oversold" and was "not likely to overcome the drug problem in the long run or on a citywide basis."[43] The rave reviews that followed the success of OPP perhaps raised expectations for what can be done to reduce street-level drug trafficking, and police departments may find themselves pressured to expand these types of programs. In the current era of high demand for drugs, they may also find themselves unable to duplicate on a broader scale what OPP was able to accomplish on New York's Lower East Side.

## Notes

[1] See, for example, the National Advisory Commission on Criminal Justice Standards and Goals (1973), National Commission on the Causes and Prevention of Violence (1969), National Advisory Commission on Civil Disorders (1968), and President's Commission on Law Enforcement and the Administration of Justice (1967a, 1967b).

[2] Drug transactions, at every level, have the potential for violence as buyers and sellers disagree over the price, quality, and quantity of drugs changing hands (McBride, 1981; McCoy et al., 1978). The property crimes of robbery and burglary are also associated with drugs because drug users—especially addicted ones—may turn to crime to support their habits. Researchers disagree over the magnitude of this drug-crime connection (Ball et al., 1981; Inciardi, 1979; Inciardi and Chambers, 1972; Goldman, 1978a; Moore, 1977), but it is well accepted that drug users are responsible for a substantial amount of property crime.

[3] In January 1984, the *Los Angeles Times* ran a front-page story of "the most open heroin market in the nation," with a picture of customers lining up to buy drugs on New York's Lower East Side. See, *Los Angeles Times*, January 8, 1984, p. 1.

[4] According to Paul Goldstein et al. (1984), illegal drugs are increasingly being marketed under "brand names" applied by the seller as a way of creating user loyalty. Goldstein lists hundreds of names which have recently turned up on packets of heroin and cocaine in New York City—names like "evening delight," "dragon lady," "temptation," "magic blue," "prophecy," "black death," etc.

[5] In fact, a New York City police officer told me of driving through the Lower East Side with his family and how his wife and children urged him to stop so they could participate in what they assumed was one of the many ethnic festivals which occur on the streets of New York during the summer.

[6] There are three regular precincts on the Lower East Side; the 5th, the 7th and the 9th. The Pressure Point area included sections from all three of these precincts but did not fully encompass all of the streets from any of them.

[7] These statistics are based on data provided by the New York City Police Department.

[8] In 1974, the police reported approximately 525,000 index crimes; in 1980, 720,000, and in 1984, 600,000. Throughout this period there were several increases and decreases, but at no point did the amount of reported crime decline to 1974 levels. (Data obtained from New York City Police Department.)

[9] Drug arrests were given a low priority in other cities as well. According to Herbert Jacob (1984), narcotic arrests peaked in the early 1970s; after this time, serious crimes made up a growing proportion of all arrests.

[10] According to Kleiman (1986), drugs bought on the streets of the Lower East Side made it as far as Lynn, Massachusetts where they were then sold in open street operations not unlike those in New York.

[11] See *New York Eagle*, December 2, 1983 (p. 7).

[12] "Is This Any Place for Children?" by Murray Weissetal, *New York Daily News*, July 31, 1983, p. 1.

[13] See *New York Tribune*, April 30, 1984 (p. 1) for such comments by some Lower East Side residents. This is also the position taken by Jagna Sharff (1985). She claims that the drug traffic, which initially served to "push out" much of the older, immigrant population, was, by 1984, "the last obstacle to gentrification" and invasion by the "yuppies." Her position is that drug dealing was tolerated by the police when the neighborhood was in decline (pre-gentrification) but became the object of police attention once property values began to increase. Beecher et al. (1981) and Farmer (1984) point out that official responses to crime are almost always "political," in that they respond to some interests over others and are particularly influenced by business interests in the community.

[14] In meetings with the community, the police receive more complaints of "street conditions"—loud music, rowdy youth, derelicts, street vendors, prostitutes, and the like—than they do of serious crime. Citizens want and expect the police to take care of these problems and Commissioner Ward decided to give them a much higher priority than did his predecessors. He was particularly influenced by the work of Wilson and Kelling (1982) suggesting that renewed attention to street conditions in deteriorating neighborhoods may also have an impact on serious crime.

[15] There are some problems in directly comparing dispositions from federal court with those of state court because the charges themselves are not identical and the time periods for which data are available are not the same. But even a rough comparison of outcomes suggests much tougher treatment in the federal system. In federal court, almost 80 percent of convicted felons were sentenced to imprisonment, with fewer than 10 percent of those serving less than one year. In state court, 66 percent of those convicted on felony charges went to jail, and almost half of them were given a year or less. At the indictment stage, the disparities are even greater between the two systems. In the federal system 126 felony indictments resulted from 161 felony arrests. In state court, fewer than one-fifth (131 out of 716) of felony arrests resulted in a felony indictment. Federal statistics are from the United States Attorney's Office, Southern District of New York. For state data, see note 26.

[16] From the police perspective, the advantage of DATs is that they can be processed more quickly, letting officers return to the streets rather than spend hours processing the arrest, transporting prisoners to detention, and waiting for arraignments to be completed.

[17] When a person issued a DAT fails to show up for the court appearance, the court will issue an arrest warrant, but the warrants division of the police department has been understaffed and unable to "track down" all defaulted DATs. Often the police will catch defaulted DATs when the person is arrested again; this time, they will not quality for DAT and will remain locked up until appearing in court to face the accumulated charges.

[18] These are very similar to the police tactics which Symanski (1981) reports are widely used against prostitution. Because the police would be able to make only a few arrests each night, they can more effectively control prostitution through "harassment" than "arrest."

[19] The constitutionality of such tactics remains questionable, and there have been some complaints by Lower East Side residents who felt they were unjustly harassed by the police. However, a study sponsored by the police department a few months after OPP began found general public acceptance of the police tactics being used.

[20] After one year, Pressure Point forces were reduced slightly from approximately 240 to 200 officers. At times, the force was reduced further as officers regularly assigned to OPP were temporarily assigned to other tasks (parades, sporting events, concerts, etc.). Skolnick and Bayley (1986) warn that for innovative strategies to be effective, the integrity of the deployment must be maintained and the tendency to "pull" officers for other assignments must be avoided.

[21] The nighttime hours between 2 a.m. and 6 am. became especially popular because OPP forces were at their lowest. Because much of the population was asleep at this time, citizen complaints were uncommon and sales could occur without much threat of arrest.

[22] Drug users reported that some sellers responded to OPP by refusing to sell "single bags" ($10 or $20 worth) and requiring buyers to buy in bundles of ten. Drug buyers would have to pool their money, send one person to make the buy, and then distribute the packets among themselves. This change increased the risk to buyers (because it required them to congregate on the street and make these arrangements) but decreased the risk to sellers by allowing them to distribute the same amount of drugs in a shorter period of time.

[23] This conclusion was unanimous among everyone interviewed, including police officers, business people, community residents, drug users, and taxi drivers familiar with the community.

[24] Data gathered by the New York State Substance Abuse Services shows no increase in the Methadone Maintenance population during this period. This may be because most methadone

clinics have a waiting list for entrance into the program, but there was also no change in the number of people on the waiting lists.

[25] One Lower East Side police officer who lived in Harlem reported a noticeable increase in the volume of drug trade there and claimed to have seen some well-known "street people" from the Lower East Side in Harlem for the first time after OPP began.

[26] These data come from Criminal Justice Agency (CJA) Follow-up Report on Criminal Court Outcomes. The agency only analyzed court outcomes for those arrested during the first month of Pressure Point; there is, at this point, no way of knowing if the courts became more or less lenient as time went by. These data also fail to include the court outcomes of defendants who had their cases heard in federal court.

[27] Of the remaining 47 convicted felons receiving jail time, 14 received a sentence of 1–3 years, 26 got 2–4 years and 7 were given longer sentences; the most severe sentence was 6–15 years, given to one person.

[28] See Follow-up report on Criminal Court and Supreme Court Outcomes, Tables 3 and 4. These tables include data from all arrestees who pled guilty in the criminal court.

[29] City of New York, Police Department News Release No. 17, March 20, 1984.

[30] Not included in this section is an examination of how OPP affected the drug users who are also a part of the community. Some of the users I spoke to were pleased with the results of OPP because they, too, felt the situation had gotten out of hand and were especially glad to see fewer out-of-town buyers on the street. Paul Goldstein (1985) reports that buying drugs became more dangerous after OPP when many selling operations moved indoors. Other users report a decrease in the quality of drugs and an increase in price.

[31] "The Fortunes of the Lower East Side are Rising," by William Greer, *New York Times*, August 4, 1986, p. 6E.

[32] According to Robert Ponte (1985), a shortage of both office and residential space in Manhattan has led to an increase in property values all over the city and the rapid development of areas that, just a few years ago, were abandoned to the poor. For example, on Avenues A and B, in the heart of OPP, new co-op units offering "moderately priced housing" in the $200,000 to $300,000 range are being developed. See "Lower East Side Buildings Rehabilitated," by Diane Shaman, *New York Times*, April 1, 1988, p. A18.

[33] This seemed to be a particular problem in the Public Housing Project where even citizens who dislike the drug trade are often personally connected to those involved; they want the drug trade gone, but without their friends and relatives being arrested. Some residents also expressed fear of retaliation and were reluctant to give even anonymous tips to the police. In some communities, money from the drug trade circulates within the community itself, again making residents reluctant to assist the police.

[34] OPP forces did conduct some surveillance operations in unmarked cars, but in uniform, leaving them quite visible to anyone looking for them.

[35] The Police Department will not release information about undercover operations, so it is impossible to compare the number of undercover operations in the early and later stages of OPP. However, OPP patrol supervisors claimed that, over time, they began to receive much less backup from the undercover units.

[36] Several researchers have shown this link between resident use of the streets and crime. When crime (or fear of crime) increases in a neighborhood, residents tend to stay off the streets as much as possible, weakening informal social controls, and perhaps causing an even greater increase in crime (Wilson, 1985; Conklin, 195; DuBow et al., 1979). Jane Jacobs (1961)

strongly suggests policies that encourage resident use of public areas as a strategy fighting crime.

[37] OPP was not based on a carefully developed "master plan." It was put into motion within a month of Commissioner Ward's appointment, after gathering together several people with knowledge of the Lower East Side's drug problem. Many operational decisions got made on an "as needed" basis.

[38] These three policing organizations in New York have not always cooperated with each other and have sometimes competed with each other for arrests. The success of OPP may facilitate additional joint efforts in the future.

[39] The only exception I could uncover was an interview with Dr. Robert Newman who admonished the police department for not providing advance warning (and seeking input from) the local drug treatment establishment before beginning the operation (CBS News, March 11, 1984).

[40] See "Crack Dealers Returning to Streets Narcotics Teams had Swept Clean," by David E. Pitt, *New York Times*, December 5, 1988, p. 1.

[41] See, for example, "East Side Drug Patrol's Tactic: Stare," by Selwyn Raab, *New York Times*, September 5, 1989, p. B3.

[42] Cornish and Clarke (1987) show that displacement is not the inevitable result of police pressure, in part because not all criminals are sufficiently mobile or sufficiently skilled to alter their criminal activity. At this point, however, there appears to be no shortage of new personnel willing to become involved in street-level drug trafficking whenever police pressure deters any number of current dealers.

[43] "Ward Calls Drug Units Panacea," by David E. Pitt, *New York Times*, November 30, 1988, p. B1.

# References

Ball, J., L. Rosen, J. Flueck & D. Nurco (1981). "The Criminality of Heroin Addicts: When Addicted and When Off Opiates." In J. Inciardi (ed.). *The Drugs-Crime Connection*. Beverly Hills: Sage.

Beecher, J., R. Lineberry & M. Rich (1981). "The Politics of Police Response to Urban Crime." In D. Lewis (ed.). *Reactions to Crime*. Beverly Hills: Sage.

Belenko, S. (1981). Drugs and the Criminal Justice System: The Processing and Impact of Drug Cases in New York. Paper prepared for the New York State Heroin and Alcohol Abuse Study.

Beschner, G. & W. Brower (1985). "The Scene." In B. Hanson et al. (eds.). *Life with Heroin*. Lexington, MA: Lexington Books.

Black, D. (1980). *The Manners and Customs of the Police*. New York: Academic Press.

Bradbury, K., A. Downs, and K. Small (1982). *Urban Decline and the Future of American Cities*. Washington, DC: The Brookings Institute.

Chein, I. et al. (1964). *The Road to H: Narcotics Delinquency and Social Policy*. New York: Basic Books.

Clark, R. (1970). *Crime in America*. New York: Simon and Schuster.

Clarke, R. (1983). "Situational Crime Prevention: Its Theoretical Basis and Practical Scope." In M. Tonry and N. Morris (eds.). *Crime and Justice: An Annual Review of Research*. Chicago: University of Chicago.

Conklin, J. (1975). *The Impact of Crime*. New York: Macmillan.

Cornish, D. & R. Clarke (1987). "Understanding Crime Displacement: An Application of Rational Choice Theory." *Criminology*, 25: 933–947.

DuBow, F. et al. (1979). *Reactions to Crime: A Critical Review of the Literature*. Washington, DC: U.S. Justice Department.

Engstad, P. & J. Evans (1980). "Responsibility, Competence and Police Effectiveness in Crime Control." In R. Clarke and J. Hough (eds.). *The Effectiveness of Policing*. Farnborough, England: Gower.

Farmer, D. (1984). *Crime Control: The Use and Misuse of Police Resources*. New York: Plenum Press.

Gardiner, J. (1970). *The Politics of Corruption: Organized Crime in an American City*. New York: Russell Sage.

Garmire, B. (1972). "The Police Role in an Urban Society." In R. Steadman (ed.). *The Police and the Community*. Baltimore: Johns Hopkins Press.

Goldman, F. (1981). "Drug Abuse, Crime, and Economics: The Dismal Limits of Social Choice." In J. Inciardi (ed.). *The Drugs-Crime Connection*. Beverly Hills: Sage.

Goldstein, H. (1975). *Police Corruption*. Washington, DC: Police Foundation.

____. (1977). *Policing a Free Society*. Cambridge, MA: Ballinger.

____. (1979). "Improving Policing: A Problem-Oriented Approach." Crime and Delinquency, 25: 236–258.

Goldstein, P. (1985). "Impact of Pressure Point on the Drug Subculture." Paper presented at Pressure Point Conference, New York University School of Law, November 22.

Goldstein, P. et al. (1984). "The Marketing of Street Heroin in New York City." *Journal of Drug Issues*, 553–566.

Greenberg, S., W. Rohe & J. Williams (1985). *Informal Citizen Action and Crime Prevention at the Neighborhood Level*. Washington, DC: U.S. Department of Justice.

Hanson, B. (1985). "Introduction." In B. Hanson et al. (eds.). *Life with Heroin: Voices from the Inner City*. Lexington, MA: Lexington Books.

Inciardi, J. A. (1979). "Heroin Use and Street Crime." Crime and Delinquency, 335–346.

Inciardi, J. & C. D. Chambers (1972). "Unreported Criminal Involvement of Narcotic Addicts." *Journal of Drug Issues*, 2: 57–64.

Jacob, H. (1980). *Crime and Justice in Urban America*. Englewood Cliffs, NJ: Prentice-Hall.

____. (1984). *The Frustration of Policy: Responses to Crime by American Cities*. Boston: Little, Brown, and Company.

Jacobs, J. (1961). *The Death and Life of Great American Cities*. New York: Random House.

Jacoby, J. E., N. A. Weiner, T. P. Thornberry & M. E. Wolfgang (1973). "Drug Use in a Birth Cohort." In *National Commission on Marijuana and Drug Abuse*,

*Drug Use in America: Problem in Perspective*. Washington, DC: Government Printing Office.

Johnson, B. D. (1984). "Empirical Patterns of Heroin Consumption Among Selected Street Heroin Users." In G. Serban (ed.). *The Social and Medical Aspects of Drug Abuse*. Spectrum Publications.

Johnson, B. D. & D. S. Lipton (1984). "The Law, Criminal Justice System, and Treatment/Rehabilitation System in New York State (USA)." In Francesco Bruno, *Combatting Drug Abuse and Related Crime*. Rome: United Nations Social Defense Research Institute.

Kleiman, M. (1986). "Bringing Back Street-Level Heroin Enforcement." Unpublished manuscript, Program in Criminal Justice Policy and Management, John F. Kennedy School of Government, Harvard University.

Knapp, W. (1972). *Report of the Commission to Investigate Alleged Police Corruption*. New York: George Braziller.

Luksetich, W. & M. White (1982). *Crime and Public Policy: An Economic Approach*. Boston: Little, Brown, and Company.

MacGillis, D. & ABS News (1983). *Crime in America*. Radnor, PA: Chilton.

McBride, D. (1981). "Drugs and Violence." In J. Inciardi (ed.). *The Drugs-Crime Connection*. Beverly Hills: Sage.

McCoy, C. B. et al. (1978). *The Social Cost of Treatment Denial*. Final Report to the National Institute on Drug Abuse.

McNamara, J. (1976). "Impact of Bureaucracy on Attempts to Prevent Police Corruption." In A. Niederhoffer & A. Blumberg (ed.). *The Ambivalent Force*. Hinsdale, IL: Dryden Press.

Moore, M. (1973). "Policies to Achieve Discrimination in the Effective Price of Heroin." *American Economic Review*, 63 (May).

___ . (1977). *Buy and Bust*. Lexington, MA: D.C. Heath.

___ . (1983). "Controlling Criminogenic Commodities: Drugs, Guns, and Alcohol." In J. Q. Wilson (ed.). *Crime and Public Policy*. San Francisco: ICS Press.

Mulgrav, J. (1985). *Operation Pressure Point: A Community Perspective*. Paper prepared for New York City Police Department, January.

National Advisory Commission on Civil Disorders (1968). *Report of the National Advisory Commission on Civil Disorders*. Washington, DC: U.S. Government Printing Office.

National Advisory Commission on Criminal Justice Standards and Goals (1973). *A National Strategy to Reduce Crime*. Washington, DC: U.S. Government Printing Office.

National Commission on the Causes and Prevention of Violence (1969). *Law and Order Reconsidered*. Washington, DC: U.S. Government Printing Office.

Palmer, S. (1973). *The Prevention of Crime*. New York: Behavioral Publications.

Phares, D. (1979). "Heroin, Society, Public Policy: The Infernal Triangle." In R. Baker & F. Mayer (eds.). *Evaluating Alternative Law-Enforcement Policies*. Lexington, MA: Lexington Books.

Ponte, R. (1985). "Manhattan's Real Estate Boom." *New York Affairs*, 8,4: 18–31.

President's Commission on Law Enforcement and the Administration of Justice (1967a). *The Challenge of Crime in a Free Society*. Washington, DC: U.S. Government Printing Office.

___. (1967b). *Task Force Report: The Police*. Washington, DC: U.S. Government Printing Office.

___. (1967c). *Task Force Report: Science and Technology*. Washington, DC: U.S. Government Printing Office.

Reuter, P. and M. Kleiman (1986). "Risks and Prices: An Economic Analysis of the Drug Markets." In M. Tonry and N. Morris (eds.). *Crime and Justice: An Annual Review of Research*. Chicago: University of Chicago.

Reiss, A. (1971). *The Police and The Public*. New Haven: Yale University.

Rubinstein, J. (1973). *City Police*. New York: Farrar, Straus and Giroux.

Sagarin, E. and D. MacNamara (1972). "The Problem of Entrapment." In R. Dahl and G. Dix (eds.). *Crime, Law and Justice Annual 1972*. Buffalo: William S. Hein, pp. 358–380.

Saunders, C. (1970). *Upgrading the American Police*. Washington, DC: Brookings Institute.

Sharff, J. (1985). "Operation Pressure Point and Gentrification of the Lower East Side." Paper presented at Pressure Point Conference, New York University School of Law, November 22.

Sherman, L. (1974). *Police Corruption: A Sociological Perspective*. New York: Anchor Press.

___. (1986). "Policing Communities: What Works?" In A. Reiss and M. Tonry (eds.). *Communities and Crime*. Chicago: University of Chicago.

Silberman, C. (1978). *Criminal Violence, Criminal Justice*. New York: Vintage.

Skolnick, J. and D. Bayley (1986). *The New Blue Line*. New York: Free Press.

Smith, D. C. (1982). "Police." In C. Brecher and R. Horton (eds.). *Setting Municipal Priorities, 1982*. New York: Russell Sage Foundation.

Symanski, R. (1981). *The Immoral Landscape: Female Prostitution in Western Societies*. Toronto: Butterworth.

U.S. Department of Justice (1978). *The Nation's Toughest Drug Law: Evaluating the New York Experience*. Washington, DC: U.S. Government Printing Office.

Waldorf, D. (1973). *Careers in Dope*. Englewood Cliffs, NJ: Prentice Hall.

Walker, S. (1977). *A Critical History of Police Reform: The Emergence of Professionalism*. Lexington, MA: D. C. Heath.

Wilson, J. Q. (1968). *Varieties of Police Behavior*. Cambridge: Harvard University.

___. (1972). "The Police in the Ghetto." In R. Steadman (ed.). The Police and the Community. Baltimore: Johns Hopkins Press.

___ . (1985). *Thinking About Crime*, Revised Edition. New York: Vintage.

Wilson, J. Q. and G. Kelling (1982). "Broken Windows: The Police and Neighborhood Safety." *Atlantic Monthly*, 249: 29–38.

# 13

# Drug Enforcement's Double-Edged Sword
## An Assessment of Asset Forefeiture Programs

## J. Mitchell Miller
## Lance H. Selva

In his 1989 inaugural address, President George Bush solemnly promised the country that the drug scourge would be eliminated. Despite the president's optimism and the pumping of $9.5 billion into the federal anti-drug effort in 1990, it is apparent that widespread drug abuse persists. Early indications suggest that the 1990s will witness a drug catastrophe even greater than in the past (Currie 1993; "Drug War Victory" 1991; Zimring and Hawkins 1992).

Many observers have characterized the current anti-drug effort, known familiarly as the "war on drugs," as a failed public policy (Bugliosi 1991; Elsasser 1990; Kleiman 1992; Trebach 1987; Wistosky 1990; Zimring and Hawkins 1992). Officially declared by the Reagan Administration in 1982, this publicly supported crusade against drug abuse and narcotics trafficking

Reprinted by permission of the Academy of Criminal Justice Sciences from *Justice Quarterly*, Vol. 11 No. 2, 1994.

was supposed to succeed where the supply reduction-oriented policies of the 1970s had failed. The war on drugs initially featured a pluralistic approach, incorporating an unprecedented amount of resources for enforcement, education concentrating on prevention of use, and treatment. Eradication of both foreign and domestic drug crops and interdiction of illicit substances at U.S. borders were added quickly to the enforcement strategy (Kleiman 1989). These methods, however, seemed to be futile; they called into question the efficacy of the present policy (Reuter and Kleiman 1986). Indeed, many measurable indicators of illicit drug activity demonstrate the ineffectiveness of this drug war strategy. Street-level prices of cocaine, for example, either have dropped or have remained relatively constant over the past decade, suggesting a consistent supply (Drug Enforcement Administration [DEA] 1992). More telling is the estimated prevalence of drug use issued by the Bureau of Justice Statistics: in spite of efforts to reduce demand, it reports, the American appetite for mood-altering substances remains insatiable (Bureau of Justice Statistics 1991).

Persistent public concern about the lack of success prompted policy makers to consider alternative strategies (Walker 1992). In attempts to find a magic bullet for drug control policy, suggestions ranged from the legalization of marijuana, cocaine, and even heroin to the death penalty for traffickers and solicitors (Inciardi 1991). After a long and heated debate in Congress, compromise overcame controversy to produce the 1988 Anti-Drug Abuse Bill, which largely continues to direct and shape the present drug enforcement strategy.

The 1988 Anti-Drug Abuse Bill created new legal tools to handle the special enforcement problems presented by crack cocaine, gang-related violence, and domestic marijuana production, all of which appeared to be increasing steadily (Weisheit 1991). The bill provided for additional allocation of resources for equipment and manpower, as well as stiffer legal penalties for drug law offenders. It also created an Asset Forfeiture Fund. This fund is modeled after the Racketeer-Influenced and Corrupt Organizations (RICO) and the Continuing Criminal Enterprise statutes as well as the Federal Criminal Forfeiture Act of 1984, which legalized seizing the fruits of criminal activities (Moore 1988).

The Asset Forfeiture Fund is much more than a depository for income generated by liquidating seized assets, whether cash, automobiles, jewelry, art, or real estate. It is the central component in a reciprocal relationship between law enforcement agencies and federal and state treasury departments, from which the attorney general may authorize

> payment of any expenses necessary to seize, detail, inventory, safeguard, maintain, advertise or sell property under seizure or detention pursuant to any law enforced. . . . Payments from the fund can be used for awards for information

or assistance related to violation of criminal drug laws. . . . Deposits to the fund will be from the forfeiture of property under any law enforced or administered (Lawrence 1988:2).

The Asset Forfeiture Fund was created with the intention of helping law enforcement agencies to combat drug lords whose wealth gave them refuge from traditional enforcement tactics. Proponents were optimistic that seizing assets would limit the amount of working capital available to drug dealers, thereby reducing their ability to facilitate criminal activity (Drug Policy Foundation 1992; Fried 1988).

The fund calls on federal agencies to form special units for conducting operations to make seizures. Most state law enforcement agencies and several metropolitan police departments soon noted the monetary benefits of the fund and copied the federal approach, making asset seizure and forfeiture a sweeping narcotics policing strategy (United States Department of Justice 1988). Like any legal innovation, however, it had the potential for unintended consequences.

Critics contend that seizing assets and money has become a primary concern of vice divisions in smaller enforcement agencies, to the exclusion of traditional enforcement goals of deterrence and punishment (Stuart 1990; Trebach 1987). The routinization of seizure and forfeiture, others allege, has prompted enforcement agencies to develop new strategies of narcotics policing that are directed more toward asset hunting than toward reducing illegal drug use (Miller 1991; Trebach and Zeese 1990). Furthermore, this new policing strategy appears to be increasingly intrusive. A number of journalistic accounts describe civil liberties violations related directly to asset forfeiture enforcement (Jacobs 1992; Morganthau and Katel 1990). A series published by the Pittsburgh Press, titled *Presumed Guilty: The Law's Victims in the War on Drugs* (Schneider and Flaherty 1991), portrays the frequent, severe victimization of ordinary citizens through forfeiture. These excellent reports, based on reviews of 25,000 DEA seizures and 510 court cases, reveal that "enormous collateral damage to the innocent" is the effect of a new standard of presumed guilt. Other information on asset forfeiture comes from legal critiques dissecting the language of the 1988 Anti-Drug Abuse Act and surveying its feasibility as an effective drug enforcement initiative (Goldstein and Kalant 1990; Krauss and Laezear 1991). No grounded studies have been conducted, however, to examine asset forfeiture in the field and to assess whether it is fair practice or foul play.

This study is an empirical examination of asset forfeiture as a tool of drug enforcement policy. It differs from previous work in this area in that it examines the implementation of the laws from within forfeiture programs, explaining experientially rather than speculatively why and how one aspect of the drug war has gone astray. We begin with a survey of the literature, focusing on the legal basis of forfeiture policy and describing the extent of its use. This section also highlights major criticisms regarding problematic aspects of asset forfeiture programs. This discussion is followed by an explanation of the study. Next, we present observations. We conclude with an assessment of asset forfeiture.

## Background

An initial assessment of the 1988 Anti-Drug Abuse Bill might suggest that it is little more than an intensification of preexisting laws and enforcement programs. Most of the provisions are either replicas or renovations of previous initiatives, but closer examination of the component establishing the Asset Forfeiture Fund reveals new developments. A brief survey of the use of forfeiture in the United States provides a framework for examining these recent changes.

The seizing of assets, both as an enforcement tactic and as a sanction, was practiced long before the creation of the 1988 Anti-Drug Abuse Bill. Historically a felony was defined as a crime for which a person could be required to forfeit all property (Reid 1991). The power of forfeiture was recognized and approved by the American colonies and was used by the First Congress of the United States to confiscate smuggling, pirate, and slave ships (Greek 1992; Myers and Brzostowski 1982). Hundreds of forfeiture laws have been created and are now enforced by both state and federal governments.

The strategy of asset forfeiture was first used against drug dealers in 1970, when persons operating a trafficking organization were required to forfeit illegally acquired profits and assets according to the Comprehensive Drug Abuse Prevention and Control Act of 1970 (*United States Code* V.21). Subsequently Congress authorized federal attorneys to file *in rem* actions, civil lawsuits staking the government's claim to property and money related to the illicit drug industry. This step potentially enabled the government to obtain legal possession of property and currency even despite dismissal of criminal charges based on a legal technicality such as a faulty search warrant or a *Miranda* rights violation. In addition, prosecutors enjoyed the reduced burden of proof required under civil law; a simple preponderance of the evidence, as opposed to the "beyond a reasonable doubt" standard recognized in criminal courts.

The consequences were considerable. During 1979, the first full year of implementation, the DEA seized close to $10 million in assets; this figure reached $54.4 million in 1981 (Myers and Brzostowski 1982). In 1983 more than $100 million in cash and property was forfeited to the government (Stellwagen 1985); an astronomical $460 million was forfeited in 1990 (Bureau of

Justice Statistics 1991). Despite these impressive statistics, advocates of asset forfeiture considered the power to be seriously underutilized.

In the early 1980s all states were seizing illicit substances during routine narcotics operations, but few were following the federal example of seizing drug profits. In 1982, to encourage states that had yet to pass laws attacking the profits of drug trafficking, the DEA developed a Model Forfeiture of Drug Profits Act and published a training manual titled "Drug Agents' Guide to Forfeiture of Assets" (Myers and Brzostowski 1982). The federal agency suggested that states adopting the Act, or a similar provision, allocate revenue generated through seizure and forfeiture to drug enforcement. By 1985, 47 states had passed legislation resembling the 1982 DEA Act (Stellwagen 1985). Federal policy recommendations, formulated in a 1985 U.S. Department of Justice study of 50 prosecutors, including extending statutes to condemn additional types of property and hiring staff for financial investigations and asset management (U.S. Department of Justice 1988). The practice of returning seized money to drug enforcers was incorporated in the 1988 Anti-Drug Abuse Bill and is the heart of the controversy surrounding asset forfeiture and its offspring, a seizure-based style of narcotics policing.

The importance of the Asset Forfeiture Fund, and the element that makes it more than a mere intensification of previous seizure laws, centers on the redirection of the income produced by asset forfeiture (Osborne 1991). Before provision was made for an Asset Forfeiture Fund, income raised by liquidating assets was generally channeled into treasury departments for redistribution into the national or state budgets. Under the present provision, however, a percentage of the funds generated by asset seizures is returned from treasury departments to law enforcement agencies to supplement their budgets. In 1988, in fact, the United States Justice Department shared $24.4 million with state and local law enforcement agencies that participated in investigations and arrests producing forfeitures (Burden 1988:29). A cycle was created, which allowed narcotics operations to make seizures that could be used to finance other operations in which yet more assets might be seized.

Proponents of asset seizure claim that it is necessary for enforcing the law and could turn the tide in the war on drugs. Substantial cash seizures, they argue, cripple large drug trafficking operations. The Los Angeles County Sheriffs Department, for example, seized more than $26 million in drug money in 1987 and another $33 million in 1988 (Stuart 1990). Forfeitures have included a Chevrolet dealership, a recording studio, a thousand-acre plantation, and numerous luxury homes, cars, boats, and planes (Wrobleski and Hess 1990:429). The distribution of the proceeds varies among federal agencies and from state to state. Under Louisiana's Drug Racketeering and Related Organizations law, all property associated with illegal drug activity is subject to forfeiture. Division of the spoils in Louisiana are 50 percent to the state, 25 percent to the district attorney's office, and 25 percent to the narcotics division of the seizing law enforcement agency. The Illinois Narcotics Profit Forfeiture Act allocates 50 percent for local drug policing, 25 percent for narcotics prosecution, and 25 percent to the State Drug Traffic Prevention Fund (U.S. Department of Justice 1988).

## Problems

Success in drug work traditionally has been measured by the protection it provides society through ferreting out drugs and drug dealers, eradicating the substances, and apprehending offenders (Carter 1990; Moore 1977). The goal has been to diminish drug use and trafficking. Despite a problematic history, narcotics policing has employed strategies and tactics that at least appeared to be consistent with policy objectives (Carter and Stephens 1988; Klockars 1983; Manning and Redlinger 1977; Wilson 1961). Many of the traditional problems of drug control, such as exposure to pressures and invitations to corruption (Carter 1990; Chambliss 1988; Wilson 1978), still must be addressed, but new problems have developed since the implementation of asset forfeiture programs.

Journalistic accounts suggest that seizing assets has become a high-priority objective in drug enforcement (Dortch 1992; Shaw 1990; Willson 1990). According to Dan Garner, an undercover narcotics agent in southern California, drug enforcement success is measured by the amount of money seized:

> You see that there's big money out there, you want to seize the big money for your department. For our unit, the sign of whether you were doing good or poorly was how much money you seized, and the kind of cases you did. And my supervisor made it extremely clear that big money cases were a lot more favorable for your overall evaluation than big dope cases (Stuart 1990).

Garner and some of his fellow agents were accused of stealing drug profits during seizure operations. Their story has called attention to a growing problem, as have other highly publicized drug-related police scandals such as the Miami River murders of drug dealers by officers who stole their profits, and the arrest of more than half of the Sea Girt, New Jersey Police Department by the DEA on drug trafficking charges (Dombrink 1988).

Asset forfeiture was designed to be used against major dealers involved heavily in criminal activity. In practice, however, suspects not associated significantly with criminal activity often become the targets of operations because they have valuable assets. Under forfeiture laws, the potential value of assets strongly affects the priority of cases, thus determining who the suspects will be. The goal of raising revenue encourages selection of cases according to the suspect's resources. Targets of police surveillance thus are chosen for their resources rather than for their criminal activity, giving credence to frequent insinuations that the police facilitate crime (Block 1993; Braithwaite, Fisse, and Geis 1987; Marx 1988).

Observers argue that when narcotics officers become revenue producers, the system itself becomes corrupt (Carter 1990; McAlary 1987; Trebach 1987). As one critic points out,

> Once you focus on cash as the goal for the officers, they accept that and they forget about the ultimate goal of eliminating dope dealers. Seizure operations are simply revenue raising devices for departments, and divert officers' attention from the real goal, stopping dope (Stuart 1990).

According to one study, police in both Los Angeles and Miami routinely took assets from dealers but did not arrest them. Officers seized money from individuals and asked them to sign a disclaimer form before release. The disclaimer form stated that the suspect was not the owner of the seized money, had no knowledge of where it came from, and would not attempt to claim it. Such forms were used in investigations where money was seized but no drugs were found. The purpose, according to agency memos, "was to assist the department in gaining legal possession of the money" (Stuart 1990).

Examination of the forfeiture process from seizure to revenue highlights the steps involved in liquidating assets. Seized currency moves through the system more rapidly than do assets such as automobiles and real estate, which must be warehoused (when appropriate), advertised, and auctioned. By seizing cash, law enforcement agencies obtain their percentage of the revenue produced much sooner than by seizing property. For this reason, narcotics operations employ strategies designed to generate cash.

The "reverse sting" (Miller 1991) has emerged as the predominant choice of narcotics divisions. This type of operation features undercover agents as the sellers of drugs, rather than as buyers who seek out illicit substances. This controversial method involves negotiation, frequently through confidential informants, aimed at arranging a time and place at which undercover agents posing as drug dealers will provide felonious resale quantities of an illicit substance for a predetermined price. After the transaction has been completed, a "take-down" team of agents arrests the suspect and seizes any assets than can be associated with the deal (frequently an automobile) as well as any cash involved. The reverse sting is the preferred approach because agents can control and calculate the amount of money a deal will involve before they commit time and resources.

Traditional tactics, such as executing search warrants, often may produce arrests and confiscation of illegal substances, but no certain cash seizure. Narcotics enforcement is becoming a business, in which officers and equipment are allocated so as to maximize profits rather than to control or eradicate drugs. Efficiency is measured by the amount of money seized rather than by the impact on drug trafficking. In achieving efficiency, however, law enforcement has so misused the power of seizure that the Supreme Court recently has limited the scope of forfeiture laws.

In *Austin v. United States* (1993) the high court examined whether the Excessive Fines Clause of the Eighth Amendment applies to forfeitures of property. Although the court declined an invitation to establish a multifactor test for determining whether a forfeiture is excessive, it held that the principle of proportionality serves as a basis by which lower courts may decide individual cases. Thus the court determined that the government exacted too high a penalty (forfeiture of a home, $4,500, and an auto body shop) for the offense (sale of two grams of cocaine). Also, in *U.S. v. A Parcel of Land* (1993), some protection was provided to innocent owners of property related to the drug industry. Although these cases may slow the momentum of future asset-gathering operations, they address only a few of the real and potential dangers presented by forfeiture laws. Observations of undercover reverse sting operations point out these dangers and evidence the contradictions of such an approach.

## The Study: A Year Under Cover

The data for this study come from the observations and experiences of one of the authors, who assumed the role of confidential informant in undercover narcotics operations in a southern state. This position provided a rare opportunity to examine, through covert participant observation, the clandestine work of narcotics operations units and to observe undercover narcotics agents, typically an inaccessible subject group.

While the researcher was a graduate student in a criminal justice program, he became friendly with fellow students who were drug enforcement agents. They invited him to participate in narcotics cases as a confidential informant. Although these fellow graduate students enabled his initial entry, the researcher then interacted with drug agents who did not know him and who had no knowledge of his research objectives. The label confidential informant should not be misconstrued; the position typically involves undercover work more often than the revealing of privileged knowledge to narcotics agents. The primary functions of a confidential informant are negotiating with and manipulating suspects so as to involve them in reverse sting operations.

The sense of police fraternity (Wilson 1961) is intensified in narcotics units, making them neither open nor receptive to research. As a confidential informant, the researcher was not accepted fully in the group. Nevertheless, his position allowed him to penetrate the hidden activities of narcotics operations and provided an excellent vantage point for conducting a study of drug enforcement. Informants interact with agent and criminal alike, often serving as a communication link between the two. This position allows proximity to the thoughts, feelings, motives, and strategies of both agents and suspects, thus permitting an investigation of asset forfeiture as implemented at the street level.

The researcher remained in this position for one year; he participated in 28 narcotics cases with agents and officers from very small city police departments, larger county sheriffs departments, urban and metropolitan forces, and two state law enforcement agencies. Here a case is defined operationally as a series of events that culminated in arrest, seizure of assets, or both. Cases often overlapped because they ranged in duration from a few days to several months. The events of each case were recorded upon leaving the various field settings, maintained in separate files, and updated as each case progressed.

As a "complete-member-researcher" (Adler and Adler 1987), the author conducted "opportunistic research" (Ronai and Ellis 1989) by studying phenomena in a setting in which he participated as a full member. This method also has been called "disguised observation" (Erikson 1967). Its distinguishing feature is that the research objectives are not made known to others in the field setting. The use of disguised or covert observational techniques often has been regarded as ethically controversial, as evidenced by the "deception debate" (Bulmer 1980; Galliher 1973; Humphreys 1970; Roth 1962). Participants in the debate tend to assume one of two polarized positions: moralistic condemnation or responsive justification. Opponents of this method hold that covert strategies should be banned from social science research (Erikson 1967). Their major objection is that these techniques often violate basic ethical principles such as informed consent, invasion of privacy, and the obligation to avoid causing harm to subjects. Specifically, the critics allege that misrepresentation can cause irreparable damage to subjects, to the researcher, and to science by evoking negative public scrutiny and by making subject populations wary of future researchers (Galliher 1973; Polsky 1967).

Justifications for the use of covert techniques have been presented on both practical and philosophical levels. One practical argument is that persons engaged in illegal or unconventional behavior, such as drug dealers and users, simply will not submit to or participate in study by overt methods. Similarly, those in powerful and authoritative positions, such as drug enforcement agents, have been considered secretive and difficult to observe openly (Shils 1975). From a philosophic perspective, Denzin (1968) argues, following Goffman (1959), that all researchers wear masks and ethical propriety thus depends on the context. Denzin suggests that:

the sociologist has the right to make observations on anyone in any setting to the extent that he does so with scientific intents and purposes in mind (1968:50).

The basis for disguise in this study, however, is "the end and the means" position stated first by Roth (1962) and later by Homan (1980). That the end may justify the means also is acknowledged by the British Sociological Association, which allows the covert approach "where it is not possible to use other methods to obtain essential data" (1973:3); such is the case in the present situation. We believe that the benefits of investigating and reporting on this expensive and dysfunctional drug enforcement strategy outweigh its potential costs. Failure to study how this strategy is implemented on the street would condemn other citizens to the misfortunes and abuses we describe below. In addition, scarce resources in the war on drugs would continue to be misused.

Drug enforcers' use of asset forfeiture has been questioned by the press and media so frequently and with such intensity that scholarly examination is warranted. The very nature of the allegations, however, has prompted the police fraternity to close ranks, thus making disguised entry a necessity. To rule out study of covert behavior, whether by the powerful or by the powerless, simply because it cannot be studied openly imposes artificial limits on science and prevents study of what may be important and consequential activities in society. The propriety and the importance of research activities always must be judged case by case. In this particular case, abandoning the study because it could not be conducted with overt techniques would cause the potential misconduct and betrayal of public trust by government officials to remain unexposed. We hope others will agree not only that the end justifies the means in the context of this research, but that it takes ethical precedence.

## Observations: Some Typical Cases

The following examples of cases involve acts and decisions by narcotics agents that illustrate several troubling aspects of asset forfeiture. These concern the impact of forfeiture on both the type of cases selected for undercover operations and the function of covert policing in society.

The researcher first came to understand how cases were assigned priority while he was working with the police department of a medium-sized city in 1989. Still unaware of the profit-seeking nature of narcotics divisions, he began undercover work by "feeling out" possible deals and meeting with an undercover agent to discuss potential cases. The researcher mistakenly believed that a large quantity of drugs or a "known" dealer made a case desirable, and accordingly proposed two possible deals. The first deal involved 2 1/2 pounds of marijuana that a dealer was willing to sell to the researcher's buyer (the agent). The second involved a factory worker who was shopping for a half-pound of marijuana to resell to friends and co-workers. The agent asked the researcher to note the license plate numbers of the suspects' vehicles. The researcher believed the plate numbers were to be used for gathering information such as the suspects' ages, addresses, and arrest records. The primary purpose, however, was to learn whether the suspect owned the vehicle or whether a lien holder was involved. This information enabled the agent to determine the amount of equity in a suspect's vehicle.

The equity in a vehicle represented potential profit that officers could expect to receive if the vehicle was seized. If a person whose car had been seized had a clear title, he or she was likely to lose the car. It would be sold later at auction, and the seizing agency would receive a percentage of the money. If a person was still making payments, the situation was more complex. Normally the defendant was given the option of making a "contribution" to the arresting department's drug fund, equal to the level of equity, in exchange for the seized vehicle.

The agent in charge of this case compared the two proposed deals in order to assess which one would generate more income. The first case involved five times as much marijuana as the second. Also, by working the first deal, officers would take 2 1/2 pounds of marijuana out of circulation because the dealer would be selling. The seller was a full-time drug dealer with two prior drug-related convictions, and was on probation at the time of this case. The suspect in the second deal had no arrest record and appeared to be a relatively small-time user who hoped to make a modest profit by selling quarter-ounce bags of marijuana. Although the first deal seemed more serious, the second would guarantee seizure of at least $700 when the suspect purchased drugs from the agent. In addition, the latter suspect owned a truck, whereas the professional dealer had only a little equity in a late-model sports car. The officer explained that the first deal simply was not profitable and would not be pursued.

The researcher was instructed to arrange for the latter suspect to meet the "seller." When he expressed concern that the officer was encouraging the suspect to commit a crime, the officer justified the operation by contending that the suspect would secure marijuana elsewhere and eventually would become a major dealer. In this way, according to the officer, the problem would be "nipped in the bud" because the suspect would be deterred from future criminal activity. The purchase was consummated with the agent, the suspect was arrested, and his cash and vehicle were seized.

This case provided the agent's department with a small profit. The buyer may or may not have been deterred from future criminal behavior. On the other hand, no drugs were taken out of circulation, and the buyer might never have acted on his intentions to purchase a felonious quantity of drugs if the researcher and the agent had not presented him with such an opportunity.

The strategy involved in this case was termed a "reverse" sting because the visual undercover function of buying narcotics was the opposite of this arrangement: here, officers became sellers. This strategy was preferred by every agency and department with which the researcher was associated because it allowed agents to gauge potential profit before investing a great deal of time and effort. Reverses occurred so regularly that the term *reverse* became synonymous with the word *deal*.

This case was not an isolated incident; it was one of many such cases in which the operational goal was profit rather than the incapacitation of drug dealers. The pursuit of profit clearly influenced policies on case selection.

The researcher was told that only exchanges involving a certain amount of money or narcotics would be acceptable. It was apparent that these guidelines came from supervisors who did not want squads to work comparatively small cases or those of low monetary value, when more profitable options existed. These standards proved to be contrary to the notion of taking distributors off the street.

The drug trade, an illicit market, is similar to licit markets in several ways. One likeness is natural price regulation through the mechanics of supply and demand (Manning and Redlinger 1977). Upon seeing a large bust, supervisors tended mistakenly to believe that the drug markets in their jurisdictions were flooded with a particular substance. Consequently they imposed limits for agents and informants. Ironically, the arrest that prompted the decision was often an isolated incident that did not accurately reflect local drug-trading activity.

These limits were a constant source of annoyance for both the researcher and the officers with whom he worked. One case, in which the researcher and an agent had spent a week preparing a suspect for a deal, provides a revealing example.

The researcher had established a relationship with the suspect, having bought marijuana from him on one occasion and cocaine on another. The suspect was informed that he could discuss business with the researcher's connection, who could supply quantities of marijuana at a low price. Having gained the suspect's confidence and whetted his appetite for a substantial bargain, the researcher arranged a conference between his supplier (an undercover agent) and the suspect. A deal was struck whereby the agent would sell two pounds of marijuana to the suspect for $2,500. The deal was canceled before the transaction, however, because the agent's supervisor decided that only reverses of five pounds or more would be worked. The researcher was told to give the suspect a reason why the deal could not take place.

After two unproductive weeks, the supervisor realized that he had been unrealistic in setting a five-pound limit. He lowered the limit to the previous level of one pound and then ordered the agent to try to recover the deal he had canceled two weeks earlier. The deal could not be saved, however, because the suspect no longer trusted the researcher. The undercover work and the money spent on compensating the researcher had been wasted. In addition, the suspect, a recidivist with criminal intent, remained free to solicit illicit substances.

Another case that was lost because of imposed limits involved a well-known suspect whom an agent had kept under surveillance for more than a year. The suspect, a college student, dealt primarily in "ECSTASY," a hallucinogenic drug in tablet form. The agent told the researcher that previously he had served a search warrant at the suspect's apartment, but had found nothing to warrant an arrest. The student had abused the agent verbally and threatened to sue his department for harassment. Later the researcher learned when and where this suspect was to deliver a quantity of ECSTASY and marijuana. Although the agent wanted to arrest this suspect, largely for revenge, his supervisor was reluctant to pursue the case because it was not regarded as profitable.

Episodes such as these not only involved nonenforcement of narcotics laws, but also promoted cynicism among officers, a troublesome aspect of police work (Carter 1990; Manning 1980). The ever-changing limits on deals magnified this problem as some officers began to question the nature and the true purpose of their occupation.

Other drug agents, however, demonstrated acceptance of asset forfeiture operations. When asked why a search warrant would not be served on a suspect known to have resale quantities of marijuana in his apartment, one officer replied: "Because that would just give us a bunch of dope and the hassle of having to book him (the suspect). We've got all the dope we need in the property room. Just stick to rounding up cases with big money and stay away from warrants."

Selecting cases on the basis of potential gain creates another problem, one that not only causes neglect of obligatory police functions but also tampers with civil rights. To raise revenue, asset-gathering operations must focus on suspects with money and other resources. Large-scale dealers could not have achieved their status without connections and suppliers. Their ties and their discretion make them largely inaccessible to seizure operations because they are not easily "reversible." Many of these dealers value safety more than profit, and work by selling drugs on credit in an operation known as "fronting." They recognize the legal advantage of keeping cash separate from illegal drugs. The big dealers do not make natural suspects for seizure strategies, nor are they easy prey. Consequently agents take the suspects they can get, namely lower-level dealers and ordinary users who fall victim to enterprising informants.

Another incident involved a 19-year-old male college sophomore, who came under surveillance while making routine deliveries of various drugs in a certain county jurisdiction. To obtain information, the researcher arranged and made an authorized purchase of two ounces of marijuana from the suspect. This individual turned out to be a "mule," a person who transports drugs but usually does not make buys or negotiate deals. The regular procedure in situations such as this was to arrest the suspect and then coerce him into cooperating with law enforcement by setting up the bigger dealer with whom he was working.

The researcher was surprised when the agent requested that a meeting be arranged with the suspect. A few days later, the researcher brought the suspect to a bar where the agent was waiting. The agent, having gained the suspect's confidence through conversation and by paying for drinks, persuaded him to secure a personal loan from a bank by using his vehicle as collateral so that he might purchase five pounds of marijuana. The ploy was successful and the suspect was arrested a few days later. This student was not searching for a large quantity of drugs, nor did he view himself as a dealer until the agent showed him how to become one. Thus, at times, undercover policing actually may promote crime by manipulating individuals who are naive, suggestible, or corruptible. Such activity not only victimizes ordinary people but also affects the conduct of police and their function in society.

## The Impact of Forfeiture on Police Conduct

The following example demonstrates how the seizure motive can undermine police interest of service to the community. The suspect, one of the larger "players" whom the researcher encountered, dealt in marijuana, barbiturates, cocaine, and stolen property. The researcher had conducted two "buy-walks" with the suspect in order to establish a relationship. A buy-walk occurs when officers or their assistants purchase illegal substances, but officers do not make an arrest so that they may observe a situation and determine whether it will lead them higher in a drug ring's hierarchy.

The state agent wanted to reverse the suspect, but realized that a reverse strategy was impractical for this situation. The alternative was to serve a search warrant that ideally would occur when the suspect possessed a large amount of cash that could be seized. As a result, the researcher was required to stay in close contact with the suspect for two days; during that time the dealer received a quarter-kilogram of cocaine, a large shipment. This shipment was worth about $7,000 in bulk and as much as $13,000 on the street. The researcher relayed this information to the agent in charge of the operation.

In this case the researcher felt that the only decision to be made was when the warrant should be served. He believed that the narcotics division of the involved state agency would wish to intervene before the drugs could be resold. Proper police procedure does not mandate that agents act immediately on information which makes an arrest possible. If that were so, valuable periods of surveillance could not be conducted. The researcher, however, was surprised when he was instructed to observe the suspect's transactions to determine the rate at which the cocaine was being resold. Less drugs meant more cash, and the agent's objective was to seize currency rather than cocaine. The case was successful as to proceeds, but perhaps not in view of the quantity of cocaine that officers knowingly permitted to reach consumers. This incident illustrates that a focus on revenue requires police to compromise law enforcement in a manner that may harm rather than protect society.

The pressure created by a demand for productivity created competition among agents from nearby jurisdictions. This was magnified in rural county agencies that also had a city or town police force. Agents consequently became "turf conscious," regarding negatively the arrests of mutual suspects by agents from other agencies because those agents had taken away potential profit and had nullified the time and effort invested in surveillance. Thus operations often disintegrated because of a general lack of interagency cooperation, and numerous suspects were left at large.

One large case collapsed for this reason. A well-known drug dealer, who traded crack and cocaine in a small rural town, had been frequenting a neighboring jurisdiction to visit a woman with whom the researcher became acquainted. The suspect had been delivering drugs on weekly visits and was said to always have a large supply on his person. A city narcotics agent arranged for the researcher and a second undercover informant, a female posing as the researcher's date, to meet with the suspect for a small party at a residence approximately two miles from the city limit, the agent's jurisdictional boundary. The researcher notified the agent when the suspect was coming and described the route he would take.

The researcher and his associate noticed that the suspect possessed a kilogram of cocaine and had an unknown amount of cash in a gallon-sized plastic freezer bag. They attempted to manipulate the dealer into entering the city police department's jurisdiction by suggesting various bars that the group might patronize. The suspect refused to go, and the deal stalled.

Other agents learned what was happening by monitoring surveillance equipment, hidden wires fixed to each informant, but they were powerless to act because of the jurisdictional dilemma. Nothing prevented them, however, from contacting the county sheriff's department or notifying the state agency, who might have conducted a vehicle stop. Even so, the agents took no action, and the suspect slipped away with his bag of money and cocaine.

Even in cases involving children's welfare, officers sometimes failed to notify other agencies. In one such case, officers of a state agency monitored the daily activities of a marijuana and cocaine dealer for a long period because he was a vital link in an interstate drug ring. On one occasion, while the researcher was waiting with the suspect late at night for a phone call regarding a shipment of cocaine, he saw the suspect overdose; he had been injecting cocaine repeatedly for two hours. The man came staggering from a bathroom and muttered something unintelligible as he walked toward a patio. He forgot to open a sliding glass door and rammed his body through the glass, cutting his face and arms badly. His wife called for an ambulance and then revealed that he had overdosed twice before.

Less than a week later, the researcher was invited to a party to celebrate the suspect's release from the hospital. The party was disrupted when a friend of the suspect brought warning of a possible raid, thus prompting the suspect to retreat to a motel room with his wife and her 12-year-old son from a previous marriage. Suffering from intense paranoia, they remained there for eight days where the researcher visited them twice.

The boy in this family had failed three grades in school and was permitted to smoke pot and drink beer. The case was unfolding in late September, when he should have been attending school. This issue was raised by the suspect's wife, who had received warnings of legal action due to the boy's excessive absences. Furthermore, during this period, the suspect traveled with his wife to a bordering state to secure drugs, leaving the youth alone in the motel room for two days.

The researcher relayed the details of this situation to the agents working the case, who listened with indifference. The researcher recommended that the agents contact the Department of Human Services (DHS), but was told that such action would only disrupt the case; DHS would be notified after an arrest was made.

This case dragged on for another month before the suspect was arrested in a marijuana field in another county. When the researcher inquired about the boy, two agents explained that the time required to contact a social worker and complete the paperwork associated with that step could be better spent in making another case.

During the summer of 1990, the researcher spent several weeks concentrating on locating marijuana patches. This task was difficult because of the secretive nature of marijuana farming and the suspicion among farmers who previously had lost crops to thieves. To induce growers to reveal the location of their crops, the researcher joined suspects in planting other patches, thus becoming a "partner." This act fostered a common bond, which often produced the information that agents desired. The researcher observed that marijuana growers took a great deal of pride in their work and often bragged about their botanical abilities. When he expressed doubt about the truthfulness of growers' claims, occasionally they showed him a patch as proof of their cultivation skills.

One eradication case demonstrated how the objective of raising revenue undermined the police functions of apprehending criminals and enforcing narcotics laws. The researcher traveled with a suspect to a rural county, while six state agents in three vehicles tailed the suspect's truck to the site where the researcher had visited twice. Another group of state agents, the "take-down" team, waited in the woods at the edge of a marijuana field. This was the researcher's largest case in terms of the number of agents involved, the amount of marijuana (approximately 50 pounds), and the potential value of the plants. The marijuana grew in three loosely connected rectangular patches, each containing approximately 30 plants 12 to 16 feet high.

The researcher and the suspect arrived at the location and hiked two miles to reach the patches. This period was very suspenseful because armed, camouflaged agents were filming every move. The suspect was armed with a semiautomatic shotgun and a nine-millimeter pistol; the researcher carried a rifle. The possibility of gunfire and the size of the deal created a great deal of anxiety.

The suspect had come to the patches on this occasion to fertilize the plants with a liquid nitrogen solution. After he and the researcher had tended to about half of the plants, agents emerged from the brush, pointing automatic weapons. Both the suspect and the researcher were ordered to lie on the ground, and were handcuffed. To protect the researcher's identity, the agents subjected him to everything that was done to the suspect, such as frisking and interrogating. The agents cut down the plants, seized the suspect's firearms, took approximately $300 in cash, which was in his wallet, and another $200 from the glove box in his truck. A quick records check on the truck showed that the grower did not own it; thus seizure of this vehicle was an unattractive option.

After taking everything of value, the agents ordered the grower to enter his truck and leave, without formally arresting him for cultivating marijuana. In effect they appeared to rob the suspect. When the researcher inquired about this questionable use of discretion, an agent replied that the grower was subject to being indicted at a later date. The suspect had not been charged formally when this study was concluded.

In several cases that the researcher observed, members of the law enforcement community compromised legitimate police functions to secure profits. This last case is significant because the pursuit of higher goals was completely abandoned. Usually the objectives of seizure operations were disguised and mixed with traditional activities, including arrests, but in this case the taking of assets was displayed boldly as the foremost concern.

## An Assessment of Asset Forfeit

Before asset forfeiture policies were established, narcotics cases were assigned priority by the amount of drugs involved and the level of threat to society posed by suspects. The observations made here, however, show that asset seizure has become the primary objective of drug enforcement. The problematic nature of asset forfeiture policy became apparent when the development of specific narcotics cases was observed. Before the procedural stage of the observed cases, the fundamental function of narcotics divisions was made clear to officers and agents through supervisors' decisions as to which cases would be pursued.

Selection of cases on the basis of seizure policy creates two basic problems. First, the process of raising revenue through asset forfeiture often requires police to concentrate on cases that offer little or no direct social benefit. Second, the suspects involved in these cases often are not engaged in serious criminal activity. Their personal profiles differ greatly from those of the drug lords, for whom asset forfeiture strategies were designed.

Equally disturbing is the effect of asset-hunting operations on police conduct; they elevate both the image and the reality of the private soldier over those of the public servant. Too often the tactics required to generate regular seizures conflict with the ideals of protecting and serving the public. A situation has developed, which allows narcotics supervisors to choose justifiably between strategies that produce revenue and those which acknowledge the demands of justice.

The recent Supreme Court decisions have done little to alter the present approach of forfeiture programs. Both *Austin v. United States* (1993) and *U.S. v. A Parcel of Land* (1993) set limits on forfeiture, thus protecting citizens' civil liberties. These restrictions, however, will not necessarily limit the scope of victimization and intrusion; they may even worsen the present condition. The principle of proportionality, for example, confines law enforcers to less property per seizure, but may invite more frequent application of the tactic so as to maintain revenue levels already fixed in agency budgets.

In certain cases, asset forfeiture has proved to be a valuable enforcement tool. This potential benefit, however, must be weighed against unfavorable consequences. This study addresses what recently has been considered a primary question concerning forfeiture laws: "What impact will asset forfeiture have on police operations and management?" (Holden 1993:1). It is apparent that asset forfeiture is already being institutionalized within law enforcement;

this process is influencing its disposition. Although the narcotics units observed in this study were confined to one general locale, the mid-south, neither empirical studies nor journalistic accounts suggest that seizure-based policing tactics differ elsewhere. Certainly, further examinations of asset forfeiture programs should be pursued. Interrelated topics to be addressed include comparative analysis of the levels of assets seized by federal and state agencies, by regions of the country; the relationship of forfeiture to the fiscal autonomy of the police (Miller and Bryan); the soundness of conceptualizing forfeiture as legitimized police deviance; and selective targeting by race and class.

The redirection of narcotics enforcement is manifested theoretically in broader implications for the entire interaction of law enforcement with society at large. The inherent contradictions of asset seizure practices have surfaced as highly controversial civil liberties violations which increasingly have eroded our sense of fairness and have caused drug enforcers to subordinate justice to profit. This insidious redirection is rooted in and propelled by American values of success, specifically profit. Societal and governmental opposition rarely succeeds in deterring means of income generation. The enforcers' inability to combat the pervasive illicit drug market does not justify legal mechanisms whereby law enforcement agencies share the wealth of drug trafficking under the guise of "service" to society.

Asset forfeiture has given drug enforcers a powerful incentive to maintain and manage economic mechanisms that allow the illegal drug market to continue. In this market, the drug enforcers and the drug traffickers become symbiotic beneficiaries of the "War on Drugs." Ironically, in its failure to reduce the marketing of illegal drugs, drug enforcement has succeeded in profiteering. Unfortunately, continued "success" in this area portends further and more widespread subversion of our ideals of fairness and justice.

## References

Adler, P. A. and P. Adler (1987) "The Past and Future of Ethnography." *Journal of Contemporary Ethnography* 16:4–24.

Block, A. (1983) "Issues and Theories on Covert Policing." *Crime, Law and Social Change: An International Journal* (special issue) 18:35–60.

Braithwaite, J. B. Fisse, and G. Geis (1987) "Covert Facilitation and Crime: Restoring Balance to the Entrapment Debate." *Journal of Social Issues* 43:5–42.

British Sociological Association (1973) *Statement of Ethical Principles and Their Application to Sociological Practice.*

Bugliosi, V. T. (1991) *Drugs in America: The Case for Victory.* New York: Knightsbridge.

Bulmer, M. (1980) "Comment on the Ethics of Covert Methods." *British Journal of Sociology* 31:59–65.

Burden, O. P. (1988) "Finding Light at the End of the Drug War Tunnel." *Law Enforcement News*, December 15, pp. 8.

Bureau of Justice Statistics (1991) *Sourcebook of Criminal Justice Statistics*. Washington, DC: National Institute of Justice.

Carter, D. L. (1990) "Drug Related Corruption of Police Officers: A Contemporary Typology." *Journal of Criminal Justice* 18:85–98.

Carter, D. L. and D. W. Stephens (1988) *Drug Abuse by Police Officers: An Analysis of Policy Issues*. Springfield, IL: Thomas.

Chambliss, W. (1988) *On the Take: From Petty Crooks to Presidents*. Bloomington: Indiana University Press.

Currie, E. (1993) *Reckoning: Drugs, the Cities, and the American Future*. New York: Hill and Wang.

Denzin, N. (1968) "On the Ethics of Disguised Observation." *Social Problems* 115:502–504.

Dombrink, J. (1988) "The Touchables: Vice and Police Corruption in the 1980s." *Law and Contemporary Problems* 51:201–32.

Dortch, S. (1992) "356 Marijuana Plants, House, Weapons Seized." *Knoxville News-Sentinel*, August 29, pp. 1.

Drug Enforcement Administration (1992) *Illegal Drug Price/Purity Report*. Washington, DC: Drug Enforcement Administration.

Drug Policy Foundation (1992) "Asset Forfeiture: Fair Practice or Foul Play?" (Film) *Drug Forum*, Date Not Available

Elsasser, G. (1990) "A Just Cause: Washington Group Wages War on the War on Drugs." *Chicago Tribune*, May 24, pp. 13.

Erikson, K T. (1967) "Disguised Observation in Sociology." *Social Problems* 14:366–72.

Fried, D. J. (1988) "Rationalizing Criminal Forfeiture." *Journal of Criminal Law and Criminology* 79:328–36.

Galliher, J. F. (1973) "The Protection of Human Subjects: A Reexamination of the Professional Code of Ethics." *The American Sociologist* 8:93–100.

Goffman, E. (1959) *The Presentation of Self in Everyday Life*. New York: Doubleday.

Goldstein, A. and H. Kalant (1990) "Drug Policy: Striking the Right Balance." *Science*, September 28, pp. 9–13.

Greek, C. (1992) "Drug Control and Asset Seizures: A Review of the History of Forfeiture in England and Colonial America." In Thomas Mieczkowski (ed.), *Drugs, Crime, and Social Policy*, pp. 4–32. Boston: Allyn & Bacon.

Holden, R. N. (1993) "Police and the Profit-Motive: A New Look at Asset Forfeiture." *ACJS Today* 12:2.

Homan, R. (1980) "The Ethics of Covert Methods." *British Journal of Sociology* 3146–59.

Humphreys, L. (1970) *Tearoom Trade: Impersonal Sex in Public Places*. New York: Aldine.

Inciardi, J. A. (1991) *The Drug Legalization Debate*. 2nd ed. Newbury Park, CA: Sage.

Jacobs, D. (1992) "Police Take $700 from Man, Calling It Drug Money." *Knoxville News-Sentinel*, February 23, pp. 1.

Kleiman, M. A. R. (1989) *Marijuana: Costs of Abuse, Costs of Control*. New York: Greenwood.

———. (1992) *Against Excess: Drug Policy for Results*. New York: Basic Books.

Klockars, C. (1983) *Thinking about Police*. New York: McGraw-Hill.

Krauss, M. B. and E. P. Laezear, eds. (1991) *Searching for Alternatives: Drug-Control Policy in the United States*. Stanford, CA: Hoover Institution Press.

Lawrence, C. C. (1988) "Congress Clears Anti-Drug Bills." *Congressional Quarterly Weekly Report*, October 29, pp. 3145.

Manning, P. K. (1980) *The Narc's Game: Organizational and Informational Limits on Drug Enforcement*. Cambridge, MA: MIT Press.

Manning, P. K. and L. J. Redlinger (1977) "Invitational Edges of Corruption: Some Consequences of Narcotic Law Enforcement." In P. Rock (ed.), *Drugs and Politics*, pp. 279–310. Rutgers, NJ: Transaction Books.

Marx, G. (1988) *Undercover: Police Surveillance in America*. Los Angeles: Twentieth Century Fund Books.

McAlary, M. (1987) *Buddy Boys: When Cops Turn Bad*. New York: Putnam's.

Miller, J. M. (1991) "Inside Narcotics Policing Operations." Master's thesis, Middle Tennessee State University.

Miller, J. M. and K. Bryant "Predicting Police Behavior: Ecology, Class, and Autonomy." *American Journal of Criminal Justice*.

Moore, M. (1977) *Buy and Bust: The Effective Regulation of an Illicit Market in Heroin*. Lexington, MA: Lexington Books.

———. (1988) "Drug Trafficking." In *Crime File*, pp. 1-4. Washington National Institute of Justice.

Morganthau, T. and P. Katel (1990) "Uncivil Liberties? Debating Whether Drug War Tactics Are Eroding Constitutional Rights." *Newsweek*, April 29, pp. 18–21.

Myers, H. L. and J. Brzostowski (1982) "Dealers, Dollars, and Drugs: Drug Law Enforcement's Promising New Program." *Drug Enforcement* (Summer): 7–10.

Osborne, J. (1991) *The Spectre of Forfeiture*. Frazier Park, CA: Access Unlimited.

Polsky, N. (1967) *Hustlers, Beats, and Others*. New York: Anchor.

Reid, S. T. (1991) *Crime and Criminology*. San Francisco: Holt, Rinehart, and Winston.

Reuter, P. and M. A. R. Kleiman (1986) "Risks and prices." In M. Tonry and N. Morris (eds.), *Crime and Justice: An Annual Review of Research*, pp. 289–340. Chicago: University of Chicago Press.

Ronai, C. R. and C. Ellis (1989) "Turn-Ons for Money: Interactional Strategies of the Table Dancer." *Journal of Contemporary Ethnography* 18:271–98.

Roth, J. A. (1962) "Comments on Secret Observation." *Social Problems* 9:283–84.

Schneider, A and M. P. Flaherty (1991) "Presumed Guilty: The Law's Victims in the War on Drugs." *Pittsburgh Press*, August 11–16.

Shaw, B. (1990) "Fifth Amendment Failures and RICO Forfeitures." *American Business Law Journal* 28:169–200.

Shils, E. A. (1975) In *Center and Periphery: Essays in Macrosociology*. Chicago: University of Chicago Press.

Stellwagen, L. D. (1985) "Use of Forfeiture Sanctions in Drug Cases." *Research in Brief* (July): ___.

Stuart, C. (1990) "When Cops Go Bad." (Film) *Frontline*, July 18.

Trebach, A. S. (1987) *The Great Drug War*. Washington, DC: Drug Policy Foundation.

Trebach, A. S. and K. B. Zeese (1990) *Drug Prohibition and the Conscience of Nations*. Washington, DC: Drug Policy Foundation.

United States Department of Justice (1988) *Research Brief*. Washington, DC: National Institute of Justice.

Walker, W. O. (1992) *Drug Control Policy: Essays in Historical and Comparative Perspective*. University Park: Pennsylvania State University Press.

Weisheit, R. A. (1991) "Drug Use among Domestic Marijuana Growers." *Contemporary Drug Problems* 17:191–217.

Willson, E. (1990) "Did a Drug Dealer Own Your Home? (Criminal assets may be seized)." *Florida Trend*, February, pp. 6–9.

Wilson, J. Q. (1961) *Varieties of Police Behavior*. Cambridge: Harvard University Press.

____. (1978) *The Investigators: Managing the F.B.I. and the Drug Enforcement Administration*. New York: Basic Books.

Wistosky, S. (1990) *Beyond the War on Drugs: Overcoming a Failed Public Policy*. Buffalo: Prometheus Books.

Wrobleski, H. M. and K. M. Hess (1990) *Introduction to Law Enforcement and Criminal Justice*. St. Paul: West.

Zimring, F. E. and G. Hawkins (1992) *The Search for Rational Drug Control*. New York: Cambridge University Press.

## Cases Cited

*Austin v. United States* 113 S Ct. 2801 (1993)

*U.S. v. A Parcel of Land* 113 S. Ct. 1126 (1993)

# 14

# The Military as Drug Police
## Exercising the Ideology of War

## Peter B. Kraska

## Introduction: Metaphorically Speaking. . .

Metaphors help us make sense of confusing and complex phenomena by associating those phenomena with something we can easily relate to and comprehend. The "war on drugs" metaphor furnishes society with what must be an appealing association that simplifies our thoughts and actions related to controlling substance abuse. The consequences of thinking about the substance abuse problem and what we should do about it as *war* should not be underestimated. Metaphors provide the framework for constructing and perceiving reality; in Morgan's terms, "metaphor has a formative impact on language, on the construction and embellishment of meaning, and on the development of theory and knowledge of all kinds" (Morgan, 1993:277). As applied here,

This is a revised version of a chapter titled "Militarizing the Drug War: A Sign of the Times," in P. B. Kraska (ed.), *Altered States of Mind: Critical Observations of the Drug War* (1993). New York: Garland Publishing.

the drug-war metaphor provides the theoretical/ideological backdrop that helps shape our mainstream drug control approach.

Nowhere is this connection more evident than in the recent "militarization" of drug control activities. It seems that where the war metaphor was once intended to be interpreted and used figuratively, current drug-war trends demonstrate a literal application—literal to the point that Congress, at the urging of President Bush, assigned the Department of Defense a key role in administering all drug-related interdiction efforts. The military currently conducts drug control operations in foreign countries, on the high seas, at our borders, and, with increasing regularity, within the United States. Violating a long-standing principle of democratic governance, military soldiers and civilian police often collaborate in these operations, blurring their traditionally distinct roles. The Pentagon, in struggling to legitimate itself in the post-cold war environment, has made clear their long-term commitment to the "drug war."

The purpose of this chapter is to explore the development of using the military as drug law enforcers and to uncover this phenomenon's ideological underpinnings. After reviewing the terms "militarization" and "militarism," I present a historical accounting of the military's involvement, followed by a critical-interpretive analysis of the construction and legitimation strategies used to establish the need for and legitimate the use of the armed forces. The conclusion explores this phenomenon's significance for trends in drug control efforts—particularly the emerging relationship between the military, the police, and the criminal justice system.

## Militarization and Militarism

In order to examine the trend of using the military as drug police we must first develop an understanding of the concepts *militarization* and *militarism*. Although criminology has some familiarity with militaristic terms and ideology, we must look to the sociology of military affairs and the area of peace research and studies for a clear discussion of these concepts. Most analyses begin with how Woodrow Wilson first popularized the term "militarism" when lecturing at West Point.

> Militarism does not consist of any army, nor even of the existence of a very great army. Militarism is a spirit. It is a point of view. It is a purpose. The purpose of militarism is to use armies for aggression. (Donovan 1970:25)

Wilson's traditional view of militarism, what Janowitz (1964) terms "designed militarism," emphasizes the military's political, economic, and ideological preeminence within the state and society. Nazi Germany is often cited as an example (Vagts 1959). As Berghahn (1982) explains, though, a more subtle but as powerful form of militarism has developed with the advent of nuclear weapons. The possibility of military action resulting in widespread nuclear destruction has created a logical reluctance to embrace outward indices of military force. However, the nuclear war threat still provides justification for the continual build-up of an enormous military apparatus. Dwight D. Eisenhower in his farewell speech warned the United States of an "immense military establishment" that fuels itself through the arms industry (Lang 1972). He termed this disturbing development the "Military Industrial Complex" (M.I.C.). The following is a list of dominant features of what we might call *contemporary militarism* (Snow 1991; Glossop 1987; Nisbet 1988; Zinn 1990; Klare 1980; Eide and Thee 1980; Kothari et al. 1987). Each of these is relevant to the militarization of drug control efforts.

- An immense and influential arms industry controlled by national and transnational corporations dependent on the military establishment's well-being.
- A military with an active hand in shaping foreign policy, especially with regards to militarizing other countries.
- A subtle, yet pervasive militaristic ideology that stresses aggressiveness and the use of force as an effective problem-solving tool, and the glorification of military power and technology as the means to supremacy.
- An overall tendency to increasingly influence internal and civilian affairs, including the military's involvement in what were traditionally seen as civilian functions (e.g., drug law enforcement).
- A perception by society that the military is a desirable evil, which forces the difficult-to-hide M.I.C. to eschew overt displays of force, weaponry, or publicity, except in times of publicly supported military conflict.

For purposes of this study, then, contemporary militarism represents a state of affairs and a set of ideological beliefs that are the guiding force, or in Wilson's terms, the "spirit," behind the process of "militarization." Militarizing the drug war, thus, is the actual application of contemporary militarism to drug control efforts, including the armed forces' involvement and the civilian forces' adoption of militaristic practices, hardware, technology, values, language, and ideology.

In order to examine the extent and significance of the military's involvement, several data- collection strategies were employed. The secrecy surrounding military activity required a mixture of traditional and unorthodox research strategies. Admiral George Gee reported to Congress that the Pentagon is "purposefully" keeping the military's visibility in the drug war as low as possible (C-Span, 1992). "Low visibility" translates into a tight lid on data and information. This research includes data collected through an analysis of over a hundred government documents and congressional hearings; in-depth interviews with military personnel (n=31); interviews with investigative reporters (N=4); observations from the field; and a collection of media accounts, including military periodicals.

## The Politics of Drug Wars: Enlisting the Military

Illicit drug control efforts have always contained an element of militaristic thinking and practices since their criminalization in the early 1900s. Defining certain types of drug use or distribution as "criminal behavior" automatically invokes the quasi-military institutions of the criminal justice system. It has only been within the last decade, however, during the U.S. government's escalation of drug control efforts, that ameliorating our substance abuse problem has been seen not only as the function of civilian law enforcement but as an appropriate role for the armed forces.

The military, in an uncoordinated fashion, began its involvement in drug control efforts in the late 1970s. Probably the first use of active duty troops was in 1977 when the Governor of Hawaii activated the National Guard to launch Operation Green Harvest (Temple 1989). Like most early programs using the military, this massive marijuana eradication effort was designed to put the marijuana industry out of business. The Coast Guard, in being responsible for maritime law enforcement, expanded its drug interdiction efforts beginning in the mid-1970s (Walter 1988). The Department of Defense has in fact been lending equipment to the Coast Guard and the U.S. Customs department to aid interdiction efforts since 1971 (Bagley 1988). The Coast Guard is actually a branch of the military, although it operates both as a law enforcement agency and military unit under the Department of Transportation during peacetime.

Except for these occasional incidents, it was not until 1978, when Congress became aware of the seemingly enormous amount of illicit drugs entering the United States through the maritime borders of Florida, that serious discussions of involving the military on a broader level were considered. On June 9 and 10 of that year, at the urging of a Florida Congressman Herbert Burke, the entire House Select Committee on Narcotic Abuse and Control traveled to Florida to hear and see firsthand what Burke termed the "drug disaster." The committee reported being "shocked" at what they found.

Almost daily, tons of marijuana and kilos of cocaine were interdicted, yet it is clear from testimony given to the committee that these seizures represent only the tip of the iceberg. . . .The committee estimates that less than 5 percent of the total contraband coming into South Florida was seized prior to the committee's hearing. . . .Illegal drug trafficking had, within the last 2 years, become the largest single commercial activity in the Florida area. (Select Committee on Narcotics, 1978:1)

The investigation focused on the economic impact this problem would have on Southern Florida and the safety of its borders—not the substance abuse problem itself. The members justified military-style measures to combat the problem by claiming that the unchecked smuggling of any contraband leads to the smuggling of "terrorist paraphernalia," which threatens national security. With the Coast Guard and U.S. Customs being plagued by outdated equipment and limited resources, the committee recommended that the military supply law enforcement officials with aircraft, boats, and electronic surveillance equipment. The members voiced their frustration at not being able to more actively involve the military by recommending to the White House a revision of the *Posse Comitatus* legislation of 1878, which prohibited the military from engaging in almost all civilian law enforcement activity.

It took only one year after Ronald Reagan's election in 1980 to relieve their frustration. Reagan assigned Vice President George Bush the task of doing something about this perceived "invasion" of drugs (Penn, 1982). He developed a military-dominated, multiagency South Florida Task Force, with a Navy Admiral (Daniel Murphy) as director of operations. By 1981, the proposed revisions of the *Posse Comitatus* law were passed, allowing the military to loan equipment to the civilian police, train law enforcement personnel, and directly assist in some aspects of interdiction efforts (Moore 1987). The revisions stopped short of giving military personnel arrest or search-and-seizure powers. Funding for this operation came primarily from Reagan's diversion of $709 million from treatment and education programs to law enforcement (Kraska 1990).

Early appraisals of these military-style operations were naively optimistic. One media report claimed that a single five-month operation raised the price of a kilo of cocaine from $5,000 to $60,000. Military hardware played a critical role:

The customs service also is benefiting from the addition of three Army Cobra helicopters, formerly used in Vietnam. The Cobras are speedy and highly maneuverable, capable of overtaking slow-moving drug planes, landing next to them and blocking the smugglers' escape. (Penn 1982)

The revision of *Posse Comitatus* and the Reagan Administration's use of the military during Bush's Southern Task Force paved the way for several joint efforts between civilian police and the armed forces between 1982 and 1985. In 1983, for example, Vice President Bush coordinated a massive program titled the National Narcotics Border Interdiction System. The program was designed to link all the military branches—Air Force, Navy, Army, and Marines—with both local and federal law enforcement agencies (Korb 1985; Moore 1987). This same year, the military began providing "training assistance" to police and military forces in several Latin American Countries (Trebach 1987; Committee on Foreign Affairs 1986) and, within the United States, several states began activating the National Guard to help with marijuana eradication programs (Temple 1989). The largest domestic marijuana destruction effort during this period was titled Operation Delta-9. Trebach (1987:149) recounts how Attorney General Edwin Meese justified this 50-state effort and its expected result:

> We are sending a strong message, both to domestic producers of marijuana and to the source countries outside our borders, that the U.S. government takes very seriously the need to attack the production of this drug. . . . The chief law enforcement officer of the nation promised that no observed marijuana plant would survive on the land of the United States.

These early beginnings of the militarization of drug control efforts, even though unprecedented, were relatively modest. The military was reluctantly involved and only provided technical and training assistance to federal police agencies and the Coast Guard. By 1985-86, however, a groundswell of support for more drastic drug control measures was growing in Congress. Concomitantly, the media began constructing an enticing theme on the cocaine and crack "crisis." The dormant "drug war" was once again resurrected, this time to unprecedented verve. Congressman Gilman captured the mood of the media and politicians during a Congressional meeting on the further repeal of the *Posse Comitatus* law:

> . . . this is a war that requires the increased use of our military to protect our nation from being destroyed by the deadly menace of drugs that have inundated every city, town and school in all of our Congressional Districts. (Subcommittee on Crime 1985:44)

Representative Charles Bennet also focused on a military solution to this rediscovered "deadly menace," claiming that ". . . it would be well if the original Comitatus legislation were repealed, outright and entirely" (Subcommittee on Crime 1985:3). His initial proposal resulted in a toned-down bill known as the Bennet Amendment. It gave the military full law enforcement powers outside the United States and would put them at the forefront of interdiction efforts. The Department of Defense (DoD), under the leadership of Casper Weinberger, protested the amendment, arguing that further military involvement in the drug war violated the sacred separation between the police and military, would be a detriment to military preparedness and would not be cost-effective (Weinberger 1988). The Pentagon's resistance helped to modify the proposed legislation, but it still lured them further into drug control activities. By late 1986, the cost of U.S. *military* interdiction activities had risen to nearly $400 million, as compared to only $4.9 million in 1982 (Moore 1987).

The "drug war" fever in 1985–86 also led to the Joint Chiefs of Staff recommending in 1985 that the military take on the task of eradicating the production and distribution of cocaine and marijuana in Latin American countries (Wilson 1985). Then in April of 1986 Vice President Bush announced that Reagan had signed a National Decision Security Directive declaring "drugs" an official threat to our "national security" (Committee on Foreign Affairs 1986). Both of these extraordinary developments were precursors of the first (publicized) U.S. military coordinated strike within an Andean nation—Operation Blast Furnace, conducted in July and August of the same year. The Bolivian government, under the threat of economic sanctions and possibly even being "decertified" by the United States, solicited help from the U.S. military for assistance in destroying coca production labs. The operation was deemed a short-term success—it curtailed the processing of coca for months—but a long-term failure, since it almost toppled the Paz Estenssoro government and coca production rose to an all time high within only a few months (Marby 1988; Committee on Foreign Affairs 1986).

In May of 1988, Congress held hearings on the role of the military in drug interdiction, resulting in the FY 1989 Defense Authorization Act (Committee on Armed Services 1988a). The act designated the Pentagon to serve as the single lead agency for the detection and monitoring of air and marine drug smugglers and to integrate the national command, control, communications, and intelligence assets for drug interdiction. Throughout these hearings Congress demonstrated its preoccupation with "calling out the troops" and having the military completely take over "drug war" operations—including suggestions for the military to set up "detention camps" (Committee on Armed Services 1988b:109).

Military officials once again exhibited some reluctance to fight the drug war, but a presidential administration and Congress now guided by the drug-war fury of 1988 dismissed their concerns as "bureaucratic footdragging." Resistance at this point was futile anyway. Several political changes combined to force the military's cooperation. Remember that the DoD under the Reagan administration wielded considerable influence. They were the focal point of Reagan's conservative administration, which nearly doubled defense spending in only a few years. Moreover, Defense Secretary Casper Weinberger worked for what could be modestly described as a laissez-faire manager, leaving him with enough clout to minimize the military's involvement in drug control activities (Weinberger 1988). The election of President Bush, however, dramatically changed the political landscape. Bush had already established himself as a militarist in drug control efforts during his vice presidency. His new Defense Secretary, Richard Cheney, who was originally a "creature of Congress" himself, did not question Bush's and Congress's penchant to enlist the military (Select Committee on Narcotics 1991b:87). The Pentagon, at the same time, recognized the increasing transparency of the "Soviet war threat" illusion. Ensuring only modest cuts in a nearly $300-billion-a-year budget would require a cooperative relationship with Congress and a willingness to adopt new roles (Abel 1990; Irwin 1988; Kenney 1989). Consequently, only four months after the passage of the Defense Authorization Act (September 18, 1988) Cheney granted the drug war "high priority" status and directed all branches of the military to draw up plans for their increased involvement (Cheney 1989).

The DoD's new "lead agency" role went a long way toward giving President Bush direct oversight of drug control efforts. He further strengthened his administrative control with the passage of a drug bill in October of 1988, creating the Office of National Drug Control Policy (ONDCP). As he did with Richard Cheney, Bush selected another ideological doppelganger to direct the new agency. Dr. William Bennett became the country's first self-proclaimed "drug czar."

A czar, of course, is an emperor or person having unlimited power over others. The term's martial connotations certainly fit well with the "drug war" rhetoric. Bennett immediately did his title justice by advancing the Bush administration's ideological stance on strengthening interdiction efforts while de-emphasizing education and treatment. He released plans in 1989 to spend an extra $270 million, in addition to the approximately $100 million already being spent, on military and some economic aid for the Andean nations—Colombia, Peru, and Bolivia—to fight drug production (Select Committee on Narcotics 1988a; Shannon 1989). Bennett simply extended the previously mentioned approach taken in Operation Blast Furnace by putting more funds into an ongoing project titled Operation Snowcap. This operation officially began in April of 1987 and was designed to provide "full-time operational capability as a follow-up to Operation Blast Furnace" (Select Committee on Narcotics 1991a:80).

Snowcap's mode of operation was and still is to suppress the cocaine supply by funding, training, and assisting the Andean nations' police and military forces in destroying cocaine production. U.S. support for these efforts came in the form of military economic aid and military hardware; Green Beret, Navy Seal, and other military advisors ostensibly used for training and transportation purposes; and, U.S. law enforcement assistance (Select Committee on Narcotics 1991a; Conniff 1992; Kirk 1991; Reynolds 1990). Bennett's plan, first disclosed by *Time* magazine in August of 1989, was to simply double what was already an unprecedented level of military involvement. He switched from the original plans that emphasized crop eradication and substitution to an approach that relied on paramilitary search-and-destroy missions of processing labs, airstrips, and storehouses (Shannon 1989).

The Bush administration remained sensitive to the negative consequences of appearing to "militarize the drug war" abroad. Their overall strategy, thus, was to minimize actual U.S. troop involvement by using them in an "advisory" capacity. By threatening economic sanctions and dangling the carrot of increased military aid, the United States was able to persuade the Andean nations to militarize, under our design, drug control activities (Klare 1990; Kawell 1991; Reynolds 1990; Kirk 1991). Bush and his advisors temporarily shelved their sensitivities, however, in late 1989 when they shocked the Andean nations by taking some rather overt military steps.

In November of 1989, two seemingly unrelated bits of information were revealed. First, the Justice Department ruled that *Posse Comitatus* revisions allowed U.S. military soldiers to legally arrest drug traffickers within their own countries (Anderson 1990). Second, in late November, it was disclosed that President Bush, under executive order, planned to send the USS *John F. Kennedy* (a carrier) and a nuclear powered cruiser to Colombia. Bush also planned to send additional ships soon thereafter in order to intensify drug interdiction efforts. The White House refused to respond to requests from the Andean nations' press for full disclosure of U.S. plans and intentions.

The actual reason for the Justice Department's ruling on military soldiers making arrests soon became clear—on December 20, 1989, the U.S. military invaded Panama and U.S. soldiers arrested Manuel Noriega for violating federal drug trafficking laws. The government of a sovereign nation had been toppled using military force under the auspices of enforcing U.S. drug laws. Then, on December 28, 1989, Press Secretary Marlin Fitzwater admitted for the first time that the United States was planning to send Navy warships to Colombia for drug interdiction purposes. The Panamanian invasion, however, had incited such criticism from Latin American countries that President Bush decided to terminate the operation (Kamen 1990; Isikoff 1990).

These incidents forced the Bush administration, the ONDCP, and Congress to avoid policies that appear to directly involve the U.S. military. In an extreme example of this approach, Bush ordered General Maxwell Thurman, the director of operations in the Panamanian invasion, to draft similar plans for a simultaneous "hemispheric drug raid" of all the Andean countries. By using these countries' police and military forces, one Defense Department analyst said, "We wouldn't pull the trigger, but we'd point the gun" (Waller et al. 1990: 16).

Dr. Bennett (the "drug czar") soon recognized, however, that successfully exporting the military model would require the United States to prove its willingness to use its military domestically. With U.S. domestic marijuana production doubling between 1985 and 1990, Bennett, in an attempt to avoid the United States' being labelled the "Yankee Hypocrites to the North" (Isikoff, 1990), persuaded Bush to order nearly 200 army and special forces troops to invade the King Range Conservation area in Northern California (Stein 1990). Operation Green Harvest illuminated the Bush administration's plans to further militarize domestic interdiction efforts. Although the bulk of National Guard activity involved marijuana eradication and border patrol missions, Bush seriously considered calling them into the streets of Washington D.C. in order to "fight drug violence" (Weinraub 1989; Sanchez 1990). The Department of Defense, in 1990, allocated over $70 million for National Guard units to conduct over 5,000 interdiction missions in all 50 states (Duncan 1991). Many financially strapped National Guard units suddenly found new lucrative new roles (Kraska 1991). Antidrug funds provided to California's National Guard, for instance, went from $1.75 million in 1989 to more than $17 million in 1991 (National Guard 1992).

## Current State of Affairs

The preceding chronology of events documents the progression of the U.S. military's involvement in the "drug war" from the 1970s to about 1990. The current state of affairs demonstrates an acceleration of this trend. By late 1990 the military fully recognized their precarious standing in the post-cold war era (the Berlin Wall came down in November, 1990). One military observer notes how the Navy views their involvement in the drug war.

> The Navy must find itself a new reason to justify spending. While the Iraqi invasion of Kuwait may have postponed the day of reckoning for the military budgets, the world of tomorrow is certain to be different. . . . The conclusion of the cold war took a reluctant bit player [in the drug war] and made it a star. This transformation was all about money; the drug war is a source of new funds. The Navy has followed a wide trail of dollars to the one "war" in town. . . . The Navy could quickly become the top cop on the maritime beat. (Abel 1990: 58-59)

Even by 1990, then, the previously mentioned hesitation of military officials to get involved had dissipated. The military even began to talk of their long-term involvement. By 1992 the military claimed that the drug war was a long-term, high-priority mission and that "we have a substantial commitment, we're in it for the long haul" (C-Span 1992; see also, Select Committee on Narcotics 1991b).

Although President Clinton de-emphasized the use of the military in the drug war during his first two years in office, he has recently (1996) appointed a military general as the country's new drug czar. The military is still conducting interdiction efforts in several different "theaters"—namely, within the United States, at or near the U.S. land/maritime borders both within and outside the United States, and within foreign countries (including at or near foreign sea borders). All branches of the armed forces are involved.

---

## Excavating Ideology: Examining Construction and Legitimation Strategies

---

These recent developments clearly demonstrate an unprecedented use of our military. The U.S. government is reacting to the abuse of certain mind-altering substances as a problem of criminality so threatening to its order that it must mobilize our armed forces to combat it. The United States has a long tradition of temporarily using military troops to quell what it defines as collective criminality during prison riots, civilian demonstrations and riots, labor strikes, or to control looting after a natural disaster (Houseman, 1986). What we have here, however, is a significant departure from a guiding tenet of democratic governance—the clear separation of a military designed to engage in war, and the civilian police who enforce the law. Even more noteworthy is how this phenomenon has silently expanded with minimal public recognition, debate, or resistance.

The task now is to examine the underlying ideological context driving this phenomenon. Specifically, this section examines the strategies used in successfully constructing and legitimating the need for and the use of the military in policing the drug problem (Deetz, Kersten, 1983; Spector, Kitsuse, 1987). The myriad of rationalizations and claims-making activities hinted in the historical development section are consolidated into three broad strategies: (1) demonizing the enemy; (2) sanitizing the enforcers; and (3) embracing the opposition. The objective here is to analyze the taken-for-granted aspects of militarizing the drug war and to decode the outward actions, policies, and interests of those involved in the construction and legitimation process (Deetz and Kersten 1983).

### Demonizing the Enemy

The construction of social problems occurs not in a vacuum but within a social and political context. This latest drug war exemplifies the reciprocal process of the political system reacting to society's outcry while at the same time orchestrating, with the aid of the media, the volume and nature of the outcry itself (Spector and Kitsuse 1987). Whether based on hysteria or fact, this process has created an image of the drug problem as "endangering" society itself.

A similar construction process occurs when gaining support for waging "real" wars. Whether it is Manuel Noriega or Saddam Hussein, "demonizing the enemy" helps to justify what would normally be unacceptable means. It does this by magnifying the differences between foe and friend so that the conflict becomes a morally righteous one, "between total good and total evil" (Zinn, 1990:71). In the drug war, mind-altering substances are defined as having seductive intentions and sinister motives, the distributors are perceived as ruthless peddlers of death and destruction, and the users are seen as criminogenic co-conspirators deserving harsh punishment.

For many claims makers, therefore, as the following passage from Congressional hearings demonstrates, only one option remains:

> There is no greater threat to the survival of our society than drugs. If the present condition continues, we will no longer be free independent citizens but people entwined and imprisoned by drugs. The military forces of this country must become more involved. (Committee on Armed Services, 1988b:112)

Demonizing the drug problem thus creates an environment whereby almost any policy on behalf of victory becomes morally acceptable. As mentioned earlier, this demonization process so intensified in 1986 that President Reagan declared illegal drugs a "national security threat" justifying the military Operation Blast Furnace, and the further involvement of all the armed forces. This strategy, then, has legitimated the broadening of the definition of what constitutes a threat to national security and the situations where military intervention is appropriate.

The military itself, however, has made it clear during the formative years of their involvement that they rejected outright this expanding definition of their role. They philosophically disagreed with using the military as cops and feared being a scapegoat for what they repeatedly described as a futile approach (Committee on Armed Services 1988a; Weinberger 1988). They even commissioned a research study conducted by the Rand Corporation to document what many already knew—interdiction, even with the military's resources, would have little impact (Reuter et al. 1988). So while the demonization tactic helped establish the importance of militarizing the drug war for others, the military did not and still has not succumbed to the tactic.

Why, then, are they now so readily accepting what they so passionately rejected? The answer is simple yet has disturbing implications—the Department of Defense now realizes the necessity in the post-cold war era of developing a *socially useful* military. Dr. William Taylor used this concept when testifying to Congress on the appropriateness of military involvement in policing narcotics (Committee on Armed Services 1988a). Taylor chastised military officials' myopia in not seeing the greater utility of fighting the drug war. The following passage discloses what he meant by the military becoming "socially useful."

> Now I think there is one more thing that the Department of Defense leadership ought to start thinking about. Defense spending has not only declined recently, it will decline because there is a declining perception of military threat in the Congress and among the American public. . . . If the DoD leadership were smart about the coming environment, they would approach the Congress with a military "social utility" argument which says that military manpower should not be further reduced because the Congress is mandating increased military involvement in the "war on drugs." They should, in fact, argue further that new funds should be appropriated for these expanded missions which are *socially useful*. (Committee on Armed Service 1988a:12–13)

In other words, Taylor recommends that the military get involved not because of the urgency of the substance abuse problem, but because it will help rebuild the military's eroding legitimacy on the fears of social problems as opposed to fears of communism. During these same hearings the military sternly opposed Taylor's position, contending that the drug problem did not threaten national security and that their efforts would only fail. Taylor's views were obviously the more prescient. As one observer put it, "the military sneered at drug interdiction—until they saw the budget crunch coming" (Magnulson 1990:23).

The point here is this: even though the military operates outwardly under the authority of the demonization tactic, in actuality they and their political supporters are tacitly exploiting the "drug crisis" in order to begin the process of substituting more socially useful threats for the now-jaded communist threat. As will be discussed later, militarizing the drug war can be viewed as only part of an even larger trend associated with the military industrial complex broadening the definition of national security and widening the military's range of legitimate activity, including that of "law enforcement" (Kothari et al. 1988; Eide and Thee 1980; Snow 1991). It is important, from the military's point of view, to maintain that they are only capitalizing on what Congress and the two presidential administrations have forced upon them. The next strategy, sanitizing the enforcers, operates to maximize the palatability of militarizing drug law enforcement.

## Sanitizing the Enforcers

Visualize for a moment National Guard soldiers, armed to the hilt, breaking into a U.S. citizen's home, searching for evidence of crack cocaine and arresting the occupants. Or picture an elite force of Green Berets and Navy Seals conducting a clandestine raid on a drug lab in Bolivia, where they destroy buildings, engage in a firefight, and capture the surviving drug insurgents. And lastly, imagine a Navy ship bearing down on a recreational yacht off the coast of Florida, firing warning shots across its bow, and detaining it while armed Navy soldiers search the entire vessel and arrest the occupants.

Each of these scenarios is of course fictitious. Except for hard-core drug war militarists, these scenes are also offensive to our sense of what constitutes proper military action. Interestingly, however, the central point of debate in the last ten years about involving the military in the drug war has been whether military soldiers could make arrests, search and seize evidence, and use force to accomplish their mission. The battle has centered around the repeal of the *Posse Comitatus* Act, originally designed to prohibit the use of the military in civilian law enforcement (Moore 1987). As of this date, despite efforts by members of Congress, the Council of Governors, the League of Mayors, and the Reagan and Bush administrations, the *Posse Comitatus* Act has been revised significantly but not repealed. Military soldiers, therefore, except under some circumstances in foreign countries, do not technically have full law enforcement powers. How, then, do we explain their high level of involvement in the drug war?

By making only minor modifications to the above scenarios we can produce more realistic scenarios, routinely occurring in the drug war. In the first scenario using the National Guard, for instance, we would still have heavily armed soldiers, and they would still be involved in law enforcement activities. Instead of military uniforms, however, the soldiers might wear t-shirts (over their flack jackets) and would stand behind law enforcement personnel in a "support" or "backup" role. They would not actually collect evidence or put on handcuffs, but they could use force to "aid" in detaining someone, and they could point to the evidence. Bocklet (1990:75) explains how in Portland,

> the traditional separation between military and police operations walks a thinner line. Portland became the first municipality to deploy Guardsmen to assist local police in drug raid operations in crack-plagued neighborhoods.

As has occurred in Washington D.C., a military helicopter and crew could also chase suspected drug violators through the city if they decided to flee, but they could only provide surveillance and/or transportation for the civilian police (Kraska 1991; Bocklet 1990). As mentioned earlier, the National

Guard has taken an even more overt law enforcement role during marijuana eradication exercises, but always with the support of civilian police.

These practices should shed light on the original question: how is it that a military prohibited by law from engaging in civilian law enforcement is so highly involved in the drug war? The answer lies in a powerful construction and legitimation tactic herein termed *sanitizing the enforcers*. The "enforcers" of course are the military themselves, and "sanitization" refers to freeing these enforcers from association with anything which might be considered undesirable or damaging. A host of innovative means are employed in order to make more palatable the government's exercise, both domestically and abroad, of its earliest and most crude assertion of its legal authority—military force (Turk 1982; Bittner 1980).

This sanitization strategy might seem constructive to the casual observer. It does restrain the military's full involvement; it maintains at least a symbolic separation between the military and civilian police activity; and, for those emersed in the militarization process, *Posse Comitatus* is viewed as substantively separating police from military activity. The concern here lies in the deceptive nature of this strategy. As evidenced in the scenarios, the sanitization techniques manage to uphold the integrity of the autonomous legal order by sustaining only the outward signs of a clear separation between military and civilian police functions. In drug-war practice, however, the demarcation between civilian police and military activity fades almost beyond recognition.

Outside the United States, specifically within the Andean nations, these types of sanitization tactics take on a unique importance. Recall how a Defense Department analyst earlier characterized the U.S. role in Operation Snowcap: "We wouldn't pull the trigger, but we'd point the gun" (Waller et al. 1990:16). Apparently the U.S. government exports to other countries that which it considers unacceptable for itself: a fully militarized drug war with nothing distinguishing civilian police from the military. "Pointing the gun" means that the United States supplies the money, weapons, expertise, transportation, and assistance both to the actual military forces of a country and to its civilian police forces. The Department of Defense's involvement has been sanctioned only because of these sanitization tactics that allow the United States to "vicariously" militarize the Andean-nation drug war. As illustrated by the uproar discussed earlier over a military carrier being sent to Colombia, whenever the United States has tried to shift from vicarious militarization to direct participation, the presence of U.S. military force becomes too conspicuous (Farah 1990; Duzan 1990; Smith 1990). In short, vicarious militarization still allows the DoD to assume a rather active role, yielding the same end result.

Sanitizing the enforcers is a deceptive yet effective strategy that contributes to the construction and legitimation of militarizing the drug war. It institutes a "win-win" situation for those with a vested interest. It maintains the technical separation between the military and civilian police when fighting the drug war, allowing both not to fully implicate each other in their mutual activities. The military wins by becoming more socially useful while artificially sanitizing itself from the enforcement of the law. As one member of the Joint Chiefs of Staff put it, "We are only in the business of putting trophies in the law enforcement showcase" (C-Span 1992). Along with these trophies, the civilian police win by receiving military hardware, training, and assistance. Indeed, the sanitization strategy enables the civilian police to communicate, act, and think militarily, while still technically retaining their civilian status.

## Embracing the Opposition

A strategy related to sanitizing the enforcers, because it enhances the palatability of militarizing the drug war, deals with how those promoting and implementing an interdiction-oriented approach to the substance abuse problem embrace its opposition's approach—demand reduction—as a means to further perpetuate the interdiction enterprise.

The interdiction approach to rectify the substance abuse problem is the theoretical/ideological underpinning of the militarization trend. The term *interdiction* means to forbid with force or state authority. When applied to drug control efforts, it refers to law enforcement activities that attempt to reduce the availability of illicit drugs through state force (i.e., the supply-side approach). It assumes that a sustained effort at targeting the source of drugs (e.g., crop eradication, lab destruction), the distribution system (e.g., maritime law enforcement, border security), and the sale of drugs (e.g., undercover buy-bust operations) will chip away at supply and eventually diminish the problem. The tools to implement supply policies consist of precisely what the military seemingly has an abundance of: military hardware/technology plus use of force capabilities (or, hardware/technology + force = control). This equation underlies the push for the armed forces' involvement and the militarization of law enforcement agencies as well. Hartlyn (1988:184) terms this approach the "containment model."

As opposed to containing and chipping away at the substance abuse problem, critics of the supply-side approach see drug interdiction efforts as only displacing and transforming it. Interdiction efforts to contain the marijuana supply, for example, have proved counterproductive by generating an enormous domestic marijuana industry (displacement) and marijuana with four times the psychoactive potency of the original, imported marijuana (transformation) (Gaines and Potter, 1993). Hartlyn (1988) terms this approach the "balloon model."

With the bulk of drug-war dollars going toward supply-side efforts and the government taking the extreme measure of using the military, one would assume that at least some evidence exists to support the containment model's efficacy and discredit the balloon model. Without discussing the voluminous literature in this area, the "overall" consensus of evidence and opinion—even according to the General Accounting Office and many drug control bureaucrats—is that the containment approach has failed and will continue to fail (Barnett 1987; Hamowy 1987; Reuter et al. 1988; Slaughter 1988; Nadelman 1988; Wistosky 1986; Trebach 1987; Kenny, 1989; Duca 1987; Committee on Armed Services 1988b; Blair 1990).

If the preoccupation with interdiction underlies the militarization of the drug war, how do those interdiction advocates and practitioners negate this condemnatory evidence and criticism? One would assume that they would quell the opposition with strong, critical rhetoric and an ardent defense of supply-side policies (Henry and Milovanovic 1991). What has developed, however, is a far more advanced strategy that initially embraces the opposition's position, admits its own limitations, and then capitalizes on the opposition's terminology to further the interdiction enterprise.

On the first account, those involved in militarizing the drug war have been able to define and react to the substance abuse problem as one of supply yet outwardly claim the best solution is one of demand. An interview with Vice Admiral James C. Irwin (1989), commander of one of two major drug task forces, represents a consistent pattern among drug control militarists of touting the necessity of supply-side efforts while upholding a reverence for demand reduction. After listing the many problems plaguing the military's drug control efforts, he states:

> But I am optimistic. It is going to take time, and we will never solve it all. And like everyone in the interdiction business will say, the ultimate solution is education. But we haven't made the required effort yet in education. (Irwin 1989:64)

Even the foremost legislative expert on military affairs, Senator Sam Nunn, in a recent congressional hearing on drug interdiction with the Joint Chiefs of Staff, criticized interdiction efforts by maintaining that demand reduction is the "only way" to curb the problem, and supply-side strategies will have only a minimal impact. He never voiced any opposition, however, to the Navy's, Marines', Army's, or National Guard's aggressive interdiction activities (C-Span 1992). Similarly, President Bush's drug czar, Martinez, after a visit to the Andean nations, admitted that the only solution to cocaine production and distribution is through "economic reorientation," not further militarizing the drug war. What came out of his visit, however, were stepped-up interdiction activities by the D.E.A., the U.S. military, and the host country's military and police forces (Select Committee on Narcotics 1991).

How do the military and other interdiction players justify their activities and budgets while waiting for demand reduction to take place? Fortunately for them, the illicit drug industry is able to "donate" an impressive amount of drugs and assets. These seizures are displayed as an indication of performance, even though they have little bearing on the efficacy of interdiction efforts (Rueter terms this the "quantity illusion") (Rueter 1988; Fuss 1989). Again, this practice functions to produce immediate results ("we're accomplishing something"), while the more substantive solution—demand reduction—is being sought.

This reverence for demand reduction brings up the second strategy which is related to embracing the opposition and helps to sustain militaristic interdiction activities: the military is beginning to develop their own variety of demand-reduction strategies based on interdiction ideology. While most people associate education and treatment with demand-reduction tactics, drug-control militarists define demand in martial ways, such as mandatory drug testing; zero-tolerance policies designed to bring pain to casual users; and boot camps, detention camps, and antidrug youth camps all run by military soldiers (Federal Bureau of Prisons 1992; The White House 1991; C-Span 1992; Kraska 1991).

In short, these are all interdiction-oriented, demand-reduction strategies. "Embracing the opposition" thus perpetuates what underlies the militarization of the drug war—an emphasis on interdiction—not by opposing but by extolling the demand-reduction virtues of its opposition.

## Streamlining the Police and Military in the Post-Cold War Era

The interdiction enterprise is further advanced by its use of martial tactics in demand- reduction efforts. What would account for what we might term the "interdiction addiction" in the government's drug control efforts? An unavoidable answer lies in recognizing how the government responds to other forms of behavior it defines as criminal. The dominant "crime control ideology" rests on the same interdiction equation as do militarized drug control efforts—use of force plus hardware/technology equals control. In sum, both embrace the metaphor of *war* and the ideology of militarism. Given these ideological leanings it seems both consistent and logical, when determining policy on the drug/crime problem, to steer toward the militarization of the police and, more importantly, the "police-ization" of the military.

Earlier we discussed how the *war* metaphor, more than just a cliché, reflects the ideological underpinnings of drug control efforts. Lakoff and Johnson (1980) note that the metaphors we use to organize our thoughts and actions mirror the values we harbor. The value-rich concept discussed earlier, contemporary militarism, may constitute the most important factor driving the militarization of the drug war. The tendency of a society to adopt the use of force as a viable problem-solving tool signals the degree to which the tenets of militarism are institutionalized in its civilian affairs, its government, and its ideological structures. Contemporary militarism emanates an ideology that stresses the use of force and domination as an appropriate means to solve problems and gain political power, while glorifying the tools used to accomplish this—military power, hardware, and technology. Militarizing drug control efforts, therefore, can be viewed as evidence of the encroachment of the military and its ideology into the thinking, discourse, and actions of those who construct, carry out, and support policies for society's problems. The legitimation strategy of embracing the opposition demonstrates the myopic focus on militaristic remedies.

Klare (1980:37) warns that the military industrial complex has an important influence on civilian affairs, including the nature of domestic order maintenance. He calls this the *national security syndrome*: "the tendency to expand the definition of 'national security' to require ever-greater control over national life." As noted earlier, the construction strategy of demonizing the enemy defined illicit drugs as posing such a serious social threat that it endangers our society's very existence. Consequently, the Reagan administration in 1986, with the blessing of Congress, took the drastic step of declaring the substance abuse problem an official threat to national security, justifying the escalation of the military's involvement in the Andean nations and within the United States itself.

It is critical to recognize that broadening the definition of "national security" to include the policing of the drug problem preceded the demise of the cold war. It would be misguided, thus, to attribute the militarization of the drug war solely as a result of the M.I.C. grasping for new threats in a post-cold war environment. The influence of contemporary militarism, therefore, stands alone as a critical sociological factor fostering this trend.

The M.I.C.'s precarious standing in the post-cold war world, though, has accelerated and deepened the trend toward militarizing drug control efforts. The United States now has a Department of Defense and its political supporters intent on making the military more "socially useful" in the post-cold war era by expanding its roles into domestic and international law enforcement. Resistance to this expansion seems minimal, partly because it is a logical extension of the nature of civilian law enforcement, and partly due to the neutralizing effects of the sanitization tactics discussed earlier.

The significance of this departure from the traditional roles of the military, police, and criminal justice system cannot be overstated. During the *war* on crime in the 1970s criminologists witnessed a similar, unprecedented development with the state expending large sums of money on the criminal justice system in order to wage a more technologically advanced fight against crime (McLauchlan, 1975). Quinney (1975) recognized this shift as signaling the development of an enormous, self-perpetuating crime control industry with militaristic undertones; he referred to it as the "criminal justice-industrial complex." Militarizing the drug war transcends what was once only an ideological link between criminal justice and militarism, and takes a small yet significant and possibly prophetic step towards incorporating the military industrial complex with the criminal justice-industrial complex. This step toward militarizing drug policies requires close scrutiny, considering that it was generated in an atmosphere of drug-war fever, has little chance of working, and violates the most basic tenets of democratic governance.

# References

Abel, A. (1989). "When Johnny Comes Marching Home." *Proceedings* 115(10): 40–45.

_____. (1990). "Hunker Down Now!" *Proceedings* 116:58–64.

Allen, S. (1990). "Hot on Their Trail: Navy, Law Enforcement Agencies Team Up to Stop Drug Smugglers." *All Hands* (June): 18–30.

America's Defense Monitor (1992). "How Much Is Enough." Washington, DC: Center for Defense Information.

Anderson, C. (1990). "Uncle Sam Gets Serious: A Report From the Front Line." *The ABA Journal* (February): 60–63.

Ault, F. (1990). "We Must Be On Drugs!" *Proceedings* 116:46–51.

Bagley, B. (1988). "The New Hundred Years War? US National Security and the War on Drugs in Latin America." *Journal of InterAmerican Studies and World Affairs* 30 (2, 3): 161–81.

Bak, D., and R. Fournier (1989). "New Weapons in the War Against Drugs." *Design News* (September 4): 117–21.

Barnett, R. (1987). "Curing the Drug-Law Addiction: The Harmful Side Effects of Legal Prohibition." In R. Hamowy (ed.), *Dealing With Drugs: Consequences of Governmental Control*. San Francisco: Pacific Research Institute for Public Policy.

Berghahn, V. (1982). *Militarism: 1861*–1979. New York: St. Martin's Press.

Bittner, E. (1980). *The Functions of Police in Modern Society*. Cambridge: Olegeschlager, Gunn, and Hain.

Blair, D. (1990). "Drug War Delusions." *The Humanist* 50(5): 7–9.

Bocklet, R. (1990). "National Guard Drug Mission Help to Law Enforcement." *Law and Order* 38(2): 71–77.

C-Span (March 26, 1992). Televised Coverage of the Senate Armed Forces Hearing on the Military's Drug-Interdiction Efforts.

Cheney, R. (1989). "Department of Defense Guidance for Implementation of the President's National Drug Control Strategy." Speech delivered to the Senate on September 18.

Coast Guard Pacific Area Public Affairs Office (1988). *Zero-Tolerance: Facts from the Coast Guard.* U.S. Coast Guard, U.S. Department of Transportation.

Committee on Armed Services (1988a). *Narcotics Interdiction and the Use of the Military: Issues for Congress.* Washington, DC: U.S. Government Printing Office.

_____. (1988b). *The Role of the Military in Drug Interdiction.* Washington, DC: U.S. Government Printing Office.

Committee on Foreign Affairs (1986). *The Role of the U.S. Military in Narcotics Control Overseas.* Washington, DC: U.S. Government Printing Office.

Conniff, R. (1992). "Colombia's Dirty War, Washington's Dirty Hands." *The Progressive* (May): 20–27.

Deetz, S., and A. Kersten (1983). "Critical Models of Interpretive Research." In L. Putman and M. Pacanowsky (eds.), *Communication and Organizations: An Interpretive Approach.* Beverly Hills: Sage.

Diaz, C. (1990). "DoD Plays in the Drug War." *Proceedings* Annual Review: 76–86.

Donovan, J. (1970). *Militarism, U.S.A.* New York: Scribner.

Duca, S. (1987). "The Ad Hoc Drug War." *Proceedings* 113 (12): 86–91.

Duzan, M. (1990). "Leave the Army Out of Colombian Anti-Drug Operations." *Wall Street Journal* (May 18): A1.

Eide, A., and M. Thee (1980). *Problems of Contemporary Militarism.* New York: St. Martin's Press.

Farah, D. (1990). "Troops' Drug War Role Questioned: Critics Wary of U.S. Push to Expand Colombian Military's Duties." *Washington Post* (July 24): A16.

Federal Bureau of Prisons (1992). *State of the Bureau 1991.* Washington, DC: U.S. Department of Justice.

Feldman, P. (1988). "Zero-Tolerance." *Los Angeles Times* (May 15): 5.

Fuss, C. (1989). "Lies, Damn Lies, Statistics, and the Drug War." *Proceedings* (December): 65–69.

Gerstenzang, J., and R. Ostrow (1985). "U.S. Launches Massive Caribbean Drug Drive." *New York Times* (November 2): 1, 3.

Glossop, R. (1987). *Confronting War: An Examination of Humanity's Most Pressing Problem.* Jefferson: McFarland and Company.

Hamowy, R. (1987). *Dealing With Drugs: Consequences of Government Control.* San Francisco: Pacific Research Institute for Public Policy.

Hartlyn, J. (1988). "Commentary on Bagley's 'The New Hundred Years War? National Security and The War On Drugs in Latin America'." *Journal of InterAmerican Studies and World Affairs* 30 (2, 3): 183–86.

Henry, S., and D. Milovanovic (1991). "Constitutive Criminology: The Maturation of Critical Theory." *Criminology: An Interdisciplinary Journal* 29 (2): 293–316.

Houseman, G. (1986). *State and Local Government: The New Battleground.* Englewood Cliffs, NJ: Prentice Hall.

Ingrwerson, M. (1990). "US Andean Plan Seen as Risky to Democracies." *Christian Science Monitor* (May 9): 1–2.

Irwin, J. (1989). "Interview: Vice Admiral James C. Irwin, Commander Joint Task Force Four." *Proceedings* 115(10): 60–64.

Isikoff, M. (1990). "U.S. Defers Antidrug Naval Plan." *Washington Post* (January 9): A6.

Janowitz, M. (1964). *The Military in the Political Development of New Nations: An Essay in Comparative Analysis*. Chicago: University of Chicago Press.

Kamen, A. (1990). "Colombian Assent to Drug-Monitoring Flotilla Seen." *Washington Post* (January 8): A8.

Kawell, J. (1991). "Troops, Not Talks in Bolivia." *The Progressive* 55(7): 27–29.

Kenny, J. (1989). "Brace Yourself, DoD, Here Comes Another Mission." *Proceedings* 115 (10): 76–77.

Kirk, R. (1991). "Oh! What a Lovely Drug War in Peru." *The Nation* (September 30): 372–76.

Klare, M. (1980). "Militarism: the Issues Today." In A. Eide and M. Thee (eds.), *Problems of Contemporary Militarism*. New York: St. Martin's Press.

_____. (1990). "Fighting Drugs With The Military." *The Nation* (January 1): 8–11.

Korb, L. (1985). "DoD Assistance in the War On Drugs." *Police Chief* (October): 57–62.

Kothari, R., R. Falk, M. Kaldor, L. Ghee, G. Deshingkar, J. Omo-Fadaka, T. Szentes, J. Silva-Michelena, I. Sabri-Abdalla, and Y. Sakamoto (1988). *Towards a Liberating Peace*. New York: New Horizons Press.

Kraska, P. (1990). "The Unmentionable Alternative: The Need For and The Argument Against the Decriminalization of Drug Laws." In R. Weisheit (ed.), *Drugs, Crime, and the Criminal Justice System*. Cincinnati: Anderson Publishing.

_____. (1991). From field interviews with members of the armed forces and police agencies.

Kufus, M. (1992). "Drug Wars." *Command: Military History, Strategy and Analysis* 18 (September-October): 18–49.

Lahneman, W. (1990). "Interdicting Drugs in the Big Pond." *Proceedings* (July): 56–63.

Lakoff, G., and M. Johnson (1980). *Metaphors We Live By*. Chicago: University of Chicago Press.

Lang, K. (1972). *Military Institutions and the Sociology of War*. Beverly Hills: Sage.

Lens, S. (1987). *Permanent War: The Militarization of America*. New York: Schocken Books.

McLauchlan, G. (1975). "LEAA: A Case Study in the Development of the Social Industrial Complex." *Crime and Social Justice* 4 (Fall-Winter): 15–23.

Mann, M. (1987). "The Roots and Contradiction of Modern Militarism." *The New Left Review* 162: 35–50.

Matthews, W. (1991a). "Military Produces Results in Drug War." *Army Times* 41 (May 13): 17.

_____. (1991b). "Lawmaker Shoots for Higher Stakes in Drug War." *Army Times* 49 (July 8): 12.

Magnulson, E. (1990). "More and More, a Real War." *Time*, January 22.

Marby, D. (1988). "The U.S. Military and the War on Drugs in Latin America." *Journal of InterAmerican Studies and World Affairs* 30 (2, 3): 53–76.

Marx, G. (1988). *Undercover Policing: Police Surveillance in America*. Berkeley: University of California Press.

Melman, S. (1991). "The Juggernaut: Military State Capitalism." *The Nation* (May 20): 649, 664.

Moore, R. (1987). "Posse Comitatus Revisited: The Use of Military in Civilian Law Enforcement." *Journal of Criminal Justice* 15:375–86.

Moore, W. (1987). "No Quick Fix." *National Journal* (November 21): 2954–59.

Nadelman, E. (1988). "The Case for Legalization." *The Public Interest* 2 (92): 3–31.

National Guard Bureau (1992). *National Guard Drug Interdiction and Counter Drug Activities*. Departments of the Army and Air Force.

Nisbet, R. (1988). *The Present Age: Progress and Anarchy in Modern America*. New York: Harper and Row.

Penn, S. (1982). "Joint Agency Effort Is Curbing Smuggling of Drugs Into Florida: Army, Navy, Planes, Help Out On Patrols." *Wall Street Journal* (August 5): 1.

Quinney, R. (1975). *Criminology*. Boston: Little Brown.

Reiss, M. (1991). "Pushing the Pentagon." *Mother Jones* 16 (4): 40.

Reuter, P., G. Crawford, and J. Cave (1988). *Sealing the Borders: The Effects of Increased Military Participation in Drug Interdiction*. Santa Monica: The Rand Corporation.

Reuter, P. (1988). "Quantity Illusions and Paradoxes of Drug Interdiction: Federal Intervention Into Vice Policy." *Law and Contemporary Problems* 51 (1): 233–52.

Reynolds, D. (1990). "The Golden Lie." *The Humanist* 50 (5): 10–14.

Sanchez, R. (1990). "D.C. Curfew Is Proposed By Barry." *Washington Post* (October 18): A4.

Shannon, E. (1989). "Attacking the Source: Bennet's Plans to Send Military Advisers to Aid Anti-Narcotics Campaigns in Peru and Bolivia Arouses Serious Worries." *Time* 134 (9): 10–12.

Select Committee on Narcotics Abuse and Control (1978). *Problems of Law Enforcement and Its Efforts to Reduce the Level of Drug Trafficking in South Florida*. Washington, DC: U.S. Government Printing Office.

Select Committee on Narcotics Abuse and Control (1991a). *Andean Strategy*. Washington, DC: U.S. Government Printing Office.

_____. (1991b). *Federal Drug Interdiction Efforts*. Washington, DC: U.S. Government Printing Office.

Sinoway, R. (1990). "Peaceful Countryside Turns Into Battlefield." *The Drug Policy Letter* 2(4): 4–6.

Skinner, J. (1990). "Narco-Guerilla Warfare: Is the U.S. Prepared?" *Defense and Diplomacy* 4: 48–53.

Slaughter, J. (1988). "Marijuana Prohibition in the United States: History and Analysis of a Failed Policy." *Columbia Journal of Law and Social Change* 21 (4): 417–74.

Smith, P. (1990). "High Political Price Exacted for Any Potential Benefits." *Los Angeles Times* (March 16): 16.

Snow, D. (1991). *The Shape of the Future: The Post-Cold War World*. New York: M.E. Sharpe.

Sommer, M. (1990). "Perils of the Drug War." *The Christian Science Monitor* (September 21): 22–23.

Spector, M., and J. Kitsuse (1987). *Constructing Social Problems*. New York: Aldine DeGruyter.

Stafford, T. (1990). "Snuffing Cocaine at its Source." *Proceedings* Annual Review: 90–91.

Stein, M. (1990). "Army Troops Join Marijuana Raids." *Los Angeles Times* (July 31): A3.

Subcommittee on Crime (1985). *Military Cooperation with Civilian Law Enforcement*. Washington, DC: U.S. Government Printing Office.

Temple, H. (1989). "The Nation's War on Drugs." *Vital Speeches of the Day* (April): 516–19.

Trebach, A. (1987). *The Great Drug War: And Radical Proposals That Could Make America Safe Again*. New York: Macmillan.

Turk, A. (1982). *Political Criminality: The Defiance and Defense of Authority*. Beverly Hills: Sage Publications.

Vagts, A. (1959). *A History of Militarism: Civilian and Military*. New York: Free Press.

Walter, C. (1988). "The Death of the Coast Guard." *Proceedings* (June): 29–33.

Waller, D., M. Miller, J. Barry, and S. Reiss (1990). "Risky Business." *Newsweek* (July 16): 16–19.

Weeks, S. (1992). "Crafting a New Marine Strategy." *Proceedings* (January): 34–38.

Weinberger, C. (1988). "Our Troops Shouldn't Be Drug Cops: Don't Draft the Military to Solve a Law Enforcement Problem." *Washington Post* (May 22): C2.

Weinner, E. (1991). "Drug 'War' Rhetoric Said to be Linked to Police Misconduct." *Drug Enforcement Report* (April 23): 8.

Weinraub, B. (1989). "Bush Considers Calling in Guard to Fight Drug Violence in Capital." *New York Times* (March 21): A1.

Weisheit, R. (1990). *Drugs, Crime, and the Criminal Justice System*. Cincinnati: Anderson Publishing.

White House (1991). *National Drug Control Strategy*. Washington, DC: U.S. Government Printing Office.

Wilson, G. (1985). "Military Urges Wider Drug War: Training Central American Teams, Blocking Transport Envisioned." *Washington Post* (June 20): A22.

Wisotosky, S. (1986). *Breaking the Impasse in the War on Drugs*. New York: Greenwood Press.

Zamichow, N. (1990). "Marines Fight Drug Smugglers in Texas With Flying Drones." *Los Angeles Times* (March 8): A28–A29.

Zinn, H. (1990). *Declarations of Independence: Cross-Examining American Ideology*. New York: Harper-Collins.

# 15

## Not Thinking Like a Lawyer
### The Case of Drugs in the Courts

## Steven Wisotsky

*The history of the narcotics legislation in this country reveals the
determination of Congress to turn the screw of the criminal machinery—
detection, prosecution and punishment—tighter and tighter.*

Alberza v. United States, 450 U.S. 333, 343 (1981)

*The world we have created as a result of the level of thinking we have done
thus far creates problems that cannot be solved at the same level at which we
created them.*

Albert Einstein[1]

## Introduction

The Supreme Court of the United States and the United States Courts of
Appeals have contributed to the generally prevailing confusion, ignorance

Reprinted by permission from the *Notre Dame Journal of Law, Ethics & Public Policy,*
Symposium on Drugs & Society, Vol. 5, No. 3, 1991.

and prejudice surrounding drug control laws and enforcement policies in this country. Rather than deciding drug law issues based upon the actual effects of drugs and drug control laws, these courts have in the main substituted rhetoric for reason and parroted the "party line" on drugs: That is, there is a need "to combat a national drug problem of epidemic proportion"[2] and that "the federal government's efforts to contain and beat back the drug scourge . . . depend importantly on convincing all Americans that drug use is as much a danger to them and to our country as is an external enemy."[3]

Few opinions combine careful reasoning and attention to evidence or empirical knowledge; we are left instead with drug law decisions based mainly on metaphors of outrage at drug users and sellers. Courts denounce the "degeneracy" of "moral perverts," and call them "vampires" or the "walking dead" engaged in "ugly" and "insidious" drug distribution offenses. Generations of scientific research, scholarly analysis, and the reports of learned commissions have been almost completely ignored. The Supreme Court of the United States has never cited the National Commission on Marijuana and Drug Abuse, the Mayor's Committee on The Marijuana Problem in the City of New York, the Panama Canal Zone Military Investigations, or any of the classic drug policy studies of Canada and Great Britain in opinions concerning drug laws.[4] Instead, the volumes of the United States Reports and the Federal Reporter[5] are filled with emotionally charged dicta mimicking the political rhetoric that has dominated drug control in the United States since its inception. Consequently, the courts have reinforced congressional determination to "turn the screw" on criminal procedure and have struck a constitutional balance in favor of law enforcement and against individual rights.[6] Courts have not advanced the cause of intelligent debate about drug policy.

## I. The War(s) on Drugs

The original war on drugs was fought by U.S. Treasury Agents in the decade following passage of the Harrison Narcotics Act of 1914,[7] which brought cocaine and opiates under federal control for the first time. A second war was organized around the Marihuana Tax Act of 1937, when Federal Bureau of Narcotics Commissioner Harry Anslinger told Congress the Act was necessary to stop the "marihuana menace" exemplified by teenage gangs who became violent and murderous after smoking marijuana.[8] A third drug war was officially declared by President Richard Nixon; in a message to Congress he portrayed drug abuse as a "national emergency." Branding it "public enemy number one," he called for a "total offensive."[9]

The drug war that currently has the eye and ear of the American public, or at least the mass media, is the one launched on October 2, 1982, by President

Ronald Reagan. In response to Congressional pressure[10] and widespread community support,[11] he committed his Administration to a War on Drugs:

> The mood towards drugs is changing in this country and the momentum is with us. We are making no excuses for drugs—hard, soft, or otherwise. Drugs are bad and we are going after them.[12]

Twelve days later, in a speech at the Department of Justice, the President pledged an "unshakable commitment . . . to do what is necessary to end the drug menace."[13]

There ensued the greatest build-up and mobilization of law enforcement resources in American history to combat drugs: the CIA, the FBI, DEA, Customs, the State Department, U.S. AID, the Coast Guard, the U.S. Navy, NASA and other services were drawn together and deployed in a futile effort to stem the tide of drugs imported into the U.S. Despite Gramm Rudham, the drug enforcement budget rose by a factor of tenfold, from about $1.2 billion in 1981 to roughly $10 billion in 1990.[14]

Congress, for its part, not only supplied the funds for this war but repealed many of the procedural protections previously guaranteed to those accused of crime, such as a presumption in favor of pretrial release on bail.[15] It also increased severely the penalties for most drug offenses, moving from long maximum prison terms to severe mandatory prison terms, and then to the death penalty for certain persons convicted as drug "kingpins" under the Continuing Criminal Enterprise Statute.[16]

Yet by the close of the decade, after numerous escalations, domestic and foreign, and billions of dollars in expenditures, the drug problem was perceived by the public, according to a Gallup poll undertaken at the request of drug "czar" William Bennett, as having gotten out of control. The public perceived drugs as the nation's number-one problem, so bad as to justify curtailment of personal freedoms.[17]

In response to this perception of crisis, President Bush, having previously pledged to stop cocaine, "the scourge of this Hemisphere," declared a further escalation in the War on Drugs. In a televised address to the nation on September 5, 1989, he announced the impending dispatch of military equipment to Colombia to support a less rhetorical war against the Cocaine Cartels of Medellin and Cali. Despite these aggressive escalations in the "War on Drugs" at home and abroad, drug suppliers enjoyed a raging bull market throughout the 1980s. Cocaine flooded into the country in multi-ton cargo shipments. Federal authorities seized 198,000 pounds in 1988, more than the total supply to the U.S. black market in 1981.[18] Marijuana, with imports pinched off by Coast Guard interdiction of "mother ships" in the Caribbean, became a major agricultural venture in the United States itself.[19]

The media incessantly reported the permeability of U.S. borders to cocaine, marijuana and heroin smugglers. The rise of drug-based urban terrorism compounded the situation. There were reports of burglaries and robberies committed by addicts in search of the next fix; drive-by shootings in the struggle for control of urban turf; and warfare between competing drug gangs armed with automatic weapons. Washington, D.C. led the list of cities in per capita "drug-related" homicides. The violence affected struggling democratic governments in Latin America, as Colombia and Peru teetered on the edge of drug-financed civil war, and at home, media accounts noted the widespread drug-money corruption in big-city police departments in Miami, New York, Chicago, and Los Angeles.

Despite the severity of the social and political problems engendered by the $100 billion black market in illegal drugs—marijuana, cocaine, and heroin—never once did any branch of the government seriously consider the soundness of the premises of the "War on Drugs." No one considered whether the "War on Drugs" "cure" may be worse than the drug abuse "disease." The only questions seriously debated have been in what way and to what extent should the existing war expand; whether to spend 10 or 12 billion dollars, whether to shoot suspected drug smuggling planes from the sky, whether to impose the death penalty upon drug traffickers who did not kill, whether to assassinate foreign traffickers beyond the reach of the U.S. justice system, whether to fully deploy military forces in drug law enforcement operations, etc.

The reason for the single-minded intensity of the crackdown mentality is simple—"drugs are bad," in the words of President Reagan, and "we are going after them." Although a catchy political sound-byte, "drugs are bad," is far from being a factual proposition. Instead it is an incoherent claim, as no meaningful statement about the effects of drugs (or alcohol) can be made without considering several fundamental variables, such as the particular drug, the dosage, frequency of use (habitual, occasional), the purpose of use (therapeutic, recreational), and the physical, personal and social circumstances of the user.

That "drugs are bad" falsely presupposes there is a bona fide distinction on health and welfare grounds between socially approved and outlawed drugs. Some Schedule I drugs, defined as drugs with high potential for abuse and no accepted use in medical practice, were in fact once accepted in medicinal use and were later banned on political and legal grounds.[20] Thus, marijuana was listed in the U.S. Pharmacopeia as a recognized medicine from 1850 to 1942; heroin was in use until 1924.[21] Conversely, socially accepted drugs, such as alcohol and tobacco are protected today by mass consumer denial. Alcohol and tobacco are not called drugs in ordinary conversation, nor are they considered controlled substances under the law. Yet the human destruction from these two drugs is enormous. Reports of the Surgeon General consistently attribute about 1,000 deaths per day—360,000 annual deaths—to lung cancer, cardiovascular disease and other diseases caused by cigarette smoking.[22] The number of alcoholics or "problem drinkers" in the United States is an estimated 10–12 million and the alcohol death toll runs around 50,000–200,000 divided roughly equally between direct morbidity (e.g., cirrhosis of the liver) and traumatic deaths (as in automobile and industrial accidents) in which drunkenness is thought to be the cause.[23]

The minimal legal controls placed on alcohol and tobacco, on the one hand, and the total prohibition on the non-medical use of marijuana, cocaine and heroin, on the other, cannot be justified by any rational assessment of the known physical or psychological effects of these drugs on the consumer or society. The literature of science and of drug policy reveals compelling evidence of the vast gulf between law and medicine in the legal status of drugs.[24] The point of this article is that the judiciary, like the political branches, has to a significant degree[25] ignored the evidence and the authorities, marching to the drum beat of the war on drugs.

## II. The Judicial Role in Drug Control

Ignorance and irrational fears have driven the drug control system from its inception with enactment of the Harrison Narcotics Act of 1914. As an abstract proposition, the irrationality of the drug control system is not especially remarkable; irrationality in the political arena is not after all surprising or unexpected. What is remarkable is the extent to which the irrationality is shared by the judicial branch, the branch institutionally committed to knowledge and reason. Even tough-minded judges at the highest levels of the federal judicial system, such as William Douglas and Hugo Black, have generally followed the crowd in this domain of drugs, embracing uncritically what J. S. Mill called "the tyranny of majority opinion."[26]

Judges who have been called upon to answer drug law policy questions arising as issues of statutory interpretation or constitutional challenge have abandoned the method of fact-based, reasoned elaboration that is the essence of thinking like a lawyer or deciding like a judge.[27] In place of careful analysis, judges have attempted to justify drug law decisions with misinformation or inflammatory rhetoric.

Indeed, there is often little difference between what is said by politicians and what is written by judges. Compare, for example, the September 12, 1989 televised speech by President Bush to the nation's schoolchildren,

> Drugs have no conscience. . . . They just murder people. Young and old, good and bad, innocent and guilty—it doesn't matter.[28]

with the drug dealer as "vampire" image of the Fifth Circuit or the opinion of the Chief Judge of the Southern District of Florida, who condemned drug dealers as "merchants of misery, destruction and death" whose greed has wrought "hideous evil" and "unimaginable sorrow" upon the nation.[29] The result of the comparison is that there is no difference between the executive and judicial branches on this drug war.

Even where the rhetoric is not so inflammatory, judges have nevertheless demonstrated that they share the fears and prejudices of the larger society. Cases reviewed here do not show a spirit of inquiry into facts but instead argument rooted in a priori assumptions. The opinions generally display indifference to facts; empiricism bows to orthodoxy. The opinions do not acknowledge gaps in information generally or in the record of the particular case under review; nor distinguish between fact and supposition; nor cite scientific studies on the properties of drugs or the economic effects of drug enforcement; nor differentiate among illegal drugs or make relevant comparisons to legal ones; nor acknowledge the secondary costs of drug enforcement arising from the black market "crime tariff";[30] nor fairly balance or otherwise attend to competing values of individual liberty and privacy. The opinions generally do not display the qualities of mind that constitute the critical judgment to be expected of judges.[31] Instead, the operative premise is that "drugs are bad," so bad that almost any law or law enforcement measure is validated.

## III. Drug Imagery in the Cases

There are two primary images in the cases on drugs. The original and still dominant theme is addiction as enslavement by drugs.[32] This imagery springs from a dark palette of words and phrases in the cases discussed below: "misery, destruction, and death"; "degradation"; "debasement"; "shameful"; "depravity"; "degeneracy"; "evil." The second major theme is drug trafficking as an "insidious crime" that reinforces the subjugation of the addict, causing crime and violence and inflicting "unimaginable sorrow" on society.

The earliest drug cases reached the Supreme Court not long after drug control (historically a matter left to the police power of the States) was federalized by the Harrison Narcotics Act of 1914. The Harrison Act made it an offense to dispense heroin, cocaine and other narcotics except on forms issued by the Commissioner of Internal Revenue. The prohibition, however, did not apply to a physician distributing drugs to a patient in the course of his professional practice. In a series of cases interpreting the Act and challenging its constitutional validity, the Supreme Court demonstrated its own "drugs-are-bad" philosophy.

In *United States v. Doremus*,[33] the Supreme Court reversed the dismissal of an indictment against a physician for violating Section 2 of the Harrison Act. The indictment alleged that Doremus unlawfully distributed to a man named Ameris 500 one-sixth grain tablets of heroin, without using the prescribed forms, and with knowledge that Ameris was addicted to the drug and was a "dope fiend." The court condemned the doctor for "gratifying his (Ameris') appetite for the drug as a habitual user thereof"[34] without considering the arguments for maintaining an addict on drugs under medical supervision—that it "may . . . become justifiable in certain cases to order regularly the minimum dose which has been found necessary, either in order to avoid serious withdrawal symptoms, or to keep the patient in a condition in which he can lead a useful life."[35]

The *Doremus* indictment was brought as part of the federal government's sustained campaign to put an end to the practice of addiction maintenance, a goal that it largely achieved by the mid-1920s. In the attack on addiction maintenance, approximately 25,000 physicians were indicted, and over 3,000 actually went to prison.[36] The hostile attitude toward drug dependence underlying that campaign comes into sharper relief in *United States v. Behrman*,[37] where a doctor prescribed take-home drugs to an addict named King as a treatment for withdrawal and provided no supervision for its use. The prescription was lawful if regarded as being in the course of the doctor's professional practice. The district court dismissed the indictment, as it did not allege a lack of good faith on the part of the doctor, and held that the statute did not prohibit prescribing maintenance doses to addicts.

Noting the legislative purpose "to confine the distribution of these drugs to the regular and lawful course of professional practice,"[38] the Supreme Court reversed. The court concluded that such "so-called prescriptions could only result in the gratification of a diseased appetite for these pernicious drugs" or an unlawful diversion of them to others by the addict, restrained only by an addict's "weakened and perverted will."[39]

The quantities of drugs involved, in *Behrman* as in *Doremus*, permitted an inference that the prescriptions were being resold on the black market. King had obtained 150 grains of heroin, 360 grains of morphine, and 210 grains of cocaine, which the court pointed out was equivalent to three thousand ordinary doses. Reinstatement of the indictment here might have been defended in light of the abuse of the professional privilege. What is remarkable is the contempt shown by the court for the addict, as though he were something less than human—possessed of a "diseased appetite" and a "perverted will." By comparison, it is difficult to imagine the Supreme Court of the United States using similar language of condemnation in determining whether other conduct constitutes murder, rape or other crime.[40]

For the next several decades, the Supreme Court made no further pronouncements on drugs. A few cases did arise in the lower federal courts, where judges further developed the theme of degradation and debasement. For example, in *Menna v. Menna*,[41] a wife alleged in a divorce suit grounds of "moral turpitude" on the part of her husband for being twice convicted of Harrison Narcotics Act violations. The court agreed that moral turpitude was established by the violations, even though the Harrison Act was a revenue statute administered by the Department of the Treasury.

The court in *Menna* stated that "it has become a matter of general knowledge that the habitual use of opium produces crime, violence, brutality and insanity."[42] The court even went so far as to adduce "proof" that drugs are criminogenic, citing the Narcotic Bureau's Report for 1937 that 63 percent of the drug law violators arrested in that year had previous criminal records. This "proof" completely dispensed with an elementary question of cause and effect: were the individuals made criminals as a result of using drugs, or were they using drugs because they were criminals?

The opinion presumes to answer the defendant's personal culpability in the divorce suit by reference to the wrongdoing of others, a form of guilt by association.[43] Even the guilt by association is deeply flawed, the moral turpitude simply assumed from the "common knowledge" that opium is harmful. That the appellant therefore committed "wicked and shameful acts" is not, in the court's view, truly open to question or in need of proof:

> There can be . . . no question of doubt in anyone's mind that the peddler of these dangerous drugs is a menace to society. Nor can there be the slightest doubt that the crime which it is the purpose of the statute to punish is one involving moral turpitude.

> An act which creates human misery, corruption, and moral ruin in the lives of individuals is necessarily so base and shameful as to leave the offender not wanting in the depravity which the words "moral turpitude" imply.[44]

This is extravagant talk for a court that needed only to decide whether the plaintiff in a divorce action had grounds for divorce by reason of the defendant having been convicted of two Harrison Act violations. The court could have rested its decision on the ground that a felony conviction, by definition, demonstrates moral turpitude. Perhaps the court could have characterized the conviction as a rebuttable presumption of moral turpitude, and examined the statute to see whether the Harrison Act violations were offenses malum in se. The court did not consider questions of strict liability or criminal intent.

More importantly, the court failed to examine the facts underlying the convictions. Did the appellant's particular criminal acts cause actual "misery, corruption and moral ruin" to some identifiable victim(s)? Did his acts create a risk of such harm, and if so, how great was that risk? The court ignored these obvious questions in its zeal to condemn a "base and shameless" "menace to society."[45]

In *Burke v. Kansas State Osteopathic Association, Inc.,*[46] the court held that Kansas law did not confer upon osteopaths, as distinct from physicians, the right to administer narcotic drugs:

> All legislation respecting the use or any limitation on the use of narcotics, is based upon the established fact that narcotic drugs are dangerous. Not that they are poisons within themselves, but are worse than poisons. Their excessive use destroys will power, ambition, self-respect, and in the end, mentality. They make men and women moral perverts. Their influence upon society is most degrading. . . .[47]

In reaching this decision, the court quoted from pop articles warning about the "drug curse," "the evils that come from drugs" and the like. The "established fact" that narcotic drugs are "worse than poisons" which make people "moral perverts" must rank among the most outrageous of anti-drug assertions in the judicial literature. Even the statement that excessive use destroys "mentality" goes beyond the pale of anything resembling reasoned legal discourse. Such language resembles a kind of hellfire-and-brimstone sermon pitting the righteous (virtuous lawmakers) against the wicked (drug users).

As in the *Menna* case, the judicial denunciations are gratuitous; the court had ample grounds on which to base its decision in the definition of osteopathy as being "fundamentally different" in its natural orientation from the practice of medicine involving the administration of drugs. Alternatively, the court might have confined its ground of decision to a simple determination of the legislative intent underlying the Kansas law.

Both *Menna* and *Burke* display an inexcusable ignorance about the effects of drugs and the nature of addiction. Unlike the early Supreme Court cases on Harrison Act issues, the courts of appeals had available to them, in addition to domestic scientific literature, the 1926 Rolleston Committee Report, the landmark study by a distinguished group of British physicians acknowledging the existence of stable addicts and approving the practice of addiction maintenance. Although the issues before the courts in *Menna* and *Burke* were different, those decisions surely could have been improved by consideration of that medical perspective. Rather than speaking in metaphors of "depravity" and "poisons," those courts could have learned that addiction may be considered a disease. The Report defined "addict" as "a person who, not requiring the continued use of a drug for the relief of symptoms of organic disease, has acquired, as a result of repeated administration, an overpowering desire for its continuance, and in whom withdrawal of the drug leads to definite symptoms of mental or physical distress or disorder."[48] Rolleston's reluctant endorsement of addiction maintenance, as a last resort, need not be accepted in order to view the addict as a person rather than as a "moral pervert" lacking "mentality." One of the ironies of these cases, containing some of the hottest anti-drug rhetoric in the reporter system, is that they were decided at a time (1939–40) when the black market in illicit drugs was at its nadir. Apparently, the fears survived an earlier societal scare.

Drug-related issues resurfaced in the Supreme Court in the 1960s. The first, *Robinson v. California*,[49] presented the constitutional validity of a California statute that made it a criminal offense for a person to be addicted to the use of narcotics. The trial court had instructed the jury that the appellant could be convicted upon a finding of his "status" or "chronic condition" as "addicted to the use of narcotics."[50] In the Supreme Court's analysis, the statute punished a person not for the use of narcotics, nor for selling, buying or possession of narcotics in California, but for being an addict—for status or condition without proof of a common law actus reus. The *Robinson* court struck the statute as cruel and unusual punishment under the Eighth Amendment.

But although the *Robinson* decision may appear to be enlightened, the court hastened to add, lest it be thought soft on drugs, "[W]e are not unmindful that the vicious evils of the narcotics traffic have occasioned the grave concern of the government."[51] The "evils" were apparently too obvious to specify. In his concurring opinion, Justice Douglas did not shy away from offering a fantastic bill of particulars on the evils of heroin:

> To be a confirmed drug addict is to be one of the walking dead. . . . The teeth have rotted out; the appetite is lost and the stomach and intestines don't function properly. The gall bladder becomes inflamed; eyes and skin turn a bilious yellow. In some cases membranes of the nose turn a flaming red; the partition separating the nostrils is eaten away—breathing is difficult. Oxygen in the blood decreases; bronchitis and tuberculosis develop. Good traits of character disappear and bad ones emerge. Sex organs become affected. Veins collapse and livid purplish scars remain. Boils and abscesses plague the skin; gnawing pain racks the body. Nerves snap; vicious twitching develops. Imaginary and fantastic fears blight the mind and sometimes complete insanity results. Often times, too, death comes—much too early in life. . . . Such is the plague of being one of the walking dead.[52]

Justice Douglas was known for his rebellious streak and his sense of humor, and the purple passage quoted above may have been intended as a parody. If taken literally, it is absurd, the print equivalent of the 1989 TV commercial showing a frying egg as "your brain on drugs." Even if there were a clinical case to exemplify the foregoing description, it would bear the same relationship to a typical heroin user as a sterno-drinking skid row bum bears to a typical social drinker.

Douglas' opinion is perhaps unique insofar as it exculpates rather than condemns the drug user. Still, his absurdly lurid and inaccurate account of heroin addiction hardly qualifies as an exemplar of lawyer-like fact-finding and analysis. Where are his sources? He cites only an article in a legal newspaper, completely ignoring the extensive body of studies about heroin addiction that had been produced in the United States and Britain. In fact, Douglas had available to him not only the Rolleston Report, but also the first Brain Report, which had been commissioned to review the Rolleston recommendations.

Brain I specifically endorsed the recommendations of the Rolleston Committee on addiction maintenance. The Committee confirmed the existence of "stabilized addicts" based upon "careful scrutiny of the histories of more than a hundred persons classified as addicts." The Brain Committee concluded that "many of them who have been taking small and regular doses for years show little evidence of tolerance and are often leading reasonably satisfactory lives."[53] This should not surprise those knowledgeable about the physiological effects of heroin: "putting aside the problem of addiction, the chemical heroin seems almost a neutral or benign substance. Taken in stable, moderate doses, it does not seem to cause organic injury, as does alcoholism over time." Longevity and good overall health are not uncommon in addicts with access to sterile needles and uncontaminated heroin.[54]

Justice Douglas did not have the benefit of the Zinberg and Trebach books when he wrote *Robinson*; he did have access to Rolleston, Brain I, the Joint Committee of the American Bar Association and the American Medical Association on Narcotic Drugs, Drug Addiction: Crime or Disease? Interim and Final Reports, 1961. Also, an extensive body of research in medical journals was available to refute the ridiculous "walking dead" metaphor. The Justice apparently did not want hard data and informed policy analysis; instead he replaced analysis with metaphor, which better suited his goal. The nature of the nonmedical source he cited, the *New York Law Journal*, a legal newspaper, indicates that he searched for the most grotesque account he could find. Douglas was able to succeed in this gross distortion of reality on the relatively safe assumption that no one would challenge it. After all, it was an "established fact" that narcotics were "worse than poisons." Given that social reality, there was no need for Justice Douglas to quote from the extensive literature of heroin addiction and treatment.

The extremism of the "walking dead" and "worse-than-poisons" rhetoric is brought into sharper relief by comparison with the rarely encountered analytical and temperate approach of the court of appeals in *United States v.*

*Moore*.[55] The court there rejected the defendant's argument that his drug addiction was a defense to drug possession charges, observing that before becoming addicted, a person's heroin use is a "freely willed illegal act."[56] After becoming addicted, an addict cannot demand exculpation on the ground that he cannot stop his drug taking because he "retains some ability to extricate himself from his addiction by ceasing to take drugs," depending upon his "strength of character."[57]

The metaphysics of free will to one side, the court's insistence in *Moore* on the legal responsibility of the addict is consistent with the premise of rehabilitation: the addict must take responsibility for becoming and staying drug free. That it has a basis in reality is demonstrated by the fact that there are millions of *former* addicts—not only of heroin but of the similarly addictive drug nicotine[58]—who have mustered up the necessary self control. This is a far distance from being one of the "walking dead" or a "moral pervert."

The concurring opinion in *Moore* by Judge Leventhal is one of the best informed and most intelligent opinions on drug policy ever published by a judge, speaking in a nuanced way of the respective roles of law enforcement and medicine in responding to drug addiction. There are yet other concurring opinions in this unique case.[59] None of them necessarily captures the elusive truth(s) about drugs and drug addiction. All of the opinions command respect as judicious and judicial. Several opinions canvass and consult the Prettyman Commission, the National Commission on Marihuana and Drug Abuse, and many other authorities on drug issues. This intelligence at work is a far cry from the rantings of the "walking dead" or "worse than poisons" language that in general dominates judicial discussions of drug issues in the cases. Unfortunately, there are few other examples of critical thought by federal judges on the drug issue.

*Turner v. United States*,[60] introduced a new, more modern theme in to the Supreme Court's cases on drugs—the "evils of drug trafficking" confused with and misstated as the "evils of drugs." In this domain, the court failed to recognize the destructive power of drug money, as distinguished from the drugs themselves. Turner was charged *inter alia* with two counts of receiving and transporting illegally imported heroin and cocaine. The Supreme Court reviewed the case with respect to the validity of the statutory presumption that the drugs in question were illegally imported, as charged in two counts of the indictment.

Justice Black, joined by Justice Douglas, dissented vigorously from the portion of the opinion upholding Turner's convictions on the other counts. The strongly worded dissent attacked the majority, listing eight separate respects in which the decision operates "to undercut and destroy" the constitutional rights of the accused.[61] However, the dissenters ironically provided a rationale for the very crackdown they denounced by assuming, without citation or analysis, that "drugs are bad":

> Commercial traffic in deadly mind-soul-and-body-destroying drugs is beyond a doubt one of the greatest evils of our time. It cripples intellects, dwarfs bodies, paralyzes the progress of a substantial segment of our society, and frequently makes hopeless and sometimes violent and murderous criminals of persons of all ages who become its victims. Such consequences call for the most vigorous laws to suppress the traffic as well as the most powerful efforts to put these vigorous laws into effect. *Unfortunately, the grave evils such as the narcotics traffic can too easily cause threats to our basic liberties by making attractive the adoption of constitutionally forbidden short-cuts that might suppress and blot out more quickly the unpopular and dangerous conduct.*[62]

Active verbs in Justice Black's opinion in *Turner*—"cripples," "dwarfs," "paralyzes," "makes"—smack of factuality. The Justice does not trouble to cite any authority for those claims. Rather, he returns to the theme that "drugs are bad," and relies on what the public "knows" and fears about drugs. This is bad medicine and bad law.

The Justice does not trouble to identify the drugs condemned as mind-body-and-soul destroyers in the opinion. Cocaine is in some respects more toxic than heroin, having a narrower range of variation between an effective dose and a lethal dose.[63] Although classified by Title 21 as a Schedule II narcotic—having a high potential for abuse and an accepted use in medical practice in the United States—it is actually a stimulant of the central nervous system similar in its action to amphetamines. It has a legitimate medical use as a topical anesthetic in ear, nose and throat surgery. In 1985, 1,223 people died from illicit cocaine use as reported by Medical Examiners from most major cities (excluding New York); an additional 20,393 persons visited hospital emergency rooms in distress from cocaine.[64] These casualties must be assessed in the context of the consumption by 12.2 million people who reported using cocaine that year.[65] The fear of cocaine looms larger than its actual threat to life and limb, primarily because celebrity overdose deaths such as those of John Belushi, David Kennedy, and Len Bias, proved to be so dramatic and shocking.

Justice Black's claims in *Turner* about cocaine were not true then and remain untrue today even though there is significantly more mortality. Therefore, it is false to say that cocaine in general "cripples intellects" and "dwarfs bodies" as stated in *Turner*. Longer-term physical and mental problems occur, often dramatically, but in unknown proportion to the total population of users.[66] Clearly, Justice Black was not concerned with empiricism but was engaged in a metaphorical exercise in asserting that drugs cripple minds, dwarf bodies or turn people into "violent and murderous criminals." The use of the anthropomorphic "they" in speaking of drugs is especially revealing: it attributes to "drugs" control over the individual. That conclusion quite falsely assumes that there is a predictable *behavioral* as opposed to physical effect from the taking of a drug.[67] Medicine can reliably predict that a person who ingests cocaine will experience an elevated heart rate and other physiological changes; no one can predict whether that person will do anything as a result of the drug.

Justice Black's claims not only lack any basis in evidence, they also defy common sense and experience. "Common knowledge" of drinking suggests that alcohol affects people in many different ways. Alcohol "makes" some people aggressive and violent, some cheerful and gregarious, some passive and drowsy, and some simply sick and non-functional. So, too, can cocaine or any other drug affecting the central nervous system vary in its effects. Further, the incidence and prevalence of harms to the user are fundamentally distinct from the "violent and murderous" trade that seeks to reap the risk premium offered by black market sales. But this distinction is never acknowledged by the dissenters in *Turner*; who simply assert that the drug traffic is "one of the greatest evils of our time."[68] If this is true, it is the result of the black market crime tariff and not the psycho-pharmacological properties of drugs themselves.

The same confusion of drug and drug traffic appeared again in *United States v. Mendenhall*,[69] one of a series of cases to reach the court arising from the use of the airport courier profile.[70] Mendenhall was stopped and questioned during a search and was told that she had a right to refuse to be searched. Because she consented, the court held that two bags containing heroin that were found on her person did not constitute a Fourth Amendment violation.

Justice Powell's concurring opinion, joined by the Chief Justice and Justice Blackmun, once again shows the power of the single, simple yet compelling idea that "drugs are bad":

> The public has a compelling interest in detecting those who would traffic in deadly drugs for personal profit. Few problems affecting the health and welfare of our population, particularly our young, cause greater concern than the escalating use of controlled substances. Much of the drug traffic is highly organized by sophisticated criminal syndicates. The profits are enormous. . . .[71]

Like Justice Black in *Turner*, Justice Powell assumes the worst about the psychopharmacology of drugs, without troubling to check his opinion against medical or pharmacological authorities. He repeatedly used the word "deadly," for example. But as applied to marijuana, this clearly is wrong. Not a single death from the pharmacological action of marijuana has ever been confirmed.

DEA Chief Administrative Law Judge Frances Young ruled in 1988 that marijuana is "far safer than many foods we commonly consume" and that its medical benefits are "clear beyond any question."[72] Marijuana's therapeutic applications include the relief of intra-ocular pressure in glaucoma sufferers and the nausea often suffered by chemotherapy patients. Yet marijuana has an outlaw legal status; it is listed along with heroin as a Schedule I drug and is thus completely outlawed in medical practice in the United States, except for experimental and research purposes.

The beating of the tom-toms of the "War on Drugs," especially the war against cocaine, has caused a kind of national amnesia about marijuana. As recently as 1972, the National Commission on Marijuana and Drug Abuse recommended that private "possession of marihuana for personal use should no longer be an offense" and that "distribution in private of small amounts of marijuana for no remuneration or insignificant remuneration not involving a profit would no longer be an offense."[73] Similar, sometimes broader, proposals to relax the drug laws came from the American Medical Association, the American Bar Association, the Consumer's Union, the National Education Association, the National Council of Churches, the American Public Health Association, the National Advisory Commission on Criminal Justice Standards and Goals and others.[74] As late as 1977, President Carter declared himself in favor of decriminalization of marijuana.

A decade later, the National Academy of Sciences reviewed the findings and recommendation of the National Commission on Marijuana and Drug Abuse. It found no "conclusive evidence" of major, long-term public health problems caused by marijuana, only "worrisome possibilities." On the question of legal control, it basically endorsed the position of the 1972 National Commission: "On balance . . . we believe that a policy of partial prohibition is clearly preferable to a policy of complete prohibition of supply and use."[75] This scientific and informed view contrasts markedly with the political and uninformed point of view embodied in the Anti-Drug Abuse Act of 1988, which states that "Congress . . . believes marijuana is a serious evil in American society and a serious threat to its people."[76]

In light of these recommendations, we cannot assume that Justice Powell meant "drugs" to refer to marijuana. He might have been referring to cocaine, a far more toxic drug and one that can be (although it is not ordinarily) deadly; but Mendenhall was arrested for heroin trafficking. Assuming that Justice Powell meant to refer only to heroin, the drug involved in the case, his use of the word "deadly" is either intended metaphorically or is irresponsibly misleading. Even though heroin has a lethal potential, heroin has benign or therapeutic purposes for the relief of pain, was at one time accepted in medical practice in the United States and Europe, and can be taken by citizens leading "satisfactory lives," as found by the Brain Committee. Heroin is unlike a deadly weapon, for example, one designed to inflict death or great bodily harm, such as a gun or a knife. To call it deadly is thus a rhetorical flourish. Although overdose death can occur, that is not heroin's intended function.

Moreover, the risk attending the use of heroin, medically supervised, is very small. Without medical supervision, the risk rises with contaminated needles, adulterated heroin, and ignorance of important purity and dose control information, for example. Even so, the annual death toll from heroin overdose is very low in relation to the millions of doses consumed: roughly 1,000 deaths per year in the DAWN reporting system,[77] out of an estimated heroin using population of 1–2 million dosing itself with varying frequencies.[78] All of these facts were readily available to Justice Powell. Neither he nor his law clerks troubled to do the research. After all, isn't it a matter of common knowledge?

Perhaps even more fundamentally wrong is Justice Powell's confusion of two entirely distinct issues: the harms that may arise from "the escalating use of controlled substances" and the harms that may arise from the traffic that is "highly organized by sophisticated criminal syndicates" reaping enormous profits. The first is a problem of drugs. The second is a problem of drug money. Many courts have confused the two issues as Justice Powell did, falsely attributing the demonstrable evils of violent black marketeering to the drugs themselves.

A case in point is *Carmona v. Ward*,[79] where the court considered the argument that mandatory life sentences meted out under New York's "Rockefeller" drug laws constituted cruel and unusual punishment in violation of the Eighth Amendment. In reviewing a conviction on habeas corpus, the court of appeals applied a tripartite proportionality test which considered the gravity of the offense, a comparison of the punishments for other crimes in New York, and a comparison of the challenged penalty to those for the same offense in other jurisdictions.

In weighing the gravity of the offense, the court rejected the argument that petitioners' drug sales should be viewed, standing alone, as isolated, relatively minor events. Instead, the court assessed them as "symptoms of the widespread and pernicious phenomenon of drug distribution."[80] The court then listed the social harms arising from drug trafficking:

1.  Narcotic addicts turn to crime—such as prostitution, drug sales and property crimes to feed their habits [a function of inflated black market prices].

2.  Drug addiction degrades and impoverishes those whom it enslaves [impoverishment is a function of inflated black market prices].

3. Addicts often commit acts of violence against police officers and other addicts because of the high stakes [a function of the large amounts of money].

4. The profits are so lucrative that police become corrupted [again, the issue is one of money].

The court concluded:

> Measured thus by the harm it inflicts upon the addict, and through him, upon society as a whole, drug dealing in its present epidemic proportions is a grave offense of high rank.[81]

While this line of argument is obviously far more sophisticated than the rhetoric of "moral perverts" or "worse than poisons," it is still not a serious job of analysis. For even if the social harms listed by the court are accepted as true, the argument evades the question of the gravity of the drug offense *per se*, as compared to the effects of prohibition. The court's litany of social harms arising from drug trafficking unwittingly makes the case for deregulation of the drug markets. The four points—apart from the moral degradation argument, which is contradicting by the "strength of character" premise of the *Moore* case—would not exist but for the black market set up by the legal prohibitions on drug transactions. Indeed, the precise claims made by the court to justify the severity of punishment would have applied to the sale of alcohol during National Prohibition, which greatly enriched bootleggers and empowered organized crime. Such claims would also apply if the sale of cigarettes—a drug as addictive as cocaine or heroin, according to former Surgeon General C. Everett Koop[82]—were to be outlawed, throwing some 52,000,000 nicotine addicts into craving and withdrawal symptoms. The *Carmona* court would conclude that the illegal sale of a familiar and once socially acceptable drug constitutes "a grave offense of high rank."

Is this line of economic and historical analysis too much to expect of a court engaged in a serious job of constitutional analysis? Relevant information was easily accessible to the court when it wrote. In response to President Nixon's declaration of war on drugs in 1972, for example, economist Milton Friedman had written about the drugs/crime connection years before *Carmona* reached the court of appeals in 1978. Friedman wrote that:

> Prohibition is an attempted cure that makes matters worse—for the addict and the rest of us. . . . [T]he individual addict would clearly be far better off if drugs were legal. Addicts are driven to associate with criminals to get the drugs, become criminals themselves to finance the habit, and risk constant danger of death and disease. Consider next the rest of us. The harm to us from the addiction of others arises almost wholly from the fact that drugs are illegal. It is esti-

mated that addicts commit one third to one half of all street crime in the U.S. Legalize drugs, and street crime would drop dramatically.

In a 1989 letter to drug czar Bennett, Freidman wrote that "[d]ecriminalizing drugs is even more urgent now. Our experience with the prohibition of drugs is a replay of our experience with the prohibition of alcoholic beverages."[83]

One might question whether a court could appropriately consider the severity of the offense absent black market effects on the assumption that the New York law violated the laws of supply and demand. But irrationality is the core concept of a substantive due process attack such as the Eighth Amendment's proportionality test as applied by *Carmona*. Judge Oakes, in his dissent, did question the wisdom of the law by citing a report that concluded "the operation of the 1973 New York drug law has had no real deterrent effect on drug abuse or on resulting felonious property crimes."[84] He made the further point that the Governor had appointed a revision committee to reconsider the mandatory sentences.

But even if the law had to be taken as a given, it was unfair to lay the effects of the massive black market in drugs at the petitioner's door on the grounds that he was a cog in a much larger machine: "New York's drug problem is a socioeconomic phenomenon or set of phenomena attributable to a great many factors with which the appellees have had nothing whatsoever to do."[85]

When *Carmona* reached the Supreme Court, Justice Marshall, joined by Justice Powell dissented from the denial of certiorari on the ground that the mandatory penalties of the Rockefeller law were disproportionately severe.

> To rationalize petitioner's sentences by invoking all evils attendant on or attributable to wisespread drug trafficking is simply not compatible with a fundamental premise of the criminal justice system, that individuals are accountable only for their own criminal acts.[86]

> To justify a stringent penalty for an act on the assumption that the act may engender other crimes makes little sense when those other crimes carry less severe sanctions than the act itself. [citation omitted] In sum, by focusing on the corrosive social impact of drug trafficking in general, rather than on petitioner's actual—and clearly marginal—involvement in that enterprise, the Court of Appeals substantially overstated the gravity of the instant charge.[87]

That same error was committed by the Fifth Circuit in *Terrebone v. Blackburn*,[88] where the defendant was convicted of distributing 22 packets of heroin to undercover narcotics agents. After receiving a mandatory life sentence under Louisiana law, Terrebone sought a federal writ of habeas corpus on the Eighth Amendment grounds raised in *Carmona*, and argued that a mandatory life sentence imposed upon an addict constituted cruel and unusual punishment. Following the same analysis as the *Carmona* court, the Fifth Circuit rejected the challenge in vivid metaphors:

> It is quite true that the trade in drugs is an *ugly enterprise* which preys upon both the physical and psychological weaknesses of man, and that this enormous danger to society may justify severe sanctions in many or most distribution cases.
>
> *It is a matter of common knowledge and it is a fact,* that social conditions in this state are adversely affected by the pervading traffic in and use of drugs. This condition is a serious menace to good social order. . . .
>
> It is no defense to this prosecution that distribution of drugs is not a violent crime and consequently punishment for this offense should not be on a par with second degree murder and aggravated kidnapping. Assuming the punishments are equal, traffic in narcotics is *an insidious crime* which, although not necessarily violent, is surely as grave. Indeed, the effect upon society of drug traffic is *pernicious* and far reaching. For each transaction in drugs breeds another and in the case of heroin the *degeneracy of the victim is virtually irreversible.* Compared to the effect of drug traffic in society isolated violent crimes may well be considered the lesser of the two evils.[89]

Following a second en banc consideration, the Fifth Circuit re-asserted its view that heroin dealing, even in small retail amounts, should be ranked for Eighth Amendment purposes as equal to or worse than violent crimes such as aggravated kidnapping or aggravated arson:

> Except in rare cases, the murderer's red hand falls on one victim only, however grim the blow; but the foul hand of the drug dealer blights life after life and, like the vampire of fable, creates others in its owner's evil image—others who create others still, across our land and down our generations, sparing not even the unborn.[90]

Grotesque and damning imagery ("foul hand" and "vampire") again masquerade as analysis and conceal completely the consensual nature of drug transactions. The responsibility of the user, or even an addict, is disregarded; it is the "drug dealing vampire" that "blights" the lives of others and "creates" more vampires, who bear no responsibility for their conduct. They are portrayed as victims, pure and simple. The distinction is crucial for policy purposes. Whereas consumers are entitled to freedom in the marketplace, victims are entitled to legal protection from their victimizers.

The court upheld "the most severe penalty for heroin dealing" among the 50 states largely because of the majority's view that Terrebone "was caught contributing to what seems generally agreed to be our country's major domestic problem: the sale and use of hard drugs."[91] The court did not cite any authority to justify its *ipse dixit*; is it really so obvious that drug trafficking is more serious than homelessness, the impoverishment of children, or the apparent decline of the public schools? The drug problem is simply assumed to be the "major domestic problem."

Assumptions like those are part of a vicious circle. Cocaine floods into the country despite vigorous law enforcement and interdiction. The social pathologies of the black market grow worse and worse. Then it is a short step to the public frustration, outrage and "call to arms" as expressed in *United States v. Miranda*,[92] where the defendant was convicted of conspiracy to import and importing 23 tons of marijuana and sought release on bond pending appeal. The court analyzed nine criteria specified by the statute then governing bail pending appeal, determined that defendant was a danger to the community, and denied bond pending appeal. Having decided the dispositive questions adversely to the defendant, the court did not rest but added an extended commentary, following the *Carmona* and *Terrebone* "thinking:"

> Drug trafficking represents a serious threat to the general welfare of this community. Drug importation and its eventual sale is directly involved in the furtherance of drug dependence and is conducive to the proliferation of crimes related thereto. National statistics on armed robbery, assault and murder have increased tremendously as narcotics addicts have sought ways to obtain funds to feed their habits.
>
> The community must be protected from violations of the law which prey on the weak of mankind. A wholesale drug peddler, such as the defendant, exploits this weakness and, in doing so, certainly poses a danger to the welfare of the community.
>
> If narcotics traffic is a social and health hazard, then every narcotics dealer is a danger to society.
>
> The call to arms, simply stated, it is time for the merchants of misery, destruction and death to be put out of business. The hideous evil wrought by these criminals through their unlawful importation and distribution of narcotics and controlled substances is unforgivable. Engulfed by their greed, these individuals have shown no concern for the thousands of lives that they have ruined and the unimaginable sorrow that they have heaped upon the people of this community, this state and this nation.[93]

In the years following *Miranda*'s call to arms, the United States escalated the current War on Drugs to unprecedented levels. *Albernaz*' "turning the screw" of the criminal justice system in drug enforcement now includes, *inter alia*, pretrial detention, mandatory and severe sentences, expanded search and seizure powers—helicopter overflights, sniffing of luggage by drug detector dogs, electronic surveillance of vehicles by concealed radio-tracking devices, warrantless searches of motor-home residences, public school students' purses, ships in the inland waterways connected to the sea, etc.—mandatory urinalysis, "zero tolerance" forfeitures of cars, planes and boats, the assessment of "civil fines" up to $10,000 and termination of government benefits for simple possession of personal use amounts.[94] Yet the drug trade flourishes, openly and notoriously, in outdoor drug markets.

The zeal born of frustration and outrage sometimes borders on vindictiveness, as reflected in anti-drug proposals that have thus far failed to become law: the Arctic Gulag proposal for convicted drug offenders;[95] the House Republican Task Force bill calling for confiscation of 25 percent of the adjusted gross income *and* net assets of anyone caught possessing illegal substances;[96] the proposal to shoot down civilian aircraft entering the United States without having filed a flight plan; the boot camp for drug users proposed by Secretary Bennett or his acquiescence in the beheading of drug dealers; and many others of this genre. On occasion, the outrage spills over into prejudice against those racially or ethnically associated in public stereotype with the drug traffic.[97]

## Drugs in Political Perspective

The foregoing examples demonstrate the strong emotional, non-rational attitudes surrounding the drug issue. The cycle of crackdown, escalation, failure and repression perpetuates itself. Judges and other policy makers do not seem to be aware that their decisions and actions arise out of preconceptions or presupposition rather than factual inquiry and reasoned study.

If these ideas are false, or at least unproved, why do they persist so strongly? They are deeply rooted in the public consciousness. Consider Musto's account:

> By 1900, America had developed a comparatively large addict population, perhaps 250,000, along with a fear of addiction and addicting drugs. This fear had certain elements which have been powerful enough to permit the most profoundly punitive methods to be employed in the fight against addicts and suppliers. . . .
>
> In the nineteenth century addicts were identified with foreign groups and internal minorities who were already actively feared and the objects of elaborate and massive social and legal restraints. Two repressed groups which were associated with the use of certain drugs were the Chinese and the Negroes. The Chinese and their custom of opium smoking were closely watched after their entry into the United States about 1870. At first, the Chinese represented

only one more group brought in to help build railroads, but, particularly after economic depression made them a labor surplus and a threat to American citizens, many forms of antagonism arose to drive them out or at least to isolate them. Along with this prejudice came a fear of opium smoking as one of the ways in which the Chinese were supposed to undermine American society.

Cocaine was especially feared in the South by 1900 because of its euphoric and stimulating properties. The South feared that Negro cocaine users might become oblivious of their prescribed bounds and attack white society.[98]

Drug control provided a point of convergence for Progressive reformers, moral crusaders, political entrepreneurs and those who were simply ignorant, fearful, and prejudiced. Under federal control, the non-rational elements soon drove out the rational; by the mid-1920s, the police model of drug control had almost completely displaced the medical model. Policing drugs not only required a drug abuse establishment, it also invited political exploitation of the drug issue, a legacy from which the United States has never recovered.

Edward Jay Epstein begins his account of political manipulation of federal drug control with Harry Anslinger. Before asking Congress for funds to expand the Bureau, he published an article entitled "Marijuana: Assassin of Youth," in which he warned of an epidemic of violent crimes committed by young people under the influence of marijuana. Unlike opium, which, he told Congress, could be good or bad, marijuana was "entirely the monster [Mr.] Hyde." In short, those who smoked it would go insane or turn violent or both. Congress responded, and over the opposition of the American Medical Association enacted the Marijuana Tax Act of 1937, empowering the federal government to police the marijuana supply. Federal suppression of marijuana was thus based on a false premise.

During World War II, according to Epstein's account, Anslinger waged a press campaign to convince the American public of the baseless charge that Japan was systematically attempting to addict its enemies, including the American people, to opium, in order to destroy their civilization. During the Korean War, Anslinger used a similar ploy. He leaked a report to the press claiming that "subversion through drug addiction is an established aim of communist China," and that the Communist Chinese were smuggling massive amounts of heroin into the United States to "weaken American resistance." Later politicians such as Senator Paula Hawkins (R. Fla.) made essentially the same claims about Cuba in 1984, i.e., that the Government of Cuba, as a matter of policy, was flooding the United States with cocaine in order to subvert our society by ruining our youth. New York Governor Hugh Carey had done essentially the same thing regarding a 1980 wave of jewelry snatching on subways and commuter trains: "The epidemic of gold-snatching in the city is the result of a Russian design to wreck America by flooding the nation with deadly heroin."[99] Of course, he presented no evidence in support of this claim.

Epstein's account of the politics of drugs extends to Presidential politics. He makes the point that Richard Nixon built his 1968 "law and order" campaign on public fear of street crime after realizing that "the menace of communism on which he built his early reputation no longer was an effective focus for organizing the fears of the American public."[100] Epstein's interpretation, if correct, is even more persuasive in the 1980s, as Presidents Reagan and Bush have presided over the apparent end of the Cold War.[101] These historical and political perspectives show that much of the conventional wisdom about drugs is rooted in decades of disinformation and manipulative rhetoric. Consider how the dark, sinister imagery must have played a decisive role in shaping contemporary public consciousness about drugs: "assassin of youth," "subversion," "Communist China," "Russian design," "national emergency," "public enemy number one." This is powerful stuff, if one accepts that the words and ideas have power.

In fact, the "killer weed" fears frightened Congress in 1937 into passing the Marihuana Tax Act and the "cocaine-crazed Negroes" frightened police departments in the pre-Depression South to trade up to .38 caliber handguns.[102] During virtually all of the twentieth century, with the possible exception of a brief *glasnost* during the 1970s, these false images of drugs have reigned unchallenged. Anslinger's bogus claims about marijuana set an enduring tone and mood. Thirty-five years later, more or less, Pennsylvania Governor Raymond Shafer, Chairman (ironically) of the President's Commission on Marijuana and Drug Abuse, held a press conference at which he announced—falsely—that a youth had taken LSD and stared at the sun until he became blind. He later admitted his scare tactic, justifying it by a desire to save people from what he was convinced was a real danger, although he had no medical evidence to support his preconception. No wonder judges have for the most part accepted what nearly everyone "knows" to be the truth about drugs. Misinformation is the norm.

## Fresh Perspectives on Drugs

Fresh perspectives on drugs may be impossible for society as a whole. Seven decades of relentless anti-drug propaganda have deprived the public of its power of critical thinking on this subject. The government, more than ever, is committed to a war on drugs almost as a categorical imperative, irrespective of whether it produces positive results. Doubting politicians are for the most part cowed into silent submission by a McCarthyite anti-drug witch hunt. Ironically, like the stopped clock that comes right twice a day, the emergence of crack-cocaine in the summer of 1986 finally conferred some plausibility upon the most outrageous claims about drugs that drug enforcement bureaucrats and allied politicians have always made. The very worst, most sensational scenarios of crack addiction seem to resemble the "walking dead" and "worse than poisons" metaphors so promiscuously used in the past, before crack was invented. The more meaningful fact—that we do not know the ratio of crack "victims" to the total population of crack users—carries no clout. One known victim is worth a thousand words of analysis, and maybe even a thousand points of light.

For these reasons, the public is probably lost to reason about popular black market drugs. Judges, one hopes, can be made to look at the evidence and listen to reason. Consider *National Treasury Employees v. Von Raab*,[103] a case that epitomizes the dialectical tension in the cases between empiricism and catechism. In that case the United States Customs Service implemented a drug testing program to screen for illegal drug use all applications in three categories. On review in the United States Supreme Court, the court affirmed that part of the judgment upholding the urinalysis testing of employees involved in drug interdiction or required to carry firearms. Justice Kennedy, carrying on the tradition of Justices Black, Powell, and others, repeated the familiar litany: "drug abuse is one of the most serious problems confronting our society today. There is little reason to believe that American work places are immune from this pervasive social problem. . . ."[104] The court concluded that "the government has demonstrated that its compelling interest in safeguarding our borders and the public safety outweigh the privacy expectations of employees. . . ."[105]

The court split 5–4. Justices Marshall and Brennan dissented. Justice Scalia, joined by Justice Stevens, wrote a separate dissent: "In my view the Custom Service rules are a kind of immolation of privacy and human dignity in symbolic opposition to drug use."[106] For Justice Scalia, drug testing of customs employees was completely unlike the testing of railroad employees involved in train accidents. In that case,[107] there was actual evidence that railroad accidents had for many years been caused by alcohol use, including a 1979 study finding that 23 percent of the operating personnel were problem drinkers.[108] But the majority opinion, "will be searched in vain for real evidence of a real problem that will be solved by urine testing of customs service employees."[109]

> What is absent in the government's justifications—notably absent, revealingly absent, and as far as I am concerned dispositively absent—is the recitation of even a single instance in which any of the speculated horribles actually occurred: an instance, that is, in which the cause of bribe-taking, or of poor aim, or of unsympathetic law enforcement, or of compromise of classified information, was drug use.[110]

Justice Scalia notes, correctly, that the true basis for the drug testing program is ideological and symbolic:

> The only plausible explanation, in my view, is what the Commissioner himself offered in the concluding sentence of his memorandum to Customs Service Employees announcing the program: "Implementation of the drug screening program would set an important example in our country's struggle with this most serious threat to our national health and security. . . ." What better way to show that the government is serious about its "war on drugs" than to subject its employees on the front line of that war to this invasion of their privacy and affront to their dignity? To be sure, there is only a slight chance that it will prevent some serious public harm resulting from service employee drug use, but it will show to the world that the service is "clean," and—most important of all—will demonstrate the determination of the government to eliminate this scourge of our society![111]

Justice Scalia concluded that this justification is unacceptable to validate an otherwise unreasonable search. He closed by rejecting the proposition that the end justifies the means.

Close analysis of this kind, so generally powerful in the law, has so far failed to carry the day on drug issues because the values at stake carry heavy baggage of emotion and symbolism. Fact, logic and reason become relatively unimportant.

## Conclusion

During the editing process, the editors raised several questions that I would like to address in question-and-answer format, by way of a conclusion.

**Q.** What difference does it make that the courts use hot rhetoric to describe drug effects when everyone knows that drugs are bad?

**A.** Drugs—referring primarily to marijuana, cocaine, and heroin, the big three in the black market by dollar volume—are neither good nor bad. They are both. They can facilitate healing[112] and provide pleasure; they can also contribute to illness, addiction or death. Drugs are not like radioactive waste, where mere proximity can be lethal. For a court to call drugs "poisons" is as irresponsibly misleading as calling kitchen knives murder weapons. With both drugs and kitchen knives, the ordinary intended purpose is benign. The dangers are those of misuse and abuse. Further, judicial demagoguery obscures the vital point that drug use is largely volitional.[113]

Unless one assumes that they are infantile or insane, drug users, like other competent adults, must be understood to be acting in what they perceive as their own best interests. Responsible public policy on drugs must begin with a pluralistic society's deference to individual self-governance and, insofar as harm to others may justify restrictions, a realistic cost-benefit analysis of the restrictions. The necessary risk assessment has been largely preempted by the prevailing imagery of misery, destruction and death.

**Q**. What practical difference does it make that the courts use loose language in speaking of drugs, drug abuse and drug trafficking?

**A**. In *The Least Dangerous Branch* (1962), Alexander Bickel argued that the true purpose of the power of judicial review was to elaborate the principles of the Constitution; otherwise, the Framers' insulation of the Supreme Court from the political branches was inexplicable. As we have seen above, the Supreme Court, and the courts of appeal, frequently address issues of principle presented by drug cases—questions of search and seizure, cruel and unusual punishment, the sixth amendment right to retain private counsel with drug money, and so on.[114]

In performing the mission of making constitutional law case-by-case, the courts have skewed the balance sharply in favor of the power of the State precisely because they are hostage to the simple false idea that drugs are bad and that the nation confronts a drug crisis. Thus, in balancing individual rights against the claims of public necessity, the scales of justice are weighted against the Bill of Rights. Accordingly, the courts have validated every important Congressional "turning of the screw" in drug enforcement. Instead of cautioning the political branches that they will be required to make a convincing factual demonstration of the basis for the war on drugs, the courts have sent a message that in the field of drug enforcement, virtually anything goes. As Justice Scalia put it in *Von Raab*, Supreme Court decisions on drugs represent "a kind of immolation of privacy and human dignity in symbolic opposition to drug use."[115] The courts, in order to discharge their role as guardian of the Bill of Rights, should be raising hard questions about the premises, and proof, that might be claimed to justify the legislative and enforcement crackdowns. But that is not intellectually possible, generally speaking,[116] so long as the tens of millions of citizens who have ever taken illegal drugs are stigmatized as less-than-human "walking dead" or "moral perverts." The result of all the anti-drug invective has been the slow death of the Bill of Rights[117] as a necessary sacrifice to the perceived exigencies of the positivist state besieged by drugs.

**Q**. What are the ethical implications of the judicial abdication of responsibility for critical analysis of governmental claims about drugs and drug abuse?

**A**. The adversary system employs a dialectical opposition of the interests of contending parties as a means of achieving truth in a particular case. In that sense, the adversary system may be considered an epistemology, a method of coming to know the truth, although it is restricted by rules of procedure and evidence that would be intolerable (or so a layman supposes) in a purely scientific inquiry. Still, the basic idea is one of aggressive inquiry into facts organized by logical methods.

But as the cases discussed above demonstrate, the courts have passively accepted unproven and often unprovable claims in reaching conclusions about drug abuse and drug trafficking. In this respect, they have damaged the ethical basis of the adversary system, converting it largely into a propaganda tool for the party line.

My colleague, Gerald Uelmen,[118] has offered a particularly revealing example of how the Court has boot-strapped political "truth" into legal doctrine. It begins with a concurrence by Justice Powell in *Mendenhall*, upholding a warrantless strip search initiated after an airport drug courier profile stop and citing a DEA source for "concern [over] the escalating use of controlled substances."[119] In *United States v. Montoya de Hernandez*,[120] the court upheld an incommunicado detention and rectal examination of a traveler, citing Justice Powell's *Mendenhall* concurrence as authority for the existence of a "national crisis in law enforcement caused by the smuggling of illicit narcotics." Finally, in the *Von Raab* case, Justice Kennedy cited the *Montoya* court's assertion of a "national crisis in law enforcement" as support for the majority's ruling in favor of the Customs' drug testing program.[121]

Apart from the incestuous sourcing of the proposition that there was a national crisis, the statement was false—or at least not provably true. NIDA's 1988 National Household Survey on drug abuse reported significant declines in nearly every category of drug abuse compared to the 1985 and 1982 surveys. For example, it noted that rates of marijuana use had been "steadily decreasing since 1979."[122] This information was well publicized in the press and available to any modestly skilled researcher who was interested in learning the facts rather than simply repeating a preconveived notion. Dean Uelmen concluded that justices "accept without skepticism . . . that a national crisis of the greatest conceivable magnitude now besets us."[123]

**Q**. How should the legal profession respond to the judicial blind spot on drugs?

**A**. There are several practical reforms that might be pursued to improve the situation described in this paper. First, lawyers must ensure that judges have the benefit of good Brandeis briefs when arguing cases with primary or secondary drug issues. There is no good reason why a skilled advocate could not make use of the kinds of materials cited in this article.[124]

By the same token, the law schools could make it a lot easier for the next generation of lawyers and judges[125] to be knowledgeable by covering basic drug issues in criminal law courses and by offering drug law and policy courses and seminars. Very few do so at present. Traditional first-year criminal law courses do not generally include drug law. One reason is that criminal law books are silent on the issue, an incredible omission in an era when nearly half of felony filings are drug law violations. The law schools have long had their own blind spot on the drug issue.[126] They could do a lot more, not only in teaching but also in sponsoring symposia and supporting faculty research on the subject. Finally, law journals should encourage the line of critical thinking represented by this symposium.[127]

A final recommendation is for more comprehensive research that has been presented here in this somewhat impressionistic account of the work of the courts. Thoughts on a research agenda follow.

---

# A Methodological Postscript and Agenda for Future Research

---

This essay does not purport to make a comprehensive survey of the attitudes of appellate judges as reflected in opinions dealing with drug issues. The sheer volume of such cases decided since 1914, and the diversity of issues they decide, would make such an undertaking impracticable. The goal here is more sharply focused: to review those decisions in the United States Supreme Court and Courts of Appeal that reveal something of the courts' method or general approach—whether based in empiricism and logic or preconception and ideology—in deciding drug policy issues.

In most, but not all, of the landmark cases, the Supreme Court had ruled for the government. Moreover, it did so in flights of rhetoric that were unnecessary to the decision of the particular issues before the court. Then, in 1981, on the eve of the contemporary War on Drugs, the court delivered a strong message about its own basic orientation. In *Albernaz v. United States*,[128] the court, in an opinion by Justice Rehnquist, held that its constitutional interpretation of the Double Jeopardy Clause would cleave to the statutory intent expressed by Congress. The latter would control the former. Statute would trump the Constitution.

Of course, *Albernaz* alone cannot speak for past courts or for future ones. But the argument of this essay—that judges when they have revealed themselves on drug policy issues have followed political rather than judicial standards of knowledge—is based on several dozen such cases. The reader might well ask to what extent is it valid to generalize from the small number of cases reviewed here to the tens of thousands that deal with some aspect of the drug issue?

The strength of this assertion must be judged against the methods that were used in selecting the cases discussed in this article. Computer searches of the Supreme Court and Federal databases were used to generate lists of cases. The top tiers of the judicial pyramid were chosen for three reasons: the landmark cases are almost all federal cases; the Supremacy Clause makes federal decisions on constitutional questions binding on the States; and the Federal Government has since 1914 been the dominant force in the field of drug regulation and law enforcement.

But the goal of this article was to cull those cases that spoke to issues of drug policy, that engaged the broader questions of a principled and effective national drug policy, and that displayed some awareness of methodological issues. (None fit the latter category.) These questions arise, if at all, when a court is asked to interpret a statute regulating controlled substances or decide a question of constitutional law bearing on drug law enforcement powers. To winnow those cases from the routine cases, search techniques were used combining "drugs" and "drug trafficking" with limiting phrases, in the same sentence or paragraph, such as "public health" or "danger to society" or "morality" or "evil" and the like. Several hundred cases thus generated were read by me and by research assistants; many turned out to contain no more than a passing reference to the search phrase. This reflects the inherent limitations of computer research, which functions best at simple word-recognition and cannot effectively isolate abstractions or concepts.

In the end, no single search phrase or combination of phrases could be relied upon to yield up the type of case sought—a case in which the opinion engaged basic issues of drug policy in *some* manner, whether hotly rhetorical or coolly analytical. Thus, I freely concede that case selection for this article was necessarily "subjective" in turning on my judgment whether an opinion fit the foregoing criteria for inclusion. I should add that these judgments were informed by more than a decade of experience reading drug law cases as author, teacher and appellate practitioner.

My students and I did not find very many cases in the Supreme Court or the federal courts of appeal that fit the policy model that we were looking for. It thus remains arguable that the lack of rhetoric in most drug cases supports the view that most federal appellate judges do a proper job of judging in most drug cases—they apply the law to the facts and eschew unnecessary statements of a political or policy-oriented character. But I think that argument misses the point. The opinions we have turned up purport to speak for whole courts, if not the entire federal judiciary. On those relatively few occasions when judges have troubled to declare themselves on matters of drug policy, they have done so, with several notable exceptions, in denunciatory language parallel to that prevailing in the political arena. And even when there are dissenting opinions, it is rare to find a judge distancing himself from the intemperate and uninformed rhetoric of his brethren.

Still, as a final point, I would like to emphasize that these observations are offered in a preliminary and tentative way. They should be tested by other researchers. I suggest a less global technique using a narrower query. It would be interesting to focus, for example, on the issue of the oft-assumed connection between drugs and other crimes, especially violent crimes. Researchers might also find it more manageable to select a smaller data base, e.g. a state jurisdiction or a federal circuit for a relatively short time frame. 1983 to the present would be most reflective of the cases decided in the crackdown atmosphere of the War on Drugs. The question to be pursued by the researchers is whether courts are employing proper decision-making techniques on a subject vitally affecting the rights of millions of persons charged with drug offense and also the rights of citizens generally.

## Endnotes

[1] S. Wisotsky, *Beyond the War on Drugs 1* (1990) (quoting A. Einstein) [hereinafter *Beyond the War on Drugs*].

[2] United States v. Property Known as 6109 Grubb Road, 890 F.2d 659, 665 (3rd Cir. 1989) (dissenting opinion). Justice Kennedy used substantially similar language to uphold the Customs Service's drug testing program in National Treasury Employees Union v. Von Raab, 485 U.S. 903 (1988).

[3] Harmon v. Thornburgh, 878 F.2d 484, 497 (D.C. Cir. 1989) (Silberman, J. concurring in part and dissenting in part). Judge Silberman thought that the majority had unduly restricted the scope of the government's drug testing program while personally expressing "grave doubts that the criminal law is the most effective way of dealing with our drug problem. . ." Id.

[4] Other learned commission reports not referred to include the *Indian Hemp Drugs Commission, Marijuana, 1893–94*; *Departmental Committee on Morphine and Heroin Addiction* (1926) [hereinafter *Rolleston Report*]; *Drug Addiction: Crime or Disease?*, Interim and Final Reports, Joint Committee of the American Bar Association and the American Medical Association on Narcotic Drugs (1961); Interdepartmental Committee, *Drug Addiction* (1961) [hereinafter *Brain I*]; Interdepartmental Committee, *Drug Addiction, Second Report* (1965) [hereinafter *Brain II*]; Advisory Committee on Drug Dependence, *Cannabis* (1968) [hereinafter *The Wooton Report*]; Canadian Commission of Inquiry, *The Non-Medical Use of Drugs, Interim Report* (1970) [hereinafter *LeDain Report*]; National Research Council of the National Academy of Sciences, *An Analysis of Marijuana Policy* (1982).

[5] Overall, the various courts of appeal have performed with greater intellectual rigor than the Supreme Court. See, e.g., United States v. Moore, 416 F.2d 1139 (D.C. Cir. 1973); The National Organization for Reform of Marijuana Laws v. Drug Enforcement Administration, 559 F.2d 735 (D.C. Cir. 1977); United States v. Kiffer, 477 F.2d 349 (2d Cir. 1973).

[6] Wisotsky, "Crackdown: The Emerging 'Drug Exception' to the Bill of Rights," 38 *Hastings L. J.* 883 (1987) [hereinfater "Crackdown"].

[7] Harrison Narcotic Act, ch. 1, 38 Stat. 785 (1914) (current version at 21 U.S.C. §§ 801-969 (1981)). See generally King, "Punishing the Sick and Jailing the Healers," 62 *Yale L.J.* 736 (1953).

[8] For accounts of the "killer weed" scenario, see Bonnie & Whitebread, "The Forbidden Fruit and the Tree of Knowledge: An Inquiry into the Legal History of American Marijuana Prohibition," 56 *Va. L. Rev.* 971 (1970), and J. Himmelstein, *The Strange Career of Marijuana: Politics and Ideology of Drug Control in America* 49 (1983).

[9] E. J. Epstein, *Agency of Fear* 178 (1977).

[10] The House Select Committee on Narcotics Abuse and Control had urged the President to declare war on drugs. *H. R. Rep. No. 418*, 97th Cong., 2d Sess. pts. 1–2, at 50 (1982).

[11] Approximately 3,000 parents' groups had organized across the nation under the aegis of the National Federation of Parents for Drug Free Youth, Gonzalez, "The War on Drugs: A Special Report," *Playboy*, Apr. 1982, at 134. Pamphlets of Informed Parents of Dade put the number of such groups at nearly 6,000 in the 1985–86 period.

[12] President's Radio Address to the Nation, 18 *Weekly Comp. Pres. Doc.* 1249 (Oct. 2, 1982).

[13] 18 *Weekly Comp. Pres. Doc.* 1311, 1314 (Oct. 14, 1982).

[14] *New York Times*, April 22, 1990, at 6E (city ed.).

[15] The Comprehensive Crime Control Act of 1984 created a presumption in favor of pretrial detention for any person accused of a ten-year drug felony. 18 U.S.C. § 3141 (1990).

[16] 21 U.S.C. § 848 (1989).

[17] A *New York Times*/CBS poll based on telephone interviews conducted September 6–8, 1989 produced similar results. Sixty-four percent cited drugs as the most important problem facing the nation—triple the percentage of July, 1989. Sixty-one percent favored drug testing of workers generally. *New York Times*, Sept. 12, 1989, at B8, col. 1.

[18] See generally *Congressional Research Service, Drug Abuse Prevention and Control: Budget Authority for Federal Programs, FY 1986*–FY 1988 (Feb. 27, 1987):

> Despite a doubling of federal expenditures on interdiction over the past five years, the quantity of drugs smuggled into the United States is greater than ever. . . . There is no clear correlation between the level of expenditures or effort devoted to interdiction and the long- term availability of illegally imported drugs in the domestic market.

See also Wisotsky, "Exposing the War on Cocaine," 1983 *Wis. L. Rev.* 1305.

[19] *Beyond the War on Drugs*, supra note 1, at xix.

[20] For the listing of schedules of controlled substances, see 21 U.S.C. § 821 (a)-(d) (1989).

[21] T. Szasz, *Ceremonial Chemistry: The Ritual Persecution of Drugs, Addicts, and Pushers* 183 (1974).

[22] *Beyond the War on Drugs*, supra note 1, at 186.

[23] Id. at 187. Directly comparable data for illegal drugs is difficult to come by because of the crudeness of the government's data collection system, the failure of the government to fund long-term research into the extent and effects of long-term non-abusive illegal drug use, and the natural reluctance of people to volunteer information of criminal conduct. The two major techniques used by the government to track illicit drug use are the National Institute of Drug Abuse Household Survey and the Drug Abuse Warning Network. See infra at nn. 77–78.

[24] One author argues quite powerfully that the differential treatment of the legal and illegal drugs arises from tradition and culture—particularly the deep-rooted psycho-social need to identify some substances as taboo—rather than any inherent properties of the drugs themselves. T. Szasz, supra note 21, at 18–25.

[25] There are of course voices of reason on the federal bench. But as in the rest of society, they appear to be a minority. For one recent example of presuppositions of the war on drugs, see the majority opinion of Justice Kennedy and the dissenting opinion of Justice Scalia in National Treasury Employees Union v. Von Raab, 485 U.S. 903 (1988).

[26] J. S. Mill, *On Liberty* 5 (1940).

[27] See K. Llewelyn, *The Common Law Tradition: Deciding Appeals* 1961); B. Cardozo, *The Nature of the Judicial Process* (1921).

[28]"Bush Gives Anti-Drug Talk to Kids," *Miami Herald*, Sept. 13, 1989, at 1A.

[29]United States v. Miranda, 442 F. Supp. 786, 795 (S.D. Fla. 1977).

[30]H. Packer, *The Limits of the Criminal Sanction* 177 (1969).

[31]See R. Aldisert, *Logic For Lawyers* (1989); W. Read, *Legal Thinking* (1986). See Also M. Rombauer, *Legal Problem Solving* (1973).

[32]The Harrison Act was motivated in substantial part by the large addict population that developed around the easy access in the U.S. to potent patent medicines. D. Musto, *The American Disease: Origins of Narcotics Control* (1973); J. Phillips & R. Wynne, *Cocaine: The Mystique and the Reality* 78–80 (1980). In both the U.S. and Europe widespread "fear and loathing" of cocaine developed not long after Freud's popularization of the drug in the 1880s. R. Byck, *The Cocaine Papers of Sigmund Freud* (1974).

[33]249 U.S. 86 (1919).

[34]Id. at 90.

[35]Ministry of Health, Departmental Committee on Morphine and Heroin Addiction, Report at 18, cited in A. Trebach, *The Heroin Solution* 85 (1982). This report, also known as the Rolleston Report, was not issued until 1926, and obviously could not have been cited by the Supreme Court in these early cases. However, the medical practices which the report endorses did exist at the time; Trebach states that the Rolleston report "codified the best of the common law of medical practice." Id. at 90. There was no good reason for the Supreme Court simply to ignore popular and professional accounts supporting the legitimacy and efficacy of addiction maintenance.

[36]King, supra note 7.

[37]258 U.S. 280 (1921).

[38]Id. at 287.

[39]Id. at 289. The district court had written earlier in a similar vein: "The so-called 'Patient' in this case was suffering from no disease except drug addiction. . . . [I]t is a well known fact, of which this court has taken notice, that drug addicts as a class are persons weakened materially in their sense of responsibility and in their power of will. . . ." Id. at 281. That generalization is certainly not a fact so well known as to dispense with the need for proof and justify the taking of judicial notice.

[40]Justices Holmes, McReynolds and Brandeis dissented. A few years later in Linder v. United States, 268 U.S. 5 (1925), a doctor was indicted for prescribing one tablet of morphine and three tablets of cocaine to a woman he knew to be addicted to these drugs in order to satisfy her craving. The Supreme Court viewed the case as a conviction for a prescription with "the sole purpose of relieving conditions incident to addiction and keeping [the patient] comfortable." It was not willing to find that Dr. Linder had "necessarily transcended" the limits of professional practice. Id. at 19.

[41]102 F.2d 617 (D.C. Cir. 1939).

[42]Id. at 618.

[43]Guilt by association is done in later cases, such as Carmona v. Ward, infra note 79, and Terrebone v. Butler, infra note 90.

[44]Id.

[45]A later case similarly cites "the common knowledge of society" that addicts are indecent people:

> The violation of the narcotic drug laws . . . is a violation of a rule which is accepted
> by all decent people as involving public policy and morals in the United States.
> The evils which the illicit narcotic traffic brings in its wake are *all well known* and

they are rightfully the subject of public abhorrence. . . . In my opinion it is clearly demonstrated that either class of offense involves moral turpitude.

It is *common knowledge* that narcotics addicts must, and will in order to obtain a supply of the drug to which they are addicted, lie, cheat or steal. Constant deception and subterfuge are necessary, if an addict is to remain at liberty and to enjoy the dubious boon of his addiction. United States v. Cisneros, 191 F. Supp. 924 (D. Cal. 1961) (emphasis added).

[46]111 F.2d 250 (10th Cir. 1940).

[47]Id. at 256.

[48]A. Trebach, supra note 35, at 92.

[49]370 U.S. 660 (1962).

[50]Id. at 662.

[51]Id. at 667.

[52]Id. at 672 (quoting *N.Y.L.J.*, June 8, 1960 at 4, col. 2).

[53]A. Trebach, supra note 35, at 104.

[54]A. Trebach, supra note 35, at 60. Norman Zinberg's research in *Drug, Set and Setting* (1984) confirms, in the United States, that a great many heroin users have developed stable, non-addictive patterns of occasional use or "chipping," over long periods of time. Many users and even addicts are employed and have stable family relationships. Compare J. Kaplan, *The Hardest Drug: Heroin and Public Policy* (1983), for an argument against legalization or even addiction maintenance.

[55]486 F.2d 1139 (D.C. Cir. 1973).

[56]Id. at 1145.

[57]Id. at 1151.

[58]Report of the Surgeon General, *The Health Consequences of Smoking: Nicotine Addiction* (1988).

[59]In dissent, Judge Wright tilted toward the drug-taker-as-victim approach of Justice Douglas: "The confirmed addict is in fact a worried, troubled, harried individual. Misery, alienation and despair, rather than pleasure and ecstasy, are the key features of his existence." 486 F.2d at 1234. His opinion is marked by compassion rather than condemnation.

[60]396 U.S. 398 (1969).

[61]Id. at 425.

[62]Id. at 426 (emphasis supplied).

[63]See L. Grinspoon & J. Bakalar, *Cocaine: A Drug and Its Social Evolution* (1976).

[64]*National Narcotic Intelligence Consumers Committee Report 9* (1989). The comparable figures for 1988 were 2,334 deaths out of some 8.2 million people who had used it that year, and 42,383 hospital emergency room visits.

[65]The National Institute for Drug Abuse, *National Household Survey* (1985) data also reported 5.8 million having used cocaine in the 30 days preceding the household survey and 22 million with lifetime experience with the drug. The reliability of such self-reporting measures is called into serious question by NIDA's 1988 National Household Survey. In 1988, reported lifetime experience had declined to 21.2 million; did the other 800,000 all die in three years, or simply deny their criminality in the fact of increasing public hostility and punitive laws?

A second doubt arises from the fact that the thirty-day use figure declined by half to 2.9 million, and the annual use figure to 8.2 million. Despite these large reported drops in the number of users, the mortality rose to 2,234 and the hospital emergency room visits rose to

42,512. It is possible that many fewer users were hard-core addicts, especially crack smokers, running much higher risks of overdose and death. Skepticism is warranted, however.

[66]The author estimates that the addiction potential for cocaine is about the same for alcohol—about 20 percent of the population of consumers. *Beyond the War on Drugs*, supra note 1, at 17–30.

[67]Id. at 17–18.

[68]A similar assumption about the relation between drugs and violence appears at United States v. Holland, 810 F.2d 1215 (D.C. Cir. 1987), where the court upheld the constitutional validity of a statute doubling the punishment for drug distribution within one thousand feet of a public or private elementary or secondary school. In moderate language, the court held that the statute was "rationally structured" to effectuate its purpose of "threatening pushers who approach our children near school with stiff penalties." Id. at 1219. The court did assume, however, without record support or citation, that such transactions "contribute directly to the violent and dangerous criminal milieu Congress sought to eliminate in the proximity of schools." Id. at 1219.

[69]446 U.S. 544 (1979).

[70]See also Florida v. Royer, 448 U.S. 438 (1980); United States v. Sokolow, 490 U.S. 1 (1989).

[71]446 U.S. at 561.

[72]In the Matter of Marijuana Rescheduling Petition, Dkt. No. 86-22, Dept. of Justice, DEA, Sept. 6, 1988.

[73]First Report of the National Commission on Marijuana and Drug Abuse, *Marijuana: A Signal of Misunderstanding* 154 (1972). The Commission also recommended that possession in public of one ounce or less of marijuana would no longer be an offense, although the drug would be "contraband subject to summary seizure and forfeiture." Id.

[74]A partial list of these "decriminalizing" organizations appears in National Research Council, Commission on Behavioral and Social Sciences and Education, Committee on Substance Abuse and Habitual Behavior, *An Analysis of Marijuana Policy* (1982) [hereinafter NRC Commission].

[75]Id. at 29.

[76]The National Academy focused its concern on the very young: "heavy use by anyone or any use by growing children should be discouraged. Although conclusive evidence is lacking of major, long-term public health problems caused by marijuana, they are worrisome possibilities, and both the reports and a priori likelihood of developmental damage to some young users makes marijuana use a cause for extreme concern." Id. Compare United States v. Rush, 738 F.2d 497, 513 (1st Cir. 1984):

> The question whether the government has an overriding interest in controlling the use and distribution of marijuana by private citizens is a topic of continuing political controversy. Much evidence has been adduced from which it might rationally be inferred that marijuana constitutes a health hazard and a threat to social welfare; on the other hand, proponents of free marijuana use have attempted to demonstrate that it is quite harmless.

See also Randall v. Wyrick, 441 F. Supp. 312, 315–16 (W.D. Mo. 1977); United States v. Kuch, 288 F. Supp. 439, 446, 448 (D.D.C. 1968).

[77]DAWN is the acronym for Drug Abuse Warning Network, a compilation of information from medical examiners and hospital emergency rooms in most Standard Metropolitan Statistical Areas. The combined figure for morphine/heroin deaths for the first nine months of 1987 was 918, excluding New York City. National Narcotics Intelligence Consumers Committee, *The NNICC Report 1987* (1988).

[78]National Institute of Drug Abuse, *National Household Survey* 29 (1985).

[79]576 F.2d 405 (2d Cir. 1978). Carmona was convicted of two counts of possession of cocaine with intent to distribute, an A-I felony with a mandatory minimum 15-year sentence. She plead to second degree felony and was sentenced to six years to life. Defendant Fowler was charged with an A-III felony, a four years to life sentence, after selling twenty dollars worth of cocaine to an undercover agent.

[80]Id. at 411.

[81]Id.

[82]Report of the Surgeon General, supra note 58.

[83]Both references are incorporated in "An Open Letter to Bill Bennett," *Wall St. J.*, Sept. 29, 1989, § 1, at 15, col. 2.

[84]576 F.2d at 447.

[85]Id. at 422.

[86]439 U.S. 1091, 1096 (1979).

[87]Id. at 1097.

[88]624 F.2d 1363 (5th Cir. 1980).

[89]Id. at 1369 (emphasis supplied).

[90]Terrebone v. Butler, 848 F.2d 500, 504 (5th Cir. 1988). The vampire language was quoted by the court in Young v. Miller, 883 F.2d 1276, 1283 (6th Cir. 1989), upholding mandatory life without parole upon a first offender under Michigan law, which punished petitioner's offense the same as first degree murder. The defendant was a 25-year-old mother of a small child.

[91]Id. at 505.

[92]442 F. Supp. 786 (S.D. Fla. 1977).

[93]Id. at 792.

[94]"Crackdown," supra note 6, at 907.

[95]H.R. 7112, 97th Cong., 2d Sess., § 2,128 Cong. Rec. 7088 (1982).

[96]*The Drug Enforcement Report* 2 (June 23, 1988).

[97]A district judge remarked that Colombians had little regard for judges, having killed 32 of them. United States v. Edwardo-Franco, 885 F.2d 1002, 1005 (2d Cir. 1989).

The Florida Highway Patrol drug courier profile alerts troopers to watch for "ethnic groups associated with the drug trade." Pollack, "Troopers Aiming at Flow on Turnpike," *Ft. Lauderdale News*, August 6, 1984, at B9.

[98]See D. Musto, supra note 32, at 5–7.

[99]E. J. Epstein, supra note 9, at 33.

[100]Szasz, "The War Against Drugs," 12 *J. Drug Issues* 115 (1982).

[101]E. J. Epstein, supra note 9, at 59.

[102]D. Musto, supra note 32, at 28.

[103]489 U.S. 656 (1989).

[104]Id. at 674.

[105]Id. at 677.

[106]Id. at 681.

[107]Skinner v. Railway Labor Executives Ass'n., 489 U.S. 602 (1989).

[108]Id. at 607.

[109]*Von Raab*, 489 U.S. at 681.

[110]Id. at 683.

[111]Id. at 686.

[112]L. Grinspoon & J. Bakalar, "Medical Uses of Illicit Drugs," in *Dealing with Drugs: Consequences of Government Control* (R. Hamowy ed. 1987).

[113]United States v. Moore, 486 F.2d 1139 (D.C. Cir. 1973).

[114]See "Crackdown," supra note 6.

[115]109 S. Ct. at 1395.

[116]There are occasional exceptions. See United States v. Verdugo-Urguidez, 856 F.2d 1214, 1218 (9th Cir. 1988): "We also must take great pains to ensure that the Constitution does not become the first casualty in the war on drugs."

[117]See, e.g., Saltzburg, "Another Victim of Illegal Narcotics: The Fourth Amendment," 48 *U. Pitt. L. Rev.* 1 (1986).

[118]Dean, Santa Clara University Law School, "When Supreme Court Justices Enlist in a War," address to the Plenary Session of the Drug Policy Foundation, Nov. 1, 1990, Washington D.C. [hereinafter Address].

[119]446 U.S. at 561.

[120]473 U.S. 531 (1985).

[121]109 S. Ct. at 1392.

[122]National Institute of Drug Abuse, *National Household Survey* 3 (1981).

[123]Address, supra note 118, at 2.

[124]See *Beyond the War on Drugs*, supra note 1, at 263 for a bibliography listing every major work of drug policy analysis published as of 1986, including congressional committee hearings, government monographs, and many other sources. Lawyers would do well to consult G. Uelmen & V. Haddox, *Drug Abuse and the Law Sourcebook* (1989). For additional information, refer to the Drug Policy Foundation, NORML, and the National Drug Strategy Network, all in Washington, D.C., which serve as clearinghouses for researchers.

[125]Judicial training institutes should also offer courses that educate judges about drug policy issues and encourage them to think critically about alternatives.

[126]Another example of neglect is that, on information and belief, 1991 was the first time that the AALS conducted a panel on drug policy since the author entered legal education in 1975. The author was a speaker at a Criminal Justice Section panel on "legalization of drugs" in January, 1991 in Washington, D.C.

[127]See also Symposium, "The War on Drugs: In Search of a Breakthrough," 11 *Nova L. Rev.* 891–1052 (1987); Symposium: "Testing for Drug Use in the American Workplace," 11 *Nova L. Rev.* 291–823 (1987); and Symposium: "Drug Decriminalization," 18 *Hoffstra L. Rev.* (1990).

[128]450 U.S. 333, 343 (1981).

# 16

## Miami's Drug Court
### A Different Approach

### Peter Finn
### Andrea K. Newlyn

America's courts are becoming increasingly clogged with drug-related cases, and many of our jails and prisons are overflowing with drug offenders. Nationwide, there were more than one million arrests for drug offenses in 1991—a 56 percent increase since 1982. Two-thirds of those arrests were for illegal possession of drugs; one-third were for manufacturing or selling drugs.[1] Dade County (Miami), Florida, is no exception to this crisis: Police arrested 9,409 individuals for drug offenses in 1991, including 6,923 for illegal possession of drugs.[2]

What makes Dade County different is its Diversion and Treatment Program, which channels almost all nonviolent defendants arrested on drug possession charges into an innovative court-operated rehabilitation program as an alternative to prosecution. Known as Miami's "Drug Court," the program expands on the traditional concept of diversion to provide a year or more of

*Program Focus,* June 1993, National Institute of Justice, U.S. Department of Justice, Office of Justice Programs.

treatment and case management services that include counseling, acupuncture, fellowship meetings, education courses, and vocational services along with strict monitoring through periodic urine tests and court appearances. Defendants who succeed in the program have their criminal cases dismissed.

Program administrators acknowledge that the Diversion and Treatment Program is much more complex—and initially more costly—than prosecution. Most of these defendants, especially if they are first-time offenders, would normally receive a few minutes of court attention and go home. But the program adds a new component to business as usual: It provides defendants with the treatment and support services that can shut the revolving door that brings the majority of drug offenders back to court again and again. Additional funds and personnel are needed to provide the required long-term services. However, Miami has shown that communities can assemble the needed resources into a total package, from initial detoxification through eventual job placement.

According to Tim Murray, director of the Metro/Dade Office of Substance Abuse Control, around 60 percent of the defendants diverted to the program in its first 3 years successfully completed the year-long regimen of urine testing, treatment, and reporting to court, or are still in treatment. Moreover, Murray reports, the program is experiencing unusually low rates of recidivism.

## Drug Court

The program's centerpiece is its Drug Court, set up in the summer of 1989 by an administrative order from Chief Judge Gerald Weatherington of Florida's eleventh judicial circuit. The Drug Court places defendants in the Diversion and Treatment Program, monitors their progress, and decides whether they have recovered sufficiently to have their cases dismissed. The result is a treatment program overseen by a court. However, not every arrestee charged with a drug offense gets the chance to participate.

### Who Is Eligible for the Program?

After booking, arrestees are screened for eligibility at the Pretrial Detention Center. To qualify, the defendant must be charged with possessing or purchasing drugs, and the State Attorney must agree to diversion. Defendants who have a history of violent crime, have been arrested for drug trafficking, or have more than two previous nondrug felony convictions are ineligible.

The program initially accepted only first-time drug offenders, but arrestees are now accepted regardless of how many times they have been charged or convicted of possession. Because of the overwhelming preference for "crack" over heroin in the county, the program was also originally limited to individuals arrested for possession of cocaine; currently defendants charged with possession of any controlled substance other than marijuana can join. Participants do not have to be current drug users—in fact, many arrestees maintain they are not addicts, to which the judge in Drug Court has been heard to retort, "Congratulations! Then you'll have a real easy time with the program."

## Choosing a Judge To Run the Drug Court

The chief and associate chief judges of Florida's eleventh circuit court knew that the Diversion and Treatment Program would never work unless the Drug Court had the right person on the bench. However, they felt they had the ideal candidate in Judge Stanley M. Goldstein, a local criminal division judge well known to them. Judge Goldstein seemed the perfect person for the job because for several years he had on his own time done volunteer work with youth drug prevention efforts in the community. In addition, as a former police officer, defense attorney, and prosecutor, Judge Goldstein had first-hand familiarity with the criminal justice system from every angle. Finally, Judge Goldstein seemed to have the personality that the job required—outspoken, hard-working, no-nonsense, and affable. Once he accepted the position, the county sent him to the National Judicial College in Reno, Nevada, to round out his preparation with courses in drug treatment and the courts.

## The Personal Touch

Except for when he is on vacation or ill, Judge Stanley M. Goldstein is the only Drug Court judge. Judge Goldstein explains the program to all new defendants, making clear that they should expect a year of treatment, that it will be difficult for them to succeed, but that everyone involved will provide them with all the assistance they need and keep pushing them to do better. Judge Goldstein tells defendants their urine will be tested regularly and they will have to return to court an average of once a month for a review of their progress. If their improvement is unsatisfactory, prosecution of the case may resume, and a conviction will usually involve jail time. Judge Goldstein then remands each consenting defendant (almost all agree to participate) to the custody of the Diversion and Treatment Program for at least 365 days.

Drug Court handles a large volume of cases—an average of 80 a day—as both new arrestees and defendants already in the program appear as called. Nevertheless, Judge Goldstein makes sure he talks with every defendant, offering a few words of encouragement for an offender who is improving nicely or initiating an extended discussion with a defendant who has been turning in "dirty" urine samples. Judge Goldstein has access to every offender's treatment records on his computer, located on the bench. If a program participant appearing before him swears to have attended every clinic appointment, the judge can use his computer to verify immediately the persons' actual attendance record. If a defendant's record turns out to be uneven or deteriorating, Judge Goldstein puts on his judicial hat and emphasizes the critical importance of showing up for every treatment appointment. Then, on a more personal level, he asks what the problem is. Judge Goldstein can be fatherly, supportive, sarcastic, or stern as the case may require: "What are you doing with your money, Louise? You're not buying food with it. What *are* you doing with it? Put on some weight!"

## Defendants Cannot Play Their Usual Games

Arrestees and program participants find they cannot manipulate the court system in the way they anticipate or may have done in the past. They cannot ask the public defender to get them off on a technicality, lie to the probation officer, or get away with feigning innocence to the judge. Defendant to judge: "I couldn't make it to the treatment center. I work odd hours and I got domestic problems. Also, I . . ." Judge, interrupting: "*I* got domestic problems, too. We *all* do! Doesn't mean you go do cocaine!" Judge Goldstein exposes defendants and justice system personnel alike to a very different experience from most courts' traditional assembly-line processing of drug possession cases: the public defender does not speak for the accused, and the prosecutor does not speak for the State. Instead, Judge Goldstein addresses each defendant directly, and he requires each defendant to respond directly to him. (On occasion, the judge—a former motorcycle patrolman—has told a defendant whose eyes wander nervously toward the public defender looking for help, "Don't look at him; he's not gonna help you.")

In Drug Court, all the justice system players are on the same team, making the same demands on the defendant and standing ready to impose the same penalties for noncompliance. In addition, in contrast to most courtrooms where different personnel may preside and prosecute at every encounter, and where defendants can try to get a better deal out of each new adversary, the faces in Drug Court remain the same. Eventually, defendants come to realize that Drug Court is a paradox: Everyone there is using the courtroom to keep the defendants out of the court system—by helping them to get off and stay off drugs.

Judge Goldstein believes one reason the program works is that the justice system personnel consistently hold defendants accountable. Whether defendants are congratulated or reprimanded for not doing well, "at least they know that someone is paying attention to what's happening to them." And because all court officers work together rather than as adversaries, Judge Goldstein believes that defendants feel responsible not only to him but to the public defender and the prosecutor as well. Drug Court becomes, in Tim Murray's words, "a very personal experience in an impersonal system."

Another reason Drug Court succeeds, in Murray's opinion, is the willingness of court personnel and treatment providers alike to take a program that appears on paper to be tightly structured and tailor it to each defendant's personality and progress. The program has three distinct phases—detoxification, stabilization, and aftercare—with testing and monitoring continuing during all three phases. . . . Counselors and the court exercise a great deal of discretion in tailoring the program to meet the needs of the "clients" (as they are often called).

## Figure 1. Diversion and Treatment Program Client Flow Chart

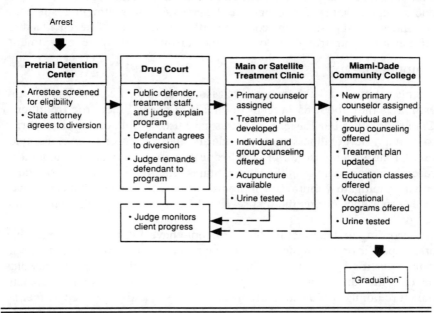

## Phase I: Detoxification

Once assigned to the Diversion and Treatment Program, clients are transferred to the county's main treatment clinic for intake processing. Clients receive all their phase I and phase II services at this facility unless they live in the southern part of the county, where they can go to a more convenient satellite clinic.

## Role of the Counselor

The primary goal of phase I is detoxification. Phase I is expected to last 12 to 14 days, but frequently continues longer if a client has trouble getting off drugs. The client's primary counselor, a licensed addiction treatment professional, makes sure the client appears every day in phase I to leave a urine specimen and then carefully tracks the test results. The counselor offers the client individual and group counseling. According to Tim Murray, many clients resist treatment for a week or two, denying they have a drug problem. On occasion, clients even try to sneak clean urine specimens into the clinic or claim they tested positive because of drugs lingering in their system. But as clients realize that program staff cannot be manipulated and are serious about helping them get off drugs, they begin to ask for treatment. If someone continues to test positive, the counselor informs the court of the client's negative attitude and strongly encourages the person to participate in treatment.

## Acupuncture

Clients are offered daily acupuncture as an aid in detoxification. Tim Murray estimates that about 85 percent of clients in phase I elect the treatment. China and other Far Eastern countries have used acupuncture for centuries to treat a variety of illnesses and provide anesthesia during surgery. Acupuncture has also been used for drug detoxification in these countries and, more recently, in some clinics in the United States. The treatment is said to reduce cravings, mitigate withdrawal symptoms, and ease the anxiety that clients typically experience during the first several days or weeks after they stop using drugs.

According to acupuncture theory, people have 136 pressure points that affect specific organs in the body. During a Miami program acupuncture session, a certified acupuncturist inserts five thin, sterile, disposable needles beneath the surface of the outer part of the ear at specific sites called acupuncture points. The needles are inserted quickly, and clients report feeling at worst a slight pinch upon insertion. This procedure is said to facilitate detoxification by causing the release of endorphins, the body's pain killers. Each session lasts 45 minutes, during which the clients appear very relaxed.

Proponents of acupuncture say that the treatment is more effective than other detoxification methods (for example, use of drugs like methadone), is inexpensive, can be administered on an outpatient basis, and makes it possible for a large number of clients to be treated simultaneously by only two or three staff members. A panel of acupuncture researchers and drug abuse treatment experts at a 1991 National Institute on Drug Abuse technical review meeting criticized the methods used to evaluate whether acupuncture really helps addicts maintain abstinence. Many panel members believed there were enough positive reports of acupuncture's benefits to justify conducting additional studies of its value as a supplement to other drug abuse treatment, particularly in light of its low cost and ease of delivery.[3]

## Treatment Planning

Another important component of phase I is the development of the client's treatment plan. Prepared jointly by the counselor and the client, the treatment plan lists realistic and measurable short-term and long-term goals the client wishes to achieve, identifies barriers to their attainment, and lists strategies for overcoming these obstacles. For example, a short- term goal might be to stay off drugs for 2 months; a barrier might be to accidentally run into former drug-using friends; and solutions could include going to group counseling sessions to find out how other addicts in recovery manage to cope with friends who are still using drugs. A long-term goal might be to become a legal secretary; an obstacle might be lack of a high school diploma; and a solution could be to enroll in a General Equivalency Diploma (GED) program.

In addition to acupuncture, the options for substance abuse treatment include group and individual counseling; fellowship meetings such as the 12-step meetings of Narcotics Anonymous and Alcoholics Anonymous, and based on a determination of need by counseling staff and the court, inpatient treatment in one of 204 publicly funded residential treatment beds in the county. Finally, clients who realize they cannot control their craving can ask to be removed temporarily from the program and incarcerated for 2 weeks to take advantage of the jail's 146 treatment beds reserved specifically for use by the Drug Court. Once detoxification is completed, they can ask the judge to return them to the Diversion and Treatment Program.

The counselor monitors client progress against the treatment plan, reassessing and adjusting it as needed to reflect new circumstances. These may range from dirty urine tests, which indicate the need for more frequent attendance at counseling sessions, to changed economic conditions that suggest exploring alternative occupational goals.

A final element of the treatment plan is a "psychosocial assessment" that provides the counselor with information about the client's needs and history for use in developing a realistic treatment plan. Typically, the psychosocial assessment includes information about the client's history of substance abuse involvement and previous treatment; social, economic, and family background; educational and health problems; and arrests, convictions and sentences (based on court records). If necessary, counselors can refer clients for psychological testing.

## Phase II: Stabilization

Clients are ready to move into phase II when Judge Goldstein believes they have shown enough progress to function successfully in a less structured treatment environment. Program rules require that clients attend all 12 scheduled sessions with their primary counselor and achieve at least 7 consecutive clean urine results before they can move into phase II. However, counselors base their recommendation on their *overall* impression of the client's ability to move on, even if that means ignoring the formal requirements for entering the next phase. Judge Goldstein, too, looks at the total picture in deciding whether he thinks a client is ready for phase II.

Clients in phase II concentrate on maintaining abstinence by attending individual and group counseling sessions and attending local fellowship meetings. Each primary counselor provides one-on-one substance abuse counseling a client may need; group therapy sessions are also conducted in the treatment clinic. Fellowship meetings are held at the clinic during the evenings as well as at many locations in the community. Clients often continue to attend acupuncture sessions on a voluntary basis once or twice a week during phase II to help them stay off drugs.

As in every program phase, counselors permit clients to decide on the treatment modalities they prefer—as long as their urine remains clean and they show up for required treatment and court sessions. For example, one client may opt for acupuncture and group counseling, while another chooses individual counseling and fellowship meetings. Clients can also change their minds about the services they want.

Phase II is scheduled to last 14 to 16 weeks, but clients can exit in 2 months or remain over a year, depending on their progress. In addition, Judge Goldstein may collaborate with treatment staff in recycling clients from phase II back into phase I if they have difficulty staying off drugs.

## Phase III: Aftercare

Treatment staff members base their decision to move a client into phase III on their overall impression of how far the individual's recovery has progressed. Attention is paid to the client's success in staying off drugs; attending counseling sessions, fellowship meetings, and court hearings; as well as progress toward achieving the goals of the individual treatment plan. Here, too, Judge Goldstein switches clients back and forth between phases II and III, depending on their progress.

## Focus on Education and Employment

Once accepted into phase III, clients change treatment sites from the main or satellite treatment clinic to one of two campuses of Miami-Dade Community College. Here, they are assigned new counselors and shift their focus from continuing their abstinence to preparing themselves academically and occupationally for the future—hence the label *aftercare*. Clients still return to court every 30 to 60 days and still provide urine specimens during phase III. In addition, they discuss with their counselors issues of maintaining sobriety that may arise now that they are no longer in the more intensive treatment atmosphere of phase II. However, the emphasis in phase III shifts to encouraging clients to do things without the help of treatment staff and to focus on the educational and vocational services they want. According to the administrator of the main treatment clinic, by the time they reach phase III, most clients have addressed many of the social and interpersonal problems caused by their drug use—lack of stable housing, poor eating habits, petty theft, and the like—and are ready to work on becoming productive members of society again.

College faculty provide the literacy training and GED classes at the on-campus Diversion and Treatment Program buildings. Program counselors encourage qualified clients to enroll in regular day classes at the schools. School financial aid counselors are available to help clients apply for financial aid. Employability skills training and job development classes are also provided to clients, along with access to current job listings, apprenticeship programs, and training programs.

If a client's urine tests start to come back positive, but the client denies using drugs, the counselor may increase the number of individual and group sessions and require more frequent testing. The counselor may also request an immediate court appearance for a client who is showing signs of trouble. First, of course, the counselor initiates a discussion about what happened and what can be done to prevent a recurrence. Whether they are having problems staying clean or not, many clients attend fellowship meetings at this stage of their recovery in addition to ongoing formal drug abuse counseling and urinalysis monitoring.

## Graduation

Phase III is slated to last 36 weeks, rounding out the anticipated year of program participation. However, some clients cycle back and forth between the final phase and phase II, while others remain in phase III well beyond the expected 8 or 9 months.

When a client no longer seems to need further monitoring or case management services, the counselor recommends discharge to the Drug Court judge, who has the final say before the prosecutor dismisses the charges. In making their decision, the counselor and judge examine the client's overall recovery, including progress in academic and vocational activities according to the treatment plan. At a final court appearance, the client is released from the program and court supervision. Diversion and Treatment Program staff then complete a discharge summary with reasons for leaving the program, progress notes, clinical assessments, and referrals.

Twelve months later, the court seals the arrest record of any client with no previous felony conviction who has not been rearrested and has paid the program fee (see below). First-time offenders can then legally report on any job application that they have never been arrested. However, police and fire departments can examine the record if the client ever applies for a job in public safety.

---

**Figure 2.  Diversion and Treatment Program Staff**

---

**Phases I & II**

**Main Treament Clinic**
- 10 full-time counselors
- 2 full-time counselors
- 3 acupuncturists
  (2 part-time)
- 3 clerks
- 1 administrator

---

**Satellite Clinic**
- 3 full-time counselors
- 1 part-time acupuncturist
- 1 supervisor
- 1 clerk

**Phase III**

**Miami-Dade Community College North Campus**
- 6 full-time counselors
- 1 full-time supervisor
- 1 clerk

---

**Miami-Dade Community College South Campus**
- 3 full-time counselors
- 1 clinical counselor
- 1 clerk

---

## A Second Chance—and More

---

Like other substance abusers in the early stages of recovery, many Diversion and Treatment Program clients have lapses involving occasional drug use without necessarily reverting to regular daily use. Program staff members estimate that at least one-third of all clients in phase I have these slips at least once. Court personnel and treatment staff do not consider these lapses to be signs of failure or inevitable precursors to a full-blown return to substance abuse. Instead, when a client's urine tests positive or a client volunteers information about slips, the counselor reviews the events that preceded the lapse to help the person recognize the feelings or events that seem to trigger renewed drug use and think of ways to cope with these warning signals. The counselor is also likely to insist that the phase I client who had a lapse begin going to individual and group counseling sessions.

When a lapse occurs during phase II or phase III, the counselor may adjust the client's treatment plan to require more frequent urine testing and move up the date of the client's next scheduled court appearance. The counselor may also insist on increased counseling or attendance at fellowship meetings. If positive test results become too frequent, the judge may reassign the client to an earlier program phase. Even if a client's urine tests are consistently or almost always negative, the counselor or the judge may impose these restrictions if there are other indications that the person's recovery is shaky or deteriorating—for example, if the client is extremely agitated, talks compulsively about drugs, reports acute tension with a family member, or misses court appearances.

Only as a last resort—and very rarely—does Judge Goldstein remove a client from the program; only he has the authority to do so. Despite repeated client lapses, failures to show up in court, and excuses for lack of progress, the judge makes every effort to find a way for treatment to work and to avert prosecution—sometimes against the treatment recommendation to discharge the person to criminal prosecution. Judge Goldstein tells these clients, "You're not getting out of this program until you get better!" Rather than expel them from the program, he often sends uncooperative clients to jail for 2 weeks if he feels they are capable of recovery but are simply not trying hard enough. For example, a middle-aged woman appeared in court with her two daughters—an 18-year-old and an infant. She had missed most of her treatment appointments and had positive urine tests on the few occasions she did show up. Judge Goldstein had her tested during the court session, and the results were positive again. The judge sent her to jail for 2 weeks for a bond violation, and the older daughter took her baby sister home.

---

### Do You Want to Go to My Hotel?

"Show me what you can do." So instructs Judge Stanley M. Goldstein of Criminal Division 51, more commonly referred to as the "Drug Court," as he leans over his bench, pen in hand, pointing to the young man before him. "Do you want to go to my hotel?" The defendant shifts nervously on his feet. He knows that "hotel" is Judge Goldstein's euphemism for jail. "No, your honor, no sir." Judge Goldstein nods, saying, "What's going on, Victor? You've missed 5 out of 12 counseling sessions? You're clean every time you go, but you're just not goin' regularly. *Go* to the program, Victor. All right. Come back in 2 weeks. I want to see some progress."

---

Tim Murray estimates that about 6 out of 10 clients who eventually grad-uate from the program spend at least 2 weeks in jail for failing to cooperate— more time than they would have spent in jail if they had plea bargained the case. As many as 3 in 10 successful clients spend 4 or more weeks in jail where they receive continuing treatment and voluntary acupuncture designed to support the Drug Court's therapeutic objectives.

The approach recognizes that some drug users experience many ups and downs before they finally recover and that criminal prosecuting is not the answer to their problems. However, a number of defendants have become vir-tually perpetual clients in the program, shuttling back and forth between phases or simply remaining in phase I. Some clients who entered the program in 1989 are still participating. As a result, treatment staff and court personnel have begun conducting case reviews of long-time clients who are failing to make progress to determine whether anything else can be done to hasten their recovery, such as placing them in residential treatment, or whether the case should be referred for traditional prosecution.

In a few cases (immediately for anyone who is rearrested), the judge removes a client if he is convinced the person cannot stop using drugs. These clients are sent to another court for disposition that usually includes jail time. Clients who fail the program may rejoin it at a later date if they can convince Judge Goldstein that they are now ready to make the effort to stay clean.

The Diversion and Treatment Program has thus resulted in comprehensive, long-range, and sometimes unexpected outcomes for Miami's drug-using offenders. Yet the program did not spring up overnight.

---

## Two Sources of Program Strength

**Comprehensive services are made available.** The program addresses the problem areas that can prevent drug users from staying clean, including illiteracy, lack of academic credentials, unemployment, lack of work experience, need for job search skills, and inadequate housing. Counselors in phase III function much like case managers, encouraging clients to exercise independence but interven-ing when necessary to line up the resources clients cannot seem to secure on their own. As one treatment administrator put it, acupuncture would not work with-out counseling, counseling would not work without job development, and job de-velopment would not work without education.

**A range of public agencies participate.** Counselors cannot provide effective case management unless there are programs with which they can link clients in need. The involvement of the community colleges is especially critical for making educational and vocational services available to clients. The County Department of Human Resources furnishes the needed treatment resources for individual and group counseling sessions. Residential care is funded by the State Department of Health and Rehabilitation Services. And all branches of the criminal justice system, from the prosecutor to the defense attorney, cooperate to make client recovery their primary goal.

# How the Program Was Developed

Dade's uncommon approach to dealing with drug offenders originated with a circuit court judge's creative thinking and the collaborative effort of many public agencies. In 1989, deeply troubled by the paralyzing effect that drug offenses were having on the Dade County court system, the Florida Supreme Court gave Judge Herbert M. Klein, associate chief judge of the eleventh circuit court, a 1-year leave of absence to come up with a comprehensive solution to the problem. After intensive study, Klein concluded that the answer lay not in finding better ways of handling more and more offenders in the criminal justice system, but in "determining how to solve the problem of larger numbers of people on drugs."

## Bringing Accountability to the System

Klein knew that offenders arrested for simple possession of narcotics were seldom held accountable for their crime. An arrestee might be locked up overnight, but the next day, after a 5-minute bond hearing before a judge, that person would typically be released pending arraignment. Three weeks later, the defendant would return to court where the public defender assigned to the case would work out a plea bargain that allowed the person to plead guilty with credit for time served (the night in jail after arrest) and go free.

Although this typical case cost the criminal justice system only a few hours in terms of police services, booking time, and recordkeeping, there was a better than even chance the offender would be rearrested and recycle through the system—eventually going to jail or prison as the felony convictions mounted or the offender began dealing drugs in order to pay for the drugs. Judge Klein developed the premise that investing a year of comprehensive treatment coupled with close surveillance in these typical cases—instead of a few hours—would pay off in the long run with reduced costs to the police, courts, and jail as more and more drug users kicked the habit.

## Involving Everyone in the Solution

Realizing that providing this level of treatment for drug offenders would require a major collaborative effort among a number of public agencies,

Klein gathered together representatives from the State attorney and public defender offices, the corrections and public safety departments, the department of human services, the county manager's office and the clerk's office, and community colleges and community organizations. Within this group, a core team was formed to design and monitor the program.

From the outset, the team agreed with Klein that to keep the criminal justice system from being inundated with drug cases, the demand for drugs had to be reduced; strategies had to extend beyond the police, courts, and jails. Following extensive discussion and testimony, the group also concluded that diverting drug arrestees into treatment could be an effective means of rehabilitation that would eventually reduce recidivism. The team reached a consensus that treatment had to include:

- A choice of several treatment modalities, including individual and group counseling, attendance at fellowship meetings, and acupuncture.
- Ancillary services, including literacy testing and education, vocational assessment and counseling, job placement services, and assistance in finding housing.
- Close monitoring of defendant progress through urine testing, adherence to an individualized treatment plan, and regular court appearances.
- The option of sentencing uncooperative defendants to jail.

In short, drug offenders would be treated as addicts, not criminals, for as long as they made a sincere effort to get off and stay off drugs.

## Overcoming Concerns and Objections

Hammering out this unusual master plan with such a wide range of agencies did not, of course, come easily or quickly. Klein was asking the criminal justice system to abandon its adversarial mode of doing business, treatment providers to increase their caseloads, and public colleges to educate recovering cocaine users. Klein ran into numerous roadblocks.

- The public defender pointed out that whereas in the past his assistants could finish a case in short order by recommending that the defendant plead to time served, under the proposed diversion-to-treatment plan they would have to carry each client for an entire year in a program in which this type of offender usually fails.
- Faculty of the two community colleges were concerned about providing services to this population on campus because students—and their parents—would not feel comfortable mingling with criminals and drug users. Some school administrators were apprehensive that drugs would be used or sold around the program buildings.

Klein emphasized to defense attorneys that treatment, not another plea bargain, was in the best long-term interests of their clients, and he pointed out that the court, not they, would have the headache of monitoring defendants' progress. Klein and Chief Judge Weatherington personally presented to the community college cabinet the case for locating phase III activities on campus. The judges explained that clients would go through extensive screening before being allowed on campus and that only clients who volunteered to take courses would be on the grounds. No one was going to be "sentenced" to campus activities. The judges received support from the deans at the community colleges, who pointed out to skeptical faculty members that the schools already had students who used drugs. Besides, it was time the colleges demonstrated their social commitment to the surrounding community by helping to solve this countywide problem. (Three years into the program, one dean reported he had yet to receive a negative comment from faculty or students about the program.)

According to Murray, one key official who did not have reservations about Klein's community strategy for handling drug offenders was U.S. Attorney General Janet Reno, then State Attorney for Dade County. Indeed, it was Reno, picking up on Klein's idea of a special court to handle drug arrestees, who proposed that the court apply a carrot-and-stick approach to drug users: Accept and complete treatment, and your case will be dismissed and your record sealed; refuse or fail, and you will be prosecuted. Reno also pushed for expanding the program to include more than just first-time offenders and to enlarge its treatment capability. Murray noted that Reno's chief complaint for the first 3 years was that the program didn't reach enough offenders.

It took 6 months of meetings and debates before Klein could overcome the team's doubts and before the members could agree on a specific program structure. The team was eventually able to reach a consensus because of a number of factors: respect for Klein's authority as a circuit court judge, his decision to charge team members with developing a mutually acceptable solution, and his appeals to the group's sense of community. A powerful contributing factor was the strong sense of urgency most team members felt about the failure of the current system in dealing with drug offenders and the conviction that a cosmetic or public relations gesture would not solve the problem.

## Program Accomplishments

Several sets of data suggest the range of the Diversion and Treatment Program's achievement.

## Participation

Tim Murray estimates that between June 1989, when the program began, and March 1993, around 4,500 defendants entered the Diversion and Treatment Program, representing about 20 percent of all arrestees in the county charged with a drug-related offense. Approximately 60 percent of all those diverted have graduated or are still in treatment, Murray reckons.

## Recidivism

Murray reports that whereas typical recidivism rates range up to 60 percent, only 11 percent of defendants who completed the program have been rearrested in Dade County on any criminal charges in the year after graduation. No follow-up information is available on participants who failed to complete the program.[4]

## Costs

The Diversion and Treatment Program's budget (including the cost of constructing the North Campus building) was $1.3 million in fiscal year 1990 (June 1, 1989, to May 31, 1990) and $1.8 million in fiscal years 1991 and 1992 after the county added $500,000 for expanded services. According to Murray, this translates into about $800 per client per year—or roughly the cost of jailing an offender for 9 days. (Of course, as noted, a majority of clients do spend at least 2 weeks in jail before they graduate.)

Most funding for the program has come from the Dade County General Fund. Acting on a suggestion from Judge Klein, Dade County commissioners developed a new method of redistributing income from traffic offense fees, thus generating some $1 million annually for the Diversion and Treatment Program. No taxes were increased, nor were funds from any county operations diverted to the program.

Startup costs to pay for urinalysis during the first program year were partially funded by a one-time contribution from the Law Enforcement Trust Fund (money realized from seized assets which, by State law, cannot be used to fund recurring expenses). The program also collects a client fee according to a sliding scale based on the defendant's ability to pay. For example, clients with gross annual incomes between $5,000 and $12,000 are assessed $500, while clients who earn $50,000 or more pay $2,500. The program has collected between $11,000 and $23,000 per month in client fees, depending on caseload levels. While fees go directly into the county general fund to be spent as the commissioners see fit, in effect the revenues make the program partially self-supporting.

## Promising Evidence

Although insufficient time has elapsed to examine long-term results, available data suggest that a majority of clients remain in the program for at least a year and are discharged on the basis of a record of negative urine tests and a behavioral profile consistent with a promise of recovery. Furthermore, the rate of rearrest 1 year after graduation is low.

According to Judge Klein, the crime reduction potential of the program is substantial. Considering that a crack addict can commit between 25 and 600 crimes a year, the decline in crimes could be significant, he points out, if these persons are drug free and employed. Research supports Klein's logic. A study of 573 substance abusers in Miami found that in a 1-year period they committed 6,000 robberies and assaults, 6,700 burglaries, 900 auto thefts, 25,000 acts of shoplifting, and 46,000 other larcenies or frauds.[5]

Two other sets of research findings also provide optimism for concluding that the program reduces drug abuse. First, several studies have shown that offenders referred to treatment by the courts have a powerful incentive to remain in treatment in order to avoid being jailed again.[6] Other research, in turn, suggests that the longer an addict remains in treatment, the better his or her chances for long-term recovery.[7] Miami's Diversion and Treatment Program seems to meet these preconditions for effectiveness. It makes use of legal coercion to motivate defendants to accept treatment, and a substantial number of diverted defendants remain in treatment a considerable length of time.

Despite these program features, many clients either fail to make progress or hang on to a precarious recovery only as long as they continue to receive services. However, for many other defendants, the combination of comprehensive services, regular monitoring, and personal attention appears to enable them to stay off drugs and avoid further entanglement with the law.

An evaluation of the program by the National Institute of Justice and the State Justice Institute is looking at whether it is possible to draw more definitive conclusions about the program's effectiveness. The evaluation is examining whether the Diversion and Treatment Program diverts cases that ordinarily would be formally adjudicated (with a resulting savings in court and jail sentences), and whether diverted defendants reduce their use of drugs, comply with other program conditions, and are rearrested less often compared with offenders who are not diverted.

## Notes

[1]Federal Bureau of Investigation. *Uniform Crime Reports for the United States, 1991.* Washington, D.C.: U.S. Department of Justice, Federal Bureau of Investigation, 1992: pp. 212–213.

[2]Computed by Abt Associates, Inc., from the 1991 Uniform Crime Reports data tape.

[3]Swan, N. "Experts Divided on Effectiveness of Acupuncture as a Drug Abuse Treatment." *NIDA Notes* (September-October 1992): 8–9.

[4]It is difficult to determine whether the low recidivism rate among program graduates indicates the program is more effective than traditional criminal processing, however, because there are no data available on the arrest rate of participants who fail to complete the program.

[5]Inciardi, J. A. *The War of Drugs*. Palo Alto, CA: Mayfield Press, 1986.

[6]Anglin, D. M. "Treatment of Drug Abuse." *Criminology*, vol. 25:359–397; Dunham, R. G. and A. L. Mauss, "Reluctant Referrals: The Effectiveness of Legal Coercion in Outpatient Treatment for Problem Drinkers." *Journal of Drug Issues*, vol. 12:5–20; Hubbard, Robert, M. E. Marsden, J. V. Rachal, H. J. Harwood, E. R. Cavanaugh, and H. M. Ginzburg. *Drug Abuse Treatment: A National Study of Effectiveness*. Chapel Hill: The University of North Carolina Press, 1989.

[7]Office of National Drug Control Policy. *Understanding Drug Treatment*, Washington, D.C.: The White House, 1990.

# 17

# Correctional Alternatives for Drug Offenders in an Era of Overcrowding

## Todd R. Clear
## Val B. Clear
## Anthony A. Braga

The antidrug movement in the United States is running on a collision course with the problem of overcrowded prisons and jails. Regardless of the sincerity with which political leadership seeks to reduce certain types of drug use, the realities of the justice system are seriously strained resources at all levels of law enforcement, prosecution and adjudication, and correctional supervision and treatment. If there is hope for the so-called war on drugs, it must be based on a realistic assessment of affordable costs.

In corrections, this means that extensive use of alternatives to traditional corrections must occur. Stated bluntly, most corrections systems in the United States are so seriously overburdened in their traditional resources of jails, prisons, and probation, that small increases in demand will constitute major management problems.

Reprinted by permission of Sage Publications, from *The Prison Journal*, Vol. 73, No. 2, pp. 178-198, © 1993 by Sage Publications, Inc.

Because of strained resources, many corrections systems have experimented with new types of alternatives to the traditional forms of corrections. The purpose of this article is to explore how the "new generation" alternatives to traditional corrections are relevant for the drug offender. The article begins with a description of the major types of correctional alternatives currently being used around the country, followed by a description of types of drug offenders and their suitability for different forms of alternatives. Drawing from research on alternatives, a set of principles in their application to offenders is then developed. The article concludes with suggested strategies for using alternative correctional forms for drug offenders.

## Major Forms of Alternatives to Traditional Corrections

Nearly every jurisdiction has experimented with one form or another of corrections alternatives in recent years. This has resulted in a rich variety of programs for offenders falling between the prison and traditional probation. A description of prototypical programs is provided below, but the reader should be aware that many versions of each of these prototypes exist, and each extant program has unique characteristics that help it fit its jurisdiction.

### Shock Incarceration

One of the newest forms of correctional alternatives involves a sentence to a "boot camp" type experience (Parent, 1989). Normally, the term is short (30 to 90 days), but the experience is intentionally harsh. Offenders are put through a regimen of long days of intense physical effort under strict discipline. In some respects, the new shock programs are a throwback to early forms of imprisonment that extolled the virtues of hard work and daily discipline. The idea of these programs is to "shock" offenders in two ways: first, by removing them from the community and, second, by subjecting them to harsh, unrelenting conditions of work.

Most shock programs target first offenders—many require no prior felony convictions—and most exclude violent or previously incarcerated offenders. In addition, most programs are limited to persons under a certain age, no older than early 20s, to have young, impressionable inmates in the programs.

### Residential Centers

Because prisons are so expensive to build, many urban areas have renovated existing buildings, turning them into part-time or full-time residential facilities. In many ways, these programs resemble the traditional work release center or halfway house. Part-time programs are the most common, and they allow the offender to be away during work hours and for some social time, returning to sleep at night. Full-time programs usually restrict the offender's ability to be away from the facility to only special occasions.

Residential centers normally incorporate a treatment regime into their programs. Commonly, they use group-based approaches such as "guided group interaction" to help offenders confront their lifestyles. They also commonly restrict their populations to specific target groups: probation failures, substance abusers, persons owing restitution, and so forth. This enables the treatment programs to concentrate on a more homogeneous population. With drug-involved offenders, residential centers have often used "therapeutic community" methods (DeLeon, 1987).

## Financial Penalties

Financial penalties such as fines, restitution, and forfeitures have recently been advanced as an alternative approach to punishment. Advocates of financial penalties argue that they are particularly well suited to a capitalist society that places importance on monetary incentives and the accumulation of wealth. Not only can the fruits of crime be eliminated through monetary sanctions, but also substantial punishment can be inflicted on offenders by imposition of a financial penalty, all without the severe costs of incarceration (Hillsman & Greene, 1992).

The aim of fines and forfeitures is essentially punitive and deterrent, not reformative. The severity of a fine can even be adjusted to the seriousness of the offense and to the offender's financial circumstances taking into consideration the amount of the offender's income and assets (called the "day fine"). Some observers have argued that, potentially, fines are very different—and much fairer—than forfeitures, which can be arbitrary and disproportionate in impact.

## Community Service

Community service—labor performed by the offender, generally for a public agency or nonprofit organization—has many attractive features: The person "pays back" to the offended community, all offenders are charged equally (in hours) regardless of their circumstances, and the cost is much less than prison (McDonald, 1992). Community service sanctioning programs have been successfully run in numerous jurisdictions around the United States.

One advantage of community service approaches has been that they provide a relatively efficient way to sanction repetitive minor offenders, such as misdemeanants. The cost of law enforcement for these offenders often outweighs the seriousness of their crimes, and community service can provide a vehicle for appropriate, inexpensive consequences for minor illegal activity.

## Conventional Probation

With caseloads often ranging from 100 to 300 offenders, most conventional probation systems do little more than monitor compliance and react to misbehavior of clients. Recently developed classification systems have allowed conventional probation supervision to focus attention on the most risky and needy clients within a caseload (Clear & Gallagher, 1983), and some research suggests that this approach can be promising with serious offenders (Markley & Eisenberg, 1987).

In many areas of the country, however, conventional probation remains a highly criticized form of correctional treatment. Some studies have shown that probationers exhibit high rates of rearrest while under supervision (Petersilia, Turner, Kahan, & Peterson, 1985), although this appears to be less true in some parts of the country than in others (Ficher, Hirschberg, & McGaha, 1987).

## Intensive Supervision Programs (ISPs)

One of the most popular new approaches is to intensify the level of probation (or parole) supervision given to offenders. Instead of the common practice of one or two face-to-face contacts each month, these ISPs require a minimum of two or three per week, including unannounced evening visits to the home. They also typically employ "back-up" controls of electronic monitoring and/ or urine testing (described below) to augment the level of surveillance (Byrne, 1990).

ISPs differ in their offender eligibility criteria and program philosophy. Many are designed to divert offenders from incarceration, and these typically will not consider offenders convicted of violent offenses. Other ISPs target the most difficult offenders already on probation or parole caseloads, and these ISPs normally do not use exclusionary criteria (Byrne, Lurigio, & Baird, 1989). Unlike their predecessors in the 1960s, most modern ISPs are unabashedly "tough" in their stance with offenders, although a handful advertise a treatment orientation.

## Electronic Monitoring

The "hottest" of the new alternatives is not a program per se but, instead, a technique applied within a program. Made possible by recent technical advances in computers and telephones, electronic monitors are devices that emit a coded signal to a receiver. When these devices are attached to the body (usually the wrist or ankle) the signal can be used to indicate the offender's whereabouts—and especially to certify that the offender is home in accordance with a curfew or court order (Schmidt, 1989).

The use of monitors is in its technical and experiential infancy, and although the early results of these programs are intriguing, there is as yet no basis to say whether they succeed. Early experiments reported considerable technical problems, although many of these problems appear to have been eradicated in revised units. They are, however, expensive, running as much as $300 per month (although most units are considerably cheaper). Many programs therefore restrict themselves to offenders who are able to pay for the equipment, those who have telephones, and those whose offenses are nonviolent.

## Urine Testing

Like electronic monitoring, urine testing is not a program but a surveillance component that can be used in conjunction with any correctional program, even incarceration. These tests not only indicate whether a person has been using a substance, but they also indicate which substances. When urine testing is done with any population, a high proportion of "hits" (indicators of substance use) is found—but this is especially true for offender groups (Wish & Gropper, 1990).

Questions have been raised about the accuracy of urine tests, but research consistently shows that when recommended procedures are followed, the test results are highly reliable. For this reason, the high level of drug use in arrested offenders (ranging across the country from 50 percent to over 80 percent) is remarkable evidence about the extensiveness of drug involvement in this population.

## Antidote Drugs

A variety of drug use suppressants exist that either reduce the desire for drugs or counteract their effects. The oldest versions are methadone, a drug that replaces the heroin urge, and Antabuse, which causes unpleasant side effects when mixed with alcohol. Both drugs have been available for decades. More recently, new drugs have been used experimentally to combat the effects of cocaine and other sources of the "high" (Anglin & Hser, 1990).

Drug use suppression is controversial. All tests of the technique find that there are limits to the success experienced in eradication of substance use—often offenders under one drug suppression regimen simply change drugs of preference (Rosenbaum & Murphy, 1984). There is also a nagging conceptual problem with using drugs to fight drugs. Nonetheless, this approach is a frequently used tool in the arsenal of drug treatment agencies, once offenders have shown a motivation to quit.

## Treatment

Although technically, all forms of intervention with drug offenders are *treatment*, the term usually denotes mental health approaches with the aim to change the offender's lifestyle. Treatment programs for drug offenders focus on the rationalizations, dependencies, and delusional thinking that feed the addictive lifestyle. They attempt, through therapeutic interaction with others, to convince the offender of the value of the wholesale lifestyle change needed to overcome drug abuse.

Treatment Alternatives to Street Crime (TASC) is a nationwide program that specializes in working with drug-abusing offenders. The program is eclectic, using numerous techniques, from direct, random urine testing to job training, counseling, and referral. Programs vary their approaches to fit local environments, but all serve as adjuncts to probation and parole operations, using specially trained staff to work with drug users.

Narcotics Anonymous (NA) and Alcoholics Anonymous (AA) are well-established self-help programs that rely on reformed users (called *recovering*) to provide support for others interested in ending their drug use. Because the program is based on the desire of the clients to change, it is entirely voluntary (although courts will often violate this by ordering attendance). Members are aware of the games that drug users play, see through their manipulations, and challenge their co-users to sustain recovery.

In-patient drug treatment programs have become more common in recent years. These programs usually have highly structured environments in which the patient proceeds through a series of stages of treatment requiring 30 to 90 days to complete. Most programs accept nonoffenders, and all are expensive. Experts believe that follow-up treatment and support are necessary if drug abusers are to stay clean after release (Wexler & Lipton, 1985).

## Jail and Prison

Although these are not truly *alternatives* as the term is commonly used, short-term prison and jail stays are an important approach to be considered in lieu of longer penalties. When incapacitation is not a consideration, short prison stays are thought to provide an incentive for the offender to avoid repeat crimes. Although evidence for the usefulness of short-term prison sentences is inconclusive, many people argue that short prison sentences are as effective as long ones for most offenders, even drug offenders (Wexler & Williams, 1986).

Jail terms, by contrast, can play an important role in reinforcing compliance with alternative programs. Nearly all alternatives programs have strict rules, and when these are broken, it is often inadvisable to revoke the offender and impose the full, original sentence. Short stays in the local jail of

24 to 72 hours in length can serve to confirm the importance of the program's rules for offenders who are otherwise doing well in the community.

## A Drug-Crime Behavior Typology

The phrase "drug offender," when used to refer to all people who both use drugs and commit crimes, and be a misleading oversimplification. The high proportion of arrestees who have used drugs prior to their crimes is evidence that not all drug-crime relationships are the same (Fagan, 1990). The optimal use of correctional alternatives requires an understanding of the nature of drug-crime behaviors and their suitability for different types of programs. This suggests the need for a typology of offenders' drug-crime relationships. A typology would allow differential assignment of offenders to correctional programs, based on the nature of the program and the offender's crime-related drug problems.

In developing such a typology, an implicit assumption is made that the purpose of correctional intervention is to prevent or control the risk of criminal recidivism. Correctional programs are interested in the drug use of offenders only insofar as drug use relates to the potential for new criminal behavior. A typology is helpful if it identifies the different ways that drugs and crime can be related and classifies offenders according to those patterns.

Using such a typology requires caution, however. Although any correctional typology has the ultimate aim of informing action about offenders, the following typology is not about *people*, but about *events*. It posits that for drug-using offenders, their criminal events vary in the way they relate to drug use. Rather than classifying people, then, this typology attempts to classify drug use and criminal events into a logical framework.

The resulting behavior types are, in actuality, stereotypes—they fit more or less well to certain offenders. Although offenders vary in their drug-crime behavior pattern, the implication is that many offenders will exhibit a high concentration of one pattern. Stereotypes are not used merely to classify offenders but are developed to decide the kind of correctional programs that might be effective for an offender and why (Chaiken & Chaiken, 1984).

It is also important to note that a behavior will sometimes change; especially, their drug-crime behavior may evolve. Correctional strategies should be designed to inhibit the continuation of this process. Interventions should aim to prevent the habituation of illicit drug involvement for the offender's current behavioral type.

## Types of Drug-Crime Behaviors

The typology recognizes that drug use and criminal behavior are two different forms of deviance, and an offender might be more, or less, committed to either. Figure 1 shows the model.

---

**Figure 1: A Model for Identifying Correctional Programs for Drug Offenders**

|  |  | Commitment to Crime | |
|---|---|---|---|
|  |  | **High** | **Low** |
| **Commitment to Drugs** | **High** | Predator | Addict |
|  | **Low** | Seller | User |

---

For linguistic ease, the stereotypes will be described for persons whose drug-crime behavior is exclusively of that type. The reader should remember our caveats stated above. There are offenders for whom a "pure type" model is simplistic, and many (perhaps most) offenders will experience a change in the drug-crime pattern of their behavior over their lifetimes. Four types of drug-crime relationships are identified. *Users* are those who have little commitment to either drugs or crime. *Addicts* are committed to drugs but not to crime. *Sellers* are committed to crime but not to drugs. *Predators* are committed to both crime and drugs. A description of the four types follows.

*Addicts.* The Addict has become so attached to drug use that his or her lifestyle is built around the acquisition and consumption of drugs (Ball, Shaffer, & Nurco, 1983; Hanson, Beschner, Walters, & Bovelle, 1985). Because Addicts are physically and/or psychologically dependent on the drug, their problem is to break the addiction and learn a substance-free lifestyle.

Because many drugs are expensive, many Addicts must engage in criminal activity to obtain money to support their drug use. Studies show that criminal behavior remains high during periods of drug use (Speckart & Anglin, 1986). Common forms of such criminality are burglary, small item theft, and drug sales, although middle-class Addicts will choose other types of crime and alcoholics commit crimes by driving (Goldstein, 1981). For Addicts, however, the criminal activity is not an end but a means (Mieczkowski, 1986).

Addicts need correctional approaches that force them (or enable them) to confront the circumstances of their abuse of drugs. Many treatment programs are based on this model. They use various techniques to demonstrate to the offender the consequences of drug use, including direct education, confrontive counseling, drug therapy, and interventions from friends and family (Platt, 1986). When treatment is successful with this person, the results are significant: A drug user is reformed and criminal activity is prevented (Ball, Rosen, Flueck, & Nurco, 1982).

*Sellers.* The essential cog in the illicit drug machine is the Seller of drugs. Among Sellers there is a hierarchy, of course, with the street salespersons occupying the lowest rung and representing the most commonly arrested type. The drug-crime connection of many of those engaged in street sales is, in fact, the Addict variety (Chaiken & Johnson, 1988).

True Sellers are involved with drugs solely (or primarily) as a way to make large amounts of money. Studies show that a small percentage of offenders arrested for drug sales or possession test negatively for drug use—these are economically motivated drug offenders engaging in business (Goldkamp, 1989). Although the business risks are high—especially in terms of the violence inherent to the drug market—the potential reward is considerable (Reuter, Macoun, & Murphy, 1990). A street Seller can make hundreds of dollars in a day; a higher-level person even more. Frequently, juveniles are used in this role to avoid processing by the adult criminal justice system.

Because the Seller has no personal commitment to drugs but has accepted the risk of crime, little drug treatment is needed. Moreover, punishment is not likely to do much good, at least for crime control. A person who is willing to risk death is probably willing to risk prison—and while he or she is incarcerated, someone else will sell in his or her place.

*Users.* Unlike Addicts, Users have little commitment to drugs, and unlike Sellers, they are basically noncriminal in lifestyle. These offenders use drugs periodically because they like the high. Their lives are otherwise more or less normal, but they come to the attention of the criminal justice system as a result of an instance of their occasional drug use (Zinberg, 1984).

The Users' main problem is that they are now identified offenders. Treatment may help forestall movement toward greater drug abuse, and it may provide the offender with information, but it can do little to prevent crime, because there is little crime to prevent. For most Users, the issue is to avoid creating problems through correctional programming.

*Predators.* Some drug-using offenders are committed to a criminal lifestyle, a lifestyle of risk and excitement, and a part of that lifestyle is extensive use of drugs (Ball, 1986). Patterns of criminal behavior will include serious, violent crimes such as rape, armed robbery, assault, and burglary—drugs are often used to generate the "courage" to commit the offense (Chaiken & Chaiken, 1990; Johnson & Wish, 1987).

For the Predator, crime and drugs are linked (as they are for the addict), but crime is not just a means, it is also an end. These criminals enjoy the thrill and fruits of criminal acts as well as the thrill of drug use.

Correctional treatment can be useful for Predators but must be undertaken with the recognition that their drug use behavior is not the central cause of criminal behavior; instead, there is a criminal orientation that needs to be overcome. Treatment will need to address both the mood-changing aspects of drugs and the criminal thought patterns and desires of the offender (Andrews, Kessling, Robinson, & Mickus, 1986).

## Principles of the Use of Correctional Alternatives

Before concluding with a discussion of the strategies for using alternatives with drug offenders, it is important to summarize prior experiences with these alternatives when used on the larger body of offenders. These experiences form a framework for developing drug offender strategies.

### Alternatives Are Susceptible to Net-Widening

The most pernicious aspect of alternatives to traditional corrections is that they frequently end up costing more tax dollars and interfering more with offenders than the programs they were designed to replace. Called *net-widening*, this means that the ultimate result of these programs is greater social control rather than reduced state involvement in cases (Austin & Krisberg, 1980). This is especially unfortunate, because these programs are normally based on the premise that they are less intrusive than traditional prison and more effective than traditional probation. Often sold as cost-effective alternatives to crowded prison systems, when these programs prove to be more expensive than the traditional system, serious questions are raised about their overall value.

There are two ways that programs widen the net. First, they may advertise that they are alternatives to prison, but instead they serve as alternatives to probation. In the typical case, judges are given authority to sentence directly to the program. Net-widening occurs when judges place borderline cases into the new programs, when most of the borderline cases otherwise would have gone to probation. The consequence is that the program is used to augment probation supervision, not to reduce reliance on incarceration. Because "new generation" programs are always more expensive than traditional probation, this means the programs fail to save tax dollars.

This problem happens in new programs when eligibility criteria are too conservative. For example, to restrict a program to nonviolent nonrecidivists, as so many of the new boot camps have done, is to invite net widening because these offenders seldom go to prison or jail anyway. To attain a diversion population, programs must be willing to accept offenders whose profiles and prior record make them likely prison candidates.

The second way that these programs can widen the net is by increasing the rate of imprisoned failures. Often, people who fail under a new program are charged an added "premium" for their failure. They receive a prison sentence of several years to make a point about the toughness of the alternative, even though their original sentence would have been much less had they not been given the alternative.

These two problems are particularly acute for drug offenders. Users seldom receive incarcerative terms. Admitting them to the alternatives is almost always going to widen the net. Addicts, on the other hand, go to prison or jail when their accompanying crimes are serious. They make good candidates for diversion, but their prognosis in these programs is problematic, although somewhat better than their prognosis in prison. Admitting them to these programs can accomplish goals of diversion and crime control, but it will guarantee a client group experiencing high levels of difficulty—dirty urines, unemployment, and so forth. Sellers and Predators are normally excluded from alternatives programs by virtue of their criminal history. In short, trying to reduce prison population through diverting drug offenders requires making difficult choices.

In addition, the experience of the alternative can actually be more intrusive than prison. Intensive supervision for 18 months, with surprise home visits, urine monitoring, a 7:00 P.M. curfew, electronic bracelets, and 120 hours of community service—many offenders might consider this worse than 6 months in jail. And there is the very real question that such close control might draw a user into further difficulty with the system, even though adjustment is otherwise adequate.

The main point is that correctional alternatives are not a fail-safe way to reduce the pressure of prisons. If they are to work as true alternatives, they must be carefully designed, with eligibility criteria that are tightly drawn to guarantee true diversion from incarceration.

## It Is Easier to Contain Costs than to Reduce Them

Much is made of the fact that alternatives are cheaper than traditional prison. When offenders assigned to alternatives are truly diverted from prison, they generally receive a less costly sentence. But this may not necessarily translate into cost savings. For one thing, the very best alternatives can approach the cost of prison. In-residence treatment and shock incarceration can be more expensive per day than traditional prison—they cost less only when the terms are shorter. ISPs, when truly intensive, can involve costs nearly half that of prison, and may be imposed for twice as long (McDonald, 1989).

A more difficult problem is that the total cost of running a prison is about the same when the prison is 90 percent full as when it is at capacity. The housing costs of a given prison (food and clothing) contribute insignificantly to the daily prison budget, but security needs, mostly in the form of personnel requirements, stay relatively stable within a range of capacity. (Conditions of extreme crowding will aggravate security costs, whereas closing unused units can eliminate some personnel needs.) No matter how extensively systems use their new alternatives, almost no states find they have vacant cells as a result.

Rather than reducing total systems costs, it is better to think in terms of cost containment, whereby expenditures on new facilities are avoided (or delayed) through the extensive use of less expensive alternatives. This strategy seems especially applicable to those drug offenders, in particular, addicts, who experience the system serially over their lifetimes (Ball et al., 1982). Costs of managing these offenders can be contained through careful use of layered alternatives, in which short treatment experiences are augmented by community control approaches (such as ISP). The long-term goal is desistance, which may require several years to achieve and may be accomplished through repeated use of alternatives that seem to fail in the short run. In this approach, program failure is accompanied by short-term consequences, including even short jail stays, followed by renewed attempts at treatment/control. If this seems an unappealing strategy, it is more desirable than longer prison stays, which cost much more and have little impact on desistance.

For Predators and Users, the concept of cost containment may not be so relevant. With Predators, their procriminal lifestyle is precisely the type on which correctional costs should be concentrated. For Users, the benefits of any system expenditures should be questioned. Sellers, on the other hand, pose a dilemma. In today's atmosphere of toughness with "pushers," it is not easy to argue for cost containment. Yet research shows, first, that these offenders are quickly replaced by other sellers after their incarceration, and, second, that they have low failure rates after release. In other words, few crimes are prevented by their incarceration.

## The Costs of Tough Enforcement Can Be Considerable

All research on the new alternatives finds that they enforce program requirements stringently and thus have high program failure rates (Petersilia, Peterson, & Turner, 1992). This result should not surprise anyone. Offenders are not a compliant group to begin with. When they are made accountable for a large number of strict rules and then are closely monitored for compliance, they often fail. On the face of it, this seems both obvious and desirable. Closer analysis raises questions about the wisdom of a strategy of unrelenting enforcement.

The process of tough enforcement in these programs involves the imposition of costly consequences for behavior that is either noncriminal (failure to comply with curfew or failure to complete community service work) or of minor seriousness (marijuana in the urine). Imposition of an original prison term for such behavior may satisfy program directors that their requirements "have teeth," but it seems to miss the point that the program's ultimate responsibility is to prevent crime and change the offender's behavior patterns, not simply to run a tight ship. When program requirements are so strict that offenders are returned to prison for rules violations despite the absence of evidence of new criminality or impending criminal conduct, both the offender and the system lose.

This is especially likely to happen with drug offenders. Addicts will fail, and they will fail frequently. Any program built on a foundation of zero tolerance for failure will find the fully successful Addict to be in a small minority. By the same token, professionals who work with Addicts know that misbehavior must be met with consequences. The strategy is normally to impose sanctions of slowly ascending seriousness in the face of "slips" for persons thought otherwise to be noncriminal. Addicts can move up and down through phases of increased urine testing, curfews, loss of privileges (such as driving), and even short jail stays several times before they finally establish a period of sobriety that can form the foundation for recovery.

When prison is thought of as a last resort, programs take the approach of working with Addicts who exhibit motivation to stay clean, even in the face of occasional slips. The idea is to decrease the incidence and frequency of the slips and reward the offender in the process. But when reincarceration is thought of as the only consequence for misbehavior, none of this sequencing is possible, and addicts fail at very high rates.

This program is all the more difficult for Users, whose involvement in the criminal justice system is essentially a result of drug laws. To enforce packages of requirements on them in a nonnegotiable fashion is to invite failure where there would otherwise be success. For Predators and Sellers, the story is quite different. Misbehavior on the part of these offenders can be interpreted as predictive of a resumption of criminal activity. In these cases, rapid and serious consequences for noncompliance with program rules may prevent crime.

## All Alternatives Impose Opportunity Costs

The popularity of alternatives to traditional corrections should not obscure the fact that the decision to invest in these programs ties up public dollars. It is the same for prisons—the decision to construct a prison means that dollars dedicated to that task cannot be spent on public health, schools, transportation, or other worthy public causes. The decision to develop alternatives may contain costs of traditional corrections, but that still means the devotion of tax dollars to that alternative.

From a broad perspective, the decision to expand alternatives for drug offenders may mean, for example, that noncorrectional treatment approaches receive less support. This certainly appears to have been the case since 1980, at least at the federal level of government. The appropriate public policy question is whether dollars put into correctional forms of treatment, traditional or nontraditional, pay off to the public more than dollars in non-custodial treatment or prevention. Insufficient information exists to answer this question, but it is certainly a question worth asking: If investing in prisons and special correctional programs means the decimation of mental health alternatives, is that a wise trade-off?

More narrowly, the problem of opportunity costs applies to the assignment of "spaces" to persons in alternatives programs. An ISP caseload, for example, has a capacity of 20 to 25 cases. It is better to place a burglar or a drug offender under such close scrutiny? The question is not merely rhetorical, for as the system begins to devote more attention to the problem of drugs, other types of offenders take a backseat in its priorities.

The question of the wisdom of focusing alternatives on drug offenders instead of other offenders is probably dependent on the type of offender being considered. It would appear unwise, for example, to use up the scarce resources of an ISP program on mere Users when the traditional probation caseload contains burglars, assaulters, and others representing a much more significant risk to the general public. Regardless of the public relations value of zero tolerance, there may be serious detriment to focusing such resources on relatively minor problems (and problem makers). By contrast, when Predators are released from prison, it would seem wise to give them the closest control available (ISP with electronic and urine monitoring, for example) instead of traditional parole. Yet many of the alternative programs specifically exclude the latter and seek the former, advertising themselves as "fighting drugs." When this occurs, there are substantial opportunity costs in the misapplication of risk management resources in correction.

## Four Strategies for Effective Use of Alternatives with Drug Offenders

A clearer understanding of the types of alternative programs available and the types of offenders to be assigned to them helps put the usefulness of alternatives into perspective. The following discussion should not be taken as a recommendation for prison in cases where no other program seems to make sense. With the exception of some Predators, no consistent evidence can be found that prison is a preferable program placement to lesser alternatives for any drug offenders. Failure rates of drug offenders in most programs are high, but failure rates after prison are just as high and may be higher. Instead, the aim should be to put the use of alternatives into a perspective that both reflects evidence about their suitability and resists overreliance on them and unrealistic expectations of them.

### Drug Offenders Should Be Assigned to Programs that Fit Their Drug-Crime Behavior

Alternatives are not equally suitable for all drug offenders. Drug offenders vary in their manageability, their risk to the community, and their compunction to commit crimes. Using the typology described earlier, program recommendations can be made reflecting the fit between the program's ordinary capacity and the drug offender's needs. A summary of such suitability is presented in Table 1.

Predatory offenders appear well suited for several of these programs, especially intensive supervision and the close control inherent in residential programs and urine monitoring (Anglin & Hser, 1990). For the most part however, Predators are not suitable subjects for diversion into these programs, for they are strong candidates for incarceration in the first place. After incarceration, Predators benefit (and the community can be protected) by the close supervision in these alternatives programs (Wexler, Lipton & Johnson, 1988).

Addicts also fit intensive alternatives well, especially when control-oriented approaches are closely coupled with treatment interventions (Anglin, 1988). Conventional probation is seldom useful for long-term Addicts. Shock approaches also appear inadvisable, because the addict's drug use is not easily susceptible to deterrence through threats. The main aim of programs for Addicts is to lengthen the periods of drug-free street time. Total abstinence is usually seen as an unreasonable goal (Wexler & Lipton, 1985).

## Table 1: Fitting Drug Offenders to Appropriate Correctional Alternatives

| Type of Correctional Alternative | Type of Offender | | | |
|---|---|---|---|---|
| | *Seller* | *Addict* | *Predator* | *User* |
| Shock incarceration | − | − | − | 0 |
| Residential programs | 0 | + | + | 0 |
| Intensive supervision | + | + | + | 0 |
| Electronic monitoring | 0 | 0 | + | − |
| Urine testing | − | + | + | − |
| Drug suppression | − | + | | 0 |
| treatment programs | − | + | + | + |

+ =Suggested as appropriate by rresearch and theory
0 =No research or theory to support this ooption.
− =Research or theory suggest this option is inappropriate.

Users, by contrast, might benefit from treatment approaches, but the heavy control approaches are liable to be counterproductive by forcing the User deeper into the criminal justice system, should there be noncompliance with program rules (Petersilia, 1987; Petersilia & Turner, 1990). For many Users, fines, community service, and conventional probation are enough to deter.

Sellers can be managed in the context of intensive supervision but are not likely to do well in other strategies. Residential programs provide an audience of potential consumers; shock approaches are unlikely to deter, given the financial incentives of the drug business. Some have argued that fines and forfeiture help to remove the financial incentives for the drug business and thus are relevant to the Seller (Cole, Mahoney, Thornton, & Hanson, 1987).

These general strategies are suggested with caution. The research on program effectiveness with drug offenders is scanty at best, and few of the studies attempt to isolate the interaction effects proposed here. The type of research needed in this area is illustrated by a RAND study that attempted to classify offenders in an ISP experiment according to the model we have proposed. Overall, offenders did no better on ISP than on regular probation (in fact, evidence suggested they may have done worse under the ISP option). However, Users had a 50 percent higher (nonsignificant) arrest rate under ISP as compared to regular probation, consistent with the model (Deschenes, Turner, &

Petersilia, 1992). (There was no difference for the other three types—a result perhaps due to small sample size, the pure control nature of the program, and the limited ability to classify offenders, post hoc.)

## Expect High Rates of Failure; Prepare Programming Options

With the exception of users, drug offenders fail at high rates in any program placement, including prison (Wish & Johnson, 1986). Working with these offenders requires a large number of options and schedules of reinforcement, with the ability to intensify or reduce controls in small increments as justified by the offender's behavior.

One implication of this caution is that if these programs are working well, they will have lots of action in relation to offenders' conduct. Programs with low failure rates are probably either lax in enforcement or are drawing too heavily from user populations that would produce high success rates.

Because alternative programs have high levels of enforcement action, they require a special type of staff and unusually consistent support from the courts. Staff need to be professionally trained and well experienced with drug users' special problems. Their expectations should be realistic, and their patience (grounded in firmness) should enable them to have credibility with the offenders they see. Courts need to encourage latitude in working with offenders, supporting approaches that maintain consistent programs of consequences. There is always a temptation to "do treatment" from the bench, but courts should resist the desire to innovate on an ad hoc basis because this usually undercuts the logic of a program.

The larger the number of alternatives, the better. It makes good public relations to present programs as "tough last stops before prison," but if this is the way the programs operate, they will be irrelevant to many drug users. Prison is a necessary option in the enforcement spectrum, especially for criminally active addicts, sellers, and predators, but its benefits are often overstated. Eventually, offenders are released, and drug programs have to begin with the progress made earlier on the street.

One way to view this system of approaches is to see traditional probation and prison as the "bookends" of a spectrum of available interventions. Strict enforcement requires that misbehaving drug users be moved off traditional probation relatively easily into nontraditional approaches but should encounter prison only as a last resort (except for Predators), and perhaps only for short periods. Offenders moving out of the courts (at sentencing) and out of prison (onto parole) should be placed initially in the approach that best fits their circumstances, not the one that has available space or is currently popular.

## There Are No "Pure" Types and No "Perfect" Programs

It goes without saying that complexity underlies any system of dealing with drug offenders, and so no perfect solution exists. In fact, many sellers are involved in other predatory crime (Spunt et al., 1987); many users stand on the brink of addiction and sell drugs to a small circle of friends (Biernacki, 1986). The drug offender types provide a heuristic device to analyze the problem, the program prototypes display general programs, but there is much overlap among them in practice (Chaiken & Johnson, 1988).

In the real world, the best program fit for an offender will not always be obvious, and all programs will have idiosyncratic strengths and weaknesses, often due to unique staff configurations. Predators will sometimes do quite well in response to an electronic monitoring program; users will occasionally fail miserably on traditional probation.

The term used to describe this situation is *technical uncertainty*—it means that the technologies for working with drug offenders are unpredictable in their outcomes. Because technical uncertainty produces frustrations for staff and system decision makers, there is a constant temptation to perceive alternatives to traditional corrections as ineffectual. The usual choice in the face of frustration is incarceration. Imprisonment has the advantage for decision makers of disengaging the decision from the feedback about its effectiveness. When drug offenders recidivate after imprisonment, it is unusual for the judge or the prosecutor to admit it was the wrong choice, even though they will be quick to do so after a similar failure under an alternative program.

If there is a secret in dealing with drug offenders, it is creative persistence with individually scripted strategies. Imprisonment has a role, but it will ultimately prove frustratingly ineffectual unless it is used appropriately in response to the right offenders and in the right situation.

## Focus on the Goal of Reducing the Pains of Drugs

In recent years, the American public has become increasingly sensitized to the harmful effects of drugs. There are many: Criminal networks, criminal acts, physical side effects, unsafe streets and lost lives are among them. These problems have fueled the war on drugs (Inciardi, 1992).

There are also harmful effects, just of the war itself. Sending people to prison seldom improves their life chances and is almost never intended to do so. When youngsters enter the criminal justice system, they face long odds of overcoming the negative impact of a record and the affiliations produced in processing their case. Removing men and women from their families can be permanently damaging to children and to their family units. Whole neighborhoods become dominated by definitions of deviance, lawbreaking, and avoiding "the man"—this changes the meaning of "growing up." In the pressure to respond to the problem of drugs, families are uprooted from public housing, draconian penalties are handed out, and irretrievable resources are committed to the problem. Almost no proposal is seen as too excessive. It is hard, sometimes, to know if the cure is more painful than the disease.

It is time to admit that a drug-free society is not now and never was a realistic aim. Whether or not it is good rhetoric, the desire for zero tolerance has fed a zealousness that overwhelms the realities of modern, urban America. A much more realistic and realizable goal must replace this unrealistic vision. The purpose of correctional intervention is to prevent crimes where possible, reduce harms to families and communities where feasible, and take reasonable steps to encourage and assist offenders to forgo drug use and related criminal activity. The aim is to reduce, in small measures, the pain experienced by all citizens, offenders and others alike, resulting from drugs in America.

## References

Andrews, D., Kessling, J., Robinson, D., & Mickus, S. (1986). The risk principle of case classification: An outcome evaluation with adult probationers. *Canadian Journal of Criminology, 28*, 377–396.

Anglin, D. (1988). The efficacy of civil commitment in treating narcotic addiction. In C. Leukefeld & F. M. Tims (Eds.), *Compulsory treatment of drug abuse*. Rockville, MD: National Institute on Drug Abuse.

Anglin, D., & Hser, Y. (1990). Treatment of drug abuse. In M. Tonry & J. Q. Wilson (Eds.), *Drugs and crime*. Chicago: University of Chicago Press.

Austin, J., & Krisberg, B. (1980). *The unmet promise of alternatives to corrections*. San Francisco: National Council on Crime and Delinquency.

Ball, J. C. (1986). The hyper-criminal opiate addict. In B. D. Johnson & E. Wish (Eds.), *Crime rates among drug abusing offenders* (Final Report to the National Institute of Justice). New York: Narcotic and Drug Research, Inc.

Ball, J. C., Rosen, L., Flueck, J., & Nurco, D. (1982). Lifetime criminality of heroin addicts in the United States. *Journal of Drug Issues, 3*, 225–239.

Ball, J. C., Shaffer, J., & Nurco, D. (1983). The day-to-day criminality of heroin addicts in Baltimore: A study in the continuity of offense rates. *Drug and Alcohol Dependence, 12*, 119–142.

Biernacki, P. (1986). *Pathways to addiction*. Philadelphia: Temple University Press.

Byrne, J. (1990). The future of intensive probation supervision and the new intermediate sanctions. *Crime & Delinquency, 36*, 6–41.

Byrne, J., Lurigio, A., & Baird, C. S. (1989). *The effectiveness of the new intensive supervision programs* (Research in Corrections, No. 5). Washington, DC: National Institute of Corrections.

Chaiken, M., & Chaiken, J. (1984). Offender types and public policy. *Crime & Delinquency, 30*, 195–226.

Chaiken, J., & Chaiken, M. (1990). Drugs and predatory crime. In M. Tonry & J. Q. Wilson (Eds.), *Drugs and crime*. Chicago: University of Chicago Press.

Chaiken, M., & Johnson, B. (1988). *Characteristics of different types of drug involved offenders*. Washington, DC: National Institute of Justice.

Clear, T. & Gallagher, K. (1983). Screening devices in probation and parole: Management problems. *Evaluation Review, 7*, 217–234.

Cole, G. F., Mahoney, B., Thornton, M., & Hanson, R. (1987). *Attitudes and practices of trial court judges toward the use of fines.* Denver: Institute for Court Management.

DeLeon, G. (1987). Alcohol use among drug abusers: Treatment outcomes in a therapeutic community. *Alcoholism Clinical and Experimental Research, 11*, 430–436.

Deschenes, E., Turner, S., & Petersilia, J. (1992). *The effectiveness and costs of intensive supervision for drug offenders* (Working paper). Santa Monica, CA: RAND.

Fagan, J. (1990). Intoxication and aggression. In M. Tonry & J. Q. Wilson (Eds.), *Drugs and crime.* Chicago: University of Chicago Press.

Ficher, M. Hirschberg, P., & McGaha, J. (1987). Felony probation: A comparative analysis of public risk in two states. *Perspectives, 11*, 6–11.

Goldkamp, J. (1989, March). *The effectiveness of drug testing in the courts.* Paper presented to the Conference on Drugs and the Courts, Denver, CO.

Goldstein, P. (1981). Getting over: Economic alternatives to predatory crime among street drug users. In J. Inciardi (Ed.), *The drugs/crime connection.* Beverly Hills: Sage.

Hanson, B., Beschner, G., Walters, J., & Bovelle, E. (1985). *Life with heroin: Voices from the inner city.* Lexington, MA: Lexington Books.

Hillsman, S., & Greene, J. (1992). The use of fines as an intermediate sanction. In J. Byrne, A. Lurigio, & J. Petersilia (Eds.), *Smart sentencing: The emergence of intermediate sanctions.* Newbury Park, CA: Sage.

Inciardi, J. (1992). *The war on drugs II.* Palo Alto, CA: Mayfield.

Johnson, B., & Wish, E. (1987). *Criminal events among seriously criminal drug abusers* (Final Report to the National Institute of Justice). New York: Narcotic and Drug Research, Inc.

Markley, G., & Eisenberg, M. (1987). *Evaluation of the Texas parole classification and case management system.* Austin: Texas Board of Pardons and Paroles.

McDonald, D. (1989). *The cost of corrections* (Research in Corrections, No. 4). Washington, DC: National Institute of Corrections.

McDonald, D. (1992). Punishing labor: Unpaid community service as a criminal sentence. In J. Byrne, A. Lurigio, & J. Petersilia (Eds.), *Smart sentencing: The emergence of intermediate sanctions.* Newbury Park, CA: Sage.

Mieczkowski, T. (1986). Geeking up and throwing down: Heroin street life in Detroit. *Criminology, 24*, 645–666.

Parent, D. (1989). *Shock incarceration: An overview of existing programs.* Washington, DC: National Institute of Justice.

Petersilia, J. (1987). *Expanding options for criminal sentencing.* Santa Monica, CA: RAND.

Petersilia, J., Peterson, J., & Turner, S. (1992). *Intensive probation and parole: Research findings and policy implications* (Working paper). Santa Monica, CA: RAND.

Petersilia, J., & Turner, S. (1990). Comparing intensive and regular supervision for high-risk probationers: Early results from an experiment in California. *Crime & Delinquency, 36,* 87–111.

Petersilia, J., Turner, S., Kahan, J., & Peterson, J. (1985). *Granting felons probation: Public risks and alternatives.* Santa Monica, CA: RAND.

Platt, J. (1986). *Heroin Addiction: Theory, research and treatment* (2nd ed.). Malabar, FL: Krieger.

Reuter, P., Macoun, R., & Murphy, P. (1990). *Money from crime.* Santa Monica, CA: RAND.

Rosenbaum, M., & Murphy, S. (1984). Always a junkie? The arduous task of getting off methadone maintenance. *Journal of Drug Issues, 3,* 527–552.

Speckart, G., & Anglin, D. (1986). Narcotics use and crime: A causal modeling approach. *Journal of Quantitative Criminology, 2,* 3–28.

Schmidt, A. (1989). Electronic monitoring of offenders increases. *NIJ Reports, 212,* 2–5.

Spunt, B., Goldstein, P., Lipton, D., Belluci, P., Miller, T., Cortez, N., Kahn, M., & Kale, A. (1987, November). *Systemic violence among street drug distributors.* Paper presented at the annual meetings of American Society of Criminology, Montreal, Canada.

Wexler, H., & Lipton, D. (1985, November). *Prison drug treatment: The critical ninety days of re-entry.* Paper presented at the annual meetings of the American Society of Criminology, San Diego, CA.

Wexler, H., Lipton, D., & Johnson, B. (1988). *A criminal justice strategy for treating drug offenders in custody.* Washington, DC: National Institute of Justice.

Wexler, H., & Williams, R. (1986). The Stay N' Out therapeutic community: Prison treatment for substance abusers. *Journal of Psychoactive Drugs, 18,* 221–230.

Wish, E., & Gropper, B. (1990). Drug testing by the criminal justice system: Methods, research, and applications. In M. Tonry & J. Q. Wilson (Eds.), *Drugs and crime.* Chicago: University of Chicago Press.

Wish, E., & Johnson, B. (1986). The impact of substance abuse on criminal career. In A. Blumstein, J. Cohen, J. A. Roth, & C. Visher (Eds.), *Criminal careers and "career criminals"* (Vol. 2). Washington, DC: National Academy Press.

Zinberg, N. (1984). *Drug, set, and setting.* New Haven, CT: Yale University Press.

# 18

# The Boot Camp Program
# for Offenders
## Does the Shoe Fit?

## Rudolf E. S. Mathias
## James W. Mathews

## Introduction

The phrase "war on crime, war against drugs" is widely heralded as the new approach to attack the complex problems of substance abuse as one of the major causes of crime, delinquency, and social disintegration. The metaphor of declaring war on such social problems embraces a political strategy that reaches out to the constituents while it gives the elected legislator an opportunity to take a firm stand as the relentless fighter against crime. By

Reprinted by permission of the Guilford Press from the *International Journal of Offender Therapy and Comparative Criminology*, Vol. 35, No. 4, pp. 322–327, 1991.

declaring "war" the stage is set to enhance the popular perception of obliterating evil and punishing the perpetrator. The high incidence of drug dependency and crime has brought public clamors that "something must be done." The political climate demands immediate action rather than time-consuming research: the boot camp presents a simple and appealing method for immediate action against convicted criminals who are substance abusers and drug dealers.

In the fight against crime, plans are developed and implemented by a quasi military strategy. This has led to the creation of the boot camp for correctional programs. Such an approach fits the "war criteria" with its command hierarchy, strict discipline and Spartan life style. It attempts by rigorous methods to punish and change the offender. The methods used to effect changes are highly varied depending on the particular if not idiosyncratic view of the current correctional administration, as well as the level of expertise and training of the staff. Frequently used methods include behavior modification techniques, sustained psychological pressures through intimidation, and "encounter sessions" aimed frequently at verbal degradation of a particular individual. One program makes reference to "ventilation therapy," "reeducative therapy" though no explanation is given as to the rationale of this "therapy" or what qualifications and training is required for the so called "therapist" (MacKenzie & Shaw, 1990).

## Some Findings on the Success Rate

Closer examination of commitments to a boot camp program indicate some success in separating the young, nonviolent first offender from the heterogeneous population of medium or maximum security prisons.

However, a boot camp program also enlarges the net to draw in those young first offenders who previously had been considered good candidates for successful supervision on probation—a markedly less costly method. Recent reports of Wisconsin's Department of Corrections indicated an overall success rate of 80 percent for probationers. In comparison, the rate of successful completion for boot camp participants in Florida was reported at 47 percent (*Chicago Tribune*, 1990). A recent *Time Magazine* article stated that in Georgia 35 percent of boot camp participants were sent to higher security prisons within three years of release (*Time Magazine*, 1989). In the most comprehensive study to date by MacKenzie and Shaw (1990) the authors compared the participants in a "shock program" for offenders called IMPACT against two other groups, i.e., the "drop outs" and the incarcerated offender in Louisiana. "For the demographic variables there were no significant differences between drop outs and shock offenders in race . . . sex . . . IQ (M =

78.1, *SD* = 13.3) or age . . ." [The intelligence test utilized in this study is not cited;] A mean IQ of 78—on most psychometric tests—would indicate that the sample was heavily skewed toward the lower end of measured intelligence quotients. Furthermore, the same study cited a drop out rate of 50 percent for Louisiana's IMPACT program (ibid.). A recent article by Caldas (1990) describes an interesting rehabilitation program in Orleans Parish Prison (Louisiana). It points out the "substantial hope of rehabilitating those few inmates fortunate enough to enter them" (i.e., intensive incarceration programs). The program described by Caldas does not specify the age range, ethnic composition, nature of offense, total length of sentence and other important variables. The program called "About Face" aims at "the development of positive attitudes and values (i.e., self-confidence, self-respect, and respect of others)." It appears akin to a military-type boot camp program. It is entered on a voluntary basis "open to non-violent offenders who have between six months and two years left of their sentences to serve."

It appears unfortunate that most descriptions of various boot camp programs do not present clear, concise data on the selection of inmates, i.e., type of offense and sentence structure, age, vocational training, degree of literacy, cultural and ethnic variables, psychometric data, physical health and emotional stability.

## Contrasting Military and Correctional Boot Camps

It appears significant that the boot camp program for offenders in the armed services has shown a high rate of success upon return to military duty. However, it is not feasible to draw comparisons since the disciplinary program in the military services lists no specific details regarding the seriousness and type of offense (*Chicago Tribune*, 1990). In the military code of conduct certain infractions considered "misconduct, unauthorized absence, failure to follow orders" have no equivalency in civilian life. In addition the military correctional program deals exclusively with a highly select group of young first offenders who had been previously screened for their physical and mental fitness. Moreover, military personnel who return from "boot camp" to duty enter a structured, stable environment which provides for the basic needs, food, shelter, clothing, employment and health care.

Program administrators of state correctional systems face entirely different problems in providing a program for first offenders who had been involved in the abuse of drugs and/or alcohol. These problems include a broad range of offenders, both male and female, a wide diversity of sociological vectors, such as educational and vocational training, physical and mental health. Finally, state administrators of prisons cannot provide the released offender with a job placement and a structured life environment.

## Unique Problems of the Correctional Boot Camp

One of the perennial problems in corrections is harnessing authority for a positive purpose; in comparison, the highly authoritarian approach of the boot camp may reinforce an unbridled use of power. As a program patterned after basic training in the military, the staff is likely to be selected on the basis of assertiveness, stamina, control and determination. Such scenario calls for "machismo" to serve as role model. Shouting, belittling, the use of profanity, denigration of individuals, all these may become major ingredients in such a program (*Chicago Tribune*, 1990). As the program develops, intrastaff rivalry may well heighten the emphasis on being the toughest member of the cadre. Thus, the focus of such an approach may shift from an offender-oriented program toward goals for staff recognition and promotion.

A question seldom asked is what emotional needs—both conscious and unconscious—are met when correctional staff members choose an assignment which requires the exercise of powerful authoritarian dominance. In numerous descriptions of boot camp programs scant attention has been given to these aspects of personal interactions which are diametrically in conflict with goals of productive living in a democratic society.

A boot camp program which relies on dominance, degradation and demeaning of the prisoners runs counter to the basic principles of learning and human behavior. The person abused is likely to become an abuser, and given the opportunity may well use these tactics upon release to the community.

Correctional staff is not immune to psychological risk. Even though staff members may initially carry out their assignments in strict adherence to defined positions of dominance as part of their duties, the pervasive use of power feeds on itself and may soon overshadow alternate behavior patterns.

For dramatic results some of the boot camps rely on the "shock therapy" of an acting scenario with the stars being the hard-nosed staff and the offenders playing the bit parts. All this produces a play in several acts. The simple question remains: just how transient are the effects of such a scenario? How long after boot camp will such influence remain effective?

Finally, a "chameleon effect" of adaptation may occur when the offender returns to the same environment which had created his set of values. When the young adult returns to the community he [she] will again be strongly influenced by peer pressure: any shift away from the value system of the moment is likely to bring rejection and exclusion from the peer group. Thus, the transient nature of human behavior is put to a test.

---

# Conclusion

---

The current assumption that boot camp is the best solution in changing the actions and behavior of offenders convicted of drug and alcohol offenses tends to minimize the complexity of social problems and interplay of individual and environmental factors. A firm schedule for work, schooling, physical fitness, vocational training are all highly desirable aspects of rehabilitation. But this should be accomplished without the blaring fanfare and noisy bravado of the "boot camp" environment.

The use of drugs and their trade is like a cancer metastasizing into all social strata and crossing every geographic boundary. Its malignant effects are spread throughout the world. The monetary gain in drug trade by itself has financed private military forces in various countries.

The concept of a "war against drugs" has strong political appeal: the metaphor implies that force alone can overcome this specific evil. The problems of drug abuse are intertwined with the vast complexities of human behavior. It is essential that we gain thorough knowledge of those geographic, cultural and socioeconomic factors which have given impetus to the current problems of alcohol and drug abuse. In this so-called war there are no clearly defined lines of battle, there are no specific zones of combat, the enemy forces are only shadows in misty and uncertain terrain.

Ironically, in this struggle the foes are also the victims. While we must stop the abuser and the trader we must also find ways to help him [or her]. The core question is just what substance abuse occurs in a particular individual in a specific environment and under what conditions?

The boot camp program heralded as a new approach in corrections will initially draw attention and support. An open and healthy attitude for program improvement is commendable; as the novelty wears off and flaws become evident enthusiasm wanes and the program may lose its appeal and political endorsement.

Thus far those programs offered in several states for participants in a boot camp program show a wide divergence in methods, design and follow-up studies. Further, the use of group therapy, counselling, behavior modification, appears almost haphazard in depth and frequency. It is difficult to envision how in some programs a small number of staff would have the expertise to function as drill instructors, role models, and therapists all in a day's work.

Incarceration per se rarely has positive effects other than being a deterrent. To establish programs based on negative reinforcement, the unbridled, unquestionable use of authority and a mentality which degrades the self image of prisoners and human values is akin to voodoo penology. The boot camp may be a rather effective approach in a closely monitored military environment where highly selected participants are returned to a structured, well-organized type of life. These productive aspects should be further studied and utilized in controlled programs.

As it stands now in settings such as state or county correctional programs the boot camp program poses serious risks. The shoe does not fit everyone.

## References

Caldas, Stephen C. "Intensive programs offer hope of rehabilitation to a fortunate few: Orleans parish prison does an about face." *International Journal of Offender Therapy & Comparative Criminology*, April 1990, 67–76.

*Chicago Tribune*. March 4, 1990.

*Chicago Tribune*. Dec. 10, 1990.

MacKenzie, D. L. (1990). Boot camp prisons: Components, evaluations and empirical issues. *Federal Probation* (Sept. 1990), 44–52.

MacKenzie, D. L. & Shaw, J. (1990). *Justice Quarterly*, 7, 125–145.

Ratcliff, B. [Major] (1988). *Corrections Today, 50*, 7.

*Time*, Oct. 16, 1989, *134*, 17–18.

# 19

# Rethinking the Drug Problem

## Jerome H. Skolnick

When first delineated in the late nineteenth century, Tourette's syndrome was regarded as a "moral" disease, an expression of deliberate mischievousness or weakness of the will. In a sudden reversal in the 1960s, when it was discovered that the drug haloperidol could suppress Tourette's symptoms, including involuntary twitching and grimacing, the disease came to be understood "as the result of an imbalance of a neurotransmitter, dopamine, in the brain." In a recent article, the neurologist Oliver Sacks discussed Tourette's as having an extraordinarily complex etiology and cure. Sacks argues, however, that no single perspective—biological, moral-social, or psychological—adequately captures the full meaning and impact of the disease.[1]

Reprinted by permission of *Daedalus, Journal of the American Academy of Arts and Sciences*, Vol. 121, No. 3, Summer 1992, pp. 133–159.

The etiology and solution to the American drug problem is possibly even more complex than that of Tourette's syndrome. Yet it has been defined at the national level as primarily a moral challenge. In September 1989, the Bush administration published its first *National Drug Control Strategy*, which set a tone and direction for drug policy which has continued throughout the Bush presidency. (Another *Strategy* was published in January 1992 with only a slightly different ordering of priorities.) The use of any drug, in whatever quantity, was attributed to the deficient moral character of individuals, or weakness of will. Drug use was said to "degrade human character," while a good society "ignores its people's character at its peril."

The high priority accorded repressive law enforcement seemed to flow naturally from the moralistic attitudes toward drug use and the role of government as expressed in the 1989 *Strategy*. Adopting the "war on drugs" as its overriding metaphor, the 1989 *Strategy* fulfilled the metaphor's promise by advocating a vast expansion of the apparatus of social control—particularly of law enforcement and prisons—into what resembles a semimartial state. Introducing the 1989 *Strategy* to America on national television, President Bush proposed that the federal government increase spending to combat drugs by $1.5 billion for enforcement and $1.5 billion for interdiction, but only by $321 million for treatment and $250 million for education. The *Strategy* advocated that billions more be spent by states, particularly to expand the criminal justice system.

While acknowledging that there is no easy, or even difficult, solution to the American drug problem, I shall argue that, like the shift in understanding Tourette's syndrome, we need a sharp reversal in our thinking regarding drugs, from a perspective centered on moral failure to a broader and more complex etiology highlighting public health and underlying social issues. The militaristic approach is, in any case, programmed to fail. Persistent dilemmas and paradoxes will undermine the capacity of law enforcement officers, at any level, to solve the drug problem.

Working narcotic police understand the limitations of law enforcement, perhaps more than anyone. I asked an experienced New York narcotics officer, a trainer of undercover operatives, whom I accompanied in 1990 to observe the drug dealing scene in New York City's Washington Heights (a major marketing center for crack cocaine), how effective narcotics enforcement was in interfering with cocaine trafficking. His succinct and evocative reply: "We're like a gnat biting on a horse's ass."

The drug problem has two facets: one is abuse and addiction of both legal and illegal drugs; the second is the crime and violence connected to illegal drug use and sale. The administration's approach to expand law enforcement in an unprecedented way has had little impact on either of these problems—except to worsen street violence—because it ignores or does not appreciate the imperatives driving people to use and sell illegal drugs; it underestimates the dilemmas faced by law enforcement in controlling the distribution and use of drugs; it is insensitive to the social and economic underpinnings of drug marketing and use in the United States; and it is oblivious to the implications of a war on drugs for the character of the nation.

## Drugs: Natural Crime or Vice?

The Bush administration's approach is built on the premise that drug dealing and use is something morally repugnant in and of itself; the solutions that flow from this premise treat people's involvement in drugs as major crimes which must be punished severely. This vision has, of course, serious implications for the workings of our criminal justice system at every level, for the police, the courts, and the prisons. Criminological theorists classically distinguish between "natural" and "regulatory" conceptions of crime. A "natural" conception of crime "embodies a sense of an act that is deeply wrong, that evokes strong communal disapproval, and that is thought to deserve, indeed to call for, a punitive sanction."[2] Ordinarily then, when we think of crime we think of homicide, rape, and assault. We think of these because all are "natural" wrongs, *mala in se*, acts that we understand, almost intuitively, to be wrong in themselves.

By contrast, under a "regulatory" conception, crime is not grounded in moral intuition. It is simply conduct prohibited by a legislature to which penalties are attached. For example, in England the law requires automobiles to drive on the left, while in the United States we drive on the right. Similarly, it might be considered *mala prohibitum* to accept bets on horse racing in a city where off-track betting is illegal (for example, New York) because accepting these bets does not conform to the regulations under which legal horse race betting is permitted. In neither of these cases, however, could the conduct that is prohibited be considered *mala in se*.

A key question that any drug strategy must address is whether the sale or use of drugs is more comparable to illegal betting (use) and bookmaking (sale) or to armed robbery and homicide. How one answers that question will in large part determine one's assessment of the nation's drug control policy. The *Strategy* rests on the moral vision that not only the sale but also the use of illegal drugs is *mala in se*. The *Strategy* accordingly advocates expanding and reshaping the criminal justice system "in an unprecedented way" with not only more police, but more "jails, prosecutors, judges, courtrooms, prisons and administrative staff."[3] The criminal justice system has, in fact, become a growth industry, yet with not nearly enough capacity to contain the more than one million inmates already incarcerated.

From the perspective of the *mala in se* theorist, environmental causes of crime and drug use are largely irrelevant, practically invisible. Since individual moral failure, or the failure of will, activates the drug problem, environmental or medical causes—poverty, unemployment, family breakdown, addiction—need not be given high priority. Punishment thus becomes the primary preferred response. From this perspective it makes sense to stigmatize the casual user as the root villain of the drug problem, since without the casual user, the seller would presumably disappear.[4]

But is the casual user the root of the drug problem? The 1989 *Strategy*'s statistical analysis suggests that attributing the drug problem to the casual user rather than the addict is a moral judgement, not analytical one. The *Strategy* itself begins with good news. Citing a July 1989 survey by the National Institute on Drug Abuse (NIDA), the *Strategy* reports that "current use of the two most common illegal substances—marijuana and cocaine—is down 36 and 48 percent respectively."[5] But it quickly moves to the bad news. Drug related crime and violence continue to rise, the *Strategy* points out, and the threat drugs pose to public health has never been greater because drugs are cheap and "available to almost everyone who wants them."[6]

Who wants drugs? The 1992 *Strategy* acknowledges that the "drug war" is a "two-front" affair.[7] It takes credit for declining use by casual and younger users but sadly reports increasing use by addicted users and those over 35. In actuality, this pattern occurred in 1989 as well. According to an earlier self-report study, casual users never did use much of the total cocaine consumed in the United States. The National Narcotics Intelligence Consumer Committee found that "heavy users" comprised 6.9 percent of the user population, yet consumed 63 percent of the cocaine in this country.[8]

This pattern is probably true of most drugs, including alcohol. One report, for example, shows that 10 percent of the population uses 57 percent of the alcohol, 20 percent of the population uses 78 percent.[9] Moreover, if as the *Strategy* reports, casual use is declining while demand for drugs rises or remains about the same, it seems clear that the addict, not the casual user, is the chief source of demand for cocaine.

Nevertheless, casual use rather than addiction is the focal point of the *Strategy*. The theory plays out something like this: addicts need treatment, but they do not contribute much to the spread of drug use. An addict is a "bottomed-out mess" and his or her drug use is therefore "not very contagious."[10] But the casual user is an attractive person "likely to have a still-intact family, social and work life."[11] More attractive than the addict, the casual user sets a bad and appealing example; therefore, his drug use "is *highly* contagious."[12]

Since, however, casual use seems to be declining, and since addicts consume most of the drugs consumed, including alcohol, a focus on the casual, more moderate, user can scarcely be justified. How can we account for it?

Three possible reasons come to mind. First, it virtually insures a measure of success, since casual drug use seems to be flagging anyhow. Second, denunciation of the casual user, who is more likely to be white and middle class, relieves the administration of accusations that the law enforcement side of the war on drugs will surely turn out to be disproportionately a war on minority sellers and users, which it surely will be. Finally, a focus on the addict would shift the priorities of drug policy away from police and punishment to treatment, rehabilitation, AIDS research, and the social and economic conditions under which treatment is most likely to work.

Yet casual use of drugs and alcohol is fairly commonplace in American society—enough so that there is almost intuitive agreement that these acts should be heavily punished. If casual use can be shown to have a practical, harmful effect, however, even if not a direct one—i.e., the "contagious" spread of the drug "disease"—the more persuasive is the justification for cracking down on an activity considered to be immoral.

The disease metaphor implies such a justification, although scarcely a compelling one. The casual user's supposed propensity to "infect" others becomes the reason for cracking down. Use, it is assumed, must inevitably lead to abuse. In actuality, the relation between use and abuse depends on the drug, the nature of the user, and the circumstances under which it is consumed. But a moralistic stance easily escalates into a legalistic one collapsing "use" with "abuse." Thus, all marijuana users become, by that definition, immoral abusers who deserve punishment.

## Alternative Views: Mala Prohibitum

Those who believe that drug use is *mala prohibitum* fall into two basic camps. One regards drug use in classic libertarian terms, as a private matter. This view is grounded in John Stuart Mill's theory of individual liberty. Mill feared the tyranny of the majority which he described as "the tyranny of the prevailing opinion and feeling."[13] He argued that society has a "tendency to impose, by other means than civil penalties, its own ideas and practices as rules of conduct on those who dissent from them." Mill believed in the sanctity of the individual, in individual independence. Most of all he feared the tendency of collective opinion to *compel* others "to fashion themselves upon the model of its own."

Mill did not deny that collective opinion had a legitimate need to interfere with individual independence. He believed that unless society found the proper limit and maintained it against encroachment, the result would be a form of political despotism. This limit is widely known among philosophers as the "harm principle." The enduring influence of *On Liberty* and its harm principle is derived less from some exquisite utilitarian summation than from

Mill's intuitions about the despotic potential of government. "The only purpose for which power can be rightfully exercised over any member of a civilized community, against his will," Mill says, "is to prevent harm to others."[14] Mill did not oppose persuading, entreating, or remonstrating with people who engage in admittedly self-destructive conduct. He believed that the criminal law, the power of government, should not be used to deter and to punish individuals in that part of conduct which "merely concerns himself."

Assuming the validity of the harm principle, what standard or principle should we employ to decide whether a particular line of potentially harmful conduct—smoking cigarettes, snorting cocaine, eating to obesity—is of sufficient concern to others to warrant the imposition of a criminal penalty? Mill is himself not entirely clear on this point, but he does make two observations which suggest how it is that such political opposites as William Buckley, Milton Friedman, and the American Civil Liberties Union can agree that drug use ought to be decriminalized.

Mill strongly opposed government interference. He believed in competition, and in competitive examinations, even though the losers might be hurt. In general, he believed in free trade and opposed governmental regulation of advertising. Nor could he be considered a powerful advocate of consumer protection. Indeed, the principle was for him not an invitation for the government to act when conduct is harmful; rather, it is a limiting principle—the government should not act unless there is demonstrable harm to others.

Nevertheless, Mill did not oppose and even encouraged government regulation where appropriate. The state of Maine had passed a 19th-century prohibition statute, and the "Maine Law" figures prominently in Mill's discussion of liberty. He recognized that those who sold alcoholic beverages— "strong drink" as he called it—had an interest in promoting sales and, contrary to popular assumptions about Mill, he was not at all opposed to regulating them. On the contrary, he saw their interest in promoting intemperance as a "real evil," justifying State restrictions.[15]

Mill, furthermore, uses the example of drunkenness to illustrate the boundaries of the harm principle. Whether someone becomes drunk or not is their business. When, however, under the influence of alcohol, the drunken person commits an act of violence against another, it becomes the government's business. Then, Mill writes:

> I should deem it perfectly legitimate that a person, who had once been convicted of any act of violence to others under the influence of drink, should be placed under a special legal restriction, personal to himself; that if he were afterwards found drunk, he should be liable to a penalty, and that if when in that state he committed another offense, the punishment to which he would be liable for that other offense should be increased in severity.[16]

In sum, the key distinction for those who stand by the harm principle is between private and public space. Mill believed that individuals should be free to gamble in their own homes or private clubs, but that public gambling should not at all be permitted.[17] A Millian liberal distinguishes between being in a state of intoxication in the privacy of one's home, thereby doing whatever harm intoxication does to oneself; and driving on public roads under the influence of drugs or alcohol. A liberal opposes, on principle, as "legal paternalism" any form of coercive legislation that seeks to protect individuals from self-inflicted harm.

A second *mala prohibitum* view regards drug use as at worst undesirable, unfortunate, even deviant, but not necessarily so socially harmful as to justify its characterization as a crime. How we should deal with it is less a matter of the principled relationship between the government and the individual than a weighing of the costs and benefits of one policy over another. In this view, drug use should regulated, not because it is a serious criminal offense, but because drug use entails external costs that society must bear. This position could be termed "post-Millian" in that it calculates the interests of society rather than the individual. This pragmatic position balances the costs against the benefits of a proposed policy. The Millian vision is broadened to include a plurality of others, including costs to community and public safety. Since the morality of a line of conduct is not dispositive, proponents might *entertain* legalization of drugs, as does George P. Schultz, who as Secretary of State led the Reagan administration's overseas crop eradication program.[18] Even Milton Friedman and William Buckley increasingly make their arguments based on the social consequences of criminalization rather than on individual freedom alone.

## The Consequential Critique

How should we think about drugs? If one accepts the underlying assumptions of the Bush administration's *Strategy*, it is difficult to argue with its combination of unprecedented punishment and moral regeneration. But if one rejects, or is even unsure of, the underlying assumptions and perceptions of the problem, we need to ask how well its proposals will work and whether alternative policies might work better, and at less cost to the values of a free society.

There is much disagreement, especially within the policy-making and academic communities, over the appropriate definition of and response to the drug problem. Advocates of repression have gained their share of supporters as the social acceptability of drug use shifted dramatically toward moral intolerance over the past two years. In an anticrime climate, politicians are responding to an electorate demanding higher penalties for drug dealing and use. However, these views, while increasingly popular, by no means represent a consensus.

Many people maintain quite different attitudes toward drug use, depending on the levels, time, place, and occasion for intoxication. They are ambivalent about the moral blameworthiness of private drug use and even of addiction, should it occur. As Herbert Packer once observed:

> The extent of disagreement about moral judgements is an obvious reason for hesitancy about an automatic enforcement of morals. There have been monolithic societies in which a static and homogeneous ethnic, religious, and class structure conduces to widely shared acceptance of a value system. But that is hardly a description of the reality of twentieth-century American society, or of its pluralistic and liberal aspirations. . . . We don't begin to agree about the "morality" of smoking, drinking, gambling, fornicating, or drug-taking, for example, quite apart from the gap between what we say and what we do. The more heterogeneous the society, the more repressive the enforcement of morals must be.[19]

If, as Packer suggests, there is no consensus that intoxication—absent tangible harm to others—is inherently despicable, then we have no intuitive sense of deserved retribution. This does not imply that drug use should never be penalized, but rather that consequentialist arguments stressing the impact of deterrence, incarceration, and rehabilitation will make more sense than moralistic ones. People will ask, "What works and what doesn't work and why?"—rather than assuming that drug use of any kind, by any consenting adult, is inherently evil. So the question becomes, how well do the law enforcement forces arrayed against drug use and dealing work in practice?

## Dilemmas of Law Enforcement

One would think that the heightened penalties and huge infusions of resources we have devoted to drug enforcement at the state and national levels would long ago have dried up the drug trade. Yet that did not happen during the 1980s and early 1990s. New York City arrest statistics tell the story. Despite efforts by dedicated and resourceful police officers, the New York narcotics scene seemed impervious to their intervention. Arrests increased every year in New York City following the introduction of crack cocaine in 1984. There were 45,000 arrests in that year, rising to 58,000 in 1986, 79,000 a year later, 89,000 in 1988 and more than 100,000 by the end of the decade. I asked then New York narcotics Chief John Hill whether these increasing arrests have been effective in stopping the problem. Chief Hill was less colorful in his language than the street detectives with whom I had been riding, but equally pessimistic. "The easiest thing to do is make an arrest," he said to me. "The hardest thing is to stop it. Enforcement will never stop it."

The "get tough" approach is essentially based on a theory of deterrence that sounds superficially persuasive. If we raise the cost of selling and using drugs by increasing penalties, it is assumed, we drive out dealers and sellers. In the abstract, the theory seems to make sense. In practice, when we delve more deeply into its workings, we can understand how and why it works far less efficiently than assumed, or, paradoxically, may even worsen the drug problem.

## Supply and Demand

The sale of drugs is economically motivated, and is thus responsive to market incentives and disincentives. The question remains as to how these operate in the context of the drug trade. The 1989 *Strategy* acknowledges that "despite interdiction's successful disruptions of trafficking patterns, the supply of illegal drugs entering the United States has, by all estimates, continued to grow."[20] Why should that have happened? One reason is that demand generates supply for drugs. Demand for drugs in the United States and Europe contributed to the growth of the cocaine business in Colombia and Peru, the world's main growers of coca.[21] A rise in production increases supply, which causes a drop in price. Price reduction in turn invigorates demand, which stimulates the whole cycle again.

## Efficient Suppliers: Survival of the Fittest

"As we have expanded our interdiction efforts," the 1989 *Strategy* states, "we have seized increasing amounts of illegal drugs. Stepped up interdiction has also forced drug traffickers to make significant operational changes . . . . Every time we disrupt or close a particular trafficking route, we have found that traffickers resort to other smuggling tactics that are even more difficult to detect."[22] This is undoubtedly true, but it argues as well against, rather than for, stepped-up interdiction.

More recently, the 1992 *Strategy* took pride in record drug seizures. It reported that in May 1991, US Customs inspectors seized a record 1,080 pounds of heroin in a cargo container arriving at San Francisco. In July 1991, the US Navy intercepted the *Lucky Star* in the Pacific. The ship was escorted to Pearl Harbor, where Customs agents seized a record 73 tons of hashish. In November 1991, US Customs and DEA agents seized, in the second largest cocaine seizure in US history, 23,641 pounds of cocaine concealed in concrete fence posts that were being delivered from Venezuela to Miami.

Should record seizures be considered an accomplishment or a concern? If we interpret the record seizures as a cutoff of the drug supply to the United States, then they are a triumph. If we believe, however, as most observers of the drug trade do, including law enforcement observers, that we interdict around 10 percent to, at most, 20 percent of the shipments of drugs to the United States, these record seizures suggest the enormity of the drug supply and the relatively efficient organization of the suppliers.

As these more efficient producers exercise greater control over markets, they may exercise monopolistic control to raise prices. Law enforcement officials may mistakenly assume that rises in the street price of drugs are a result of efficient interdiction strategies. In actuality, higher prices may bring greater profits to efficient suppliers.

Approximately 60 percent of the world's cocaine is grown in the Peruvian Andes and processed in Colombia. Late in 1991, the United States assisted the Peruvian government in asserting control over airspace by introducing and manning new radar stations at airfields at Andoas and Iquitos, two river towns in the vast Amazonian region. In the first three months of 1992, nine planes were intercepted, forcing six to land and three to crash. Yet an estimated six planes a day leave Peru carrying coca base north.[23] Thus, only nine planes out of more than 1,000, approximately 1 percent, were intercepted. Even if ten or fifteen times that number were to be intercepted, there would be minor interference with the overall enterprise. Practically, interdiction is said to "introduce another level of risk to the individual drug smuggler."[24] Yet, while defending interdiction, the 1989 *Strategy* concedes that "interdiction alone cannot prevent the entry of drugs or fully deter traffickers and their organizations."[25]

Quite an understatement. In reality, interdiction efforts face what might be called "the Darwinian Trafficker Dilemma." Interdiction undercuts the marginally efficient drug traffickers and their operations, while the fittest—the best organized, the most corrupting of authorities, the most ruthless and efficient, survive. As Stephen G. Trujillo, a former Army Ranger, Green Beret, and enforcement specialist with the Drug Enforcement Administration's Operation Snowcap wrote of his experiences the day after President Alberto Fujimori suspended the Peruvian Constitution with the army's backing, in effect, a right wing military coup: Paradoxically, the destruction of dozens of cocaine labs by US and Peruvian forces has only encouraged the coca processors to be more efficient. Smaller, more decentralized labs are processing purer cocaine in the impenetrable jungles.[26]

## The Permeability of Borders

Rand Corporation economist Peter Reuter, who studied the question of border permeability for the Department of Defense, concluded that "the U.S.-Mexico border can be crossed at many points . . . and a high value crossing can be accomplished very suddenly by a single individual in a large crowd of similar individuals . . . ."[27] Thus, the sheer number of people who make border crossings each year aggravates the problem of penetrable borders.

When the Reagan administration's war on drugs cracked down on Florida as the main entry point for cocaine, drug smugglers moved the main supply route of the product from Florida to California. I spent four days reviewing the border situation in California with the assistance of the California State Narcotics Agency. They assigned a Mexican-American agent to me in Los Angeles, to help me understand the drug scene in southern California. Through his assistance, I was able to observe DEA operations, and to interview local and federal police. As with most narcotics police, they seemed to be intelligent, energetic, and well supplied with equipment. I was told that 60 percent of the narcotics entering the United States passed through California. The Mexican border posed a major, and virtually insolvable problem, however. The Mexican-American state narcotics agent who was my guide, and who had been raised in a Los Angeles gang neighborhood, took me to a Mexican restaurant for lunch, told me about his childhood, his entry into the police, looked at me earnestly, and said with some exasperation: "Look professor, 400,000 of my people cross the border illegally every year. How can you stop a much smaller number who carry a kilo or two of cocaine on their back?"[28] None of the record seizures reported in the 1992 *Strategy*, it might be noted, were at the Mexican border.

What is the administration's justification for interdiction efforts? The 1989 *Strategy* claims that interdiction "has major symbolic and practical value."[29] The symbolic value is gained from showing foreign governments and trafficking organizations our commitment to combating the drug trade. But symbolism seems an odd reason for policy, resting neither on practical achievement nor on canons of justice. Still, much of the proposal is grounded on symbolic themes and on the appearance of determination, rather than on a careful assessment of short- and long-range outcomes.

Interdiction advocates vastly overestimate the costs that interdiction imposes on drug trafficking. Interdiction is supposed to reduce street sales by increasing smuggling costs—in effect, taxing smuggling—and thus raising the street price. This assumes that smuggling costs constitute a significant percentage of street price. But that simply is not true. It is relatively cheap to produce and refine a kilo of cocaine, perhaps around $1,000 for a kilo that might eventually retail for $250,000 when broken down into quarter- or even eight-gram units. Smuggling costs might amount to an additional few percent of the retail price. In actuality, most of the retail price of cocaine is divided among those who distribute it on this side of the border. Rand economist Peter Reuter writes, "Fully 99 percent of the price of the drug when sold on the streets in the United States is accounted for by payments to people who distribute it."[30]

Thus, if a kilo of cocaine retails for $250,000, smuggling costs account for around $2,500. A doubling or tripling of smuggling costs accordingly has a negligible impact on street price. Combined with the vastly increased production which has driven prices down, interdiction has had little, if any, positive effects—and these can be outweighed by the unanticipated side effect of strengthening drug marketing organizations.

## Drug Hardening and Demand Substitution

When the Nixon administration succeeded in reducing the supply of low potency Mexican marijuana to California in the early 1970s, agriculturally skilled drug entrepreneurs developed a high potency marijuana (sensimilla) industry in Northern California, generating a market for a drug five or more times as potent. This example is illustrative of what might be called "The Drug Hardening Paradox." The more successful law enforcement is at cutting off supply, the more incentive drug dealers have for hardening drugs—i.e., developing varieties that are more potent, portable, and dangerous. Thus, the recent crackdown by state narcotics agents on the California marijuana market has reduced its supply, but crack cocaine has emerged to replace marijuana. My colleagues and I have interviewed Oakland and south central Los Angeles youngsters who have never used marijuana, but who have used crack cocaine, which has for several years been less expensive and more available on California streets. In sum, law enforcement tactics may create more severe public health problems by generating demand for and production of more potent and dangerous drugs.

A paradox closely related to drug hardening, might be called "The Demand Substitution Paradox." Those who are interested in faster living through chemistry often find it possible to substitute one drug for another. (Most drug abusers usually ingest more than one drug.) Thus, price increases or lack of availability of one drug may activate consumers to seek out cheaper alternative drugs.

In the 1970s, marijuana was the popular drug among students. Today, it is alcohol. Thirty percent of high school seniors reported in 1991 that they had drunk heavily (five or more drinks in a row) at least once in the previous two weeks. Since alcohol is illegal for those under 21, all of this drinking was in violation of the law.

Twenty or thirty years ago, heroin was the "problem" drug in American society.[31] More recently, it has been crack cocaine, which is becoming less popular. At the same time, according to the 1992 *Strategy*, "the price of heroin has dropped, the purity has increased, seizures by law enforcement officials have increased, and there has been an upsurge in heroin emergency-room mentions in the first quarters of 1991—all, it would seem, indicative of a resurgence in drug use."[32] Although heroin users tend to be older, they are more dangerous to the public health. Heroin is consumed intravenously, and its users are thus more likely to spread the HIV virus.

If we succeed in destroying agricultural drugs through crop destruction efforts in Peru, Bolivia, and Colombia, we could find increase in the use of alternate drugs and in the supply of synthetic, designer drugs that are more potent and destructive than anything we have yet seen. These include fentanyl, for example, which is around 100 times as powerful as morphine and 20 times stronger heroin. Fentanyl's medicinal analogs, sufentanyl and alfentanyl, are 2,000 to 6,000 times stronger than morphine. These drugs produce bizarre, destructive, and unpredictable toxic effects. Fentanyl may be more widely used than we now know, since it cannot be detected by drug tests.[33]

As demand for particular drugs waxes and wanes based either on fashion or on interdiction, new drugs will be demanded by consumers and supplied by innovative entrepreneurs.

## Corruption

Whatever the latest trend in drug use, manufacturers, smugglers, and distributors can operate more efficiently by corrupting public officials. Neither the 1989 nor 1992 *Strategy* discuss corruption, another dilemma confronting law enforcement efforts in the war on drugs, although it discusses "turf battles" among federal enforcement agencies.[34] A discussion of interagency rivalry is acceptable because it is a normal and acceptable aspect of bureaucratic processes.[35]

Corruption, on the other hand, is unmentionable. Any strategy, however, which fails to consider the possibility and ramifications of increased corruption in the wake of expanded law enforcement is seriously flawed.[36]

As we attempt to pressure foreign producers, we will have to work with authorities in such countries as Colombia, Bolivia, Panama, and Peru, countries where the bribe is a familiar part of law enforcement. Thus, the State Department's Bureau of International Narcotics Matters found that Jorge Luis Ochoa, a major Colombian drug trafficker, "was able to buy his freedom through the intimidated and vulnerable Colombian judicial system."[37] Concerning Colombia, journalist Tina Rosenberg observed:

In general, the closer an institution gets to the traffickers, the more corrupt it becomes. Cocaine's new income opportunities for judges have been well documented. Prosecutors are less corrupt, but it is a matter of logistics, not morals: it is simply easier to win cases by bribing judges, or the police. . . . Policemen, the infantry in the war on drugs, are usually young men from slum neighborhoods with third grade education—exactly the profile of a drug dealer, and the line between the two tends to blur on the job.[38]

No matter how honest US drug enforcement agents operating abroad are, they may find themselves operating in a climate of official corruption. In Peru, police officers bribe their superiors to be transferred to interdiction zones, where illegal landing fees can bring $5,000. Peru's Attorney General said in March 1992, "Many policemen, instead of fighting against drug trafficking . . . are involved in it."[39]

Indeed, in Peru, the corruption is so pervasive, and so sinister—the military are also in league with and protective of the drug dealers—as to endanger the safety of American advisers and DEA agents. Stephen Trujillo describes one of several threatening incidents:

On June 15, 1990, three other DEA advisers and I accompanied the drug police to Tocache, north of the Santa Lucia base. Hovering over the municipal airfield in our helicopters, we caught soldiers red-handed as they transferred a load of cocaine base to a stash house. We landed and chased the fleeing soldiers back to their barracks, only to be surrounded by the remainder of the garrison. The soldiers raised their assault rifles, and their commander ordered us to surrender our weapons. Only adroit diplomacy of the senior DEA agent saved us.[40]

Domestic police officers are equally susceptible to the temptations of drug money. Unfortunately, we are all too familiar with legendary narcotics scandals which have plagued police departments in various cities. Perhaps the most famous have occurred in New York City where the Knapp Commission investigations reached both narcotics and other forms of vice. Patrick V. Murphy, a man with a reputation for reform, was recruited as Police Commissioner in New York in the wake of the scandal uncovered by the Knapp Commission. In his autobiography, he writes, "We ultimately discovered that the narcotics units under the previous police administration had made major contributions to the city's drug traffic. It was this area of corruption more than anything else which most shocked me."[41]

Narcotics corruption is not confined to New York City. Deputies in the Los Angeles County Sheriff's Department were recently involved in what The Los Angeles Times called "one of the worst corruption cases" in the department's history. Videotapes revealed one deputy hurriedly taking three

$10,000 bundles of $100 bills from a dealer's shoulder bag and putting them into his partner's leather briefcase.[42]

Although the possibilities of corruption exist in any form of enforcement against criminal activity, it is particularly in drug enforcement that agents and officers encounter large sums of cash and drugs with great market value. In short, corruption must be counted as one of the anticipated costs of an unprecedented expansion of drug law enforcement. As Peter Reuter recently summed up the dilemma of corruption, "The incentive to bribe criminal justice officials is positively related to the intensity of enforcement."[43]

## The Explosion of Imprisonment

The "unprecedented" expansion of police, prosecutors, and prisons implicates a third set of problems related to imprisonment. Attempting to solve the drug problem by imprisoning more drug users and sellers may, paradoxically, worsen the problem at the street level. State and federal prison populations have virtually doubled in the 1980s[44] and the rate of our prison population per 100,000 of total resident population has increased from 96 in 1970 to 228 in 1987.[45] Overcrowded jails and prisons are bulging with newly convicted criminals, and also with criminals whose probation and parole were revoked. In California, for example, the number of parole violators returned to prison between 1978 and 1988 increased by about eleven times.[46]

A likely reason for this rise is the increased frequency with which drug tests are being required of parolees.[47] Revised estimates by the California Department of Corrections project that the state's prison population will grow by more than 50 percent by the year 1994, and that the state will need to build up to twenty prisons to house the expected growth in inmate population.[48] As our advanced drug testing technology consigns more parolees and probationers to prison, we cannot continue to convict and impose longer sentences without building many new prisons.

The Bush administration's drug policy acknowledges this critical lack of prison space. It appreciates that "most state prisons are already operating far above their designed capacity."[49] It also recognizes that "many states have been forced under court order to release prisoners before their terms have been served whenever a court-established prison population limit has been exceeded."[50] The solution, however, is to encourage state governments to persuade their citizens to support new prisons. "The task of building [prisons], remains with state governments, who poorly serve their constituents when prison construction is stalled or resisted."[51]

Yet not a word appears about how to persuade citizens to pay for the continuing and rising expense of maintaining prisons, without raising state taxes to support prison construction. Furthermore, even those citizens who demand longer and more certain prison sentences are reluctant to live next door to prisons, which are being built in increasingly remote areas. Highly publicized plans for a 700-bed prison to house convicted Washington, D.C. drug dealers at Fort Meade, Maryland were embarrassingly withdrawn the day after they were announced because "there was too much public resistance,"[52] as there are near urban areas whenever a new prison site is proposed.

## Ineffective Criminal Sanctions

Even if new prisons could be constructed over financial and community objections, a more fundamental problem is the failure of criminal sanctions to achieve purported goals. One of these is the reform and correction of inmates. Imprisonment is not necessarily stigmatic, nor entirely foreboding for those who sell drugs. My students and I have been interviewing imprisoned drug dealers in California since 1989, and learned that imprisonment may bring a certain elevated "home boy" status, especially for gang youths for whom prison, and prison gangs can become an alternative site of loyalty.[53]

Moreover, imprisonment often reinforces prisoners in their troublesome behavior. Already consigned to the margins of society, prisoners join gangs, use drugs, and make useful connections for buying and selling drugs. Perhaps the penitentiary was once a place for experiencing penance. However, today's correctional institutions, overcrowded with short-term parole violators who have failed their court-mandated drug tests, often serve purposes similar to those advanced by academic and business conventions as an opportunity for "networking."[54] A recent newspaper survey of prison drug use found that it has become a "major problem," and it cited "threats to prison order, violence among inmates and corruption of guards and other employees" as among the most serious.[55]

President Bush and others have made the incarceration and execution of "drug kingpins" a focus of the drug war. When we succeed in incarcerating drug dealers in prisons, however, we encounter what I think of as the Felix Mitchell Paradox, named in honor of the West Coast's formerly most infamous drug distributor. In the mid-1980s, a federal strike force, with considerable assistance and dogged investigation by an Oakland Police vice squad, succeeded in convicting and imprisoning the East Bay's three leading drug dealers. Among these was the legendary Felix Mitchell, who, the prosecution charged, was largely responsible for Oakland's becoming a major drug dispensary, and who received a life sentence without possibility of parole in a federal district court for his drug related convictions.[56] One would expect that confining three leading drug dealers to prison would reduce the violence and other crimes related to narcotics. On the contrary, Oakland has since then experienced a continued increase in narcotics crimes and the absence of any indication that the Oakland residents perceive the community to be safer.[57] The post Felix Mitchell drug related homicide rate has proved especially vexing. Gangs competing for the Mitchell territory accounted for multiple murders, high speed chases, daytime assassinations, four assaults on police officers, and scores of other shootings. It is likely that, for the drug gangs, whatever deterrent value the criminal law has can be outweighed by the profits to be gained through expanding into the market vacuum created by the withdrawal of imprisoned suppliers.

Peter Reuter makes a similar observation about the relationship between violence and market share as an explanation for the District of Columbia's soaring homicide rate. He argues that when the supply of drug dealers exceeds the demand for drugs, "one obvious way to raise earnings is to eliminate the competition through violence."[58] The District of Columbia's soaring homicide rate cannot be attributed to inactivity of the District's police during the 1980s. Only 58 juveniles had been arrested for drug dealing offenses in 1981; by 1987 that figure had reached 1550.[59] In 1981, adult arrests—usually men in their early twenties—totalled 408; by 1987 it was 5,297.[60]

However notorious for drugs and homicides, Oakland, California and Washington, D.C. are scarcely unrepresentative. One can pick up almost any major metropolitan newspaper on any given day and read of drugs and homicide. Drugs and violence have in the 1980s and 1990s become as institutionalized a part of American life and journalism as the Vietnam War was in the 1960s, and as much of a quagmire. Thus, on April 2, 1992, the front page of The New York Times carried an article titled "From Queens to Rochester: Adrift in a World of Violence," about an 18-year-old who was arrested in a church, where he had sought sanctuary as a suspect who had killed eight people in four days. The author, Alison Mitchell, had interviewed the suspect's friends and neighbors who spoke to her of "a land in which a teen-ager sold cocaine like candy, putting an 'out' sign in his apartment window when he had run out of supplies." Increased criminal sanctions, as in the war on drugs, have little impact in the cities of America against either drug kingpins or local-level dealers. Stepped-up enforcement has usually encouraged other suppliers to enter the market or amplify their activities through violent elimination of competitors. It is time to face reality. The drug war has failed.

## What Is to Be Done?

It is easier to say what is *not* to be done than what is to be. To be avoided are the ineffectual and costly policies and the misinformation of previous decades. When we educate about drugs we need to stress reality and health values. Drug education often poses false polarities. Drugs are either harmless or will "fry your brain." The dangers of marijuana were overstated in the 1950s and 1960s. The absurd overstatements (that marijuana use leads to violent assaults) instead of discouraging use, encouraged false inferences in the opposite direction—that marijuana use posed no dangers. In fact, drug effects and side effects are complex and vary according to the chemical properties of the drug; the setting in which it is used; the potency (unfortified wine vs. distilled spirits); the quantity used; the frequency of use; and the biological, psychological, and social circumstances of the user. Many people can control their use of alcohol, cocaine, and marijuana. Others cannot.

Legalization has often been proposed as an alternative to the vast expansion of law enforcement that we witnessed during the Reagan-Bush years. Legalization is no panacea either, however. Questions to be asked about it are: what form would legalization take; are all or only some drugs to be legalized; what would be the costs and benefits and to which groups; and can legalization be reconciled with a positive moral message?

Essentially, legalization implies four models. Under the least restrictive free-market model, every drug, even cocaine and heroin, could be sold as we do aspirin, over the counter. The free-market model offers the strongest argument for legalizing. At one stroke, the free market would wipe out smuggling (drugs could be taxed), organized drug syndicates, street sales, and street violence. Scarcely less restrictive is the cigarette paradigm, regulating only as to age of purchaser. Alcohol offers a third, slightly more regulated model, while the most restrictive of the legalization models is the prescription drug paradigm, which is already employed for methadone treatment, and for treatment accorded to a vast patient population of users of tranquilizers and sleeping pills.

Marijuana offers the most plausible case for nonprohibition. Were we to regulate marijuana more tightly than we do alcohol, we would end half or more of our current drug arrests without a significant impact on public health. We would expect that more people would use marijuana, but not so many more, given the increasing concern for health and sobriety between the 1960s and the 1990s. None of this will perfectly succeed. The more controls government imposes, the greater the incentives to develop illegal markets. If we allow the sale and use of low-potency marijuana, we will stimulate illegal markets in the high-potency stuff. If we control sales to youngsters, some will surely buy on the black market, as they already do.

If Cocaine HCL (powder cocaine) were to be legalized, we would generate incentives for producing crack cocaine, that is, purified, heat-stable cocaine, suitable for smoking. "Absorbed across the pulmonary vascular bed," explain the neurologists Golbe and Merkin, "it produces a more intense euphoria and more precipitous withdrawal than Cocaine HCL and is therefore more addictive."[61]

There is thus no perfect legalization solution, but the benefits of marijuana legalization seem to outweigh the costs of enforcement. On the other hand, since crack cocaine, heroin, and phencyclidine (PCP) remain inner-city favorites, the actual and symbolic consequences of legalizing these drugs may prove disastrous, possibly generating a sharp rise in use among the truly disadvantaged, especially among teenagers already inclined to use these drugs. To be sure, these drugs are already easily obtainable, though not as easily as they would be under a legalization regime. Reasonable prudence demands that these drugs remain illegal. As John Kaplan observed in opposing cocaine legalization: "If we legalize cocaine now, how long should we wait before deciding whether we made a mistake? And if we decided that we had, how would we go about recriminalizing the drug?"[62]

The issue, however, is not only whether to legalize a drug, but how to influence the message accompanying legalization. Legalization of a vice does not necessarily connote approval or promotion of the activity, although it so often has in the United States. When Prohibition was repealed, the saloon doors were thrown open. We not only legalized distilled spirits, but the cocktail lounge and a culture of drinking along with it. When our state governments have legalized gambling—lotteries, casinos, and off-track betting—they have also, and shamelessly, promoted gambling. However, it is possible to reconcile legalization with a strong public health message. When the British legalized casinos in 1968, the purpose was to control organized crime. They did not permit casinos to advertise at all, not even with matchbooks or advertisements in the telephone directory.

Similarly, if we eliminated criminal penalties for possession of marijuana, and strictly regulated its sale, such decriminalization would need to be accompanied by a larger moral purpose—to reduce crime and violence, to enhance public health and safety through drug education and treatment, and to invigorate a sense of community. Legalization of marijuana, in sum, need not and should not imply advocacy. On the contrary, the taxed proceeds from such legalization should discourage, even while permitting, use of the drug. A slogan for legal drugs might be: "Never use cigarettes; and if you must use alcohol and marijuana, use moderately."

## A Public Health/Social Problems Strategy

On March 12, 1992, *The San Francisco Examiner*, a Hearst newspaper critical of the Bush administration's war on drugs strategy, praised Dr. Andrew Mecca, director of California's Department of Alcohol and Drug Programs for his new ideas. What are these? Presently, two-thirds of the nearly $13 billion the United States spends waging a war on drugs is allocated to interdiction and law enforcement. Only one-third goes to prevention and treatment. In the *Examiner*'s view, and in my own, these priorities should be reversed. Dr. Mecca is taking the right course but is not there yet. With a $1 billion budget to fight drugs, California is allocating 50 percent for enforcement, and 50 percent for treatment and prevention. Nevertheless, this recognition that priorities need to be shifted is the sensible direction in which to move.

I would add, however, that the public health approach needs to be supplemented by a "social problems" dimension critical to understanding the etiology of drug use and the obstacles to successful treatment prevention. The moralistic stance adopted by the Bush administration in its *Strategy* assumes a single minded moral paradigm—drug users and sellers are evil and they must be punished. But it ignores key issues: why do some communities produce street drug dealers and street violence, while others do not? How do social, economic, and psychological conditions affect drug use and sale? Why do users ingest crack cocaine? What does it mean to say that it is "addicting?"

Here are some answers: Crack cocaine, like Cocaine HCL, but unlike heroin, is psychologically, but not physiologically addicting. A drug dealer (and former user) whom I interviewed communicated the distinction vividly and clearly in nonmedical terminology:

> It's not addicting like your body craves it. You're not going to get sick . . . by not smoking. Only thing that craves crack is your mind. It's like an illusion. You hit the pipe you are whatever you want to be. . . . Say you're into music and you're basing (using crack or its chemical equivalent). You feel like you *are* James Brown or Stevie Wonder or Michael Jackson.

The above description suggests that users ingest drugs to feel euphoric, to take one out of life's circumstances, to overcome despair, hopelessness, and low self-esteem. Such feeling states can occur to individuals within any social group, but they are heightened by joblessness, poverty, and neglect. Thus, the more satisfied and engaged people are with their lives and themselves, the less likely are they to be drawn—regardless of the consequences—to the euphoric feeling states of crack cocaine. A clean and sober addict with a job will be less likely to relapse than one who is unemployed.

Total abstinence—being clean and sober—should be the treatment goal for cocaine and alcohol addictions. Oral methadone maintenance is a less desirable, but necessary, alternative for heroin addicts, especially since heroin addicts, who are physically addicted, typically ingest intravenously, and therefore are at risk for contracting and spreading the HIV virus. Whatever the treatment modality, the more an addict can count on social support through family, friends, a therapy group such as Alcoholics Anonymous, the more likely will the goal of total abstinence be achieved.

The "truly disadvantaged" are less likely to enjoy this sort of social and economic support. Such addicts live in a world—often a housing project—which cues craving as they see drugs being sold and used all around them. Treatment is often unavailable as there are no Betty Ford clinics for the desperately poor. It is in this setting, through patrol, community policing and community organization, that enforcement enjoys perhaps its greatest potential.

But even the best organized and most thoughtful local law enforcement strategies are constrained, since those who sell, as well as those who buy, are also responding to underlying economic and social conditions. Terry Williams, a sociologist who spent more than 1,200 hours studying a primarily Dominican drug gang in Washington Heights, whom he called "The Cocaine Kids," portrays them as both antisocial criminals and "struggling young people trying to make a place for themselves in a world few care to understand and many wish would go away." The kids have learned a trade. They know how to buy cocaine, cook it into crack, distribute, and sell it. Williams portrays them as entrepreneurs, interested not only in making money, but also in showing their families and friends that they can succeed at something.[63] And Phillipe Bourgeois, who studied crack dealers in New York's Spanish Harlem, challenges the assertion of culture-of-poverty theorists that the poor are socialized out of the mainstream and have different values. He concludes that:

> On the contrary, ambitious, energetic, inner-city youths are attracted to the underground economy precisely because they believe in the rags-to-riches American dream. . . . Without stretching the point too much, they can be seen in conventional terms as rugged individualists on an unpredictable frontier where fortune, fame and destruction are all just around the corner.[64]

Neither moral exhortation nor an unprecedented expansion of law enforcement, or military intervention can or should be used to address what is essentially a health and social problem. These hard-edged responses are costly to our pocketbooks and, worse, are largely counterproductive. Until we redefine the drug problem as a public health and social problem rather than as a moral failure, we make little headway in promoting the health and public safety of our citizens.

## Endnotes

[1]Oliver Sacks, "A Neurologist's Notebook," *The New Yorker*, 16 March 1992, 85.

[2]Hughes, *The Concept of Crime*, in S. Kadish, ed., *Encyclopedia of Crime and Justice* (1983), 294–95. This excellent essay goes on to develop the distinction.

[3]See the first *National Drug Control Strategy* issued by the Office of National Drug Control Policy, Executive Office of the President (Washington, D.C.: US Government Printing Office, 1989), 24. [hereinafter *Strategy*].

[4]Jaynes and Williams, eds., *A Common Destiny: Blacks and American Society* (Washington, D.C.: National Academy Press, 1989), 398.

[5]Sacks, "A Neurologists's Notebook."

[6]*Strategy*, 2.

[7]*National Drug Control Strategy: A Nation Responds to Drug Use* (Washington, D.C.: US Government Printing Office, 1992).

[8]These data are cited in Cloud, "Cocaine, Demand, and Addiction: A Study of the Possible Convergence of Rational Theory and National Policy," *Vanderbilt University Law Review* 42 (1989): 725, 752.

[9]Dean R. Gerstein, "Alcohol Use and Consequences," in Mark H. Moore and Dean Gertstein, eds., *Alcohol and Public Policy: Beyond the Shadow of Prohibition* (Washington, D.C.: National Academy Press, 1981).

[10]*Strategy*, 11.

[11]Ibid.

[12]Ibid.

[13]John Stuart Mill, *On Liberty* (London: Penguin, 1974), 9. (First published in 1859).

[14]Ibid.

[15]Ibid., 170.

[16]Ibid., 167.

[17]Ibid, 170.

[18]Even conservative policy analyst Charles Murray thinks legalization might be the answer to the drug problem. *The New York Times*, 27 November, 1989, A15, C14.

[19]H. Packer, *The Limits of the Criminal Sanction* (1968), 265.

[20]*Strategy*, 73.

[21]The notorious Peruvian guerrilla organization, the Shining Path, has become deeply involved in the narcotics business. It serves as a broker for coca growers, collects taxes from traffickers, and protects both from security sources. See, for example, *The New York Times*, 6 December 1989.

[22]*Strategy*, 73.

[23]James Brown, "Fighting the Drug War in the Skies Over Peru," *The New York Times*, 28 March 1992.

[24]*Strategy*, 74.

[25]*Strategy*, 73.

[26]Stephen G. Trujillo, "Corruption and Cocaine in Peru," *The New York Times*, 7 April 1992, Op-Ed.

[27]P. Reuter, G. Crawford, and J. Cave, "Sealing the Borders: The Effects of Military Participation," in *Drug Interdiction* 18 (1988).

[28]Skolnick, Correl, Navarro, and Raab, *The Social Structure of Street Drug Dealing*, California Bureau of Criminal Statistics Forum (Office of the Attorney General, 1988) [hereinafter *Social Structure*].

[29]*Strategy*, 74.

[30]Peter Reuter, "Can The Borders Be Sealed?" *The Public Interest* (Summer 1988): 56.

[31]For a thorough analysis of the problems posed to American society by heroin, see J. Kaplan, *Heroin: The Hardest Drug* (1983).

[32]*Strategy* (1992), 11.

[33]*Journal of the American Medical Association*, 12 December 1986, 3061.

[34]*Strategy* (1992), 11.

[35]The *Strategy* suggests that "we should be extremely reluctant to restrict within formal and arbitrary lines" the extent of bureaucratic bickering when it is attributable to the "overriding spirit and energy of our front-line drug enforcement officers . . . " *Strategy*, 8.

[36]For an account of rampant corruption in the Drug Enforcement Agency, see *The New York Times*, 17 December 1989.

[37]US Department of State, Bureau of International Narcotics Matters, *International Narcotics Strategy*, Report 86 (March 1988).

[38]Rosenberg, "The Kingdom of Cocaine: A Report from Colombia," *New Republic*, 27 November 1989, 28.

[39]Brown, "Fighting the Drug War in the Skies Over Peru."

[40]Trujillo, "Corruption and Cocaine in Peru."

[41]P. Murphy and T. Plate, "Commissioner: A View from the Top of the American Law Enforcement" (1977), 245.

[42]*The Los Angeles Times*, 24 October 1989.

[43]Peter Reuter, *On the Consequences of Toughness*, RAND Note 3347 (Santa Monica, CA: Drug Policy Research Center, 1991), 147.

[44]At year end 1988, the number of prisoners under the jurisdiction of federal or state correctional authorities reached 627,402, compared to 329,821 in 1980. This amounts to an increase of approximately 90 percent in eight years. Bureau of Justice Statistics, US Department of Justice, Bulletin, Prisoners in 1988 (1989).

[45]Bureau of Justice Statistics, US Department of Justice, Sourcebook of Criminal Justice Statistics—1988 612 (Table 6.31) (1988).

[46]See Messinger, Berecochea, Berk, and Rauma, "Parolees Returned to Prison and the California Prison Population" 13 (Table 5) (California Bureau of Criminal Statistics and Special Services Collaborative Report, 1988). In 1988, about 43 percent of the admissions to California state prisons were parole violators returned to prison by the Parole Board without a conviction for a new charge. Sourcebook 612, 11 (Table 3).

[47]Messinger, et al., 5.

[48]*San Francisco Chronicle*, 18 May 1989.

[49]*Strategy*, 26.

[50]Ibid.

[51]Ibid.

[52]*The New York Times*, 18 April 1989. Mr. Bennett has attributed the halting progress of the war on drugs to state officials who are reluctant to use state funding for new prison construction. *The Wall Street Journal*, 30 November 1989.

[53]*Social Structure*, 13.

[54]Ibid.

[55]*The New York Times*, 30 December 1989, 1.

[56]See Covino, *How the 69th Mob Maximized Earnings in East Oakland* (California: November 1985), 83.

[57]Center for the Study of Law and Society, *Courts, Probation, and Street Drug Crime: Executive Summary and Conclusions* (Final report on the Targeting Urban Crime Narcotics Task Force, 1988), 4–5, 9. [hereinafter *Executive Summary*].

[58]Peter Reuter, "The D.C. Crime Surge: An Economist Looks at the Carnage," *The Washington Post*, 26 March 1989.

[59]Ibid.

[60]Ibid.

[61]Lawrence I. Golbe and Michael D. Merkin, "Cerebral Infraction in a User of Free-Base ('Crack')," *Neurology* 36 (1986): 1602.

[62]John Kaplan, "Taking Drugs Seriously," *The Public Interest 42* (Summer 1988).

[63]Terry Williams, *The Cocaine Kids: The Inside Story of a Teenage Drug Ring* (Reading, MA: Addison-Wesley, 1989).

[64]Phillipe Bourgeois, "Just Another Night on Crack Street," *The New York Times Magazine*, 12 November 1989, 63.

# 20

# The Case for Legalization

## Ethan A. Nadelmann

What can be done about the "drug problem"? Despite frequent proclamations of war and dramatic increases in government funding and resources in recent years, there are many indications that the problem is not going away and may even be growing worse. During the past year alone, more than thirty million Americans violated the drug laws on literally billions of occasions. Drug-treatment programs in many cities are turning people away for lack of space and funding. In Washington, D.C., drug-related killings, largely of one drug dealer by another, are held responsible for a doubling in the homicide rate over the past year. In New York and elsewhere, courts and prisons are clogged with a virtually limitless supply of drug-law violators. In large cities and small towns alike, corruption of policemen and other criminal-justice officials by drug traffickers is rampant.

Reprinted by permission of the author and *The Public Interest*, No. 92, Summer, 1988, pp. 3–31, © 1988 by National Affairs, Inc.

Former President Reagan and the former first lady were not alone in supporting increasingly repressive and expensive anti-drug measures, and in believing that the war against drugs can be won. Indeed, no "war" proclaimed by an American leader during the past forty years has garnered such sweeping bipartisan support; on this issue, liberals and conservatives are often indistinguishable. The fiercest disputes are not over objectives or even broad strategies, but over turf and tactics. Democratic politicians push for the appointment of a "drug czar" to oversee all drug policy, and blame the Administration for not applying sufficient pressure and sanctions against the foreign drug-producing countries. Republicans try to gain the upper hand by daring Democrats to support more widespread drug testing, increasingly powerful law-enforcement measures, and the death penalty for various drug-related offenses. But on the more fundamental issues of what this war is about, and what strategies are most likely to prove successful in the long run, no real debate—much less vocal dissent—can be heard.

If there were a serious public debate on this issue, far more attention would be given to one policy option that has just begun to be seriously considered, but which may well prove more successful than anything currently being implemented or proposed: legalization. Politicians and public officials remain hesitant even to mention the word, except to dismiss it contemptuously as a capitulation to the drug traffickers. Most Americans perceive drug legalization as an invitation to drug-infested anarchy. Even the civil-liberties groups shy away from this issue, limiting their input primarily to the drug-testing debate. The minority communities in the ghetto, for whom repealing the drug laws would promise the greatest benefits, fail to recognize the costs of our drug-prohibition policies. And the typical middle-class American, who hopes only that his children will not succumb to drug abuse, tends to favor any measures that he believes will make illegal drugs less accessible to them. Yet when one seriously compares the advantages and disadvantages of the legalization strategy with those of current and planned policies, abundant evidence suggests that legalization may well be the optimal strategy for tackling the drug problem.

Interestingly, public support for repealing the drug-prohibition laws has traditionally come primarily from the conservative end of the political spectrum: Milton Friedman, Ernest van den Haag, William F. Buckley, and the editors of the *Economist* have all supported it. Less vocal support comes from many liberals, politicians not among them, who are disturbed by the infringements on individual liberty posed by the drug laws. There is also a significant silent constituency in favor of repeal, found especially among criminal-justice officials, intelligence analysts, military interdictors, and criminal-justice scholars who have spent a considerable amount of time thinking about the problem. More often than not, however, job-security considerations, combined with an awareness that they can do little to change official policies, ensure that their views remain discreet and off the record.

During the spring of 1988, however, legalization suddenly began to be seriously considered as a policy option; the pros and cons of legalization were discussed on the front pages of leading newspapers and news magazines, and were debated on national television programs. Although the argument for legalization was not new, two factors seem to have been primarily responsible for the blitz of media coverage: an intellectual rationale for legalization—the first provided in decades—appeared in my article in the spring issue of *Foreign Policy* magazine; more importantly, political legitimacy was subsequently bestowed upon the legalization option when Baltimore Mayor Kurt Schmoke, speaking to the National Conference of Mayors, noted the potential benefits of drug legalization and asked that the merits of legalization be debated in congressional hearings.

The idea of legalizing drugs was quickly denounced by most politicians across the political spectrum; nevertheless, the case for legalization appealed to many Americans. The prominent media coverage lent an aura of respectability to arguments that just a month earlier had seemed to be beyond the political pale. Despite the tendency of many journalists to caricature the legalization argument, at long last the issue had been joined. Various politicians, law-enforcement officials, health experts, and scholars came out in favor of drug legalization—or at least wanted to debate the matter seriously. On Capitol Hill, three or four congressmen seconded the call for a debate. According to some congressional staffers, two dozen additional legislators would have wanted to debate the issue, had the question arisen after rather than before the upcoming elections. Unable to oppose a mere hearing on the issue, Congressman Charles Rangel, chairman of the House Select Committee on Narcotics, declared his willingness to convene his committee in Baltimore to consider the legalization option.

There is, of course, no single legalization strategy. At one extreme is the libertarian vision of virtually no government restraints on the production and sale of drugs or any psychoactive substances, except perhaps around the fringes, such as prohibiting sales to children. At the other extreme is total government control over the production and sale of these goods. In between lies a strategy that may prove more successful than anything yet tried in stemming the problems of drug abuse and drug-related violence, corruption, sickness, and suffering. It is one in which government makes most of the substances that are now banned legally available to competent adults, exercises strong regulatory powers over all large-scale production and sale of drugs, makes drug-treatment programs available to all who need them, and offers honest drug-education programs to children. This strategy, it is worth noting, would also result in a net benefit to public treasuries of at least ten billion dollars a year, and perhaps much more.

There are three reasons why it is important to think about legalization scenarios, even though most Americans remain hostile to the idea. First, current drug-control policies have failed, are failing, and will continue to fail, in good part because they are fundamentally flawed. Second, many drug-control efforts are not only failing, but also proving highly costly and counterproductive; indeed, many of the drug-related evils that Americans identify as part and parcel of the "drug problem" are in fact caused by our drug-prohibition policies. Third, there is good reason to believe that repealing many of the drug laws would not lead, as many people fear, to a dramatic rise in drug abuse. In this essay I expand on each of these reasons for considering the legalization option. Government effort to deal with the drug problem will succeed only if the rhetoric and crusading mentality that now dominate drug policy are replaced by reasoned and logical analysis.

## Why Current Drug Policies Fail

Most proposals for dealing with the drug problem today reflect a desire to point the finger at those most removed from one's home and area of expertise. New York Mayor Ed Koch, Florida Congressman Larry Smith, and Harlem Congressman Charles Rangel, who recognize government's inability to deal with the drug problem in the cities, are among the most vocal supporters of punishing foreign drug-producing countries and stepping up interdiction efforts. Foreign leaders and U.S. State Department and drug-enforcement officials stationed abroad, on the other hand, who understand all too well why it is impossible to crack down successfully on illicit drug production outside the United States, are the most vigorous advocates of domestic enforcement and demand-reduction efforts within the United States. In between, those agencies charged with drug interdiction, from the Coast Guard and U.S. Customs Services to the U.S. military, know that they will never succeed in capturing more than a small percentage of the illicit drugs being smuggled into the United States. Not surprisingly, they point their fingers in both directions. The solution, they promise, lies in greater source-control efforts abroad and greater demand-reduction efforts at home.

Trying to pass the buck is always understandable. But in each of these cases, the officials are half right and half wrong—half right in recognizing that they can do little to affect their end of the drug problem, given the suppositions and constraints of current drug-control strategies; half wrong (if we assume that their finger-pointing is sincere) in expecting that the solution lies elsewhere. It would be wrong, however, to assume that the public posturing of many officials reflects their real views. Many of them privately acknowledge the futility of all current drug-control strategies, and wonder whether radically different options, such as legalization, might not prove more successful in dealing with the drug problem. The political climate pervading this issue is such, however, that merely to ask that alternatives to current policies be considered is to incur a great political risk.

By most accounts, the dramatic increase in drug-enforcement efforts over the past few years has had little effect on the illicit drug market in the United States. The mere existence of drug-prohibition laws, combined with a minimal level of law-enforcement resources, is sufficient to maintain the price of illicit drugs at a level significantly higher than it would be if there were no such laws. Drug laws and enforcement also reduce the availability of illicit drugs, most notably in parts of the United States where demand is relatively limited to begin with. Theoretically, increases in drug-enforcement efforts should result in reduced availability, higher prices, and lower purity of illegal drugs. That is, in fact, what has happened to the domestic marijuana market (in at least the first two respects). But in general the illegal drug market has not responded as intended to the substantial increases in federal, state, and local drug-enforcement efforts.

Cocaine has sold for about a hundred dollars a gram at the retail level since the beginning of the 1980s. The average purity of that gram, however, has increased from 12 to 60 percent. Moreover, a growing number of users are turning to "crack," a potent derivative of cocaine that can be smoked; it is widely sold in ghetto neighborhoods now for five to ten dollars per vial. Needless to say, both crack and the 60 percent pure cocaine pose much greater threats to users than did the relatively benign powder available eight years ago. Similarly, the retail price of heroin has remained relatively constant even as the average purity has risen from 3.9 percent in 1983 to 6.1 percent in 1986. Throughout the southwestern part of the United States, a particularly potent form of heroin known as "black tar" has become increasingly prevalent. And in many cities, a powerful synthetic opiate, Dilaudid, is beginning to compete with heroin as the preferred opiate. The growing number of heroin-related hospital emergencies and deaths is directly related to these developments.

All of these trends suggest that drug-enforcement efforts are not succeeding and may even be backfiring. There are numerous indications, for instance, that a growing number of marijuana dealers in both the producer countries and the United States are switching to cocaine dealing, motivated both by the promise of greater profits and by government drug-enforcement efforts that place a premium on minimizing the bulk of the illicit product (in order to avoid detection). It is possible, of course, that some of these trends would be even more severe in the absence of drug laws and enforcement. At the same time, it is worth observing that the increases in the potency of illegal drugs have coincided with decreases in the potency of legal substances. Motivated in good part by health concerns, cigarette smokers are turning increasingly to lower-tar and -nicotine tobacco products, alcohol drinkers from hard liquor to wine and beer, and even coffee drinkers from regular to decaffeinated coffee. This trend may well have less to do with the nature of the substances than with their legal status. It is quite possible, for instance, that the subculture of illicit-drug use creates a bias or incentive in favor of riskier behavior and more powerful psychoactive effects. If this is the case, legalization might well succeed in reversing today's trend toward more potent drugs and more dangerous methods of consumption.

The most "successful" drug-enforcement operations are those that succeed in identifying and destroying an entire drug-trafficking organization. Such operations can send dozens of people to jail and earn the government millions of dollars in asset forfeitures. Yet these operations have virtually no effect on the availability or price of illegal drugs throughout much of the United States. During the past few years, some urban police departments have devoted significant manpower and financial resources to intensive crackdowns on street-level drug dealing in particular neighborhoods. Code-named Operation Pressure Point, Operation Clean Sweep, and so on, these massive police efforts have led to hundreds, even thousands, of arrests of low-level dealers and drug users, and have helped improve the quality of life in the targeted neighborhoods. In most cases, however, drug dealers have adapted relatively easily by moving their operations to nearby neighborhoods. In the final analysis, the principal accomplishment of most domestic drug-enforcement efforts is not to reduce the supply or availability of illegal drugs, or even to raise their price; it is to punish the drug dealers who are apprehended, and cause minor disruptions in established drug markets.

## The Failure of International Drug Control

Many drug-enforcement officials and urban leaders recognize the futility of domestic drug-enforcement efforts and place their hopes in international control efforts. Yet these too are doomed to fail—for numerous reasons. First, marijuana and opium can be grown almost anywhere, and the coca plant, from which cocaine is derived, is increasingly being cultivated successfully in areas that were once considered inhospitable environments. Wherever drug-eradication efforts succeed, other regions and countries are quick to fill the void; for example, Colombian marijuana growers rapidly expanded production following successful eradication efforts in Mexico during the mid-1970s. Today, Mexican growers are rapidly taking advantage of recent

Colombian government successes in eradicating marijuana in the Guajira peninsula. Meanwhile, Jamaicans and Central Americans from Panama to Belize, as well as a growing assortment of Asians and Africans, do what they can to sell their own marijuana in American markets. And within the United States, domestic marijuana production is believed to be a multi-billion-dollar industry, supplying between 15 and 50 percent of the American market.

This push-down/pop-up factor also characterizes the international heroin market. At various points during the past two decades, Turkey, Mexico, Southeast Asia (Burma, Thailand, and Laos), and Southwest Asia (Pakistan, Afghanistan, and Iran) have each served as the principal source of heroin imported into the United States. During the early 1970s, Mexican producers rapidly filled the void created by the Turkish government's successful opium-control measures. Although a successful eradication program during the latter part of the 1970s reduced Mexico's share of the U.S. market from a peak of 87 percent in 1975, it has since retained at least a one-third share in each year. Southwest Asian producers, who had played no role in supplying the American market as late as 1976, were able to supply over half the American market four years later. Today, increasing evidence indicates that drug traffickers are bringing unprecedented quantities of Southeast Asian heroin into the United States.

So far, the push-down/pop-up factor has played little role in the international cocaine market, for the simple reason that no government has yet pushed down in a significant way. Unlike marijuana- and opium-eradication efforts, in which aerial spraying of herbicides plays a prominent role, coca-eradication efforts are still conducted manually. The long anticipated development and approval of an environmentally safe herbicide to destroy coca plants may introduce an unprecedented push-down factor into the market. But even in the absence of such government pressures, coca growing has expanded rapidly during the past decade within Bolivia and Peru, and has expanded outward into Colombia, Brazil, Ecuador, Venezuela, and elsewhere. Moreover, once eradication efforts do begin, coca growers can be expected to adopt many of the same "guerrilla farming" methods adopted by marijuana and opium growers to camouflage and protect their crops from eradication efforts.

Beyond the push-down/pop-up factor, international source-control efforts face a variety of other obstacles. In many countries, governments with limited resources lack the ability to crack down on drug production in the hinterlands and other poorly policed regions. In some countries, ranging from Colombia and Peru to Burma and Thailand, leftist insurgencies are involved in drug production for either financial or political profit, and may play an important role in hampering government drug-control efforts. With respect to all three of the illicit crops, poor peasants with no comparable opportunities to earn as much money growing legitimate produce are prominently involved in the illicit business. In some cases, the illicit crop is part of a traditional, indigenous culture. Even where it is not, peasants typically perceive little or nothing immoral about taking advantage of the opportunity to grow the illicit crops. Indeed, from their perspective their moral obligation is not to protect the foolish American consumer of their produce but to provide for their families' welfare. And even among those who do perceive participation in the illicit drug market as somewhat unethical, the temptations held out by the drug traffickers often prove overwhelming.

No illicit drug is as difficult to keep out of the United States as heroin. The absence of geographical limitations on where it can be cultivated is just one minor obstacle. American heroin users consume an estimated six tons of heroin each year. The sixty tons of opium required to produce that heroin represent just 2–3 percent of the estimated 2–3,000 tons of illicit opium produced during each of the past few years. Even if eradication efforts combined with what often proves to be the opium growers' principal nemesis—bad weather—were to eliminate three-fourths of that production in one year, the U.S. market would still require just 10 percent of the remaining crop. Since U.S. consumers are able and willing to pay more than any others, the chances are good that they would still obtain their heroin. In any event, the prospects for such a radical reduction in illicit opium production are scanty indeed.

As Peter Reuter argues elsewhere in these pages, interdiction, like source control, is largely unable to keep illicit drugs out of the United States. Moreover, the past twenty years' experience has demonstrated that even dramatic increases in interdiction- and source-control efforts have little or no effect on the price and purity of drugs. The few small successes, such as the destruction of the Turkish-opium "French Connection" in the early 1970s, and the crackdown on Mexican marijuana and heroin in the late 1970s, were exceptions to the rule. The elusive goal of international drug control since then has been to replicate those unusual successes. It is a strategy that is destined to fail, however, as long as millions of Americans continue to demand the illicit substances that foreigners are willing and able to supply.

## The Costs of Prohibition

The fact that drug-prohibition laws and policies cannot eradicate or even significantly reduce drug abuse is not necessarily a reason to repeal them. They do, after all, succeed in deterring many people from trying drugs, and they clearly reduce the availability and significantly increase the price of illegal drugs. These accomplishments alone might warrant retaining the drug laws, were it not for the fact that these same laws are also responsible for much of what Americans identify as the "drug problem." Here the analogies to alcohol and tobacco are worth noting. There is little question that we could reduce the health costs associated with use and abuse of alcohol and tobacco if we were to criminalize their production, sale, and possession. But no one believes that we could eliminate their use and abuse, that we could create an "alcohol-free" or "tobacco-free" country. Nor do most Americans believe that criminalizing the alcohol and tobacco markets would be a good idea. Their opposition stems largely from two beliefs: that adult Americans have the right to choose what substances they will consume and what risks they will take; and that the costs of trying to coerce so many Americans to abstain from those substances would be enormous. It was the strength of these two beliefs that ultimately led to the repeal of Prohibition, and it is partly due to memories of that experience that criminalizing either alcohol or tobacco has little support today.

Consider the potential consequences of criminalizing the production, sale, and possession of all tobacco products. On the positive side, the number of people smoking tobacco would almost certainly decline, as would the health costs associated with tobacco consumption. Although the "forbidden fruit" syndrome would attract some people to cigarette smoking who would not otherwise have smoked, many more would likely be deterred by the criminal sanction, the moral standing of the law, the higher cost and unreliable quality of the illicit tobacco, and the difficulties involved in acquiring it. Nonsmokers would rarely if ever be bothered by the irritating habits of their fellow citizens. The anti-tobacco laws would discourage some people from ever starting to smoke, and would induce others to quit.

On the negative side, however, millions of Americans, including both tobacco addicts and recreational users, would no doubt defy the law, generating a massive underground market and billions in profits for organized criminals. Although some tobacco farmers would find other work, thousands more would become outlaws and continue to produce their crops covertly. Throughout Latin America, farmers and gangsters would rejoice at the opportunity to earn untold sums of gringo greenbacks, even as U.S. diplomats pressured foreign governments to cooperate with U.S. laws. Within the United States, government helicopters would spray herbicides on illicit tobacco fields; people would be rewarded by the government for informing on their tobacco-growing, -selling, and -smoking neighbors; urine tests would be employed to identify violators of the anti-tobacco laws; and a Tobacco Enforcement Administration (the T.E.A.) would employ undercover agents, informants, and wiretaps to uncover tobacco-law violators. Municipal, state, and federal judicial systems would be clogged with tobacco traffickers and "abusers." "Tobacco-related murders" would increase dramatically as criminal organizations competed with one another for turf and markets. Smoking would become an act of youthful rebellion, and no doubt some users would begin to experiment with more concentrated, potent, and dangerous forms of tobacco. Tobacco-related corruption would infect all levels of government, and respect for the law would decline noticeably. Government expenditures on tobacco-law enforcement would climb rapidly into the billions of dollars, even as budget balancers longingly recalled the almost ten billion dollars per year in tobacco taxes earned by the federal and state governments prior to prohibition. Finally, the State of North Carolina might even secede again from the Union.

This seemingly far-fetched tobacco-prohibition scenario is little more than an extrapolation based on the current situation with respect to marijuana, cocaine, and heroin. In many ways, our predicament resembles what actually happened during Prohibition. Prior to Prohibition, most Americans hoped that alcohol could be effectively banned by passing laws against its production and supply. During the early years of Prohibition, when drinking declined but millions of Americans nonetheless continued to drink, Prohibition's supporters placed their faith in tougher laws and more police and jails. After a few more years, however, increasing numbers of Americans began to realize that laws and policemen were unable to eliminate the smugglers, bootleggers, and illicit producers, as long as tens of millions of Americans continued to want to buy alcohol. At the same time, they saw that more laws and policemen seemed to generate more violence and corruption, more crowded courts and jails, wider disrespect for government and the law, and more power and profits for the gangsters. Repeal of Prohibition came to be seen not as a capitulation to Al Capone and his ilk, but as a means of both putting the bootleggers out of business and eliminating most of the costs associated with the prohibition laws.

Today, Americans are faced with a dilemma similar to that confronted by our forebears sixty years ago. Demand for illicit drugs shows some signs of abating, but no signs of declining significantly. Moreover, there are substantial reasons to doubt that tougher laws and policing have played an important role in reducing consumption. Supply, meanwhile, has not abated at all. Availability of illicit drugs, except for marijuana in some locales, remains high. Prices are dropping, even as potency increases. And the number of drug producers, smugglers, and dealers remains sizable, even as jails and prisons fill to overflowing. As was the case during Prohibition, the principal beneficiaries of current drug policies are the new and old organized-crime gangs. The principal victims, on the other hand, are not the drug dealers, but the tens of millions of Americans who are worse off in one way or another as a consequence of the existence and failure of the drug-prohibition laws.

All public policies create beneficiaries and victims, both intended and unintended. When a public policy results in a disproportionate magnitude of unintended victims, there is good reason to reevaluate the assumptions and design of the policy. In the case of drug-prohibition policies, the intended beneficiaries are those individuals who would become drug abusers but for the existence and enforcement of the drug laws. The intended victims are those who traffic in illicit drugs and suffer the legal consequences. The unintended beneficiaries, conversely, are the drug producers and traffickers who profit handsomely from the illegality of the market, while avoiding arrest by the authorities and the violence perpetrated by other criminals. The unintended victims of drug prohibition policies are rarely recognized as such, however. Viewed narrowly, they are the 30 million Americans who use illegal drugs, thereby risking loss of their jobs, imprisonment, and the damage done to health by ingesting illegally produced drugs; viewed broadly, they are all Americans, who pay the substantial costs of our present ill-considered policies, both as taxpayers and as the potential victims of crime. These unintended victims are generally thought to be victimized by the unintended beneficiaries (i.e., the drug dealers), when in fact it is the drug-prohibition policies themselves that are primarily responsible for their plight.

If law-enforcement efforts could succeed in significantly reducing either the supply of illicit drugs or the demand for them, we would probably have little need to seek alternative drug-control policies. But since those efforts have repeatedly failed to make much of a difference and show little indication of working better in the future, at this point we must focus greater attention on their costs. Unlike the demand and supply of illicit drugs, which have remained relatively indifferent to legislative initiatives, the costs of drug-enforcement measures can be affected—quite dramatically—by legislative measures. What tougher criminal sanctions and more police have failed to accomplish, in terms of reducing drug-related violence, corruption, death, and social decay, may well be better accomplished by legislative repeal of the drug laws, and adoption of less punitive but more effective measures to prevent and treat substance abuse.

## Costs to the Taxpayer

Since 1981, federal expenditures on drug enforcement have more than tripled—from less than one billion dollars a year to about three billion. According to the National Drug Enforcement Policy Board, the annual budgets of the Drug Enforcement Administration (DEA) and the Coast Guard have each risen during the past seven years from about $220 million to roughly $500 million. During the same period, FBI resources devoted to drug enforcement have increased from $8 million a year to over $100 million; U.S. Marshals resources from $26 million to about $80 million; U.S. Attorney resources from $20 million to about $100 million; State Department resources from $35 million to $100 million; U.S. Customs resources from $180 million to over $400 million; and Bureau of Prison resources from $77 million to about $300 million. Expenditures on drug control by the military and the intelligence agencies are more difficult to calculate, although by all accounts they have increased by at least the same magnitude, and now total hundreds of millions of dollars per year. Even greater are the expenditures at lower levels of government. In a 1987 study for the U.S. Customs Service by Wharton Econometrics, state and local police were estimated to have devoted 18 percent of their total investigative resources, or close to five billion dollars, to drug-enforcement activities in 1986. This represented a 19 percent increase over the previous year's expenditures. All told, 1987 expenditures on all aspects of drug enforcement, from drug eradication in foreign countries to imprisonment of drug users and dealers in the United States, totalled at least ten billion dollars.

Of course, even ten billion dollars a year pales in comparison with expenditures on military defense. Of greater concern than the actual expenditures, however, has been the diversion of limited resources—including the time and energy of judges, prosecutors, and law-enforcement agents, as well as scarce prison space—from the prosecution and punishment of criminal activities that harm far more innocent victims than do violations of the drug laws. Drug-law violators account for approximately 10 percent of the roughly 800,000 inmates in state prisons and local jails, and more than one-third of the 44,000 federal prison inmates. These proportions are expected to increase in coming years, even as total prison populations continue to rise dramatically.[1] Among the 40,000 inmates in New York State prisons, drug-law violations surpassed first-degree robbery in 1987 as the number-one cause of incarceration, accounting for 20 percent of the total prison population. The U.S. Sentencing Commission has estimated that, largely as a consequence of the Anti-Drug Abuse Act passed by Congress in 1986, the proportion of federal inmates incarcerated for drug violations will rise from one-third of the 44,000 prisoners sentenced to federal-prison terms today to one-half of the 100,000 to 150,000 federal prisoners anticipated in fifteen years. The direct costs of building and maintaining enough prisons to house this growing population are rising at an astronomical rate. The opportunity costs, in terms of alternative social expenditures foregone and other types of criminals not imprisoned, are perhaps even greater.[2]

During each of the last few years, police made about 750,000 arrests for violations of the drug laws. Slightly more than three-quarters of these have not been for manufacturing or dealing drugs, but solely for possession of an illicit drug, typically marijuana. (Those arrested, it is worth noting, represent little more than 2 percent of the thirty million Americans estimated to have used an illegal drug during the past year.) On the one hand, this has clogged many urban criminal-justice systems: in New York City, drug-law violations last year accounted for more than 40 percent of all felony indictments—up from 25 percent in 1985; in Washington, D.C., the figure was more than 50 percent. On the other hand, it has distracted criminal-justice officials from concentrating greater resources on violent offenses and property crimes. In many cities, law enforcement has become virtually synonymous with drug enforcement.

Drug laws typically have two effects on the market in illicit drugs. The first is to restrict the general availability and accessibility of illicit drugs, especially in locales where underground drug markets are small and isolated from the community. The second is to increase, often significantly, the price of illicit drugs to consumers. Since the costs of producing most illicit drugs are not much different from the costs of alcohol, tobacco, and coffee, most of the price paid for illicit substances is in effect a value-added tax created by their criminalization, which is enforced and supplemented by the law-enforcement establishment, but collected by the drug traffickers. A report by Wharton Econometrics for the President's Commission on Organized Crime identified the sale of illicit drugs as the source of more than half of all organized crime revenues in 1986, with the marijuana and heroin business each providing over seven billion dollars, and the cocaine business over thirteen billion. By contrast, revenues from cigarette bootlegging, which persists principally because of differences among states in their cigarette-tax rates, were estimated at $290 million. If the marijuana, cocaine, and heroin markets were legal, state and federal governments would collect billions of dollars annually in tax revenues. Instead, they expend billions on what amounts to a subsidy of organized crime and unorganized criminals.

## Drugs and Crime

The drug/crime connection is one that continues to resist coherent analysis, both because cause and effect are so difficult to distinguish and because the role of the drug-prohibition laws in causing and labelling "drug-related crime" is so often ignored. There are four possible connections between drugs and crime, at least three of which would be much diminished if the drug-prohibition laws were repealed. First, producing, selling, buying, and consuming strictly controlled and banned substances is itself a crime that occurs billions of times each year in the United States alone. In the absence of drug-prohibition laws, these activities would obviously cease to be crimes. Selling drugs to children would, of course, continue to be criminal, and other evasions of government regulation of a legal market would continue to be prosecuted; but by and large the drug/crime connection that now accounts for all of the criminal-justice costs noted above would be severed.

Second, many illicit-drug users commit crimes such as robbery and burglary, as well as drug dealing, prostitution, and numbers running, to earn enough money to purchase the relatively high-priced illicit drugs. Unlike the millions of alcoholics who can support their habits for relatively modest amounts, many cocaine and heroin addicts spend hundreds and even thousands of dollars a week. If the drugs to which they are addicted were significantly cheaper—which would be the case if they were legalized—the number of crimes committed by drug addicts to pay for their habits would, in all likelihood, decline dramatically. Even if a legal-drug policy included the imposition of relatively high consumption taxes in order to discourage consumption, drug prices would probably still be lower than they are today.

The third drug/crime connection is the commission of crimes—violent crimes in particular—by people under the influence of illicit drugs. This connection seems to have the greatest impact upon the popular imagination. Clearly, some drugs do "cause" some people to commit crimes by reducing normal inhibitions, unleashing aggressive and other antisocial tendencies, and lessening the sense of responsibility. Cocaine, particularly in the form of crack, has gained such a reputation in recent years, just as heroin did in the 1960s and 1970s, and marijuana did in the years before that. Crack's reputation for inspiring violent behavior may or may not be more deserved than those of marijuana and heroin; reliable evidence is not yet available. No illicit drug, however, is as widely associated with violent behavior as alcohol. According to Justice Department statistics, 54 percent of all jail inmates convicted of violent crimes in 1983 reported having used alcohol just prior to committing their offense. The impact of drug legalization on this drug/crime connection is the most difficult to predict. Much would depend on overall rates of drug abuse and changes in the nature of consumption, both of which are impossible to predict. It is worth noting, however, that a shift in consumption from alcohol to marijuana would almost certainly contribute to a decline in violent behavior.

The fourth drug/crime link is the violent, intimidating, and corrupting behavior of the drug traffickers. Illegal markets tend to breed violence—not only because they attract criminally-minded individuals, but also because participants in the market have no resort to legal institutions to resolve their disputes. During Prohibition, violent struggles between bootlegging gangs and hijackings of booze-laden trucks and sea vessels were frequent and notorious occurrences. Today's equivalents are the booby traps that surround some marijuana fields, the pirates of the Caribbean looking to rip off drug-laden vessels en route to the shores of the United States, and the machine-gun battles and executions carried out by drug lords—all of which occasionally kill innocent people. Most law-enforcement officials agree that the dramatic increases in urban murder rates during the past few years can be explained almost entirely by the rise in drug-dealer killings.

Perhaps the most unfortunate victims of the drug-prohibition policies have been the law-abiding residents of America's ghettos. These policies have largely proven futile in deterring large numbers of ghetto dwellers from becoming drug abusers, but they do account for much of what ghetto residents identify as the drug problem. In many neighborhoods, it often seems to be the aggressive gun-toting drug dealers who upset law-abiding residents far more than the addicts nodding out in doorways. Other residents, however, perceive the drug dealers as heroes and successful role models. In impoverished neighborhoods, they often stand out as symbols of success to children who see no other options. At the same time, the increasingly harsh criminal penalties imposed on adult drug dealers have led to the widespread recruitment of juveniles by drug traffickers. Formerly, children started dealing drugs only after they had been using them for a while; today the sequence is often reversed: many children start using illegal drugs now only after working for older drug dealers. And the juvenile-justice system offers no realistic options for dealing with this growing problem.

The conspicuous failure of law-enforcement agencies to deal with this drug/crime connection is probably most responsible for the demoralization of neighborhoods and police departments alike. Intensive police crackdowns in urban neighborhoods do little more than chase the menace a short distance away to infect new areas. By contrast, legalization of the drug market would drive the drug-dealing business off the streets and out of the apartment buildings, and into legal, government-regulated, tax-paying stores. It would also force many of the gun-toting dealers out of business, and would convert others into legitimate businessmen. Some, of course, would turn to other types of criminal activities, just as some of the bootleggers did following Prohibition's repeal. Gone, however, would be the unparalleled financial temptations that lure so many people from all sectors of society into the drug-dealing business.

## The Costs of Corruption

All vice-control efforts are particularly susceptible to corruption, but none so much as drug enforcement. When police accept bribes from drug dealers, no victim exists to complain to the authorities. Even when police extort money and drugs from traffickers and dealers, the latter are in no position to report the corrupt officers. What makes drug enforcement especially vulnerable to corruption are the tremendous amounts of money involved in the business.

Today, many law-enforcement officials believe that police corruption is more pervasive than at any time since Prohibition. In Miami, dozens of law-enforcement officials have been charged with accepting bribes, stealing from drug dealers, and even dealing drugs themselves. Throughout many small towns and rural communities in Georgia, where drug smugglers en route from Mexico, the Caribbean, and Latin America drop their loads of cocaine and marijuana, dozens of sheriffs have been implicated in drug-related corruption. In New York, drug-related corruption in one Brooklyn police precinct has generated the city's most far-reaching police-corruption scandal since the 1960s. More than a hundred cases of drug-related corruption are now prosecuted each year in state and federal courts. Every one of the federal law-enforcement agencies charged with drug-enforcement responsibilities has seen an agent implicated in drug-related corruption.

It is not difficult to explain the growing pervasiveness of drug-related corruption. The financial temptations are enormous relative to other opportunities, legitimate or illegitimate. Little effort is required. Many police officers are demoralized by the scope of the drug traffic, their sense that many citizens are indifferent, and the fact that many sectors of society do not even appreciate their efforts—as well as the fact that many of the drug dealers who are arrested do not remain in prison. Some police also recognize that enforcing the drug laws does not protect victims from predators so much as it regulates an illicit market that cannot be suppressed, but can be kept underground. In every respect, the analogy to Prohibition is apt. Repealing the drug-prohibition laws would dramatically reduce police corruption. By contrast, the measures currently being proposed to deal with the growing problem, including better funded and more aggressive internal investigations, offer relatively little promise.

Among the most difficult costs to evaluate are those that relate to the widespread defiance of the drug-prohibition laws: the effects of labelling as criminals the tens of millions of people who use drugs illicitly, subjecting them to the risks of criminal sanction, and obliging many of these same people to enter into relationships with drug dealers (who may be criminals in many more senses of the word) in order to purchase their drugs; the cynicism that such laws generate toward other laws and the law in general; and the sense of hostility and suspicion that many otherwise law-abiding individuals feel toward law-enforcement officials. It was costs such as these that strongly influenced many of Prohibition's more conservative opponents.

## Physical and Moral Costs

Perhaps the most paradoxical consequence of the drug laws is the tremendous harm they cause to the millions of drug users who have not been deterred from using illicit drugs in the first place. Nothing resembling an underground Food and Drug Administration has arisen to impose quality control on the illegal-drug market and provide users with accurate information on the drugs they consume. Imagine that Americans could not tell whether a bottle of wine contained 6 percent, 30 percent, or 90 percent alcohol, or whether an aspirin tablet contained 5 or 500 grams of aspirin. Imagine, too, that no controls existed to prevent winemakers from diluting their product with methanol and other dangerous impurities, and that vineyards and tobacco fields were fertilized with harmful substances by ignorant growers and sprayed with poisonous herbicides by government agents. Fewer people would use such substances, but more of those who did would get sick. Some would die.

The above scenario describes, of course, the current state of the illicit drug market. Many marijuana smokers are worse off for having smoked cannabis that was grown with dangerous fertilizers, sprayed with the herbicide paraquat, or mixed with more dangerous substances. Consumers of heroin and the various synthetic substances sold on the street face even more severe consequences, including fatal overdoses and poisonings from unexpectedly potent or impure drug supplies. More often than not, the quality of a drug addict's life depends greatly upon his or her access to reliable supplies. Drug-enforcement operations that succeed in temporarily disrupting supply networks are thus a double-edged sword: they encourage some addicts to seek admission into drug-treatment programs, but they oblige others to seek out new and hence less reliable suppliers; the result is that more, not fewer, drug-related emergencies and deaths occur.

Today, over 50 percent of all people with AIDS in New York City, New Jersey, and many other parts of the country, as well as the vast majority of AIDS-infected heterosexuals throughout the country, have contracted the disease directly or indirectly through illegal intravenous drug use. Reports have emerged of drug dealers beginning to provide clean syringes together with their illegal drugs. But even as other governments around the world actively attempt to limit the spread of AIDS by and among drug users by instituting free syringe-exchange programs, state and municipal governments in the United States resist following suit, arguing that to do so would "encourage" or "condone" the use of illegal drugs. Only in January 1988 did New York City approve such a program on a very limited and experimental basis. At the same time, drug-treatment programs remain notoriously underfunded, turning away tens of thousands of addicts seeking help, even as billions of dollars more are spent to arrest, prosecute, and imprison illegal drug sellers and users. In what may represent a sign of shifting priorities, the President's Commission on AIDS, in its March 1988 report, emphasized the importance of making drug-treatment programs available to all in need of them. In all likelihood, however, the criminal-justice agencies will continue to receive the greatest share of drug-control funds.

Most Americans perceive the drug problem as a moral issue and draw a moral distinction between use of the illicit drugs and use of alcohol and tobacco. Yet when one subjects this distinction to reasoned analysis, it quickly disintegrates. The most consistent moral perspective of those who favor drug laws is that of the Mormons and the Puritans, who regard as immoral any intake of substances to alter one's state of consciousness or otherwise cause pleasure: they forbid not only the illicit drugs and alcohol, but also tobacco, caffeine, and even chocolate. The vast majority of Americans are hardly so consistent with respect to the propriety of their pleasures. Yet once one acknowledges that there is nothing immoral about drinking alcohol or smoking tobacco for non-medicinal purposes, it becomes difficult to condemn the consumption of marijuana, cocaine, and other substances on moral grounds. The "moral" condemnation of some substances and not others proves to be little more than a prejudice in favor of some drugs and against others.

The same false distinction is drawn with respect to those who provide the psychoactive substances to users and abusers alike. If degrees of immorality were measured by the levels of harm caused by one's products, the "traffickers" in tobacco and alcohol would be vilified as the most evil of all substance purveyors. That they are perceived instead as respected members of our community, while providers of the no-more-dangerous illicit substances are punished with long prison sentences, says much about the prejudices of most Americans with respect to psychoactive substances, but little about the morality or immorality of their activities.

Much the same is true of gun salesmen. Most of the consumers of their products use them safely; a minority, however, end up shooting either themselves or someone else. Can we hold the gun salesman morally culpable for the harm that probably would not have occurred but for his existence? Most people say no, except perhaps where the salesman clearly knew that his product would be used to commit a crime. Yet in the case of those who sell illicit substances to willing customers, the providers are deemed not only legally guilty, but also morally reprehensible. The law does not require any demonstration that the dealer knew of a specific harm to follow; indeed, it does not require any evidence at all of harm having resulted from the sale. Rather, the law is predicated on the assumption that harm will inevitably follow. Despite the patent falsity of that assumption, it persists as the underlying justification for the drug laws.

Although a valid moral distinction cannot be drawn between the licit and the illicit psychoactive substances, one can point to a different kind of moral justification for the drug laws: they arguably reflect a paternalistic obligation to protect those in danger of succumbing to their own weaknesses. If drugs were legally available, most people would either abstain from using them or would use them responsibly and in moderation. A minority without self-restraint, however, would end up harming themselves if the substances were more readily available. Therefore, the majority has a moral obligation to deny itself legal access to certain substances because of the plight of the minority. This obligation is presumably greatest when children are included among the minority.

At least in principle, this argument seems to provide the strongest moral justification for the drug laws. But ultimately the moral quality of laws must be judged not by how those laws are intended to work in principle, but by how they function in practice. When laws intended to serve a moral end inflict great damage on innocent parties, we must rethink our moral position.

Because drug-law violations do not create victims with an interest in notifying the police, drug-enforcement agents rely heavily on undercover operations, electronic surveillance, and information provided by informants. These techniques are indispensable to effective law enforcement, but they are also among the least palatable investigative methods employed by the police. The same is true of drug testing: it may be useful and even necessary for determining liability in accidents, but it also threatens and undermines the right of privacy to which many Americans believe they are entitled. There are good reasons for requiring that such measures be used sparingly.

Equally disturbing are the increasingly vocal calls for people to inform not only on drug dealers but also on neighbors, friends, and even family members who use illicit drugs. Government calls on people not only to "just say no," but also to report those who have not heeded the message. Intolerance of illicit-drug use and users is heralded not only as an indispensable ingredient in the war against drugs, but also as a mark of good citizenship. Certainly every society requires citizens to assist in the enforcement of criminal laws. But societies—particularly democratic and pluralistic ones—also rely strongly on an ethic of tolerance toward those who are different but do no harm to others. Overzealous enforcement of the drug laws risks undermining that ethic, and encouraging the creation of a society of informants. This results in an immorality that is far more dangerous in its own way than that associated with the use of illicit drugs.

## The Benefits of Legalization

Repealing the drug-prohibition laws promises tremendous advantages. Between reduced government expenditures on enforcing drug laws and new tax revenue from legal drug production and sales, public treasuries would enjoy a net benefit of at least ten billion dollars a year, and possibly much more. The quality of urban life would rise significantly. Homicide rates would decline. So would robbery and burglary rates. Organized criminal groups, particularly the newer ones that have yet to diversify out of drugs, would be dealt a devastating setback. The police, prosecutors, and courts would focus their resources on combatting the types of crimes that people cannot walk away from. More ghetto residents would turn their backs on criminal careers and seek out legitimate opportunities instead. And the health and quality of life of many drug users—and even drug abusers—would improve significantly.

All the benefits of legalization would be for naught, however, if millions more Americans were to become drug abusers. Our experience with alcohol and tobacco provides ample warnings. Today, alcohol is consumed by 140 million Americans and tobacco by 50 million. All of the health costs associated with abuse of the illicit drugs pale in comparison with those resulting from tobacco and alcohol abuse. In 1986, for example, alcohol was identified as a contributing factor in 10 percent of work-related injuries, 40 percent of suicide attempts, and about 40 percent of the approximately 46,000 annual traffic deaths in 1983. An estimated eighteen million Americans are reported to be either alcoholics or alcohol abusers. The total cost of alcohol abuse to American society is estimated at over 100 billion dollars annually. Alcohol has been identified as the direct cause of 80,000 to 100,000 deaths annually, and as a contributing factor in an additional 100,000 deaths. The health costs of tobacco use are of similar magnitude. In the United States alone, an estimated 320,000 people die prematurely each year as a consequence of their consumption of tobacco. By comparison, the National Council on Alcoholism reported that only 3,562 people were known to have died in 1985 from use of all illegal drugs combined. Even if we assume that thousands more deaths were related in one way or another to illicit drug abuse but not reported as such, we are still left with the conclusion that all of the health costs of marijuana, cocaine, and heroin combined amount to only a small fraction of those caused by tobacco and alcohol.

Most Americans are just beginning to recognize the extensive costs of alcohol and tobacco abuse. At the same time, they seem to believe that there is something fundamentally different about alcohol and tobacco that supports the legal distinction between those two substances, on the one hand, and the illicit ones, on the other. The most common distinction is based on the assumption that the illicit drugs are more dangerous than the licit ones. Cocaine, heroin, the various hallucinogens, and (to a lesser extent) marijuana are widely perceived as, in the words of the President's Commission on Organized Crime, "inherently destructive to mind and body." They are also believed to be more addictive and more likely to cause dangerous and violent behavior than alcohol and tobacco. All use of illicit drugs is therefore thought to be abusive; in other words, the distinction between use and abuse of psychoactive substances that most people recognize with respect to alcohol is not acknowledged with respect to the illicit substances.

Most Americans make the fallacious assumption that the government would not criminalize certain psychoactive substances if they were not in fact dangerous. They then jump to the conclusion that any use of those substances is a form of abuse. The government, in its effort to discourage people from using illicit drugs, has encouraged and perpetuated these misconceptions—not only in its rhetoric but also in its purportedly educational materials. Only by reading between the lines can one discern the fact that the vast majority of Americans who have used illicit drugs have done so in moderation, that relatively few have suffered negative short-term consequences, and that few are likely to suffer long-term harm.

The evidence is most persuasive with respect to marijuana. U.S. drug-enforcement and health agencies do not even report figures on marijuana-related deaths, apparently because so few occur. Although there are good health reasons for children, pregnant women, and some others not to smoke marijuana, there still appears to be little evidence that occasional marijuana consumption does much harm. Certainly, it is not healthy to inhale marijuana smoke into one's lungs; indeed, the National Institute on Drug Abuse (NIDA) has declared that "marijuana smoke contains more cancer-causing agents than is found in tobacco smoke." On the other hand, the number of joints smoked by all but a very small percentage of marijuana smokers is a tiny fraction of the twenty cigarettes a day smoked by the average cigarette smoker; indeed, the average may be closer to one or two joints a week than one or two a day. Note that NIDA defines a "heavy" marijuana smoker as one who consumes at least two joints "daily." A heavy tobacco smoker, by contrast, smokes about forty cigarettes a day.

Nor is marijuana strongly identified as a dependence-causing substance. A 1982 survey of marijuana use by young adults (eighteen to twenty-five years old) found that 64 percent had tried marijuana at least once, that 42 percent had used it at least ten times, and that 27 percent had smoked in the last month. It also found that 21 percent had passed through a period during which they smoked "daily" (defined as twenty or more days per month), but that only one-third of those currently smoked "daily" and only one-fifth (about 4 percent of all young adults) could be described as heavy daily users (averaging two or more joints per day). This suggests that daily marijuana use is typically a phase through which people pass, after which their use becomes more moderate.

Marijuana has also been attacked as the "gateway drug" that leads people to the use of even more dangerous illegal drugs. It is true that people who have smoked marijuana are more likely than people who have not to try, use, and abuse other illicit substances. It is also true that people who have smoked tobacco or drunk alcohol are more likely than those who have not to experiment with illicit drugs and to become substance abusers. The reasons are obvious enough. Familiarity with smoking cigarettes, for instance, removes one of the major barriers to smoking marijuana, which is the experience of inhaling smoke into one's lungs. Similarly, familiarity with altering one's state of consciousness by consuming psychoactive substances such as alcohol or marijuana decreases the fear and increases the curiosity regarding other substances and "highs." But the evidence also indicates that there is nothing inevitable about the process. The great majority of people who have smoked marijuana do not become substance abusers of either legal or illegal substances. At the same time, it is certainly true that many of those who do become substance abusers after using marijuana would have become abusers even if they had never smoked a joint in their life.

## Dealing with Drugs' Dangers

The dangers associated with cocaine, heroin, the hallucinogens, and other illicit substances are greater than those posed by marijuana, but not nearly so great as many people seem to think. Consider the case of cocaine. In 1986 NIDA reported that over 20 million Americans had tried cocaine, that 12.2 million had consumed it at least once during 1985, and that nearly 5.8 million had used it within the past month. Among those between the ages of eighteen and twenty-five, 8.2 million had tried cocaine, 5.3 million had used it within the past year, 2.5 million had used it within the past month, and 250,000 had used it weekly. Extrapolation might suggest that a quarter of a million young Americans are potential problem users. But one could also conclude that only 3 percent of those between the ages of eighteen and twenty-five who had ever tried the drug fell into that category, and that only 10 percent of those who had used cocaine monthly were at risk. (The NIDA survey did not, it should be noted, include people residing in military or student dormitories, prison inmates, or the homeless.)

All of this is not to deny that cocaine is a potentially dangerous drug, especially when it is injected, smoked in the form of crack, or consumed in tandem with other powerful substances. Clearly, tens of thousands of Americans have suffered severely from their abuse of cocaine, and a tiny fraction have died. But there is also overwhelming evidence that most users of cocaine do not get into trouble with the drug. So much of the media attention has focused on the small percentage of cocaine users who become addicted that the popular perception of how most people use cocaine has become badly distorted. In one survey of high school seniors' drug use, the researchers questioned recent cocaine users, asking whether they had ever tried to stop using cocaine and found that they couldn't. Only 3.8 percent responded affirmatively, in contrast to the almost 7 percent of marijuana smokers who said they had tried to stop and found they couldn't, and the 18 percent of cigarette smokers who answered similarly. Although a similar survey of adult users would probably reveal a higher proportion of cocaine addicts, evidence such as this suggests that only a small percentage of people who use cocaine end up having a problem with it. In this respect, most people differ from monkeys, who have demonstrated in experiments that they will starve themselves to death if provided with unlimited cocaine.

With respect to the hallucinogens such as LSD and psilocybic mushrooms, their potential for addiction is virtually nil. The dangers arise primarily from using them irresponsibly on individual occasions. Although many of those who have used one or another of the hallucinogens have experienced "bad trips," others have reported positive experiences, and very few have suffered any long-term harm.

Perhaps no drugs are regarded with as much horror as the opiates, and in particular heroin, which is a concentrated form of morphine. As with most drugs, heroin can be eaten, snorted, smoked, or injected. Most Americans, unfortunately, prefer injection. There is no question that heroin is potentially highly addictive, perhaps as addictive as nicotine. But despite the popular association of heroin use with the most down-and-out inhabitants of urban ghettos, heroin causes relatively little physical harm to the human body. Consumed on an occasional or regular basis under sanitary conditions, its worst side effect, apart from addiction itself, is constipation. That is one reason why many doctors in early twentieth-century America saw opiate addiction as preferable to alcoholism, and prescribed the former as treatment for the latter when abstinence did not seem a realistic option.

It is important to think about the illicit drugs in the same way we think about alcohol and tobacco. Like tobacco, many of the illicit substances are highly addictive, but can be consumed on a regular basis for decades without any demonstrable harm. Like alcohol, most of the substances can be, and are, used by most consumers in moderation, with little in the way of harmful effects; but like alcohol, they also lend themselves to abuse by a minority of users who become addicted or otherwise harm themselves or others as a consequence. And as is the case with both the legal substances, the psychoactive effects of the various illegal drugs vary greatly from one person to another. To be sure, the pharmacology of the substance is important, as is its purity and the manner in which it is consumed. But much also depends upon not only the physiology and psychology of the consumer, but also his expectations regarding the drug, his social milieu, and the broader cultural environment— what Harvard University psychiatrist Norman Zinberg has called the "set and setting" of the drug. It is factors such as these that might change dramatically, albeit in indeterminate ways, were the illicit drugs made legally available.

## Can Legalization Work?

It is thus impossible to predict whether legalization would lead to much greater levels of drug abuse, and exact costs comparable to those of alcohol and tobacco abuse. The lessons that can be drawn from other societies are mixed. China's experience with the British opium pushers of the nineteenth century, when millions became addicted to the drug, offers one worst-case scenario. The devastation of many native American tribes by alcohol presents another. On the other hand, the legal availability of opium and cannabis in many Asian societies did not result in large addict populations until recently. Indeed, in many countries U.S.-inspired opium bans imposed during the past few decades have paradoxically contributed to dramatic increases in heroin consumption among Asian youth. Within the United States, the decriminalization of marijuana by about a dozen states during the 1970s did not lead to increases in marijuana consumption. In the Netherlands, which went even further in decriminalizing cannabis during the 1970s, consumption has actually declined significantly. The policy has succeeded, as the government intended, in making drug use boring. Finally, late nineteenth-century America was a society in which there were almost no drug laws or even drug regulations—but levels of drug use then were about what they are today. Drug abuse was considered a serious problem, but the criminal-justice system was not regarded as part of the solution.

There are, however, reasons to believe that none of the currently illicit substances would become as popular as alcohol or tobacco, even if they were legalized. Alcohol has long been the principal intoxicant in most societies, including many in which other substances have been legally available. Presumably, its diverse properties account for its popularity—it quenches thirst, goes well with food, and promotes appetite as well as sociability. The popularity of tobacco probably stems not just from its powerful addictive qualities, but from the fact that its psychoactive effects are sufficiently subtle that cigarettes can be integrated with most other human activities. The illicit substances do not share these qualities to the same extent, nor is it likely that they would acquire them if they were legalized. Moreover, none of the illicit substances can compete with alcohol's special place in American culture and history.

An additional advantage of the illicit drugs is that none of them appears to be as insidious as either alcohol or tobacco. Consumed in their more benign forms, few of the illicit substances are as damaging to the human body over the long term as alcohol and tobacco, and none is as strongly linked with violent behavior as alcohol. On the other hand, much of the damage caused today by illegal drugs stems from their consumption in particularly dangerous ways. There is good reason to doubt that many Americans would inject cocaine or heroin into their veins even if given the chance to do so legally. And just as the dramatic growth in the heroin-consuming population during the 1960s leveled off for reasons apparently having little to do with law enforcement, so we can expect a levelling-off—which may already have begun—in the number of people smoking crack. The logic of legalization thus depends upon two assumptions: that most illegal drugs are not so dangerous as is commonly believed; and that the drugs and methods of consumption that are most risky are unlikely to prove appealing to many people, precisely because they are so obviously dangerous.

Perhaps the most reassuring reason for believing that repeal of the drug-prohibition laws will not lead to tremendous increases in drug-abuse levels is the fact that we have learned something from our past experiences with alcohol and tobacco abuse. We now know, for instance, that consumption taxes are an effective method of limiting consumption rates. We also know that restrictions and bans on advertising, as well as a campaign of negative advertising, can make a difference. The same is true of other government measures, including restrictions on time and place of sale, prohibition of consumption in public places, packaging requirements, mandated adjustments in insurance policies, crackdowns on driving while under the influence, and laws holding bartenders and hosts responsible for the drinking of customers and guests. There is even some evidence that government-sponsored education programs about the dangers of cigarette smoking have deterred many children from beginning to smoke.

Clearly it is possible to avoid repeating the mistakes of the past in designing an effective plan for legalization. We know more about the illegal drugs now than we knew about alcohol when Prohibition was repealed, or about tobacco when the anti-tobacco laws were repealed by many states in the early years of this century. Moreover, we can and must avoid having effective drug-control policies undermined by powerful lobbies like those that now protect the interests of alcohol and tobacco producers. We are also in a far better position than we were sixty years ago to prevent organized criminals from finding and creating new opportunities when their most lucrative source of income dries up.

It is important to stress what legalization is not. It is not a capitulation to the drug dealers—but rather a means to put them out of business. It is not an endorsement of drug use—but rather a recognition of the rights of adult Americans to make their own choices free of the fear of criminal sanctions. It is not a repudiation of the "just say no" approach—but rather an appeal to government to provide assistance and positive inducements, not criminal penalties and more repressive measures, in support of that approach. It is not even a call for the elimination of the criminal-justice system from drug regulation—but rather a proposal for the redirection of its efforts and attention.

There is no question that legalization is a risky policy, since it may lead to an increase in the number of people who abuse drugs. But that is a risk—not a certainty. At the same time, current drug-control policies are failing, and new proposals promise only to be more costly and more repressive. We know that repealing the drug-prohibition laws would eliminate or greatly reduce many of the ills that people commonly identify as part and parcel of the "drug problem." Yet legalization is repeatedly and vociferously dismissed, without any attempt to evaluate it openly and objectively. The past twenty years have demonstrated that a drug policy shaped by exaggerated rhetoric designed to arouse fear has only led to our current disaster. Unless we are willing to honestly evaluate our options, including various legalization strategies, we will run a still greater risk: we may never find the best solution for our drug problems.

## Notes

[1] The total number of state and federal prison inmates in 1975 was under 250,000; in 1980 it was 350,000; and in 1987 it was 575,000. The projected total for 2000 is one million.

[2] It should be emphasized that the numbers cited do not include the many inmates sentenced for "drug-related" crimes such as acts of violence committed by drug dealers, typically against one another, and robberies committed to earn the money needed to pay for illegal drugs.

# 21

## Legalization
### A High-Risk Alternative in the War on Drugs

## James A. Inciardi
## Duane C. McBride

Ever since the passage of the Harrison Act in 1914, American drug policy has had its critics (see Lindesmith, 1965; King, 1972; Musto, 1973). The basis of the negative assessments has been the restrictive laws designed to control the possession and distribution of narcotics and other "dangerous drugs," the mechanisms of drug law enforcement, and the apparent lack of success in reducing both the *supply of* and the *demand for* illicit drugs.

During 1988, concerns over the perceived failure of American drug policy spirited a national debate over whether contemporary drug control approaches ought to be abandoned, and replaced with the decriminalization,

Reprinted by permission of Sage Publications, from *American Behavioral Scientist*, Vol. 32, No. 3, pp. 259–289, © 1989 by Sage Publications, Inc.

if not the outright legalization, of most or all illicit drugs. Most vocal in supporting legalization have been Ernest van den Haag (1985), professor of jurisprudence and public policy at Fordham University; Ethan A. Nadelmann (1987, 1988a, 1988b) of the Woodrow Wilson School of Public and International Affairs at Princeton University; free-market economist Milton Friedman (Friedman and Friedman, 1984); Gary S. Becker (1987), professor of economics and sociology at the University of Chicago; and freelance writer Harry Schwartz (1987).

The arguments posed by the supporters of legalization seem all too logical. *First*, they argue, the drug laws have created evils far worse than the drugs themselves—corruption, violence, street crime, and disrespect for the law. *Second*, legislation passed to control drugs has failed to reduce demand. *Third*, you cannot have illegal that which a significant segment of the population in any society is committed to doing. You simply cannot arrest, prosecute, and punish such large numbers of people, particularly in a democracy. And specifically in this behalf, in a liberal democracy the government must not interfere with personal behavior if liberty is to be maintained. And *fourth*, they add, if marijuana, cocaine, heroin, and other drugs were legalized, a number of very positive things would happen:

1. Drug prices would fall.

2. Users could obtain their drugs at low, government-regulated prices and would no longer be forced to engage in prostitution and street crime to support their habits.

3. The fact that the levels of drug-related crime would significantly decline would result in less crowded courts, jails, and prisons, and would free law enforcement personnel to focus their energies on the "real criminals" in society.

4. Drug production, distribution, and sale would be removed from the criminal arena; no longer would it be within the province of organized crime, and therefore, such criminal syndicates as the Medellin Cartel and the Jamaican posses would be decapitalized and the violence associated with drug distribution rivalries would be eliminated.

5. Government corruption and intimidation by traffickers as well as drug-based foreign policies would be effectively reduced, if not eliminated entirely.

6. The often draconian measures undertaken by police to enforce the drug laws would be curtailed, thus restoring to the American public many of its hard-won civil liberties.

To these contentions can be added the argument that legalization in any form or structure would have only a minimal impact on current drug use levels. Apparently, there is the assumption that given the existing levels of access to most illegal drugs, current levels of use closely match demand. Thus there would be no additional health, safety, behavioral, and/or other problems accompanying legalization. And, finally, a few protagonists of legalization make one concluding point. Through government regulation of drugs, the billions of dollars spent annually on drug enforcement could be better utilized. Moreover, by taxing government-regulated drugs, revenues would be collected that could be used for preventing drug abuse and treating those harmed by drugs.

The argument for legalization seems to boil down to the basic belief that America's prohibitions against marijuana, cocaine, heroin, and other drugs impose far too large a cost in terms of tax dollars, crime, and infringements on civil rights and individual liberties. And while the overall argument may be well intended and appear quite logical, it is highly questionable in its historical, sociocultural, and empirical underpinnings, and demonstrably naive in its understanding of the negative consequences of a legalized drug market.

Within the context of these opening remarks, what follows is an analysis of the content of legalization proposals combined with a discussion of the more likely consequences of such a drastic alteration in drug policy.

## The Incomplete Content of Drug Legalization Proposals

At the outset, current legalization proposals are not proposals at all! Although legalizing drugs has been debated ever since the passage of the Harrison Act in 1914, never has an advocate of the position structured a logical and concrete proposal. Any attempt to legalize drugs would be extremely complex, but proponents seem to proceed from a simplistic "shoot-from-the-hip" position without first developing any sophisticated proposals. Even in 1988, amid the clamor for legalization, there was still no specific proposal on the table. And in this regard, there are many questions that would need to be addressed, including:

1.  What drugs should be legalized? Marijuana? Heroin? Cocaine? And if cocaine is designated for legalization, should proposals include such coca products as crack and other forms of freebase cocaine? Should the list include *basuco* (coca paste), that potent and highly toxic processing derivative of the coca leaf? There are other drugs to be considered as well. Which hallucinogenic drugs should be legalized? LSD? Peyote? Mescaline? What about

Quaaludes? Should they be returned to the legal market? And let's not forget *ecstasy* and the various designer drugs. In short, which drugs should be legalized, according to what criteria, and who should determine the criteria?

2. Assuming that some rationally determined slate of drugs could be designated for legalization, what potency levels should be permitted? Like 80, 100, and 151 proof rum, should marijuana with 5 percent, 10 percent, and 14 percent THC content be permitted? Should legalized heroin be restricted to Burmese No. 3 grade, or should Mexican "black tar" and the mythical "China White" be added to the ledger?

3. As with alcohol, should there be age limits as to who *can* and *cannot* use drugs? Should those old enough to drive be permitted to buy and use drugs? And which drugs? Should it be that 16-year-olds can buy pot and Quaaludes, but have to wait until 18 for cocaine and crack, and 21 for heroin?

4. Should certain drugs be limited to only those already dependent on them? In other words, should heroin sales be restricted to heroin addicts and cocaine sales limited to cocaine addicts? And if this approach is deemed viable, what do we say to the heroin addicts who want to buy cocaine? In other words, do we legalize heroin and cocaine sales but forbid speedballing? And then, what about drug experimenters? Should they be permitted access to the legal drug market? And assuming that these issues can be decided, *in what amounts* can users—regardless of their drugs of choice—purchase heroin, cocaine, marijuana, Quaaludes, and other chemical substances?

5. Where should the drugs be sold? Over the counter in drug and grocery stores, as is the case with many pharmaceuticals? Through mail-order houses? In special vending machines strategically located in public restrooms, hotel lobbies, and train and bus stations? In tax- supported "drug shacks," as representative Charles Rangel (*Drug Abuse Report*, May 17, 1988:7) satirically asked? Should some, or all, of the newly legalized drugs be available only on a prescription basis? And if this be the case, should a visit to a physician be necessary to get a prescription? And for how many tabs, lines, lids, bags, rocks, joints, or whatever, should prescriptions be written? How often should these prescriptions be refillable?

6. Where should the raw material for the drugs originate? Would cultivation be restricted to U.S. lands, or would foreign sources be permitted? Coca from Bolivia and Peru, or from all of South America

and Java, as well? Marijuana from Colombia and Jamaica? Opium from Mexico, Laos, Thailand, or from the "Golden Crescent" countries of Iran, Afghanistan, and Pakistan? Should trade restrictions of any type be imposed—by drug, amount, potency, purity, or by country? Should legalization policies permit the introduction of currently little- known drugs of abuse into the U.S. from foreign ports, such as *qat* from Yemen, *bekaro* from Pakistan, and *mambog* from the Southeast Asian countries?[1]

7. If drugs are to be legalized, should the drug market be a totally free one, with private industry establishing the prices, as well as levels of purity and potency? What kinds of advertising should be permitted? Should advertisements for some drugs be allowed, but not others? Should Timothy Leary and Manuel Noriega be permitted to endorse certain drugs or brands of drugs as part of advertising programs?

8. If drugs are to be legalized, what types of restrictions on their use should be structured? Should transportation workers, nuclear plant employees, or other categories of workers be forbidden to use them at all times, or just while they are on duty?

9. As is the case with alcohol, will certain establishments be permitted to serve drugs (and which drugs) to their customers? And similarly, as is the case with cigarettes, should there be separate drug-using and non-drug-using sections in restaurants, on planes and trains, and in the workplace? As with coffee and cigarette breaks, should users be permitted pot and coke breaks as part of their union contracts or employer policies?

10. For any restrictions placed on sales, potency levels, distribution, prices, quantity, and advertising in a legalized drug market, what government bureaucracy should be charged with the enforcement of the legalization statutes? The Federal Bureau of Investigation (FBI)? The Drug Enforcement Administration (DEA)? The Food and Drug Administration (FDA)? The Bureau of Alcohol, Tobacco, and Firearms (ATF)? State and local law enforcement agencies? Or should some new federal bureaucracy be created for the purpose? Going further, what kinds of penalties ought to be established for violation of the legalization restrictions?

There are likely many more questions. In short, the whole idea of even articulating a legalization policy is complex. Not only have legalization proponents failed to answer the questions, they have yet to even pose them. Moreover, anyone attempting to structure a serious proposal highlighting the beneficial expectations of a legalization policy would find little support for his or her arguments in either published research data or clinical experience. By contrast, there are numerous legitimate arguments against the legalization of drugs, all of which have considerable empirical, historical, pharmacological, and/or clinical support.

## Some Public Health and Behavioral Consequences of Drug Use

Considerable evidence exists to suggest that the legalization of drugs would create behavioral and public health problems to a degree that would far outweigh the current consequences of the drug prohibition. There are some excellent reasons why marijuana, cocaine, heroin, and other drugs are now controlled, and why they ought to remain so. What follows is a brief look at a few of these drugs.

*Marijuana.* There is considerable misinformation about marijuana. To the millions of adolescents and young adults who were introduced to the drug during the social revolution of the 1960s and early 1970s, marijuana was a harmless herb of ecstasy. As the "new social drug" and a "natural organic product," it was deemed to be far less harmful than either alcohol or tobacco (see Grinspoon, 1971; Smith, 1970; Sloman, 1979). More recent research suggests, however, that marijuana smoking is a practice that combines the hazardous features of both tobacco and alcohol with a number of pitfalls of its own. Moreover, there are many disturbing questions about marijuana's effect on the vital systems of the body, on the brain and mind, on immunity and resistance, and on sex and reproduction (Jones and Lovinger, 1985).

One of the more serious difficulties with marijuana use relates to lung damage. The most recent findings in this behalf should put to rest the rather tiresome argument by marijuana devotees that smoking just a few "joints" daily is less harmful than regularly smoking several times as many cigarettes. Researchers at the University of California (Los Angeles) reported early in 1988 that the respiratory burden in smoke particulates and absorption of carbon monoxide from smoking just one marijuana joint is some four times greater than from smoking a single tobacco cigarette (MacDonald, 1988). Specifically, it was found that one "toke" of marijuana delivers three times more tar to the mouth and lungs than one puff of a filter-tipped cigarette; that marijuana deposits four times more tar in the throat and lungs and increases carbon monoxide levels in the blood fourfold to fivefold.

There seem to be three distinct sets of facts about marijuana its apologists tend to downplay—if not totally ignore—about its chemical structure, its "persistence-of-residue" effect, and its changing potency.

*First*, the *cannabis sativa* plant from which marijuana comes is a complex chemical factory. Marijuana, which is made up of the dried leaves and flowering tops of the plant, contains 426 known chemicals, which are transformed into 2,000 chemicals when burned during the smoking process. Seventy of these chemicals are *cannabinoids*, substances that are found nowhere else in nature. Since they are fat-soluble, they are immediately deposited in those body tissues that have a high fat content—the brain, lungs, liver, and reproductive organs.

*Second*, the fact that THC (delta-9-tetrahydrocannabinol), the active ingredient and most potent psychoactive chemical in marijuana, is soluble in fat but not in water has a significant implication. The human body has a water-based waste disposal system—blood, urine, sweat, and feces. A chemical such as THC that does not dissolve in water becomes trapped, principally in the brain, lungs, liver, and reproductive organs. This is the "persistence-of-residue" effect. One puff of smoke from a marijuana cigarette delivers a significant amount of THC, half of which remains for several weeks. As such, if a person is smoking marijuana more than once a month, the residue levels of THC are not only retained but also building up—in the brain, lungs, liver, and reproductive organs.

*Third*, the potency of marijuana has risen dramatically over the years. During the 1960s the THC content of marijuana was only two-tenths of one percent. By the 1980s the potency of imported marijuana was up to 5 percent, representing a 25-fold increase. Moreover, California *sinsemilla*, a seedless, domestic variety of marijuana, has a THC potency of 14 percent. In fact, so potent is sinsemilla that it has become the "pot of choice" both inside and outside the United States. On the streets of Bogotá, Colombia, sinsemilla is traded for cocaine on an equal weight basis (*Street Pharmacologist*, May/June 1988:5).

*Fourth*, and finally, aside from the health consequences of marijuana use, recent research on the behavioral aspects of the drug suggests that it severely affects the social perceptions of heavy users. Findings from the Center for Psychological Studies in New York City, for example, indicated that adults who smoked marijuana daily believed the drug helped them to function better—improving their self-awareness and relationships with others (Hendin et al., 1987). In reality, however, marijuana had served to be a "buffer," so to speak, enabling users to tolerate problems rather than face them and make changes that might increase the quality of their social functioning and satisfaction with life. The study found that the research subjects used marijuana to avoid dealing with their difficulties, and the avoidance inevitably made their problems worse—on the job, at home, and in family and sexual relationships.

This research documented what clinicians had been saying for years. Personal growth evolves from learning to cope with stress, anxiety, frustration, and the many other difficulties that life presents, both small and large. Marijuana use (and the use of other drugs as well, including alcohol), particularly among adolescents and young adults, interferes with this process, and the result is a drug-induced arrested development (see DuPont, 1984).

*Cocaine.* Lured by the Lorelei of orgasmic pleasure, millions of Americans use cocaine each year—a snort in each nostril and the user is up and away for 20 minutes or so. Alert, witty, and with it, the user has no hangover, no lung cancer, and no holes in the arms or burned- out cells in the brain. The cocaine high is an immediate, intensively vivid, and sensation-enhancing experience. Moreover, it has the reputation for being a spectacular aphrodisiac: It is believed to create sexual desire, to heighten it, to increase sexual endurance, and to cure frigidity and impotence.

Given all these positives, it is no wonder that cocaine has become an "all-American drug" and a multibillion-dollar-a-year industry. It permeates all levels of society, from Park Avenue to the ghetto: Lawyers and executives use cocaine; baby boomers and yuppies use cocaine; college students and high school dropouts use cocaine; police officers, prosecutors, and prisoners use cocaine; politicians use cocaine; housewives and pensioners use cocaine; Democrats, Republicans, Independents, and Socialists use cocaine; barmaids and stockbrokers and children and athletes use cocaine; even some priests and members of Congress use cocaine.

Yet the pleasure and feelings of power that cocaine engenders make its use a rather unwise recreational pursuit. In very small and occasional doses it is no more harmful than equally moderate doses of alcohol, but there is a side to cocaine that can be very destructive. That euphoric lift, with its feelings of pleasure, confidence, and being on top of things, that comes from but a few brief snorts is short-lived and invariably followed by a letdown. More specifically, when the elation and grandiose feelings begin to wane, a corresponding depression is often felt, which is in such marked contrast to users' previous states that they are strongly motivated to repeat the dose and restore the euphoria. This leads to chronic, compulsive use. And when chronic users try to stop using cocaine, they are typically plunged into a severe depression from which only more cocaine can arouse them. Most clinicians estimate that approximately 10 percent of those who begin to use cocaine "recreationally" will go on to serious, heavy, chronic, compulsive use (Grabowski, 1984; Kozel and Adams, 1985; Erickson et al., 1987; Spita et al., 1987).

To this can be added what is known as the "cocaine psychosis" (Weiss and Mirin, 1987:50–53). As dose and duration of cocaine use increase, the development of cocaine- related psychopathology is not uncommon. Cocaine psychosis is generally preceded by a transitional period characterized by increased suspiciousness, compulsive behavior, fault finding, and eventually paranoia. When the psychotic state is reached, individuals may experience visual and/or auditory hallucinations, with persecutory voices commonly heard. Many believe that they are being followed by police or that family, friends, and others are plotting against them. Moreover, everyday events tend to be misinterpreted in ways that support delusional beliefs. When coupled with the irritability and hyperactivity that the stimulant nature of cocaine tends to generate in almost all of its users, the cocaine-induced paranoia may lead to violent behavior as a means of "self-defense" against imagined persecutors.

Not to be forgotten are the physiological consequences of cocaine use. Since the drug is an extremely potent central nervous system stimulant, its physical effects include increased temperature, heart rate, and blood pressure. In addition to the many thousands of cocaine- related hospital emergency visits that occur year to year, there has been a steady increase in the annual number of cocaine-induced deaths in the United States, from only 53 in 1976 to almost 1,000 a decade later. And while these numbers may seem infinitesimal when compared with the magnitude of alcohol and tobacco-related deaths, it should be remembered that at present only a small segment of the American population uses cocaine.

*Crack.* Given the considerable media attention that crack has received since the summer of 1986, it would appear that only a minimal description of the drug is warranted here. Briefly, *crack*-cocaine is likely best described as a "fast-food" variety of cocaine. It is a pebble-sized crystalline form of cocaine base, and has become extremely popular because it is inexpensive and easy to produce. Moreover, since crack is smoked rather than snorted, it is more rapidly absorbed than cocaine—reportedly crossing the blood-brain barrier within six seconds (Inciardi, 1987a)—creating an almost instantaneous high.

Crack's low price (as little as $3 per rock in some locales) has made it an attractive drug of abuse for those with limited funds, particularly adolescents. Its rapid absorption initiates a faster onset of dependence than is typical with cocaine, resulting in higher rates of addiction, binge use, and psychoses. The consequences include higher levels of cocaine-related violence and all the same manifestations of personal, familial, and occupational neglect that are associated with other forms of drug dependence.[2]

*Heroin.* A derivative of morphine, heroin is a highly addictive narcotic, and the drug historically most associated with both addiction and street crime. Although heroin overdose is not uncommon, unlike alcohol, cocaine, tobacco, and many prescription drugs, the direct physiological damage caused by heroin use tends to be minimal. And it is for this reason that the protagonists of drug legalization include heroin in their arguments. By making heroin readily available to users, they argue, many problems could be sharply reduced if not totally eliminated, including the crime associated with supporting a heroin habit; the overdoses resulting from problematic levels of heroin purity and potency; the HIV (human immunodeficiency virus) and hepatitis infections brought about by needle-sharing; and the personal, social, and occupational dislocations resulting from the drug-induced criminal life-style.[3]

The belief that the legalization of heroin would eliminate crime, overdose, infections, and life dislocations is for the most part delusional, for it is likely that the heroin use life-style would change little for most American addicts, regardless of the legal status of the drug. And there is ample evidence to support this argument—in the biographies and autobiographies of narcotics addicts (Anonymous, 1903; Burroughs, 1953; Fisher, 1972; Hirsch, 1968; Street, 1953; Rettig et al., 1977), in the clinical and ethnographic assessments of heroin addiction (Fiddle, 1967; Gould et al., 1974; Rosenbaum, 1981), and in the treatment literature (Smith and Gay, 1971; Nyswander, 1956; Platt, 1986; Peele, 1985). And to this can be added the many thousands of conversations conducted by the authors with heroin users during the past two decades.

The point is this. Heroin is a highly addicting drug. For the addict, it becomes life consuming: It becomes mother, father, spouse, lover, counselor, confidant, and confessor. Because heroin is a short-acting drug, with its effects lasting at best four to six hours, it must be taken regularly and repeatedly. Because there is a more rapid onset when taken intravenously, most heroin users inject the drug. Because heroin has depressant effects, a portion of the user's day is spent in a semistupified state. Collectively, these attributes result in a user more concerned with drug-taking than health, family, work, or anything else.

As a final note to this section, and perhaps most importantly, recently completed research by professors Michael D. Newcomb and Peter M. Bentler (1988) of the University of California at Los Angeles has documented the long-term behavioral effects of drug use on teenagers. Beginning in 1976 a total of 654 Los Angeles County youths were tracked for a period of eight years. Most of these youths were only occasional users of drugs, using drugs and alcohol moderately at social gatherings, whereas upwards of 10 percent were frequent, committed users. The impact of drugs on these frequent users was considerable. As teenagers, drug use tended to intensify the typical adolescent problems with family and school. In addition, drugs contributed to such psychological difficulties as loneliness, bizarre and disorganized thinking, and suicidal thoughts. Moreover, frequent drug users left school earlier, started jobs earlier, and formed families earlier, and as such, they moved into adult roles with the maturity levels of adolescents. The consequences of this pattern included rapid family break-ups, job instability, serious crime, and ineffective personal relationships. In short, frequent drug use prevented the acquisition of the coping mechanisms that are part of maturing; it blocked teenagers' learning of interpersonal skills and general emotional development.

---

## Drugs, Street Crime, and the Enslavement Theory of Addiction

---

For the better part of the current century there has been a concerted belief in what has become known as the "enslavement theory of addiction"—the conviction that because of the high prices of heroin and cocaine on the drug black market, users are forced to commit crimes in order to support their drug habits (Inciardi, 1986:145–173). In this regard, supporters of drug legalization argue that if the criminal penalties attached to heroin and cocaine possession and sale were removed, three things would occur: The black market would disappear, the prices of heroin and cocaine would decline significantly, and users would no longer have to engage in street crime in order to support their desired levels of drug intake. Yet there has never been any solid empirical evidence to support the contentions of enslavement theory.

From the 1920s through the close of the 1960s, hundreds of studies of the relationship between crime and addiction were conducted.[4] Invariably, when one analysis would support enslavement theory, the next would affirm the view that addicts were criminals first, and that their drug use was but one more manifestation of their deviant life-styles. In retrospect, the difficulty lay in the way the studies had been conducted, with biases and deficiencies in research designs that rendered their findings to be of little value.

Research since the middle of the 1970s with active drug users in the streets of New York, Miami, Baltimore, and elsewhere, on the other hand, has demonstrated that enslavement theory has little basis in reality, and that the contentions of the legalization proponents in this behalf are mistaken (Inciardi, 1986:115–143; Johnson et al., 1985; Nurco et al., 1985; Stephens and McBride, 1976; McBride and McCoy, 1982). All of these studies of the criminal careers of heroin and other drug users have convincingly documented that while drug use tends to intensify and perpetuate criminal behavior, it usually does not initiate criminal careers. In fact, the evidence suggests that among the majority of street drug users who are involved in crime, their criminal careers were well established prior to the onset of either narcotics or cocaine use.

## Some Cost/Benefit Considerations of Legalization

An explicit, or at least considerably implicit, assumption of the legalization argument is that the purported benefits of legalization (reduced crime, corruption, criminal justice system costs, and increased tax revenues) will far outweigh any costs that may ensue (increased drug use and its consequences, if any). In particular, any increases in the use of the legalized substances will be insignificant, and thus there will be only minimal increases in the costs of health care and public safety. Given this, it would appear that the prolegalization lobby believes that since marijuana, cocaine, crack, heroin, and other illegal drugs are so widely available, to a significant extent there is market demand saturation. While hard evidence of the validity of this assumption is anything but apparent, there are a variety of historical and empirical data that seriously contradict its basic contention.

At the outset, it should be noted that national and local surveys clearly indicate that young people perceive fairly open access to most illegal substances. Consider, first, some findings from one of the more recent surveys of America's high school seniors, conducted each year by the Institute for Social Research at the University of Michigan. Among those surveyed in 1986 for example, just over 50 percent reported that access to cocaine was easy, with 85 percent suggesting the same for marijuana, and 22 percent reporting the same ease of access to heroin (Bachman et al., 1987). By contrast, less than one-third of the nation's high school seniors reported that it was probably impossible to obtain any of these drugs. In addition, similar perceptions of easy access to drugs have been found even among small-town and rural mid-American high school students (McBride et al., 1988). As such, the assumption of ease of access appears to have a reasonable basis in empirical data.

The more important question revolves around the assumption that legalization will have minimal impact on use, that most or all those who would use drugs are now doing so. Such an assumption appears to ignore one of the most powerful aspects of American tradition: the ability of an entrepreneurial market system to create, expand, and maintain high levels of demand.

As noted previously, specific legalization proposals do not exist at present. As such, there has never been any serious discussion of how the issues of advertising and marketing might be handled. However, if the treatment of such *legal* drugs as alcohol and tobacco are used as models of regulatory control, then it is reasonable to assume an application of free speech rights to legalized drugs. And this indeed would be logical; for after all, the drugs would be *legal* products. And similarly, it would not seem unreasonable to assume that the American market economy would become strongly involved in expanding and maintaining demand for the legalized substances. The successes of tobacco and alcohol advertising programs are eminently conspicuous. The linking of smoking with women's rights has been masterful. The linking of alcohol with the pursuit of happiness after work, in recreational activities, and in romantic liaisons has been so effective that during 1987 alone, Americans spent some $71.9 billion on beer, wine, and distilled spirits (*Drug Abuse Update*, June 1988:5).

In an America where drugs are legal, how far will advertisers go? Will they show students, executives, and truck drivers—overworked and faced with tight schedules and deadlines—reaching for a line of cocaine instead of a cup of coffee? Will cocaine be touted as the mark of success in an achievement-oriented society? Will heroin be portrayed as the real way to relax after a harried day? Will the new "Marlboro man" be smoking marijuana or crack instead of tobacco? These are not fanciful speculations, for there are many controlled substances that are regularly advertised, even if only in the medical media. Regardless, the focus of advertising is to market a product by creating and maintaining demand.

The issue, then, of whether the market is saturated fails to recognize the ability of a free enterprise system to expand demand. And there are epidemiological data that confirm that there is considerable room for increasing the demand for drugs. Estimates projected from the National Institute on Drug Abuse's (1986:5) most recent household survey of drug abuse suggest that only 10 percent of the population ages 12 years and older are "current users" (use during the past month) of marijuana and only 3 percent are current users of cocaine. The survey also demonstrated, however, that the majority of adolescents and young adults are current users of the major available legal drug—alcohol—and that in all, there are no less than 60.3 million current users of cigarettes and more than 113 million users of alcohol. To assume that the legalization of drugs would maintain the current, relatively low levels of drug use when there are high rates of both alcohol and tobacco use seems rather naive. Moreover, it considerably underestimates the advertising industry's ability to create a context of use that appears integral to a meaningful, successful, liberated life.

Another point should be added here. It was noted above that there is the general "perception" that drugs are readily available. Yet perceptions are one thing. There are times when the real world is something very different.

This may indeed be the case regarding cocaine. While some 50 percent of the students surveyed in 1986 believed that access to cocaine was easy, for example, data from the household surveys conducted by the National Institute on Drug Abuse (NIDA) provide some interesting insights. As indicated in Table 1, for example, *most people in the general population have never had a chance to use cocaine.* Moreover, this proportion has remained fairly stable over the seven-year period of the three NIDA surveys. What this suggests is that cocaine is not really all that available within the general population, but that if it were, usage rates would likely be much higher.

**Table 1. Trends in Percent of Respondents Reporting Chance to Use Cocaine  (U.S. household population, age 12 years and older)**

|                               | 1979  | 1982  | 1985  |
|-------------------------------|-------|-------|-------|
| No chance to use cocaine      | 81.1% | 75.5% | 79.4% |
| Chance but did not use        | 10.1% | 12.6% |  8.8% |
| Chance and did use cocaine    |  8.8% | 11.8% | 11.8% |

Source: Rouse (1988).

If the assumption of a minimal increase in drug use as the result of legalization is not valid and there indeed occurs a significant escalation in use, then the presumed cost/benefit ratio is dramatically affected. Already the estimated health care and lost productivity costs for alcohol use alone approach $90 billion annually (*Time*, May 30, 1988:14). How much greater will these be if the use of other toxic substances increases, particularly cocaine?

## Legalization and the Drugs/Violence Connection

There seem to be three models of drug-related violence—the psychopharmacologic, the economically compulsive, and the systemic (Goldstein, 1986). The *psychopharmacological model of violence* suggests that some individuals, as the result of short-term or long-term ingestion of specific substances, may become excitable, irrational, and exhibit violent behavior. The paranoia and aggression associated with the cocaine psychosis fits into the psychopharmacological model, as does most alcohol-related violence.

**Figure 1. Trends in Marijuana Use**

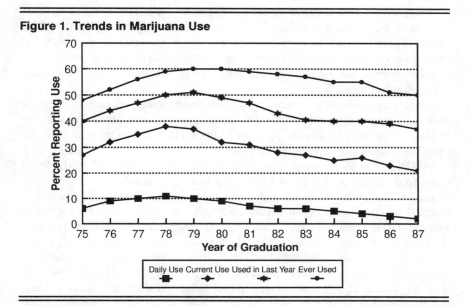

**Figure 2. Trends in Cocaine Use**

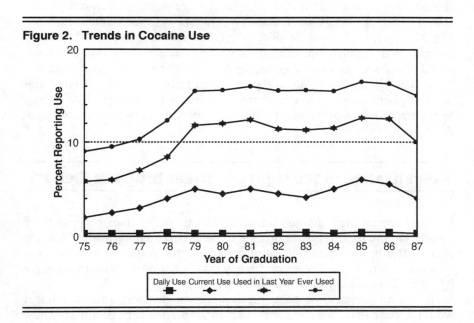

The *economically compulsive model of violence* holds that some drug users engage in economically oriented violent crime to support drug use. This model is illustrated in the many studies of drug use and criminal behavior that have demonstrated that while drug sales, property crimes, and prostitution are the primary economic offenses committed by users, armed robberies and muggings do indeed occur.

The *systemic model of violence* maintains that violent crime is intrinsic to the very involvement with illicit substances. As such, systemic violence refers to the traditionally aggressive patterns of interaction within systems of illegal drug trafficking and distribution.

It is the systemic violence associated with trafficking in crack in the inner cities that has brought the most attention to drug-related violence in recent years. Moreover, it is concern with this same violence that focused the recent interest on the possibility of legalizing drugs.[5] And it is certainly logical to assume that if heroin, cocaine, and marijuana were *legal* substances, systemic drug-related violence would indeed decline significantly. But, too, there are some very troubling considerations. *First*, to achieve the desired declines in systemic violence, it would require that crack be legalized as well. For after all it is in the crack distribution system that much of the drug-related violence is occurring. *Second*, it is already clear that there is considerable psychopharmacologic violence associated with the cocaine psychosis. Moreover, research has demonstrated that there is far more psychopharmacologic violence connected with heroin use than is generally believed (Goldstein, 1979: 126; McBride, 1981; Inciardi, 1986:135). Given that drug use would certainly increase with legalization, in all likelihood *any declines in systemic violence would be accompanied by corresponding increases in psychopharmacologic violence*. The United States already pays a high price for alcohol-related violence, a phenomenon well documented by recent research (Collins, 1981). Why compound the problem with the legalization of additional violence-producing substances?

## Legalization in the Light of Current Drug Use Trends

It would appear that agitation for such a drastic policy change as would be involved in the legalization of drugs is in great part an outgrowth of frustration. "After having spent billions of dollars on interdiction, education, prevention, treatment, and research," many ask, "what do we have to show for it?" *What indeed do we have to show for it?*

To many, the response being offered here might seem a bit odd, but it would appear that to a measurable extent, America is beginning to show some very positive gains in its war on drugs, at least in the middle class. Consider the data. *First*, there is the National Institute on Drug Abuse's annual survey of high school seniors, conducted each year by the University of Michigan.[6] As indicated in Figure 1, for example, marijuana use has been on a steady decline since its peak usage levels at the close of the 1970s.

Whereas 60.4 percent of high school seniors in 1979 had used marijuana at least once in their lives, by 1987 that figure had dropped to 50.2 percent. Even sharper declines are apparent with regard to use in the past year and current use (any use in the past 30 days). Perhaps the most significant drop has been in the daily use of marijuana, from a high of 10.7 percent in 1978 to 3.3 percent in 1987.

*Second*, the results of the 1987 survey also reflected the first significant drop in the use of cocaine after a decade of rising trends in use. As indicated in Figure 2, the survey found a decrease of about one-third—from 6.2 percent in 1986 to 4.3 percent in 1987—in the proportion of seniors who said they were current users of cocaine, and a decline of about one-fifth, from 12.7 percent to 10.3 percent, in seniors who had used the drug at least once in the past year. The proportion of seniors who had "ever used" and who used "daily" also declined.

*Third*, no trend data are available in these surveys regarding crack, but the 1987 figures suggest that crack use may not be all that widespread within America's high school population: 5.6 percent reported having ever tried crack, 4 percent reported having used it in the past year, 1.5 percent reported current use, and only .2 percent indicated the current daily use of the drug.

*Fourth*, focusing on a different population, since 1980 the University of Michigan survey team has been collecting data on drug use among college students. As indicated in Table 2, the proportion of college students reporting "any use during the past year" declined since 1986 and overall. Marijuana use has been on a steady decline in this population since 1980, and cocaine use experienced a major drop in 1987. Moreover, the use of all other drugs declined when comparing 1980 with 1987. There were .1 percent increases from 1986 to 1987 in the proportions using heroin and LSD, but these changes were minimal and not statistically significant.

*Fifth*, there are other data indicative of declining drug use in the general population. NIDA's National Household Surveys on Drug Abuse tend to confirm the findings of the high school surveys. In addition, there are the worldwide surveys of American military personnel (Burt and Biegel, 1980; Bray et al., 1983; Bray et al., 1986). In 1980, 27 percent of all military personnel reported using an illicit drug during the past 12 months, but this dropped to 19 percent in the 1982 survey and to 9 percent by 1985.

**Table 2. Trends in Drug Use During the Past Year Among American College Students**

| | Percent Who Used in the Last 12 Months | | | | | | | |
| | 1980 | 1981 | 1982 | 1983 | 1984 | 1985 | 1986 | 1987 |
|---|---|---|---|---|---|---|---|---|
| Marijuana | 51.2 | 51.3 | 44.7 | 45.2 | 40.7 | 41.7 | 40.9 | 37.0 |
| Cocaine | 16.9 | 15.9 | 17.2 | 17.2 | 16.4 | 17.3 | 17.1 | 13.7 |
| LSD | 6.1 | 4.6 | 6.3 | 4.2 | 3.7 | 2.2 | 3.9 | 4.0 |
| Heroin | .4 | .2 | .1 | .0 | .1 | .2 | .1 | .2 |
| Other opiates | 5.1 | 4.4 | 3.8 | 3.8 | 3.8 | 2.4 | 4.0 | 3.1 |
| Barbiturates | 2.9 | 2.8 | 3.2 | 2.2 | 1.9 | 1.3 | 2.1 | 1.2 |
| Methaqualone | 7.2 | 6.5 | 6.6 | 3.1 | 2.5 | 1.4 | 1.2 | .8 |
| Tranquilizers | 6.9 | 4.8 | 4.7 | 4.6 | 3.5 | 3.5 | 4.4 | 3.8 |

NOTE: For other opiates, barbiturates, methaqualone, and tranquilizers, only use that was not under a physician's orders is included here.

In short, drug using behavior in the general population is changing. Just as important, research documents a decreasing peer support for most drug use. As indicated in Table 3, in 1978 some 43.5 percent of the nation's high school seniors disapproved of occasional marijuana use; by 1987 this has increased to over 71.6 percent. Drugs such as LSD, barbiturates, and heroin had smaller but consistent increases in disapproval ratings. These data vividly demonstrate not only that peer group support can change, but also that it has—quite markedly.

## Legalization and Underclass Population Control

As the protagonists of legalization might wish to point out, the high school senior data and the national household survey data reflect stable populations. These data do not include dropouts, transients, the homeless, members of deviant subcultures living "on the street," so to speak, prison inmates, and other groups of people not readily accessible through standard survey techniques, and that it is reasonable to assume that drug use is higher in these populations. It is likely, furthermore, that drug use, and crack use in particular, is higher among high school dropouts in urban areas than in other segments of the population. In fact, for decades, research has been documenting that illegal drug use tends to be concentrated in America's inner cities (Faris and Dunham, 1925; Illinois Institute for Juvenile Research, 1953;

**Table 3: Trends in Proportions of High School Seniors Disapproving of Drug Use (percentages disapproving)**

| | Class of 1978 | Class of 1979 | Class of 1980 | Class of 1981 | Class of 1982 | Class of 1983 | Class of 1984 | Class of 1985 | Class of 1986 | Class of 1987 |
|---|---|---|---|---|---|---|---|---|---|---|
| *Q: Do you disapprove of people (who are 18 or older) doing each of the following?* | | | | | | | | | | |
| try marijuana once or twice | 33.4 | 34.2 | 39.0 | 40.0 | 45.5 | 46.3 | 49.3 | 51.4 | 54.6 | 56.6 |
| smoke marijuan[a] occasionally | 43.5 | 45.3 | 49.7 | 52.6 | 59.1 | 60.7 | 63.5 | 65.8 | 69.0 | 71.6 |
| smoke marijuana regularly | 67.5 | 69.2 | 74.6 | 77.4 | 80.6 | 82.5 | 84.7 | 85.5 | 86.6 | 89.2 |
| try LSD once or twice | 85.4 | 86.6 | 87.3 | 86.4 | 88.8 | 89.1 | 88.9 | 89.5 | 89.2 | 91.6 |
| take LSD regularly | 96.4 | 96.9 | 96.7 | 96.8 | 96.7 | 97.0 | 96.8 | 97.0 | 96.6 | 97.8 |
| try cocaine once or twice | 77.0 | 74.7 | 76.3 | 74.6 | 76.6 | 77.0 | 79.7 | 79.3 | 80.2 | 87.3 |
| take cocaine regularly | 91.9 | 90.8 | 91.1 | 90.7 | 91.5 | 93.2 | 94.5 | 93.8 | 94.3 | 96.7 |
| try heroin once or twice | 92.0 | 93.4 | 93.5 | 93.5 | 94.6 | 94.3 | 94.0 | 94.0 | 93.3 | 96.2 |
| tale herion occasionally | 96.4 | 96.8 | 96.7 | 97.2 | 96.9 | 96.9 | 97.1 | 96.8 | 96.6 | 97.9 |
| take heroin regularly | 97.8 | 97.9 | 97.6 | 97.8 | 97.5 | 97.7 | 98.0 | 97.6 | 97.6 | 98.1 |
| try amphetamines once or twice | 74.8 | 75.1 | 75.4 | 71.1 | 72.6 | 72.3 | 72.8 | 74.9 | 76.5 | 80.7 |
| take amphetamines regularly | 93.5 | 94.4 | 93.0 | 91.7 | 92.0 | 92.6 | 93.6 | 93.3 | 93.5 | 95.4 |
| try barbiturates once or twice | 82.4 | 84.0 | 83.9 | 82.4 | 84.4 | 83.1. | 84.1 | 84.9 | 86.8 | 89.6 |
| take barbiturates regularly | 94.3 | 95.2 | 95.4 | 94.2 | 94.4 | 95.1 | 95.1 | 95.5 | 94.9 | 96.4 |
| try one or two drinks of an alcoholic beverage (beer, wine, liquor) | 15.6 | 15.8 | 16.0 | 17.2 | 18.2 | 18.4 | 17.4 | 20.3 | 20.9 | 21.4 |
| take one or two drinks nearly every day | 67.7 | 68.3 | 69.0 | 69.1 | 69.9 | 68.9 | 72.9 | 70.9 | 72.9 | 74.2 |
| take four or five drinks nearly every day | 90.2 | 91.7 | 90.8 | 91.8 | 90.9 | 90.0 | 91.0 | 92.0 | 91.4 | 92.2 |
| have five or more drinks once or twice each weekend | 56.2 | 56.7 | 55.6 | 55.5 | 58.8 | 56.6 | 59.6 | 60.4 | 62.4 | 62.0 |
| smoke one or more packs of cigarettes per day | 67.0 | 70.3 | 70.8 | 69.9 | 69.4 | 70.8 | 73.0 | 72.3 | 75.4 | 74.3 |

Schmid, 1960; Chein et al., 1964; Inciardi, 1974; Dai, 1937; McBride and McCoy, 1981). But this is hardly a reason to legalize drugs. On the contrary, it is perhaps the primary justification for rejecting *all* legalization proposals.

A timeless feature of cities has been concentrated poverty. Concentrations of poverty appear in all metropolitan areas and are greatest in inner cities. Moreover, poverty in American cities tends to be more concentrated among the members of minority groups than among whites. As such, minority group membership and living in the ghetto tend to go hand in hand across the American urban landscape. Numerous explanations for this situation have been offered: that cities tend to attract the poor, many of whom cannot or will not help themselves and therefore create and sustain the conditions of their own degradation (Banfield, 1974); that in great part many of the poor adapt to their impoverished conditions by creating a set of attitudes and behaviors that tend to perpetuate poverty—the so-called "culture of poverty" thesis (Lewis, 1961); that the cause of poverty is not with the poor but with the systematic limitation of opportunity imposed by the wider society (Ryan, 1971); that attempts by the urban poor to improve their economic power are hindered by "ghetto colonialization"—the ownership of ghetto businesses by persons from outside the ghetto (Aldrich, 1973; Blauner, 1969); and that the wider society encourages the persistence of poverty because it has positive functions, providing (a) an underclass to do the "dirty work" of society, (b) a pool of low-wage laborers, (c) a place where less qualified members of the professions can practice, (d) a population that can be exploited by businesses and served by social agencies, and (e) a reference point to justify the norms and behavior patterns of the wider society (Gans, 1972). And there are other reasons for urban poverty and its persistence that have been put forth. Whatever the reasons, it seems to be generally agreed that part of the problem lies in the wider society—that the American social structure has economically disenfranchised significant portions of its urban inner cities.

Urban ghettos are not particularly pleasant places in which to live. There are vice, crime, and littered streets. There is the desolation of people separated culturally, socially, and politically from the mainstream. There are the disadvantages of a tangle of economic, family, and other problems—delinquency, teenage pregnancy, unemployment, child neglect, poor housing, substandard schools, inadequate health care, and limited opportunities. There are many modes of adaptation to ghetto life (see McCord et al., 1969). A common one is drug use, perhaps the main cause of the higher drug use rates in inner cities. And it is for this reason that the legalization of drugs would be a nightmare.

The social fabric of the ghetto is already tattered, and drugs are further shredding what is left of the fragile ghetto family. A great number of inner city families are headed by women, and for reasons that are not all that clear, women seem to be more disposed to become dependent on crack than men.

In New York City since 1986, this led to a 225 percent increase in child neglect and abuse cases involving drugs, and a dramatic rise in the number of infants abandoned in city hospitals and those born addicted or with syphilis, as well as a surge in children beaten or killed by drug-addicted parents (*New York Times*, June 23, 1988; A-1).

Within this context, the legalization of drugs would be an elitist and racist policy supporting the neocolonialist views of underclass population control. In a large sense, since legalization would increase the levels of drug dependence in the ghetto, it represents a program of social management and control that would serve to legitimate the chemical destruction of an urban generation and culture.

## Legalization and Public Opinion

A "democracy," in the most literal sense, is government by the people as a whole, rather than by any section, class, or interest group within it. And because America is a democracy, the legalization of drugs would be an inappropriate policy to implement at the present time. It may be introduced, tendered, and presented, and it may be pondered, debated, argued, and contested. But alas, in the final analysis, it must be put to pasture because the American people simply don't want it. Even the legalization or decriminalization of marijuana has only minimal support within the general population. Consider the data.

(1) In Gallup surveys conducted from 1969 through 1985, people were asked: "Do you think the use of marijuana should be made legal, or not?" The responses were as follows (*Gallup Poll*, June 20, 1985).

### Legalization of Marijuana

| Year of Survey | Favor | Oppose | No Opinion |
|---|---|---|---|
| 1985 | 23% | 73% | 4% |
| 1980 | 25% | 70% | 5% |
| 1979 | 25% | 70% | 5% |
| 1977 | 28% | 66% | 6% |
| 1973 | 16% | 78% | 6% |
| 1972 | 15% | 81% | 4% |
| 1969 | 12% | 84% | 4% |

(2) Surveys of college freshmen conducted each year by the American Council on Education (*San Diego Union*, April 10, 1988:C-5) have found that the overwhelming majority of students are opposed to the legalization of marijuana. For example:

Proportion of College Students *Opposed*
to the Legalization of Marijuana

| Class of: | Percent |
|-----------|---------|
| 1976 | 53.4 |
| 1977 | 51.8 |
| 1978 | 53.3 |
| 1979 | 52.8 |
| 1980 | 51.1 |
| 1981 | 47.1 |
| 1982 | 50.5 |
| 1983 | 53.9 |
| 1984 | 60.7 |
| 1985 | 66.0 |
| 1986 | 70.6 |
| 1987 | 74.3 |
| 1988 | 77.1 |
| 1989 | 78.2 |
| 1990 | 78.7 |
| 1991 | 80.7 |

(3) In an ABC News poll conducted in 1986,[7] respondents were asked about the legalization of several drugs. The responses were as follows:

| | Favor | Oppose | No Opinion |
|---|---|---|---|
| • Do you favor or oppose legalizing the possession of small amounts of marijuana for personal use? | 24% | 75% | 1% |
| • Do you favor or oppose legalizing the possession of small amounts of cocaine for personal use? | 5% | 94% | <.5% |
| • Do you feel that all drugs should be made legal? | 4% | 96% | - |

(4) In a *Parents Magazine* poll conducted in 1978,[8] an even broader spectrum of questions about legalization was asked. For example:

| | Yes | No | Not Sure |
|---|---|---|---|
| • Do you think prescription drugs such as Valium or amphetamines should be legally available to any adult who wants them? | 29% | 65% | 6% |

|  | *Yes* | *No* | *Not Sure* |
|---|---|---|---|
| • Do you think marijuana should be legally available to any adult who wants it? | 14% | 81% | 5% |
| • Do you think cocaine or crack should be legally available to any adult who wants it? | 2% | 97% | 1% |
| • Do you think other illegal drugs, such as heroin, should be legally available to any adult who wants them? | 2% | 96% | 2% |

Most recently, the findings of a *Washington Post* (June 26, 1988:C1, C4) poll of 1,012 randomly selected adults interviewed during the period June 15–19, 1988, demonstrated that even at a time when drug-related violence was receiving the most and highly negative media attention, the legalization option was overwhelmingly rejected. Specifically, some 90 percent of those surveyed indicated opposition to legalizing drugs. Furthermore, as indicated in Figure 3, most supported the harsh punishment of anyone convicted of selling cocaine.

**Figure 3.** *Washington Post* **Poll Responses to the Question: "Do you think that people convicted of selling cocaine should be given the death penalty, life imprisonment, a long jail term, or a short jail term."**

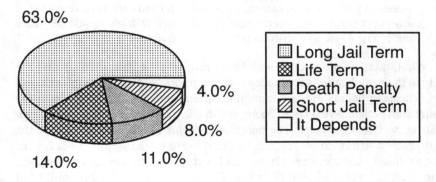

63.0%

4.0%

8.0%

14.0%    11.0%

☐ Long Jail Term
⊠ Life Term
▨ Death Penalty
▨ Short Jail Term
☐ It Depends

---

# Discussion

---

Perhaps a useful philosophical framework for analyzing the issue of the legalization of drugs is contained in John Stuart Mill's noted essay *On Liberty*, first published in 1859. Mill, an eighteenth-century philosopher and economist, played a significant role in defining both British and American concepts of individual liberty and the proper limitation of government intrusion into individual behavioral choice (Mill, 1863, 1921).

Mill's utilitarian ideals might argue that drugs should be legalized if the benefits in doing so would outweigh the harms causes by drug use. The liberty principle implies that government has no right to interfere with adult behaviors that do not harm others. Government may educate, it may inform, and it may even cajole, he argued, but its laws must not restrict individual choice, even if the actions in question may be harmful to the individual involved. Whether implicitly or explicitly, all arguments for the legalization of drugs draw upon these principles.

In considering this framework, it should be remembered that from Mill's perspective, government can legitimately interfere with adult behavioral choice *only if* there is ample evidence of *actual* (not potential) harm to others. Even then, he added, interference must be restricted to individuals actually *doing* the harm, and not extend to those having the *potential* for doing harm. Or as Mill (1921) put it:

> I deem it perfectly legitimate that a person, who had once been convicted of any act of violence to others under the influence of drink, should be placed under a special legal restriction personal to himself.

What, then, might be done with Mill's principles of utilitarianism and liberty in their implications for the legalization of drugs? Both principles underlie American beliefs in the common good and individual liberty. From the utilitarian perspective it could be argued that drugs should be legal if the benefits outweighed the costs. The perceived *benefits* of legalization include the redirection of law enforcement to "real" crime, reductions in levels of drug-related violence, street crime, and corruption, increased tax revenues, and the protection of civil liberties. The costs include the probability of increased drug use and its consequent social, physiological, psychological, and public safety costs.

Although the benefits of legalization are only *potential*, the costs are readily apparent in existing levels of illegal drug use. American society already pays a rather high tariff as a result of the public health, safety, and violence problems associated with drug use—both legal and illicit. This would necessarily increase when levels of drug consumption increase through legalization. Furthermore, and quite simply, there is no reason to believe that the real costs of legalization would outweigh the potential benefits for the public good. Existing data do not support the utilitarian benefit of legalization.

The issues raised by Mill's principle of liberty are more complex. As noted earlier, integral here is the argument that government has no right to protect citizens from their own harmful choices. To do so represents a denial of basic civil rights. Interference is justified only when behavioral choice actually—not potentially—harms others, since all human action may unintentionally harm others. In addition, Mill suggests that the government may individualize laws. That is, when certain people are found to have harmed others as the result of drug use, *then* and only then may they be denied any further use. This aspect of Mill's perspective is apparent in the parole and probation conditions in many jurisdictions that prohibit alcohol use by persons convicted of alcohol-related violent crimes (Inciardi, 1987b:633, 657).

Within this context, Mill's principle of liberty fails to support the legalization of drugs. The weight of evidence would seem to argue that the harm to others is *actual*, not potential. For example:

(1) *Crime.* The research discussed earlier in this essay demonstrates that there are significant psychopharmacological and behavioral relationships between cocaine use and violent behavior. These relationships transcend the situational context emerging from cocaine's illegality. The weight of evidence is that violence to others is a *general* consequence of chronic cocaine use.

(2) *Public health and safety costs.* Marijuana, cocaine, crack, and other illegal drugs have demonstrably major health consequences in and of themselves. Additional health consequences are associated with specific modes of ingestion, particularly with the use of unsterile needles, injection sites, and addict life-styles. Any policy change that increases consumption would also increase the health costs and public safety problems associated with drug use on the highway and in the workplace. Currently, American society pays a considerable health and safety price for current levels of chemical consumption. To be the victims of impaired drivers and transportation workers, or of inflated insurance and health care costs as the result of drug consumption, constitutes *actual*, rather than potential harm.

(3) *Practical considerations.* One might well argue that these contentions are mere possibilities of harm rather than inevitable, integral results of drug consumption. As such, drugs should be legal for all except those who have already caused actual harm through drug-taking. Such a view is of only idealistic merit, however, for the enforcement of individual consumption bans would present an application nightmare in densely popu-

lated and highly mobile postindustrial societies. In all likelihood, enforcement would result in exactly the violations of liberty with which Mill was most concerned.

(4) *The denial of freedom.* To a very great extent, arguments for the legalization of drugs emerge from concerns over the widespread use of drugs in the ghetto. Yet to legalize drugs and thereby make them more available would likely result in a further chemicalization of America's inner cities. As such, rather than extending legitimate economic opportunity and quality education and housing—the basic tools for the exercising of liberty—to inner city residents, the legalization of drugs would actually reduce opportunity and choice.

(5) *The will of the people.* The unfettered pursuit of chemically based happiness has never been viewed by the courts as a constitutional right. Furthermore, knowledge and experience has led the American public to conclude that adding to the pharmacopoeia of already legal substances would not benefit society. Survey after survey shows an increasing lack of support for legalization.

But if not legalization in the light of a problematic "war" on drugs, what then?

It is eminently sensible to strengthen the supply-side programs aimed at keeping heroin, cocaine, marijuana, and other illegal drugs out of the country. However, the emphasis of federal policy has been a bit lopsided. Between 1981 and the passage of the Anti-Drug Abuse Act of 1986, federal funding for drug treatment was cut by 40 percent (Inciardi, 1988). The result included sharp reductions in the available number of treatment slots, overcrowded treatment centers, and the turning away of tens of thousands of drug abusers seeking help. Then, of the $1.7 billion authorized by the 1986 legislation, almost 80 percent was earmarked for enforcement efforts. Moreover, much of the $363 million Congress targeted for state education and treatment programs became bogged down by the red tape of an entrenched bureaucratic process.

The difficulty lies in the fact that allocating resources for warring on drugs is always more of a political rather than a commonsense process. Arrests and seizures are easy to count, making for attractive press releases and useful political fodder. And in recent years the figures were indeed dramatic. Reporting on the number of persons in treatment is far less impressive to a constituency. But the tragedy of it all is that the waiting time for treatment entry in some cities is up to a year.

In the final analysis, drug abuse is a complicated and intractable problem that cannot be solved with quick-fix approaches tended to by politically appointed boards. Deploying more patrol boats in the Caribbean or diverting additional high-technology military hardware will not guarantee an end to or even a slowing of the war. Intercepting drugs at the borders or cutting off illegal drugs at their sources are praiseworthy goals, but they are likely impossible ones. And pressuring source countries into compliance with U.S. objectives is also an elusive task, even when there is willingness.

Thus, if total elimination of the supply of drugs is impossible, then more attention must be focused on the demand side of the equation. For after all, without drug users there would be no drug problem. The weapons here are treatment and education, initiatives that seem to be both working and failing—working for some but failing for others.

*On the treatment side*, many drug users seeking help are unable to find it, for, as noted earlier, treatment resources fail to match the demand. This problem is easily solved by a financial restructuring of the war on drugs. For the many thousands of users in need of help but unwilling to enter treatment programs, compulsory treatment may be in order.

*On the education side*, it is already clear that American youths are beginning to turn away from drugs. Moreover, surveys by the University of Michigan's Institute for Social Research suggest that this trend will continue. But all of these positive indicators relate only to mainstream American teenagers. Crack-cocaine is now tragically abundant in inner-city neighborhoods throughout the country. The antidrug messages from government, schools, parent groups, sports figures, and the entertainment media are either not reaching, or have little meaning to, ghetto youth. Like the situation with treatment, the bottom line involves a restructuring of ideas, resources, and goals.

## Notes

[1]*Qat* (also known as khat, chat, jimma, and mirra) is the evergreen shrub *Catha edulis*, the leaves and buds of which are either chewed or brewed into a beverage. Qat engenders stimulant effects similar to, but milder than, those of amphetamines, and psychic dependence has been known to develop. *Bekaro*, the seed of the Tula tree (*Pterigota alata*), is well known in many parts of India and Pakistan as an effective opiate substitute. *Mambog*, a thick syrup made from the tropical Asian shrub *Mitragyna speciosa*, is a hallucinogenic drug with stimulant effects similar to cocaine. (See Weir, 1985; Emboden, 1979).

[2]For example, see *New York Times*, March 7, 1987: 29, 32; *New York Times*, June 23, 1988: A1, B4.

[3]This point of view is most thoroughly articulated in Trebach (1982).

[4]For bibliographies and analyses of the literature on drugs and crime, see Austin and Lettieri (1976) and Greenberg and Adler (1974).

[5]See, *Time*, May 20, 1988: 12–19; *USA Today*, May 18, 1988: 10A; *Drug Abuse Report*, April 6, 1988: 7–8; Wilmington (Delaware) *News-Journal*, April 3, 1988: E2; *Newsweek*, May 30, 1988: 36–38; *Fortune*, June 20, 1988: 39–41; *New York Times*, June 2, 1988: A26.

[6]These surveys have been conducted since 1976, and the data reported here have been drawn from three sources: Johnston et al. (1986), Bachman et al. (1987), and a University of Michigan News and Information Services release (January 12, 1988).

[7]National telephone survey of 2,326 persons ages 16 and over, August 14–26, 1986. Data provided by Roper Center, Storrs, Connecticut, June 15, 1988.

[8]National telephone survey of 1,003 adults conducted for *Parents Magazine* by Kane, Parsons & Associates, May 2–20, 1987. Data provided by Roper Center, June 26, 1988.

# References

Aldrich, H. E. (1973). "Employment opportunities for blacks in the black ghetto: the role of white-owned business." *Amer. J. of Socio.* 78 (May): 1403–1425.

Anonymous (1903). *Twenty Years in Hell, or the Life, Experience, Trials, and Tribulations of a Morphine Fiend.* Kansas City, MO: Author's Edition.

Austin, G. A. and D. J. Lettieri (1976). *Drugs and Crime: The Relationship of Drug Use and Concomitant Criminal Behavior.* Rockville, MD: National Institute on Drug Abuse.

Bachman, J. G., L. D. Johnston, and P. M. O'Malley (1987). *Monitoring the Future: Questionnaire Responses from the Nation's High School Seniors.* Ann Arbor: University of Michigan, Institute for Social Research.

Banfield, E. C. (1990). *The Unheavenly City Revisited.* Prospect Heights, IL: Waveland Press.

Becker, G. S. (1987). "Should drug use be legalized?" *Business Week* (August 17): 22.

Blauner, R. (1969). "Internal colonization and ghetto revolt." *Social Problems* (Spring): 393–408.

Bray, R. M., L. L. Guess, R. E. Mason, R. L. Hubbard, D. G. Smith, M. E. Marsden, and J. V. Rachel (1983). *Highlights of the 1982 Worldwide Survey of Alcohol and Nonmedical Drug Use Among Military Personnel.* Research Triangle, NC: Research Triangle Institute.

Bray, R. M., L. L. Guess, R. E. Mason, R. L. Hubbard, D. G. Smith, M. E. Marsden, and J. V. Rachel (1986). *Highlights of the 1985 Worldwide Survey of Alcohol and Nonmedical Drug Use Among Military Personnel.* Research Triangle, NC: Research Triangle Institute.

Burroughs, W. (1953). *Junkie.* New York: Ace.

Burt, M. R. and M. M. Biegel (1980). *Worldwide Survey of Nonmedical Drug Use and Alcohol Use Among Military Personnel: 1980.* Bethesda, MD: Burt Associates.

Chein, I., D. L. Gerard, R. S. Lee, and E. Rosenfeld (1964). *The Road to H: Narcotics, Delinquency, and Social Policy.* New York: Basic Books.

Collins, J. J. [ed.] (1981). *Drinking and Crime: Perspectives on the Relationships between Alcohol Consumption and Criminal Behavior.* New York: Guilford.

Dai, B. (1937). *Opium Addiction in Chicago.* Shanghai: Commercial.

DuPont, R. L. (1984). *Getting Tough on Gateway Drugs.* Washington, DC: American Psychiatric Press.

Emboden, W. (1979). *Narcotic Plants.* New York: Macmillan.

Erickson, P., E. M. Adlaf, G. F. Murray, and R. G. Smart (1987). *The Steel Drug: Cocaine in Perspective.* Lexington, MA: Lexington Books.

Faris, R. E. L. and H. W. Dunham (1925). *Mental Disorders in Urban Areas.* Chicago: University of Chicago Press.

Fiddle, S. (1967). *Portraits From a Shooting Gallery.* New York: Harper & Row.

Fisher, R. (1972). *The Lonely Trip Back.* New York: Bantam.

Friedman, M. and R. Friedman (1984). *Tyranny of the Status Quo.* San Diego: Harcourt Brace Jovanovich.

Gans, H. J. (1972). "The positive functions of poverty." *Amer. J. of Socio.* 78 (September): 275–289.

Goldstein, P. J. (1979). *Prostitution and Drugs.* Lexington, MA: Lexington Books.

Goldstein, P. J. (1986). "Homicide related to drug traffic." *Bull. of the New York Academy of Medicine,* 62 (June): 509–516.

Gould, L., A. L. Walker, L. E. Crane, and C. W. Litz (1974). *Connections: Notes from the Heroin World.* New Haven: University Press.

Grabowski, J. [ed.] (1984). *Cocaine: Pharmacology, Effects, and Treatment of Abuse.* Rockville, MD: National Institute on Drug Abuse.

Greenberg, S. W. and F. Adler (1974). "Crime and addiction: an empirical analysis of the literature, 1920–1973." *Contemporary Drug Problems* 3: 221–270.

Grinspoon, L. (1971). *Marijuana Reconsidered.* Cambridge: Harvard Univ. Press.

Hirsch, P. (1968). Hooked. New York: Pyramid.

Hendin, H., A. P. Haas, P. Singer, M. Ellner, and R. Ulman (1987). *Living High: Daily Marijuana Use Among Adults.* New York: Human Sciences Press.

Illinois Institute for Juvenile Research and the Chicago Area Project (1953). Report of the Chicago Narcotics Survey. Unpublished manuscript.

Inciardi, J. A. (1974). "The vilification of euphoria: some perspectives on an elusive issue." *Addictive Diseases: An International Journal* 1: 241–267.

Inciardi, J. A. (1979). "Heroin use and street crime." *Crime and Delinquency* (July): 335–346.

Inciardi, J. A. (1986). *The War on Drugs: Heroin, Cocaine, Crime, and Public Policy.* Palo Alto, CA: Mayfield.

Inciardi, J. A. (1987a). "Beyond cocaine: basuco, crack, and other coca products." *Contemporary Drug Problems* 14 (Fall): 461–492.

Inciardi, J. A. (1987b). *Criminal Justice.* San Diego: Harcourt Brace Jovanovich.

Inciardi, J. A. (1988). "Revitalizing the war on drugs." *The World & I* 3 (February): 132–139.

Johnson, B. D., P. J. Goldstein, E. Preble, J. Schmeidler, D. S. Lipton, B. Spunt, and T. Miller (1985). *Taking Care of Business: The Economics of Crime by Heroin Users.* Lexington, MA: Lexington Books.

Johnston, L. D., P. M. O'Malley, and J. G. Bachman (1986). *Drug Use Among American High School Students, College Students, and Other Young Adults, National Trends through 1985.* Rockville, MD: National Institute on Drug Abuse.

Jones, H. C. and P. W. Lovinger (1985). *The Marijuana Question.* New York: Dodd, Mead.

King, R. (1972). *The Drug Hang-Up: America's Fifty-Year Folly.* New York: W. W. Norton.

Kozel, N. J. and E. H. Adams [eds.] (1985). *Cocaine Use in America: Epidemiologic and Clinical Perspectives.* Rockville, MD: National Institute on Drug Abuse.

Lewis, O. (1961). *The Children of Sanchez.* New York: Random House.

Lindesmith, A. R. (1965). *The Addict and the Law.* Bloomington: Indiana University Press.

MacDonald, D. I. (1988). "Marijuana smoking worse for lungs." *J. of the Amer. Medical Association* 259 (June 17): 3384.

McBride, D. C. (1981). "Drugs and violence" pp. 105–123 in J. A. Inciardi [ed.] *The Drugs-Crime Connection.* Beverly Hills: Sage.

McBride, D. C. and C. B. McCoy (1981). "Crime and drug-using behavior: an areal analysis." *Criminology: An Interdisciplinary J.* 19 (August): 281–302.

____. (1982). "Crime and drugs: the issues and the literature." *J. of Drug Issues* (Spring): 137–152.

McBride, D. C., P. Mutch, and A. Julian (1988). *Substance Use and Abuse Prevalence Survey of High School Students in South Western Michigan: A Report to the State of Michigan Human Resources Commission.* Berrien Springs, MI: Andrews University.

McCord, W., J. Howard, B. Friedberg, and E. Harwood [eds.] (1969). *Life Styles in the Black Ghetto.* New York: W. W. Norton.

Mill, J. S. (1863). "Utilitarianism," *Frazer's Magazine.* London: Parker, Son & Bourn.

Mill, J. S. (1921). *On Liberty.* Boston: Atlantic Monthly Press.

Musto, D. F. (1973). *The American Disease: Origins of Narcotic Control.* New Haven: Yale University Press.

Nadelmann, E. A. (1987). "The real international drug problem." Presented at the Defense Academic Research Support Conference, "International Drugs: Threat and Response," National Defense College, Defense Intelligence Analysis Center, Washington, DC (June 2–3).

Nadelmann, E. A. (1988a). "U.S. drug policy: a bad export." *Foreign Policy 70* (Spring): 83–108.

Nadelmann, E. A. (1988b). "The case for legalization." *Public Interest 92* (Summer): 3–31.

National Institute on Drug Abuse (1986). "Overview of the 1985 household survey on drug abuse." *NIDA Capsules* (October 26): 5.

Newcomb, M. D. and P. M. Bentler (1988). *Consequences of Adolescent Drug Use: Impact on the Lives of Young Adults.* Newbury Park, CA: Sage.

Nurco, D. N., J. C. Ball, J. W. Shaffer, and T. F. Hanlon (1985). "The criminality of narcotic addicts." *J. of Nervous and Mental Disease* 173: 94–102.

Nyswander, M. (1956). *The Drug Addict as a Patient.* New York: Grune & Stratton.

Peele, S. (1985). *The Meaning of Addiction.* Lexington, MA: Lexington Books.

Platt, J. J. (1986). *Heroin Addiction.* Malabar, FL: Robert E. Keiger.

Rettig, R. P., M. J. Torres, and G. R. Garrett (1977). *Manny: A Criminal Addict's Story.* Boston: Houghton Mifflin.

Rosenbaum, M. (1981). *Women on Heroin.* New Brunswick, NJ: Rutgers University Press.

Ryan, W. (1971). *Blaming the Victim.* New York: Vintage.

Schmid, C. F. (1960). "Urban crime areas: part II." *Amer. Socio. Rev.* (October). 655–678.

Schwartz, H. (1987). "We can't win the war, let's make drugs legal." *USA Today* (October 12): 12A.

Sloman, L. (1979). *Reefer Madness: The History of Marijuana in America.* Indianapolis: Bobbs-Merrill.

Smith, D. E. [ed.] (1970). *The New Social Drug: Cultural, Medical, and Legal Perspectives on Marijuana.* Englewood Cliffs, NJ: Prentice-Hall.

Smith, D. E. and G. R. Gay [eds.] (1971). *It's So Good, Don't Even Try It Once.* Englewood Cliffs, NJ: Prentice-Hall.

Spitz, H. I. and J. S. Rosecan (1987). *Cocaine Abuse: New Directions in Treatment and Research.* New York: Brunner/Mazel.

Stephens, R. C. and D. C. McBride (1976). "Becoming a street addict." *Human Organization*, 35: 87–93.

Street, L. (1953). *I Was a Drug Addict.* New York: Random House.

Trebach, A. S. (1982). *The Heroin Solution.* New Haven: Yale University Press.

van den Haag, E. (1985). "Legalize those drugs we can't control." *New York Times* (August 8): 22.

Weir, S. (1985). *Qat in Yemen: Consumption and Social Change.* London: British Museum Publications.

Weiss, R. D. and S. M. Mirin (1987). *Cocaine.* Washington, DC: American Psychiatric Press.